MW01713127

English, The Aussie Way

A Fun Guide to Australia's Colourful Phrases, Words, and Expressions

By
Lynne Maree Walsh

Strategic Book Publishing and Rights Co.

Strategic Book Publishing and Rights Co., LLC
USA | Singapore
www.sbpra.com

For information about special discounts for bulk purchases, please contact Strategic Book Publishing and Rights Co., LLC. Special Sales, at bookorder@sbpra.net.

ISBN: 978-1-61897-544-7

This book is dedicated to Sarah, Jeromé, Yoko,

Florian, Anna Maria, and Gregory.

The English language, as used in Australia today, is rich in clever and colourful descriptions. It has been influenced by words, sayings, and idioms from foreign shores, creating a unique language. Some elements of Aboriginal languages were also adopted, mainly for flora and fauna and place names, as well as some localised terms and slang. There are no regional dialects as such, only minor idiomatic and descriptive variations.

Aussie English is informal, with diminutives and nicknames used commonly to indicate familiarity. We have a collective fondness for either shortening or lengthening someone's name. There are no hard and fast rules as to whether a name is shortened or lengthened, but generally, if the name is long it's shortened and if the name is short it is lengthened. For example, the surname Jones would change to Jonesey, Smith to Smithy, Robert to Robbo, Jonathon to Jonno (almost never Jonny), and Michael to Mike or Mick. Full names are most often reserved for formal occasions only. Some examples of diminutives are: barbie, ambo, and cabbie.

Many quintessential Australian words and phrases are outdated and have disappeared from everyday use, while others are still commonplace in rural settings or specific regions. Others remain in use nationally and others are constantly emerging. For this book, I have chosen the most common colloquialisms used throughout Australia today.

The Aussie accent is consistent throughout the land, except for some minor regional variations in vowel sounds. It often relies on tone to convey different meanings. Our manner of speech is also informal, and could very well be termed lazy. It's our habit to combine two or three words to make one, for example: waddya—what do you, or dunno—(I) don't know. Visitors from foreign shores, even those with a good grasp of formal English, often find it difficult to understand the vernacular.

One does not have to look far to find information on Australian colloquialisms. In fact, there are many Internet sites and books dedicated entirely to that subject. There are also many formal books on the topic, which include documented origins of the entries, as well as exclusive language dictionaries devoted to formal English.

I would like to point out that this book is not a formal dictionary, nor does it contain a mere handful of Aussie expressions. It simply describes conversational English as spoken in Australia today.

Contained herein and listed alphabetically are standard English idioms, phrases, and phrasal verbs coloured with unique Aussie expressions, informal terms, and idiomatic single words. Each entry has one or more synonyms or idiomatic use of the word(s), and almost all entries have one or more example sentences. I have been very selective with derogatory and/or vulgar terms, with the exception of a few entries.

To break the monotony of listed words I have included snippets of information on places of interest, as well as some of Australia's unique flora and fauna, in the main body of text or at the end of many chapters. Also listed are capital cities and states, the floral emblems of each state, as well as iconic products, brands, foodstuff, habits, sporting terminology, and all things Australian.

For cross-referencing, all listed head words and phrases are in bold text.

A

ABC: Australian Broadcasting Corporation—Australia's national television and radio broadcasting service

Aborigine: an indigenous person

(it's) about time: 1) at last/finally ~ *It's about time you cleaned your room!*

2) the right time/moment to do something ~ *It's about time we leave.*

about time too: expressed when something will/has finally happened ~ *I hear they're going to widen the road here. And about time too!* *also: and not before time

about to: on the verge of; intending to ~ *We're about to leave.*

not about to: not intending or likely to ~ *I'm not about to tell everyone.*

above all: more so than anything else ~ *But above all, tell the truth.*

above and beyond: greater than the required amount/more than is required ~ *1a) Firefighters worked above and beyond the call of duty. 1b) It sold for $1 million above and beyond the expected selling price.*

(stay/keep) abreast of: 1) maintain knowledge of something ~ *She listens to the radio to stay abreast of the latest news.*

2) keep even with something ~ *He had to swim fast to stay abreast with the others.*

acacia/wattle: Commonly known in Australia as wattle, the genus *acacia* belongs to the family *mimosaceae*. It is a small tree or shrub with yellow or white flowers. There are about 1,000 species of acacia found in Australia. The Golden Wattle is Australia's national floral emblem, and Wattle Day is celebrated on September 1 each year.

acreage: an area of land measured in acres

ACT: Australian Capital Territory—the capital territory of the Commonwealth of Australia. It is the smallest self-governing internal territory. It is enclosed within New South Wales.

act as if/like: behave in a specific way ~ *1a) Mary acted as if she was the one in charge. 1b) She was acting like an idiot.*

act the fool: act stupidly, foolishly; be disruptive ~ *He's always acting the fool in class.*

act for/on behalf of: represent someone ~ *A solicitor is acting on her behalf.*

act of God: an instance of uncontrollable natural forces in operation ~ *Some consider it an act of God.*

act on: take action accordingly ~ *I acted on your advice and rested for a few days.*

act up: misbehave ~ *The baby has been acting up all day!* *also: play up

balancing/juggling act: a situation in which someone is doing several different things at the same time ~ *Trying to coordinate everything most days is a balancing act.*

(get/be) in on the act: to want to participate in something current/popular in order to share the benefits ~ *The advertising campaign was so successful that everyone else wanted to get in on the act.*

in the act of: in the process of ~ *The thief was caught in the act of breaking into a car.* *also: caught in the act

get one's act into gear: get oneself organised ~ *If you don't get your act together and finish packing you're going to miss your flight.* *also: get one's act together: get it together

vanishing act: to suddenly disappear (especially to avoid doing something) ~ *He always does a vanishing act when it's time to clean up.*

ad/advert: advertisement

ad lib: speak publically without a prepared script ~ *I hadn't prepared a speech, so I had to ad lib.*

Adelaide: the capital city of South Australia

add fuel to the fire/flames: aggravate/worsen the situation ~ *You'll only be adding fuel to the fire if you publish this.*

add insult to injury: become more upset/embarrassed ~ *To add insult to injury, my friends laughed at me when I slipped in the mud!*

add up/add something up: 1) make sense; be plausible/ reasonable ~ *His version of events just didn't add up.*

2) put two or more numbers together to reach an expected total ~ *Could you please add up these figures?*

3) amount of expense/size ~ *He wasn't earning much money and the bills just kept adding up.*

add together: 1) (when cooking) mix all the ingredients in a bowl ~ *The recipe says to add together the sugar, milk, and eggs.*

2) determine the sum of ~ *What's the total if you add the figures together?*

add up to: amount to/constitute ~ *It all adds up to a conspiracy to overthrow the government.*

admin: administration ~ *I work in admin.*

Aerogard: a nationally famous brand of outdoor insect repellent that is applied to the skin.

aggro: aggressive ~ *He sometimes gets a bit aggro if he's been on the booze.*

turn up the aggro: be more aggressive

aha: [spoken] expression of surprise/ discovery ~ *Aha! There it is!*

ahead of: in a superior/advanced position/place; early ~ *1a) We arrived ahead of the others. 1b) They arrived at their destination ahead of time.*

ahead of the pack/field: more successful/advanced than the competition ~ *The technology they use puts them way ahead of the field.*

(get the) go-ahead: receive approval/approval to do something ~ *The boss gave me the go-ahead to start the project.* *also: get the green light

air grievances: complain/make a public complaint ~ *The town meeting will give residents a chance to air their grievances.*

air out: 1) place something outside to freshen it ~ *I took the mats outside to air them out.*

2) allow fresh air into a room ~ *We opened all the windows so as to air out the house.*

airy-fairy: vague/unknowing ~ *She was a bit airy-fairy about tonight's plans.*

Akubra: Made from rabbit fur felt, the iconic, Akubra wide-brimmed hat is an important part of Australian culture in rural areas. It is the unofficial standard headwear used by horsemen, stockmen, farmers and graziers, and an important part of traditional outdoor clothing in the Australian bush.

Alice Springs: a major city in the Northern Territory in central Australia, often called the Alice.

alive and well/kicking: 1) still in existence/functioning ~ *Community spirit is alive and well in this town.*

2) alive and healthy ~ *I've been absent from the organization for a while, but I'm still alive and kicking!*

all about: concerning ~ *What was that all about?*

all along: from the beginning; the entire time ~ *I knew all along she was lying.*

all but: almost ~ *My memories of it are all but forgotten.*

all in all: generally ~ *All in all it was a successful campaign.*

all the more: even more; with even better reason for doing something ~ *I think my eyesight's getting worse. All the more reason to get my eyes checked.*

all of: used to emphasise the amount/extent/size of something ~ *1a) It took him all of two seconds to do. 1b) It's going to cost all of $500 to repair it.*

all out: using one's own resources/strength ~ *The Lions went all out to win.*

all over: 1) everywhere ~ *Clothing was scattered all over the place.*

2) typical of a person mentioned ~ *I expect that what she'd do. That's Lilli all over.*

3) completely finished ~ *I'm glad it's all over.*

4) in reference to one's body ~ *I was shaking all over.*

all over somebody like a rash: touching and engaging in bodily contact with someone you like ~ *It was embarrassing. He was all over her like a rash.*

all round: in all respects ~ *It was a good day all round.*

all told/in all: altogether; the total number ~ *All told, about 200 people attended.*

all too often/easy/few: greatly; a case to the extreme ~ *Unfortunately it's something that happens all too often.*

. . . and all: including everything/everyone ~ *I've decided to cancel the picnic, with the bad weather and all.*

at all: to any extent; in any way; period ~ *I don't like it at all.*

not all there: [informal] lacking in intelligence ~ *I'm not sure that he's all there.*

for all . . . : in spite of; despite ~ *For all its faults, it's a nice place to live.*

of all something/someone: that something is surprising/unlikely ~ *I never expected to see Sam, of all people, there.*

something of all: the best/worst etc. of something ~ *That was the best of all holidays.*

along for the ride: accompany someone/be present somewhere for sheer pleasure/fun; for no particular reason ~ *My sister's the one performing. I'm just along for the ride.* *also: go/come along for the ride

along the way: 1) at some time during a process/procedure ~ *The tour offers a wonderful experience, with the promise of making many new friends along the way.*

2) at a time in the past ~ *We lost contact with each other somewhere along the way.*

along the lines of: similar in type/similar to ~ *I can't remember exactly what was said, but it was something along the lines of the companies merging.* *also: along those lines

along with: in addition to/together with/inclusive/also/as well as ~ *1a) Bring your sister along with you. 1b) She brought something to drink along with some snacks.*

all along: 1) the entire period of time ~ *I knew all along that you were hiding there.*

2) for the entire length/stretch of area ~ *Wildflowers grew all along the river bank.*

be along: will soon arrive/come ~ *1a) You go ahead; I'll be along soon. 1b) The bus should be along any minute now.*

get along: 1) have a good relationship with someone ~ *Sally and Linda get along well with each other.* *also: get on/get on with

2) leave/depart ~ *I'd better be getting along or I'll be late.* *also: get going; run along

3) live/manage one's life independently ~ *She's getting along just fine in her new surroundings.*

go along with: concur/agree with someone/something ~ *1a) I'll go along with what Peter said. 1b) His plan was a bit dubious, but we went along with it anyway.*

help along: assist someone to move/advance ~ *Linda helped her little sister along with her homework.*

hurry (someone) along: 1) walk/travel quickly ~ *We hurried along to get out of the rain.*

2) cause/make someone move faster ~ *Hurry them along, will you, or we'll be late!*

pass along: give/relay/send something to someone ~ *Could you please pass the message along to Greg?*

pull along: move (a heavy load) by pulling ~ *The suitcase had wheels so she was able to pull it along.*

move along: continue moving; move away ~ 1a) *An officer was positioned to keep the crowd moving along.* 1b) *The traffic moved along a slow pace.*

run along: a spoken request to leave/go/depart ~ *Run along, little dog—this is not your home.*

saunter along: walk slowly/casually ~ *Tired and weary, we sauntered along homeward.*

scurry/scamper along: run nimbly/quickly along something ~ *The spider scurried along the branch.*

tag along after/behind/with someone: follow/go along with someone ~ 1a) *Do you mind if I tag along with you?* 1b) *The kids tagged along with us on the bushwalk.*

tear along: travel very quickly ~ *Cars regularly tear along this stretch of road.*

all but: nearly/almost ~ *I'll be home soon, I'm all but finished here at the office.*

all dressed up: be dressed in one's best clothes ~ *Little girls love to get all dressed up.*

all ears: be listening intently ~ *What have you got to tell me? I'm all ears.*

all for: in agreement ~ *I'm all for the proposed changes.*

all hands on deck: a spoken announcement for everybody to commence work/activity ~ *Due to the busy day ahead, the boss called for all hands on deck.*

all heart: generous/considerate/kindly (often said sarcastically about someone who displays very little kindness) ~ *Gee, thanks—you're all heart.*

all in a day's work: an ordinary/usual task/activity ~ *1a) I don't really like doing it, but it's all in a day's work. 1b) Being lowered out of a helicopter is all in a day's work for a rescue officer.*

all in all: a spoken indicator that all aspects/everything has been considered (usually used at the beginning of a sentence) ~ *1a) All in all it's a good proposal. 1b) All in all the show was a success!*

all in the head: imaginary ~ *His illness is all in the head.*

all over: 1) everywhere ~ *I've looked all over for it.*

2) finished (never to occur again) ~ *The marriage is all over.*

all over bar the shouting: that the outcome is certain ~ *The game's all over bar the shouting.*

all shook up: worried; emotionally upset ~ *The incident left her all shook up.*

all talk (and no action): talk/boast/brag about doing something but never actually do it ~ *He's all talk when it comes to actually doing something about the problem.*

all the best: [spoken] to wish someone a good future ~ *Goodbye, all the best!*

all the time: continuously; habitually; very often; repeatedly ~ *He whistles all the time.*

all the time in the world: having unlimited time ~ *Don't hurry—you've got all the time in the world to finish.*

all time: ever ~ *He's the greatest writer of all time.*

all told: with everything considered/included/counted ~ *All told it cost $400.*

all up: in total ~ *1a) All up it cost me $100. 1b) I worked for ten hours all up.*

all very well: acceptable/okay/good but not good enough ~ *1a) It's all very well for you to say that, but you don't know all the facts. 1b) It's all very well to have a gas heater, but you need an outlet to connect it to.*

all washed up: the end of a career ~ *His long career is all but washed up.*

all's/all is well: that the situation is okay; there are no problems ~ *We had a few problems at the start, but all's well now.*

at all: whatsoever/in the least/in any way ~ *I'm not at all interested!*

in all: considering everything; all being counted; altogether ~ *1a) In all, there are twenty applicants. 1b) I bought two hats in all.*

all-round/rounder: someone with many (varied) skills/talents ~ *He is a good all-round sportsman.*

be-all and end-all: the ultimate/most important/best of ~ *1a) He's so vain, he thinks he's the be-all and end-all. 1b) It was the be-all and end-all of concerts.*

almighty: very big/loud ~ *We heard this almighty crash!*

along the lines of: similar to/in type ~ *The lyrics were something along the lines of the poem we learned in class.* *also: along those lines

along the way: 1) over a distance from A to B ~ *I lost my umbrella somewhere along the way.*

2) during a period of time ~ *Apart from being a fine musician for twenty years, Janet has acquired many other skills along the way.*

along with: in addition to; together with ~ *1a) Do you want to come along with us? 1b) You'll find it in the top drawer, along with pens and pencils.*

alright already: a spoken exclamation of impatience ~ *Alright already—I'm coming!*

ambo(s): ambulance officer(s)

ammo: ammunition

amounts for nothing: of something/someone to be worthless; of something done in vain ~ *So, are you saying all the work we've done amounts for nothing?* *also: counts for nothing

amount to: equal in total; meaning/value/effect ~ *1a) Unfortunately all the donations didn't amount to much. 1b) She'll never amount to much if she continues to take drugs.*

amp: sound amplifier

anchors: the brakes on a vehicle *see also: hit the anchors

ancient history: outdated facts ~ *That secret is ancient history.*

angel: a kind-hearted, caring person ~ *Thanks for doing that—you're an angel.*

ankle-biters: very young children/babies

per annum: annually/by the year ~ *I make four payments per annum.*

another thing: something very different ~ *Playing recreational sport is one thing, but playing professionally is another thing altogether.* *see also: another cup of tea; something else

antsy: nervous/fidgety/restless ~ *I always get antsy before a job interview.*

(to have) ants in one's pants: be very excited/fidgety/ impatient ~ *The children were jumping around like they had ants in their pants.*

(the) ant's pants: the best/ultimate ~ *She thinks she is the ant's pants!* *also: bee's knees; cat's whiskers

any tick of the clock: very soon ~ *They'll be here any tick of the clock.*

any way: by whatever means/method ~ *You may complete the task any way you want.* *also: by any means

anybody's guess: something uncertain or unknown ~ *How it got here is anybody's guess.*

anyone who's anyone: important people ~ *Anyone who's anyone could be seen at the event.*

anything but: not at all; by no means ~ *The result's anything but good.*

anything goes: a situation where there are no rules/anything is acceptable ~ *In this sporting contest, almost anything goes.*

anything to do with: of having no association/connection ~ *1a) They didn't have anything to do with the project. 1b) I don't want anything to do with them.*

do anything/nothing for: be unaffected by something/someone ~ *1a) I'm afraid it does nothing for me. 1b) That outfit does nothing for her.*

for anything: never; under no circumstances ~ *I wouldn't change my situation for anything in the world.*

like anything: to a greater degree/very much ~ *I ran like anything to get there on time.*

ANZAC: 1) Australian and New Zealand Army Corps

2) Australian or New Zealand Army Corps soldier

ANZAC Day: A national day celebrated each year on April 25 to honour soldiers who fought for Australia in any conflict.

Anzac biscuit: Originally called soldiers biscuits, these oat cakes were created by the mothers, wives, and girlfriends of Australian soldiers. Concerned that their soldier sons and brothers were deprived of nutrients, they created a biscuit with as much nutritional value as possible. They used ingredients that did not spoil so that they remained edible after the long sea voyages. The biscuits were packed in airtight tins to ensure they remained crisp. Anzac biscuits are still popular today, but the commercially made biscuits are not as tasty as ones made at home.

Apple Isle: Tasmania, Australia's island state and southernmost state.

apple of one's eye: something/someone held very dear ~ *His little daughter was the apple of his eye.*

she's apples/okay/right/sweet: [spoken] reply meaning everything's alright/okay ~ *Do you need some help? No thanks, she's apples.*

upset the apple cart: ruin/spoil someone's plans; throw proceedings into disarray ~ *He upset the apple cart by arguing with everyone.*

April fool: the unsuspecting victim of a practical joke played on April Fool's Day

April Fool's Day: April 1, a day (up to midday) to play practical jokes on someone

arm in arm: of people to have their arms hooked together/ entwined ~ *The lovers strolled arm in arm along the river bank.*

Arnhem Land: A large Aboriginal reserve in the far north of the Northern Territory of Australia, it is a vast, untamed region with breathtaking scenery. It is an all-Aboriginal land, requiring permission from outsiders to visit the reserve—a place where the indigenous inhabitants are happy to share their culture and traditions with the outside world.

Arnott's Biscuits: Beginning in 1865, Arnott's is now one of the largest food companies in the Asia-Pacific region, and a nationally iconic company. Its more popular products includes Tim Tams, Milk Arrowroot, and SAO biscuits.

around: in/near one's current location/vicinity ~ *We waited around until the shop opened.*

(go/run) around in circles: 1) make no progress; go nowhere in a discussion ~ *I've been driving around in circles looking for her house.*

2) waste time and effort doing something ~ *This discussion is going around in circles.*

around the clock: all day and all night; continuously ~ *We've been working around the clock to get finished.*

around the corner: 1) in the very near future ~ *Summer is just around the corner.*

2) nearby ~ *I live around the corner from her.*

around the track: one lap of a race track ~ *The cars raced around the track.*

around the traps: a regular visiting place; haunt ~ *Where's John? I haven't seen him around the traps for a while.*

arse: [coarse slang] bottom/bum/buttock/backside

arse around/about:[coarse slang] act foolishly ~ *We'll never finish the work if you two don't stop arsing around.*

arse about face: [coarse slang] a change in direction/back to front/turned around ~ *When he saw the trouble ahead, he turned arse about face.*

arse over turkey: [slang] fall with a rolling motion ~ *He was running and fell arse over turkey.* *also: head over heels

arsey: unusually lucky ~ *You won again! Geez, you're arsey.*

arvo: afternoon ~ *What are you doing this arvo?*

as a rule: usually/in general ~ *1a) As a rule, I go for a walk before brekkie. 1b) They meet for coffee once a week, as a rule.*

as a result of: because of; due to ~ *The accident happened as a result of negligence.*

as far as: the degree/extent to which ~ *1a) As far as I know it's been postponed. 1b) As far as I'm concerned the matter's closed. 1c) We went as far as possible along the road.*

as is: in its current state/condition; without changes/ modifications ~ *I bought it as is.* *also: as stands

as it is: already; actually (contrary to other beliefs) ~ *I've got enough to do as it is without doing any extra work.*

as it were: *see: so to speak *also: insofar as

as much as: 1) an equal; indefinite amount ~ *1a) I have as much work to do as you. 1b) You can eat as much as you like.*

2) even though/despite ~ *As much as I like visiting this town, I could never live here.*

as such: intrinsically; in itself; per se ~ *Although it was raining, the temperature, as such, remained high.*

as the crow flies: in a direct/straight line ~ *It's ten kilometres north as the crow flies.*

ASAP: as soon as possible

asking a bit much: ask someone to do too much; do something difficult ~ *She wants me to take all the equipment, but I think that's asking a bit much.* *also: asking too much

asking for it: looking for trouble ~ *You're asking for it if you behave like that.*

asking price: the price for an item set by the seller ~ *What's the asking price for the painting?*

asleep on the job: lazy/idle at work ~ *If I catch you asleep on the job again you're fired!*

ass: [informal] a foolish/stupid person *see also: make an ass/fool of oneself

astronomical: numerically large ~ *My last phone bill was astronomical.*

at a glance: almost immediately ~ *At a glance it appeared the lake was empty.*

at a loss: confused/uncertain/bewildered/emotional ~ *She was at a loss as to how it happened.*

at a price: for a large cost ~ *He can fix it, but at a price.*

at a push: complete a task/job; do something within a time-frame/with difficulties ~ *The report will be finished Tuesday morning, or Monday evening at a push.*

at a rate of knots: at great speed/quickly ~ *The boat was coming towards us a great rate of knots.*

at any price/cost: for whatever cost/price; under any terms ~ *He wants to succeed at any cost.*

at any rate: anyhow; anyway; whatever happens ~ *Bad weather might be a problem, but we'll still go at any rate.* *also: in any case

(at) arm's length: 1) at a distance ~ *I held the phone at arm's length.*

2) (to) not become too friendly with someone ~ *I always felt he kept her at arm's length.*

at (the) crack of dawn: daybreak/at first light ~ *We left at the crack of dawn.*

at ease: relaxed/comfortable; free from trouble ~ *His comforting words make me feel at ease.*

at hand: close/nearby; within reach ~ *Have you got those scissors at hand?* *also: close/near at hand; at one's fingertips

at home with: accustomed to, comfortable with someone/a place ~ *Mary feels at home with Tom's family.*

at it: busy doing something; actively engaged ~ *I've been at it all day!*

at it (again): pursuing an activity ~ *1a) The dog's been at it again—digging up my flowers! 1b) I see our neighbour is at it again—working on his boat.*

at large: *see: on the loose

at long last: finally ~ *At long last we arrived home!*

at present: now ~ *I'm busy at present.*

at (the) risk (of): of something in jeopardy/danger ~ *1a) I'll be putting my career at risk by doing this. 1b) At the risk of losing my job, I'll testify in court.* *also: at stake

at sixes and sevens: mixed up; confused ~ *With so much on offer, I'm at sixes and sevens.*

at someone/one: nag/remind/hassle someone ~ *1a) Mum's been at me about getting my hair cut. 1b) I've been at my husband about doing some maintenance around the house.*

at the hands of: occur as a result of someone's action ~ *He died at the hands of his attacker.*

at the drop of a hat: almost immediately ~ *If offered a free holiday, I'd go at the drop of a hat.*

at the mercy of: defenceless; in the power of another force ~ *We were at the mercy of the storm in our little boat.*

at the helm: in a position of control/power ~ *The business was a success with Steve at the helm.*

at work: 1) at one's place of work ~ *I don't usually ring her at work unless it's an emergency.*

2) in the process of working ~ *He's busy at work right now, but he'll be free later today.*

be at something: be doing something; working ~ *She's been at the job for three years.*

'attaboy: [spoken] exclamation of encouragement/approval ~ *'Attaboy—you can do it!*

ATM: Automatic Teller Machine

call something to someone's attention: make someone notice/recognise/be aware of something ~ *1a) May I call to your attention the size difference? 1b) Thank you for bringing this to my attention.* *also: bring to attention; call someone to attention; draw to attention

centre of attention: the focus of someone's attention ~ *Our cute little kitten is always the centre of attention.*

get/grab someone's attention: attract the attention of someone; draw someone's attention ~ *I tried to grab the waiter's attention.*

hold someone's attention: keep someone interested; keep their attention ~ *The movie didn't hold my attention for long.*

pay attention: watch/consider/listen to something/someone with interest ~ *1a) I'd like you to all pay close attention. 1b) I didn't pay attention to the details.*

attention-getting: appealing; likely to attract attention ~ *She wore this attention-getting outfit.* *see also: eye-catching

Aussie: anything relating to Australia/being Australian ~ *. . . a dinkum Aussie hamburgers.*

Aussie battler: *see: battler

Aussie Rules: Australian Rules Football *see also: football

(great) Aussie salute: the action of waving the hand to shoo flies away from your face

Australia Day: January 26 is Australia Day. It is the biggest day of celebration in the country, when residents gather to celebrate the nation, reflect on what it's like being Australian, what the nation has achieved, and what it can be proud of. It is observed as a public holiday in all states and territories.

'ave a go: a spoken expression of encouragement; to attempt something ~ *Go on—'ave a go!*

to no avail: *see: for nothing

away with the fairies: to not concentrate/daydream ~ *Can you remember anything I said, or were you away with the fairies?*

awful: a great/extreme amount of something ~ *1a) She earns an awful amount of money. 1b) It's taken an awful amount of time to finish the project.*

awfully: very ~ *That was awfully nice of her to help him.*

axe: 1) terminate; cancel a plan/project/program ~ *It was decided to axe the television program due to poor ratings.*

2) dismiss from duty ~ *Poor Sue was given the axe.*

B

back away: walk backwards; retreat; draw away from ~ *I froze, then slowly backed away from the snarling dog.* *also: back off

back down: retreat from a discussion or argument ~ *I know I'm right, I won't back down.* *also: back off

back o' Bourke: any place far away from populated areas ~ *They bought a farm out the back o' Bourke.* *also: back of beyond; Woop Woop; the sticks

back on deck: back at work ~ *I'll be back on deck next week.*

back out (of): retreat from a promise/deal ~ *They're threatening to back out of the deal.*

back to square one: revert to/be in the same situation as before ~ *The deal fell through; now we're back to square one.*

back stab: a treacherous, dishonest, or unfair action or remark designed to cause hurt/harm to someone ~ *After all the work I've done to help set up his business, he back stabs me by giving the contract to someone else.* *also: stab someone in the back

back up: 1) support someone/something ~ *They provided financial back up for the project.*

2) move in reverse ~ *I've driven past it—I'll have to back up a bit.*

3) accumulate ~ *The traffic was backed up for miles.*

at the back of my mind: describes something you intend to do but keep forgetting about ~ *All week it's been at the back of my mind to call you.*

behind one's back: secretly/without knowledge; in one's absence ~ *They all talked about him behind his back.*

break one's back: do much physical hard work ~ *I nearly broke my back trying to lift it.*

get back at/get someone back: retaliate; take revenge ~ *I'll get back at you one day.*

get one's back up: become angry due to someone's actions ~ *She really gets my back up sometimes!*

on one's back: resting/idle; in bed due to illness ~ *I've been on my back all week with the flu.*

(get) on someone's back: to persistently annoy/harass someone about something until action is taken ~ *They've been on my back about giving up smoking.* *also: get up someone; get on someone's case

out the back: at the rear of a house/building ~ *You'll find him out the back somewhere.*

(give someone/receive) a pat on the back: congratulate someone/be congratulated ~ *You deserve a pat on the back for your all the work you've done today.*

pay someone back: return a favour; return money to someone ~ *Thanks for the loan. I'll pay you back next week.*

back and forth: 1) backwards and forwards; side to side; up and back ~ *She paced back and forth waiting for news.*

2) discuss/argue unresolvedly ~ *They argued back and forth for an hour.*

back-to-back: 1) without interruption; consecutively ~ *He performed back-to-back concerts.* 2) stand with backs touching ~ *They stood back-to-back to see who was taller.*

backside: bum; buttocks; bottom

backyard: fenced area at the rear/back of a house ~ *The kids are playing in the backyard.*

bad/rotten apple: a bad person within a group of good people ~ *There was only one bad apple amongst them.*

bad blood: long-time hatred between groups/individuals ~ *There's has been bad blood between the two families for twenty years.*

bad break: bad luck; misfortune

bad dream: nightmare; an event one would rather forget ~ *I keep hoping I'm going to wake up and find it's all a bad dream.*

bad/sore loser: someone who cannot readily accept defeat

bad news: someone or something likely to cause trouble ~ *Don't get involved with him; he's bad news.*

bad turn: to have sudden and unexpected bad health ~ *Jane had a bad turn last night and is now in hospital.*

badly off: financially poor; destitute

not too badly off: (said in the negative) to be reasonably wealthy ~ *I'm sure he can afford it, he's not too badly off.*

bags: 1) [spoken] request to make the first choice ~ *I bags the blue one.*

2) lots of money ~ *She can afford an expensive holiday, she's got bags of money.*

bail out: make an early retreat from a situation ~ *They decided to bail out of the sinking boat.*

bail (someone) out: rescue someone from an unsatisfactory situation ~ *I'll bail you out if you get into trouble.*

bail up: 1) detain under guard (in order to rob)

2) retain in position by guarding ~ *I was bailed up in the street by a viscious dog.*

3) hold/detain in conversation ~ *My neighbour bailed me up for twenty minutes.*

bait (someone): tease/trick someone in fun

ball of muscle: physically strong/powerful ~ *There's no fat on him anywhere; he's just a ball of muscle.*

on the ball: alert; knowledgeable; up-to-date ~ *She was on the ball spotting that mistake.*

balls-up: a bungled action/task ~ *The whole event was a total balls-up; there was little preparation and nobody knew what to do.*

go ballistic: become suddenly enraged ~ *He went ballistic when he saw the damage that had been done.*

bamboozled: puzzled; confused ~ *The instructions completely bamboozled him.*

bananas: insane/crazy/mad/excited ~ *1a) Mum went bananas when she saw the mess. 1b) They walked onto the stage and the crowd went bananas.* *also: troppo

banana bender: a humorous term for someone who lives in Queensland

band together: join/unite as a group to achieve something ~ *Government leaders banded together to help victims of the disaster.*

Band-aid: an adhesive dressing used to cover wounds

Bandicoot: Bandicoots are small, rat-like marsupials found throughout Australia. They live in a wide variety of habitats and eat mainly insects, spiders, and grubs.

bang against: strike/hit against something ~ *I tripped and banged my head against the wall.*

bang away (at): strike the keys of a piano; computer ~ *He banged away at the computer until 1 a.m.*

bang goes: [spoken] it's what you say when the opportunity to do something is lost ~ *I have to work back tonight, so bang goes my dinner date.*

bang in the middle: precisely in the centre ~ *The table was bang in the centre of the room.* *also: smack bang in the middle

bang into: bump/knock into something ~ *She lost control of the bike and banged into the fence.*

get a bang out of: derive pleasure/excitement from ~ *Some people get a bang out of doing that sort of thing.*

with a bang: spectacularly/impressively ~ *The event went off with a bang.*

bang something up: extensively damage something ~ *He banged up the car last night.*

bang-up: excellent/very good ~ *She did a bang-up job with the meal.*

bang-on: exactly correct; on target ~ *Your estimation was bang-on.*

bangers: sausages

bank job: (commit) a bank robbery ~ *He was accused of committing a bank job.*

bank on: rely/depend/count on ~ *You can bank on them for continual support.*

Banksia: The Banksia is a genus in the *Proteaceae* family. It is an iconic Australian flower, a popular nectar-producing garden plant and an important food source for bats, possums, birds, rats, and bees. It is recognised by its characteristic flower spikes.

break the bank: something so expensive it depletes funds in a bank account ~ *Any extra expenses incurred right now will break the bank.*

(won't) break the bank: that something is not be too expensive; affordable ~ *Buying it won't break the bank.*

bar: 1) the counter inside a pub/hotel where one purchases drinks ~ *I'll meet you at the bar at 8 p.m.*

2) with the exception of ~ *Everyone, bar three, attended the meeting.*

can't/won't stand a bar of: be intolerant of someone/ something ~ *1a) I dislike him intensely—in fact, I can't stand a bar of him! 1b) I won't have a bar of that behaviour in my house!*

barbie: barbecue; BBQ.

barbecue stopper: A topic of conversation that is interesting or controversial enough to halt proceedings at a barbie.

barge in: enter without permission/noisily ~ *He barged in to the meeting and demanded attention.*

bark orders: speak harshly/loudly at someone ~ *My boss has been barking orders at everyone all day.*

bark up the wrong tree: pursue the wrong meaning/direction/ purpose of something ~ *You're barking up the wrong tree if you think I have anything to do with it.*

barney: an argument/fight

barra: barramundi (fish)

(give someone) both barrels: deliver a forceful/aggressive verbal assault ~ *When Dad found out what I did, he gave me both barrels.* *refers to a double-barrelled shotgun *also: let someone have it

bash: 1) try/attempt something ~ *Go on, give it a bash.*

2) a big party ~ *We're having a bit of a bash next weekend.*

blind as a bat: having very poor vision ~ *Without my glasses I'm as blind as a bat.*

battle: struggle or fight with something/someone ~ *1a) She battled against the strong current. 1b) The army battled against the enemy.*

battle for something: fight to gain something ~ *We had to battle for our rights.*

battle it out: fight/argue until a conclusion is reached; until the end ~ *1a) The opposing players battled it out on the tennis court. 1b) They battled their differences out in court.*

have a battle/fight on one's hands: to face opposition; resistance ~ *I'm going to have a battle on my hands when I tell her she can't go.*

right-royal battle/time/fight: intense; difficult; hard-fought battle ~ *1a) I had a right-royal time trying to get it working again. 1b) The small argument turned into a right-royal battle.*

(Aussie) battler: someone who works hard for most of their life, but still struggles financially

go/drive someone batty/bonkers: annoy/irritate something; be annoyed/irritated by someone/something ~ *1a) That high-pitched alarm is driving us all bonkers. 1b) I'd go batty working at a computer all day.* *also: go mad/nuts/ crazy; drive/be driven up the wall

be around: 1) remain/stay in the same vicinity ~ *If you need me I'll be around this part of the mall for the next half hour.*

2) pay someone a visit; go to a pre-determined destination ~ *I'll be around at 5 p.m. to pick you up.*

3) remain alive; stay living ~ *I'm going to fight this illness—I plan to be around for a long time yet.*

be here till the cows come home: a long time; at length ~ *At the pace you're working we'll be here till the cows come home.*

be in it: participate; become involved in; show an interest in doing something *sometimes said in the negative ~ *I asked her if she'd join the committee, but she wouldn't be in it.*

be long: be absent/away for a long time ~ *1a) I'm going to the shops now—I won't be long. 1b) I've nearly finished—I won't be long.*

be rough on: treat someone/something harshly ~ *The superior officer was rough on the new recruits.*

be with you in a tick: [spoken] a way of telling someone you will be with them soon ~ *Could you come here please? okay, I'll be with you in a tick.*

beak: [informal] magistrate

bear arms: carry weapons ~ *All the gang members were bearing arms.*

bear the brunt (of): receive the full force; the worse part; the greater/larger amount of something bad ~ *1a) The houses in the outer suburbs bore the brunt of the storm. 1b) Unfortunately, I bore the brunt of his anger.*

bear down: advance threateningly/menacingly ~ *A severe storm is bearing down on us.*

bear fruit: yield results; yield fruit (of a plant/tree) ~ *1a) Finally her hard work and effort was starting to bear fruit. 1b) I don't expect our new apple tree will bear fruit for a few years.*

bear a grudge (against someone): continue to feel angry/ unfriendly/resentful towards someone/something that has upset you ~ *I don't think they could ever become friends—she still holds a grudge against him.*

bear a resemblance to: to look like someone ~ *She certainly bears a resemblance to her grandmother.*

bear up: for someone to remain mentally strong; be able to sustain/support someone/something ~ *1a) How's Jim bearing up after the accident? 1b) The storm cover is bearing up well against the strong wind.*

bear with: endure; be patient with someone/something ~ *If you could just bear with me for a moment—I'm nearly finished.*

grin and bear it: endure something under difficulties; suffer in silence ~ *There wasn't much he could do about the verbal attack, he just had to grin and bear it.* *also: take it on the chin

more than one can bear/stand: too much of something troublesome that one can endure ~ *The tragic news is more than I can bear.*

beat: defeated; exhausted; weary ~ *I've worked hard all day—I'm beat.* *see also: dead beat; dead tired

beat the clock: finish/complete something before due time; a deadline ~ *We had to work quickly to beat the clock.*

beat around/about the bush: work slowly; delay your action/ response ~ *Stop beating around the bush and tell me what happened!*

beat it: [spoken] a harsh way of telling someone to go away; get lost ~ *You're not supposed to be in this area; you'd better beat it!*

beat hands down: win overwhelmingly/easily ~ *I beat him hands down in a card game.* *also: beat the pants off; beat the socks off; beat the hell out of

beat into: punch/hit; use physical violence towards someone ~ *.. and beat into the other guy.*

beat oneself up: mentally punish/berate oneself over past actions/deeds ~ *You shouldn't beat yourself up for not making the finals—you can try again next time.*

beat (them) all: surpass/out-do anything of a similar nature ~ *The manner and speed he completed the job beat them all.*

beats me: [spoken] expression that means "I don't know" ~ *Why would they do that? Beats me!*

what beats/gets (me) . . . : [spoken] expression of amazement; said when something can't be understood, mostly followed by "is" ~ *1a) What beats me is that nobody was informed of the changes. 1b) What gets me is why they did it.*

badly/soundly beaten: 1) be thoroughly defeated ~ *We were soundly beaten in our soccer game today.*

2) physically bashed ~ *The poor fellow was badly beaten in a fight.*

beat/bash up: cause/inflict severe physical damage by striking/ punching/kicking ~ *Poor John got beaten up last night.*

beat-up: dilapidated; worn out; in poor condition ~ *He happily drives a beat-up old car.*

downbeat: depressed/gloomy; pessimistic ~ *He's very downbeat since his work proposal was rejected.*

upbeat: happy/cheerful; optimistic

beaut/beauty/bewdy: a congratulatory cry; very good; great; fantastic *often preceded by—you (little); what a (little); she's/he's/it's a (little) ~ *1a) I discovered this beaut coffee shop nearby. 1b) You little bewdy—my horse won! 1c) Your new car's a little beauty.* *also: you beaut; you beauty

bedridden: confined to bed ~ *I was bedridden with the flu.*

(a) beef: a complaint ~ *What are you beefing about? What's your beef?* 2) - description and example sentence needs to begin on a new line.

beef up: 1) become greater; strengthen ~ *They were forced to beef up security after a robbery.* 2) have more body fat/muscle ~ *The skinny teenager went to the gym to beef himself up.*

beeline: direct route/course ~ *She made a beeline for the handsome young man.*

been around: very experienced/knowledgeable; in existence ~ *1a) You can trust his advice, he's been around in the business for a while. 1b) The species has been around for thousands of years.*

been badly done by: to have been treated unfairly ~ *He felt badly done by when he was missed for promotion.*

been had: to be tricked

be landed with: encumbered; forced to endure ~ *I've been landed with the job of telling her the bad news.*

been up to: been doing; occupied with something ~ *What have you been up to today?* *also: get up to

Beer glass names and sizes:

285 ml/10 fl oz: Sydney/Canberra/Perth: middy/half pint

Darwin: handle

Brisbane/Melbourne: pot

Adelaide: schooner/pint

Hobart: ten ounce pot/425 ml/15 fl oz

Sydney/Canberra/Darwin/Brisbane/Melbourne/Perth: schooner

beer gut: a large stomach on a man, usually from drinking too much beer

behind someone's/one's back: do something secretly ~ *The kids made funny faces behind his back.*

behind bars: in jail ~ *There was relief at knowing the murderer would be behind bars for the rest of his life.*

behind closed doors: in private/secretly ~ *All the major decisions are made behind closed doors.*

behind the eight ball: in a difficult situation; be unable to progress in a task ~ *The change in plans for the project has put us behind the eight ball.*

behind the wheel: driving; in control of a car/vehicle/boat ~ *Don't get behind the wheel if you've been drinking.*

come from behind: advance/improve one's position ~ *The team came from behind to win the game.*

die behind the wheel: die in a car accident ~ *Too many young adults die behind the wheel.*

get behind someone: encourage/help someone's cause ~ *They wanted to get big businesses behind them in a charity event.*

leave behind: fail/forget to bring someone/something with you ~ *Here, take this, we don't want to leave it behind.*

behind: a person's bottom; bum ~ *I slipped and fell on my behind.*

put something behind (you): forget about; choose not to remember something ~ *I hardly think about it anymore. I've put it all behind me.*

believe in: accept as truth/as fact; have trust/faith in something ~ *1a) To succeed one has to believe in themselves. 1b) I don't believe in magic.*

believe it or not: something that is surprising/amazing but true ~ *1a) Believe it or not, she's ninety years old! 1b) Believe it or not, they've changed their plans again.*

believe me: (spoken) to emphasise that something is true ~ *1a) Her version of the event is not true—believe me! 1b) Believe me, it was terrifying!*

(I) believe so: (I) guess/expect/suppose/think that something is true ~ *Did he really do that? I believe so!*

hard to believe: something not easy believed ~ *It's hard to believe what just happened.* *also: hard to swallow

I do believe: a spoken statement reaffirming one's opinion/the facts ~ *1a) I do believe his business will do well. 1b) I do believe they're in love.*

would you believe it: a spoken statement emphasizing something unbelievable/shocking/terrible ~ *1a) Would you believe it—after all that preparation the project's been cancelled! 1b) Would you believe it, they both got top marks in the exam!*

you'd better believe it: [spoken] an emphatic yes/without any doubt ~ *Did we really win the lottery? You'd better believe it!*

you wouldn't believe . . . : [spoken] expression of amazement ~ *You wouldn't believe what happened to me today!*

bellyache: stomach pains; a verbal complaint ~ *I'm tired of listening to you bellyache about the work we have to do.*

belly button: one's navel

bellyful: (to have had) enough of something ~ *I've had a bellyful of your complaining!*

below the belt: unfair; sneaky ~ *That comment was below the belt.*

belt[1]: hit/punch someone ~ *He belted him on the chin.*

(a) belt[2]: 1) a quantity/swig of alcohol

2) a leather strap to hold one's trousers/pants up.

belt[3]: move/run/drive very quickly and recklessly ~ *1a) I was about to cross the road when this car came belting around the corner. 1b) The horse escaped the enclosure and belted across the paddock.*

belt up: 1) [spoken] an angry request for someone to stop talking ~ *Oh, will you belt up!*

2) the action of putting on a seat belt ~ *Everyone in the car should be belted up before we proceed.*

(a) belting: 1) a beating; thrashing; physical punishment ~ *He gave him a belting.*

2) a bad loss in a sporting contest ~ *I got belted.*

bend over backwards: go to great trouble to do a good deed ~ *They bent over backwards to help me.*

bend the rules: change the rules to suit ~ *He's been known to bend the rules to gain the advantage.*

bend the truth: distort the truth ~ *Don't believe everything he tells you, he's known to bend the truth.*

we'd/I'd/you'd best be . . . : ought/should be doing something ~ *1a) Well, we'd best be going if we want to catch that bus. 1b) You'd best be good while I'm away.* *also: better be

beside your/her/himself: distraught/overcome with worry ~ *She was beside herself with worry.*

best of all: the most outstanding/attractive/desirable/ suitable, etc. ~ *I liked that one the best of all.*

best man: the bridegroom's attendant

best wishes: an expression of hope for someone's happiness or welfare written at the end of a letter

at best: at the most/favourably ~ *It travels at a top speed of ten kilometres an hour at best.*

at the best of times: something that is not good in the most favourable circumstances ~ *I don't play well at the best of times.*

(be) at your best: performing as well/effectively as possible ~ *1a) He's playing at his best. 1b) I'm never at my best at this time of day.*

(be) for the best: [spoken] that the outcome/results of a bad situation will be good ~ *I know you don't want them to go, but it's for the best.*

give something your best: do something the best you can ~ *It was tough, but I gave it my best.*

had best/better be . . . : [spoken] that someone/something should do/be something ~ *1a) It's late, we'd best be leaving. 1b) Your excuse had better be good!*

make the best of something: do whatever you can to make a poor/bad situation tolerable/better ~ *The equipment we were given is inadequate, but we just have to make the best of it.*

the best of the best: the best people in a group; type of a particular thing ~ *The gala event attracted the best of the best in the entertainment industry.*

the best part of: the most/majority of ~ *I've been driving for the best part of the day.*

with the best of them: as much/well as anyone ~ *He'll be there playing with the best of them.*

bet quids: bet a lot of money that something will/won't happen ~ *I'll bet quids they don't come.* *also: bet one's bottom dollar

(you) bet your life: [spoken] a way of saying that you're certain something is true/will happen ~ *You bet your life I'm coming to your performance.* *also: bet your boots; bet your bottom dollar

you bet: [spoken] an emphatic yes ~ *You bet I'll be there!* *also: you betcha

better be . . . : that one/someone ought/should be doing something/do as asked ~ *1a) I'd better be going now or I'll be late. 1b) You'd better be home on time!*

better half: one's husband or wife (one half of a couple) ~ *Is your better half coming?* *also: the other half

better late than never: a saying that means that it is better to arrive late than not arrive at all ~ *I should have arrived fifteen minutes ago, but better late than never.*

better off: at an advantage ~ *You're better off staying there until the storm passes.*

better still: more satisfactorily ~ *I passed the exam, and better still, I got top marks!* *also: even better

better than nothing: something that is not satisfactory without there being an alternative choice ~ *It's not the result I wanted, but it's better than nothing.*

change for the better: an improvement in a situation/ condition of something ~ *1a) The building renovations are certainly a change for the better. 1b) Rethinking the plan will be a change for the better.*

get the better of: defeat; overcome someone/something ~ *He was in front nearly all of the race, but his opponent got the better of him and won.*

go one better: have a better result; be better than someone *often a statement to challenge someone ~ *One hundred push-ups is pretty good, but I'll go one better and do 150.* *also: do one better

beyond a doubt: of something so certain that it cannot be argued about/doubted ~ *The jury proved her guilty beyond a doubt.*

beyond a shadow of a doubt: without question; unequivocally; certainly ~ *She's the best in the business, beyond a shadow of a doubt!* *also: without a shadow of a doubt

beyond help: unable to be saved ~ *The badly injured animal was beyond help.*

beyond one/someone: too difficult to understand/ comprehend; incomprehensible/baffling/confusing ~ *1a) Why anybody could do such a thing is beyond me! 1b) The complex operating instructions are beyond the trainees.* *also: beyond me how/what/why; beyond belief

beyond question: have no doubts about; not in doubt ~ *His knowledge of the subject is beyond question.*

beyond recognition: totally unrecognizable ~ *It was destroyed beyond recognition.*

beyond reproach: above criticism; perfect; ideal ~ *His manners are beyond reproach.*

beyond the call of duty: do much more than is expected ~ *She often goes beyond the call of duty by working overtime if we get busy.* *also: above and beyond the call of duty

bible: any book/reference seen as/accepted as an essential text/authority on any topic/subject ~ *This comprehensive book is considered the bible of cookbooks.*

bickies: 1) biscuits (sweet or savoury) ~ *Come to my place for tea and bickies.*

2) money *also: bikkies

(big) bickies: lots of money ~ *That sports car would have cost big bickies.* *also: big bucks

bicycle: push bike/bike

biffo: physical/verbal conflict ~ *It was a clean game apart from a bit of biffo in the first half.*

big time: very much; a lot ~ *Thanks—I owe you big time.*

be big of someone to do something: a way to say that someone has been kind/generous ~ *That was big of them to do that.* *also used sarcastically if someone has been less than kind or generous

be big on something: be greatly interested in something/ enjoy something a lot ~ *I'm not big on spicy food.* *often used in the negative

in a big way: to a higher degree/greatly ~ *Their contributions over the years have helped us in a big way.*

too big/hot to handle: beyond one's capabilities; a difficult undertaking ~ *I'll have to get the experts in to fix the problem; it's too big for us to handle.*

what's the big idea: [spoken] a way of asking someone why they did/said something they probably shouldn't have done/said ~ *What's the big idea of you borrowing the car without asking?*

big-hearted: a generous person

big-note oneself : boastfully promote/exaggerate one's achievements ~ *I see Paul's been running around town big-noting himself again.*

bike: motorcycle; bicycle

biker: someone who rides a motorcycle

bikie: a member of a motorcycle club/gang

fit the bill: be suitable for a particular purpose ~ *This computer you're showing us doesn't quite fit the bill.*

foot the bill: pay the expenses/costs ~ *The boss said he'll foot the bill for this meal.*

billabong: a waterhole; a body of water fed from the main stream of a river

billy can: a small metal tin with a lid and handle used to boil water over an open fire

billyoh: an unimaginably large amount ~ *It's pouring like billyoh.*

Billy Tea: popular brand of tea

billy tea: tea made in a billycan

bin: rubbish/garbage container ~ *Throw it in the bin!*

bingle: a minor car accident

bird's-eye view: the view as seen from above

bit: 1) amount; degree; portion; some; slightly ~ *I don't like it one bit!*

2) a moment; brief period of time ~ *Wait a bit before commencing.*

3) somewhat ~ *It's a bit cold in here!*

(a) bit of this and a bit of that: small portions of; a different selection of something ~ *The food choices were numerous so I had a bit of this and a bit of that.* *also: some of this, (and) some of that

bit by bit: gradually; slowly; small steps at a time; in stages ~ *Bit by bit they completed the project.*

(a) bit of alright: a spoken statement indicating one's appreciation of another person ~ *I like Steve—he's a bit of alright.*

a bit much: excessive; over the top ~ *All that gaudy decoration's a bit much.* *also: a bit rich

do (his/her/my) bit: contribute one's share; do one's part ~ *We do our bit for the environment by recycling our household rubbish.* *also: do your part

bite the dust: 1) fall heavily to the ground ~ *The soldier bit the dust when he heard gunfire.* 2) (mechanical) cease operating ~ *My old car finally bit the dust.*

a bite to eat: a snack; small quantity of food ~ *Let's grab a bite to eat before we go.*

bits and pieces: small miscellaneous items ~ *What are all these bits and pieces used for?*

bitumen: asphalt; tar (road surface)

bizzo: 1) something inconsequential ~ *I don't understand all that bizzo he's talking about.*

2) unknown/incidental/random items ~ *What's all this bizzo on the floor?*

blab: to disclose confidential information ~ *Don't go blabbing to Mum about what happened.*

blabbermouth: a person who discloses confidential information ~ *I wouldn't tell Jack that secret, he's a big blabbermouth.*

black and blue all over: skin discolouring from bruising ~ *He was black and blue all over after falling off the ladder.*

black as the ace of spades: very black ~ *Her hair is as black as the ace of spades.*

Black Friday: Friday the thirteenth, an unlucky day for the superstitious.

Black-necked stork: Commonly known as a Jabiru, the Black-necked stork is Australia's only stork. Found primarily in Queensland, these beautiful white birds have glossy green-black heads, necks, tails, and lower wings. They stand at about 1.2 meters high.

black sheep of the family: an outcast/non-conformist ~ *John's the black sheep of our family.*

black eye: discoloration; bruising around the eye caused by a punch/blow *also: bruiser

give someone a black eye: punch someone in the face ~ *The town bully gave him a black eye.*

black out: to faint; become unconscious ~ *I don't remember what happened before I blacked out.*

black spot: a dangerous section of roadway; a place on a road where accidents frequently occur

black tie: formal dress code ~ *You'll need to wear a tuxedo; it's a black tie event.*

Black Stump: an imaginary place in a very remote area far from civilization ~ *How far is it? Oh, from here to the Black Stump.* *also: Timbuktu

blackout: a temporary loss of electricity/power/lighting ~ *We had a blackout during last night's storm.* *also: power outage

blah blah blah: et cetera, et cetera; talk incessantly/non-stop

give someone a blank look: to not comprehend what has been said ~ *When I asked her what happened, she just gave me this blank look.*

blast: [spoken] exclamation of annoyance; frustration ~ *Oh blast, I forgot my car keys!*

blast someone: *see: blast hell out of

a blast: a good/great time ~ *The party was a blast!*

blast hell out of: severely reprimand/scold someone ~ *I'll blast hell out of them when they get home.*

blazes: 1) a severe dismissal; to get lost; go far away ~ *You can go to blazes for all I care!*

2) an expression of intense anger/frustration ~ *What the blazes have you done?!*

bleary eyed: be affected by lack of sleep ~ *I'm a bit bleary eyed today—I only had about four hours sleep last night.*

blend together: mix evenly (with something else) ~ *The recipe says to blend together the milk and eggs.*

blessed (bless + ed): an intensifier ~ *I've got no blessed time for your silly antics!* *also: blasted

blessing in disguise: an experience/situation that appears to be bad, when in fact it is good ~ *Losing her job was a blessing in disguise.*

blimey: [spoken] exclamation of surprise/amazement ~ *Blimey, look at that!*

blinkers: direction indicators on a vehicle

blind: intoxicated; drunk ~ *They got blind drunk last night.*

blind as a bat: very blind; unable to see the obvious ~ *I didn't see it. I must be as blind as a bat.*

blind date: an arranged date between two people who have never met

block: 1) one's head ~ *If he does that one more time I'll knock his block off!*

2) a rectangular land area bounded by roads ~ *His fitness regime includes jogging around the block ten times.*

block of flats: a building divided into separate living units; an apartment complex/building

do (one's) block: become very angry ~ *I hope he doesn't do his block when he finds out the bad news.*

off (one's) block: [informal] mad/crazy/angry

blockout: skin cream to prevent sunburn *also: sunscreen/ sunblock

bloke: male/man ~ *I like Tim. He's a good bloke.*

bloodbath: an indiscriminate massacre/slaughter ~ *The events that took place could only be described as a bloodbath.*

blood, sweat, and tears: much effort; suffering ~ *A lot of blood, sweat, and tears went into making that.* *also: sweat blood

(your) blood's worth bottling: if someone tells you your blood's worth bottling, it means they are paying you a compliment or showing their appreciation ~ *Thanks for that. Your blood's worth bottling.*

young blood: young people to revitalise/bring fresh ideas ~ *The company employed young blood in the marketing/ advertising department to refresh and boost sales.*

bloody: [coarse slang] possibly the most used adjective to emphasize almost anything; any situation good or bad ~ *1a) You got top marks—bloody terrific! 1b) I've worked bloody hard all day. 1c) This bloody thing won't work!*

bloody oath: [coarse slang] [spoken] 1) absolutely/certainly ~ *1a) Bloody oath I'll be there! 1b) Bloody oath it is!*

bloody hell: [coarse slang] an expression of frustration; anger; amazement ~ *Bloody hell, what are you doing?!*

blotto: very drunk ~ *They were blotto last night.*

blow away: 1) for the wind to carry someone/something away ~ *A strong gust of wind blew it away.*

2) to kill/murder by gunfire

3) to be shocked/overwhelmed with emotion ~ *Her performance blew me away.*

blow hot and cold: to change one's opinion on a matter ~ *She blows hot and cold as to whether or not to marry him.*

blow in: arrive unexpectedly for a (usually) short visit ~ *Her relatives blew in for the weekend.*

blow it: lose an opportunity ~ *I blew my chance at being picked for the team!*

blow me down: [spoken] expression of utter amazement; surprise; disbelief ~ *Well, blow me down—I never expected to see you here!* *also: well, I'll be

blow one's mind: amaze; surprise; overwhelm ~ *The concert is guaranteed to blow your mind.*

blow one's own trumpet: boast; brag about one's successes ~ *She's got where she is in her career because she always blows her own trumpet and get noticed by the right people.*

blow one's top: to become very angry; lose your temper ~ *Mum blew her top when she saw the damage to the car.* *also: blow a fuse/gasket/stack

blow out of proportion: exaggerate; make bigger ~ *By the time the news reached him it had been blown out of proportion.*

blow over: be gone; forgotten; waned; eased ~ *By next week this will have all blown over.*

blow up: 1) explode with anger ~ *He'll probably blow up when I tell him how much money I spent.*

2) mechanical failure/break down ~ *The engine blew up right at a busy intersection.*

blow something up: 1) fill with air ~ *They blew up the balloons for the party.*

2) make larger; expand something ~ *I had the photograph blown up.*

blow up in one's face: unexpectedly fail; cause emotional hurt ~ *If he's not careful, his plan to play a trick on Steve could blow up in his face.*

blow wide open: expose corrupt practises or secrets ~ *The witness claimed to have information that would blow the case wide open.*

(be) blown away/blow one away: be overwhelmed; intensely affected by something ~ *1a) Her piano recital blew me away. 1b) I was blown away by his kindness.*

come to blows: engage in physical combat; begin to fight ~ *The debate escalated and they came to blows.*

blow-up: a sudden outburst of temper; a sudden argument ~ *Peter and Adam had a big blow-up.*

blower: telephone

blowy: windy ~ *It sure is blowy today.*

blowies: blowflies

bludge: be extremely lazy/evade work ~ *He preferred to bludge all day rather than work.*

2) take or borrow something ~ *Can I bludge a cigarette off you?*

3) an easy job ~ *This job's a real bludge.*

4) impose oneself on others ~ *Since Phil lost his job he's been bludging on his parents.*

bludger: a lazy, idle person who lives by the financial support of others ~ *I don't want that bludger staying in this house!*

blue: a physical fight; verbal argument ~ *We had a bit of a blue, but all's good now.*

Bluebottle: Found floating in colonies, these sea creatures are swept onshore by winds. They appear as a bottle-shaped sac with tentacles dangling below. They are blue in colour and the tentacles will cause a sharp, painful sting if they come in contact with the skin. They are common along the east coast.

bluey: 1) legal summons/order for a traffic infringement ~ *She copped a bluey for speeding.*

2) common name given to an Australian kelpie (cattle-dog)

blue blood: pertaining to royalty

blue blooded: describing someone appearing to be noble, aristocratic

bluff one's way: achieve something by maintaining a pretense ~ *1a) I bluffed my way in. 1b) Although she passed the exam, she bluffed her way through.*

blunder: gross mistake/error

board shorts: swimming shorts

boardies: board shorts

board something up: secure/cover/enclose with panels/ boards ~ *We boarded up the windows as a precaution against the approaching cyclone.*

go by the board: fail; be ruined; lost ~ *That procedure went by the board years ago.*

on board: 1) working for a company/involved in a project ~ *It's good to have someone with your expertise on board.*

2) aboard an aeroplane/ship/plane/train ~ *If you haven't got a ticket you won't be allowed on board.*

take on board: consider an opinion/idea; process/ comprehend information ~ *1a) I've taken your ideas on board and I'll give you a verdict tomorrow. 1b) By the third lecture of the day I was hardly taking anything on board.*

Bob's your uncle: [spoken] expression used to emphasise how easily a task/job is achieved ~ *You just press this button, and Bob's your uncle— the door opens!*

bob up: emerge/appear unexpectedly ~ *Swimming in the surf, a surfboard suddenly bobbed up in front of me.*

bobby pin: a hair clip/pin *also: hair pin

bodgie job: a task/job completed in an unprofessional, inferior manner ~ *He did a bodgie job of fixing the chair.*

bogan: someone lacking in manners/education/intelligence; having a low social status

bogged down: to have a heavy/excessive workload; be overloaded ~ *I'll be late home tonight—I'm bogged down with paperwork.*

boil the billy: boil the water to make a cup of tea ~ *Now that we've made camp, let's boil the billy for a cuppa.*

boil(s) down to: reduced to the most basic point; summarized ~ *1a) I like everything on offer, but ultimately it boils down to cost. 1b.) The information would be better understood if it was boiled down to a couple of paragraphs.*

boil up:1) the inflammation of emotions ~ *Having witnessed what they'd done, his anger boiled up inside him.*

2) cook/heat to boiling point ~ *I'm boiling up a pot of soup for dinner.*

booby-trap: 1) a practical joke for an unsuspecting person

2) an explosive device designed to be triggered/ignited by an unsuspecting person

boofhead: 1) an idiot ~ *He's a nice enough bloke, but a bit of a boofhead.*

2) a person with a large head

bolt out of the blue: a sudden, unexpected occurrence/ thought ~ *The idea came to me like a bolt out of the blue.*

bolt upright: strictly straight upright ~ *She sat bolt upright in bed after hearing a strange noise in the night.*

bone dry: very dry ~ *The intense heat had made the ground bone dry.*

bonzer/bonza: terrific; great; wonderful ~ *What a bonzer night we had!*

boo-boo: mistake; error

boogie board: A small lie-on board to ride the waves in the surf.

book something: make a reservation; purchase tickets for a movie/show ~ *1a) I've booked a table at the restaurant for Saturday. 1b) Jack said he'll book the tickets for the show.*

be/get booked: have traffic charges recorded against one/someone ~ *He'll go to jail if he's booked for drunk driving once more.*

booked up: to be fully booked with appointments/customers ~ *I tried to reserve a table at the restaurant, but they were booked up.* *also: fully booked; booked solid

do the books: record the financial information of a business ~ *An accountant helps me do the books.*

go by the book: do as the rules/instructions state ~ *He gave no favours. Everything was done by the book.*

in his/her/(my) book: in one's/someone's opinion ~ *In my book it should never be prepared that way.*

in the good/bad books: to be in or out of favour with someone; that someone is pleased/angry with you (always used in the plural) ~ *I'm in her bad books at the moment because I wouldn't let her go to the party.*

on someone's books: have one's professional details recorded with an agency/company ~ *The company has a lot of casual employees on their books.*

(to) book someone: officially note the details of someone who has broken the law ~ *He got booked for speeding.*

throw the book at someone: incur as many charges against someone as possible ~ *The judge threatened to throw the book at Jim if he committed the crime again.*

bookie: bookmaker

bookmaker: a person whose occupation it is to accept bets and pay out winning bettors (as on a horse race)

bookworm: someone who constantly reads

boomerang: a crescent-shaped object that, when thrown, will return to you *used as a hunting or recreation tool

boot: 1) storage compartment found at the rear of a car (a trunk in the U.S.)

2) give something a hard kick ~ *He booted the ball clear over the fence.*

boot out: force/send/remove someone forcibly from a place ~ *1a) He was booted out for bad behaviour. 1b) My game was not up to standard and I got booted out of the team.* *also: give someone the boot

boot up: begin; start operating a computer

hang up one's boots: retire from playing sport ~ *He's getting too old to play footie; he should hang his boots up.*

put the boot in: violently attack someone by repeatedly kicking them when they are on the ground ~ *They were brawling, and when he fell the other started putting the boot in.*

shake in one's boots/shoes: trembling/shaking in fear or anxiety ~ *I was so scared that I was shaking in my boots.*

the boot/shoe is on the other foot: a situation is reversed; the person who was at a disadvantage now has the advantage ~ *The boot's on the other foot now that I have your weapon.*

to boot: in addition; besides; as well ~ *1a) I bought this travel case from John and he threw in a carry bag to boot! 1b) Not only was the weather cold when we went camping, it rained to boot.*

too big for one's boots: a person acting/behaving as if they are more important/clever than they really are ~ *Since her promotion she's become too big for her boots and has been bossing everyone around.*

booze: alcohol/wine/beer/spirits

booze bus: In Australia, drivers may be stopped at any point along any road by a police officer for what police term a RBT, or random breath test, which involves testing a driver's blood alcohol level. For an operation involving a large number of police (typically 10-20) at a fixed location, a bus is used to conduct the testing. The bus used for the testing has come to be known as a booze bus.

boozed: drunk/intoxicated

(been) on the booze: having consumed alcohol ~ *He's a terrible hangover from being on the booze all night.* *also: on the grog/turps

booze-up: a party where lots of alcohol has been consumed ~ *I've a hangover from that big booze-up we had last night.*

bored to tears: to be totally/absolutely bored ~ *1a) Her speech bored me to tears. 1b) We were all bored stiff.* *also: bored silly/stiff/out of one's brains/out of one's mind

boss: humorous term for a wife/husband ~ *I'm not sure what our plans are this weekend—I'll have to ask the boss.*

boss someone around: give orders; instruct others in what to do ~ *My older brother thinks he can boss me around.*

bossy: domineering

bossy boots: someone who is domineering/gives orders ~ *She's become a bossy boots since she was promoted.*

make a botched job of something: to ruin through clumsiness; repair or mend clumsily; make or perform clumsily ~ *He made a botched job of it.* *also: botch something

bottle neck: the narrowing of a passageway/roadway; a point of congestion ~ *Two lanes of traffic were closed off, causing a bottle neck.* *also: traffic jam.

bottle shop: 1) a section of a hotel where one can purchase alcohol to take away

2) liquor shop *also: bottl'o

bottle up: to repress one's feelings ~ *He's naturally shy, and tends to keep his emotions bottled up.*

chief cook and bottle washer: a person in charge of doing almost every job ~ *When you run your own small business you're the chief cook and bottle washer.*

crack open (a bottle): open a bottle of wine/champagne ~ *Let's crack open the champers.*

(have a) battle with the bottle: someone with a drinking problem/habit who is having problems trying to kick the habit ~ *She's now sober after a long battle with the bottle.*

hit the bottle: drink alcohol to excess (usually to forget one's troubles) ~ *He's been hitting the bottle a bit since his wife left him.* *also: hit the grog/booze/turps

bottom line: 1) the main/essential point ~ *The bottom line is that we all will lose money.*

2) the final result/statement ~ *What's the bottom line on the figures?*

3) the last figure on a financial statement/bill; the lowest price for something ~ *The bottom line on the quote is $2,000.*

bottom of the barrel: the lowest possible quality ~ *By the time I got there, all that was left was bottom-of-the-barrel goods.*

bottoms up: [spoken] an informal drinking toast ~ *Here's to us, bottoms up!*

get to the bottom of something: discover the truth about a situation; try to better understand the cause of something ~ *1a) The journalist promised to get to the bottom of the scandal. 1b) Before I can make a decision, I need to get to the bottom of the problem.*

rock bottom: 1) one's emotional health/well-being being at its lowest; be emotionally spent ~ *He hit rock bottom after his business collapsed.*

2) the lowest possible price offered ~ *The store was offering rock bottom prices on all furniture*

3) have very little cash/money ~ *My finances are at rock bottom since losing my job.*

bounce around: 1) to move something up and down ~ *The rough road made all the equipment in the back of the truck bounce around.*

2) discuss something in order to make a decision ~ *We bounced a few ideas around before making any final decisions.*

bounced cheque: a dishonoured check from an account that has insufficient funds ~ *The business no longer accepts personal cheques because too many of them bounce.*

bounce back: 1) regain strength/power/health; make a recovery ~ *1a) The intense treatment for the injury had him bouncing back in no time. 1b). After a succession of losses, the team bounced back to win the tournament.*

2) rebound ~ *The ball hit the wall and bounced back to me.*

bounce off: 1) rebound off something ~ *The sunlight bounced off the car window and into my eyes.*

2) discuss something with someone to get their opinion ~ *He bounced his plan off the other committee members.*

bound and determined: very committed/determined/ dedicated to something ~ *The detective was bound and determined to catch the killer.*

bound and gagged: to have one's hands and feet tied and mouth gagged/covered ~ *The robbery victims were found bound and gagged.*

bound for: headed for a specific destination; be certain to achieve something ~ *1a) They'll be bound for Africa this time next week. 1b) Having succeeded thus far the team was now bound for glory.*

bound in: covered in/with ~ *The old book was bound in leather.*

bound to: be certain; destined to do something ~ *1a) The accident was bound to happen. 1b) She's bound to do a good job. 1c) They're bound to have a good time.*

bound up in: deeply involved; concerned with something/ someone ~ *1a) He's so bound up in his new girlfriend he's forgotten about his friends. 1b) I somehow found myself bound up in their troubles.*

bound with: tied with something ~ *The victim's hands were bound with rope.*

in leaps and bounds: progress/move forward/grow rapidly/in large movements ~ *She's improving in leaps and bounds.*

out of bounds: a restricted; forbidden; off-limits area beyond a boundary; an area beyond the playing field ~ *1a) This area is out of bounds. 1b) ... kicked the ball out of bounds.*

'bout: about

bowser: petrol pump; a mechanical pump that delivers fuel/petrol

the box: a television set

boxed in: surrounded; having no means of escape ~ *The cars on either side had me boxed in.*

(oh) boy: 1) [spoken] exclamation of surprise; mild anger; nervousness ~ *1a) Boy, I'm really nervous about my speech. 1b) Boy, is all this just for me? 1c) Boy—what a fantastic view!*

boys in blue: male police officers

mummy's boy: A young adult male who is not totally independent of his mother and who relies on her for support/an allowance.

boy oh boy: an exclamation of excitement; wonder; amazement ~ *Boy oh boy, will you look at that!*

the boys: a group of males ~ *He's down at the local having a drink with the boys.*

BO: body odour

brain-teaser: riddle; puzzle; problem to test one's intellect

brains: the main organiser/planner/thinker ~ *Sally is the brains behind this project.*

brainwave: a sudden, inspirational idea

brainy: clever; smart; intelligent ~ *Ask Joan, she's the brainy one.*

branch off: divide away from; separate off something ~ *1a) The road branches off to the right at this intersection. 1b) A smaller group of bushwalkers branched off from the main group.*

branch out: diversify/expand and go into new areas/fields ~ *The business has branched out and we now manufacture a variety of products.*

brass: 1) coin money ~ *Sorry, I can't lend you two dollars, I've got no brass on me at the moment.*

2) senior management ~ *I've got a meeting with the top brass this morning.*

brass razoo: a non-existent coin having no value/worth ~ *1a) I don't have a brass razoo. 1b) It's not worth a brass razoo.*

brawl: a physical fight (usually between many people) ~ *The gangs were brawling in the street.*

all-in brawl: a fight involving many people ~ *What started as a punch-up between two players soon became an all-in brawl.*

bread: [informal] money ~ *She doesn't earn a lot of bread working with that company.* *see also: dough

bread roll: a small, individual round of bread *also: bun

bread-winner: the person who works to support the family ~ *He couldn't afford to be sick; he was the sole bread-winner.*

break away (from): escape/be free from physical restraint; of a piece of something to break away from the whole ~ *1a) He managed to break free from his attacker. 1b) A panel broke away from the main structure.*

break bread: eat (a meal) together

break camp: pack up the equipment and leave a campsite

break down: 1) fail to function; cease to be operable/ functioning ~ *I'm late because the car broke down.*

2) emotionally upset/distressed ~ *She broke down when she heard the bad news.*

3) divide into sections/parts ~ *The lesson will be broken down into four sections.*

4) decompose ~ *The infected wound started to break down.*

5) break apart (physically) ~ *The fireman broke down the door of the burning house.*

break open a coldie: to open a cold can of beer ~ *Thirsty, he broke open a coldie.* *also: crack a tinnie

break even: having no advantage/disadvantage; that no money was gained or lost ~ *He broke even after a day at the races.*

break in/into: 1) enter illegally/forcibly (with intent to steal/rob; commit illegal acts) ~ *Thieves broke into the shop and stole the goods.*

2) begin to do something ~ *2a) I broke into a sweat after running for only one minute. 2b) He is known to suddenly break into song.*

break off: remove a piece from the main part ~ *The handle broke off the door.*

break off with someone: end/sever a romantic relationship ~ *Did you know Craig and Anne broke off their engagement?* *also: break up

break the ice: begin an informal conversation with a shy person ~ *She told a few jokes to break the ice.*

break the law: act contrary to; fail to obey a law ~ *Well, if you break the law you will suffer the consequences.*

break out: 1) escape from jail ~ *The prisoner was planning a break out.*

2) erupt suddenly ~ *The crowd broke out in wild applause.*

3) serve refreshments/food ~ *I'm hungry—let's break out the snacks.*

break a record: outdo; surpass a previous record ~ *He broke the world record on his third attempt at high jump.*

break someone's heart: cause emotional upset/ disappointment ~ *It broke his heart to see his home in ruins.*

break through something: advance through an obstruction/ barrier ~ *The angry crowd broke through the security fence.*

break up: 1) to laugh uncontrollably ~ *We just broke up laughing listening to his hilarious story*

2) disintegrate ~ *The rocket began to break up as it entered Earth's atmosphere.*

break wind: expel intestinal gases *also: fart

(an) even break: a fair/equal chance/opportunity as other people ~ *My innovative product is good. All I need is an even break to demonstrate its potential.*

give me a break: [spoken] expression of exasperation ~ *1a) Give me a break will you—I'm doing the best I can! 1b) Not more work—give me a break!*

lousy break: receive bad luck; have an unpleasant experience ~ *Unfortunately, I got a lousy break and didn't qualify for the finals.*

break-and-enter: unlawfully enter a premises/house with criminal intent ~ *He was charged by police for break-and-enter and robbery.*

(a) breath of fresh air: something/someone new; different; exciting ~ *Listening to Jenny's new ideas is like a breath of fresh air.*

catch one's breath: 1) resume normal breathing

2) rest/recover after physical exercise ~ *Please wait a minute while I catch my breath.*

hold one's breath: wait for something (in anticipation) ~ *I held my breath waiting for the answer.*

(don't) hold one's breath: don't expect something to happen ~ *She said she'd be here at 10 a.m., but don't hold your breath.*

in the same breath: make two conflicting/opposite statements ~ *He said he liked living here, but in the same breath said he was homesick.*

out of breath: gasping for air; wanting air ~ *I was out of breath after running up that hill.*

save/waste one's breath: speak/say something that will be ignored/have no effect ~ *1a) Save your breath—I don't want to hear excuses. 1b) It's a waste of breath talking to him—he won't listen.*

takes one's breath away: a physical response at seeing something wonderful/impressive ~ *The amazing scenery took my breath away.*

under one's breath: say something so quietly that it cannot be heard by others ~ *He was mumbling something under his breath.*

with bated breath: wait with excited/anxious anticipation ~ *We waited with bated breath.*

breathe a word: reveal a secret ~ *Don't breathe a word about this to anyone.*

breathe easy: relax; stop worrying ~ *We can breathe easy now the exams have finished.*

breathing space: pause to relax/rest/think ~ *Stop questioning me about it. I need some breathing space.*

breeze: an easy task ~ *This job's a breeze.*

breeze in (and out): enter a place in a confident/carefree manner ~ *1a) I hadn't seen her for six months, when she suddenly breezes in* *and makes herself at home. 1b) I didn't even get to talk to him, he just breezed in and breezed out again.*

breeze through: 1) complete a task rapidly/easily ~ *I breezed through the exam.*

2) travel rapidly through a place ~ *We didn't stop there, we just breezed through.*

breezeway: a covered walking area between buildings

brekky/brekkie: breakfast ~ *What's for brekkie?*

bric-a-brac: assorted/miscellaneous small items ~ *The room was filled with bric-a-brac.*

brickie: bricklayer

bride-to-be: a woman engaged to be married; preparing for her wedding

bright spark: 1) someone intelligent/clever ~ *The new student's proving to be a bright spark.*

2) a sarcastic way to describe someone who has good intentions but makes dumb mistakes ~ *Who's the bright spark that locked the car keys in the house?*

brighten up: 1) for the sky to become lighter ~ *After all that rain the sky is finally brightening up.*

2) for one's/someone's mood to lift ~ *I have some news that will brighten up your day.*

3) for a room/space to become brighter/fresher ~ *Those pictures have brightened up the room.*

bring about: cause/make happen ~ *She brings about her own misery.* *also: give rise to ~ *The new rules brought about many complaints.*

bring into line: 1) manipulate someone to conform ~ *Hopefully the harsh penalty will bring the teenager into line.*

2) make equal ~ *The increases will bring rural nurses salaries into line with the national wage.*

bring it on: [spoken] when one is ready to begin a competition/ fight ~ *I'm ready—bring it on!*

bring someone/something around: 1) revive after unconsciousness ~ *We were able to easily bring him around after he fell.*

2) convince someone to agree with you ~ *He's not convinced that the product will work, but I'm sure I'll be able to bring him around.*

3) present/show someone/something to another person ~ *3a) I'll bring the car around later. 3b) She brought her new boyfriend around to meet us.*

bring someone up to date: to inform/update the facts ~ *I'll bring you up to date on the new developments.* *also: bring up to speed

bring something up: 1) raise an issue/subject ~ *I'll bring it up at the next meeting.*

2) raise children ~ *They did a great job of bringing up the children.*

bring to mind: cause something to be remembered; to remember; recall something ~ *To mind, I don't remember that ever being here.* *also: call to mind

bring together: cause to become linked/joined ~ *1a) It took a tragedy to bring Peter and Jane together. 1b) The event brought together all the previous winners.* *also: gather together

brrr: [spoken] what you say when you're cold ~ *Brrr—it's cold out here!*

Brisbane: the capital city of the state of Queensland

Brissie: Brisbane

broke: having no money ~ *I can't afford to go; I'm broke.*

(flat) broke: utterly broke *also: stone-cold broke

brolly: umbrella

browse through: quickly look at written/printed material ~ *I had a quick browse through the magazine while I was waiting.*

brumby: wild horse

brunch: combined breakfast/lunch meal usually eaten in the late morning

brush aside: ignore/dismiss; push/sweep out of the way ~ *1a) Seeing him restored my faith and I was able to brush away any doubts*

I had. 1b) I had to brush aside the overhanging branches to clear the path. *also: brush off

brush away: remove something/someone with a brushing action ~ *Any dirt can easily be brushed away.*

brush by/past: come so close as to almost/lightly touch ~ *The bird came so close I could feel it brush past my face.*

brush something down: clean/groom fabric/clothing ~ *My coat was covered in lint, so I had to brush it down.*

brush something off: remove by brushing ~ *I brushed the grass off.*

brush over: deal lightly; give a brief account of something ~ *1a) He brushed over the unimportant facts. 1b) I haven't got a lot of time so I'll brush over the boring parts.*

brush up on something: improve one's knowledge on a subject; revise one's skills ~ *1a) I need to brush up on what we learned earlier on in the year if I want to pass the exam. 1b) You should brush up on your technique if you want to play in the tennis tournament.*

brush up against someone/something: touch lightly in passing ~ *I brushed up against the newly painted wall.*

(have a) brush with death: experience an instance of nearly dying ~ *After a brush with death, she is more appreciative of each new day.* *also: a near-death experience

bubbly: 1) a happy, bright person ~ *She's got a bubbly personality.*

2) champagne ~ *Let's break out the bubbly to celebrate.*

buck: 1) dollar ~ *It cost me thirty bucks.*

2) go against/oppose directly ~ *Her new fashion designs buck the trend.*

buck up: cheer up; become happier ~ *1a) She's been sad all day, but she's bucked up since you arrived. 1b) Come on, buck up, it can't be all that bad.*

big bucks: lots of money ~ *It cost us big bucks to have it repaired.*

bang for your buck: value; returned effort (for money spent) ~ *I guarantee this motorcycle will give you more bang for your buck.*

earn/make a fast/quick buck: earn money dishonestly or with little effort ~ *I know a good way to earn a fast buck.*

bucks party: a men's-only party held in honour of a man about to be married

buck naked: completely naked ~ *He was sitting there buck naked!*

bucket down: describes very heavy rainfall ~ *It's bucketing down.*

bucket list: a list of things to do before someone/one kicks the bucket

kick the bucket: die ~ *I may be old and in poor health, but I'm not ready to kick the bucket just yet.*

buckle under: yield to pressure

buckle up: put on one's seat belt in a car ~ *Buckle up everyone—we're about to leave.*

Buckley's (chance): little hope/slim chance of something happening ~ *You've got Buckley's of getting there on time.*

Buckley's and none: of having absolutely no chance at all ~ *Your chances of borrowing some money are Buckley's and none.*

Budgerigar: Native to Australia, the budgerigar is considered one of the most popular caged birds in the world. *also known as a parakeet

budgie: a budgerigar

budgie smugglers: humorous term for a man's Speedo swimming costume

break the budget: exceed the allotted amount of money kept for specific needs or purposes ~ *Buying that dress will break the budget.*

bug: 1) annoy/harass someone ~ *Oh, will you stop bugging me!*

2) a bacterial infection ~ *I've some type of bug.*

3) a fault/defect ~ *The new electrical system still has a few bugs in it.*

bug off: [spoken] coarse command to get lost; go away

bugger: [informal] 1) someone/something considered unpleasant; difficult ~ *He's a bugger to work for.*

2) an affectionate/humorous term for someone ~ *Tom's a funny little bugger.*

3) [spoken] exclamation of annoyance/disappointment *often preceded by—*what a* or followed by *it* ~ *3a) What a bugger—it's broken! 3b) Bugger it, I missed the train!*

bugger around/about: [informal] waste time; act foolishly ~ *If you don't stop buggering around we'll be late.*

bugger off: [spoken informal] request to go away; get lost ~ *Oh, bugger off will you!*

bugger something up: [informal] ruin; spoil; make dysfunctional ~ *Don't let John try and fix it, he'll just bugger it up.*

bugger all: [informal] little or nothing at all ~ *1a) He got bugger all pay for a hard day's work. 1b) I've done bugger all today. 1c) You ate most of the food, leaving me with bugger all!*

not give a bugger: [informal slang] to not care in the slightest ~ *I don't give a bugger what they think!*

buggered: [informal] 1) physically exhausted ~ *I can't take another step—I'm buggered!*

2) broken down; ruined beyond repair ~ *You'll have to throw it away—it's buggered!*

(I'm) buggered if . . . : [spoken informal] means that 1) you don't know something ~ *Where did they go? Buggered if I know.*

2) you certainly won't/can't do something ~ *I'm buggered if I'm going to lend him any money again!*

Well, I'll be buggered: [spoken informal] expression of amazement ~ *1a) They won? Well, I'll be buggered! 1b) Well, I'll be buggered—look who's here!* *also: well, bugger me!

build up: 1) accumulate ~ *The debts have been building up.*

2) bolster ~ *Today's win really built up her confidence.*

3) develop/increase in degrees/stages ~*They slowly built up the business to the success it is today.*

(like a) bull at a gate: do a task/job quickly/recklessly (without really thinking about you're actually doing) ~ *You're making mistakes because you're going at it like a bull at a gate.*

bully (someone): cause intentional harm to others either by verbal or physical assault and exclusion; manipulate; coerce or threaten violence ~ *The young schoolboy was bullied into stealing goods for a gang.*

bum: [informal] backside/bottom/arse

2) bludger; tramp; vagrant ~ *Steve's a lazy beach bum who spends his days surfing.*

3) an obnoxious/incompetent/insignificant person ~ *I want nothing to do with that bum.*

bum around: [informal] be idle; have no particular plans ~ *I've done nothing but bum around all week.*

give a bum steer: give incorrect directions/instructions to someone ~ *I'm still lost, he must have given me a bum steer.*

bummer: [spoken informal] expression of dismay *often preceded by what/it's a ~ *What a bummer you can't come.*

bump into: meet by chance ~ *You wouldn't believe who I bumped into today.* *also: run into

bump someone off: murder someone ~ *He was bumped off by a rival gang member.*

bump up: to greatly increase the price of something ~ *The oil companies often bump up the price of fuel during the holiday period.*

bumper: a great quantity/plenty of something ~ *1a) Bumper crowds were reported at Sydney's beaches today. 1b) Due to good rain, we harvested a bumper crop this year.*

bumper-bar: impact/collision protection device at each end of a motor vehicle

bumper-to-bumper: slow-moving traffic; cars end-to-end ~ *The traffic was bumper-to-bumper for one kilometre.*

bunch: a group of people ~ *A whole bunch of us met for lunch.*

bunch up: form a bunch/bundle/clump ~ *He looked and found the bedclothes all bunched up at the end of the bed.* *also: bunch together

bundle of nerves: very nervous ~ *I was a bundle of nerves before the exam started.*

bundle up: 1) dress very warmly ~ *Everyone was bundled up against the cold night air.*

2) make/wrap into a bundle ~ *He bundled up his possessions and quickly left.*

Bundy rum: Bundaberg rum; a popular rum made in the Queensland city of Bundaberg ~ *I'll have a Bundy and Coke please, barman.*

bung it on: feign/exaggerate an injury so as to get attention/ to be relieved of a duty ~ *I think he's just bunging it on to stay home from school.*

'burbs: suburbs/suburbia

burn away: 1) burn until there is nothing left ~ *The big logs have burned away, leaving nothing but embers.*

2) burn slowly ~ *I looked and saw all the little candles burning away.*

burn down: 1) burn with decreasing intensity ~ *Wait for the flames to burn down before roasting marshmallows.*

2) be destroyed by fire ~ *Their house burned down to the ground in the bushfire.*

burn up: 1) become angry/upset ~ *Her hurtful comments burned me up.*

2) travel at speed ~ *The cars burned up the race track.*

3) burn completely/utterly ~ *The old timber house burned up quickly.*

4) have a temperature ~ *You're burning up—you need to see a doctor.*

burning issue: a serious, urgent problem

burnt out: describes any structure that has been severely burnt on the inside, but retains an outer shell/perimeter ~ *All that was left of the getaway car was a burnt out shell.*

burnt to a crisp: something so burnt it has become crispy ~ *I left the pizza in the oven for too long, and it was burnt to a crisp.*

burst through: penetrate something ~ *1a) The armed robbers burst through the front door. 1b) The sun burst through the clouds.*

bush/bushland: 1) wilderness areas/national parks containing Australian native trees, plants, shrubs and native wildlife ~ *I have a beautiful view of the bush from my house.*

2) an area far from populated cities ~ *I'm leaving Sydney and going to live in the bush.*

bush tucker: any animal and plant food native to Australia. *also: bush food

bush walk: the Australian term for hiking in the wilderness

bushed: be physically exhausted ~ *I'm bushed; let's rest for a while.*

bushfire: the Australian version of a forest fire; wildfire

bushie: farmer; person who makes a living from farming

bushranger(s): criminal/criminal gangs who terrorised the inhabitants of the bush in nineteenth century Australia

business as usual: continue as before after a delay/ disturbance ~ *It didn't really affect us, so it was business as usual.*

get down to business: start doing what needs to be done ~ *Let's eat first and then get down to business.*

have no business: have no right to do something ~ *You had no business being there!*

in business: operating/operational ~ *1a) We just need to sign the papers and we're in business. 1b) The competitive market makes it hard to stay in business.*

in the business of: engaged in ~ *1a) We're in the business of making toys. 1b) I'm not in the business of cheating.*

go about your business: do the things you usually do ~ *Everyone was going about their business as if nothing happened.*

make (something) your business: concern yourself with something ~ *She makes it her business to meet and greet all the passengers as they board the ship.*

mind your own business/beeswax: [spoken] terse way of telling someone to stop interfering in things that don't concern them ~ *Mind your own business; this has nothing to do with you!* *also: mind your own beeswax

(be) minding one's own business: to concern yourself with what is of interest to you ~ *I was sitting there minding my own business when someone came over and started abusing me.*

risky business: something involving danger/risk; the chance of failure ~ *Trading on the stock market is somewhat of a risky business.*

open for business: for a restaurant/shop/business to be operational ~ *1a) We're open for business Tuesday to Saturday. 1b) Now that the renovations are finished, we're open for business again.*

(go) out of business: to have ceased operating as a business ~ *Sadly, the financial crisis has forced many stores to go out of business.*

unfinished business: matters of importance yet to be discussed/dealt with ~ *I'll be there soon. I have some unfinished business to attend to first.*

busted: broken/ruined ~ *I need to buy a new drill; my old one's busted.*

(get) busted: get caught doing something wrong ~ *They got busted trying to steal a car.*

(be) busting: have an urgent need to go to the toilet

busybody: an interfering person ~ *She always wants to know what we're doing. She's a real busybody.* *see also: sticky beak

butcher: one who prepares and sells meat

butcher shop/butchery: a shop in which meat and poultry is sold

butt: 1) the remains of a cigarette ~ *He carelessly discarded the butt.*

2) [informal] buttocks; bum; bottom

butt in: interfere; interrupt a conversation ~ *She tried to butt into our conversation.*

butter (someone) up: praise/flatter someone in order to gain a favour ~ *Try to butter Dad up so I can borrow the car.*

button your lips: [spoken] a way of telling someone to be quiet; to not speak

button up: 1) fasten all the buttons on one's coat jacket

2) close your lips/don't speak *see: button your lips

buoy up: support/encourage someone; make someone happy ~ *His funny jokes buoyed her up.*

buy it: accept/believe something ~ *I don't buy his excuse.*

buy into: purchase a share/interest/membership in something ~ *Our application to buy into the club was rejected.*

buy one's way somewhere: bribe someone to do something ~ *1a) It's believed he bought his way into the academy. 1b) The soldier tried to buy his way out of the army.*

buy out: purchase an owner's/partner's share/interest in an enterprise ~ *He bought out his brother's share in the house.*

buy up: purchase all the goods; everything on offer ~ *They bought up all the bread rolls in the shop.*

buzz: 1) rumour/gossip ~ *Have you heard the latest buzz going round the office?*

2) exhilaration ~ *I get a buzz out of skydiving.*

3) a telephone call ~ *Give me a buzz tomorrow.*

buzz around: move around very quickly ~ *1a) I'll do a quick buzz around to see if I can find it. 1b) A little plane's been buzzing around all morning.*

buzz off: a request to get lost; go away ~ *Oh, will you buzz off!*

by a long shot: that something is not true ~ *They're not ready yet, not by a long shot.*

by and large: generally/mostly ~ *By and large that's what you'd expect to pay for that model car.* *also: for the most part

by chance: without planning; accidentally ~ *We met by chance on a tour bus.*

by no means: not at all; no way (used to emphasize a negative statement) ~ *Jane's health is much better, but by no means is she ready to work again.*

by the book: to follow the rules/method exactly as required ~ *He's very fussy; he does things by the book.*

by the way: incidentally; in addition ~ *1a) By the way, what time are we leaving? 1b) By the way, you left the door unlocked when you went out.* *also: by the by

by way of: 1) as a method/means ~ *We positioned it by way of rolling.*

2) the route taken/via/through ~ *They went to London by way of Paris.*

C

cab: taxi

first cab off the rank: the first to do something/be chosen for something ~ *I was the first cab off the rank to be interviewed.*

cabbie: cab/taxi driver

cactus: totally ruined; dead; beyond help ~ *I'm afraid this old computer is cactus.*

café: *see: coffee shop

piece of cake: an easy task/job ~ *Fixing it was a piece of cake.*

call: a telephone call ~ *1a) I'll call you later today. 1b) Yes, I'll take the call.*

call a meeting: request a meeting be held; initiate a meeting ~ *Authorities called an urgent meeting to discuss the situation.*

call around: visit someone/be visited by someone ~ *I called around to see you, but you weren't home.*

2) make a succession of phone calls ~ *I'll call around and tell everyone the news.* *also: call in

call attention to: make something be noticed/known/observed ~ *The tour guide called attention to a famous painting.*

be called away: leave a particular place to go to another place ~ *1a) The doctor got called away and won't be back until later. 1b) I called my children away from the road.*

call back: 1) ask/direct someone to come back ~ *I'll have to call them back—they've forgotten something.*

2) return someone's earlier telephone call ~ *Lucy's busy right now, she'll call you back later.*

3) return (later) to visit/see someone ~ *No one's home—I'll call back tomorrow.*

call for: 1) a necessary/appropriate requirement ~ *The recipe calls for two eggs.*

2) arrive at a place to collect someone/something ~ *A courier will soon be calling for the parcel.*

3) a demand for attention/action on something ~ *The event calls for greater action by the government.*

call forth/forward: call/request someone to step forward/to the front ~ *I'd like to call forth all the witnesses.*

call in: request a consultation with a professional ~ *I think it's time to call in the experts to fix the computer.*

call in sick: telephone one's workplace to say you are sick and will not be coming to work ~ *Three staff members called in sick today.*

call it a day: cease activity temporarily or for the day ~ *We've worked hard—it's time to call it a day.* *also: pack it in (for the day); call it quits

call it a night: end/cease activity (at night) and go to bed ~ *I'm really tired—I think I'll call it a night.*

call it quits: 1) stop doing something ~ *Their relationship had gone from bad to worse, so they decided to call it quits.*

2) agree that a debt has been paid ~ *You bought lunch, so if I buy the tickets we can call it quits.*

3) resign/quit ~ *That's it, I've had enough. I'm calling it quits!*

call off: postpone; cancel ~ *We had to call off the picnic because of the rain.*

call on somebody: 1) visit someone ~ *I called on Sandra on the way home.*

2) ask someone to do something ~ *I was called on to make a speech.*

call on something: use particular skills/talents ~ *I had to call on all my technical skills to fix it.*

call the roll: read aloud people's names from a list to make sure they're in attendance/present ~ *The first thing our teacher does is call the roll.* *also: roll call

call the shots: exercise authority; be in charge/command ~ *Don't forget—I call the shots.* *also: call the tune

call to someone: shout to get someone's attention ~ *I called out to them, but they didn't hear me.*

call to a halt: declare a proceeding/procedure finished/ended ~ *The speaker called the meeting to a halt because everyone was arguing.* *also: call a halt to

call to arms: a summons to engage in active hostilities/warfare

(answer) the call of nature: respond to the need to go to the toilet

call up: call someone on the phone ~ *Call Gary up and see if he wants to come.*

close call: a narrow escape from danger ~ *Phew, that was a close call!* *also: a close shave; near miss

calm down: relax; become calm ~ *Calm down—arguing with him now is not going to achieve anything.*

Canberra: Located in the northern end of the Australian Capital Territory, Canberra is the capital city of Australia and is Australia's largest inland city. It is Australia's only planned city, and is the seat of the country's government. Canberra is the site of Parliament House, the High Court of Australia, and is also the location of many cultural and social institutions of national significance.

can't stand: can't tolerate someone/something ~ *I can't stand him!*

can't win: what is said when nothing goes right ~ *First the shop was shut, then I ran out of petrol. I just can't win!*

campervan: a motor home; self-contained travel van

cap in hand: humbly/respectfully ~ *He stood there, cap in hand, asking for money.* *also: hat in hand

(to) cap it off: to complete; complement something ~ *That's a great outfit, but I think a scarf will really cap it off.*

car crash: a road traffic incident involving one vehicle colliding with another or with a stationary object *also: motor vehicle accident; car accident

caravan park: Found throughout Australia, these parks provide a variety of accommodation facilities for holiday makers, including permanent on-site caravans or cabins, as well as sites to park a caravan or campervan.

card: a funny, amusing person ~ *Steve's a real card.*

cards: playing cards

on the cards: likely to occur/happen; probable ~ *With all the recent political unrest, an early election is on the cards.*

play one's cards right: act cautiously/sensibly/cleverly ~ *If you want a promotion you have to play your cards right.*

put one's cards on the table: be completely honest; open; straightforward ~ *I've put all my cards on the table—I have no secrets.*

cardie: cardigan

cark it: [informal] 1) for machinery to totally break down/become unusable ~ *My old car has finally carked it.*

2) [informal] to die

carry a tune: sing tunefully ~ *Fred would never win a singing competition—he just can't carry a tune.*

be/get carried along/with/by something: be moved/transported with something as it moves/travels ~ *They let the boat get carried along by the gentle current.*

carry around: 1) retain thoughts/ideas/memories in one's head ~ *She's been carrying her father's memory around for years.*

2) physically hold/carry/retain something/someone on one's person ~ *I've been carrying this heavy coat around all afternoon.*

get carried away with/by: 1) become emotional/excited; overenthusiastic in doing a task ~ *I got a bit carried away and cut his hair very short instead of just trimming it.*

2) be physically moved/transported to another place ~ *The current carried us away from the beach and out to sea.*

carry off: 1) succeed/be successful at doing something ~ *Although he'd never hosted such a big event, he managed to carry it off without any problems.*

2) remove/take something ~ *Thieves broke into the clubhouse and carried off all the sporting equipment.*

carry on: 1) endure/keep ~ *After all the difficulties he's had, I don't know if he'll be able to carry on for too much longer.*

2) act stupidly/foolishly; misbehave ~ *2a) If you don't stop carrying on like that you'll hurt yourself. 2b) I do wish you wouldn't carry on like that.* *also: carry on like a pork chop/an idiot; carry on a treat

carry on regardless: keep going/continue ~ *The rain had set in, but we carried on regardless.*

carry on (with): continue doing something ~ *Ignore the distraction—just carry on!*

carry something on: continue with a tradition ~ *The family has carried on the tradition for many years.*

carry out: perform; complete a job/assignment/activity ~ *1a) He was given a medal for bravely carrying out his duties. 1b) All the kids had a task to carry out.* *also: carry through

carry over: 1) extend/continue; postpone to another location/period of time/particular time ~ *Their knowledge of farming has carried over for generations.*

2) transfer a sum/figures to a new column/page ~ *The sum from this column of figures has carried over to the next page.*

carry something along: take something with oneself/someone ~ *We had to carry the equipment along with us.*

cart something: to carry an item with difficulty ~ *You don't expect me to cart that up that hill, do you?*

cart away: remove/take elsewhere ~ *We needed two trucks to cart everything away.*

(a) case of: an instance of; an occurrence of an illness ~ *1a) It is a case of mistaken identity. 1b) She has a bad case of the flu. 1c) I had a bad case of nerves before the performance.*

by the case: of bottles of drink/wine etc. purchased in a box of one dozen ~ *It's cheaper to buy wine by the case.*

in case: if; in the event of something happening ~ *1a) I'll bring an umbrella in case it rains. 1b) I'll take some extra cash, just in case.*

cash in hand: payment/wages paid in cash ~ *We got paid cash in hand for doing the job.*

cash in on: earn/gain a profit, sometimes at someone else's loss/expense ~ *Now's a good time to cash in on your investments.*

cold, hard cash: notes and coins, not cheques or credit ~ *They paid me in cold, hard cash.*

cashed-up: have plenty of money at hand; have lots of money to spend ~ *1a) I don't need to use the ATM—I'm already cashed-up. 1b) The investment plan is designed to lure cashed-up retirees.*

Cassowary: This large flightless bird—the second largest in the world—is found in tropical north Queensland. They are known to display aggressive behaviour towards humans, resulting in serious injury or death. They are identified by their striking blue neck and horn-like crest. They are fast runners and good swimmers.

cast a line: reel out/throw a fishing line into the water ~ *We watched as the fishermen cast their lines.*

cast a spell: intrigue/enchant/delight someone ~ *She seems to have cast a spell on him.*

cast aside: desert; dispose of; reject/discard ~ *Casting aside any inhibitions, he plunged into the water with the rest of them.*

cast doubts (on/over): cause to doubt ~ *Poor attendance has cast doubt on the show's future.*

cast one's mind back: try to remember/recall something ~ *Cast your mind back to this time last year—what were we doing?*

cast open: open with force ~ *They cast open the doors to allow eager shoppers to enter.* *also: throw open

catch a ride/lift: travel in someone else's car ~ *Can I catch a lift with you to work?*

catch breath: 1) regain normal breathing after an activity; regain one's composure ~ *I had to stop and catch my breath.*

2) momentarily stop breathing after receiving a surprise/fright *also: take one's breath away ~ *The raw beauty took my breath away.*

catch a cold: be infected with a common respiratory virus ~ *I think I caught your cold.*

catch forty winks: have a short sleep/nap ~ *I think I'll catch forty winks before going out tonight.* *also: grab forty winks

catch fire: ignite/burn with flames ~ *Suddenly, the whole house caught fire.*

catch hold of: seize/grasp something ~ *I couldn't quite catch hold of it.*

catch a movie/show/act: attend/see ~ *I managed to catch a Broadway show when I was in New York.*

catch off guard: be surprised; surprise someone ~ *1a) Her question caught me off guard. 1b) Authorities were hoping to catch the thieves off guard.*

catch on: 1) grasp the meaning of; understand something ~ *It's a difficult concept, but it won't take him long to catch on.*

2) become popular, trendy ~ *I don't think this new fashion trend will catch on very quickly.*

catch out: 1) be in an unpleasant situation you're not prepared for ~ *Dress appropriately; you don't want to get caught out by bad weather.*

2) trick someone into making a mistake ~ *Some of the questions are designed to catch you out, so be prepared.*

catch red-handed: be discovered/caught committing a wrongdoing ~ *He was caught red-handed breaking into the premises.* *also: catch someone in the act; spring someone

catch sight of: see something/someone unexpectedly/suddenly ~ *I caught sight of it as it darted between the trees.*

catch someone/be caught at a bad time: attempt to deal with/speak to someone at an inconvenient time ~ *1a) Can I talk to you about the proposal—or have I caught you at a bad time? 1b) Sorry, you've caught me at a bad time. Can I call you tomorrow?*

catch someone's eye: gain someone's attention through eye contact ~ *He's trying to catch the waiter's eye.*

catch up (with): 1) meet with someone again in the future ~ *Bye! I'll catch up with you soon.*

2) reach a person who is ahead of you ~ *We ran as fast as we could to catch up with the others.*

catch a wave: ride a wave ~ *I caught the next wave into shore.*

catch you later: [spoken] farewell/goodbye/we'll meet again soon ~ *Bye! I'll catch you later.*

catch-22: a no-win situation/a set of problems that is impossible to escape from

a good catch: the most suitable person to be romantically involved ~ *He ought to marry her; she's a good catch.*

cater for: provide food/services; whatever is wanted or needed ~ *1a) The restaurant caters for everyone. 1b)The program caters for adults of every ability.*

cater to: be attentive/minister to ~ *The butler catered to his every need.*

cattle dog: an Australian-bred herding dog for controlling cattle *also known as Queensland Blue Heeler, Blue Heeler, Red Heeler, kelpie

exercise caution: be very careful/cautious ~ *Please exercise caution when using this machinery.*

C.E.O: chief executive officer of a company/organization

(a) cert: something certain ~ *He was a cert to win.*

chain up: secure something; bind an animal in chains ~ *1a) The gate was all chained up. 1b) I'll chain the dog up.*

chain smoker: someone who smokes one cigarette after another

fall off the chair: be so amused/surprised/amazed at something ~ *When I heard what had happened I nearly fell off the chair.*

chalk and cheese: to be different in every way ~ *They might be sisters, but they're like chalk and cheese.*

chalk up: to score/earn; record something ~ *They chalked up 500 kilometres on their trip.*

chalkie: school teacher

champers: champagne

chances are: it is likely that; the likelihood is ~ *Chances are she'll make a full recovery.* *see also: slim chance

fat chance: very little or no chance ~ *Fat chance you'll have of borrowing any money off Dad.* *also: ghost of a chance/Buckley's chance

fighting chance: an opportunity to succeed (but with effort) ~ *Because of your generous donation, the innovative business now has a fighting chance.*

given half a/the chance: (be) allowed the smallest of opportunities; accept/take up a small opportunity ~ *1a) Given half the chance, I'd do things differently. 1b) He could certainly have done better if he'd been given half a chance.*

(on the) off chance: random/slight possibility ~ *1a) I'll give it to you now, on the off chance I don't see you tomorrow. 1b) There's an off chance that I might promoted.*

slim chance: slight/small opportunity ~ *There's a slim chance that I might stay an extra day.*

(has/is in with) a sporting chance: a reasonable/fair opportunity ~ *He has a sporting chance of being elected.* *also: in with a sporting chance ~ *I can't predict the outcome, but he's in with a sporting chance.*

stand a chance: have no opportunity; possibility of success ~ *1a) She doesn't stand a chance of winning. 1b) You wouldn't stand much of a chance of surviving a fall from that height.* *also: ghost of a chance

take a chance/risk: do something that involves risk ~ *1a) I took a chance crossing the river. 1b) I could get injured doing it, but it's a chance I have to take. 1c) I'm not going to do it—I don't want to take any chances.*

change: coins ~ *Have you any lose change?*

change for the better: improved/made better ~ *1a) This weather's a change for the better. 1b) Her attitude is certainly a change for the better.*

change for the worse: decline/regress/worsen ~ *He's changed for the worse for joining that gang.*

change hands: change ownership from one to another ~ *The business changed hands last month.*

change one's mind: have a different opinion; think differently about something ~ *1a) I've changed my mind—I'll take this one instead. 1b) If you ever change your mind, let me know.*

chap: man; fellow; bloke ~ *He's a nice young chap.*

character: an unusual/interesting/odd person ~ *Jim's certainly a bit of a character.*

charged up: *see: revved up

chase around: follow/pursue someone/something closely ~ *1a) Our dog loves chasing a ball around the yard. 1b) Their favourite game is to chase each other around.*

chase away: force someone/something to go away ~ *Our dog chases away any cats that stray into the yard.*

chase down: follow/pursue someone/something in order to catch them ~ *The police chased the thieves down and captured them.*

chase up: find/locate/search for ~ *I'd better chase up that missing file.*

give chase: chase someone/something ~ *The policeman spotted the thief and gave chase.*

chat: an informal conversation ~ *We had a nice little chat.*

chat (someone) up: talk flirtatiously with ~ *He's always chatting up the girls.*

chatterbox: someone who never stops talking ~ *June, across the road, is real chatterbox.*

cheap and nasty: inferior; cheaply manufactured ~ *I thought it would break easily, it was cheap and nasty.*

cheap as chips: very cheap ~ *Socks were as cheap as chips at that shop, so we bought a dozen pairs.*

cheap thrill: excitement that doesn't take much effort ~ *They roamed the streets looking for some cheap thrills.*

on the cheap: at a low cost ~ *It was built on the cheap.*

check back (with): make inquiries at a later time ~ *I'll check back with you this afternoon.*

check in: give one's name; register into a hotel ~ *We were able to check in to a cheap hotel.*

check on/up on/in on: scrutinize/inspect/investigate something/someone ~ *1a) I'll just check on the dinner to see if it's cooked. 1b) First, I have to go home and check up on the children to see if they're okay. 1c) I'll check in on you tonight.*

check something in: record the return of something; record incoming goods/stock ~ *1a) It's my job to check in the library books when they are returned. 1b) It's Sam's job to check in the new books.*

check something out: 1) pay close attention; look closely at something ~ *1a) Check out the fine detail on the dress. 1b) Wow, check this car out!*

2) record outgoing goods/stock ~ *Could you please check out the goods to the delivery driver?*

check through something: examine goods/items/papers/written work ~ *1a) The customs officer checked through our luggage. 1b) I'll check through my work for any spelling errors.*

check with: make enquiries; ask someone about something ~ *First, you'd better check with the manager.*

checkout: the exit point in a shop where you pay for goods

check-up: a physical examination ~ *In order to stay healthy, one should have a regular check-up.*

cheek: nerve/rudeness/impudence ~ *1a) What a cheek! 1b) She had the cheek to ask us to pay for it.*

(give) cheek: be rude or impudent ~ *Don't give me cheek!*

cheer someone up: make someone happy/be made happy ~ *1a) My friends came over to cheer me up. 1b) These flowers should cheer her up.*

cheerio (then): [spoken] a way of saying goodbye ~ *Cheerio, I'll see you next week.*

cheers: a salute to good health

cheese(d) off: be angry; annoyed; exasperated ~ *I was cheesed off by his actions.*

chew on it/chew it over: seriously consider /think about something ~ *Let me chew it over before I give you an answer.*

chew someone out: reprimand/admonish someone ~ *Jim did something terribly wrong and the boss really chewed him out.*

chewie/chewy: chewing gum

chick flick: a movie more suited to the female viewer

be a chicken/chicken out: show cowardice; be afraid/scared/ frightened ~ *1) I'm such a chicken when it comes to touching insects. 1b) I was going to go skydiving, but I chickened out at the last minute.*

chill out: relax; calm down; be stress free ~ *1a) She took a long walk to chill out after a stressful day. 1b) Chill out, will you—let me explain!*

chinwag: a long conversation ~ *Alison and I had a good chinwag.*

chip(s): 1) crisps; potato chips ~ snack contained within a sealed bag *also: chippies

2) representing money at a casino

chip away at: 1) break off/remove small pieces by hitting with a tool ~ *He demolished it by chipping away at the edges.*

2) reduce/make less powerful ~ *Rebels in the gang have been chipping away at his authority.*

chip in: make a monetary contribution ~ *We all chipped in to buy Megan a birthday present.*

chip off the old block: describes a son who shares the same characteristics/mannerisms/looks as his father

spit chips: (to be) very angry ~ *I was spitting chips when I heard what happened.*

when the chips are down: a difficult, critical time ~ *Even when the chips are down, he can still smile.*

chippie/y: carpenter

chirpy: cheerful/happy ~ *You're very chirpy this morning.*

chit-chat: small talk; gossip

chockers/chock-a-block: crammed full; overcrowded ~ *1a) We couldn't board the bus. It was absolutely chockers. 1b) The bin was chock-a-block with rubbish.* *also: chock full

chokkie bikkies: chocolate biscuits

choked up: be emotionally affected and unable to speak ~ *I got all choked up when I heard the story.*

choof off: leave/depart ~ *It's 5 p.m., I'd better choof off.*

chook: 1) domestic fowl/chicken ~ *This chook hasn't laid any eggs for a few days.*

2) affectionate term for an older woman ~ *Aunt Maud's a great old chook.*

chop and change: change one's opinion about something ~ *The customer was always chopping and changing her ideas about the colour scheme.*

chop-chop: [spoken] request to hurry up ~ *Come on, chop-chop, let's go!*

chopper: helicopter

chuck: 1) throw ~ *Chuck it over here!*

2) vomit ~ *He chucked everywhere after eating bad food.*

chuck a u-ey: make a sudden U-turn when driving ~ *Just chuck a u-ey here.*

chuck a left: make a quick left-hand turn when driving

chuck a right: make a quick right-hand turn when driving

chuck a sickie: pretend to be sick so as to have a day off work ~ *I think he's just chucking a sickie so he can go to the beach.* *also: take a sickie

chuck a wobbly: have a tantrum/a show of anger *also: throw a wobbly/tantrum/turn/fit/tizzy; spit the dummy

chuck out: throw away/discard; forcibly evict ~ *1a) What will I do with it? Oh, just chuck it out. 1b) The troublemakers were chucked out of the nightclub.* *also: chuck away; throw out; throw away

chummy: friendly ~ *The two of them soon became chummy.*

chunder: [informal] to vomit

cicada: These singing insects, found throughout Australia, can be heard in great numbers during the days through summer. Together, the noise they create is deafening to the human ear, but they make the noise to avoid being eaten by birds.

ciggies: cigarettes ~ *I'll just have a quick ciggie before we leave.*

circle around: move/travel in a circular direction ~ *The birds circled around us a few times before flying away.*

clam up: refuse to talk ~ *I tried to get her to tell me, but she just clammed up.*

clamp down: become stricter (with a rule/law) ~ *Police are going to clamp down on speeding drivers.*

clamber up: climb with difficulty using hands and feet ~ *They clambered up the rock face.*

clanger: blunder/faux pas

drop a clanger: unwittingly say something that embarrasses or upsets someone ~ *I dropped a clanger by asking Sue where her husband was when they'd been divorced three months.*

clapped out: worn out; dilapidated ~ *She drives this clapped out old car.*

classy: elegant/superior ~ *We ate at a really classy restaurant.* *also: swish

clean: someone not to be doing/carrying anything illegal ~ *The police searched him, but he was clean.*

clean bill of health: confirmation of good health; condition ~ *The doctor gave me a clean bill of health.*

(make) a clean break (from): break away/disconnect totally from something ~ *To stay up-to-date, the company made a clean break from using outdated technology.*

clean forgot: entirely forget something ~ *I'm sorry, I clean forgot the appointment.* *also: plumb forgot

clean something/someone out: 1) illegally remove items from a place/premises ~ *Thieves broke into the house and cleaned me out.*

2) empty and clean a space/cupboard ~ *I spent all day cleaning out the garage.*

3) have nothing left (of something) ~ *The kids cleaned me out of all my spare change.* *see also: clear out[1]

clean record: of someone having no legal history of any wrongdoings or involvement in illegal/criminal activities ~ *He was let off with a caution because of his clean driving record.*

clean up: 1) make tidy/orderly; wash clean ~ *1a) I've a big mess to clean up. 1b) He has to clean up his room before he goes anywhere.*

2) be rid of undesirable persons/features ~ *The top golfer easily cleaned up the competition.*

3) make a large profit; win lots of money ~ *I cleaned up at last night's poker game.* *also: tidy up

clean up one's act: *see: lift one's game

clean as a whistle: extremely clean ~ *After a good wash it's as clean as a whistle.* *also: squeaky clean

come clean: tell the truth; confess ~ *It's best if you come clean and tell us what really happened.*

clean-cut: of a male to look neat/tidy/well groomed ~ *She prefers a clean-cut guy rather than someone unshaven and with untidy hair.*

spring-clean: thoroughly clean a space/room/house in springtime

clear as a bell: hear/understand/comprehend perfectly ~ *1a) I can hear you clear as a bell. 1b) Their instructions were as clear as a bell.*

clear as mud: confusing/misleading instructions/directions (often said humorously); something not easily understood ~ *The directions Fred gave me are as clear as mud.*

clear away: remove the contents; take items away to make a free space/area ~ *We have to clear away the equipment before we can leave.*

clear off: quickly depart; go away ~ *The thieves cleared off before the police arrived.*

clear out: 1) *see clean out.

2) pack one's belongings and permanently leave/depart a place ~ *I arrived home to find they'd cleared out.*

clear the air: 1) make stale air fresh/cool ~ *I opened the windows to clear the air.*

2) explain a misunderstanding; a confusing issue ~ *To clear the air, she met with staff to discuss the new arrangements.*

clear the way: prepare for; make ready for something ~ *His victory in suing the corporation cleared the way for others wanting to do the same.* *also: pave the way

clear up: 1) put something in place/make orderly ~ *There was a lot of clearing up to do after the guests had left.*

2) for the weather to become sunny/bright ~ *The weather's finally clearing up.*

3) solve a mystery/explain ~ *I'm glad we cleared up the misunderstanding between us.*

4) for an illness to ease/lessen ~ *This cream should clear up the skin rash.* *also: clear away

(get the) all clear: receive a signal/report that all is good ~ *The doctor's given me the all clear to return to work.*

cliff-hanger: 1) a close contest ~ *The game was a cliff-hanger; the teams were equal until the last minute.*

2) (in fiction) a suspenseful/dramatic situation occurring at the end of an episode, chapter, or scene ~ *This episode was a real cliff-hanger—I can't wait to watch the next one.*

(the) clink: prison; jail

clobber: 1) bash someone ~ *He got clobbered about the head.*

2) clothing ~ *He wore his best clobber to the party.*

3) lose badly in a sporting contest ~ *Our team got clobbered today.*

clock up: 1) reach a total ~ *He's clocked up more than fifty points for the club.*

2) record a distance travelled ~ *We clocked up more than a thousand kilometres on our journey.*

clog up: become obstructed ~ *Leaves can easily clog up your gutters.*

close up[1]: (klōz) 1) block/obstruct a passage/path ~ *A boulder closed up the cave's entrance.*

2) of a business to cease operating ~ *After twenty years in business they decided to close up shop.*

3) bring two edges together/into contact ~ *The wound should soon start to close up.*

close up[2]: (klōs) very near/close ~ *1a) Close up he's much more handsome. 1b) You can see the detail if you look close up.*

too close (klōs) **for comfort**: feel discomfort when a misfortune/threat is dangerously close ~ *That was a little too close for comfort.*

close-knit: loyal; united ~ *It's a close-knit community.*

clot: [informal] foolish, stupid person

clothesline: cord/rope strung between two points above the ground, used to attach recently washed clothes *see also: Hills Hoist

clothes-peg: a plastic/wooden clip to fasten wet clothes on to a clothesline

cloud over: for the sky to fill with clouds ~ *We cancelled the picnic when the sky started to cloud over* *also: cloud up

have one's head in the clouds: fantasise/daydream; be unaware of what's happening ~ *He's been walking around with his head in the clouds since he met her.*

carry clout: exert power; influence; importance; authority ~ *He carries a lot of clout.*

clock on: record one's arrival at work by means of an automated recording clock ~ *He clocked on at 10:00 a.m.*

clock off: record one's departure from work by means of an automated recording clock ~ *It happened just as everyone was clocking off.*

clock something: record as reaching a specified rate/time ~ *The speedster was clocked doing 130 kmh.*

clock up: 1) accrue ~ *He has clocked up over thirty years of service.*

2) achieve a victory ~ *The Tigers have clocked up their second win of the season.*

around the clock: all day and night ~ *Staff here work around the clock.*

watch the clock: wait anxiously/impatiently for time to pass ~ *He sat watching the clock waiting for their return.*

clown around: act foolishly ~ *Oh, will you stop clowning around!*

clucky: a woman eager to have children *also: broody

clue (someone) in: reveal, explain the facts ~ *I'll clue you in later.*

clued up: become informed of the facts ~ *Before we continue, is everybody clued up as to what they have to do?*

clueless: ignorant of the facts ~ *I'm clueless as to why they did it.*

haven't (got) a clue: *see: clueless ~ *I haven't got a clue as to what's happening.*

cluey: well informed; smart; intelligent ~ *Jane will be able to understand it, she's pretty cluey.* *also: know what's what

clutter up: fill a space in a disorderly way ~ *All the sporting equipment is cluttering up the garage.*

coast: where the ocean meets the land ~ *We're going to the coast for our holidays.*

the coast is clear: a signal that it is safe to proceed ~ *The coast is clear—you can come out now.*

Coat-hanger: [informal] Sydney Harbour Bridge

Sulphur-crested Cockatoo: Identified by its distinct sulphur-yellow crest and the yellow underside of its wings and tail, this large, white parrot is a familiar sight throughout Australia, and is quite at home in both rural and suburban areas. Its loud, distinctive screech is also readily identifiable.

cocky: 1) cockroach

2) cockatoo

3) a farmer

4) confident/self-assured ~ *He's a cocky young man.*

co-ed: co-educational—a mixed gender school

coffee shop: a place where coffee is sold and consumed; café (coffee shop is the more common conversational term used, whereas café is usually used in reference to the name of the establishment) ~ *1a) I'll meet you at the corner coffee shop. 1b) That new coffee shop is called Joe's Café.* *also: café; coffee lounge

coin a phrase: invent a phrase/term ~ *I'm not sure who exactly first coined the phrase "A fish out of water."*

cold: a viral throat infection ~ *I hope I didn't give you my cold.*

cold comfort: little encouragement/sympathy/consolation ~ *His apology was cold comfort to the victim.*

cold feet: loss of courage/nerve ~ *She got cold feet before giving her speech.*

(go) cold turkey: an abrupt withdrawal from drugs or alcohol ~ *The hardest, but the best, way to give up smoking is to go cold turkey.*

in cold blood: without mercy/feeling ~ *He was killed in cold blood.*

out cold: be unconscious ~ *The fall knocked him out cold.* *see also: knock cold

cold-hearted/cold-blooded: lacking emotion/feeling ~ *The cold-blooded killer was sent to jail.* *also: unkind; mean; unsympathetic

coldie: an icy cold can/bottle of beer *also: a cold one

Coles: Coles Supermarkets—national supermarket chain

comb through: thoroughly examine something ~ *I combed through everything, but still couldn't find it.*

come through: do what is required/anticipated ~ *I didn't expect that he could do it, but he came through in the end.*

come a cropper: (to) fall heavily ~ *She came a cropper off her horse.*

come a long way: 1) (to have) travelled a great distance ~ *Simon's come a long way to be with us today.*

2) (to have) improved greatly; progressed ~ *He's come a long way since he started his business ten years ago.*

come across: 1) find; discover by accident ~ *We explored the town and came across a little antique shop.* *also: happen across

2) communicate successfully ~ *She was very nervous and her speech didn't come across very well.*

comes across (as): appears/seems ~ *Her new boyfriend comes across as a nice guy.*

come adrift: be separated/unattached from something ~ *The trailer has come adrift from the car.*

come again?: [spoken] a way of asking someone to repeat what they said ~ *Sorry, I can't hear you. Come again?*

come along: 1) develop/improve ~ *How's the project coming along?*

2) come/go with someone ~ *You can come along with us if you like.*

3) appear ~ *We got on the next train that came along.*

come apart: break into pieces; disintegrate ~ *1a) It was so old it came apart in my hands. 1b) It comes apart for easy storage.*

come around: 1) regain consciousness ~ *It took a while for him to come around after his operation.*

2) visit someone ~ *You can come around any time.*

3) realise/accept someone else's ideas/way of thinking ~ *She eventually came around to my point of view.*

4) for a regular event to happen again ~ *The school holidays have come around again.*

come as you are: go somewhere in the clothes one is wearing ~ *Don't worry, just come as you are.*

come at: 1) make a threatening advance toward/attack someone ~ *The attacker came at me with a knife!*

2) attain/succeed/achieve/touch ~ *I couldn't come at eating some of the food that was offered.*

(come) at a price/cost: the disadvantages/negative aspects of achieving something ~ *1a) I can do that job for you—but at a price. 1b) Their freedom came at a price.*

come away from: 1) fall/break off something ~ *A brick has come away from the wall.*

2) move away from something ~ *Come away from there!*

come away with: journey/travel with someone ~ *Steve and Jan are coming away with us this weekend.*

come back: return to a place/someone ~ *1a) I'll come back later. 1b) I knew he'd soon come back to her.*

come between: 1) interfere with; cause disagreement between two people ~ *I'll never let anyone come between us.*

2) be placed/positioned between something ~ *July comes between June and August.*

3) be prevented from achieving/getting something ~ *He was determined that nothing would come between him and his career goal.*

come by: 1) obtain/acquire/find/get something ~ *How did you come by that large amount of money?*

2) visit a place ~ *You can come by the office and collect it.*

3) method of transport ~ *I commute by train.*

come close (klōs): 1) almost reach/attain/do something ~ *1a) I came that close to quitting. 1b) He came so close to winning.*

2) be almost correct in an approximation; almost equal someone/ something ~ *2a) I didn't even come close to estimating the total cost. 2b) Sandra's knowledge on the subject doesn't even come close to yours.*

come down on: 1) harshly berate/admonish/punish someone ~ *I know Dad would come down on me if I ever took drugs.*

2) fall on top of someone/something ~ *The wall almost came down me!*

come back down to earth: think realistically/practically ~ *An outright rejection brought him back down to earth.*

come down like a ton of bricks: severely criticise/berate ~ *I warn you, if you do it again I'll come down on you like a ton of bricks.*

come down with (something): experience the symptoms of an illness ~ *I feel awful. I think I'm coming down with the flu.*

come forward: offer information about something ~ *Police are urging any witness to please come forward.*

come from: originate/derive from ~ *1a) Where did this come from? 1b) Our neighbours come from Western Australia.*

come full circle: return to the original state/position/beginning ~ *After a varied career, things have come full circle and I now own the company I was first employed with.*

come good: improve ~ *My broken leg is finally coming good.*

come in: 1) enter a place ~ *1a) He came in through the back door. 1b) I'll come in next week to see you.*

2) [spoken] invitation/request (for someone) to enter ~ *Please, come in.*

come in(to) contact with: touch/communicate with something/ someone ~ *1a) The device is designed to stop the electrical wires coming into contact with anything else. 1b) I often come into contact with them.*

come in handy: describes something that will be useful ~ *Here, take this umbrella, it might come in handy.*

come into: acquire/receive/inherit ~ *She came into a lot of money when her uncle died.*

come into one's/its own: realise one's potential/capabilities ~ *After many difficult years, Steve had finally come into his own as a teacher.*

come into play: be an influencing factor ~ *All their skills came into play during the rescue operation.*

come off it: [spoken] stop joking; stop talking nonsense ~ *1a) Oh, come off it—it didn't happen like that! 1b) Come off it, Jack—you're just as guilty as all of us! 1c) Come off it—you're not serious, are you?* *also: come off the grass; get real

come off second best: be defeated; come in second to someone/something ~ *He was inexperienced and came off second best in the fight.*

come on¹: [spoken] cheer of encouragement ~ *Come on, you can do it!*

come on²: 1) used to placate someone ~ *Come on, it can't be all that bad.*

2) expressed when you don't believe what someone has said/done ~ *Oh, come on, who's going to believe that story?*

3) used to tell someone to hurry up ~ *Come on, or we'll be late!*

come on strong: 1) act/speak forcefully/aggressively ~ *He came on a bit strong with his sales pitch.*

2) make forceful romantic advances ~ *We only just met, but already he's coming on strong and wanting to be intimate.*

come out: 1) be revealed/emerge ~ *The truth will come out in the inquiry.*

2) (to) exit a place ~ *Everyone came out via the back door.*

come out in the wash: 1) be eventually revealed/become clear ~ *The truth is sure to come out in the wash during the investigation.*

2) of a stain/dirt to wash out of clothing ~ *Hopefully the stain should come out in the wash.*

come out with: express/tell/utter ~ *Children often come out with the funniest things.*

come out of the woodwork: appear out of nowhere/materialise ~ *All I did was mention free ice cream and the kids came out of the woodwork.* *also: come out of nowhere

come out on top: succeed/win ~ *Sam came out on top, as expected.*

coming right up: [spoken] ensuing; soon to be delivered/served ~ *1a) The feature movie will be coming right up after the commercial break. 1b) Dinner's coming right up.*

come over: 1) move over/above something ~ *It's come over all cloudy.*

2) visit someone/be visited by someone ~ *Our friends are coming over for dinner tonight.*

3) for one's behaviour/action/feelings to change/be altered ~ *I don't know what came over me, I don't usually act this way.*

come round: agree with/accept the facts ~ *After much persuasion he finally came round to my way of thinking.*

come to[1]: 1) reach a certain place/spot ~ *Turn left when you come to the top of the hill.*

2) develop into *also: amount to ~ *I don't think these clouds will come to much.*

3) involve/include ~ *When it comes to a fine dining experience, they offer nothing but the best.*

4) approach someone/a place ~ *Come to me if you need advice.*

5) recall/remember something ~ *I can't think of her name right now, but I'm sure it'll come to me.*

come to[2]: wake up; become conscious ~ *She hasn't come to after the operation as yet.*

come to the boil: for liquid to reach boiling point ~ *Has the water come to the boil yet?*

come to blows: begin to physically fight ~ *The argument worsened, and they ended up coming to blows.*

come to a close/end: end/finish something; progress to an end ~ *1a) The meeting has come to a close. 1b) Our journey is coming to a close.*

come to fruition: reach maturity; have the desired outcome; be successful ~ *Her years of hard work building her career have finally come to fruition.*

come to a full/dead stop: stop fully ~ *1a) Suddenly the car came to a dead stop. 1b) All conversation came to a stop when they walked into the room.*

come to grief: 1) suffer physically/mentally ~ *The race car driver came to grief during the last lap.*

2) fail ~ *Their marriage came to grief after only one year.*

come to grips with: understand/comprehend something difficult ~ *She was unable to come to grips with the tragedy.* *also: come to terms with

come to a halt/standstill: for proceedings/something to slow down and temporarily stop ~ *A minor road accident caused the traffic to come to a halt.*

come to harm: get hurt/injured/harmed ~ *Various safety measures are in place so we don't come to harm.*

come to a head: reach a crisis point in a situation ~ *The ill feeling between them came to a head today, resulting in a huge argument.*

come to life: be energised/awakened/aroused/animated ~ *1a) Visual and audio enhancements made the dinosaurs come to life. 1b) The party really came to life when the band started playing.*

come to much: 1) amount to a large amount of money ~ *The bill didn't come to much considering all the food we ate.* *also: count for much

2) be important/meaningful ~ *Their relationship didn't come to much.* *also: amount to much

come to realise: begin to understand/comprehend something ~ *I've only just come to realise how generous he is.*

come to terms with: accept/reconcile/confront ~ *He's finding it hard to come to terms with the tragedy.*

come to attention: a military command to stand erect, with eyes to the front, arms to the sides, and heels together ~ *The troops were commanded to come to attention.*

come to one's/someone's attention: become aware of/notice something ~ *1a) A very serious matter has just come to my attention. 1b) Your bad behaviour has come to the director's attention.*

come(s) to mind: for a thought/idea to be remembered ~ *1a) Just write the first word that comes to mind. 1b) A funny thought just came to mind.* *also: bring to mind; spring to mind; cross one's mind

come to think of it: [spoken] on reflection; when one has just remembered/thought of something ~ *1a) Now I come to think of it, it was last Friday, not Thursday. 1b) Come to think of it, I don't know where it is.*

come to this: have this result; result in this situation (either in a positive or negative way) ~ *Who'd have thought our original ideas on the project would ever come to this.*

come together: 1) merge ~ *This is where the two rivers come together.*

2) form a united group ~ *All the missing pieces of the story were coming together and he began to understand things a lot better.*

come through: 1) move from one area into another area; enter an area/room ~ *The doctor will see you now—please come through.*

2) approve/accept something ~ *The building application has finally come through.*

3) support/assist someone in a time of need ~ *You can depend on Paul; he always comes through as promised.*

come true: happen/materialize as expected; become real ~ *1a) At first this achievement was only a dream, but it's finally come true. 1b) I thought my dreams would never come true.*

come under: be classed/classified in an index ~ *The term "bee keeper" would come under the heading of apiarist.*

come under fire: 1) suffer a verbal attack ~ *The politician came under heavy fire when he revealed the new proposals.*

2) be under attack by bullets ~ *We came under fire from the gunmen.*

come unglued/unstuck: for a plan to fall apart/fail ~ *Their plan soon came unstuck.*

come up: 1) arise/manifest ~ *I'll have to cancel the appointment, something's come up.*

2) rise in rank/status ~ *Pete's come up in the world since then.*

3) rise above the horizon ~ *She likes to watch the sun come up.*

4) draw near/approach ~ *The wild animal came right up to me.*

5) something about to happen ~ *There's a meeting coming up next week.*

6) travel in a perceived northerly direction; move in an upward direction ~ *6a) My sister's coming up from Melbourne tomorrow. 6b) There are too many stairs, so I'll come up in the lift.*

come up for air: have a rest; take a break (from strenuous work/activity) ~ *I've been working hard all morning—I need to come up for air.*

come up heads: for a tossed coin to fall and display the side showing the head ~ *I called "tails," but it came up heads.*

come/rise up through the ranks: secure a leadership position by working through a sequence of lower positions ~ *She's come up through the ranks to become the chief executive of the company.*

come up to: of something to reach a certain height; mark; place ~ *1a) The top of her head comes up to his shoulders. 1b) Water came up to the top of the door.*

come up to expectations: be as good as expected ~ *The movie didn't come up to my expectations.*

come up to standard: be equal to; meet the expected requirement/standard/quality ~ *The repair work on the car didn't come up to standard.* *also: be up to standard

come up trumps: surprisingly complete an activity successfully; have a good result ~ *John came up trumps by securing front row tickets to the show.*

come up with: 1) find something/improvise ~ *1a) The coach was able to come up with a replacement player. 1b) He came up with some jobs to be done.*

2) develop an idea ~ *Travis came up with a fantastic plan.*

comfy: comfortable ~ *She found a comfy spot in the garden to read.*

common knowledge: facts/information that most people are aware of ~ *Oh, that's common knowledge.*

compo: compensation/monetary compensation ~ *He's off work on compo, due to a work-place accident.*

con: deceive/cheat/swindle for monetary gain ~ *1a) It's just a big con to get your money. 1b) I'd advise you not to do business with him, he'll con you out of all your money.*

con artist: one who is practises conning people

be conned into (something): be tricked into doing something ~ *Many people were conned into investing in a fraudulent company.*

conjure up: make an idea/imagine appear in one's mind ~ *The music conjures up images of a fast flowing river.*

conk out: collapse; break down with exhaustion; fail ~ *The old engine finally conked out.*

cooee: [spoken] a call used to attract attention ~ *Cooee! Can anybody hear me?*

within cooee: within calling distance ~ *1a) Our house is within cooee of the centre of town. 1b) You'd better fill up here, because you won't find a petrol station within cooee of where you're going.*

cook something up: 1) make plans/arrangements ~ *I'm not sure what, but they're cooking up something.*

2) invent a story/lie to achieve the desired result ~ *He cooked up a story to stay out of trouble.*

cool: 1) first rate; excellent ~ *His new car is really cool!*

2) acceptable; okay ~ *That type of behaviour is not cool!*

3) actual (without exaggeration) ~ *It cost a cool $2 million.*

4) composed/calm/relaxed ~ *It's best to stay cool in this situation.*

5) moderately cold ~ *I enjoy relaxing outside on cool evenings.*

cool down/off: 1) calm one's temper ~ *I'll speak to him after he cools off.*

2) make one's body temperature colder ~ *They jumped in the water to cool down.*

cool it: [spoken] request/plea for calm/order ~ *Cool it, will you! You won't achieve anything by getting upset.*

keep one's cool: maintain one's composure; stay calm; think clearly ~ *He's only trying to provoke you— it's best to keep your cool and walk away.* *also: keep a cool head; stay cool

lose one's cool: become upset/angry ~ *He provoked me so much I lost my cool and punched him.*

cooped up: be confined in a small space/area ~ *I have been cooped up in the house all weekend.*

cop/copper: [informal] policeman/policewoman

cop car: [informal] police patrol vehicle

cop an eyeful: 1) get a full view/good look at something ~ *Everyone copped an eyeful when her bikini top came off in the surf.*

2) a quantity of something going into one's eye ~ *I copped an eyeful of juice when I squeezed the orange.*

cop a beating/hiding: receive physical punishment; suffer the consequences

cop/get it: 1) receive a verbal punishment ~ *You're going to cop it from Mum when you get home!*

2) receive something unfavourably ~ *The storm missed us, but many houses in the next suburb copped it.*

cop the lot: get/receive everything/the full force of something ~ *Our town copped the lot from a bad storm.*

cop out: give up; quit; withdraw from doing something ~ *She's copping out of the job because it's too difficult.*

cop shop: [informal] police station

cop it sweet: 1) accept the consequence/penalty ~ *I know what I did was wrong, I just have to cop it sweet.* *also: take it on the chin

2) receive unexpected luck ~ *The students copped it sweet by being allowed to go home early.*

copycat: someone who imitates or copies another person

cordial: a fruit-based, non-alcoholic beverage diluted in water

cossie: swimming costume *also: swimmers; bathers; togs; swim suit; bathing costume; trunks

cost the earth: extremely expensive ~ *It would have cost the earth.* *also: cost a mint/packet

cosy up to: 1) snuggle up against someone for warmth ~ *The children cosied up to their mother.*

2) try to influence someone/gain favour ~ *Seeking dispensation, he cosied up to the authorities.* *also: cosy up to

cot: baby's bed

cotton on to: 1) comprehend; understand something ~ *I'm only just cottoning on to what's happening.*

2) find out; discover something ~ *They haven't cottoned on that we're here.*

cough up: 1) hand over; relinquish (goods/money) ~ *I had to cough up $200 to have it repaired.*

2) confess/disclose information ~ *The suspect finally coughed up to the authorities.*

3) expectorate; spit up

couldn't care less: an expression of indifference ~ *I couldn't care less about what they say about it—it's the truth.*

couldn't hack it: be unable to tolerate something any longer; unable to maintain doing something ~ *I couldn't hack the job, so I quit.*

council clean-up: A day when councils collect unwanted bulky household goods. Residents put the goods near the roadside for collection the weekend before the designated collection day.

count: consider something/someone to have value/worth/ importance ~ *I count her as a close friend.*

count against: regard as a negative against someone ~ *I hope this situation won't count against my good attendance record.*

count among: regard/consider/include someone in a group of others ~ *1a) After what happened I count myself as one of the lucky ones. 1b) She counts Steve as one of her closest friends.* *also: count as

count blessings: regard/consider one's/someone's good luck ~ *We're counting our blessings after escaping the avalanche.*

count for: be valid/worth something (said in the negative) ~ *Sometimes the effort I put into doing something counts for very little.* *also: count for much; come to much

count heads: count the number of people in attendance ~ *There should be thirty people here, but the head count showed only twenty-eight.*

count on something/someone: rely; depend on ~ *1a) You can count on Steve to remember to bring everything. 1b) Can I count on you to bake a special cake?*

count one/someone in: include/involve someone ~ *Don't forget to count me in when you finalise the number of people attending.*

count one/someone out: note someone as not being included/ involved ~ *You can count me out—I've already seen that movie.*

count oneself lucky: consider; believe oneself to be lucky ~ *Count yourself lucky you didn't go. It was a disaster.*

something/someone doesn't count: consider something worthless/unimportant ~ *His vote doesn't count.*

out for the count: be in a deep sleep ~ *Nothing could have woken me last night—I was out for the count.*

count up: total/add the amount of people/things ~ *I'd best count up the items that need to be sent.*

count up to: recite/list numbers in order to a specified/unspecified number ~ *My three-year-old can count up to twenty.*

lose count of: fail to remember the amount of times something has happened ~ *1a) Don't lose count of the number of the number of sheep already shorn. 1b) I've lost count of the times I've been asked that question.*

course of action: a plan ~ *After inspecting the damage, they decided the best course of action was to make immediate repairs.*

until the cows come home: do something/be somewhere for a long time ~ *At the rate you're going, we'll be here until the cows come home.*

cow-cocky: dairy farmer

cover charge: extra money (a fixed amount) added to the restaurant or nightclub bill for extra services or entertainment ~ *The admission price is relatively cheap, but there's a big cover charge.*

cover for someone: substitute/replace someone; do someone's work in their absence ~ *Julie will cover for me when I'm on holidays.*

cover ground: 1) traverse a given distance ~ *We were able to cover much more ground when the terrain was flat.*

2) discuss/write about a topic/subject ~ *We will be covering a lot of ground in today's lecture.*

covered in/with: be/spread over the surface of something ~ *1a) He came home covered in mud. 1b) I found the cake covered in ants.*

cover one's tracks: leave no clues; go undetected ~ *The thieves covered their tracks well.*

cover up: hide/conceal from view; keep secret ~ *He tried to cover up his involvement in the crime.*

cover up for someone: lie to conceal someone else's wrongdoing ~ *He knew his friend would be in big trouble so he covered up for him.*

blow one's cover: reveal someone's true identity; concealment ~ *They blew his cover when they realised he was an imposter.*

take cover: seek shelter ~ *We took cover from the heavy rain and hailstones.*

crack a joke: tell a joke ~ *He cracked jokes all night.*

crack a smile: smile slightly; give a small smile ~ *Although she was sad, she managed to crack a smile at her friend's funny jokes.*

crack down on: take severe measures/action on something ~ *The police are going to crack down on speeding drivers.*

crack (it): decipher/solve; interpret something ~ *I can't crack the puzzle.*

crack of dawn: at the first light of day; daybreak ~ *We're leaving at the crack of dawn.*

crack on to someone: pursue a romantic interest ~ *Tim was trying to crack on to her all night.*

crack the big time: finally find success ~ *His music now has international recognition. Finally, he'd cracked the big time!*

crack up: 1) laugh heartily ~ *Sam's jokes crack me up.*

2) mentally break down ~ *The strain is too much—I think she's cracking up.*

cracker: 1) a firework that explodes with a cracking sound

2) a thin, dry savoury biscuit

a cracker of: superlative—great/good/fantastic ~ *What a cracker of a party it was!*

not worth a cracker: useless/worthless ~ *The little gadget is not worth a cracker.*

cracking: exciting; fast ~ *We walked at a cracking pace.*

get cracking: a request to act quickly/hurry up ~ *Come on, get cracking! We have to leave soon.*

Cradle Mountain: Part of the Tasmanian Wilderness World Heritage Area, Cradle Mountain provides a range of environments to explore, including icy streams, rugged mountains, ancient forests, glacial lakes, and plenty of wildlife. It is one of the most popular natural areas in Tasmania.

crank: someone with a bad temper ~ *I'm a bit of a crank in the mornings.*

crank up: 1) get a machine started/warmed up; begin a process ~ *As soon as I crank up the computer, we'll begin.*

2) increase the volume/output ~ *Let's crank up the music and get this party going!*

cranky: angry/ bad tempered ~ *I'm really cranky with her for doing that.*

crap: 1) something inferior/shoddy/second-rate ~ *These cheap toys are really crappy.*

2) miscellaneous clutter/junk ~ *Will you get all your crap out of the car?!*

3) insolent/boastful talk; lies ~ *Don't listen to her, she's talking crap!*

crash: 1) fail financially ~ *Many investors were affected when the stock market crashed.*

2) fall asleep quickly ~ *I was so tired I just crashed when I got home.*

3) go to sleep ~ *Can I crash at your place after the party?*

4) enter a party/function uninvited ~ *A few people tried to crash the party.* *see also: gate crasher

crash through: break through something forcefully/at speed ~ *The out-of-control vehicle crashed through the wall of the house.* *also: smash through

craze: popular trend/activity ~ *I can't keep up with the latest craze.*

crazy about: infatuated/in love with somebody ~ *She's crazy about him!*

creature comforts: familiar things that makes one feel comfortable; at ease ~ *Shelley would prefer to stay at a motel rather than go camping—she likes her creature comforts too much.*

creature of habit: someone who keeps the same daily ritual ~ *Tom, being a creature of habit, buys the paper at 10 a.m. every day.*

creep: an undesirable/despicable person who inspires fear ~ *Stay away from him, he's a real creep.*

creep up: move gradually towards someone/something ~ *The water level is slowly creeping up.*

creep up on: *see: sneak up

the creeps: the sensation/feeling of fear; horror; unpleasantness ~ *Just thinking of spiders gives me the creeps.* *also: the willies/jitters/horrors

creepy crawlies: crawling insects ~ *Creepy crawlies give me the jitters.*

Cricket: Cricket is a bat-and-ball sport played by two teams consisting of eleven players each. It is played on an oval-shaped grassy field. It's been an established team sport for hundreds of years, and is played by over 100 countries around the world. It is followed with passion in many different countries.

crikey: [spoken] expression of astonishment/amazement ~ *Crikey! Look at the size of that!* *also: by cripes

crim: criminal

criminal record: a list of a person's criminal convictions ~ *She has a record a mile long.*

croc: crocodile

crook: 1) dishonest; illegal ~ *Don't have any dealings with him. He's a crook.*

2) unsatisfactory; bad; unpleasant ~ *The food was good but the service was crook.*

3) ill, sick ~ *3a) Geez mate, you're looking a bit crook. 3b) I've got a crook knee.*

go crook (on): become angry with; berate someone ~ *He went crook on her for coming home late.*

crooked /'krʊkɪd/: 1) a dishonest; fraudulent person ~ *No one trusted the crooked salesman.*

2) not straight ~ *That picture's crooked.*

crooked as a dog's hind leg: very crooked

crop up: arise; happen suddenly/unexpectedly ~ *Sorry I'm late, I had to deal with some problems that cropped up at the last minute.*

crossed lines: confusing; conflicting information ~ *We must have our lines crossed, I thought we were meeting today.* *also: have lines crossed

cross (one's/someone's) mind: to suddenly think of someone/ something ~ *1a) A disturbing thought just crossed my mind. 1b) It never crossed her mind that she might have upset everyone.* *also: entered one/someone's head

double cross: betrayal; an act of betrayal ~ *He double-crossed her by revealing her illegal activities to the authorities.*

crowd around: flock/swarm/gather around something ~ *The children crowded around to hear the story.*

crowd together: pack tightly (together) ~ *When you plant the flowers you need to crowd them together for effect.* *also: bunch together; jam together; pack together

crumpet: A small round bread with holes in one side, eaten hot with butter and sweet or savoury toppings.

not worth a crumpet: utterly worthless ~ *This gadget I bought is not worth a crumpet.*

crumple(d) up: wrinkled/scrunched/creased ~ *All his clothes were all crumpled up at the bottom of the bag.*

cruise around (in/on): ride/drive in a vehicle/boat; walk around aimlessly ~ *1a) We just cruised around the streets enjoying the sights. 1b) We spent the day cruising around the harbour on Steve's boat.*

crust: job; livelihood ~ *What do you do for a crust?*

cry one's eyes out: cry profusely ~ *I cried my eyes out when I heard the sad news.*

(for) crying out loud: [spoken] exclamation of surprise; anger; shock; annoyance ~ *1a) For crying out loud—shut the door! 1b) I've already done it, for crying out loud!*

far cry from: unalike; very different ~ *The city was a far cry from how the advertising brochure described it.*

in full cry: loudly/noisily ~ *The army of men rampaged in full cry through the town.*

cubbyhole: a comfortable, confined space/area; small room ~ *The children were having fun playing in the cubbyhole.* *also: cubbyhouse

cuddle up: *see: snuggle up

off-the-cuff: spontaneous/informal/unprepared ~ *1a) He was overheard making an off-the-cuff remark about the performance.* *also: speak off-the-cuff

cupcake: individual small cakes made in batches (one cupcake = one serving)

cup of tea: 1) a drink of tea

2) an enjoyable activity or scene ~ *2a) A hot bath on a cold night is just my cup of tea. 2b) Skydiving is not my cup of tea.* *also: not my thing (used in the negative)

cuppa: *see: cup of tea[1] ~ *Let's meet later for a cuppa.*

curly (one): a difficult problem; question; situation ~ *He asked me a curly question.*

curl up: to bend one's body (with one's knees almost touching the chin); roll into a ball/coil ~ *1a) The cat spent the day curled up in the chair. 1b) The dry, dead leaf was curled up at the edges.*

curl up and die: humorous expression for extreme embarrassment/ discomfort ~ *I could have curled up and died when I realised the embarrassing blunder I'd made.*

cushy: an easy task/job *pronounced as in "push" ~ *I wish I could have a cushy job like yours.*

(a) cut above: describes something of higher quality than another ~*1a) His suits are a cut above everyone else's. 1b) She thinks she's a cut above her work colleagues.*

cut back: 1) reduce spending ~ *You'll have to cut back spending if you want to save for a holiday.*

2) reduce the time/hours spent doing a job/task ~ *Ill health forced her to cut back her hours.*

cut corners: take shortcuts; use inadequate, cheap equipment ~ *Your good reputation in the industry will be compromised if you cut corners.*

cut in: 1) interrupt a conversation ~ *1a) I was talking to John when Sue rudely cut in. 1b) It's bad manners to cut in on someone's conversation.*

2) move quickly in front of/behind someone whilst driving ~ *The driver cut in front of me, forcing me to slam on the brakes.*

cut it/things fine: leave a small margin of time to do something ~ *Allowing ten minutes to get there is cutting it fine, don't you think?*

cut that/it out: [spoken] command to stop acting foolishly/stop doing something (for humorous or serious situations) ~ *1a) Oh would you please cut that out! 1b) Just cut it out, will you!!*

cut lunch: sandwiches ~ *I take a cut lunch to work to save money.*

cut(s) no ice: to have no conviction/influence on one/someone ~ *His excuse cuts no ice with me.*

cut out for: well suited to/qualified to do something ~ *I'm not cut out for this type of work.*

cut the crap: [spoken] request for someone to speak the truth/stop talking nonsense ~ *Why don't you just cut the crap and tell me the truth?*

cut through: 1) penetrate by cutting/slicing ~ *The sharp edge cut through the outer layers.*

2) travel across/pass over ~ *2a) The cyclist cut through the traffic to reach her destination on time. 2b) The plane cut a path through the sky.* *also: slice through

(be) cut up: be extremely upset; distressed ~ *She was cut up about her pet rabbit dying.*

clear-cut: certain; leaving no doubt ~ *They were able to provide clear-cut evidence in court.*

D

dab hand (at): expert; skilled at/adept ~ *She's a dab hand at cooking.*

daddy longlegs: a harmless house spider which has long, thin legs

dag: friendly term for an amusing/likable but slightly eccentric person ~ *I can't believe he did that. He's such a dag.*

daily grind: routine activities/work ~ *It's been difficult getting back into the daily grind after the long holiday.*

Daintree Rainforest: Covering an area of approximately 1,200 square kilometres, the Daintree Rainforest is north of Cairns in tropical Far North Queensland. It is home to the largest range of plants and animals on earth, and is over 135 million years old. This World Heritage-listed rainforest offers a wonderful outdoor experience that few other places in the world can offer.

daks: trousers/pants ~ *Nice daks!*

damper: This Australian bread is made traditionally from flour, water, and salt and then kneaded, moulded, and cooked in the coals of an open fire. Today's recipe includes butter, milk, and self-rising flour.

dance the night away: to dance all night ~ *What a romantic night—after dinner we danced the night away.*

dash away/off/out: leave quickly ~ *He's dashed off to the bank.*

dash someone's hopes: put an end to; ruin someone's dreams/aspirations/hopes ~ *Her hopes of making the team were dashed when she injured her ankle.* *also: have one's hope dashed

dashed if I know: [spoken] said when you don't know the answer/reason for something happening ~ *Dashed if I know where it went!*

do one's dash: to have missed a chance/opportunity to do something ~ *You've done your dash, now you'll have to wait another month before you can try it again.*

make a dash for: run/move quickly towards something/someone ~ *He made a desperate dash for the exit.*

damage: cost; expense ~ *What's the damage to fix it?*

damn: 1) an expletive ~ *Damn! The car won't start.*

2) very little; nothing; worthless ~ *It's not worth a damn—throw it away.*

3) excellent ~ *It's a damn good wine.*

dare say: suppose; think that something is likely/possible ~ *I dare say it will rain.*

(I) dare you (to): [spoken] what you say when challenging someone to do something ~ *I dare you to touch it!*

don't dare (to): be afraid to do something ~ *I don't dare touch it.*

don't (you) dare: [spoken] a stern warning telling someone not to do something ~ *Don't you dare do that!*

how dare you: [spoken] expression of indignation ~ *How dare you speak to me like that!*

dark horse: a person of unknown capabilities/qualities ~ *That new candidate is a bit of a dark horse.*

darn/drat: [spoken] a mild expletive ~ *Darn! I missed the bus.*

darnedest: a most remarkable/unusual/strange thing ~ *It was the darnedest thing I'd ever encountered.*

Darwin: capital city of the Northern Territory

Darwin stubbie: a large beer bottle

to date: until now ~ *I've visited the museum three times to date.*

day and night: all the time; continuously ~ *The premises is guarded day and night.*

days are numbered: limited time; time coming to an end ~ *His days as a popular recording artist are numbered.*

day by day: gradually; a little at a time ~ *Her health is improving day by day.*

day in, day out: every day/on a daily basis ~ *Day in, day out he keeps the same routine.* *also: days on end; day after day

day of rest: Sunday

a day off: a day where you don't work; don't do a particular task ~ *I'm taking a day off to see the doctor.*

a day out: a day where you go somewhere for pleasure/fun ~ *We had a day out at the zoo.*

all in a day's work: that something you do is part of your normal routine ~ *I don't mind doing it, it's all in a day's work for me.*

an off day: a day where you don't perform to your ability/usual standard ~ *I had an off day today and scored badly in golf.*

any day now: soon ~ *They should be arriving any day now.*

as plain as day: that something is easy to hear/see/understand ~ *I can see you as plain as day.*

call it a day: decide/agree to stop doing something ~ *It's too hot to work now, let's call it a day.*

field day: a day of great pleasure—especially at the expense of someone else ~ *Journalists had a field day with the scandal.*

from day one: from the first day; the beginning ~ *I knew from day one that this was the job for me.*

in somebody's day: in earlier times; when somebody was young ~ *1a) Not many people owned televisions in Grandma's day. 1b) He was a great artist in his day.*

in this day and age: now; in modern times ~ *You don't see cars like that in this day and age.*

live day to day: be concerned with the present and not the future ~ *Having survived a serious illness, she lives day to day.*

make a day of (it): extend an enjoyable activity to last the whole day ~ *We took a picnic lunch with us to the beach and made a day of it.*

make somebody's day: to make someone feel good on a particular day ~ *That news has really made my day.*

have/not have all day: to have/not have much time ~ *1a) It's a tedious job, but I've got all day to finish it. 1b) Will you hurry up. I haven't got all day!*

not my/somebody's day: what is said when nothing seems to go right ~ *It's just not my day. First, a water pipe burst, and then the car wouldn't start.*

. . . of the day: 1) existing at a particular period of time ~ *Travis is officer of the day.*

2) food served on any particular day in a restaurant ~ *The soup of the day is . . .*

on a daily basis: every day ~ *This equipment needs to be cleaned on a daily basis.*

one day: 1) an unspecified time in the future ~ *I'll get round to finishing it one day.* *also: some day; one of these days

2) a particular day in the past ~ *She walked out one day, never to be seen again.*

one of those days: a day where everything went wrong ~ *Sorry I'm late, it's been one of those days!*

take things one day at a time: to deal with issues as they happen/occur (don't consider a future time) ~ *Your recovery will be slow, so it's best to take things one day at a time.*

the other day: recently ~ *I heard about that the other day.*

these days: used to describe the present when comparing with the past ~ *I don't seem to have energy these days.*

to the day: the exact day ~ *I've been working here ten years to the day.*

to this day: even now, after time has passed ~ *To this day nobody knows what became of him.*

day-to-day: ordinary/commonplace ~ *Tired of the day-to-day routine, he booked an adventurous holiday.*

daydream: think happy/pleasant thoughts ~ *I must have been daydreaming—I can't remember you saying that.*

daylight savings: (also known as summer time) the setting forward of clocks by one hour from October to March

dawn on: to suddenly realise something ~ *I started getting ready for work when it dawned on me that it was Sunday!*

dead: 1) (intensifier) certain/sure ~ *I'm dead certain it was him.*

2) uneventful/slow ~ *Business was dead today.*

3) unexciting/boring ~ *The party was dead so I came home early.*

dead ahead: directly/immediately ahead/in front of ~ *Suddenly something appeared on the road dead ahead of us.*

dead beat: thoroughly exhausted/very tired ~ *I can't walk any further, I'm dead beat.* *also: dead on one's feet; dead tired

deadbeat: a lazy/useless person ~ *That deadbeat father makes his children do all the work around the home.*

dead and buried: an issue that is totally finished/closed and not to be discussed again ~ *This issue should be dead and buried.*

dead as a dodo: very dead; a long time dead; non-functioning ~ *It's is as dead as a dodo.* (A dodo is an extinct bird.)

dead duck: describes someone who, potentially, will be severely punished for something ~ *If you go anywhere near there again you're a dead duck!*

dead giveaway: something revealing; obvious ~ *His moustache was a dead giveaway.*

dead heart: the dry centre of Australia

dead heat: having no obvious winner; where the competitors finish at exactly the same time ~ *The race was a dead heat.*

dead loss: someone who/something considered worthless/useless ~ *Although they had high hopes, the project turned out to be a dead loss.*

dead on: exactly; precisely ~ *I arrived dead on time.*

dead ringer (for): someone who looks/appears exactly like someone else ~ *She's a dead ringer for that movie star.*

dead set: [spoken] when someone is certain about something ~ *1a) I won't change my mind—I'm dead set about it. 1b) Dead set—I didn't do it!*

dead silence: for there to be absolute silence ~ *There was dead silence when he walked into the room.*

dead straight: very straight ~ *It was a dead straight road.*

dead to the world: in a deep sleep ~ *I tried to wake her, but she was dead to the world.* *also: fast asleep

(be in) dead trouble: in serious trouble ~ *I'm gonna be in dead trouble when my parents get home.*

dead wrong: completely/utterly wrong ~ *You're dead wrong about it.*

wouldn't/would never be seen caught dead: that someone will never do something/be seen doing something ~ *1a) I'd wouldn't be caught dead wearing something like that! 1b) She'd never be seen dead with them. 1c) You wouldn't catch me dead doing that!*

leave for dead: abandon someone/a living creature because you assume they're dead

deadly: 1) extremely accurate ~ *The shooter's aim was deadly.*

2) strong/intense so as to possibly cause death ~ *The storm hit with a deadly force.*

3) as to cause death ~ *Those mushrooms are deadly, don't eat them!*

deadpan: expressionless ~ *She didn't see the humour, her expression remained deadpan.* *also: poker-faced

deaf as a doornail/post: very deaf ~ *You'll have to shout, she's a deaf as a doornail.*

deal in: 1) buying and selling/trading ~ *Harry deals in real estate.*

2) show interest in something ~ *He doesn't deal in criminal activities.*

deal with: 1) take action on an issue ~ *1a) I'll deal with you later. 1b) I don't want to have to deal with that aspect of it.*

2) do business with ~ *They're a good company to deal with.*

dirty deal: receive an unfair deal ~ *Don't buy from him. He gave me a dirty deal on my car.*

big deal: [spoken] exclamation of scorn/indifference ~ *So, you missed the bus—big deal!*

no big deal: [spoken] 1) that something done was not troublesome ~ *Helping them was no big deal.*

2) for something not to be a problem ~ *Missing one lesson is no big deal.*

a done deal: a final agreement/decision ~ *It's not a done deal until the paperwork's been signed.*

great deal: describes something/an act that is held in high regard ~ *1a) His continued support means a great deal to me. 1b) This special gift means a great deal them.*

good/great deal of: much effort/quantity ~ *1a) I spent a good deal of time trying to fix it. 1b) We spent a great deal of money on repairs.*

make a big deal (out of something): recognise (an event/ something) as important/special (also said in the negative) ~ *1a) We always make a big deal out of their yearly visit. 1b) It's my birthday today, but I don't want to make a big deal out of it.*

what's the deal?: [spoken] what's the plan/what's happening ~ *What's the deal with tonight's party? What time is everyone coming?* *also: what's the go?

what's the big deal: [spoken] a way of asking ~ 1) all's okay/ there's nothing to worry about ~ *The damage is minimal, what's the big deal ?*

2) that something is unimportant/trivial ~ *What's the big deal—I'm just going to the beach with my friends!*

oh dear: [spoken] expression of dismay/disappointment/shock ~ *1a) Oh dear—that's terrible news! 1b) Oh dear, look what's happened!* *also: dear, oh dear; dearie me; dear me; my, oh my; good grief

dice with death: do something risky/dangerous ~ *You'd be dicing with death if you went into the lion's cage at the zoo.* *also: cheat death

at death's door: close to dying; gravely ill *also: on one's death bed

be the death of: someone/something is causing you a lot of troubles/worries ~ *It would be the death of me if ever I had to leave this house.*

do something to death: repeat to the point of becoming monotonous/boring; lose impact due to overuse ~ *Vampire movies have been done to death.*

put to death: to execute/kill (as a sanctioned punishment) ~ *He was ordered to be put to death by his captors.*

sick to death: to an extreme degree ~ *I'm sick to death of hearing the same tune!*

death-trap: something extremely dangerous ~ *That unused mine, it's a death-trap.*

deck someone: punch someone to the ground ~ *They were arguing when suddenly the big bloke just decked the little guy.*

all hands on deck: in attendance/present ~ *It's going to be very busy, so it's all hands on deck.*

decked out in: be clothed/dressed ~ *He was decked out in his best clobber to go to the party.*

demo: demonstrate (an action) ~ *I don't know how it works. Can you give me a demo?*

dense: lacking in intelligence; stupid

dero/derro: [slang] a derelict person

devil of a . . . : extremely difficult/frustrating/hellish ~ *1a) I had a devil of a time trying to fix it. 1b) They had a devil of a job building it.*

Devonshire Tea: tea served with hot scones and a side dish of whipped cream and jam

dicey: dangerous/risky; of an uncertain outcome ~ *They were unsure whether to continue—the bridge looked a bit dicey.*

dicky: faulty/weak/unsound ~ *This old radio still works, but it's a bit dicky.*

dickhead: [coarse slang] fool/idiot

diddle someone: swindle; cheat ~ *A con artist diddled him out of all his money.*

diddly-squat: something worthless; a small amount of something ~ *He knows diddly-squat about it.*

didgeridoo: a long, tubular, wooden wind instrument

dja'ava?: shortened form of "did you have a . . . ?" ~ *Dja'ava good weekend?*

didn't bat an eyelid: showed no reaction/emotion ~ *She didn't bat an eyelid when she saw a large spider in her room.*

didn't know what hit him/her/me: be completely surprised/ confused/shocked ~ *She didn't know what hit her when she was told the bad news.*

die: to be extremely embarrassed/shocked ~ *1a) I nearly died when I saw him covered in blood. 1b) I died with embarrassment when I fell over in front of everyone.*

die by one's own hand: (to) commit suicide

die laughing: collapse on the floor in laughter ~ *We died laughing at John's antics.*

die with one's boots on: 1) die whilst fighting (in a battle; for a worthy cause)

2) die while actively working (in one's profession) ~ *Carol loves her job so much she says she'll never retire, but die with her boots on.*

diff: difference (only used in this form if preceded by "what's the . . .") ~ *What's the diff? They both look the same to me.*

different kettle of fish: a different issue/matter/situation ~ *What you're proposing is a different kettle of fish, it's got nothing to do with this issue.*

dig in: spoken signal to begin eating ~ *Come on everyone—dig in!*

dig one's heels in: remain stubborn/refuse to yield ~ *I'm going to dig my heels in in this matter—you won't change my mind.*

dig up: 1) find by digging in the earth/ground ~ *They dug up an old watch in the sand.*

2) reveal/discover something ~ *I'll see what information I can dig up.*

digger: a returned soldier/serviceman from World War I

dilly-dally: waste time/stall/dawdle ~ *Stop dilly-dallying or you won't finish on time!*

dime a dozen: cheap/abundant/commonplace ~ *Books are a dime a dozen at the flea market.* *dime: ten-cent coin in U.S. currency

dimwit: a stupid/unintelligent person *also: dim-witted

ding-dong: 1) a foolish/stupid person

2) a physical fight ~ *It was a ding-dong fight.*

Dingo: a wild dog of Australia found in all states except Tasmania

dinkum: genuine/authentic ~ *They are dinkum Aussies.* *also: dinky-di

dirt cheap: very inexpensive ~ *They're dirt cheap at the markets.*

hit the dirt: fall to the ground ~ *He hit the dirt hard after being thrown from the saddle.*

dirty book/movie: pornographic/obscene ~ *We were expecting something else, but in fact it was a dirty movie.*

dirty tricks: corrupt; underhanded activities ~ *I see Sam is up to his dirty tricks again.*

play a dirty trick: unfairly/unkindly trick someone; make a bad joke ~ *He played a dirty trick on me in the classroom and the teacher blamed me!*

dirty word: obscene/vulgar/swear word *also: four-letter word

dirty work: an unpleasant job or task ~ *Why don't you get someone else to do your dirty work?*

(give/get) a dirty look: a look of contempt/disgust ~ *She gave him a dirty look then walked away.*

have a dirty mind: tending to have lewd/vulgar/obscene thoughts ~ *That's not what I meant; you've just got a dirty mind.* *also: have one's mind in the gutter

dish out: give/deal out/dispense advice or punishment/abuse ~ *1a) Dan's dishing out bad advice again. 1b) The teacher is good at dishing out punishment.*

dish the dirt on: reveal intimacies/spread gossip ~ *For $5,000 she was prepared to dish the dirt on her ex-lover.*

dish up: serve food ~ *Everyone come to the table—I'm going to dish up the dinner.* *also: serve up; plate up

a dish: a very attractive person ~ *1a) That new guy in accounts is rather dishy. 1b) Wow, what a dish!* *also: dishy

at someone's disposal: make available for one/someone to use whenever/however they wish ~ *We had a car at our disposal.*

ditch something: 1a) discard/abandon ~ *He ditched me for someone else! 1b) The crook ditched the gun in the river.*

2) make an emergency landing in the ocean ~ *The pilot was forced to ditch in the ocean.*

(the) ditch: humorous term for the Tasman Sea (between Australia and New Zealand)

ditch out: leave/abandon after making plans/committing to something ~ *Tony ditched out on us when he found out how much work was to be done.*

across the ditch: on the other side of the Tasman Sea ~ *It's but a short flight across the ditch.*

last ditch: place of last defence; last resort ~ *... made a last ditch effort to escape.*

divvy up: share/portion out ~ *They divvied up the winnings between them.*

DIY: Do-It-Yourself

do: 1) party/event ~ *We're having a big do at our place on Saturday.*

2) hairstyle/hairdo ~ *Hey, I like the new do!*

do a 180: turn around 180 degrees and go in the opposite direction ~ *When I called my dog he did a 180 and ran back to me.*

do a 360: do a 360 degree turn/turn in a complete circle ~ *The car skidded and did a 360.*

do an about face: reverse one's opinion/decision/course of action ~ *The authorities did an about face on a previous ruling.*

do away with: throw away/discard ~ *Finally I can do away with the walking stick.*

do it the hard way: do something in a difficult manner/way ~ *You're doing it the hard way like that. Let me show you an easier way.*

do (one's) block: lose your temper/have an angry outburst ~ *I did my block when I came home and found the mess everyone had made.*
*also: do one's nana

do (one's) dough: to foolishly spend money; lose money through gambling ~ *No more spending for me, I've done my dough.*

do (oneself) in: commit suicide

do the honours: perform a pleasant task/duty ~ *May I do the honours and present the awards?*

do the right thing: make a respectful decision; honour someone's beliefs ~ *She did the right thing by telling the authorities.*

do the world of good: benefit greatly; do good ~ *A holiday will do you the world of good.*

do up: 1) restore/renovate something ~ *We're going to do up the old house then sell it.*

2) fasten/close something ~ *The outfit will look better if you do up your jacket.*

do without: manage without something ~ *I can do without your help, thank you.*

do you mind: [spoken] indignant reply to something said/done ~ *Do you mind? I was sitting there!*

do/would you mind: [spoken] a polite way to ask/request something ~ *1a) Do you mind if I smoke? 1b) Would you mind closing the window? 1c) Would you mind not saying that?* *also: is it okay/alright; may/can I

(I) don't **mind if I do**: [spoken] a polite way to say "yes please" ~ *Would you like some more tea? Don't mind if I do.*

if you don't mind: 1) [spoken] a polite request ~ *If you don't mind, I'd like to have a rest now.*

2) [spoken] an angry rebuke ~ *I'd like to do it my way—if you don't mind!*

3) [spoken] a polite way of saying "yes, thank you" ~ *Would you like some help? Yes, if you don't mind.*

dob someone in: inform against ~ *1a) Close friends would never dob each other in. 1b) Someone dobbed him in to the authorities.*

(just) what the doctor ordered: the exact/precise thing needed/required ~ *A cold beer on a hot day is just what the doctor ordered.*

dodgy: untrustworthy/unreliable/risky/suspicious ~ *The deal seems a bit dodgy to me.*

doggie-bag: a container supplied by a restaurant for leftover/ uneaten food that the customer may take home

go to the dogs: deteriorate/degenerate ~ *This house used to be kept in good condition, but over the past six months it has really gone to the dogs.*

dole: social security benefits; monetary payment from the government given to people who are unemployed

dole-bludger: an unemployed person who continues to receive the dole, but has no intention of working

bottom dollar: all one's money (to the last coin) ~ *I bet your bottom dollar it won't work.*

doll up: (of a woman) to dress in her best clothes ~ *She got dolled up to go to the party.*

domestic (dispute): threatening/violent/abusive act inflicted by one member of a household on another

a done deal: [spoken] what you say when you seal a deal ~ *So, is it a done deal?*

done and dusted: successfully/fully completed ~ *There's no need to worry about doing it—it's all done and dusted.*

done for: doomed to destruction/death ~ *We're done for now—the boat's sinking!*

done in: exhausted; worn out ~ *I'm done in—I need a rest.*

done like a dinner: utterly defeated ~ *How did the game go? Oh, we got done like a dinner.*

the done thing: socially acceptable/normal practice ~ *Sending your hosts a thank you note is the done thing.*

not the done thing: something not socially acceptable ~ *Smoking during a meal is not the done thing.*

done to a T: perfectly completed ~ *The pies were done to a T.*

done with: finished with/doing something ~ *I'm done with drinking and gambling.*

all done: to have finished doing something ~ *1a) Are you all done? 1b) We're done here.*

been there, done that: to have had the same experience; been in the same predicament ~ *I understand why you're worried, I've been there, done that.*

now you've done it: 1) [spoken] interjection at someone's clumsiness/ineptness ~ *Now you've done it. It's broken!*

2) when someone has upset someone else ~ *Now you've done it—you insulted her and she's crying.* *also: you've done it now ~ *You've done it now—you missed out because your application was late.*

I've/you've done it: [spoken] congratulatory cry uttered when a difficult task/activity has been accomplished ~ *You've done it! You won!*

(be/get it) over and done with: complete/finish a difficult/ awkward task ~ *I prefer to get the housework over and done with early so I can relax.*

donkey's years: a very long time ~ *I haven't seen him for donkey's years.*

don't hold (your) breath: [spoken] don't wait in anticipation for something that might not or won't ever happen ~ *She said she'd be finished tomorrow, but don't hold your breath.*

don't know if one is Arthur or Martha: to be very busy ~ *There's too much happening right now, I don't know whether I'm Arthur or Martha.*

don't make me laugh: [spoken] expression of ridicule/scorn ~ *Don't make me laugh—you know Dad won't let us do that!*

doona: quilted bed cover; duvet

(from) door to door: from one house to another (along a street) ~ *Police went door to door in the hope of finding more leads to the crime.*

answer the door: open the door ~ *Could you answer the door?*

behind closed doors: do something in secret ~ *They discussed the deal behind closed doors.*

close (its) doors: cease trading/operating ~ *Tough competition is forcing many smaller outlets to close their doors.* *also: shut up shop

darken someone's door: visit a place (unwelcomed) ~ *Alan is such a vile person I don't want him to ever darken my door again!*

get a foot in the door: have the opportunity to achieve success in your career ~ *I've got my dream job in publishing, but it took me two years to get a foot in the door.*

keep the wolf from the door: have enough money to exist ~ *She works two jobs to try to keep the wolf from the door.*

leave the door open: allow for the possibility of something further to happen ~ *He left the door open for discussion.*

open the door to something: provide an opportunity for advancement; to make something possible ~ *Doing the degree will open the door to a range of career choices.*

(be) a doormat: someone who meekly submits to dominance; open to mistreatment by others ~ *Sadly, she's become somewhat of a doormat to her domineering husband.*

slam the door in someone's face: rudely reject/dismiss someone ~ *He wanted to discuss it with them but they slammed the door in his face.*

to the door: directly to one's/someone's premises ~ *The parcel was delivered to my door the next day.*

dooverlackie: a name given to unknown items/objects ~ *What does this dooverlackie do?*

a doozy of: outstanding/crazy/extraordinary/bizarre/daunting /difficult ~ *1b) Wow, that's a doozy of a hat you've got there! 1b) Man, I've got a doozy of a headache!*

double-cross someone: contradict a prior agreement; betray/ deceive someone ~ *She double-crossed me be telling the authorities!*

double or nothing: double the outcome of a previous bet or cancel the bet ~ *How much do you want to bet? Double or nothing.*

double(d) over: bent over in laughter or pain ~ *The cramps were so severe I was doubled over in pain.* *also: bent over

double up: share quarters; have two people sharing space/area designed for one ~ *There's only one bicycle, so we'll have to double up.*

on the double: immediately/without delay ~ *I'll be there on the double.*

double-decker: a bus with an upstairs and downstairs

double-Dutch: gibberish; nonsense; unintelligible speech ~ *He's talking double-Dutch.*

double-park: to park (in the street) alongside another car

dough: [informal] money *also: bread/moolah

down: sad; dejected; gloomy ~ *He was feeling down because he missed out on the team selection.*

down something: drink or eat something quickly ~ *... downed a sandwich before racing out the door.*

down at heel: poor; impoverished

down in the dumps/mouth: miserable/sad/depressed/dispirited ~ *She's really down in the dumps since she lost her job.*

down the drain: lost/wasted ~ *All the effort I put into the failed project has gone down the drain.*

(further) down the track: later on; in the near future ~ *We'll do more renovations further down the track.* *also down/along the line

down to last dollar: having very little money ~ *I'd lend you the bus fare, but I'm down to my last dollar.*

down tools: finish/cease work for the day ~ *It's time to down tools and go home.*

Down Under: [informal] Australia ~ *We're heading Down Under for the holidays.*

downhill: of something deteriorating/worsening ~ *Her health seems to have gone downhill since I last saw her.*

downright: utter; to an extreme degree ~ *That was downright rude of her to say that!*

down-to-earth: realistic; matter-of-fact; without pretence; honest ~ *He's a down-to-earth, hard-working citizen.*

(a) drag: something tedious/boring ~ *The job's a real drag.*

take a drag: inhale smoke from a cigarette ~ *He took a long drag of his cigarette before announcing his decision.*

drag away: push/pull away from something ~ *She didn't want to leave, so we had to drag her away.*

drag on: last/persist for a long time ~ *His speech dragged on for too long.*

dragged into: be convinced to do something you don't want to do ~ *I didn't want to go, but I was dragged into it.*

Bearded Dragon: Bearded dragons are one of the most popular species of reptiles found in Australia. Being common, most Australians are familiar with them or have seen them in the wild. There are a variety of species found throughout Australia.

drag queen: a male who dresses in women's clothes and acts like a female

no drama(s): [spoken] means that something you did for someone was no trouble ~ *Thanks for doing that. It was no drama.* *see also: no worries

drape around: casually hang/wrap something over something ~ *She draped the shawl over her shoulders.*

draw a blank: 1) get no reply/response ~ *I asked her if she knew the answer, but she drew a blank.*

2) be unable to remember/recall something ~ *I tried to remember his name, but I drew a blank.*

draw blood: cause to bleed; bleed ~ *The bite drew blood.*

draw conclusions: make a judgement after considering the information ~ *Without wanting to draw conclusions, it seems they are guilty.*

draw out: coax/persuade ~ *She was unable to draw out the frightened cat from its hiding place.*

draw the short straw: be chosen for; have to do the least enjoyable task/duty ~ *Jack, you drew the short straw. You have to clean the bathroom this time.*

draw straws: a method of selection to decide which member of a group will be first to perform a task ~ *We'll draw straws to see who goes first.*

draw the line: set/define limits ~ *1a) I don't mind them going to the party, but I draw the line at them coming home at 3 a.m. 1b) I draw the line when it comes to lending money to my friends.*

draw up: 1) compose/write; formulate/devise a formal contract/ proposal ~ *I'll have the contact drawn up by tomorrow.*

2) halt/bring to a stop ~ *The car drew up in front of the building.*

(go) back to the drawing board: revise/re-think one's plans/ strategies; start something over again ~ *We had to go back to the drawing board when the project failed.*

drawn out: prolonged; never ending ~ *1a) I got bored listening to his drawn out speech.*

dream up: invent; imagine something ~ *She dreamt up a plan to save the company.* *also: think up

wouldn't dream of: would never consider doing something (often a humorous response) ~ *1a) Don't do anything stupid while we're gone. Oh, I wouldn't dream of it. 1b) I wouldn't dream of doing anything that will upset the proceedings.*

dreaming: believing in/imagining something unrealistic ~ *You must be dreaming if you think she'll go out with you.*

dredge up: locate; unearth/reveal after an investigation/search ~ *1a) They dredged up the body from the river bed. 1b) She dredged up some unfavourable facts about the organization.*

dress up: get dressed in one's best clothes ~ *We got dressed up for the occasion.*

dressed to the nines: to be very well dressed; overdressed ~ *Jane, as usual, came dressed to the nines.* *also: dressed to kill; spruced up; spiffed up

dressing down: give/receive a severe reprimand ~ *Mum gave me a dressing down after I arrived home after 2 a.m.*

dressing gown: bathrobe

dribs and drabs: in small amounts at irregular intervals ~ *People arrived at the party in dribs and drabs.*

drift along/around: 1) float/be carried along ~ *The boat drifted along with the strong current.*

2) travel with no direction/aim ~ *After finishing his studies he drifted from job to job.*

drift apart: for people to gradually lead separate lives/lose personal contact ~ *We were once close friends, but we've drifted apart over the years.*

drift in: of something/someone to gradually/slowly continue on/move into an area ~ *1a) The boat drifted in to the shore. 1b) The crowd drifted in to the auditorium.*

drift off/out: move slowly away ~ *1a) The crowd soon drifted out of the building. 1b) Free from its anchor, the boat drifted off to sea.* *also: drift away

drift off to sleep: fall asleep gradually ~ *I drifted off to sleep watching TV.*

drift towards: slowly move towards someone/something ~ *Something was drifting towards the boat.*

drift with the tide/wind: travel/move about aimlessly ~ *He has no place he calls home—he just drifts with the tide.*

get one's/someone's drift: understand/comprehend what is being said/implied ~ *I thought I'd explained it properly, but he didn't seem to get my drift.* *also: Do you get my drift? Do you understand what I mean? *see also: getting at

if you get my drift: [spoken] a way of confirming; making sure that someone has understood/comprehended what you said (sometimes said as a threat) ~ *If we see you here again there might be trouble, if you get my drift.*

drifter: one who moves aimlessly throughout an area

know the drill: know the usual procedure; what needs to be done in a situation ~ *I needn't tell you what needs to be done—you know the drill.*

drink: 1) a body of water ~ *The sailboat tipped and they all ended up in the drink.*

2) drink alcohol ~ *It is not advised to drink then drive.*

drinks: a party/gathering where no food is served ~ *We're having a few people over for drinks on Sunday if you want to come.*

drink someone under the table: drink more alcohol than someone at any one time ~ *Oh, I could easily drink him under the table.*

drink to someone/something: *see: propose a toast

drink too much: regularly drink too much alcohol ~ *I'm worried about Steve, lately he's been drinking too much.* *also: drink like a fish; (be) a heavy drinker

drink up: [spoken] call to fully consume one's drink ~ *1a) Drink up, everybody, the bar is about to close. 1b) Drink up, everybody, there's more wine coming.*

drink (something) down: consume/drink all (of the drink in the glass) ~ *Here, drink this medicine down.*

drink-drive: to drive a vehicle whilst under the influence of alcohol ~ *He was jailed on a drink-driving charge.*

drive around: 1) drive/be driven in a vehicle ~ *I can drive you around to Ted's house.*

2) steer/propel a vehicle around something ~ *I had to drive around the block to find a parking space.*

drive someone/be driven around the bend: cause someone to go crazy/be caused to go crazy ~ *His incessant questions drove me around the bend.* *also: drive me nuts/crazy; around the twist; up the wall

drive away: leave (a place) in a vehicle ~ *The car pulled up beside us then drove away.*

drive someone/something away: repel; cause something/someone to leave a place ~ *We built a scarecrow to drive the birds away from the grapevines.*

drive someone/one to drink: be the reason someone drinks alcohol to escape their frustrations (often used humorously) ~ *You're driving me to drink!*

drive to distraction: cause someone to be unable to function/think properly ~ *That constant loud banging is driving me to distraction!*

drive through (a place): travel without stopping from one side of a town/city to the other ~ *We didn't have time to stop so we just drove through all the little towns.*

drive-through: the service window at a restaurant/fast food outlet where one can remain in the car to order their food

Driza-bone: Originating from the term "dry as a bone," Driza-bone is a company that makes full-length waterproof riding coats and clothing mainly worn by rural dwellers.

drop: 1) punch someone to the ground in a fight ~ *He was so drunk I could have easily dropped him.*

2) end a relationship ~ *When she discovered he was seeing another girl, she dropped him.*

3) (in tennis) to lose a set ~ *She only dropped two sets in the tournament.*

drop a hint: give a clue ~ *I don't know the answer—could you drop me a hint?*

drop a line: send a brief letter to someone ~ *I'll drop you a line when I get there.*

drop away: of the ground to slope downwards ~ *Here, the land drops away to a sheer cliff.*

drop in (on): pay someone a casual visit ~ *I'll drop in you next week.* *also: drop by/around

drop it: [spoken] a way of asking someone to stop talking about a particular subject ~ *I've heard enough. Just drop it, will you!*

drop like flies: get sick/faint; die in great numbers ~ *Due to the extreme heat, people watching the concert were dropping like flies.*

drop of rain: quantity of rain ~ *We haven't had a drop of rain since last month.*

drop of: a small measure of liquid (to drink) ~ *I like a drop of wine with dinner.*

drop off: 1) fall asleep ~ *He drops off watching TV on the lounge most nights.*

2) a humorous term for die ~ *Our pet bird dropped off his perch.*

3) a weakening/decline in numbers ~ *Business has dropped off in the last week.*

drop something/someone off: leave someone/something at a particular place ~ *I'll drop you off at the station at 5 p.m.*

a wee drop: a very small measure of liquid (to drink) ~ *I'll have just a wee drop, thanks.*

drought: a long period of time without significant rainfall

in a drought: experience drought conditions ~ *This area of land has been in a drought for one year.*

drover: A drover is an experienced stockman who moves livestock over long distances, usually in search of better feed or water during a drought. A traditional team of drovers numbered seven people—the boss, four stockmen/women, a cook, and a horse-trailer, whose job it was to move ahead and set up the night camp. A person who accompanies a mob of cattle on a transport train to a new location is called a cattle-train drover. Queensland is now the only state that runs cattle trains. Traditionally, drovers rode on horseback, but these days drovers are assisted with modern equipment such as trucks, all-terrain vehicles, and motorcycles.

(in) droves: in great numbers ~ *Tourists came in droves to see the spectacular garden.*

druggie: [informal] a drug addict; habitual drug user

drum up: entice/lure/obtain ~ *It's useful marketing tool to drum up business.*

(a) drunk: someone who drinks too much alcohol ~ *That old drunk must live permanently at the pub.*

as drunk as a skunk: extremely drunk ~ *I was as drunk as a skunk last night and now I have a killer hangover.*

dry: dry ginger ale (mixer drink) ~ *I'll have a brandy and dry please, barman.*

dry off: become dry; dry oneself ~ *He dried off by the roaring fire.*

(the big) dry: a prolonged period of drought ~ *We were hoping the predicted rain will put an end to the big dry.*

dry as a bone: very dry

dry up: 1) stop being available ~ *The organization will collapse if the funds dry up.*

2) become completely dry ~ *The dams will soon dry up if the drought continues for much longer.*

duck in/out/under: 1) momentarily go in/out of (a space/an area) ~ *He's just ducked out for a minute.*

2) quickly go underneath something ~ *It's easier to just duck under the fence.* *also: slip out

(a) dud: something worthless/faulty; counterfeit ~ *This cheap radio's a dud.*

duds: pants; trousers

dump: 1) dispose of/get rid of something ~ *The assailant dumped the weapon in the river.*

2) a squalid, run down house/building ~ *You should see the dump he lives in!*

3) end a relationship ~ *She dumped me for someone else!*

dummy: 1) baby's pacifier

2) store mannequin

3) [derogatory] someone unintelligent/stupid/dumb

dung: animal poo/droppings

dunno: [informal] I don't know ~ *1a) I dunno where it is. 1b) Oh, I dunno!*

dunny: [informal] toilet *also: lav (lavatory)/throne/toot/loo

dunny paper: toilet paper

durry: [informal] cigarette

dwindle away: diminish/shrink in size/quantity ~ *The crowd slowly dwindled away.*

dying for/to: long to/yearn for something ~ *1a) I'm dying for a coffee. 1b) I'm dying to meet him.*

E

each to their own: that one should respect someone's ideas/likes and dislikes ~ *It's not the type of music I'd listen to, but each to their own.*

Wedge-tailed Eagle: The Wedge-tailed eagle is Australia's largest living bird of prey, and one of the largest eagles in the world. It is found throughout mainland Australia, Tasmania, and Southern New Guinea.

believe one's ears: what you say when you can't believe what you're hearing ~ *I couldn't believe my ears when they announced Sue as the winner.*

easy on the ears: a pleasant/gentle sound ~ *This music is easy on the ears.*

prick one's ears up: listen attentively/with interest ~ *My ears pricked up when I heard your name mentioned.* *also: prick up one's ears; all ears

earlier on in the piece: at an earlier time in a process/activity ~ *Why didn't you tell me earlier on in the piece that you hate flying?*

early bird: 1) someone who gets out of bed early

2) someone who arrives before anyone else

(an) early mark: permission to leave school/class early/before the usual finishing time, usually preceded by have or take ~ *You got all the questions right, so you can have an early mark.*

earshot: within hearing distance ~ *It's okay, you don't have to whisper—he's out of earshot.*

ear-splitting: painfully loud ~ *She let out this ear-splitting scream.*

cost the earth: (be) very expensive ~ *It must have cost the earth.* *also: a packet

what/how/who on earth: a spoken exclamation to show extreme surprise/anger/confusion ~ *1a) What on earth is that thing? 1b) How on earth did you do that? 1c) Who on earth could have done such a horrible thing?* *also: what in the world

ease away: 1) move slowly away from something ~ *The train eased away from the platform.*

2) slowly diminish ~ *A good soak in a hot spa eased away the muscle pain.*

ease off: become less intense; abate ~ *I'll leave when the rain eases off.*

ease up: put less urgency/pressure on something/someone ~ *You should ease up on her to get top grades in school.*

at ease: relaxed/comfortable; free from anxiety/worry ~ *1a) She feels at ease when she is with them. 1b) He's at ease when he's performing on stage.*

2) a command to troops to assume a relaxed position

easy as pie: easy to do; easily done ~ *It's as easy as pie to do.* *also: easy as ABC; easy as falling off a log; easy done; easy peasy; dead easy

easy does it: [spoken] request to be moderate; do something carefully ~ *Easy does it—it's very fragile.*

easy money: 1) money earned using minimum effort ~ *It's a boring job, but it's easy money.*

2) money obtained by fraud/deception

easy pickings: items/goods readily obtained ~ *In summer there are easy pickings to be had from careless tourists.*

(an) easy target/prey: someone gullible/unsuspecting ~ *He's such an easy target to play tricks on.*

(that's) easy for you to say: [spoken] used to tell someone that something may be easy/simple for them but it's not easy/simple for you ~ *That's easy for you to say, you don't face the same difficulties as I do.*

easy street: be financially secure; have no money worries ~ *We've been living on easy street since winning the lottery.*

easy to come by: readily available; easily obtained/purchased/found ~ *1a) Romance novels are easy to come by. 1b) Please don't break them, they're not easy to come by.*

easy to see: something obvious; not difficult to understand/comprehend ~ *1a) It's easy to see you've done this before. 1b) It's easy to see you're sisters.*

go easy (on): 1) use sparingly ~ *Go easy on the butter, that's all there is.*

2) show leniency ~ *Go easy on him, it wasn't all his fault.* *also: go soft on

take it/things easy: relax; be careful/calm ~ *1a) After such a busy week, I'm going to take it easy all weekend. 1b) It's been such an ordeal for you, why don't you go home and take things easy for a while.*

(take the) easy way out: choose the easiest way to be free of a difficult situation ~ *Quitting now would be the easy way out.*

easy-going: relaxed; calm; nonchalant ~ *Ted's pretty easy-going, I'd talk to him about it.*

eat and run: eat quickly then leave ~ *I hate to eat and run, but I've a train to catch.*

eat away at/into: gradually harm/destroy (physically/mentally) ~ *1a) His guilty conscience had been eating away at him for quite some time. 1b) Termites have eaten away the main support beam.* *also: gnaw away/at/into; nibble away

eat out of someone's/one's hand: be compliant/submissive; dominated by another ~ *The group commander soon had even the most rebellious recruits eating out of his hand.*

eat someone/one alive: 1) angrily criticise/berate someone ~ *Don't get into an argument with him, he'll eat you alive.*

2) be bitten repeatedly by an insect ~ *The mozzies will eat you alive if you camp by the creek.*

eat through: erode/eat something from one surface area to the other; make a hole in something ~ *1a) Termites have eaten through the framework. 1b) Acid ate through the metal.*

[1]**eat up**: [spoken] invitation to begin eating; to continue eating ~ *1a) Come on everybody—eat up before the food goes cold. 1b) I want you to eat up all your vegetables.*

[2]**eat up**: 1) for a thought/idea to consume a person ~ *He was eaten up with guilt.*

2) show enthusiasm for/appreciate something ~ *The audience ate up every word he said.*

Echidna: Found both in Australia and New Guinea, the Echidna is the most primitive mammal on earth. Its spines cover the top of its body and it has long, sharp claws, enabling it to dig for ants or to burrow into the earth for protection. They use their noses to find food, and use their long, sticky tongues to catch ants, insects, and worms.

eco: ecological ~ *We have a good ecosystem in place.*

egg on: encourage/incite/urge; cause to act ~ *Egged on by the crowd, the runner sprinted ahead to win the race.*

either way: whatever the result; whatever happens (positive or negative) ~ *1a) Let me know either way about the job. 1b) I don't know how we'll do it, but either way it'll get done.* *also: in any event; in any case; come what may; at the very least

EFTPOS: Electronic Funds Transfer at Point of Sale

elbow grease: physical effort ~ *It's going to take some elbow grease to clean this!*

elbow room: space to move ~ *The new office gives me more elbow room.*

eleventh hour: the last possible chance to take action/do something ~ *The director called for an eleventh hour change to the script.*

(if) all else fails: [spoken] in the event of something failing ~ *If all else fails, I'll get a part-time job.*

'em:[informal] them ~ *Just put 'em here, thanks.*

empties: empty beer bottles ~ *The empties can go in this bin.*

Emu: Standing 1.5 to 2 meters tall and with an average weight of thirty-six kilograms, the emu is a large flightless Australian bird and the world's third largest bird. They have three toes and long legs, enabling them to run very fast. They feed on leaves, grass, and small insects and live all over Australia in grasslands. The emu is featured on Australia's coat of arms.

end it all: commit suicide/end the suffering ~ *He was so overcome with grief he wanted to end it all.*

end with: conclude/finish something ~ *1a) I'd like to end the meeting by asking everyone to thank our special guest. 1b) The concert ended with a solo performance by the lead pianist.*

end up: 1) make an alternate ending to a plan ~ *1a) The weather was so bad we ended up coming home. 1b) We've no destination in mind so I'm not sure where we'll end up.*

2) reach/find oneself at a destination/place; situation/predicament ~ *2a) He'll soon end up in jail if he continues with his criminal ways. 2b) She began her career as an accountant and ended up being a doctor.* *also: finish up; land up; wind up; end up doing/becoming

at an end: having reached the end; having come to a stop; finished ~ *Our work here is at an end.* *also: come to an end ~ *Sadly, our wonderful journey has come to an end.*

at the end of one's tether: of having lost all patience; at the limits of one's endurance ~ *With four young children housebound because of the rain, I'm at the end of my tether!* *also: at wit's end

be at the receiving end: be the recipient/target of an unpleasant action/effect ~ *I found myself at the receiving end of my boss's bad mood, just because I was five minutes late.*

in the end: ultimately/eventually/conclusively ~ *We had a few minor problems, but it turned out alright in the end.*

(the) living end: something outrageous; the utmost in any situation ~ *I can't believe how rude Jane is sometimes—she's just the living end!*

make ends meet: survive financially ~ *He didn't earn much and often found it hard to make ends meet.*

no end: many/a great deal/amount ~ *We had no end of problems getting the motor to start.*

no end in sight: 1) no foreseeable finish/conclusion ~ *It seems there is no end in sight to the conflict.*

2) something plentiful ~ *There was no end in sight to the parade.*

on end: 1) non-stop/without stopping ~ *We talked for hours on end.*

2) upright with one end facing downwards ~ *Please place the books on end.*

(to the) ends of the earth: anywhere; eternity ~ *She loved him so much she would go to the ends of the earth to be with him.*

dead end: 1) a road/street that has one entrance/exit point ~ *The road is a dead end.*

2) a futile/useless job ~ *I'll have to find other work. I'm going nowhere in this dead end job.*

enough to make a grown man cry: said of something so amazing/horrific that a man would cry ~ *The horror of the situation was enough to make a grown man cry.*

enough to sink a battleship: extreme excess; too much of something ~ *We brought enough supplies to sink a battleship.*

enough to wake the dead: a very loud din/noise ~ *That music is loud enough to wake the dead!*

enough is enough: [spoken] expression of intolerance/exasperation at something sufficient for the purpose ~ *Enough is enough—stop arguing! I've had it with your bickering.*

Enzed: [informal] N.Z./New Zealand

Esky: portable, insulated container

etc.: et cetera

eucalypts: Eucalypts are the dominant trees of established areas of the country and are the defining tree of Australia. There are over 800 species that have adapted to nearly every environment. They are commonly called gum trees.

eureka: [spoken] exclamation of discovery; success ~ *Eureka! I found it.*

even as we speak: just now at this moment ~ *They should be arriving even as we speak.*

even if it kills me: a pledge; determination to complete something ~ *I'll get this finished today, even if it kills me.*

even out: become equal; level/even ~ *1a) Right now this team has the most points, but in time it will even out. 1b) This surface needs to be evened out—it's sloping downwards.*

even so: nevertheless/despite everything ~ *You claim that it definitely wasn't there, but even so I'll look again.*

even up: make something equal/balanced/level ~ *Winning the last few points has evened up the score.*

get even (with): equalise the score; get revenge ~ *He always beats me at cards, but I'll get even with him someday.*

even-stevens: equal in a competition; in amounts ~ *1a) The two runners are even-stevens. 1b) We'll split the money even-stevens.*

in the event of: on the chance; if something should happen ~ *The picnic will be cancelled in the event of rain.*

ever so: exceedingly ~ *He touched it ever so gently.*

every bit: in every aspect/way ~ *He's every bit as good as some veteran competitors.*

every inch of the way: for the duration/until the end ~ *He supported her every inch of the way.*

every man and his dog: all people/everyone ~ *Every man and his dog were there.* *also: every Tom, Dick, and Harry

every man for himself: to look after your own interests; go without assistance ~ *When the boat started sinking it was every man for himself.*

every so often: occasionally ~ *Every so often I have to stop and rest.*

every which way: in all directions ~ *The wind blew the leaves every which way.*

everything but the kitchen sink: almost everything (including unnecessary items) ~ *He brought everything but the kitchen sink with him when he went on holidays.*

ex: former ~ *Pam's an ex-student of this school.*

explain away: make excuses; minimize by explanation ~ *She tried to explain away the missing money.*

explore every avenue: look at all possibilities ~ *I'll have to explore every avenue before I can give you an answer.*

eyes are bigger than (one's) stomach: describes someone greedy, who wants more than they can eat ~ *I can't eat another bite—my eyes are bigger than my stomach.*

eyes fall out of (one's) head: expressed when seeing something amazing/wonderful/frightening ~ *My eyes nearly fell out of my head when I saw her diamond ring.*

eye off: regard/observe someone/something with interest ~ *1a) Looking for a suitable gift, he eyed off the jewellery on display. 1b) Sarah spent the entire time eyeing off the handsome newcomer.*

eyes glued to: to watch intently ~ *Her eyes were glued to the television all night.*

all eyes are/will be on: that everyone is watching; showing interest in someone/something ~ *All eyes will be on the tennis tonight.*

bat an eye(lid): show no concern/worry ~ *He didn't bat an eyelid when I told him.*

cast an eye over: look at something quickly/make a quick assessment ~ *Could you cast an eye over this report?*

couldn't believe (my/his/her) eyes: [spoken] expression of amazement ~ *I couldn't believe my eyes when I say how much she'd changed.*

cry one's eyes out: cry excessively, with great sadness ~ *I cried my eyes out when I heard the bad news.*

easy on the eyes: someone/something pleasant to look at ~ *He's easy on the eyes.*

feast eyes on: look at something/someone with great enjoyment/ pleasure ~ *She feasted her eyes on the cakes displayed in the window.*

for your eyes only: privileged/classified information meant to be seen by one person ~ *No one else is to read this—it's for your eyes only.*

from/out of the corner of one's eyes: see/notice something briefly, but not clearly ~ *I saw something move out of the corner of my eye.*

get/give someone the eye: send eye signals/communicate visually to indicate romantic interest ~ *That handsome guy over there is giving me the eye.*

got/have eyes in the back of (one's) head: can see everywhere at once ~ *I know what you're doing, I've got eyes in the back of my head.*

have an eye for: have the ability to notice a particular type of thing/appreciate distinctions ~ *Having an eye for detail is a necessary skill for an art buyer.*

have one's eye on: 1) show romantic interest in someone ~ *She's had her eye on Steve for a long time.*

2) observe/watch someone/something closely/with interest ~ *2a) I've got my eye on you, so you'd better behave. 2b) I've had my eye on that ring for a while now.* *see also: eye off

in the blink of an eye: of something to happen in an instant/very quickly ~ *I can't tell you the details, it all happened in the blink of an eye.*

in one's/someone's eyes: in one's/someone's opinion ~ *1a) They're the better team in my eyes. 1b) In Sue's eyes, Paul can do no wrong.*

in one's mind's eye: in one's memory/imagination ~ *In my mind's eye, the house was two-storey.* *also: for memory ~ *For memory, she had fair hair and blue eyes.*

keep an eye on: watch someone/something carefully/intently ~ *1a) He kept an eye on his children whilst they played near the river. 1b) We need to leave soon, so keep your eye on the time.* *also: keep a close eye on

keep an eye out: be watchful; look out for; look for someone/something ~ *I don't know where it is, but I'll keep an eye out for it.* *also: keep (one's) eyes peeled ~ *Tom will be exiting through those gates, so keep your eyes peeled for him.*

lay eyes on: see something/someone; see for the first time ~ *1a) I never want to lay eyes on him again. 1b) He loved her the first time he laid eyes on her.* *also: set eyes on

make eyes at someone: flirt seductively ~ *That handsome guy across the room is making eyes at you!*

more than meets the eye: something/someone is more difficult/complex than first appears ~ *You might think Jack's very shy, but there's more to him than meets the eye.* *also: more to it than that

only have eyes for: be interested/attracted to one thing/person ~ *They only have eyes for each other.*

open one's eyes to something: cause to realise/understand/develop an interest in something ~ *1a) Having such an injury has opened his eyes to the mobility problems facing disabled persons. 1b) Politicians need to open their eyes to needs of the homeless.*

(can't/don't) take eyes off: 1) be unable to stop looking at something ~ *She couldn't take her eyes off him!*

2) a spoken instruction to watch someone/something closely at all times ~ *Don't take your eyes off of it!*

turn a blind eye (to): pretend to not see/ignore something ~ *The corrupt policeman turned a blind eye to the drug deal.*

with open eyes: with full awareness/knowledge ~ *He embarked on the journey with open eyes.*

see eye to eye: agree with someone ~ *Luckily we saw eye to eye on the project.*

don't see eye to eye: have different opinions/be unable to compromise ~ *We've don't see eye to eye on that topic.*

the naked eye: (see) unassisted by optical instruments ~ *It's too small to see with the naked eye.*

under someone's watchful eyes: something observed/watched very closely/carefully ~ *The child was safe under the watchful eyes of his parents.*

bright-eyed and bushy-tailed: full of energy; alert/active ~ *After a good sleep I was bright-eyed and bushy-tailed.*

eye-catching: conspicuous; attention getting; visually attractive ~ *Stan wore an eye-catching yellow jacket to the party.*

eye-opener: a revealing; surprising happening/event ~ *The lecture was a real eye-opener.*

eyewitness: one who has seen something with their own eyes ~ *There were no eyewitnesses to the accident.*

shut-eye: a period of sleep ~ *I'm going home to get some shut-eye.*

wide-eyed: 1) credulous/innocent ~ *Back then I was a wide-eyed youngster.*

2) of having one's eyes open in wonderment ~ *The kids watched the fireworks in wide-eyed wonder.*

F

face: a familiar person/representative ~ *1a) He's a well-known face around here. 1b) She's the face of a well-known cosmetic company.*

face the fact: confront the (often undesirable) truth ~ *She had to face the fact that she might never walk again.* *also: face up to; face it ~ *Let's face it, we're broke!*

face the music: accept the consequences/punishment ~ *He couldn't postpone it any longer, he decided to confess his crime and face the music.*

can't face (up to) something/someone: be unable to confront a task/someone because it's difficult or unpleasant ~ *1a) Embarrassed by what happened, I couldn't face everyone. 1b) I can't seem to face up to the big cleaning task.*

do an about-face: have a complete change of mind ~ *The authorities did an about-face and accepted our proposal.*

(have a) long face: have a sad look ~ *What happened, why the long face?*

not just a pretty face: to be attractive as well as talented ~ *She's not just a pretty face, she also a cattle farmer.*

off one's/someone's face: of someone very drunk or affected by drugs ~ *He was so off his face he didn't know where he was.*

staring one in the face: for something to be obvious/visible yet unable to be seen ~ *I stood there for five minutes looking for it, but it was staring me right in the face.*

facts and figures: relative/precise information ~ *Peter's here to provide the facts and figures.*

a fact of life: something unavoidable that's always there or always true ~ *High unemployment seems to be a fact of life these days.*

get your facts right/straight: [spoken] that you should have the correct information before you criticise or argue with someone ~ *Make sure you get your facts straight before you make accusations.*

in fact: [spoken] used when you're adding further information ~ *I love it here; in fact, I'd like to move here one day.*

in actual fact: [spoken] used to emphasise something that is surprisingly true ~ *In actual fact, they were right.* *also: in point of fact

the facts of life: the physiological functions involved in sex and reproduction

the fact remains that . . . : that despite what has happened, something remains true ~ *I know he didn't cause the accident, but the fact remains that he shouldn't have been driving.*

fade away: gradually disappear/diminish; become less bright ~ *1a) The memory of it has all but faded away. 1b) If she doesn't start eating properly she'll fade away to nothing. 1c) As the sun begins to rise, the stars fade away.*

fair dinkum: honest/true/genuine; for real ~ *1a) Fair dinkum—we had the best fun ever! 1b) I didn't do it—fair dinkum! 1c) It's fair dinkum Aussie beer.*

fair's fair: [spoken] that something should be accepted, because it's fair ~ *Fair's fair, it's your turn to mow the lawn. I did it last time.*

fair go: 1) a reasonable chance/opportunity ~ *Oh, give him a fair go.*

2) an appeal for fairness ~ *Come on, fair go, why do I have to do all the work?!* *also: fair suck of the sauce bottle; fair suck of the sav; fair crack of the whip

fairy bread: Sliced white bread spread with margarine or butter and covered with sprinkles or hundreds and thousands which stick to the spread. It is typically cut into squares or triangles and is commonly served at children's birthday parties.

fairy tale: a fabricated story ~ *It is just a fairy tale.*

fall apart at the seams: 1) for something to disintegrate/break apart/break down ~ *This coat is so old it's beginning to fall apart at the seams.*

2) suffer mentally ~ *Poor old Tom just fell apart at the seams when his wife died.* *also: fall to bits/pieces; fall in a heap; come apart at the seams

fall asleep: go to sleep ~ *I was so tired I fell asleep instantly.*

fall asleep at the wheel: to fall asleep whilst driving

fall back on: resort to another plan; a familiar situation ~ *1a) He has his nursing profession to fall back on. 1b) I have my family to fall back on if I get into financial difficulties.*

fall behind: 1) move more slowly (than someone) so you are behind them ~ *Tired from walking, she fell behind the others in the group.*

2) make less progress (than someone) ~ *Due to constant interruptions, I've fallen behind in my work.*

3) fail to pay for something/make a payment at the agreed time ~ *After losing his job, he soon fell behind in the rent.*

fall by the wayside/way: of something halted/failing to continue ~ *Due to the extreme heat, many competitors fell by the wayside.*

fall flat: of a joke/entertainment failing to have the desired effect ~ *My attempt at a joke fell flat.*

fall for: 1) be attracted to and start loving someone ~ *She's really fallen for him.*

2) be tricked/deceived ~ *I can't believe you fell for that old trick!* *also: fall into

fall foul of: be in/get into trouble with someone ~ *By disobeying a direct order, the soldier fell foul of his commanding officer.*

fall ill: become sick/ill ~ *I fell ill in the first week of my holiday.*

fall in a heap: collapse with physical/mental exhaustion ~ *Exhausted after completing the marathon, he fell in a heap after crossing the finishing line.*

fall in line: assume a predetermined formation/order ~ *The troops were ordered to fall in line ready for inspection.* *also: fall into line

fall in with: form a relationship with someone/a group of people ~ *Steve fell in with a group of students who shared an interest in horses.*

fall into disrepair: a structure in a broken/damaged state ~ *Unoccupied for many years, the house had fallen into disrepair.*

fall into place: of a problem to be solved satisfactorily; of events to occur as anticipated ~ *1a) After weeks of investigation, all the details of the crime slowly fell into place. 1b) I know you're confused with the process, but everything will soon fall into place.*

fall/get into the wrong hands: for something or information to be in the possession of the wrong person/people ~ *Make sure the information doesn't fall into the wrong hands.*

fall into something: collapse/drop on/in something ~ *I fell into bed, then fell into a deep sleep.*

fall into step: start walking/walk alongside someone; walk in unison ~ *Wanting to introduce himself, he fell into step beside her and struck up a conversation.*

fall into a trap: be deceived/tricked into believing/doing something ~ *Many people fell into the trap believing their money was safely invested.*

fall off the back of a truck: goods of questionable origin; stolen goods ~ *The stall owner was accused of selling goods that had fallen off the back of a truck.*

fall on deaf ears: be unheard (intentionally) ~ *All our complaints have fallen on deaf ears.*

fall on hard times: experience financial difficulties ~ *They fell on hard times after their business collapsed.*

fall over: stumble and fall down; topple and fall ~ *I fell over and hurt myself.*

fall over backwards: do everything possible to please someone ~ *The host fell over backwards to please his guests.*

fall over oneself: be very eager/enthusiastic about doing something ~ *He was falling over himself trying to impress her.*

fall prey to: become a victim of something/someone ~ *1a) The young deer fell prey to the hungry tiger. 1b) Alas, many vulnerable people fell prey to the con-man's scam.*

fall short (of): fail to reach the standard/level/amount of something ~ *The money we raised fell short of the target.*

fall through: collapse/fail ~ *Unfortunately the building proposal fell through.*

(almost/nearly) fall off the chair: what one might say when amazed/surprised ~ *I nearly fell off the chair when she told me what really happened.* *also: fall through

fall under: 1) be categorised/included ~ *Soccer falls under the code of ball sports.*

2) be mesmerised by something/someone ~ *So enchanting was she, James fell under her spell almost at once.*

(a) fall(ing) out: a disagreement/dispute with someone ~ *We haven't spoken for over a month since we had a falling out.* *also: fall out with someone

false step: an improper/unwise action ~ *I'll give you another chance—but one false step and you're out of the team.*

fancy: desire/want something ~ *I quite fancy the red one.*

fancy that: [spoken] interjection of surprise/amazement ~ *You live here now—well, fancy that!*

fancy oneself: to have a big ego; think highly of oneself ~ *I think he rather fancies himself as the next leader of the country.*

fancy-free: unencumbered; free of a relationship ~ *She's been running round fancy-free since their divorce.*

far and wide: great distances/from far places ~ *1a) Their journey took them far and wide. 1b) People came from far and wide to see the show.* *also: near and far

far away: 1) a great distance from a fixed point ~ *They moved far away from the city.*

2) distance in time ~ *I suddenly realised next month is not all that far away.*

far be it for me to say: that one would not presume to know something ~ *Far be it for me to say, but are you sure you're using the correct method?*

far out: [spoken] exclamation of amazement/astonishment/ wonder ~ *Far out! This view is amazing!*

far gone: in an advanced state/condition ~ *Unfortunately the injured bird was too far gone to be saved.*

by far: much/considerably; to a great degree ~ *1a) It's the shorter route by far. 1b) He's the better player, by far!* *also: far and away

few and far between: rare; scarce; scattered ~ *You'll have trouble finding one—they're few and far between.* *also: rare as hens' teeth; rare on the ground

go far: 1) succeed/achieve much ~ *She'll go far with a talent like that!*

2) be effective; extend in range/importance ~ *Their contribution will go far toward helping the needy.*

how far: to what extent/distance/degree ~ *1a) How far did you travel? 1b) I'm not sure how far I can trust her. 1c) They're not sure how far the damage extends.*

so far: up till now; to this point/extent ~ *1a) So far, twenty people have accepted. 1b) You can only take the issue so far.* *also: thus far

so far, so good: that progress is being made ~ *How's the project going? So far, so good.*

faraway: remote/dreamy/dazed ~ *I can tell she's in love. She's got that faraway look in her eyes.*

far-fetched: unlikely/exaggerated ~ *I think her ideas are sometimes a little far-fetched.*

far-flung: remote; wide-ranging ~ *They're moving to some far-flung place in the middle of nowhere.*

far-out: odd/eccentric/unconventional ~ *Some of his ideas are a bit too far-out for my liking.*

fart around: act foolishly; waste time ~ *If you don't stop farting around we'll be late!*

fat lot of good/use that is/was: that something done/said was useless/worthless ~ *A fat lot of good that was asking you to help—I've done all the work!*

fathom something: understand/comprehend ~ *I just can't fathom his reasoning.*

do yourself a favour: a hint that someone should abandon bad habits/do something positive for themselves ~ *Do yourself a favour and give up smoking.*

(be) fazed: be intimidated/upset/disturbed ~ *I've seen it all. Nothing fazes me.*

feast or famine: to have too much or too little of something ~ *Last month was the driest in 30 years, and this month's been the wettest in 50 years. It's either a feast or famine.*

no mean feat: not easy to achieve ~ *Building it was no mean feat.*

(the) feds: the police

fed up: angry/frustrated/annoyed ~ *I'm fed up with having to do all this work on my own!* *also: sick to the back teeth

(a) feed: a wholesome meal ~ *She was so happy to get home and have a good feed.*

feed someone a line: make an excuse that might or might not be true ~ *She fed me a line about her car not starting as her excuse for being late.*

feel a bit off: feel slightly unwell ~ *Sorry, I'm not coming; I'm feeling a bit off.*

feel at home: relaxed at ease; comfortable in a situation ~ *The staff at the hotel really made us feel at home.*

feel it in one's bones: intuitively know something is about to happen ~ *I'm sure something's happened to them. I can feel it in my bones.*

feel like: have a desire/want to do something ~ *1a) I don't feel like doing anything this weekend. 1b) What do you feel like doing tonight?* *also: feel up to ~ *I don't feel up to going out tonight.*

feel one's way around: proceed cautiously/carefully; become familiar with one's surroundings/situation ~ *1a) The lights went out and we had to feel our way around to get to the exit. 1b) I haven't worked there for long. I'm still feeling my way around.*

feet first: do something thoughtlessly/recklessly ~ *He embarked on the project feet first and then found himself in financial trouble.*

dead on (one's) feet: totally exhausted; unable to stand ~ *I have to sit down—I'm dead on my feet.*

drag (one's) feet: deliberately work/act; complete something at a slow pace ~ *The player was warned about dragging his feet during the game.*

get/have itchy feet: to be restless; have the need to make changes ~ *He was getting itchy feet at work, and so began looking for another job.*

have two left feet: be awkward/clumsy, usually when dancing

land on one's feet: survive/succeed after a difficult situation ~ *Due to a positive attitude, he managed to land on his feet after the company collapsed.*

rushed off one's feet: to be very busy ~ *We were rushed off our feet at work.*

think on one's feet: to make good decisions without prior planning ~ *As a rescue worker, you must be able to think on your feet*

in one fell swoop: all at the same time ~ *We went to one big shop and bought everything in one fell swoop.*

fella/fellow: man/bloke/male/guy ~ *He's such a nice fellow.*

sit on the fence: have a neutral opinion about something

fence sitter: someone who has a neutral opinion

fend off: deflect something/someone; prevent something from happening ~ *1a) She managed to fend off the attacker. 1b) He was left to fend off questions.*

fiddle around: waste time doing something unimportant ~ *I spent the weekend fiddling around at home.* *also: fiddle about

fiddle with: 1) move; touch something nervously ~ *He fiddled with his tie whilst waiting for his test results.*

2) make an unskilled attempt at fixing/repairing something ~ *He relaxes by fiddling with old, broken radios.*

fit as a fiddle: in very good health ~ *He's as fit as a fiddle. He should be able to run the race easily.*

fiddle-faddle: nonsense ~ *He's just talking fiddle-faddle.*

fiddlesticks: an expression of disagreement ~ *Oh, fiddlesticks—that's not true!*

fiddly: small and awkward to use/handle ~ *It was fiddly trying to build it because of all the small pieces.*

field questions: answer questions from an audience/reporter ~ *He spent the second half of the presentation fielding questions from the audience.*

field day: 1) a time of unrestrained pleasure/fun/excitement ~ *Reporters would have a field day if they heard about the embarrassing government blunder.*

2) a day in rural areas dedicated to displaying and demonstrating farm machinery

lead the field: be in a commanding position; ahead of the competition (in business) ~ *1a) He is leading the field at this stage of the Tour de France. 1b) This team leads the field in medical research.*

play the field: have many romantic relationships ~ *He would rather play the field than settle down with one girl.*

far afield: far away ~ *You can find this type of insect as far afield as Russia.*

fess up: admit your guilt ~ *He finally fessed up to stealing the goods.*

fierce: extreme ~ *There was a fierce wind blowing.*

fifty-fifty: equal amounts; half and half ~ *We'll split our winnings fifty-fifty.*

fifty-fifty chance: an equal chance ~ *You have a fifty-fifty chance of guessing which hand it's in.*

fight dirty: use unfair tactics ~ *Be careful competing against him, he's known to fight dirty.*

fight fire with fire: use the same method/tactics as the other person to equal the score or gain advantage ~ *He'll soon find out I can fight fire with fire.*

fight like cats and dogs: to constantly argue with someone, but remain friendly ~ *My children fight like cats and dogs, but are still good friends.*

fight tooth and nail: argue strenuously to win; retain your possessions or rights ~ *They fought tooth and nail to stop developers buying their land.*

fight a losing battle: to be in a situation that offers little chance of success ~ *I fought tooth and nail to stop the developers, but now I'm fighting a losing battle.*

figure in: include/consider someone/something ~ *The issue of where the funds were coming from didn't figure in their plans.*

figure on: make a guess; an estimation ~ *1a) I'm figuring on twenty people attending. 1b) I didn't figure on James and Cleo coming.*

figure something/someone out: solve/understand why something happens, or why someone does something ~ *I can't figure it/him/her/them out.*

figure something out: create an idea/plan ~ *I'm not sure what sort of entertainment we'll have, but I'll figure something out.*

figure up: reckon/add/compute the amount of ~ *The bill figures up to $100.*

file something (away): retain/archive records; retain information in one's head ~ *1a) One of your tasks is to file the patients' records. 1b) That information is filed in my head.*

fill one's face: eat excessively; enthusiastically ~ *No more for me, thanks, I've already filled my face.*

fill someone in: provide further information; elaborate ~ *Tomorrow, I'll fill you in on what was said at the meeting.*

fill-in: substitute; stand-in; temporary replacement ~ *Our class had a fill-in teacher today.*

filter through: 1) slowly pass/seep through something ~ *The water will be much clearer after it has filtered through the gravel.*

2) for information to gradually reach others ~ *News of the disaster soon filtered through to neighbouring communities.*

filthy: 1) nasty/vile ~ *She gave me a filthy look. 1b) He played a really filthy trick on her.*

2) to an extreme extent ~ *They're filthy rich.*

3) covered/smeared in filth; disgustingly dirty ~ *Your clothes are filthy!*

find one's way around: become familiar with unfamiliar surroundings ~ *I've never been here before, but I managed to find my way around.*

find one's way somewhere: find/discover how to get from one place to another ~ *Just point me in the right direction and I'll be able to find my way there.*

find out: discover/learn ~ *1a) I'd like to find out who did it. 1b) What did you find out while you were there?*

fine/fine then: an interjection to indicate indifference at what someone is doing/going to do ~ *Fine then—go ahead and do it, see what I care!*

fine by/with: that something is acceptable; agreeable ~ *It's fine by me if you go to the party.*

fine line: a small, difficult to detect distinction ~ *There's a fine line between love and hate.*

fine mess: an awkward/unpleasant/difficult situation ~ *Well, this is a fine mess you've got us into.*

fine print: very small writing on a contract (designed to go unnoticed) ~ *Make sure you read the fine print before you sign any contract.* *also: small print

cut a fine figure: to look elegant/well-dressed ~ *Steve cuts a fine figure in that suit.*

finger food: small portions of food that can easily be held in one's fingers, usually served at an event where no meal is provided

get one's fingers burnt: have a bad experience from an unsuccessful action ~ *We got our fingers burnt and lost a lot of money.*

keep one's fingers crossed: a superstitious action to guard against bad luck or hope for good luck ~ *Good luck! I'll keep my fingers crossed for you.*

lift a finger: make no effort to help/provide assistance when necessary ~ *She's so lazy! She never lifts a finger to help with the housework.*

pull one's finger out: begin/speed up activity after a period of inactivity/delay ~ *If she doesn't pull her finger out, the project won't be finished on time.*

slip through one's fingers: lose an opportunity; fail to take advantage of an offer ~ *Take up the offer—you can't let an opportunity like this to slip through your fingers.*

snap one's fingers: the act of striking your middle finger against your thumb to make a clicking sound

five-finger discount: If someone tells you they got a five-finger discount, it means they stole the goods.

finish up: *see end up; wind up

fire (someone): dismiss them from their job ~ *Unfortunately, I had to fire him.* *also: be fired; get the sack

fire away: [spoken] signal to begin talking/to ask questions ~ *I'm ready for questions, so fire away.*

fire off: 1) discharge a gun/weapon ~ *He fired off a few warning shots.*

2) write and send a letter (in anger) ~ *I fired off a letter of complaint to the mayor.*

fire up: 1) arouse/excite one's enthusiasm/passion ~ *The exciting new project has her all fired up.*

2) ignite/light a fire ~ *Let's fire up the barbie and cook some snags.*

draw fire: cause people to attack or criticise you because of something you did ~ *His harsh comments drew fire from the governing body.*

fan the fire/flame: make a situation worse; cause anger/bad feelings to increase ~ *1a) Her hurtful comments are just fanning the fire. 1b) The riot fanned the fire of racial tension.*

get on like a house on fire: to have a good relationship/close friendship with someone ~ *They get on like a house on fire.*

hold fire: to stop shooting ~ *The rebels agreed to hold their fire.*

hold your fire: [spoken] command for someone to stop shooting/ wait until you begin shooting

line of fire: the path of a missile/bullet ~ *They took a wrong turn and found themselves right in the line of fire.*

on fire: 1) alight/burning ~ *The entire building is on fire.*

2) doing/performing well ~ *Pete's certainly on fire scoring two goals in a row.*

open fire: begin shooting at someone/something ~ *The army came into enemy territory and insurgents opened fire on them.*

play with fire: act recklessly; take foolish risks ~ *You'll be playing with fire if you try to steal Nick's girlfriend.*

return fire: to shoot back at the person shooting at you ~ *He heard the pop, pop, pop of a rifle and quickly returned fire.*

first and foremost: something more important than anything else ~ *First and foremost, I would like to thank everybody for coming tonight.* *also: first things first

first cab off the rank: be the first to do something; volunteer for selection ~ *I'm nervous at being first cab off the rank to perform.* *also: first in line

first come, first served: The first person/people to arrive will be dealt with in strict order ~ *Tickets will be available on a first come, first served basis.*

first of all: before doing anything else ~ *There's a lot to do, but first of all we have to finish this.*

first up: before anyone/any item on an agenda ~ *1a) First up on the stage to perform is Carol Smith. 1b) We have a great night's viewing here on the Nine Network, and first up is the tennis.*

first-hand: directly see/experience something from the original source ~ *1a) She gave a first-hand account of the accident. 1b) I can tell you first-hand what happened.*

fish and chips: popular take-away food consisting of fish deep-fried in either batter or breadcrumbs, and potato chips (fries) *also: fish 'n chips

fish out of water: feel/be uncomfortable in new, unfamiliar surroundings/situations ~ *I have an outdoor job and I would feel like a fish out of water working in an office.*

drinks like a fish: someone who drinks a lot of alcohol (usually beer)

fishy: something suspicious/odd/questionable happening ~ *Something fishy is going on here.*

fistful: a handful ~ *He had a fistful of money!*

fit around: wrap/enclose around something ~ *It won't fit around it. It's too short.*

fit as a fiddle: very fit/healthy ~ *These exercises will have you fit as a fiddle.*

fit for a king: of something top quality; luxurious ~ *Our hotel room was fit for a king.*

fit in: 1) belong in a group/community ~ *It didn't take us long to fit in to the neighbourhood.*

2) accommodate something/someone ~ *2a) The package didn't fit in the letterbox. 2b) I'm rather busy, but I think I can fit our meeting into my schedule.*

fits like a glove: of clothing to fit snugly; to fit one's body perfectly ~ *It fits me like a glove.*

fit out: provide/furnish with something ~ *The apartment was fitted out with brand new furniture.*

fits and starts: short periods of activity with long periods of inactivity ~ *It took him months to build because he could only work on it in fits and starts.*

fit the bill: have the necessary experience/qualities/suitability ~ *Unfortunately your qualifications don't quite fit the bill for this appointment.*

fit together: put/touch the parts of something together; of something to conform in shape to another ~ *The parts fit together easily.* *also: join together

pink fit: 1) a temper tantrum; an outburst of rage (where one's face turns red/pink) ~ *Dad had a pink fit when he found out I had a tattoo.*

2) do something under any circumstance ~ *I wouldn't eat that in a pink fit.*

see fit: make an informed decision (to do something) ~ *1a) I'll leave it to you to deal with them in whichever way you see fit. 1b) Make any corrections as you see fit.*

be in fits (of laughter): laugh uncontrollably ~ *I was in fits listening to his story.*

five-star: the grade/excellence/quality of a service ~ *The service was five-star.*

fix (it): ensure something happens ~ *I fixed it so we can travel together.*

fix someone up: 1) arrange to do something for someone ~ *I know a good builder I could fix you up with.*

2) introduce a possible love interest ~ *Matchmaker Sue tried to fix John up with Janet.*

3) pay back money owed ~ *Thanks for the loan, I'll fix you up tomorrow.*

fix something: 1) illegally tamper/interfere with something for financial gain ~ *They were accused of fixing the company's books.* 2) mend something ~ *Jack can fix anything.*

fix something up: repair/mend/refurbish/improve something~ *1a) He loves nothing better than fixing up old cars. 1b) The house needs some fixing up, but it's affordable.*

have/get one's fix: a dose of a drug; anything that brings pleasure ~ *1a) The druggie went to his dealer for his weekly fix. 1b) I usually have my coffee fix at about 10:30 in the morning.*

in a fix: be in a difficult predicament/situation ~ *He's in a fix because of a business deal that went wrong.*

fizzle out: a gradual decline in quality after a good beginning ~ *The storm started out strong, then just fizzled out to nothing.*

FJ Holden: The FJ Holden was one of a range of motor vehicles produced in Australia by General Motors-Holden's from 1953 to 1957. It was the second model of an all-Australian car manufactured by Holden. The FJ was the car that cemented Holden's position as the country's most popular car, and they are now a celebrated piece of Australiana.

flag down: wave/signal/indicate that someone/something should stop ~ *They flagged down a taxi.*

flag-fall: the upfront fee to hire a taxi

flake out: fall asleep; collapse from physical exhaustion ~ *I was so exhausted after the marathon I came home and flaked out.*

flap around: 1) of something to move up and down in a flapping motion ~ *The sheets were madly flapping around in the breeze.*

2) move about in a fluster/frenzy/panic ~ *The startled birds were flapping around our heads.* *also: flutter around/about; flitter about

in a flap: of someone to be panicked/flustered ~ *Mum was in a real flap trying to get dinner ready before the guests arrived.* *also: in a tizz

flare up: 1) when a situation/emotions become inflamed/ intensify/erupt ~ *There was much opposition to the proposed development and tempers soon flared at the public meeting.*

2) for a flame/fire to re-ignite/intensify ~ *Strong winds caused the smouldering fire to flare up.*

flat as a board: very flat *also: flat as a pancake

flat on one's face: 1) to fail miserably at something ~ *I fell flat on my face at the audition.*

2) fall forward in an outstretched position ~ *Tripping, I fell flat on my face.*

flat broke: having no money ~ *I can't by anything today, I'm flat broke.*

flat out: 1) extremely busy ~ *I've been flat out all day!*

2) quickly ~ *He ran flat out to get there.* *also: flat chat

block of flats: a building with separate living units *also: an apartment complex

flatmate: someone who shares accommodation *also: roommate

flatten someone: overpower/defeat in a physical fight ~ *The tall, large man easily flattened his smaller opponent.*

flats: low-heeled shoes

flea market: market place where second-hand goods are bought and sold

flesh and blood: 1) a person's blood relatives/kin ~ *You shouldn't treat her like that; after all, she is your own flesh and blood.*

2) human (real as opposed to fantasy) ~ *The young boy finally came to realise that his hero is flesh and blood.*

flick through: look quickly through a book/magazine/leaflets/ papers ~ *I only have time to flick through it now, I'll read it properly later.* *also: leaf through

give someone/something the flick: 1) to end a relationship ~ *Finally, I gave that no-hoper the flick.*

2) kick a habit/addiction ~ *Poor health was the main reason I gave cigarettes the flick.*

the flicks: a film/movie showing at the cinema ~ *We're going to the flicks tonight. Are you coming?*

catching flies: have your mouth open when you're asleep (as if to catch flies)

a fling: a brief love affair ~ *He could never commit himself to anyone, his love life was a series of flings.*

flip one's lid: suddenly become very angry ~ *He's going to flip his lid when he finds out.*

flip (you) for it: toss a coin to decide the outcome ~ *I'll flip you to see who goes first.* *also: toss you for it

flippers: swimming fins worn on the feet when scuba diving or snorkelling

flipside: the only other alternative ~ *The flipside of the argument is that we'll be rich.*

float around: 1) information suspended in or moving through space ~ *There's a rumour floating around that the building is to be demolished.*

2) move from place to place at random ~ *I'm not exactly sure where, but she's floating around here somewhere.*

flock to: gather somewhere in great numbers ~ *1a) Everyone flocks to the beach on hot days. 1b) Fans flocked to the watch the game.* *also: flock together

flog something: 1) dispose of; sell quickly at a reduced price ~ *He flogged all his possessions because he was moving overseas.*

2) beat severely/abusively ~ *They accused the jockey of flogging his horse during the race.*

3) publicize/promote aggressively ~ *I saw her there flogging her new book.*

(be) floored: be amazed/stunned by something ~ *1a) He was floored by her incredible beauty. 1b) I was floored by such insensitivity.*

(a) flop: of something to fail miserably ~ *The movie was a total flop.*

flora/fauna: native plants/animals

Floral Emblems of Australia:

Commonwealth of Australia: Golden Wattle

Australian Capital Territory: Royal Bluebell

New South Wales: Waratah

Northern Territory: Sturt's Desert Rose

Queensland: Cooktown Orchid

South Australia: Sturt's Desert Pea

Tasmania: Tasmanian Blue Gum

Victoria: Common Heath

Western Australia: Red and Green Kangaroo Paw

go with the flow: agree with a decision ~ *I'm easy, I'll just go with the flow.* *also: swim with the tide

(the) flu: influenza

flush away: wash away (with water) *see also: wash away

fly: move/travel quickly (on land) ~ *1a) I didn't realise how late it is, I'd better fly. 1b) Pete's new sports car really flies. 1c) This car flew around the corner and nearly knocked me over.*

fly away: take flight ~ *Without warning, all the birds suddenly flew away.*

(pass with) flying colours: get good marks in a test/exam ~ *She passed the with flying colours!*

(to have) flown the coop: 1) of one's children to have left the family home ~ *The house is empty now that all the kids have flown the coop.*

2) of a bird to escape/flee from an enclosure

flying fox: Australian native fruit bat whose face resembles a fox

fly off the handle: lose your temper/become angry ~ *He flew off the handle for no apparent reason.* *also: fly into a rage

fly on the wall: an unnoticed observer ~ *I'd love to be a fly on the wall when he tells her the news.*

there are no flies on . . . : someone astute/quick ~ *You've finished already? Yep, there are no flies on me.*

wouldn't hurt/harm a fly: to be so gentle/kind as to not upset/ injure anyone/anything ~ *My dog looks aggressive, but he wouldn't hurt a fly.*

wouldn't have the foggiest: [spoken] response when you don't know the answer to something ~ *I wouldn't have the foggiest idea where they went.* *also: wouldn't have a clue; have no idea

fold up: to double something over; to fold/collapse for storage ~ *The table folds up for easy storage.* *also: fold away

(to) follow someone: understand what's being said ~ *I'm sorry, I don't quite follow you.* *see also: do you follow me; do you get my drift; are you with me

follow in one's footsteps/tracks: assume someone's role/ occupation; follow someone's example ~ *She followed in her father's footsteps and became a doctor.*

follow one's nose: 1) be guided by instinct ~ *Despite having no formal training, she followed her nose and was successful in her chosen career.*

2) continue in a straight line ~ *Just follow your nose until you get to the school.*

follow suit: copy an action/idea ~ *When one restaurant offered a healthier menu, the others soon followed suit.*

follow through with: continue an activity/task/plan until it's finished ~ *The company needs to follow through with the proposed changes.*

follow up: 1) take further action on something already done ~ *It was now up to detectives to follow up the lead.*

2) check someone's health to make sure a medical procedure has been effective ~ *I'll need to see you in two weeks for a follow-up appointment.*

be fond of: like and care about something/someone very much ~ *1a) I'm very fond of my grandmother. 1b) I'm not really fond of spicy food.* *also: have a fondness for

(have) fond memories: to remember someone/something with great happiness/pleasure ~ *I have fond memories of holidays by the sea.* *also: think fondly of

fool around: act in a silly way ~ *The boys missed most of the lesson because they were fooling around.*

fool with something/someone: tamper/meddle with something ~ *Someone's been fooling with the TV remote and now it won't work.* *also: monkey with something

foot it: walk somewhere ~ *We had to foot it home after the car broke down.* *also hoof it

foot the bill: pay for something ~ *Dad kindly offered to foot the bill for the meal.*

get off on the right foot: make a good start ~ *I need to come prepared for the interview because want to get off the right foot.*

get off on the wrong foot: make a bad start ~ *I got off on the wrong foot in my new job by making a big mistake.*

have/got one's foot in the door: an opportunity to advance one's goals ~ *Her job with the company gave her a foot in the door to her preferred career.*

have/got one's foot in the grave: [informal] near to death; expected to die (humorous)

my foot: [spoken] exclamation of disbelief/contradiction ~ *Easy to assemble—my foot! It took us nearly all day to put it together.*

on foot: to walk ~ *The rescuers set off on foot to look for the lost child.*

put a foot wrong: to make no mistakes; do no wrong ~ *He hasn't put a foot wrong since a prior warning.*

put one's best foot forward: make a good start/first impression ~ *This interview is important, so put your best foot forward.*

put one's foot down: 1) be firm/resolute; exert authority ~ *I'm putting my foot down this time and denying your request.*

2) accelerate quickly ~ *He put his foot down to escape the police.*

put one's foot in it: say/do something embarrassing ~ *I really put my foot in it by mentioning the trip. I didn't know it was a surprise!* *also: put one's foot in one's mouth

set foot in: enter a place ~ *I hope they never set foot in this place again!*

set foot on: stand (on the ground) ~ *After being on a boat for two days, they were glad to set foot on land again.*

the shoe is on the other foot: the roles of people in a situation have been reversed

underfoot: in the way; at one's feet ~ *With three young children underfoot there's no such thing as quiet time.*

play footsies (with someone): secretly touch someone's feet under the table to show sexual interest in that person ~ *I'm sure they were playing footsies during the meeting.*

football: *see: footy

footy: There are four football codes played in Australia: rugby league, rugby union, Australian rules, and soccer, which is identified as such so as to not to be confused with the other codes. Soccer, in most parts of the world, is called football. Rugby league and rugby union are played, and are more popular spectator sports, in the eastern parts of Australia, and Aussie rules is played and the more popular spectator sport in the southern and western parts of Australia. Soccer is the national sport. Footy is the common terminology used, with the *T* almost pronounced as a *D*.

for: share an interest in doing something ~ *1a) Who's for a game of footy? 1b) I'm all for the proposed changes.*

for all I care: [spoken] when you're indifferent to something/ unconcerned ~ *Do what you like for all I care!*

forever and a day: eternity/ever ~ *It's going to take me forever and a day to clean up this mess.*

for good: finally/for all time ~ *This time I'm determined to give up smoking for good.*

for keeps: 1) forever ~ *He gave it to me for keeps.*

2) seriously/permanently ~ *This time we're playing for keeps.*

for my part: concerning me ~ *For my part, I'm happy for you to go to the party.*

for real: [spoken] a way of confirming that someone meant what they said ~ *What? You don't like it! Are you for real?*

for starters: firstly/in the first instance ~ *For starters, it's too cold to go swimming.*

for sure: unquestionably/certainly ~ *I'll be there for sure.*

for the world: do something under any circumstances ~ *I wouldn't do it for the world.*

fork out/over: pay for something (often unwillingly) ~ *I had to fork out $100 for repairs.*

fossick around: search without method ~ *I'll fossick around and see if I can find it.*

Fosters: famous brand of beer

(have a) foul mouth: swear; use obscene language ~ *She might be attractive, but unfortunately she has a foul mouth.*

foul up: ruin/spoil/bungle ~ *1a) I fouled up my speech. 1b) The arrangements got fouled up so we came home early.*

four-wheel drive: 4x4 off-road vehicle; a vehicle powered by four wheels

fraction of: a part/portion of a whole figure/amount ~ *1a) They sell them elsewhere for a fraction of the price. 1b) You can fly there in a fraction of the time it takes to drive.*

frame someone: fraudulently incriminate an innocent person ~ *He believed he was being framed for the murder.* *also: frame-up

Fraser Island: Found along the southern coast of Queensland, World Heritage-listed Fraser Island is the largest sand island in the world. It's over 123 kilometres long and covers an area of 184,000 hectares. This exceptionally beautiful place plays host to sand dunes, some of which reach to 200 metres in height, rainforests growing on sand dunes, white beaches, over one hundred freshwater lakes, coloured sand cliffs, and crystal clear creeks. Some natural inhabitants include dingoes, wallabies, snakes, lizards, flying foxes, and river turtles, as well as over 350 bird species.

frazzled: be in a state of nervous/physical fatigue ~ *Having the kids indoors all day has left him somewhat frazzled.*

freak out: to react alarmingly/overreact to something ~ *1a) She's going to freak out when she finds out she's won an overseas trip. 1b) I freak out when I see spiders.*

Fred Nurks: a name used for anonymity; the average man in the street

free and easy: uninhibited/informal/casual ~ *He's lived a free and easy life since he won all that money.*

freebie: to gain/obtain anything for free ~ *They were handing out freebies to promote a new product.*

free-for-all: a gradual decline in law and order ending in verbal or physical violence ~ *What began as a public debate soon turned into a free-for-all between opposing groups.*

freeze up: 1) be unable to move/speak/continue due to being anxious/nervous ~ *I hope I don't freeze up when I make my speech.*

2) become so cold as to stop working ~ *Where I live, we have to cover the taps at night so they don't freeze up.*

fresh as a daisy: physically and mentally rested ~ *She returned to work fresh as a daisy after a long holiday.*

fresh out of . . . : 1) having just run out supplies (of something) ~ *I'm fresh out of bananas, will an apple do?* *also: clean out of

2) to have recently come from a place/situation ~ *The new employee is fresh out of college.*

freshen up: revive/renew/make fresh/brighten something/ oneself ~ *1a) The workers freshened up before dinner. 1b) She freshened up the house before the guests arrived.*

strike up a friendship: become friends with someone ~ *I struck up a good friendship with a fellow traveller.*

frighten off/away: scare something/someone away/off ~ *1a) A recent attack in a local park frightened off many visitors. 1b) Oh, you frightened it away.*

frightfully: very/extremely ~ *This meal is frightfully good.*

no-frills: of something that includes the most basic features; of equal quantity but not quality ~ *She was happy to buy cheaper, no-frills supermarket products.*

fritter away: foolishly waste money/time/an opportunity ~ *She frittered away her inheritance.*

from A-Z: including everything; from beginning to end/start to finish ~ *The book is titled* The A-Z of Astronomy.

from all walks of life: from all of society ~ *People from all walks of life attended the conference.*

from bad to worse: a gradual deterioration/decline in someone/something ~ *The situation has gone from bad to worse.*

from head to toe: from the top of one's head and down to the toes ~ *He was covered head to toe in mud.*

from point A to point B: from one place to another ~ *I don't care what type of car I drive, as long as it gets me from point A to point B.* *also: A to B

from top to bottom: thoroughly ~ *I've searched the house from top to bottom and I still can't find it!*

front up: make an appearance somewhere ~ *1a) He just fronted up to the counter and demanded to see you. 1b) She had the courage to front up to her accuser.*

front-page: of news/information worthy of being on the front page of a newspaper ~ *The story of the disaster is, of course, front-page news.*

fuddy-duddy: describes someone old-fashioned/conservative ~ *He didn't mean it like that, he's just an old fuddy-duddy.*

full: intoxicated; drunk ~ *He got full at the party and made a fool of himself.*

(on) full alert: be fully ready to act immediately ~ *With predicted high temperatures this weekend, firefighters are on full alert.*

full blast: of great force; the highest volume ~ *1a) He turned the stereo up full blast. 1b) The winds hit us full blast.*

(in) full flight: having gained momentum in an activity/movement ~ *Watching the orchestra perform in full flight is mesmerizing.*

full force: the maximum power/capacity ~ *1a) The community felt the full force of the storm. 1b) The full force of her anger took him by surprise.*

full house: filled to capacity (with people) ~ *It was a full house for opening night of the new show.*

full of: filled with something ~ *1a) The bucket is full of water. 1b) She was full of hatred.*

full of crap: of someone to say things that are not true (to impress someone); be uninformed on a subject ~ *I don't believe what he says half the time, because he's full of crap.* *also: full of shit (impolite); full of it

full of beans: be filled with energy; spirited ~ *She's usually full of beans. I don't know why she's so listless today.* *also: full of life

full of holes: to have many faults/flaws; a plan/argument easily challenged/scrutinized ~ *His story was full of holes.*

(at) full pelt: as fast as possible ~ *They ran full pelt to get there on time.* *also: full bore; full speed

have a full plate: have a busy schedule ~ *I'd like to help you with it, but I've got too much of full plate.* *also: have a lot on one's plate

full steam ahead: make an energetic, enthusiastic start ~ *Now that preparations are out of the way, it's full steam ahead.* *also: full speed ahead

full strength: the greatest amount/quantity/power/dilution ~ *1a) I want the team to be at full strength for the final. 1b) It's full strength cleaning liquid, so use with care.*

full strength beer: beer with a full alcohol content, as opposed to "light" beer

(at) full stretch: to work as strenuously as possible ~ *The firemen were working at full stretch to put out the blaze.*

(in) full swing: fully underway; moving quickly/efficiently; at the highest level of operation ~ *By ten, the party was in full swing.*

full throttle: with as much energy/speed as possible (in a car) ~ *The motor was running at full throttle.*

(be) full of oneself: egotistical/conceited ~ *He's so full of himself!*

fuming: extremely angry ~ *He was positively fuming when he found his car had been badly damaged.*

fun and games: 1) difficulties; problems with a process ~ *We had fun and games trying to catch the escaped rabbit.*

2) make mischief; have fun ~ *They had fun and games with a water pistol.*

barrel of fun: of someone very funny/amusing ~ *We never stopped laughing—he's a barrel of fun.* *also: barrel of laughs

for the fun of it: for no reason other than for fun ~ *I'm not particularly interested in cars, but I went for the fun of it.* *also: for the hell of it

make fun of: tease/ridicule someone/something ~ *They made fun of her artwork.* *also: poke fun at

not all fun and games: that something has a serious side ~ *He soon found out that owning a boat was not all fun and games.*

Funnel-web spider: Found in eastern and southern areas of Australia, the Funnel-web is among the world's deadliest spiders. These large, black spiders may range in size from 1.5 cm up to more than 5 cm long. They live in burrows in the ground, sheltered positions in tree trunks, or stumps above the ground. With a fearsome reputation, the Sydney Funnel-web is probably the most notorious of all spiders. If threatened it will behave aggressively by rearing up and displaying its long fangs. The male will sometimes wander into houses looking for a cool, dark place to beat the heat or to look for a mate. If they fall into water, they can survive for many hours. The Sydney Funnel-web has the most toxic venom to humans than any other spider. Their bites can cause serious injury or death, but *no* deaths have occurred since the introduction of antivenin.

funnily enough: odd/strange/curious as it seems ~ *I was just about to say that, funnily enough.* *also: strangely enough; strange as it may seem/be; the funny thing is . . .

funny fellow: someone strange/odd/weird ~ *He's a bit of a funny fellow.*

funny feeling: a strange/odd perception/awareness/sensation; premonition ~ *1a) I have a funny feeling that something bad is going to happen. 1b) I have a funny feeling in my stomach.*

very funny: [spoken] response to something done/said that *isn't* funny ~ *You made me spill it—very funny!*

funny bone: A contradictory reference to a spot on your elbow that, if knocked or hit, hurts very much.

furphy: a false rumour/urban myth

fussed: concerned/worried ~ *I'm not fussed about which pub we go to tonight.*

fusspot: one who fusses

G

gaga: silly; mad; crazy; besotted ~ *Meeting their favourite rock group sent the girls gaga.*

Galah: 1) pink and grey native Australian bird

2) a silly; foolish person ~ *He made a galah of himself at the party.*

gallivant around: to travel around seeking pleasure ~ *She's gallivanting around the country.*

gamble away: lose all of something by gambling ~ *She gambled away her inheritance.*

(the) game's up: someone's trickery/deceit has been discovered ~ *Okay, the game's up—we know what you're up to.*

(the) aim of the game: the purpose/reason for doing something; the means to an end ~ *The aim of the game is to capture all your opponent's playing pieces.*

fair game: someone/something considered as a justifiable target for ridicule/attack ~ *The quiet, shy boy was considered fair game by the bully.*

off one's game: be unable to reach a usual standard; lack interest in doing something ~ *He blamed an illness as a possible reason for being off his game.*

make a game of: ridicule/make fun of something ~ *Don't make a game of it—this is a serious issue.*

play games with: act deceitfully/evasively ~ *Don't play games with me—I know that's not what happened.*

gander: look/observe something ~ *Here, have a gander at this!* *see also*:* squiz; sticky beak

gang up on: make a verbal or physical attack as a group ~ *He was too scared to walk home in case the bullies ganged up on him.*

garage sale: a sale of one's unwanted household possessions (usually held out of the garage)

garbage guts: humorous term for someone who eats a lot of food at any one time

garbo: garbage/rubbish collector

gas bag: gossip/talk non-stop ~ *We had a good gas bag.*

gasbag: one who gossips; talks non-stop ~ *Sue's a bit of a gasbag.*

gate crash: attend a party/social occasion uninvited

gather around: assemble/collect/come together ~ *Gather around, everyone, I've an important announcement to make.*

gather up: collect; take and lift up ~ *I have to gather up all my things before we leave.*

gawk: stare at with wonder ~ *What are you gawking at?*

g'day: form of greeting (pronounced with a hard *G*) ~ *G'day, how ya goin'?*

geared up: ready/prepared ~ *We're getting geared up for the party.*

gee/gee whiz: [spoken] an exclamation of surprise/amazement; disappointment ~ *1a) Gee, I didn't know that. 1b) Oh, gee whiz—how come I didn't get one?*

gee-gee: child's talk for horse (pronounced with a soft *G)*

g/jeez: exclamation of surprise/dismay/admiration ~ *1a) Geez, what are you doing here?! 1b) Geez, I'm feeling crook. 1c) Geez, what a nice car!*

geezer: 1) an old, often eccentric, man (pronounced with a hard *G*) ~ *Who's that old geezer you were talking to?*

2) request for someone to look at something ~ *Hey—come and have a geezer at this!*

gem: an outstanding person or thing ~ *1a) What a gem of an idea! 2) Thanks, you're a gem.*

gently does it: [spoken] reminder for someone to take care with what they're doing ~ *Gently does it—if you use too much pressure it will break.*

gents: 1) gentlemen ~ *Ladies and gents, can I have your attention please?*

2) men's public toilet ~ *Jim has gone to the gents, he'll be back soon.*

get: 1) comprehend; understand something ~ *I must have explained it dozens of times, but he just doesn't get it.*

2) seek revenge ~ *Just you wait—I'll get you for that!*

3) instruct someone to do something ~ *Don't worry, I'll get Jack to do it.*

get a buzz: be amused/entertained by doing something ~ *I really get a buzz out of helping the needy.*

get a hold of: 1) grasp/grab/hold something ~ *It's just out of my reach—I can't quite get a hold of it.*

2) speak with someone on the phone ~ *I phoned your office yesterday, but I couldn't get hold of you.*

get a hold of oneself: [spoken] a way of telling someone to control their emotions ~ *Stop panicking! Get a hold of yourself—we're okay!*

get a load of: [spoken] request to listen closely; have a look at something ~ *Get a load of this!*

get a word in edgewise: get the chance to speak ~ *I tried to say something, but I couldn't get a word in edgewise.*

get a wriggle on: what you say when you're asking someone to hurry up ~ *You'd best get a wriggle on or we'll be late.* *also: get a move on

get about: be mobile/active/walking after a period of rest/illness ~ *I see Terry's getting about a lot better now that his leg's healed.*

get an invite: receive an invitation ~ *I got an invite to her party.*

get around: 1) go around/bypass/evade something/someone ~ *We couldn't get around a fallen tree.*

2) walk/go from place to place ~ *He's on crutches and can't get around very well.*

3) (of news) to be released/become known ~ *The story of his ordeal soon got around.*

get around to: eventually begin or finish a task ~ *I'll get around to finishing it one day.*

getting at: imply/suggest; make understandable ~ *Just what are you getting at?*

get at it: touch/reach something ~ *I want to be able clean that mark on the wall, but I can't get at it.*

get away: 1) leave someplace; escape; break free ~ *1a) They managed to get away from their attackers. 1b) She talked on and on, and I couldn't get away from her.*

2) go somewhere ~ *I hope to be able to get away for the weekend.* *also: get away from it all

get away with: escape detection ~ *She thought she could get away with cheating in the exam.* *also: get away with murder

get (it) back (to): 1) continue with a task/job ~ *I can't talk now. I have to get back to work.*

2) restore something to its original state/condition ~ *Unfortunately, I was unable to get it back to its original condition.*

3) give something back to someone ~ *I'll get it back to you next week.*

4) tell someone your verdict/decision on something ~ *I'll get back to you later with my decision.*

get booked: be charged by police for a driving offence ~ *I got booked for speeding last night.*

get by: cope/manage/survive ~ *1a) She wasn't sure how she'd get by after her husband died. 1b) We don't make much money, but we get by.*

get down: 1) descend/come down ~ *Get down from there—you might fall!*

2) write something ~ *I'd like to get down in writing the story you just told me.*

get even: seek revenge ~ *He vowed to get even with him some day.*

get going: start moving; leave/depart; make progress ~ *Come on—get going or you'll be late!* *also: move/push along

get it going: start the mechanical operation of something ~ *The motor's stalled and I can't get it going again.*

get a grip: recover one's self-control ~ *Get a grip, will you!*

get a hold of yourself: [spoken] a way of telling someone to gain control of their emotions/calm down ~ *Get a hold of yourself! It's not as bad as it seems.* *also: get a grip

get hold of: locate/find someone/something ~ *1a) Can you tell me where I might get hold of a copy of that book? 1b) I tried to get hold of you yesterday, but no one was home.*

get in: arrive at home/work; for a train/bus/plane to arrive ~ *1a) What time did you get in last night? 1b) The plane gets in at 6 p.m.*

2) become involved with a group of people ~ *He got in with the wrong crowd at school.*

3) be accepted in a club/organization/group; be accepted to study somewhere ~ *You have to pass a difficult exam to get into that school.*

4) enter a premises ~ *How did you get in here?*

5) be elected into politics ~ *The Liberal Party got in again.*

get in someone's way: physically block someone's passage; impede someone's progress/vision (knowingly or unknowingly) ~ *1a) A big truck got in my way and I missed the turnoff. 1b) I know he means well, but he's getting in my way and slowing my progress.*

get into: become involved/interested in ~ *1a) You'll get into trouble if you do that. 1b) Young boys have been getting into mischief at school.*

get into a knot: become agitated ~ *He's getting himself into a knot over nothing.*

get into strife: be in trouble for doing something ~ *You'll get into strife if mum sees you doing that.*

get something: 1) retrieve something ~ *I'll go and get it for you.*

2) understand/comprehend something ~ *I didn't get the joke.*

get it all out in the open: reveal the truth/the facts ~ *Knowing he was already in trouble, he decided it was best to get it all out in the open.* *also: get it off one's chest

get (something) out of the way: 1) physically move something from a pathway/passage ~ *It's blocking the doorway—could you please get it out of the way?*

2) finish/complete a job/task ~ *I can relax once I get this job out of the way.*

get it/this/things straight: to understand clearly what's being said ~ *1a) Let me get this straight, I've just painted it blue and now you want it green?! 1b) Get it straight—you're not going skydiving!*

get mixed up in: become (involuntarily) involved in something ~ *Somehow, I got mixed up the argument.*

get nowhere: show no progress; achieve little or nothing ~ *You'll get nowhere doing it like that. Here, let me show you how it's done.*

get off: escape punishment for a wrongdoing ~ *She somehow managed to get off paying the fine.* *also: get off scot-free; get off easy

get off my back: [spoken] a harsh request for someone to stop annoying/pestering you ~ *Get off my back, will you! I'm doing the best I can.* *see also: get on someone's back

get on: 1) be friendly with someone ~ *Jack and Sandy get on really well.* *also: get on like a house on fire

2) manage/cope ~ *How are you getting on after the accident?*

3) become older/advanced in years ~ *He's getting on in years.*

get on one's/someone's nerves: be irritated/angered by someone/something ~ *1a) His attitude really gets on my nerves. 1b) She does it just to get on his nerves.* *also: get on one's goat

get on to: 1) make contact by telephone ~ *I tried to get on to you earlier, but you weren't home.*

2) make a start at; begin a job/task ~ *I'll get on to it soon.*

get on with (it): continue with what you're doing ~ *Don't waste time talking, get on with it!*

get one's lines/wires crossed: a communication mix-up ~ *I think we got our lines crossed. I thought we were supposed to meet at 11 a.m.*

get one's money worth: be satisfied with the value of something ~ *I've really got my money's worth from this old car.*

get/have one's own way: manipulate someone so they'll do what you want ~ *I'll ask Dad—I can usually get my own way with him.*

get out: 1) for information to be told to everyone ~ *I don't want this secret to get out.*

2) [spoken] command to leave ~ *Get out!*

3) leave/exit a premises ~ *They can't get out, I've locked the door.*

4) [spoken] expression of disbelief ~ *You won a holiday?! Get out!*

get out and about: visit somewhere/go places; be socially active; leave the house ~ *We like to get out and about on the weekends.*

get out of (doing something): make an excuse to be excluded from doing something you don't want to do ~ *My little sister Jane always manages gets out of doing the housework.*

get out of (it): personal satisfaction; benefits of doing something ~ *1a) What are your expectations of the course—what do hope to get out of doing it? 1b) A career advancement is what I hope to get out of it.*

get out of my sight: [spoken] an angry way of telling someone to go away ~ *Get out of my sight! I'll speak to you when I've calmed down.*

get out of the wrong side of the bed: an often humorous way to describe why someone is angry ~ *What's wrong with you this morning? Did you get out of the wrong side of the bed or something?*

get over something: recover (physically/mentally) ~ *Rick's very upset about what happened, but he'll get over it.*

get rid of: remove/discard/throw something away ~ *I'm getting rid of it next week.*

get round (it): solve a problem/overcome a difficult situation ~ *There was a problem with the delivery, but we managed to get round it.*

(don't) get someone/oneself started (on something): mention a subject that someone/one's emotional about ~ *Whatever you do, don't get Greg started on boats or you'll never shut him up.*

get side-tracked: get distracted from a conversation/task ~ *I got side-tracked and can't remember what we were talking about.*

get someone up: wake/arouse someone from sleep and tell them to get out of bed ~ *You ought to get Daniel up or he'll be late for school.*

get someone's back up: make someone angry ~ *He gets my back up when he says things like that.*

get started on something: begin to work on a task/job ~ *I can't wait to get started on the project.*

get stuck into something: begin a task/work enthusiastically ~ *We'd better get stuck into it or we'll never finish.*

get stuck into someone: berate/scold/criticize/assault someone ~ *Mum got stuck into me for coming home at 2 a.m.*

get sucked in: be conned; tricked; cheated ~ *I really got sucked into their joke.*

get/start the ball rolling: be the first to do/begin something ~ *I'll get the ball rolling by asking your names.*

get the gist of: understand the main essence/meaning of something ~ *It took me a while to understand how it's done, but I'm finally getting the gist of it.*

get the message across: convey a message ~ *1a) They hoped the graphic TV advertisement would get the "don't drink and drive" message across to teenagers. 1b) He didn't get the message across very well.*

get the munchies: become hungry ~ *I get munchies at this time every day.*

get the okay: get permission to do something ~ *Finally got the okay to start building their house.* *also: get the all clear/the green light/the nod/the go ahead

get the sack/axe/chop: be fired/dismissed from your job ~ *Did you hear Sue got the sack yesterday?* *also: get sacked; get/give someone the boot

get there: 1) arrive (at your destination) ~ *I probably won't get there until 5 p.m.*

2) fulfil one's goal; complete something ~ *We've still got a lot of work to do, but we'll get there.*

get this: [spoken] it's what you say when you want someone to listen to you ~ *Get this, everybody: I've just heard we might be getting wage rise!*

get to one/someone: be affected by something ~ *1a) That constant tapping noise is getting to me. 1b) This movie always gets to me.*

get through something: 1) endure hardship; troubles ~ *So distraught was he that he wondered how he would get through this difficult time.*

2) finish a task completely ~ *I finally got through the study assignment.*

get through to: 1) make someone comprehend what is being said ~ *I can't seem to get through to him how important it is.*

2) reach someone on the telephone ~ *Maybe they're not at home—I can't get through to them.*

get up: [spoken] command to get out of bed ~ *Come on, time to get up—it's late!*

getup: (clothing) outfit ~ *That's a pretty fancy getup you're wearing!*

get-up-and-go: one's energy; vigour; enthusiasm ~ *She's got a lot of get-up-and-go for someone her age.*

get up steam: gather momentum; summons energy ~ *She stopped to get up steam before completing the final stage of the hill climb.*

get up to: do; occupy oneself; spend one's time ~ *What did you get up to yesterday?*

get with it: 1) [spoken] a way of telling someone to concentrate; be more aware ~ *Come on, get with it! We've got more work to do.*

2) [spoken] be up-to-date/knowledgeable about current trends ~ *Get with it, Mum, that style's been out of fashion for ages!*

get your arse into gear: [spoken slang] a crude way of telling someone to get ready/organised ~ *Come on, get your arse into gear, we're leaving in ten minutes.*

getting at: the main point of an argument/the message one wants to convey ~ *What I'm getting at is . . .*

getting on: advancing in age/years ~ *He's getting on a bit now and can no longer do the things he used to.*

(it) takes (some) getting used to: that one/someone needs to become accustomed to something ~ *1a) Adjusting to a new environment takes some getting used to. 1b) Eating spicy food takes getting used to.*

gimme: give me ~ *Gimme that.*

gin and tonic/G&T: a popular alcoholic drink containing gin and tonic water ~ *I'll have a G&T, thanks, barman.*

(the) girls: a group of female friends ~ *I'm going out with the girls tonight.*

give a toss: be unconcerned; uncaring about something ~ *I don't give a toss about what people think of me.* *see also: give two hoots; give a shit

give anything/nothing away: refuse to reveal the facts/a secret ~ *I've been trying to find out what the exciting announcement will be but no one's giving anything away.*

give in to something/someone: yield to an opposing influence; agree to something after initially opposing it ~ *I finally gave in to Mum's nagging and had my hair cut.*

give it/something a rest: stop doing something ~ *1a) You haven't stopped talking all morning—why don't you give it a rest. 1b) I've been working on this all morning—I think I'll give it a rest for now.*

give it to one/someone straight: reveal the facts honestly ~ *Doctor, I'd like you to give it to me straight. How serious is my illness?*

give one/someone a break: 1) [spoken] request for someone to stop annoying/harassing you ~ *Give me a break, will you—I'm doing the best I can!*

2) consider someone's appeal/request/achievements ~ *She's proven herself, so let's give her a break and include her in the team.*

3) [spoken] said when you know that someone's trying to trick you ~ *Give me a break—I know that's not what happened.*

give/offer one's condolences: express your sympathy with someone who is grieving ~ *We offer our deepest condolences to those affected by the tragedy.*

(something) gives one the creeps/horrors/shivers/willies: describes something that evokes a strong feeling of revulsion/fear in someone ~ *1a) Just looking at spiders gives me the horrors. 1b) That weird man over there gives me the willies.*

give one's word: make a solemn promise to someone ~ *I will not tell anyone. I give you my word.*

give oneself away: reveal/make something known about yourself ~ *I'm going to give myself away here by admitting I secretly like her.*

give oneself up: surrender to ~ *He was urged to give himself up.*

give and take: mutual compromise/cooperation ~ *For this joint project to succeed, there has to be a of give and take on everyone's behalf.*

give or take: more/less of; plus or minus a specified amount/space/length/weight/quantity of something ~ *I should be there in about an hour, give or take ten minutes.*

give someone a buzz: call someone on the phone ~ *I'll give you a buzz when I get home.*

give someone a fair go: provide a reasonable opportunity for someone to do something ~ *He's worked hard, so we should give him a fair go and hire him for the job.*

give someone a hand: help/assist someone with something ~ *Would you like me to give you a hand to finish it?*

give someone a (big) hand: a spoken request for the audience to clap/applaud someone's performance/act ~ *Everyone, please give a big hand to the Candy Sisters Singers.*

give someone a hard time: 1) make things difficult for someone/give someone grief ~ *For reasons unknown, my boss gave me a hard time at work today.*

2) mock/tease/criticise someone (humorously) ~ *My friends all gave me a hard time about my haircut.* *also: give someone heaps/hell

give your respects: send your greetings to someone ~ *Please give my respects to your parents.*

give someone a hoy: 1) [shouted] so as to get someone's attention ~ *Hoy! We're over here!*

2) call someone on the phone ~ *I'll give you a hoy next week.*

give someone/something a wide berth: 1) avoid someone ~ *People often gave him a wide berth because of his strange appearance.*

2) allow plenty of space between yourself and something ~ *The truck needed space to turn, so I gave it a wide berth.*

give something a whirl: give something a try ~ *I've never done it before, but I'm willing to give it a whirl.*

give in: yield/admit defeat ~ *I give in. What's the answer?*

give in to: accept that you cannot win/accept defeat ~ *1a) Authorities finally gave in to public pressure and changed the ruling. 1b) She refused to give in, and went on to win the match.*

give/get marching orders: be dismissed; fired; sacked; axed from one/someone's job ~ *Two staff members were given their marching orders for misconduct.*

give someone the run around: purposely inconvenience/mislead someone; act evasively ~ *He gives me the run around whenever I ask him about it.*

give something away: 1) reveal information or facts that should be kept secret ~ *Don't tell Sue our plans, she's sure to give them away.*

2) show an emotion or quality that you're trying to hide ~ *His face gave nothing away.*

3) give something to someone for free ~ *As a promotion, the company gave away free movie tickets.*

give the game away: retire from playing your chosen sport or career ~ *1a) He suffered too many injuries so he decided to give the game away. 1b) Do you still work in advertising? No, I gave the game away last year.*

give two hoots: be indifferent/unconcerned about something ~ *I don't give two hoots about what people think of me.* *also: give a damn; give a toss; couldn't care less

give (it) your all: do something the best you can; try as hard as you can to do something ~ *1a) We lost to a stronger team, but we gave it our all. 1b) It doesn't matter if you come first or last, as long as you give your all.*

give up: 1) admit defeat/failure ~ *I've given up trying to get her to change her mind.*

2) stop doing something you do regularly ~ *I don't think he'll ever give up smoking.*

give up the ghost: 1) for machinery to cease working ~ *My old car finally gave up the ghost.*

2) to die ~ *After a prolonged illness, the old man finally gave up the ghost.*

3) lose motivation/the will to do something ~ *She's given up the ghost following many unsuccessful attempts to play the guitar.*

give way: for a structure to collapse/yield ~ *The chair I was sitting on suddenly gave way.*

give way to: 1) allow other cars to go before you when driving ~ *When turning you must give way to oncoming traffic.*

2) supersede something/be replaced by something newer ~ *Smaller businesses gave way to bigger corporations.*

3) surrender strong emotions ~ *Excitement gave way to sadness when the siren signalled the end of the game. Our team had lost.*

give what for: strong reprimand/scolding ~ *She did what? I'll give her what for when I see her!*

give-and-take: mutual cooperation/agreement ~ *There was a lot of give-and-take between them, but they finally agreed on a deal.*

what gives: [spoken] a way of asking "what happened" or "why" ~ *You promised me a ticket, but gave it to Jack! What gives?*

gizmo: an unidentifiable small device/gadget/piece of equipment ~ *They were amazed by the funny looking gizmos in the computer workshop.*

Gladwrap: plastic food wrap

glam: glamorous ~ *You're looking very glam tonight!*

glammed up: dress glamorously ~ *The excited young teenager got all glammed up for her first big date.*

glance around: look quickly around ~ *She glanced around the room looking for her friends.*

at first glance/sight: the moment you first see someone/something ~ *At first glance it appeared she was naked.*

glasses: eyeglasses; spectacles/specs ~ *He can't see a thing without his glasses.*

globe-trotting: to travel to different parts the world ~ *She spends almost six months of the year globe-trotting.*

glued to the box: to watch television intently or for long periods ~ *He sits glued to the box every Saturday.*

glued to the spot: be unable to move because you're frightened/ shocked/mesmerised by what you're seeing ~ *They stood there, glued to the spot.*

gluggy: a sticky, thick-textured substance ~ *Whenever she tries to make custard she always ends up with a gluggy mess.*

go about: 1) undertake a task in a particular way ~ *Think carefully about how you should go about the task before you begin.*

2) do something you usually do ~ *The victim was going about her usual business when she was attacked.*

go about it the wrong way: the wrong way/method of doing/ saying something ~ *You won't get the results you want because you're going about it the wrong way.*

go after: chase/pursue /try to catch someone ~ *The policeman had no choice but to go after the thief.*

go ahead: proceed/begin/start to do something ~ *1a) We decided to go ahead with the plan. 1b) Please, go ahead and use my phone.*

go ahead of: go before someone ~ *He went ahead of me on the bushwalk.*

go along: 1) accompany someone somewhere ~ *I was asked if I'd like to go along to the party.*

2) continue to happen/develop ~ *Everything was going along well until it started to rain.*

3) proceed/travel ~ *Go along this road for a bit, then turn right when you get to the park.*

go along with: agree with something/someone ~ *1a) I didn't go along with what they said. 1b) The majority of residents didn't go along with the council's proposed changes.*

go(ing) around: 1) visit a person/place ~ *I'm going around to Mike's place for a while.*

2) for information/an illness to travel from one person to another ~ *2a) There's a rumour going around that Steve's leaving. 2b) Take precautions, the flu's going around.*

3) move/travel in a circular motion ~ *The racing cars are going around the track.*

4) enough of something for everyone ~ *There weren't enough books to go around.*

go astray: 1) to wander off the path/route ~ *Not wanting to go astray, they were careful to follow the trail.*

2) get lost/misplaced ~ *Pens have a habit of going astray in this office.*

3) to turn bad/go wrong ~ *3a) My plans went astray. 3b) Their marriage went astray after only a year.*

4) fail reach a destination ~ *The letter I sent him went astray.*

go away: 1) [spoken] a command/request for something/someone to move away from you ~ *Go away!*

2) move away from a person or place ~ *You'd best go away from there, it's dangerous.*

3) leave for a short period of time ~ *We're going away for three weeks.*

4) of something to stop existing/be noticeable ~ *This rash won't go away.*

go back for: return to a place to get something/someone ~ *I'd left my wallet at home, so I had to go back for it.*

go back to: 1) return to a person/place/subject/activity ~ *1a) I don't like it here, let's go back. 1b) I didn't think he'd ever go back to her after they separated. 1c) I'm now well enough to go back to work. 1d) At last, he was able to go back to what he was doing.*

2) for something to have existed since/for a particular time ~ *2a) Some of these buildings go back to the eighteenth century. 2b) Our friendship goes back a long way.*

3) return to school after a break ~ *The kids go back to school next week.*

4) the clocks go back when daylight saving finishes ~ *Don't forget to put your clocks back tonight.*

go before: of a matter/person to be considered before an authority/judge/committee ~ *1a) The proposal will go before the committee tomorrow. 1b) He's due to go before the judge next week.*

go begging: 1) for unsold goods/items to sell at a discount price ~ *Mostly everything's been sold, but there's still plenty of books going begging.*

2) for many jobs/positions to still be vacant ~ *It's hard to find jobs in certain fields, but there are many hospitality jobs going begging.*

go belly up: for a business to fail/fold up ~ *Struggling financially, the business eventually went belly up.*

go berserk: to go wildly mad/crazy with excitement or anger ~ *1a) The crowd went berserk when the singer came on stage. 1b) The effect of alcohol and drugs made him go absolutely berserk.*

go bush: retreat to/live in a remote rural area for an extended period of time ~ *His idea of relaxation is to go bush for a couple of months.*

go by: 1) for time to pass ~ *The day's gone by so quickly.*

2) for something to move in and out of one's line of vision ~ *They sat on the riverbank and watched the boats go by.*

3) to move past or stop at a place for a short time ~ *I'll go by the supermarket before I come home.*

go by something: 1) consider/be guided by what someone said/suggested/wrote ~ *1a) If we go by Jane's instructions we shouldn't have any trouble finding it. 1b) Going by this map, the building should be on our left.*

2) use an alias ~ *He often goes by the name of Bigsy.*

go down: 1) be remembered or recorded ~ *He went down in history as one of Australia's greatest Olympic swimmers.*

2) receive a prison sentence ~ *They'll go down for a long time for their crime.*

3) to occur/happen ~ *What's going down?*

4) something easily swallowed ~ *These large tablets don't go down easily.*

5) travel/journey in a southerly direction ~ *We're going down to Melbourne next week.*

go down the wrong way: describes what happens when food that's been swallowed begins to enter the breathing tube

(to not) go down well: information received unfavourably ~ *Plans to demolish the building didn't go down to well with local residents.*

go too far: of something said or done to be inappropriate/upsetting ~ *This time your silly pranks have gone too far.*

go for: 1). attack someone/something ~ *The dog looked like it was about to go for me.*

2) have a liking/fondness for something ~ *I don't really go for that type of music.* *see also: go in for

3) be sold for a particular amount of money ~ *The house went for more than $3 million at auction.*

4) choose something in particular ~ *I'm going for the fish and chips. What about you?*

5) engage in an activity ~ *5a) I'm going for a walk. 5b) Would you like to go for a drive?*

go for a burn: go for short drive in a car ~ *Chris took us for a burn in his new sports car.*

go for broke: invest everything/take a big risk/put great effort into doing something ~ *He was very determined, so he decided to go for broke and invest all his savings into purchasing the house.*

go for it: [spoken] enthusiastic encouragement for someone to try hard ~ *If you want to try out for the team, go for it then, you've got the talent.*

go for your life: [spoken] expression of encouragement

go, go, go: hectic non-stop activity ~ *I'll be glad to have a rest. It's been go, go, go all week.*

go hell for leather: go/travel very fast ~ *I had to go hell for leather to catch up with them.*

go in: 1) enter a place/space ~ *1a) We'll go in the front door. 1b) Here's where the water goes in.*

2) participate/take part in an event ~ *I'm going in four events at the swimming carnival.*

go in for: have/not have an interest in something ~ *I don't go in for that type of music.*

go it alone: do something alone/independently ~ *John can no longer accompany me on the journey, so I'll have to go it alone.*

go jump in the lake: [spoken] a rude dismissal ~ *After the way you treated me you can just go jump in the lake!* *also: go jump!

go/sell like hot cakes: said of things that sell very quickly and in great numbers ~ *The books went like hot cakes.*

go off: 1) of food to go bad/become spoiled ~ *This milk smells bad, I think it's gone off.*

2) lose interest in doing something ~ *I've gone off eating fish.*

go off at someone: [spoken] reprimand angrily ~ *She just went off at me for nothing.*

go off half-cocked: act prematurely/without thinking ~ *It won't do you any good to go off half-cocked when you confront him about it.*

go off with a bang: of something to be very successful ~ *The party went off with a bang.*

go on: 1) to act/behave stupidly ~ *I wish you wouldn't go on like that.*

2) talk endlessly about something ~ *He could go on about that topic for hours if you let him.*

3) take place/occur ~ *What's going on here?*

4) continue doing something ~ *We can go with our work after lunch.*

5) [spoken] request to continue ~ *Go on, what were you saying?*

6) [spoken] encouragement for someone to try/do something ~ *6a) Go on, try it—you'll like it. 6b) Go on—you can do it!*

go on and on: 1) talk endlessly about something ~ *He went on and on about his new car.*

2) something never ending/endless ~ *I thought we'd never get there—the road seemed to go on and on forever.* *also: rattle on; ramble on; go on forever

go one better: outperform; outdo someone; improve on someone else's effort ~ *He went one better than his neighbour and built a bigger swimming pool.*

go out: 1) of a light/flame to become extinguished/non-functioning ~ *The power went out during the thunderstorm.*

2) in a romantic relationship ~ *Bill and Wendy have been going out for about three years.*

3) do something for pleasure/entertainment ~ *We're going out for dinner tonight.*

go out of one's way: 1) make a special effort to do something for someone ~ *Steve often goes out of his way to help his neighbour.*

2) divert from the set route ~ *You have to go out of your way to get there, but it's worth it.*

go over: 1) review something ~ *I'll go over the report with you when you've finished reading it.*

2) repeat/rehearse an action/activity ~ *Let's go over the dance steps again until we get it right.*

go over one's/someone's head: 1) approach a higher authority to get results ~ *I'll have to go over her head to air my complaint.*

2) difficult to understand/comprehend ~ *His joke went straight over my head.*

go overboard: do or say something excessive/unreasonable ~ *1a) We went overboard when we ordered the food—there's so much left over. 1b) He's not one to go overboard with praise.*

go places: likely to succeed ~ *With a great voice like that, I'm sure she'll go places.*

go the distance: endure; carry a course of action until finished ~ *I wasn't fit enough to go the distance in the marathon.*

go through: 1) endure difficult times ~ *The poor fellow went through a terrible ordeal.*

2) examine/search a space/area ~ *I've gone through all the cupboards and I can't find it.*

3) rehearse/practise something ~ *3a) The director wants us to go through the opening scene once more. 3b) She went through the usual morning routine of making school lunches.*

4) to go through processes/stages in a procedure ~ *It goes through various cleaning and sorting stages before it's packaged.*

5) pass from one area to another ~ *The road takes you right through the middle of the town.*

6) use/spend/eat all of something ~ *He went through most of his weekly wage in three days.*

go through someone: 1) use someone as an intermediary ~ *You'll have to go through Mark to get it approved.*

2) be digested too quickly; have a laxative effect ~ *That spicy food has gone right through me!*

go through the roof: 1) when the cost/price of something increases greatly ~ *The price of petrol has gone through the roof.*

2) to get very angry ~ *He's going to go through the roof when he sees the damage you've done to the car.* *also: hit the roof

go through with: finish/complete something as planned/promised (often said in the negative) ~ *It's too risky. I don't think I can go through with it.*

go to billyo: [spoken] a rude dismissal

go to any/great lengths: do whatever's necessary to achieve something ~ *She went to great lengths to ensure their safety.*

go to one's head: 1) suffer from the effects of alcohol (feel dizzy) ~ *That champagne has gone to my head.*

2) to feel proud/egotistical ~ *She's never let her celebrity status go to her head.*

go to town: lose your inhibitions; become carefree have a fun time ~ *They went to town after finishing their exams.*

go (well) together: for two or more things to complement each other ~ *1a) The scarf and the shoes go well together. 1b) The curtains don't go well with the carpet.* *also: go well with

go too far: behave unreasonably; exaggerate/do something to the excess ~ *1a) I think we've gone too far with the decorations. 1b) He went too far with that tasteless joke.*

go troppo: Behave strangely, lose your mind. The phrase was first used by Australian troops in the Pacific during the Second World War, and arose from the idea that long exposure to tropical conditions affected your sanity.

go under: 1) of a business to collapse; fail ~ *The poor economy was the main reason his business went under.*

2) sink below the water surface ~ *Filling quickly with water, it took only minutes for the boat to go under.*

go underground: hide from authorities ~ *The criminals went underground to avoid capture.*

go up: 1) to increase ~ *1a) The price of petrol is always going up. 1b) His weight's gone up slightly.*

2) travel in a northerly direction ~ *I'm going up north for the holidays.*

3) being built ~ *There's a new house going up next door.*

4) move upwards ~ *We watched the balloon go up higher and higher.*

go up in smoke/flames: 1) destroyed/ruined ~ *Now she's injured, her chance to compete has gone up in smoke.*

2) to burn quickly and completely ~ *They could do nothing but watch the building go up in flames.*

go with: accompany someone somewhere ~ *Can I go with you to the party?*

always on the go: always moving/busy doing something ~ *He never stays still, he's always on the go.*

from the word go: from the start of something ~ *We've had nothing but problems with the project from the word go.*

give it a go/whirl: try/experience something/attempt to do something ~ *I've never ridden a horse, but I'd like to give it a go.*

make a go of: make a serious attempt at doing something ~ *She's never done this type of work before, but she's really making a go of it.*

the go: [spoken] a way of asking what's happening ~ *What's the go with your holiday plans?*

that's the way it goes: [spoken] to accept the inevitable/that that is how things are/happen ~ *I'm sorry you missed out on selection, but that's just the way it goes.*

there you go: [spoken] 1) what you say when you recognise someone's achievement ~ *There you go, you did it!*

2) [spoken] used when giving/handing something to someone ~ *There you go, here's your coffee.*

touch-and-go: of a precarious/uncertain situation or outcome ~ *His injuries were so serious it was touch-and-go as to whether he would survive.*

goalie: goalkeeper in football/soccer

Goanna: Goannas, or monitors, are a distinctive group of lizards ranging in size from 12 cm to 1.3 metres (not including the tail). These carnivores find their food by searching across the landscape. In Australia, goannas have evolved into over twenty species. They have grown in numbers in Australia due to the fact that there were few medium-sized carnivores to compete with.

act the goat: to behave in a foolish, stupid manner ~ *He's always in trouble for acting the goat.*

old goat: [informal] a foolish old man ~ *Don't listen to his nasty comments, he's just a silly old goat.*

goat country: rough/steep/inaccessible terrain

gob: [slang] one's/someone's mouth ~ *Will you shut your gob!*

gobble up: devour; eat quickly/entirely ~ *The bird gobbled up the worm.*

gobbledegook: nonsense; unintelligible jargon ~ *This report is gobbledegook.*

gobsmacked: to be utterly amazed/astonished/speechless ~ *I was gobsmacked when I heard what happened!*

God knows when: uncertain time in the future ~ *God knows when we'll get there.* *also: who knows when

God knows where: an unknown place ~ *God knows where it went.* *also: who knows where

God only knows: no one but God knows ~ *Where is he? God only knows!* *also: who knows

goer: someone/something who/that works energetically ~ *That racehorse is a real goer.*

goes in one ear and out the other: of something to be heard and understood but soon forgotten ~ *Whatever I say to her just seems to go in one ear and out the other.*

goes for: [spoken] of something said about one person/thing to be also true for someone/something else ~ *You need to pay better attention in class, Tim—and the same goes for the rest of you.*

(it) goes without saying: [spoken] when something obvious needs no explanation ~ *It goes without saying that night follows day.*

goggles: eyewear for swimming

goin' [informal] going ~ *How's it goin'?*

going thing: a current, popular trend/fashion/ fad ~ *Shoulder pads were the going thing in fashion during the 1980s.*

going-over: 1) a severe beating ~ *His opponent gave him a good going-over.*

2) give something a full/thorough examination ~ *The mechanic gave the engine a much-needed going-over.*

goings-on: strange, odd happenings/behaviour ~ *Lately there's been some strange goings-on in that section of the reserve.*

on-going: a continuing event/procedure ~ *She's having on-going medical treatment.*

golden rule: the most important rule that never should be broken ~ *The golden rule when using this equipment is to use protective eyewear at all times.*

gold mine: 1) a profitable business/enterprise ~ *She has turned it into a goldmine.*

2) someone/something that provides/has a resource of something required ~ *You'll find a goldmine of information on their website.*

gone bung: of equipment to fail ~ *The TV suddenly went bung.*

gone bust: (of a business) to go bankrupt

gone to pack: describes something that is in bad shape/condition ~ *He has little pride in his house, he's let it go to pack.* *also: gone to the dogs

gone with the wind: of something disappeared/lost ~ *I don't know where it is, it's just gone with the wind.*

a goner: doomed; beyond help/recovery ~ *It was too late to save the blazing building—it was a goner.*

(a) gong: an award ~ *She got a gong for her community service.*

gonna: [informal] going to ~ *What are we gonna do?*

(I'm) good: [spoken] a way of saying that everything's okay/alright ~ *Did you hurt yourself? No—I'm good.*

(as) good as done: almost completed/finished/accomplished ~ *Have you finished it yet? No, but it's as good as done!*

(as) good as new: 1) revived ~ *I'm as good as new now that I'm rested.*

2) something restored/functioning as new ~ *My old bike's as good as new after Dad fixed it.*

good as gold: well behaved ~ *He's been as good as gold.*

2) in good working order ~ *My knee's been as good as gold since the operation.*

good enough for: of something adequate/suiting the purpose ~ *1a) The service wasn't exceptional, but it was good enough for me. 1b) Don't be so fussy—if it's good enough for me it's good enough for you!*

good for: adequate/suitable for something ~ *This piece of junk is only good for the bin!*

good for nothing: someone/something deemed useless; worthless ~ *The phone's good for nothing since it fell in the water.*

good grief: a mild expression of annoyance; surprise ~ *Good grief! What's that?*

(a) good many: quite a lot/few ~ *A good many residents attended the meeting.*

goodonya/yer: [informal] good on you – an expression of congratulations ~ *That's fantastic! Goodonya!* *also: good one; 'onya

good riddance: [spoken] a rude way of saying goodbye to someone undesirable/unwanted ~ *Good riddance (to you)!*

good sort: describes an attractive, well-presented woman ~ *Greg's new girlfriend's a good sort.*

make good: 1) fulfil/implement an agreement/promise ~ *She made good on her promise to help us.*

2) accomplish/carry out a procedure ~ *They made good their escape.*

3) repay/recompense ~ *He made good on the IOU.*

4) become successful ~ *She's a small town girl who made good as an international model.*

many a (something): a large number of people or things ~ *There are many a good books to be found in the library.*

no good: 1) worthless ~ *Throw them away, they're no good.*

2) verbally expressed when hearing bad/sad news ~ *You've broken your leg—that's no good.*

3) a predicted negative outcome ~ *I fear no good will come of the situation.*

4) planning/doing something bad/illegal ~ *I'm certain they're up to no good.*

5) a hopeless/worthless situation ~ *It's no good asking, she'll only say no.*

6) an unsuitable/inconvenient time ~ *Tomorrow's no good, I'm busy all day.*

fat lot of good that was: [spoken] to say that an action/idea was worthless/useless; a waste of time ~ *A fat lot of good that was washing the car earlier today, it's raining now.*

too good to be true: of something suspiciously unbelievable ~ *Their offer/deal sounds too good to be true.*

good-for-nothing: an idle/worthless/lazy person ~ *I wouldn't employ that good-for-nothing, lazy gardener.*

goodie/y: 1) the morally good character/hero of a movie/film ~ *That actor seems to always play the goodie.*

2) an expression of delight ~ *Oh goody, my favourite chocolates!*

goodies: treats ~ *Grandma always brings us lots of goodies when she visits.*

goodie/y-goodie/y: a law-abiding/virtuous citizen ~ *She's such a goody-goody and never gets into trouble in class.* *also: goody two-shoes

goodies and baddies: the good and the bad characters in the movie/film/story ~ *Of course, crime stories always have goodies and baddies.*

goodie bag: a bag containing small presents/gifts ~ *All the guests were given a little goodie bag.*

goodness: [spoken] exclamation of (a pleasant) surprise ~ *Goodness—are those flowers for me?*

goodness gracious: [spoken] exclamation of frustration/ annoyance/ mild anger ~ *Goodness gracious—what a mess!*

good-oh: [spoken] okay; an expression of approval; concludes a conversation ~ *Good-oh, we'll meet at 3 p.m. at the coffee shop. See you then.*

come across with the goods: deliver/pay money owing ~ *He hasn't come across with the goods yet.*

goof off: be lazy/idle/waste time ~ *All he's done all day is goof off.*

goof up: make an error/blunder ~ *It's important this is done properly, so don't goof up!*

goofy: someone/something silly/stupid/clumsy ~ *The goofy circus clowns are always the favourite attraction for children.*

googy egg: (said to children) a chicken's egg

gorblimey: [spoken] mild oath; expression of amazement/surprise ~ *Gorblimey, have a look at this!*

gosh: [spoken] an expression of amazement/surprise/annoyance ~ *Gosh! I didn't mean for that to happen.*

goss: gossip ~ *What's happening. What's the goss?*

go-slow: a protest action against an employer/organisation whereby workers deliberately slow down production ~ *Workers staged a go-slow protest against new work regulations.*

(what's) got into: [spoken] when trying to understand someone's change in mood/behaviour ~ *1a) I don't know what's got into him lately. 1b) What's got into you? Why are you so angry?*

(you) got me: [spoken] 1) is what you say when you don't know something ~ *You got me there—I don't know the answer.*

2) pretence (in a game) at being injured/shot at ~ *Ahhh—you got me!*

gotcha: 1) [spoken] got you; used to confirm that you have understood what someone has told you ~ *We'll meet at 3 p.m. at the park. Gotcha.*

2) exclaimed when capturing something/someone ~ *He yelled "gotcha" when he finally caught the escaping dog.*

gotta: [informal] got to ~ *1a) I've gotta go now. 1b) You've gotta be joking!*

GP: medical general practitioner/doctor

GPO: General Post Office. The main post office found in the centre of any major city. It's used as a base marker in measuring the true distance found on road maps from one place to another.

gran: grandmother/granny/grandma

grandad: grandfather/pop/poppy

granny flat: a small unit/flat for independent living either set within or set apart from the main house ~ *She lives in a granny flat at the back of my parents' house.*

Granny Smith apple: This is a popular, green-skinned apple named after Maria Smith, an orchardist (fruit grower) who began cultivating them in her Sydney orchard in 1868. They are the chosen apple for stewing or for use in baking apple pies.

The Great Barrier Reef: This popular tourist destination is the world's largest coral reef system, which is composed of over 2,900 individual reefs and 900 islands, and stretches for over 2,600 kilometres. It is located in the Coral Sea, off the coast of Queensland. It can be seen from outer space and is the world's biggest single structure made by living organisms. It is a World Heritage Site.

great one for: describes someone who habitually does something different/out of the ordinary ~ *He's a great one for losing his keys.*

greatest thing/invention since sliced bread: a new invention regarded as exceptional/noteworthy/outstanding ~ *She thinks the Internet is the greatest thing since sliced bread.*

greedy guts: *see: garbage guts

green light: permission/approval to do something ~ *The council has finally given us the green light to start the home improvements.*

have a green thumb: someone who is a skilled gardener ~ *Anne has a green thumb; why don't you give your sick plant to her?*

green with envy: when you're very jealous ~ *He was green with envy when we told him we'd bought a new boat.*

greengrocer: a fruit and vegetable seller

greenie: environmentalist/conservationist

greens: vegetables ~ *I try to encourage my kids to eat their greens.*

grey matter: [informal] one's brains/intellect

grey nomad: a retired person who spends their time travelling the countryside in a van/bus/motorhome

grin from ear to ear: to smile widely ~ *She was grinning from ear to ear when she heard the good news.* *also: (give a) cheesy grin

grind away: work/study laboriously ~ *1a) He ground away the outer rock core to get to the gemstone. 1b) She's grinding away at her math homework.*

grind to a halt: of a system/process to gradually slow down to a stop ~ *An accident caused traffic to grind to a halt.* *also: come to a grinding halt

grind up: reduce something to small pieces/pulverise ~ *1a) Grind up the seeds and sprinkle them on top. 1b) She ground up the beans before making the coffee.*

lose one's grip: 1) fail to maintain/keep control of one's mental ability/function ~ *He has lost his grip on reality.*

2) lose hold of something ~ *If he loses his grip he's doomed.*

grog: alcohol ~ *The food's supplied, but we have to bring grog.*

BYOG: bring your own grog ~ 1) a written instruction on an invitation to a private function/party that means you're expected bring alcohol

2) signage outside a restaurant indicating diners can bring their own wine and beer

groggy: giddy/unsteady ~ *He was feeling groggy from the anaesthetic.*

grog shop: a shop that sells alcohol *see also: bottle/liquor shop

(a) grot: someone dirty/unkempt ~ *He's a nice guy, but he's a bit of a grot.*

grotty: describes something/someplace filthy/untidy/dirty/messy

give ground: yield/cede territory ~ *He was going to stay where he was—he would not give ground.*

break new ground: 1) advance beyond previous achievements/ success ~ *They're breaking new ground with this new engine.*

2) do something that hasn't been done before ~ *Scientists have broken new ground in the field of medical research.*

go to ground: hide ~ *The criminal went to ground to avoid capture.*

lose ground: make no progress ~ *The racing car driver lost ground when his car skidded off the track.*

old stamping ground: the place you grew up in; a place where you lived for a length of time; a place of good memories ~ *I know the area well—it's my old stamping ground.*

on shaky ground: to be in an unstable/uncertain situation ~ *Their marriage is on shaky ground.*

from the ground up: build/create something from nothing to reality/finality ~ *It's been rebuilt from the ground up.*

lay the groundwork: provide the fundamentals; create a foundation; do the preliminary work ~ *This high school science course lays the groundwork for tertiary education.*

grow on one/someone: gradually begin to accept/agree with someone/something ~ *Ted's new plan has grown on me and I can now see its merits.*

grow out of: 1) become too tall to fit into your clothes ~ *He grew out of his new pants in four months.*

2) abandon practices as one matures ~ *She was hoping her son would soon grow out of his lazy habits.*

3) develop and grow outwards from something ~ *Rampant weeds were found growing out of the pavement.*

grow up: 1) the process of maturing/growing in size ~ *He's grown up a lot since I last saw him.*

2) arise/come into existence ~ *New suburbs are growing up all over the place.*

3) [spoken] what you tell someone who is being childish ~ *Just grow up! You're not a child any more.*

grub: 1) food

2) humorous description of a dirty child ~ *Look at you, you grub!*

grub's on: [spoken] a call to come and eat ~ *Come on everybody - grub's on!*

grundies: *see: undies

guard against: be alert/protect against someone/something ~ *1a) The building had a security system to guard against theft. 1b) She wore a thick coat to guard against the cold wind.*

be on guard: be vigilant/alert; think or behave carefully ~ *Be on guard for snakes—there are many in this area.* *also: be on the lookout

catch off guard: be surprised/surprise someone ~ *1a) My rival caught me off guard and won the race. 1b) The shop owner was caught off guard and robbed of nearly everything.*

drop/lower one's guard: relax one's vigilance; become vulnerable ~ *Once he realized they could be trusted, he dropped his guard and began talking.*

guide away: steer/direct/lead something away from something ~ *Someone was posted to guide traffic away from the accident scene.*

gum tree: the common name for a eucalypt tree

gumboots: waterproof rubber boots *UK Wellington boots/Wellies

stick to one's guns: stand firm/have confidence in your beliefs/convictions ~ *I'm sticking to my guns on this issue!*

gung-ho: eager/enthusiastic ~ *It's his gung-ho attitude that helps him achieve his goals.*

gurgler: sink/drain hole

(go down the) gurgler: if money/work has gone down the gurgler, it has been wasted/lost ~ *If you quit the course now, that'll be $500 down the gurgler.*

gut(s): 1) stomach/abdomen ~ *He has a big gut.*

2) bravado/nerve/daring ~ *It takes a lot of guts to do what he's doing.*

3) the essential/main/core workings ~ *The guts of the machine are contained within this section.*

gut ache: stomach pain ~ *I've had a gut ache all day.*

gut feeling: an instinctive feeling/response ~ *I've got a gut feeling something's gone wrong.*

gutless: lacking courage/power ~ *1a) It was a gutless attack on a defenceless person. 1b) He was unimpressed by the car's gutless performance.*

gutsy: of having courage/power/bravado ~ *The singer was praised for her gutsy performance.*

bust one's guts: do excessive physical work; work hard/make a big effort ~ *1a) I busted my guts moving the furniture. 1b) I busted my guts to get here on time.* *also: work one's guts out

have a gutful: to have had enough of something/someone ~ *I've had a gutful of your complaining.*

have/got the guts: to have or not have the courage/nerve/bravado to do something ~ *I haven't got the guts to do it.*

guzzle: to drink; consume greedily/urgently ~ *He guzzled his drink.*

H

be in the habit of: habitually do something ~ *I'm not in the habit of doing that.*

get into the habit (of): begin/form a habit ~ *I've got into the habit of staying up late.*

good/bad habit: to have a good/bad habit ~ *Regular exercise is a good habit to get into. Smoking, on the other hand, is a bad habit.*

out of habit: do something without thinking what you're doing ~ *I mostly do it out of habit.* *also: from force of habit

habit-forming: something that can easily can become a habit ~ *Don't take up smoking, it's very habit-forming.*

hack (it): tolerate/endure/cope with an issue/situation ~ *I can't hack this job any more.*

had it: 1) to be exasperated/annoyed ~ *I've had it with your bad behaviour!*

2) non-functioning/beyond repair ~ *I think my old car has finally had it.*

3) exhausted/tired ~ *I'd had it after running the marathon.*

had one/a few too many: to have consumed too much alcohol ~ *You've had a few too many beers by the looks of you.*

had up for: accused or convicted ~ *He was had up for assault.*

hair's breadth: very small measure of something ~ *I won by a hair's breath.*

hairpiece: toupee/wig

keep out of someone's hair: stay away from someone to avoid trouble or avoid bothering them ~ *I'd keep out of her hair if I were you—she's had a bad day.*

let one's hair down: relax/act freely ~ *I've worked hard all week, so I'm going to let my hair down tonight.*

not have a hair out of place: to look tidy/well-groomed ~ *She never has a hair out of place.*

hairdo: hairstyle ~ *Did you see Linda's new hairdo?* *see also: 'do

hair-raising: a thrilling/frightening/exciting/terrifying experience ~ *That was certainly a hair-raising river crossing!* *also: hairy

. . . and a half: used to emphasise that something was bigger/better/more powerful ~ *Wow—that was a game and a half. I'm thoroughly exhausted!*

half the battle: the most difficult/important part of a process/ procedure ~ *Winning their support was half the battle.*

(given) half a chance: that someone/something will do something if they had the opportunity ~ *Give him half a chance and he'd eat it all.*

half dead: 1) thoroughly exhausted ~ *I'm half dead after doing all that work.* 2) almost dead ~ *That spider won't hurt you, it's half dead.*

half decent: 1) partially dressed (so as not to be embarrassed) ~ *Don't look—I'm only half decent!*

2) mediocre; better than expected *see also: not half bad

half a dozen: six of something ~ *1a) The recipe calls for half a dozen eggs. 1b) I have half a dozen or so varieties of roses growing in the garden.*

half your luck: [spoken] expression of congratulations ~ *You won an overseas trip! Half your luck!*

half a minute: a very short period of time ~ *I'll be there in half a minute.*

halftime: a short break in the middle of a sporting game ~ *The score at halftime was nil all.*

(that's) not the half of it: that there's more bad news to come ~ *That's not the half of it—not only did we not catch any fish, I lost my good fishing rod overboard!*

half-baked: incomplete/impractical ~ *1a) I'm not sure his half-baked plan will work. 1b) I don't believe his half-baked excuse.*

half-hearted: lacking enthusiasm/interest ~ *1a) She made a half-hearted attempt at helping me. 1b) Their response was only half-hearted.*

go halves: share the cost/workload ~ *Let's go halves so we can order the large pizza.*

ham it up: overact; exaggerate one's emotions/actions ~ *You can trust Joe to make everyone laugh. He's always hamming it up.*

go at hammer and tongs: do something with much enthusiasm/ energy ~ *He worked hammer and tongs to get the job finished on time.*

hand around: pass something to everyone in attendance/present ~ *The ring was handed around for everyone to admire.*

hand back: return something back to someone by hand ~ *Could you hand it back to me when you've finished with it?*

hand down: 1) bequeath something to someone ~ *He handed down his rare book collection to his son.*

2) announce/declare an official court verdict ~ *The judge handed down a guilty verdict.*

(work) hand in glove: of people to work cooperatively/closely ~ *They worked hand in glove to complete the project.* *also: hand in hand

(go) hand in hand: 1) of two people holding hands ~ *Together, they strolled hand in hand.*

2) exist/happen together ~ *The two components go hand in hand.*

hand in: 1) submit something by hand ~ *I have to hand the assignment in tomorrow.*

2) give something to a person in authority ~ *She handed in the money she found to police.* *also: hand in something

(have one's) hand in the till: steal money from your employer ~ *She was fired after being caught with her hand in the till.*

hand it to: [spoken] give credit to someone ~ *You've got to hand it to them, they know what they're doing.*

hand over: release/relinquish something ~ *1a) Jim handed over control to his successor. 1b) Okay, hand it over!*

hand out: distribute/give out to a group of people ~ *Please hand these out.*

hand over fist: to lose/make/exchange money very quickly/ rapidly ~ *They made money hand over fist.*

hand the hat around: take up a collection of money ~ *Steve handed the hat around to buy them a wedding present.* *also: pass the hat around

hands off!: [spoken] warning that means don't touch ~ *The beer in the fridge is mine—so hands off!* *see also: keep your hands off

by hand: manually/with the hands ~ *The dishwasher's broken so I have to wash up by hand.*

close at hand: within reach/nearby ~ *I keep my phone close at hand.* *also: near at hand

firm hand: to have strong control (with good intentions) ~ *It took John's firm hand to turn the company's losses into profits.*

force someone's hand: 1) compel someone to act prematurely ~ *She changed her game plan after forcing her opponent's hand in the first set.*

2) force someone to reveal their plan/strategy (as in a card game) ~ *Workers forced the director's hand by threatening to strike.*

free hand: 1) to have/not have both hands occupied ~ *I'm busy right now, but I'll help you as soon as I have a free hand.*

2) be given complete control over something ~ *The director gave me a free hand to complete the artwork.*

get/lay one's hands on someone/something: 1) threaten physical punishment ~ *If I ever get my hands on him he'll be sorry he ever did it.*

2) physically hold/obtain something/someone ~ *2a) She bought everything she could get her hands on. 2b) He reads every book he can lay his hands on.*

give someone a (helping) hand: help/assist someone ~ *Here, let me give you a hand with the luggage.* *also: lend (someone) a hand ~ *Can you lend me a hand with this?*

give someone/get a hand up: physically assist someone/be assisted to a standing position or to climb up to a higher position ~ *Steve gave me a hand up over the steep rocks.*

have a hand in something: be involved in/take part in an activity/doing something ~*1a) He denied it, but the police believed he had a hand in the robbery. 1b) She had a hand in making the business a success.*

have one's hands full: to be fully occupied/very busy ~ *1a) They've certainly got their hands full looking after all those children. 1b) I don't think he'll be able to help you, he's got his hands full at the moment.*

(have to) hand to it to someone: give recognition/credit ~ *I've got to hand it to Jack, he alone was responsible for making the business profitable.*

have one's hands in one's pockets: to be always spending money ~ *We had a terrific holiday, but I always had my hand in my pockets buying this and that.*

in good hands for something to be safe/secure ~ *Your children will be in good hands with us.* *also: in safe hands

in the palm of one's hands: to have complete control over someone ~ *The magician had his audience in the palm of his hand.*

know (it) like the back of your hand: to be thoroughly familiar with a procedure/route/system so as to not need guidance ~ *I know this route like the back of my hand.*

in one's/someone's hands: be responsible for/manage/control something ~ *1a) The business is now in the hands of the new owners. 1b) At the close of day I had excess goods on my hands. 1c) If the police don't control the demonstrators they'll soon have a riot on their hands.*

one's hands are tied: have no immediate control of a situation ~ *I'm waiting for further orders, but at the moment my hands are tied, so I can't help you.*

out of one's hands: for something to be no longer in your control ~ *There's nothing I can do. It's out of my hands.*

try one's hand at: attempt to do something for the first time ~ *I'd like to try my hand at sailing.*

turn (their) hand to: be adept at a new skill without experience/ prior learning ~ *With her artistic talent, she could turn her hand to anything.*

hands-free: of equipment/devices that can be used without the use of hands

hand-me-down(s): second-hand clothing; clothing passed from one person to another ~ *She often wore her older sister's hand-me-downs.*

handpicked: of something/someone to be carefully chosen for a particular purpose ~ *She was handpicked for the lead role in the movie.*

hand-to-hand: at close proximity/quarters ~ *They engaged in hand-to-hand combat.*

empty-handed: having gained/acquired nothing; bearing nothing ~ *1a) The police arrived, forcing the thief to run off empty-handed. 1b) The shop didn't have what she wanted so she came back empty-handed.*

heavy-handed: 1) use severe tactics to obtain results ~ *He had to use a heavy-handed approach to prevent the business from folding.*

2) overestimate the quantity/amount needed ~ *The cook was a bit heavy-handed with the chilli.*

3) use a powerful approach ~ *The punishment the court imposed was rather heavy-handed.*

off-hand: performed or expressed without preparation ~ *I can't remember all the details off-hand.* *also: off-hand remark

handful: describes something/someone troublesome/difficult to control ~ *My five young children are a handful to look after.*

handle (something): manage/cope/deal with a difficult situation ~ *1a) He quit his job because he couldn't handle the intense pressure that came with it. 1b) I thought she handled herself really well in the final interview.*

handle with kid gloves: treat carefully/tactfully/sensitively/gently ~ *He's still quite sensitive, so you ought to handle him with kid gloves.* *also: treat with kid gloves

handout: money received from someone/charity ~ *Being unemployed, he relies on handouts from the government.*

handy: 1) of something easily accessible; within reach ~ *It's always good to keep tissues handy when you have a cold.*

2) skilled/capable/adept with the hands ~ *My neighbour is handy at fixing anything around the home.*

handyman: someone employed to do odd jobs/small repairs

hang a left/right: (when driving) to suddenly turn left/right ~ *Just hang a left here.*

hang about: linger in an immediate area for a period of time ~ *1a) We were early so we hung about until the doors opened. 1b) The smoke from the fire hung about for days.* *also: hang around

hang around with: mix/associate with ~ *I don't like the people he's hanging around with.* *also: hang together

hang back/behind: linger behind/stay towards the back of an area ~ *Assessing the situation, he hung back from the crowd before deciding what to do.*

hang by . . . : be suspended at the end of rope/chain: dangle in the air ~ *1a) The timber was hanging at the end of the crane's steel cable. 1b) Her severed fingertip was hanging by a thread.*

hang five: [spoken] a way of telling somebody to wait a while/be patient ~ *Hang five—I'll be ready in a minute.*

hang in there: [spoken] encouragement to keep trying/persevere; be patient ~ *I know it's been tough, but hang in there, it'll be worth it in the end.* *also: hang on in there

(to) hang loose: be/behave relaxed ~ *I think I'll just hang loose this weekend.*

hang on: 1) [spoken] wait; stop ~ *1a) Hang on, that's not true. I never said that! 1b) Hang on, I forgot my keys.*

2) hold tightly ~ *Hang on to it now. Don't let it go.*

3) keep believing that a bad situation will have a good ending ~ *She hung on to the hope that her seriously ill child would recover.*

hang on every word: listen intently/carefully to what someone is saying ~ *Madly in love, he hung on to her every word.*

hang on for grim death: hold fast/firmly/tightly to something ~ *They hung on for grim death on the roller coaster ride.*

2) maintain one's position/status ~ *They've just managed to hang on to the lead.*

hang on something: to depend on something (happening) ~ *Whether or not we proceed all hangs on what decisions are made today.*

hang one's head: to suffer shame/humility ~ *He hung his head in shame.*

hang out for: wait with great anticipation ~ *1a) I'm hanging out for my big holiday. 1b) I've been hanging out for a coffee all morning.*

hang out at: spend time at a particular place ~ *We mostly hang out at the beach in summer.*

hang out with: spend relaxation time with someone/a group ~ *The five of them usually hang out together.*

hang the expense/cost: [spoken] that you're not concerned about the cost of something ~ *Hang the expense—this is a special celebration!*

hang up: 1) end a telephone call/put the receiver down ~ *She hung up on me!*

2) suspend something by placing on a hanger/hook/peg ~ *You can hang your clothes up in the cupboard.*

(have a) hang-up: to have an emotional pre-occupation ~ *1a) I don't see a future in this relationship unless we discuss your hang-ups. 1b) She doesn't have any hang-ups about her appearance.*

get the hang of (something): become proficient/skilled at/master an activity ~ *It took a while, but I soon got the hang of it.*

hangover: the after-effects/ill feeling from drinking too much alcohol ~ *We had a great night—but I've got one helluva hangover!*

hankie/hanky: handkerchief

hanky-panky: devious/mischievous activity; non-serious sexual play ~ *There was a bit of hanky-panky going on between them.*

happen upon: find/discover by chance ~ *I happened upon this quaint little tea shop in the arcade.* *also: chance (up)on; come upon

happen to be: be somewhere by chance/accident when something happened ~ *1a) Luckily I just happened to be there when he fell. 1b) I happened to be driving past at the time you were leaving.*

happy as Larry: to be very happy ~ *He's as happy as Larry in his new job.* *also: happy as a pig in mud; a happy little vegemite

happy-go-lucky: carefree/happy/cheerful/unconcerned ~ *He's a pretty happy-go-lucky bloke. Nothing much bothers him.*

a hard act to follow: a performance so good that it will be difficult to match/beat ~ *Last year's final between the Tigers and the Bears will be a hard act to follow.* *also: tough act to follow

hard-and-fast: strict/non-negotiable ~ *The company operates under hard-and-fast rules.*

(as) hard as nails: tough/unyielding ~ *He's as hard as nails. I don't think he'll consent.* *also: as tough as nails

hard at it: (be) working diligently ~ *How's the project coming along? Oh, I've been working hard at it all day.* *also: hard at work

hard cash: money as opposed to a cheque or credit card ~ *I paid them in hard cash.* *also: cold, hard cash

(be) hard on someone: be strict/cruel/harsh ~ *Don't be too hard on him. It wasn't all his fault.*

hard slog: laborious/tedious work/process ~ *We got there in the end, but it was a hard slog.*

hard stuff: dangerous drugs/strong liquor/alcohol ~ *He started out using soft drugs, but now he's onto the hard stuff.*

hard to come by: of something difficult to obtain ~ *These rare books were really hard to come by.*

hard to fathom: difficult to understand/comprehend ~ *Her reasons for doing it are hard to fathom.*

hard to swallow: difficult to accept ~ *The news was hard to swallow.*

hard up: to be temporarily short of money ~ *I'd like to be able to buy it, but I'm a bit hard up for cash this week.*

do something the hard way: 1) use a difficult/time consuming method to do something ~ *You're doing it the hard way. Here, let me show you an easier method.*

2) accomplish something without help ~ *She's achieved status within the industry by doing things the hard way.*

no hard feelings: [spoken] a way of telling someone that you are not angry with them after a disagreement ~ *I just want to let you know that there are no hard feelings.*

hard-hearted: mean/cruel/unfeeling

hare-brained: foolish/irrational/reckless ~ *I don't think her hare-brained scheme will work.*

in/out of harm's way: be in/out of danger; in a dangerous situation ~ *He moved the injured man out of harm's way.*

has-been: someone/something that's no longer fashionable/popular ~ *He's too much of a has-been to successfully revive his music career.*

make a hash of: ruin something ~ *He made a complete hash of the dinner.*

hash it out: discuss details about something with others ~ *We finally came to an agreement after hashing it out all afternoon.*

(I'll) eat my hat: you will be greatly surprised if something you say can't happen does happen ~ *If they win today, I'll eat my hat.*

at the drop of a hat: without hesitation ~ *You have to give me more notice, I can't just go at the drop of a hat.*

wear a different hat: assume different roles/jobs/responsibilities ~ *During the week she wears her clerk's hat, and on the weekends she puts on her dance teacher's hat.*

hat trick: three consecutive wins/successes ~ *If the team wins the final again this year, it will be a hat trick for them.* *In cricket: to dismiss three consecutive batsmen by bowling three consecutive balls.

hate to be in someone's shoes: to not want to be in someone's situation/predicament ~ *I'd hate to be in his shoes.*

mad as a hatter: describes someone silly/crazy/mad ~ *You won't get a sensible word out of him—he's as mad as a hatter.*

haul up: 1) bring before the authorities for reprimand/judgment ~ *The criminal was hauled up before the court.*

2) drag/pull/draw with force ~ *The fishermen hauled up the net.*

haunt: a favourite/frequently visited place ~ *1a) That little wine bar on South Street is my favourite haunt. 1b) I found him at his usual haunt.*

(to) have a ball: have a great time doing something ~ *It was so much fun—we had a ball!*

have a bo-peep: take a quick look at something ~ *Will you quickly have a bo-peep at this before you go?*

have a flutter: have a small bet/wager ~ *I had a flutter at the races.*

have a go at someone: verbally attack/severely berate ~ *Mum had a go at me for leaving the place in a mess.*

have a go at something: attempt to do something ~ *I'd like to have a go at skiing one day.* *also: have a bash at

have a heart: show mercy/compassion ~ *Have a heart—give to the poor and needy.*

have a spell: have a short rest ~ *I'm having a bit of a spell before I continue.*

have a turn: to suddenly feel giddy/dizzy/unwell ~ *She was taken to the hospital after having a funny turn.*

have it out: have an earnest discussion to settle a problem ~ *No, I don't want to talk about it later, we should have it out right now!*

have kittens: get angry/upset ~ *Dad will have kittens when he sees what happened to the car.*

have someone on: 1) trick/fool/deceive/tease someone ~ *You did what? You're having me on!*

2) accept a challenge ~ *I'll have you on any day.*

have a big head: to be conceited/vain

have got a bone to pick: a way of telling someone you want to talk to them about something they've done wrong ~ *I've got a bone to pick with you about your recent bad behaviour.*

have got a card up one's sleeve: to have a secret advantageous plan to be used later ~ *He thinks he's going to win, but I've got a card up my sleeve that will give me enough points to win.* *also: have got a trick/ace up one's sleeve

have got a good head on one's shoulders: (be) practical/sensible/smart ~ *You can depend on Jane to do a good job, she's got a good head on her shoulders.*

have/got a job ahead of . . . : to have a difficult task/job to fulfil ~ *With all those trees to plant, he sure has a job ahead of him.* *also: have your work cut out

have got a lot going for: describes someone who has the potential to succeed ~ *He's still an amateur player, but he's got a lot going for him.*

have/got a nerve: to be shameless/brazen/bold ~ *She's got a nerve speaking to the boss like that.*

have/got a screw loose: to be slightly mad/crazy/insane ~ *Anyone who does that must have a screw loose.*

have/got enough on one's plate: to have many commitments ~ *Sorry, I can't join the committee, I've got enough on my plate at the moment.*

have half a mind to: [spoken] seriously consider doing something ~ *I've got half a mind to tell your parents what you did.* *also: have a good mind to

have it coming: deserve punishment ~ *He's complaining about the severity of the sentence, but he had it coming to him.*

have got it easy: [spoken] be in a comfortable situation/be fortunate ~ *Eddie's got it easy—he does the paperwork while everyone else does all the running around.*

have/got it in for one/someone: (to) bear a grudge for (for known or unknown reasons) ~ *I don't know what I've done, but the boss seems to have it in for me all week.*

have it in one/someone: have the skill/ability to do something difficult ~ *I can't believe she did it! I didn't think she had it in her.*

have/got no time for: show no interest/dislike someone/something ~ *I've no time for that kind of behaviour.*

have/got one's feet on the ground: remain sensible/practical ~ *She might be famous, but she manages to keep her feet on the ground.*

have one's hands tied: be powerless to act ~ *My hands are tied until the contract expires.*

have/got one's head in the clouds: someone idealistic/unrealistic ~ *She must have her head in the clouds if she thinks she'll become instantly famous.* *also: airy-fairy

(to) not have one's head screwed on properly: make a stupid decision; do something irrational ~ *I can't think why he did it. He mustn't have had his head screwed on properly.*

have/got one's heart in one's mouth: be scared/frightened/nervous/anxious ~ *My heart was in my mouth as I watched on helplessly.*

have one's heart set on something: to sincerely/deeply want/need to do something ~ *1a) She had her heart set on marrying him from the moment they met. 1b) He has his heart set on going to uni when he finishes school.*

have one's lines/wires crossed: 1) have a miscommunication ~ *We must have our lines crossed—I thought it was on Saturday, not Sunday.*

2) if the phone lines are crossed you are talking to the wrong person

have one's sights set on: be focused on a specific goal/aim ~ *He has his sights set on becoming a pilot when he finishes school.*

have one's wits about one: be alert/watchful; think clearly ~ *You have to have your wits about you when you do this type of work.*

have someone over a barrel: exert influence/power over someone; have someone at your mercy ~ *He won't make any wrong moves because he knows I have him over a barrel.*

have something on the brain: to be obsessed with something ~ *Her sports-mad brother only has football on the brain.* *also: have something in one's head

have the ball in one's court: take action/make a decision (in a process); respond/reply to a previous action ~ *He was given an ultimatum, now the ball is in his court.*

have the floor: to be the person speaking in a debate/discussion ~ *The company director has the floor.*

haven't the heart: to not have courage/daring/conviction to do something ~ *She didn't have the heart to tell him his performance was terrible.*

have the/a knack: have a natural talent/ability for doing something ~ *He's got a knack for handling snakes.*

have the (whole) works: to include all the optional extras ~ *The hotel has a pool, a spa, a sauna—the works!*

have the world at one's feet: be destined to succeed ~ *The talented young musician has the world at her feet.*

have/got to be kidding: [spoken] an exclamation of disbelief/ surprise ~ *You're going to do what?! You've got to be kidding.* *see also: got to be joking

have it all one's/someone's way: to do what you want despite opposition ~ *I know you're unhappy with our decision, but you can't always have it your way.*

have luck on one's side: that you were favoured in a particular situation ~ *I must have had some luck on my side when they chose me for the job.*

have one's work cut out: have a difficult job/task to complete ~ *There's a lot of weeds to clear—we're going to have our work cut out for us.*

have oneself/someone on: delude/fool oneself/someone ~ *1a) She's having herself on if she thinks she'll win. 1b) You're not really in trouble—I was only having you on.*

have time on one's side: have enough/plenty of time to do something ~ *He was lucky he had time on his side to complete the difficult project.*

have/get/gain the upper hand: obtain a superior/dominant position ~ *Scoring an early goal has given them the upper hand.*

haven't a clue: to be completely ignorant/baffled ~ *I haven't a clue where we're going.* *also: hasn't got a clue; don't have a clue

have a way with . . . : to have a talent/aptitude for doing something ~ *Jenny seems to have a way with children. She'd make a good childcare worker.*

have a weakness for: be fond of; like or enjoy something/someone ~ *She has a weakness for injured animals.*

have-a-chat: [informal] humorous name given to someone who talks a lot ~ *It's Jane, otherwise known as have-a-chat.*

(go) haywire: for something/someone to go wrong/malfunction/ behave incorrectly ~ *The computer suddenly went haywire.*

head and shoulders above: far superior in every way ~ *He's head and shoulders above everyone else in regards to analytical capability.*

head away from: turn/move away from something ~ *The storm was coming towards us, then it started heading away.*

head back: begin the return journey; go back to the starting point ~ *It's getting dark, we should head back home.* *also: start back

head down, bum up: to work diligently/hard (to complete a task/job) ~ *It's exam time soon, so you need to put your head down and bum up.*

head for: aim for/move towards something ~ *They're headed for the beach.*

have a head for figures: have a natural ability to do maths/ arithmetic ~ *Whoever undertakes the role needs to have a good head for figures.*

head for the hills: [spoken] to depart quickly, flee to higher ground

head off: depart/leave ~ *We'd better head off or we'll be late.*

head on down: leave to go to your desired destination ~ *1a) We're going to head on down to the pub now. 1b) We're going to Sydney first, then we head on down to Melbourne.*

head over heels: 1) to fall completely and utterly in love ~ *She fell head over heels in love with him.*

2) to fall with your head near the ground and your legs in the air ~ *I tripped and fell head over heels.* *also: arse over tit (slang)

head start: (get/have/give) an early start/an advantage/handicap ~ *1a) His opponents were skilful so he gave them a head start. 1b) The job will give her a head start in her career.*

heads will roll: that certain people will suffer the consequences of their actions ~ *Government officials promised that heads will roll following a damning report on what happened.* *also: have someone's head

head up (to): travel in a general northerly direction ~ *We're heading up to Brisbane during the holidays.*

all in one's head: something imagined ~ *Julie said there was a free concert in the city today, but I think it's all in her head.*

do it standing on one's head: do something easily ~ *Oh, that's easy! I can do it standing on my head.*

get (it) through your head: to accept/understand something ~ *I wish you'd get it through your head that I don't want to go!*

get out of one's head: be unable to forget about something/ someone ~ *I can't get that song out of my head.*

get one's head around: be unable to understand/comprehend something ~ *I just can't seem to be able to get my head around this mathematical concept.*

get one's head together: organise one's thoughts ~ *I'll give you an answer later. I can't seem to get my head together right now.* *also: gather one's thoughts; think properly; get one's act together; get it together

from head to toe: from the top of one's head to one's feet ~ *He was covered in sand from head to toe.* *also: top to bottom; top to tail

have a good head on (one's/someone's) shoulders: to be smart/intelligent

have a swollen head: have a big ego/sense of self-importance ~ *Being chosen for the job has given him a swollen head.*

have rocks in one's head: that someone is making stupid decisions ~ *1a) He must have rocks in his head if he thinks he can climb up there. 1b) They must have rocks in their heads if they think it will work.* *also: need your head examined; be off your head

hold one's head (up) high: remain proud/dignified ~ *After proving the sceptics wrong she could now hold her head high.*

in over one's head: be in a situation that is difficult to control/ manage ~ *I volunteered to manage the project, but right now I'm in over my head.*

keep one's head above water: survive financially ~ *With the rising cost of living and an average wage, I'm only just keeping my head above water.*

knock it/something on the head: discontinue doing something because of difficulties ~ *They knocked the plan on the head.*

laugh your head off: to laugh heartily ~ *We laughed our heads off all night.*

need (it) like a hole in the head: to not want/need something ~ *1a) We need a pet snake like we need a hole in the head. 1b) I needed this to happen like I need a hole in the head.*

need one's head read: (usually said jokingly) to tell someone they need to see a psychiatrist ~ *I don't know why she did that. She must need her head read.*

off one's head: 1) to be angry ~ *She went off her head when she found out what he's done.*

2) to act in a crazy/stupid/aggressive manner whilst under the influence of drugs or alcohol ~ *Stay away from him, he's off his head.*

off the top of one's head: without careful preparation/thought/investigation ~ *I'm not sure exactly how far away it is, but off the top of my head I guess it's about five kilometres.*

put our/their heads together: two or more people combining to discuss a plan/problem ~ *We put our heads together and came up with a workable plan.*

use one's head/loaf/noodle: think logically/clearly/cleverly ~ *The puzzle's not that difficult, you just need to use your noodle.*

headache: someone/something that causes misery/ trouble ~ *With all the problems that have arisen, this project has become a headache.*

give someone heaps: 1) mercilessly tease someone ~ *My friends gave me heaps for my embarrassing gaffe.*

2) [spoken] words of encouragement to someone before they face their opponent ~ *Good luck - give 'em heaps!*

hear about: learn/hear of something ~ *1a) Did you hear about what happened to Sally? 1b) Yes, I heard about it this morning.*

hear from: get word/a message from someone *1a) Have you heard from Peter? 1b) I haven't heard from Jane for a few months.*

hear hear: [spoken] an expression of agreement ~ *His speech was followed by cries of hear hear!*

hear of: find out that something has happened ~ *1a) I was sad to hear of her death. 1b) I've never heard of that breed of dog.*

hear (someone) out: listen to/hear all of what someone has to say ~ *You need to hear me out so you can understand exactly what happened.* *also: hear something through

hear the last of: to no longer have to listen to something ~ *Hopefully we've heard the last of his boring speeches.*

hear things: to hear imaginary noises ~ *There's no one at the door—you must be hearing things.*

hear out: [spoken] protest when someone interrupts your speech ~ *Please hear me out!*

at heart: one's true/deep feelings ~ *He seems tough, but he's a good bloke at heart.*

from the bottom of one's heart: with deep/sincere appreciation ~ *I love you from the bottom of my heart.*

break someone's heart: make someone very sad ~ *Her decision has broken his heart.*

close to one's heart: something that concerns/deeply interests you ~ *Conservation is an issue that's close to my heart.* *also: near/dear to one's heart

have a change of heart: to change your mind ~ *Mum's had a change of heart and is letting me go.*

know off by heart: know something by memory ~ *I know the words to this song off by heart.*

take (it) to heart: consider something seriously ~ *Don't take it to heart.*

heart and soul: utterly/completely ~ *She put her heart and soul into the song.*

heart attack: a severe/serious/sudden malfunction of the heart (often uttered in exaggeration when one has received a shock) ~ *Don't scare me like that—you nearly gave me a heart attack!*

heart isn't in it: to feel disinterested/unenthusiastic about doing something ~ *I've decided to quit the course—my heart's not in it.*

heart missed a beat: a physical reaction when receiving a sudden surprise/shock ~ *My heart missed a beat when I saw how handsome he was.*

heart of gold: describes someone generous/kind/thoughtful/ sincere ~ *He may look rough in appearance, but he's got a heart of gold.*

heart of the matter: the core/main aspect of a situation ~ *Money was at the heart of the matter.*

heartthrob: someone who is the object of desire/infatuation ~ *The teenage girls were thrilled to meet their heartthrob.*

heart-to-heart: an earnest/intimate talk between two people ~ *I think it's time we had a heart-to-heart.*

heart-warming: emotionally pleasing ~ *It was a most heart-warming story.*

half-hearted: do something with little effort/enthusiasm/interest job ~ *My son made a half-hearted attempt to clean his room.*

hard-hearted: lacking in feelings/unsympathetic/pitiless

heat up: 1) become active/more intense ~ *The competition is heating up.*

2) become hotter ~ *The weather is starting to heat up.*

put the heat on: 1) coerce/persuade someone to do something ~ *The detectives put the heat on the prisoner to confess.*

2) begin to perform better (in a competition), forcing the opposition to match you ~ *The Tigers have won three games in a row, which is putting the heat on the Bears.*

give the heave-ho: physically throw out/discard something/ someone (often preceded by "old") ~ *The car was beyond repair so I gave it the old heave-ho.*

heaven forbid: what is said when you hope something won't happen ~ *Heaven forbid if we break it.* *also: heaven help us

heaven knows: *see: God only knows

heavens/heavens above: [spoken] exclamation of surprise/ annoyance/frustration/excitement ~ *1a) Oh heavens above, where did it go? 1b) Heavens above! Are those lovely flowers for me?*

in seventh heaven: very happy/content ~ *I'm in seventh heaven when I'm here with you.*

what/who/how in heaven's name: [spoken] used to strongly emphasise a question ~ *What in heaven's name is that?* *also: the heck; what on earth

what the heck: [spoken] to mean who cares/it doesn't matter ~ *What the heck—let's do it!*

heck of a . . . : [spoken] intensive ~ *1a) I've had a heck of a time trying to find you! 1b) That's one heck of a big storm coming this way!* *also: hell of a . . .

heebie-jeebies: an intense feeling of horror/revulsion/ nervousness ~ *1a) This place gives me the heebie-jeebies. 1b) I only have to look at spiders and I get the heebie-jeebies.*

kick one's heels up: act/behave freely/unrestrained/carefree/ joyously ~ *I intend to kick up my heels at tonight's party.* *also: kick up one's heels

turn on one's heel: depart/leave quickly and suddenly ~ *Jim turned on his heel and walked the other way.*

down-at-heel: having a shabby appearance; destitute ~ *He had a rather down-at-heel appearance.*

at the height of: the strongest/most forceful/intense aspect of something ~ *1a) She's at the height of her career. 1b) To refuse their offer would be considered the height of rudeness. 1c) Most damage occurred at the height of the storm.*

hell: 1) anything troublesome/difficult/unpleasant ~ *It's hell trying to walk in these high-heeled shoes.*

2) [spoken] mild oath/expression of annoyance/frustration/anger ~ *Oh hell! I hate it when this happens.*

3) penance/punishment ~ *You'll have hell to pay for what you've done.*

hell bent: determined to do something ~ *She was hell bent on going to university.*

all hell broke loose: a sudden eruption of mayhem/disruption ~ *Rival gang members appeared on the scene, then all hell broke loose.*

been to hell and back: to have had an extremely bad experience ~ *I've been to hell and back with fighting this illness.*

come hell or high water: [spoken] make a firm; obstinate decision despite opposition/difficulties ~ *I'll make sure I'm there, come hell or high water.*

for the hell of it: for no particular/apparent reason/on a whim ~ *We went just for the hell of it.*

get the hell out (of): [spoken] intensive; quickly leave/depart a place/situation ~ *1a) Quickly, get the hell out—the building's on fire! 1b) I'm scared—let's get the hell out of here!*

give someone hell: severely reprimand/punish someone ~ *1a) I expect Dad will give me hell for coming home so late. 1b) We won, but the other team gave us hell.* *see also: give someone a hard time

go like a bat out of hell: go as fast as possible ~ *He drove like a bat out of hell to get the injured man to hospital.* *also: go hell for leather

go to hell: [spoken] severe dismissal ~ *I won't be intimidated by him—he can go to hell for all I care!*

go through hell: to have a very unpleasant time ~ *She's been through hell these past couple of months.*

haven't a hope/chance in hell: to have no hope/chance/ opportunity to do something ~ *I haven't a hope in hell of climbing up there.* *see also: Buckley's chance

like hell: 1) strongly disagree/oppose something ~ *Like hell you will!*

2) move very quickly ~ *We ran like hell!*

play hell with: cause grief/affect someone/something ~ *The cold weather plays hell with my arthritis.*

what the hell: [spoken] an expression of anger/impatience/disgust ~ *What the hell do you think you're doing?*

when hell freezes over: at no time ever/never ever ~ *Only when hell freezes over will I stop loving you.*

hell to pay: to face serious consequences/repercussions for doing something ~ *There will be hell to pay if they come home too late.*

help oneself: take something with or without permission ~ *1a) Please, help yourself to a drink. 1b) He broke into the house and helped himself to all their valuables.*

help out: bear the burden/be of help in a particular situation ~ *It was very kind of Tim to help us out in our time of need.*

hem in: confine/surround and restrict space/movement ~ *The cottage was hemmed in by a white picket fence.*

hen's night/party: a party held in honour of a woman about to be married. It is usually held days before the wedding, and attended only by females.

here: indicates that one is available to help right here and now ~ *1a) Here, I'll help you do it. 1b) Here, I can fix it for you.*

'ere: [informal] here ~ *Come 'ere!*

here and now: in this place at this time ~ *Let's get this issue sorted right here and now!*

here and there: in various/different places ~ *We didn't have a specific destination, we just walked here and there.* *also: here, there, and everywhere ~ *I've driven here, there, and everywhere today.*

here goes: [spoken] just before attempting/beginning something exciting/daring/unpleasant ~ *Here goes. One, two, three, JUMP!* *also: here we go

here goes nothing: [spoken] indicates a lack of confidence/a doubt in one's ability to do something (even though you're going to do it anyway) ~ *I'm not sure I know how to fix it, but here goes nothing.*

here's to . . . : expressed to honour someone/propose a toast to someone/wish someone well ~ *Here's to your promotion.*

here to stay: something/someone considered/accepted as staying permanently ~ *1a) Digital technology is certainly here to stay. 1b) No one could convince him to move—he was here to stay.*

here today, gone tomorrow: said of something non-permanent/lasting for a short time ~ *Most new fashion trends are often here today, gone tomorrow.*

here we go again: [spoken] exclamation of annoyance/frustration that something unpleasant will be repeated ~ *Here we go again, more traffic delays!*

here you go: [spoken] this is for you/here is what you wanted/the thing you asked for/the thing you're looking for ~ *1a) Here you go—a nice cuppa to warm you up. 1b) Here you go, this is what we're looking for.*

from here on (end): from now on/hereinafter/from this time onwards ~ *From here on end we're on our own.*

I'm out of here: [spoken] that one is going/leaving immediately ~ *Bye, I'm out of here.* *also: outta here

neither here nor there: of something unimportant/irrelevant ~ *Whether or not you want to do it is neither here nor there.*

same here: [spoken] I agree/me too ~ *I wouldn't mind going there one day. Same here.*

Hervey Bay: A three and a half hour's drive north of Queensland's capital city of Brisbane, Hervey Bay is a popular tourist destination. It has a sub-tropical climate, an abundance of natural assets, as well as being the main access point to Fraser Island. It is also recognised as the whale watch capital of the world.

(get) het up: become excited/angry/upset ~ *She's all het up over the senseless slaughter of the animals.*

heyday: a prosperous; exciting time in one's life ~ *They were a popular rock band in their heyday.*

hey-presto: announces a surprising/magic achievement ~ *You just walk under the sensor and "hey presto," the lights come on!*

hide: gall/nerve/impudence ~ *You've got a hide saying that!*

hide away: conceal/hide oneself/something somewhere ~ *1a) You've got to come out sometime—you can't just hide away forever. 1b) I hid them away.*

hide behind: conceal oneself behind someone/something ~ *The police found the suspect hiding behind a shed.*

hide and seek: child's game where someone hides and others have find him/her

hide nor hair: not a vestige/trace of something/someone ~ *I haven't seen hide nor hair of Fred since last Sunday.*

thick hide: to not be personally offended/be able to accept criticism ~ *You can give me your honest opinion, I've got a thick hidc.* *also: thick skin

(a) hiding: be thoroughly beaten/defeated ~ *1a) The champion boxer gave his last opponent a hiding. 1b) Our team copped a hiding in last week's game.*

hidey-hole: a small space/place of refuge *also: cubby-hole

hi-fi: high fidelity stereo sound system

higgledy-piggledy: jumbled/mixed up/disordered/out of place ~ *Toys were strewn higgledy-piggledy across the room.*

high and dry: stranded/helpless ~ *They cancelled the deal at the last minute, leaving us high and dry.*

highs and lows: to experience extremes of emotion/a succession of good and bad experiences ~ *I've experienced some highs and lows in my career.*

high and mighty: for someone to have a sense of arrogance/self-importance ~ *Just ignore his high and mighty remarks.*

high as a kite: under the influence of/affected by drugs/alcohol ~ *It's useless trying to make sense of what he's saying, he's as high as a kite.*

high hopes: be confident that something will go well/be successful ~ *She is a good player, and has high hopes of being selected to play in the national team.*

high time: the appropriate time to do something ~ *It's high time I began to study in earnest for the exams.*

high up: 1) holding a senior/important position ~ *I'm not sure of his position, but I know he's high up in the organization.*

2) at a great height/altitude ~ *We could see monkeys high up in the treetops.*

hightail it: leave/depart very quickly ~ *The troublemakers hightailed it out of there when they saw the police.*

highway robbery: blatant overcharging ~ *Fifty dollars? That's highway robbery!*

(price) hike: a rapid increases in costs/prices ~ *Once again there's going to be another petrol price hike.*

take to the hills: run to high ground and hide ~ *When the criminals heard the police were after them they took to the hills.*

Hill's Hoist: In 1946, a man named Lance Hill devised a rotary clothesline in his backyard and it was called the Hill's rotary hoist. Since its beginnings, and until today, you will almost certainly find a

Hill's hoist in any given backyard. It is one of Australia's biggest success stories, and is now part of Australian folklore.

. . . to the hilt: completely/fully/to the utmost/entirely ~ *1a) They were armed to the hilt. 1b) We're in debt to the hilt.* *also: armed to the teeth

hinges on: depend entirely on something ~ *Whether we continue or not all hinges on the weather.*

hippo: hippopotamus

hit: reach a particular amount/level/ age/place ~ *1a) She's having a big party when she hits forty. 1b) The car was hitting speeds of up to 200 kms/hr. 1c) Turn right when you hit the shopping centre.*

hit (for): ask someone to lend you money ~ *Can I hit you for $20 until tomorrow?*

hit a raw nerve: upset someone/be upset (especially if it's about a sensitive issue) ~ *The decision to close the community centre has hit a raw nerve with many residents.* *also: touch a raw nerve

hit a rough patch: to experience a difficult time/that things aren't going well ~ *The golfer had hit a rough patch with his game and was scoring badly.* *also: have a rough trot

hit back: start to play well against an opponent who is winning ~ *The Tigers hit back by scoring two quick goals.*

hit back at: attack/criticise someone who has criticised you ~ *He hit back at its critics by winning the competition.*

hit someone back: deliberately hit someone because they hit you ~ *Well, she hit me so I hit her back.*

hit for six: to be utterly surprised ~ *The team's surprise loss in the final has really hit them for six.*

hit someone for something: ask someone for something (a loan/favour) ~ *I can't afford it so I'll see if I can hit Dad for a loan.*

(be) hit hard: be affected by something ~ *1a) She's been hit hard by her mother's death. 1b) Residents in the southern suburbs were hit hardest by the storm.*

hit home: to suddenly realise the seriousness/urgency of something ~ *After seeing the extensive damage to his car, it really hit* *home how lucky he was to not be seriously injured or killed in the crash.*

hit it off: of people to meet and quickly form a good relationship ~ *They'd only just met but they hit it off instantly.*

hit list: 1) list of people to be killed for criminal or political reasons ~ *He was at the top of the terrorist's hit list for nearly two years.*

2) a target for attack/elimination ~ *Which services are on the government's hit list?*

(it) hit me: to suddenly think of/realise something ~ *I was wondering why there was so little traffic on the road, then it hit me that it was a public holiday.*

hit the anchors/skids: suddenly apply the brakes on a car ~ *A dog ran out in front of me so I hit the anchors.*

hit the big time: to reach a particular state ~ *Her career was slow to take off, but she hit the big time.*

hit the books: begin/make a start at studying ~ *I'd better hit the books today or else I won't pass the exams.*

hit the bottle: start drinking a lot of alcohol (often as a way of coping with personal problems) ~ *He hit the bottle rather heavily when he lost his job.* *also: took to the bottle; hit the grog/booze

hit the ground running: begin a venture/activity actively/ enthusiastically ~ *There hasn't been much time to think about anything else—I've pretty much hit the ground running with this project.*

hit the headlines: gain media attention/appear in the news ~ *She first hit the headlines last year when she led a protest march.*

hit the jackpot: finally find success/win lots of money ~ *After a string of failed productions the theatre company finally hit the jackpot with its current production.*

hit the nail on the head: say something that's exactly right/true; describe something exactly ~ *I think Steve hit the nail on the head when he said the team's morale was low.* *also: be right on the money

hit the road: depart/leave ~ *We'd better hit the road or we'll be late.* *also: hit the trail

hit the roof: explode with anger/lose one's temper ~ *He hit the roof when he learned of the trouble his son had caused.*

hit the spot: something having the required effect ~ *That meal hit the spot.*

hit the town: to go out and have fun ~ *We're going to celebrate by hitting the town.*

hit up: inject a narcotic drug ~ *He hits up every day.*

hit on/upon: to suddenly have an idea/thought ~ *We hit on the idea of having a double celebration.*

hit where it hurts most: cause the maximum/most upset to someone ~ *The nasty public comments hit him where it hurts.*

(be) a hit: of something to be a success/be popular ~ *The party clown was a hit with the kids.*

(be) hit with something: 1) present/receive surprising news ~ *He's still in shock after being hit with some bad news.*

2) give/receive something ~ *Would you like beer or wine? Hit me with a beer, thanks!*

3) issue/be issued with a fine/penalty ~ *They hit me with a $50 late payment fine.*

(all) in one hit: all at once/at one time/in one attempt ~ *We managed to move all the furniture in one hit.*

didn't know/never knew what hit him/her/them: 1) be unaware of impending danger and consequently be killed ~ *The accident was so sudden, the poor people in the car wouldn't have known what hit them.*

2) be shocked/surprised ~ *2a) She didn't know what hit her when she heard the bad news. 2b) He won't know what hit him when he realises how much work there is to do.*

hit-up: an informal practice session/warm-up before beginning a tennis match ~ *The game hasn't started yet—the players are still hitting-up.*

hit-and-miss: of something not planned/organised/unpredictable/ inconsistent ~ *It's a bit hit-and-miss as to how many players we have each week.* *also: hit 'n miss

hit-and-run: a car accident in which the driver at fault leaves the scene without stopping to offer assistance, so as to escape prosecution ~ *The police are looking for a white van believed to have been involved in a hit-and-run accident last night.*

get hitched: to get married ~ *I never thought Peter would ever get hitched.*

Hobart: Dating from 1804, Hobart is the capital of the state of Tasmania, and the second oldest capital city of Australia, exceeded in age only by Sydney. It is a city set in beautiful natural settings, and home to historic buildings, museums, parks and gardens, as well as family and adventure activities. It is also the destination city for sailors competing in the annual Sydney to Hobart Yacht Race held on the December 26.

hobble around: walk with difficulty/unsteadily ~ *He had to hobble around on his injured foot.*

hoe into: 1) begin to eat heartily ~ *Showing little regard for manner, they hoed into the food.*

2) verbally abuse; attack ~ *I don't know what's up, but she just hoed into him as soon as he got home.*

go the whole hog: the fullest extent/everything ~ *I'm going to go the whole hog and order a hamburger with the lot.*

hogwash: meaningless talk/nonsense/lies ~ *The excuse he gave is just a lot of hogwash!*

hoity-toity: arrogant/pretentious/**s**nobbish ~ *She's gone all hoity-toity since her promotion.*

hold something against someone: to let someone's past actions affect your current attitude ~ *You've had some minor traffic infringements, but we won't hold that against you.*

hold back: 1) avoid doing something ~ *I had trouble holding back my emotions.*

2) withhold information ~ *She was scared of the consequences so she held back vital information.*

3) restrain someone/something from getting at/to someone/something else ~ *Police held back the angry protestors.*

hold down: 1) maintain a job/rank ~ *She's been unable to hold down many jobs since the accident.*

2) hold someone/something to prevent from rising/moving ~ *They had trouble holding down the offender.*

hold off: 1) delay/postpone ~ *1a) Hopefully the rain will hold off for a while. 1b) She held off calling him.*

2) keep someone at a distance ~ *He didn't know how long he could hold off his attackers.*

hold it: [spoken] command to cease/stop/wait ~ *1a) Hold it—that's far enough! 1b) Hold it—where do you think you're going?*

(have a) hold on someone/something: 1) a full understanding/comprehension ~ *I now have a hold on how it all works.*

2) a domineering, restraining bond/force ~ *I don't know what he sees in her, but she seems to have a hold on him.*

hold on: 1) [spoken] stop/wait ~ *Hold on, I'm coming!* *also: hold your horses

2) wait to speak to someone on the telephone ~ *I'm holding on for Mr. Smith.*

3) [spoken] tell someone to think or listen ~ *Hold on—that's not what happened!*

4) remain calm/patient in a dangerous situation ~ *You'll have to hold on until help arrives.*

5) grasp/hold on to something ~ *The child held on to his father's hand.*

hold one's head up high: remain proud/dignified ~ *She held her head up high despite losing.*

hold one's own: be successful/competent in a particular situation ~ *He's struggling a bit, but he's holding his own.*

hold out: 1) defend a place that's being attacked ~ *The defenders were able to hold out for a day.*

2) continue to be enough/exist ~ *We have enough emergency supplies to hold out for a month.*

3) hold something out so someone can reach it ~ *I held out the bread for the bird to eat.*

hold out on: to keep something secret/not tell someone something ~ *His story was convincing, but I think he's holding out on me.*

hold out for: wait patiently to get what you want ~ *I'm holding out for a better job offer.*

hold someone to it: [spoken] confirmation that someone will fulfil a promise/agreement ~ *I promise I'll return it next week. Okay, I'll hold you to it.*

hold the fort: look after something/do something for someone while they're away/busy ~ *I'm holding the fort while the manager is away.*

hold the line: [spoken] what you say if you are speaking to someone on the telephone and you want them to wait ~ *You wish to speak to Mr. Brown? Could you please hold the line?*

hold together: 1) remain intact/keep from falling apart ~ *This old, worn jacket won't hold together for much longer.*

2) stay together under difficult circumstances ~ *Throughout the ongoing conflict he desperately tried to hold the family together.*

holds the key: that something/someone provides an explanation/ solution to a mystery ~ *Police were convinced the abandoned garage held the key to the man's disappearance.*

hold up: 1) be delayed ~ *Sorry I'm late, I was held up in traffic.*

2) steal by threatening with a gun or weapon ~ *The convenience store was held up by three masked men.*

3) hold something in a high position (so as to be seen) ~ *She held up her hand to answer the question.*

4) support someone/something ~ *A large beam was needed to hold up the ceiling.*

5) remain mentally strong in a difficult situation ~ *He seems to be holding up quite well since his wife died.*

hole: 1) a predicament/dilemma ~ *He's got himself into a bit of a hole with the business deal.*

2) a wretched/derelict place/town ~ *The eastern quarter of the city's a real hole.*

hell hole: an extremely frightening place/circumstance ~ *The little jail cell could only be described as a hell hole.*

made/put a hole in (it): consume/use a great amount of money/food/drink ~ *The urgent repair job needed on the house has put a hole in our savings.*

(be) holed up: take refuge/hide somewhere ~ *The police believe the criminals are holed up somewhere in this vicinity.*

hollies/hols: holidays ~ *1a) Where are you going for your hols? 1b) How were the hollies?*

holus-bolus: everything all at once/completely ~ *He ate the worm holus-bolus!*

holy cow/dooley/mackerel: [spoken] exclamation of astonishment /amazement ~ *1a) Holy cow, did you see that?! 1b) Holy mackerel—look at the size of it!*

bring home: realise the full significance of something; make something clear/understandable ~ *The accident brought home the dangers of drinking and driving.*

broken home: a home in which the parents are divorced or separated ~ *The number of children coming from broken homes is increasing.*

eat someone out of house and home: to eat/consume lots of food ~ *My teenage son and his friends often eat me out of house and home.*

make oneself at home: [spoken] an invitation for someone to sit down and relax ~ *Please, make yourself at home.*

home stretch/strait: in the final/last stages of a task/race ~ *The project's taken a long time, but we're finally in the home stretch.*

home and hosed: complete something successfully ~ *Only one more leg of the journey and we'll be home and hosed.*

home away from home: a house that has the same comfortable feel as your own home ~ *This hotel is like a home away from home.*

home truths: facts that are difficult/painful to accept ~ *I've had to tell him some home truths about her.*

homebody: someone who prefers to stay in and around the home ~ *She doesn't go out much, she's a bit of a homebody.*

do one's homework: research a topic/be prepared ~ *She made sure she did her homework on the company before the job interview.*

honestly: 1) [spoken] expression of mild anger; annoyance ~ *Honestly—I just can't understand why you do that all the time!*

2) a way of saying that you're speaking the truth ~ *I don't know. Honestly!*

honest to God: [spoken] used to emphasise one's sincerity/honesty ~ *Honest to God, I don't know what happened!*

honest-to-goodness: real/authentic ~ *His book gives an honest-to-goodness account of the life of an early settler in Australia.*

honker: one's nose ~ *He's always hated his big honker.*

hoodwinked: cheated/tricked/misled ~ *I was hoodwinked into believe her story was true.*

hooey: nonsense/lies ~ *The story he told is a lot of hooey!*

hoof: [informal] foot

hoof it: walk somewhere ~ *We had to hoof it the rest of the way after the car broke down.*

hoo-ha: fuss/bother; disturbance/outburst ~ *He didn't realise the article he wrote would cause so much hoo-ha.*

hooks: [informal] one's fingers

hook up (to): 1) assemble/wire a mechanism ~ *Would you like some help hooking up your new computer?*

2) connect to a source of power ~ *We just need to hook it up and it's ready to go.*

hook up with: 1) be linked/joined romantically ~ *Did you hear James has hooked up with Sarah?*

2) meet or associate with someone ~ *Unfortunately she got hooked up with the wrong crowd.*

by hook or by crook: achieve your goal by whatever means possible ~ *I'm going to finish this tonight, by hook or by crook!*

(be) hooked: be captivated by/addicted to/obsessed with something ~ *She's hooked on Italian food.*

hooker: [informal] prostitute

hooligan: troublemaker/thug/ruffian/lout

hoon: (young) male who speeds and drive recklessly in customised vehicles

hooray: [spoken] exclamation of joy/delight; an applause/a cheer ~ *1a) Hooray—no school today! 1b) Hooray- we won!*

hooroo: [spoken] goodbye/see you later

(a) hoot: something/someone that is fun/funny ~ *The show was a real hoot!*

don't care/give two hoots: be indifferent to/not care about something ~ *I don't care two hoots what they say about me.* *also: don't give a hoot

hooter: 1) one's nose ~ *He was conscious of his big hooter.*

2) a piece of equipment such as a siren/alarm/bell that makes a loud warning sound ~ *Ahead by one point, the team was relieved to hear the hooter that signalled the end of the game.*

hop (in): quickly move in or out of something ~ *Hop in the car and I'll give you a lift home.*

hop to it: [spoken] request to move/act quickly ~ *Hop to it or you'll be late!* *also: jump to it

hop, step, and a jump: a short distance ~ *It's not far, just a hop, step, and a jump.*

hop up/in/on: quickly/energetically spring/jump up onto or off something ~ *The cat suddenly hopped up onto my lap.*

hopping mad: very angry ~ *I was hopping mad when I heard what had happened.*

lock horns with someone: disagree/argue with someone ~ *The company directors locked horns with each other over the issue.*

on the horns of a dilemma: be confronted with two equally unpleasant options

(a) horror: an unpleasant person ~ *1a) What a little horror he is—I'm glad he's not my child. 1b) He's been a horror to do business with.*

horror of horrors: [spoken] exclamation of something unpleasant happening/about to happen ~ *I felt something on my leg, and horror of horrors, it was a huge spider!* *also: to my horror

the horrors: *see the creeps

one horse town: a very small town with few residents ~ *This is much different from the one horse town he grew up in.*

horse around: *see: fool around

horse sense: common sense

horse shoe: a good luck symbol

horseplay: rough/boisterous play

hot on the heels of: following closely behind ~ *The police were hot on the heels of the thief.*

got the hots for: to like someone very much (so as to begin a serious relationship) ~ *Jack's really got the hots for Sue.*

go hot and cold all over: to suffer a shock and feel that your body is hot and cold at the same time ~ *When I saw his horrific injuries, I went hot and cold all over.*

in hot water: to be in trouble/difficulties ~ *1a) He got into hot water over the business deal. 1b) She began to ascend the cliff face and soon found herself in hot water.*

too hot to handle: of something difficult to get involved with or talk about ~ *It's one topic most politicians find too hot to handle.*

hot and bothered: be upset/agitated/flustered ~ *Paul stormed out of the fiery meeting all hot and bothered.*

hot on the trail: in close pursuit of someone/close to discovering/finding someone ~ *The detectives were now hot on the trail of the suspect.*

hot property: something much wanted/heavily in demand ~ *1a) The actress was hot property and sought after by all the film studios bosses. 1b) Their newest technology device instantly became hot property.*

hot stuff: anything/anyone deemed exciting/unconventional/daring ~ *Her performances are hot stuff.*

hot under the collar: very angry ~ *He began to get hot under the collar as the debate intensified.*

hot tempered: *see hothead

crash hot: (said in the negative) to feel/look unwell; of being under par ~ *Are you okay? You don't look too crash hot.*

2) someone's appearance ~ *Wow, you look pretty crash hot!*

3) to be unskilled/inept ~ *I can dance well, but my singing's not that crash hot.*

hot off the press: something that's just been printed ~ *This information is hot off the press.*

hothead: someone who is quickly/easily angered

hot up: of an event/situation to become exciting ~ *The competition is hotting up.*

on the house: free/gratis ~ *The drinks are on the house.*

household name: someone/something very well-known ~ *She is a household name in Australia.*

housewarming: an occasion where hosts celebrate occupancy of a new dwelling/house

hover around/about: the act/state of lingering/waiting near/ fluctuating around a given point ~ *1a) The helicopter hovered around for five minutes. 1b) Photographers hovered around the entrance waiting for them to emerge. 1c) The temperature is hovering around 30ºC.*

how about: used when offering something to someone; suggesting something ~ *1a) How about we go to the beach? 1b) How about Jim, is he coming?*

how about it: [spoken] used when asking some their thoughts/ feelings about something ~ *1a) I think we should to go to the pub for lunch. How about it? 1b) How about we meet tomorrow at 5 p.m. to discuss it? *also: how 'bout*

how about that: [spoken] exclamation of amazement/triumph ~ *1a) You caught the biggest fish! Well, how about that! 1b) How about that—we grew up in the same street!* *also: howzat!; how's them apples!

how are things: [spoken] informal greeting asking how things are with someone ~ *I haven't seen you for a while. How are things?* *also: how's things; how are you keeping; how are you going; how goes it; how's tricks

how come: why/why is it so/what is the reason ~ *How come you have to leave so early?*

how things stand: the current status quo/situation/state of affairs ~ *I need to know how things stand between the two of you.*

how ya goin': [informal spoken] standard greeting meaning "how are you?" ~ *Hi! How ya goin'?*

howdy, stranger: [spoken] humorous greeting between two people who haven't seen each other in a long time *often complemented with—long time, no see

hubby: husband

huddle together/around: crowd/gather closely together in a group ~ *Everyone huddled around the fire for warmth.*

huffy: irritated/annoyed/offended/sulky ~ *He was a bit huffy when he found out the truth.*

in a huff: in a state of annoyance/anger ~ *I don't know what was said, but she left in a huff.*

hullo: [spoken] exclamation of surprise/discovery/astonishment; questioning/contempt ~ *1a) Hullo—what's this?! 1b) Well, hullo—that's obvious!*

humdinger: someone/something exceptionally good ~ *That's a humdinger of a car you've got there.*

humdrum: monotonous/boring ~ *I thought her performance was a bit humdrum.*

hundred percent: totally/absolutely/certainly/completely ~ *I'm a hundred percent certain we're doing the right thing.*

hundreds and thousands: tiny balls or strands of multi-coloured sugar, sprinkled over ice cream desserts or party foods

hundred-to-one: a very small/remote chance/possibility ~ *The horse had a hundred-to-one chance of winning.*

hunk: an attractive man ~ *The girls were busy checking out all the hunks at the party.*

hunky-dory: okay/alright/fine ~ *Everything's hunky-dory.*

hurl around: toss/fling carelessly/with force ~ *Many passengers were hurled around in the accident.*

hurl away: throw something with great force/energy ~ *Rescuers hurled away rocks and debris to get to the victims.*

hurry away: leave/depart in a hurry ~ *The thief hurried away from the scene of the crime.*

hurry up: [spoken] proceed/act/move with haste ~ *Hurry up or we'll be late!* *also: hurry along.

hush up: 1) [spoken] command to be quiet/silent ~ *Will you two hush up!*

2) supress mentioning something ~ *It was important they kept their illegal doings hushed up.*

hush-hush: of something to be confidential/secret; not to be discussed with other people ~ *They're keeping details of the project hush-hush at the moment.*

hustle and bustle: a state of excitement/busyness/activity ~ *I love the hustle and bustle of a big city.*

hyped up: overly excited/stimulated/hyperactive/enthusiastic ~ *Everyone was all hyped up prior to opening night of the show.*

hysterical: extremely funny/ridiculous ~ *His comedy routine is absolutely hysterical.*

(in) hysterics: to be laughing uncontrollably ~ *He had us in hysterics all day.*

I

Ibis: Ibises are a group of long-legged wading birds. They have long, down-curving bills and usually feed as a group. Straw-necked ibises are the most abundant and widespread of Australia's ibises, breeding in colonies of up to two million birds.

ice-block: water-based ice confectionary on a stick

ice cream: milk-based confectionary on a stick

keep on ice: suspend progress on a plan for an indefinite period ~ *I've kept my travel plans on ice until I've finished the course.*

icing on the cake: an added benefit to something already good ~ *Receiving an award at the end was the icing on the cake.*

get the idea: (to) understand something not expressed directly ~ *Okay, I get the idea, you want me to keep it secret.*

get the wrong idea: be mistaken about something/believe something that's not true ~ *You should explain your actions to them so they don't get the wrong idea.*

idle away: spend time relaxing/doing nothing ~ *I idled away the afternoon under a shady tree.*

idle rich: well-off people who can spend time enjoying themselves rather than working

if worse comes to worst: if the plan/situation becomes more serious ~ *If worse comes to worst we'll walk home with the others.*

if you ask me: in my opinion (whether asked for or not) ~ *If you ask me, I think the design is ugly.*

iffy: suspicious/dubious/questionable ~ *Their grand plan all sounds iffy to me.* *also: suss

ill-gotten: of something obtained illegally/dishonestly ~ *They lived a life of luxury on their ill-gotten gains.*

well, I'll be: [spoken] exclamation of surprise/amazement ~ *Well, I'll be—look who's here!*

I'll drink to that: [spoken] said when you agree with/support an opinion/decision ~ *I say we should donate the winnings to charity. I'll drink to that!*

I'll/I'd get shot: [spoken] that you will be in serious trouble for doing/saying something ~ *I'd get shot if I used Dad's car without asking.*

I'll have you know: [spoken] said to emphasise that what you're saying is true/factual ~ *I'll have you know that it was me who did the hard work, not anyone else.*

I'll tell you what: [spoken] that you are offering a proposal/plan *always used at the beginning of a sentence ~ *I'll tell you what, let's wait a few more days and see what happens.*

I'm easy: [spoken] that you don't mind what choice is made ~ *I'm easy—I don't mind which pub we go to.*

in a bad way: for someone to be in poor health ~ *He's been in a bad way since the accident.*

in a dither: be in a confused/panicked/flustered state ~ *She was running around in a dither before her dinner guests arrived.* *also: in a flap; in a spin

in a knot: in an anxious/worried state ~ *She got herself in a knot on the morning of the exam.*

in a spot of bother: to be experiencing minor difficulties/problems ~ *I'm in a spot of bother with this—can you help me?* *also: in a bind/pickle/fix

in deep: in serious trouble; in a difficult situation ~ *I'm in deep this time.*

in for: guaranteed to receive/get/have ~ *1a) She's in for a big surprise! 1b) We're in for a big storm this afternoon.*

in for it: to know you're going to be in trouble for your actions ~ *She knew she would be in for it when her mother got home.*

in force: 1) in great strength/numbers ~ *His family came in force to see his debut performance.*

2) a law or rule that is applied/operational ~ *The special traffic laws will be in force for five weeks.*

in a good light: for someone's actions to be viewed favourably or unfavourably ~ *Your previous charity work will be seen in good light in future job applications.*

in good nick: in good health/condition ~ *1a) Paul always keeps his vintage car in good nick. 1b) I try to keep myself in good nick.*

in good time: eventually/before the estimated arrival time ~ *1a) Don't worry, you'll find out in good time. 1b) If we leave now we'll get there in good time.*

in good with someone: in someone's favour ~ *I'm in good with the restaurant owner, mention my name and he'll look after you well.*

in hand: 1) be holding something/in one's possession ~ *I have the tickets in hand.*

2) under control ~ *The police have the situation firmly in hand.*

in heaven: a state of bliss ~ *I feel like I'm in heaven when I'm in the spa.* *also: in seventh heaven

in high places: of people in upper levels of business/government/organisations/society ~ *I'll make sure your protest gets heard, I know people in high places.*

in it (for): profits/advantages ~ *Before I approve the proposal, I need to know if there's anything in it for me.*

(be) in it to win it: that in order to win something you must first enter the draw/competition ~ *If you want the prize money you've gotta be in it to win it.*

in it up to one's neck/eyeballs/ears: deeply involved/fully occupied in something ~ *Of course he denied knowing about the scam, but everyone knew he was in it up to his ears.*

in luck: fortunate/lucky ~ *You're in luck—there's one ticket left.*

in on (it): take part/be involved in something planned ~ *1a) Are you in on our plan or not? 1b) It seems everyone was in on the secret, except me!*

in one ear and out the other: forget something as soon as you've heard it ~ *It doesn't matter how many times I tell her, it just goes in one ear and out the other.*

in one's own right: as a result of one's own efforts/claims/ qualifications ~ *She was a millionaire in her own right.*

(be) in one's element: in a suitable/familiar/enjoyable situation ~ *She's in her element when she's painting.*

in season: of fruit and vegetables growing abundantly and ready to eat

in someone else's/one's shoes: to be in someone else's unfortunate predicament/situation ~ *Boy, I sure wouldn't like to be in her shoes right now!*

in step with: 1) agree/conform with what others are doing or saying ~ *She's always in step with the latest fashion trends.*

2) walk/march/dance simultaneously/in rhythm with someone else ~ *The soldier was berated for marching out of step.*

in strife: in trouble ~ *My brother's in strife again for coming home late.*

in the air: 1) something which people have a shared/similar feeling about ~ *You could feel the excitement in the air as everyone waited for the results.*

2) in a state of suspension ~ *He threw the ball high in the air.*

in the bag: assured/secured success ~ *With such a big lead he's got the tournament in the bag.*

(be) in the black: to have a small amount of money in the bank and be debt free

in someone's eyes: in someone's opinion ~ *In the manager's eyes, she can do no wrong.*

in the clear: 1) free of blame/not guilty of a crime ~ *The police deemed the suspect to be in the clear, so they let him go.*

2) out of danger ~ *Her recovery's been good so far, but she's not yet in the clear.*

in the clink: in jail ~ *He's been in the clink for ten years.*

in the dark: in a state of ignorance/uninformed ~ *They kept me in the dark about what they'd planned.*

in the doldrums: miserable/gloomy/sad ~ *I don't know what happened, but she's been in the doldrums all day.*

in the drink: in the water ~ *We all got thrown in the drink when the boat capsized.*

in the family way: to be pregnant ~ *My sister is in the family way.*

(live) in the fast lane: of a lifestyle that is exciting/competitive/risky ~ *Sadly it's the price he paid for living in the fast lane.*

in the firing line: to be in a position where you can be criticised/attacked/blamed for something ~ *He's often in the firing line because of his outspoken remarks.*

in the flesh: in person ~ *The young teenager was excited to meet her idol in the flesh.*

in someone's/one's good books: in someone's favour ~ *She was in Mum's good books again after spending time doing the housework.*

in the interim: meanwhile/an intervening time ~ *You can stay here in the interim.*

in the know: possessing inside/secret information ~ *Why don't you ask Steve, he's in the know about everything that happens around here.*

in the lap of luxury: living luxuriously/comfortably ~ *They've been living in the lap of luxury since they won all that money.*

in the limelight: be the focus of attention (especially in the media) ~ *She has a big ego, and loves nothing more than being in the limelight.* *also: in the spotlight

in the main: mostly ~ *In the main, the results were promising.*

in the making: of something in the process of growing/developing/being made ~ *He's a star in the making.*

in the middle of nowhere: in a very remote area or place ~ *We got lost and ended up in the middle of nowhere.*

in the middle of something: otherwise busy/occupied ~ *The phone always seems to ring right when I'm in the middle of doing something.*

in the offing: probable/likely to happen soon ~ *The company has several changes in the offing.*

in the picture: be informed/involved in a given situation/activity ~ *I'll call Pam and put her in the picture.*

in the pink: in good health ~ *It's good to hear you're in the pink, considering how ill you've been.*

in the pipeline: in a state of being planned/prepared ~ *I've heard the company has some exciting new developments in the pipeline.*

in the poo: [informal] in trouble ~ *Uh oh, now I'm in the poo!* *also: in the shit

in the public eye: have the public's attention; be well known ~ *Her job as a politician often puts her in the public eye.*

in the red: to have a negative bank balance/be in debt ~ *Now that she has a good job, her bank balance is no longer in red.*

in the right: correct; of having the support of reason/law ~ *He wanted to defend the charges in court, because he knew he was in the right.*

in the right place at the right time: be in the right location to take advantage of an opportunity ~ *I was working in the right place at the right time and received the offer to work overseas.*

in the running: 1) have a chance to win/of placing well in a competition ~ *He's now in the running to play in the national team.*

2) enter a contest as a competitor ~ *Stella is now in the running to be mayor.*

in the same boat: be in a similar situation/predicament ~ *He's always complaining about struggling to pay the bills, but we're all in the same boat.*

in the same league: equal in skill/proficiency ~ *This restaurant isn't in the same league as the one up the street.*

in the same vein: alike/similar ~ *This, her third novel, is written in the same vein as her first.*

in the throes of: in the midst/middle of doing something ~ *We were in the throes of cooking dinner when the power went out.*

in the wars: to have received/been involved in a succession of minor injuries/misfortunes ~ *I've certainly been in the wars this week. I've got a cut on my arm and a badly bruised knee.*

in a way: to some extent ~ *That it happened like that is good in a way.*

in the way: obstruct/hinder ~ *I can't move because you're in the way!*

in the way of: to be not much of a particular thing ~ *There wasn't much in the way of gardening tools.*

in the wind: of something certain/likely to occur wind ~ *Some big changes were in the wind.*

in the wings: wait in readiness to do something/become active ~ *The corporation has a few prospective managers in the wings.*

in the works: of something under development/being planned ~ *The project has been in the works for six months.*

in the world: ever/anywhere/any place ~ *1a) Where in the world did you get that? 1b) He's considered the greatest golfer in the world.*

(the) in thing: anything current/popular ~ *Those clothes are the in thing this season.*

(be) in touch: 1) in communication/contact with someone ~ *Bye, I'll be in touch with you soon.*

2) possess up-to-date knowledge; intuitive awareness ~ *The politician is always in touch with the needs of the voters.*

in writing: in written form so as to be binding/legal ~ *You'll need to put your statement in writing.*

inclined to/towards: favour; have a preference for something ~ *He's inclined to sleep in on weekends.* *also: have a propensity towards

that way inclined: likely to behave/have similar thoughts as others ~ *Yes, I'm a bit that way inclined.*

not that way inclined: not likely to behave/have similar thoughts as others ~ *Sally likes to get drunk when she goes out, but I'm not that way inclined.*

inch by inch: gradually ~ *Inch by inch he crept closer to his quarry.* *also: bit by bit; little by little

every inch: entirely/in every way/completely ~ *1a) I searched every inch of the room and I still couldn't find it! 1b) She's every inch a dancer.*

not budge/move an inch: stubborn; unable to be persuaded ~ *We tried to coax the frightened cat down, but he wouldn't budge an inch.*

(come) within an inch (of): 1) at the point of doing something ~ *They came within an inch of winning.*

2) be near/close to death ~ *He was beaten to within an inch of his life.*

indifferent to: be apathetic; show no concern or interest ~ *At times, those in power seem indifferent to the needs of the people.*

info: information

in-house: work/activity conducted within an organisation ~ *The company provides in-house training.*

innings: in cricket ~ 1) each of two or four divisions of a game during which one side has a turn at batting

2) a player's turn at batting ~ *Steve played his greatest innings.*

(to have had) a good innings: to have had a long and fulfilling life ~ *He wasn't worried too much about the diagnosis. At eighty-six, he reckoned he'd had a pretty good innings.*

ins and outs: intricate workings of a process/detailed facts about something ~ *I can drive a car, but I don't know the ins and outs of how the motor works.*

inside: in jail/prison ~ *He's been inside for ten years.*

inside information: true/confidential information/facts ~ *Police received inside information about the robbery, enabling them to make an arrest.*

inside out: completely/thoroughly ~ *They know the procedure inside out.*

invite: (an) invitation ~ *Did you get an invite to Jan's party?*

IOU: I owe you ~ a written confirmation of a debt; promissory note ~ *Can I give you an IOU until tomorrow?*

iron oneself out: to get totally drunk; intoxicated ~ *Unfortunately, Tom ironed himself out again last night.*

iron ore: Iron ore is Australia's fourth largest minerals earner. About ninety percent of its annual production is exported to steel markets in Australia. Roughly ninety-eight percent of Australia's iron ore mines can be found in the Hammersley Range in the Pilbarra region of northwest Australia.

iron out a few wrinkles: resolve issues/problems ~ *One more rehearsal should iron out any wrinkles before opening night.*

iron someone out: resolve/settle any disputes ~ *They'll need to iron out their differences if the project is to succeed.*

itchy feet: to have a strong urge/desire to travel/do something different ~ *After living in the same town for two years she began to get itchy feet.*

itsy-bitsy: tiny/small amount/size ~ *Don't tell me you're scared of an itsy-bitsy spider!*

J

Jabiru: Established as a mining town in the 1970s and situated within Kakadu National Park, Jabiru is the only Australian town set inside a national park. It is now the main service area within the park, and it is a great starting point for excursions into Kakadu. It offers a range of accommodation and facilities.

(get the) jack of: get tired/fed up with someone/something ~ *1a) I've had the jack of your bad behaviour! 1b) I've had the jack of working in this heat. I'm finished for the day.*

jack up: 1) refuse to comply/resist ~ *Workers jacked up when asked to do something they weren't trained to do.*

2) raise prices ~ *Fuel companies regularly jack up the price of petrol.*

3) lift an object such as a car with a jack ~ *He jacked up the car to change the tyre.*

jackeroo: apprentice male farm worker

jack-of-all-trades: someone skilled at many jobs

in a jam: be in a difficult predicament; be in some trouble ~ *Jane wondered how she got herself in such a jam.*

traffic jam: congested, slow-moving traffic

jam-packed: filled to capacity; overcrowded ~ *I had to stand all the way. The train was jam-packed.*

jammies: pyjamas *also: jim-jams; pj's

jazz up: add colour; enhance; make more interesting ~ *He sure jazzed up this room with some colourful artwork.* *also: spruce up

jazzy: colourful/vibrant ~ *1a) That's a jazzy shirt you're wearing. 1b) We've got a jazzy party happening!*

Jellyfish: Most jellyfish found in Australian waters are harmless, jelly-like creatures with umbrella-type bodies and flowing tentacles. These stingers can inflict pain if their tentacles come in contact with your skin, like bluebottles, and some, like the box jellyfish found in the waters in tropical, far-north Queensland, can kill a person in minutes from a single swipe of their tentacles.

jerk away: snatch/quickly pull away from something ~ *Feeling something sharp, he jerked his hand away.*

jiff/jiffy: a short period of time ~ *Hold on—I'll be there in a jiffy!*

jiffy bag: 1) a thick/strong envelope used to send items through the post

2) a small, multipurpose carry case mainly used to carry toiletries and personal items

jillaroo: an apprentice female farm worker

jitterbug: a tense/nervous/anxious person

(get the) jitters: to become tense/anxious/worried/nervous ~ *Despite being a seasoned performer, she always gets the jitters before the show begins.*

(have one's) job on the line: (to) have a good chance of losing your job ~ *When the companies merge its almost certain some jobs will be on the line.*

lie down on the job: perform one's job/duties poorly *also: go to sleep on the job

jocks/jockeys: men's underpants

jocks and socks: men's underpants and socks ~ *We usually give Dad jocks and socks for Father's Day.*

Joe Bloggs/Blow: hypothetical average/typical man ~ *It's not something the average Joe Blow could afford.*

joey: baby kangaroo

jog someone's/one's memory: that something causes you to remember something ~ *The news story jogged my memory of a similar incident that happened ten years ago.* *also: ring a bell

join forces: work together with someone else/a group in order to support each other ~ *Emergency workers joined forces to free the trapped man.*

join in (with): participate (with a group of people) in an activity ~ *1a) We persuaded Carol to join in. 1b.) I didn't feel like joining in. 1c) Feel free to join in the chorus.* *also: take part

join the club: [spoken] a way of expressing sympathy for a common experience ~ *You've got the flu? Join the club. I've been in sick with it all week.*

join the queue: [spoken] when others/someone else is waiting to do the same thing as you are ~ *We're all waiting for the bank to open, so join the queue.*

join up: enlist for military service

case a joint: to inspect a place carefully when planning a robbery/break-in ~ *The robbers decided to case the joint to find the best escape route.*

(a) joke: a fiasco; a ridiculous/poorly managed situation (often preceded by "what a") ~ *1a) The government's proposal to fix the problem is a joke! 1b) Today's meeting was a joke. Nothing was achieved and it was a waste of everyone's time!*

(it's a) joke Joyce: [spoken] a way of saying that you were joking (the words "it's a" are understood, not uttered) ~ *Joke Joyce—there's not really a big spider on your back.*

beyond a joke: that something that was funny is now serious/unacceptable ~ *His antics have gone beyond a joke.*

broad/dirty joke: an indecent/rude/obscene joke ~ *I won't let my children listen to his dirty jokes.*

crack/make a joke: say something funny ~ *The presenter tried to make us feel at ease by cracking jokes.*

(be) no joke: of something to be unpleasant/difficult ~ *Trying to exist under these conditions is no joke.*

play a joke/trick: act; do something in a fun way to make someone look silly ~ *He played a joke on his sister by hiding all her clothes.* *also: pull a prank

practical joke: a trick/prank intended to cause embarrassment/ discomfort ~ *The boys took great pleasure in playing a practical joke on their friend.*

sick joke: an unpleasant joke ~ *She told some sick joke about someone dying.*

take a joke: to be able or not to accept a practical joke ~ *Bill didn't think that was very funny—but then, he could never take a joke.*

the joke's on . . . : said when a person who was trying to ridicule someone else is now being laughed at

(be) joking: [spoken] a way of expressing disbelief ~ *They've turned down our application? You've got to be joking!* *also: got to be kidding

joker: a funny/amusing person ~ *You'll like him. He's a bit of a joker.*

practical joker: one who plays practical jokes

jolly good: very good ~ *You did a jolly good job.*

jolly well: [spoken] used to emphasise what you're saying when annoyed/angry ~ *You can jolly well walk home!*

joshing: good natured teasing/joke in a playful way ~ *. . . just joshing—your haircut looks good.*

journo: journalist

joy-ride: a pleasure ride in a stolen car

J.P. : Justice of the Peace, a public official

jumble up: all mixed together; no longer in proper order ~ *Somebody searched the files and jumbled them up.*

jumbo: 1) [informal] an elephant

2) big/oversized ~ *1b) We flew on a jumbo jet. 1b) He ate a jumbo-sized packet of chips in one go!*

one jump ahead: do something before someone else; be at an advantage ~ *She always seems one jump ahead of me.*

jump at: seize an opportunity ~ *1a) He jumped at the job offer. 1b) She jumped at the chance to go to her dream destination.*

jump down one's/someone's throat: harshly criticise someone (without warning) ~ *He jumped down my throat before knowing all the facts.*

jump out of one's skin: physically react to a fright ~ *When he suddenly appeared in that scary outfit, I nearly jumped out of my skin!*

jump start: start a car engine by using power from a battery in another car using special cables

jump the gun: start/begin something before the appropriate time ~ *She was disqualified from the race for jumping the gun.*

jump the queue: move/push into a queue ahead of others; receive preferential treatment

jump to conclusions: evaluate/judge/decide something without full knowledge of the facts ~ *Don't jump to conclusions, it could have been her brother that was with her.*

jump up and down: to show excitement/anger/enthusiasm ~ *She was jumping up and down with excitement at meeting her idol.*

jumper: a warm winter garment made of wool *also: sweater; pullover

junk food: unhealthy food (usually take-away) considered to have a low nutritional value

junk mail: unwanted advertising material delivered to your letterbox

junk shop: a shop selling second-hand goods

junkie: a drug addict addicted to hard drugs

just a sec/tick/minute: in a very short time ~ *1a) I'll be finished in just a sec. 1b) Are you ready yet? Yes, I'll be with you in just a minute.*

just about: almost/nearly ~ *Dinner is just about ready.*

just as: at a specific moment ~ *It started raining just as I arrived.*

just as something (as): equally good/bad, etc. ~ *1a) It's just as big. 1b) They're just as bad as each other.*

just like/the same as: almost identical to something; in exactly the same way ~ *1a) You look just like your mother. 1b) It's just the same as mine.*

just like that: [spoken] used to indicate how quickly/easily something happens (usually said in conjunction with a clicking of the fingers) ~ *1a) It disappeared, just like that! 1b) You could lose your job, just like that.*

just my luck: [spoken] that something bad will happen because you're unlucky ~ *It would be just my luck for it to rain when we go camping.*

just not on: [spoken] emphatic denial/refusal; expression of distaste/displeasure ~ *1a) What they've asked me to do is just not on! 1b) That kind of behaviour is just not on!*

just now: a moment ago ~ *I heard them talking about it just now.*

just quietly: what you say (almost whispered) if you tell someone your opinion and you want it to be kept secret ~ *Just quietly, I don't like her new hair style.*

just so: of something done in a particular manner; things arranged precisely/exactly ~ *1a) He has to arrange his tools just so. 1b) It's important you follow the procedure just so.*

just the thing: exactly what's needed/required ~ *1a) This cup of tea is just the thing. 1b) This desk is just the thing we need for the room.*

could/might/may just: that something is likely to; could possibly happen ~ *1a) Well, I might just do that. 1b) It just may work.*

it's just that . . . : [spoken] used to give a specific reason for something ~ *It's not that I don't like him, it's just that he's not the type of bloke I'd marry.*

not just: not only ~ *It's not just John, we all feel the same about it.*

not just any: used to emphasise that whoever/whatever is important; has special qualities ~ *It's not just any old car, it's the first of its type to manufactured in this country.*

not just yet: not now, but soon ~ *I will be going, but not just yet.*

K

ks: kilometres ~ *It is about 20 ks from here.*

Kangaroo: The kangaroo is one of Australia's most iconic animals. It is a marsupial mammal and it is a macropod, which means "big foot." There are over sixty different species, and kangaroos of different types live in all areas of Australia. The kangaroo and the emu are represented on the Australian coat of arms.

The Kangaroos: Australia's national Rugby League football team

kangaroo bar: a specially designed, sturdy car bumper bar intended to minimise the impact and potential damage to a vehicle if you collide with a kangaroo

keel over: suddenly fall down ~ *A few of the soldiers standing in formation keeled over in the heat.*

on an even keel: to be balanced/steady ~ *The new manager was able to get the project back on an even keel.*

keep a close eye on: watch something/someone carefully ~ *Not wanting to put themselves in danger, the golfers kept a close eye on the approaching storm.*

keen as mustard: eager/enthusiastic ~ *He was as keen as mustard to begin.*

keen on someone: attracted to someone ~ *I hear Dave's keen on Sarah.*

keep a low profile: avoid attracting attention to yourself; be inconspicuous ~ *The celebrity was keeping a low profile after unwanted recent media attention.*

keep a promise: do what you said you would ~ *You can always rely on Sandy to keep a promise.*

keep a secret: (to) not tell anyone ~ *Can you keep a secret?*

keep a straight face: maintain a neutral facial expression; try not to smile ~ *I couldn't keep a straight face when Jack fell in the water.*

keep a stiff upper lip: to not show your emotions when faced with adversity

keep a tight grip/hold on something: control in a strict way ~ *The government needs to keep a tight grip on spending.*

keep an ear to the ground: be alert to new/updated information; listen for news ~ *I'll keep an ear to the ground for any updates on what's happening.*

keep fit: exercise to stay healthy ~ *For Mack, jogging is the best way to keep fit.*

keep in line: make sure someone behaves properly ~ *The rookie teacher had trouble keeping the unruly students in line.*

keep in touch: maintain communication ~ *We don't see each other often, but we always manage to keep in touch.*

keep it down: [spoken] request to keep quiet ~ *Keep it down—I'm trying to sleep!*

keep it up: continue doing something; maintain a level of quality ~ *Good work Paul—keep it up!*

keep on about: continue talking about something ~ *The discussion's finished—don't keep on about it.*

keep on doing something: continue to do something/do something again and again ~ *1a) Many went to see what was happening outside, but I just kept on with my work. 1b) He keeps on making the same mistake.*

keep on keeping on: persist/persevere against all odds ~ *The poor, tired old engine just keeps on keeping on.*

keep one's chin up: stay cheerful/optimistic in a difficult situation ~ *Keep your chin up, you can try for selection next year.*

keep/hold one's end up: adequately perform one's share/part of the load/job/task ~ *The new job's challenging, but he's managing to hold his end up.*

keep one's feet on the ground: remain practical/realistic about a situation ~ *Despite the sudden rise to fame she still keeps her feet on the ground.*

keep hands off: [spoken] warning to not touch/stay away from someone/something ~ *1a) Keep your hands off the wet paint! 1b) That piece of cake is mine—so keep your hands off!*

keep one's head: remain calm/sensible in a difficult situation ~ *He kept his head when the fire started and quickly ushered the children to a safe place.* *also: keep one's cool

keep one's nose to the grindstone: work diligently ~ *He kept his nose to the grindstone all year and got the promotion he wanted.*

keep your wits about you: be alert/aware of the situation/your surroundings ~ *You have to keep your wits about you whilst doing this job, or else you could suffer serious injuries.*

keep someone guessing: deliberately withhold information ~ *The story line keeps you guessing the whole way through.*

keep someone waiting: cause/make someone to wait for you to arrive/do something ~ *1a) She kept us waiting for twenty minutes. 1b) I need an answer by tomorrow, so don't keep me waiting.*

keep us/me on (their/my) toes: stay alert/focussed ~ *The teacher always give us something challenging to keep us on our toes.*

keep (close) tabs on: watch someone or something closely ~ *They didn't have enough evidence to make an arrest, so all the police could do was keep tabs on him.*

keep to: 1) honour an agreement/rule ~ *You should keep to the speed limit.*

2) remain/stay on the path/track/road ~ *Keep to the track or you could easily get lost.*

keep to oneself: stay alone; shun the company of others ~ *The new, shy student mostly keeps to herself.*

keep track of: be informed/fully aware of something happening ~ *1a) I can't keep track of my sister's new boyfriends. 1b) I've got to remember to keep track of the time so I don't miss my appointment.*

keep up (with): 1) stay level/equal with someone or something ~ *1a) He couldn't keep up with the other runners. 1b) Wages are failing to keep up with inflation.*

2) remain informed about something ~ *I like to keep up with the latest news.*

keep up with the Jones's: match/equal someone's success/ lifestyle/wealth ~ *I think he was trying to keep up with the Jones's when he bought that car.*

keep your eyes peeled: watch carefully for ~ *The lifeguards kept their eyes peeled for any swimmers who were in trouble.*

keep your hat/hair/shirt on: [spoken] request to stay calm; don't panic ~ *Keep your shirt on—we'll get there on time.*

for keeps: 1) permanently ~ *We're moving there for keeps.*

2) an indefinite period ~ *It's yours for keeps.*

keg: barrel of beer

kelpie: an Australian sheep dog used to muster sheep or cattle

keyed up: in a state of nervous excitement ~ *The players are all keyed up and ready to play.*

kick around: ponder/consider something ~ *I'll kick around a few ideas and let you know tomorrow.*

kick in: of something to take effect ~ *It took a while for the medication to kick in.*

kick in the arse/bum/pants: [informal] 1) receive a setback/ disappointment ~ *Losing at this stage of the competition was a kick in the pants for the team.* *also: kick up the arse/bum/pants

kick off: commence/begin ~ *When does it kick off?*

kick on: continue beyond the official finishing time ~ *Most people left early, but we kicked on until 3 a.m.*

kick oneself: reprimand/reproach yourself for doing/saying something stupid ~ *I'm kicking myself for not going.*

kick over: of an engine/motor to start ~ *The engine won't kick over.*

(get a) kick in the teeth: be treated badly/unfairly by someone who should be supporting you ~ *Losing the contract was a kick in the teeth.* *also: kick in the guts

kick someone out: unceremoniously eject/remove someone ~ *He got kicked out of the team for his actions.*

kick the habit: end a habit, such as smoking ~ *He found it hard to kick the habit.* *also: break the habit

kick up a stink/fuss: protest vigorously/complain angrily ~ *They kicked up a stink when asked to leave.*

get a kick out of: get enjoyment/pleasure from doing something ~ *She gets a kick out of helping others.*

kid around: behave in a silly way; joke with someone ~ *Relax, we're just kidding around.*

kid sister/brother: a younger sister/brother ~ *Andrew's my kid brother.*

kid(s) stuff: 1) anything seen as suitable for children only ~ *There's lots of kids' stuff happening at the fair.*

2) an act/task viewed as something childish/immature/easy to do ~ *This bit's only kids' stuff—it'll soon get more complicated.*

kid oneself: deceive/delude oneself ~ *I'd be kidding myself if I thought I could achieve all that.*

I kid you not: [spoken] a way of saying that you are serious; that you are not joking ~ *The crocodile was at least three metres long—I kid you not!*

only/just kidding: to be joking/teasing; not serious ~ *I'm only kidding—there's not really a huge spider on your back!*

you're kidding: [spoken] expression of disbelief/outrage ~ *They won 50-0? You're kidding!* *also: you're joking; you must be kidding

kiddie: young child

kiddo: form of address from an older person to a younger person ~ *How are you, kiddo?*

kill for . . . : be willing to go to extremes to do something ~ *I'd kill for a cold drink right now.*

kill off: extinguish/eliminate/kill ~ *The main character in the story gets killed off in the last chapter.*

kill switch: an emergency safety cut-off device to completely cease/abort machinery operation; bring to a sudden stop

kill time: do something to keep you occupied while you are waiting for something to happen ~ *There was a transport delay so I killed time at the shopping mall.*

kill with kindness: overdo one's effort to be kind ~ *I think I kill my plants with kindness by overwatering them.*

. . . killing me: what you say when something's hurting you ~ *My feet are killing me.*

make a killing: achieve financial success ~ *He made a killing at the races.*

won't kill you: that something is not as unpleasant or difficult as it seems ~ *A bit of hard work won't kill you.*

dressed to kill: intentionally wear clothes to attract attention ~ *She went to the party dressed to kill.*

go in for the kill: prepare to destroy or kill something/someone ~ *He'd stalked his prey, now he was going in for the kill.*

killer instinct: have a determination to succeed; be fiercely competitive ~ *He'll succeed in whatever he does because he's got that killer instinct.*

kind of: somewhat/rather ~ *Do you like it? Kind of—I'm not quite sure.*

kind of things: a specific group ~ *He bought office supplies, all those kinds of things.*

all kinds of: a variety ~ *They sell all kinds of confectionary.*

be the kind (to): a particular type of person ~ *1a) He's not the kind of person to do something like that. 1b) She's not the marrying kind.*

in kind: 1) of payment for goods/services as opposed to money ~ *They repaid in kind with boxes of home-grown fruits and vegetables.*

2) with the same thing; in the same way ~ *They responded in kind by denying them access.*

nothing of the kind: 1) not at all like something previously mentioned ~ *It's billed as a serious drama, but it's nothing of the kind.*

2) [spoken] emphatic denial ~ *I did nothing of the kind!*

of a kind: similar; rudimentary ~ *They had rigged up a heating system of a kind.*

one of a/its kind: unique; unlike anything/anyone else ~ *1a) Nobody does it like our Mary. She's one of a kind. 1b) It's the only one of its kind in Australia.*

something of the kind: used to refer to something already mentioned ~ *I thought something of the kind would happen.*

2) something/someone similar ~ *2a) It's like a giant cauldron or something of the kind. 2b) He's an accountant, or something of the kind.*

two of a kind: similar in nature/characteristics ~ *They're two of a kind, both fishing fanatics!*

kinder/kindy: kindergarten

king hit: a surprise, sharp blow/punch powerful enough to make someone fall to the ground (one that often has fatal consequences)

king's ransom: a large sum of money ~ *He's asking a king's ransom for his house.*

kiss and make up: reconcile an argument ~ *They often argue but they always kiss and make up.*

kiss of life: *see: mouth-to-mouth

kiss something better: comfort someone (usually a child) by kissing the injured/sore area as a way to remove pain

kiss something goodbye: [spoken] said when you realise that something you've lost can't be recovered ~ *I kissed my hat goodbye when it fell into the water.*

blow someone a kiss: used to indicate an intended kiss from a distance when bidding farewell, it is done by touching the palm of your hand lightly with your lips, and then blowing across your hand towards the intended person

the whole kit and caboodle: everything/the whole lot ~ *The prize is not just golf clubs, but includes all accessories - the whole kit and caboodle.* *also: the whole box and dice; the whole shebang; the works

kitchen tea: a pre-wedding party where female guests bring a kitchen item as a wedding gift

go fly a kite: *see: beat it

Kit-Kat: popular chocolate bar

Kiwi: [informal] a New Zealander; a small flightless New Zealand bird

Kleenex: popular brand of tissues

knackered: utterly exhausted/tired ~ *That was hard work. I'm knackered!* *see also: buggered

knee-high to a grasshopper: the height of a small child ~ *I used to play that game when I was knee-high to a grasshopper.*

knickers: women's underwear; panties

get your knickers in a knot: become angry/upset ~ *There's no need to get your knickers in a knot, everything's under control.*

knick-knacks: *see bits and pieces

knife-edge: a situation in which the outcome/results are uncertain ~ *Right now the election results are on a knife-edge.*

knock something/someone: condemn/criticise/find fault ~ *1a) Don't knock my cooking. I'd like to see you do better! 1b) No wonder he feels dejected, you're always knocking him.* *often used humorously/sarcastically

knock around/about with: associate/socialise with ~ *On weekends I usually knock around with my school friends.*

get knocked around/about: become damaged through physical force/constant use ~ *It's been knocked around a bit, but it still does the job.* *also: battered around/about

knock (something) back: 1) drink very quickly ~ *You knocked that back pretty quickly.*

2) refuse an offer/application ~ *The council knocked back the building application.*

knock something down: 1) reduce the price of something by persuasion ~ *I knocked him down to $50 for the lot.*

2) push/cause something/someone to fall down ~ *The force of the impact knocked him to the ground.* *also: knock over

3) demolish a building ~ *We're going to knock the old house down and build a new one.*

knock someone for six: completely overwhelm/upset someone ~ *Their decision knocked me for six.*

knock off: 1) cease work ~ *What time do you knock off work?*

2) reduce in price ~ *I knocked $10 off because it was damaged.*

4) rob/hold up a bank ~ *The thieves knocked off two banks before they were caught.*

knock something off: 1) complete a task/job easily and quickly ~ *I should be able to knock this job off in no time.*

2) steal something ~ *Someone knocked off my camera!*

knock it off: [spoken] a way of telling someone to be quiet/stop doing something (often said humorously) ~ *Will you two knock it off!*

knock someone off: kill someone; kill an animal ~ *1a) He got knocked off by a rival gang member. 1b) The hunter only managed to knock off a few rabbits.*

knock something on the head: put a stop to a plan/idea/proposal ~ *We had to knock our plans to go camping on the head because of the rain.*

knock oneself out: make a great effort to do something ~ *I knocked myself out trying to get it finished on time.* *also: see reason

knock one's socks off: be amazed/impressed ~ *Her performance knocked my socks off.* *also: knock you off your feet; blow you away

knock someone out: 1) hit/bash and cause unconsciousness ~ *It took just one powerful punch from the boxer to knock his opponent out.*

2) cause someone to go to sleep before an operation; cause drowsiness ~ *It won't take long for the anaesthetic to knock you out.*

3) be eliminated from competition ~ *The team was knocked out in the second round of the competition.*

knock over: *see knock down

knock sense into someone: encourage someone to think sensibly/logically ~ *I tried to knock some sense into her, but she insists on going.*

knock the wind out of: cause physical injury so someone has trouble breathing ~ *The heavy fall knocked the wind out of me.*

knock together/up: prepare; construct something in a hurried/ unplanned manner ~ *1a) She easily knocked together a meal for her unexpected dinner guests. 1b) The farmer knocked up a temporary fence in the meantime.*

knock 'em dead: [spoken] a way of wishing someone luck before a performance/a game ~ *Good luck. Knock 'em dead!*

knocked up: [slang] to be pregnant

knockout: be amazed by something/someone ~ *She gave a knockout performance!*

knockabout: someone rowdy/boisterous; with a carefree attitude

know all too well: to have knowledge; an understanding of something ~ *1a) He knows all too well what will happen if he fails the exams. 1b) He knows all too well what it's like to be poor.*

know a thing or two: be well informed; knowledgeable ~ *1a) Ask Jim, he knows a thing or two about snakes. 1b) After twenty years of teaching mathematics, I think I know a thing or two about algebra.* *also: know a trick or two

know all the lurks and perks: benefits/profits resulting from an unethical scheme ~ *After working in the gambling industry for twenty years, he knows all the lurks and perks.*

know better: be wise/experienced enough not to do something wrong; to behave responsibly ~ *1a) I thought you knew better than to do that! 1b) Young children don't know any better than to run onto the road. 1c) She tried to tell me it was a rare gem, but I knew better.*

know (it) backwards: be familiar with something ~ *1a) I know the route from Adelaide to Melbourne backwards. 1b) She knows the dance routine backwards.* *also: know it inside out; know it off pat; know like the back of my hand

know one's place: be aware of one's social standing/order/rank and behave accordingly ~ *He would never challenge her decision, he knows his place.*

know someone from a bar of soap: to not know what someone looks like; be unable to recognise someone ~ *You'll have to point her out, I wouldn't know her from a bar of soap.*

know who's who: to know everyone's job/position/standing within an organisation ~ *Before you begin working here, you need to know who's who.*

knows next to nothing: to know very little about something ~ *He claims he can fix motors, but in fact he knows next to nothing about them.*

knows no bounds: be limitless/unrestricted ~ *1a) His knowledge of science knows no bounds. 1b) Their love knows no bounds.*

you know: [spoken] 1) used for emphasis ~ *You know, I really don't want to go out tonight.*

2) used after a pause in conversation when you're thinking about what to say next ~ *The office is right next door to the—you know—the big international hotel.*

3) used before you begin to talk about someone/something in particular (to prompt the listener's memory) ~ *You know that job my brother applied for? Well—he got it!*

4) used when you're being more specific about something ~ *Have you seen the scissors? You know, the special heavy-duty ones.*

know-all: someone who claims to know everything but in fact knows very little ~ *Jack's a real know-all—he contradicts everything I say.*

knuckle down: apply oneself to a task/job ~ *I'd better knuckle down and study hard, or I won't pass the exams.*

knuckle sandwich: a closed-fist punch to the mouth (said humorously) ~ *If you don't keep quiet I'll give you a knuckle sandwich.*

knucklehead: fool; idiot

Koala: One of Australia's best known animals, the iconic koala is represented when promoting Australia to the tourist industry. The name koala comes from an Aboriginal word meaning "no drink." They get their fluids through eucalyptus leaves, which they feed on. Eucalyptus leaves are the only food they consume, with some exceptions. Koalas are found all over eastern Australia.

Kookaburra: The laughing kookaburra is a large member of the kingfisher family of birds, and is instantly recognisable by its shape and by its voice. A family or group of kookaburras may sing together, producing a loud and familiar *koo—koo—koo—koo—kaa—kaa—kaa—kaa* sound. They often talk or sing to other kookaburras in nearby trees in the early mornings. They feed on mostly insects and worms, but their large beaks enable them to eat small snakes, frogs, and mammals. They kill large prey by bashing it against tree branches or on the ground.

kooky: kookaburra (pronounced as in "cook")

L

L's: learner driver licence

L-plates: An *L* sign displayed at the front and back of a car/vehicle to indicate a learner driver

Australian Labour Party: a social-democratic political party

the ladies (room): toilet/bathroom ~ *Excuse me while I go to the ladies.* *also: powder room

Lady Muck: fictitious name given to a woman who has a pretentious manner or thinks they're better than others ~ *Who does she think she is—Lady Muck?*

(get) laid off: lose your job because of a shortage of work ~ *The company laid off twenty workers last month.* *also: retrenched

laid up: incapacitated/confined because of illness ~ *I've been laid up all week with the flu.*

laid-back: relaxed in manner/not easily excited/unhurried ~ *It's his laid-back manner that makes him good to work under.* *also: easy going

lairy: gaudy/flashy/loud ~ *I've got some lairy pants to wear to the costume party.*

lamington: a sponge cake square dipped in melted chocolate then covered in shredded, dry coconut

land a blow: connect with a punch ~ *The boxer had trouble landing a blow to his opponent.*

land a deal: secure a contract/agreement ~ *After two hours of negotiations, we finally landed a deal.*

land a job: win/secure a job ~ *He landed a job in the marketing department.*

land of nod: to be sleeping ~ *She's deep in the land of nod.*

land on one's feet: of the situation to improve after a difficult time ~ *After a rough time, he's finally landed on his feet with this job.* *also: fall on one's feet

in the land of the living: humorous term for being alive

landslide victory: to win an election by an overwhelming majority ~ *Opinion polls are predicting a landslide for the Labor Party in next week's election.*

lap up: delight in; enjoy something ~ *My dog laps up all the attention you can give him.*

at large: 1) not yet captured/at liberty ~ *One of the escapees is still at large.*

2) in general/as a whole ~ *He was talking about the population at large.*

larrikin: a mischievous but likable person (male) ~ *He's a bit of a larrikin, but he raises a lot of money for charity every year.*

lash out: 1) physically or verbally attack ~ *Local residents lashed out at council's plan to demolish the centre.*

2) spend money freely ~ *We lashed out on dinner at an expensive restaurant.*

at last: [spoken] finally ~ *I did it—at last!*

at long last: finally, after a long period of time ~ *I've finished, at long last!*

at the last moment: when it's almost too late ~ *He changed his mind at the last moment.*

last but not least: importantly, despite being mentioned last ~ *And last but not least, I'd like to thank my parents for all the support they've given me.*

last resort: the final option/choice ~ *In an emergency, you will be asked to abandon ship only as a last resort.*

. . . if it's the last thing I do: [spoken] used to emphasise a determination to do something ~ *I'm determined to finish it, if it's the last thing I do!*

the last I heard . . . : [spoken] used when you're giving the latest information that you know about a particular subject ~ *The last I heard they were living in Canada.*

the last/final straw: the final in a string of mishaps that pushes one's endurance/patience beyond the limit ~ *She's said some nasty things, but those insults were the last straw!* *also: the final straw

the last/final word: 1) the final utterance in a debate/argument ~ *My brother always wants to have the last word.*

2) the power of authority in an ultimate decision ~ *The CEO has the last word in all major decisions.*

the last thing you want/need: something that you certainly don't want ~ *Bad weather is the last thing I need right now.*

last-ditch effort: a desperate, final attempt to do something ~ *He made a last-ditch effort to pull him from the raging river.*

latch on to: 1) hold onto/attach to something ~ *The baby gorilla was firmly latched on to his mother's back.*

2) begin to understand something ~ *It took him a while to latch on to what was being said.*

of late: lately/recently ~ *I've been getting bad headaches of late.*

(the) latest: the most recent news/gossip/information ~ *What's the latest on the bush fire situation?*

lather up: apply soap to form suds to one's body ~ *I'd just finished lathering up when the water went cold.*

in a lather: agitated/anxious/nervous ~ *He was in a lather about the interview.*

(a) laugh: 1) a ludicrous/ridiculous situation ~ *It was so poorly organized, it was a laugh.*

2) something/someone amusing ~ *You'll like him. He's a real laugh!*

laugh at yourself: to not take yourself too seriously—especially if you fail at an attempt to do something

laugh one's head off: laugh loudly and vigorously ~ *It was so funny. I laughed my head off.*

laugh off: dismiss false reports/rumours as a joke ~ *He laughed off reports that he was about to retire.*

(be) laughing: to feel smug/happy about something; to have a sense of achievement at completing a difficult task ~ *The last rapids are difficult, but once you get past them you're laughing.*

laughing gear: one's mouth ~ *Here, wrap your laughing gear around this.*

laughing stock: an object of ridicule ~ *You'll be the laughing stock of the party if you wear that!*

laugh up one's sleeve: laugh at someone secretly, often unkindly ~ *He feigned interest in their abstract art creation, but he was laughing up his sleeve.*

for a laugh: for enjoyment as opposed to a serious purpose ~ *We decided to go, just for a laugh.*

not know whether to laugh or cry: have mixed emotions about a bad situation ~ *When it all collapsed I didn't know whether to laugh or cry.*

(have) the last laugh: achieve success after earlier criticism ~ *We got the last laugh when we won the contract.*

you have to laugh: that a situation is so appallingly bad that all you can do is laugh

laugh-a-minute: someone/something entertaining/funny (sometimes used humorously to mean someone/something is not funny) ~ *Steve is a laugh-a-minute guy who's always good to be around.*

(a) law unto oneself: one who ignores established rules/who makes up their own rules ~ *He always ignores the speed limit, but then he thinks he's a law unto himself.* *also: above the law

in the eyes of the law: considered by authorities as legal/illegal ~ *In the eyes of the law you are at fault.*

the long arm of the law: the far reaches of lawful authority ~ *They thought they had gotten away with the crime, but the long arm of the law caught up with them.*

get on the wrong side of the law: be in trouble with the police for doing something illegal ~ *What he was doing was risky, and he soon found himself on the wrong side of the law.*

lawn: an area of short, regularly cut grass

lawn mower: hand- or power-operated machine for cutting grass

lay aside: put something down and to the side ~ *He laid aside his work to deal with other important issues.*

lay charges: officially accuse someone of a crime ~ *Police have the suspect in custody and expect to lay charges later today.*

lay claim to: state that something belongs to you ~ *Both countries lay claim to the origins of the recipe.*

lay down the law/rules: create and assert rules/restrictions to be upheld in a private domain ~ *He laid down the law about what type of behaviour was acceptable and what was unacceptable.* *also: read the riot act

lay something down: give up/surrender ~ *Police convinced the gunman to lay down his weapon.*

lay a hand on: touch someone (with intent to harm) ~ *If you lay a hand on me I'll call the police!*

lay (one's) hands on: 1) acquire/obtain something ~ *Where did you lay your hands on such a rare book?*

2) locate; find by physical touch ~ *I've looked everywhere, but I just can't seem to lay my hands on the contract.*

lay into: verbally or physically attack someone ~ *The guy laid into him in a frenzied attack.*

lay it on the line: be truthful about something ~ *You're going to have to lay it on the line and tell them what's happened.*

lay/put something on the line: put something/someone at risk ~ *1a) Firefighters lay their lives on the line almost every day. 1b) In doing so, she'll be putting her career on the line.*

lay low: avoid being seen/noticed ~ *1a) I'm not feeling well so I'm going to lay low for a while and get some rest. 1b) The thieves decided to lay low after robbing the bank.*

lay off: 1) [spoken] request for someone to stop doing something ~ *Oh, lay off him will you! He doesn't need your lectures right now.*

2) end someone's employment ~ *The company had to lay off workers because of the economic crisis.*

lay on: supply; provide goods/services ~ *Her parents are going to lay on all the food for the event.*

lay (something) out: display/reveal something ~ *1a) She laid out the clothes she would wear the next day. 1b) Steve laid out the plans for the next month's agenda.*

lay someone out: knock unconscious; knock to the ground ~ *The big guy laid him out cold!*

lay to rest: inter/bury someone ~ *The family laid their mother to rest.*

lay waste: leave something in ravaged/ruined state ~ *A bushfire lay waste to the small community.*

lay-by: a system by which goods are paid for in small instalments over a period of time ~ *It was expensive, so she put it on lay-by for a couple of months.*

layabout: an idle, lazy person ~ *I've never seen him do any work. He's nothing but a layabout.* *also lazybones

laze about: spend time relaxing ~ *I spent the afternoon just lazing about watching TV.*

lead someone astray: 1) deceive someone; falsify facts ~ *The insurance company led me astray as to what the house was covered for.*

2) teach someone bad habits; influence in a negative way ~ *His new friends are leading him astray.* *also: lead down/up the garden path

lead back to: to return to a place ~ *This path eventually leads back to the campsite.*

lead to believe: cause to believe something untrue; imply something (to someone) ~ *1a) We were led to believe the meeting would be held here. 1b) I've been led to believe the companies will merge.*

lead down to: the destination of a path/trail in a downhill direction ~ *This trail leads down to the river.*

lead forth: proceed/continue ahead; precede someone ~ *The commander led forth the army.*

lead someone on: *see: lead someone astray; lead someone up the garden path

lead up to: the destination of a path/route in an uphill direction ~ *This bush track leads up to the road.*

lead the way: 1) lead someone/a group of people ~ *I don't know the route, you should lead the way.*

2) be innovative/achieve success then show others how to do it ~ *It's a country that leads the way in conservation.* *see also: lead the field

follow the lead: follow someone's direction/guidance ~ *I'm not sure exactly where we're going, I'm just following the lead.*

lead-foot: a person who drives too fast (pressing heavily on the accelerator)

leak out: of information to become known ~ *News of the merger soon leaked out.*

leak through: for a liquid to permeate/seep through something ~ *Water leaked through the basement.*

leap at: accept an opportunity to do something ~ *I'd leap at the chance to work overseas.* *also jump at

leap into action: suddenly/quickly begin doing something ~ *The firemen leapt into action when the alarm sounded.* *also: swing into action

learn a thing or two: learn bits of information about something ~ *Apart from learning safe driving techniques, we also learned a thing or two about how an engine works.*

learn the hard way: learn from an unpleasant experience; learn from your mistakes ~ *He learned the hard way that it was a stupid thing to do.* *also: learn a lesson

learn the ropes: learn how to do an activity/task ~ *The job's not that difficult, it shouldn't take you long to learn the ropes.*

leave alone: leave unchanged/undisturbed/untouched ~ *1a) Please leave me alone. 1b) I told you to leave it alone!*

leave (lying) around: carelessly leave something somewhere ~ *1a) He leaves his clothes lying around everywhere. 1b) Kids' toys were left lying around the room.*

leave aside: ignore facts; keep in reserve ~ *1a) Let's leave that information aside for a minute and concentrate on this. 1b) Leave these ingredients aside until the end of the cooking process.*

leave behind: 1) depart and fail/forget to bring something/ someone ~ *I left my keys behind.*

2) to purposely not take someone/something with you ~ *We didn't have room, so we had to leave it behind.*

3) turn one's back on a previous lifestyle ~ *He left behind a life of crime for a better life in a new country.*

leave one cold: be unaffected/disappointed/disinterested in something ~ *Her attitude left me cold.*

leave for: depart to go somewhere ~ *I leave for Adelaide on Tuesday.*

leave in someone's hands: give control/responsibility of someone/ something to someone ~ *I'll leave it in your capable hands.*

leave in the lurch: abandon someone ~ *She left him in the lurch, and he had to finish it all on his own.*

leave it at that: do or say no more ~ *We've said enough. Let's leave it at that.*

leave it to . . . : rely on someone to do something ~ *He left it to Jack to finish the work.*

leave it with me: [spoken] that you will take care of/look after an issue/problem ~ *Leave it with me for a few days and I'll get it sorted out.*

leave of absence: a period of time you're absent from your workplace ~ *Jim's on leave of absence until next week.*

leave on the shelf: (of a woman) to be considered too old to get married ~ *Still single at forty, she felt she'd been left on the shelf.*

leave out: 1) omit/disregard/ignore someone/something ~ *I left some bits of the story out.*

2) leave something out of something ~ *He left his bicycle out in the rain.*

leave out in the cold: to be excluded from shared information/ facts ~ *Everyone else seems to know what's happening, but I've been left out in the cold.*

leave for dead: 1) outrun someone in a race, leaving them far behind ~ *He started strongly, but his competitors soon left him for dead.*

2) leave someone to die ~ *The gang assaulted him and left him for dead in a dark alley.*

leave something for someone: bequeath something to someone ~ *My aunt said she'd leave her antique clock to me when she dies.*

leave the door open: allow for further action/change ~ *She rejected our proposal, but left the door open for further discussions.*

leave the nest: of your children to live away from the family home ~ *All but one of my children have left the nest.*

leave nothing to chance: plan something carefully so as to avoid something going wrong ~ *I've brought clothes for all weather. I'm not leaving anything to chance.*

leave to one's own devices: let someone do something unsupervised/without assistance ~ *I usually leave my kids to their own devices when they're playing.*

leave well enough alone: avoid correcting/changing/fixing something that is already satisfactory

leave oneself (wide) open: 1) fail to protect oneself from ridicule/criticism ~ *I know the criticism was harsh, but you left yourself wide open.*

2) remain willing to consider ~ *Jim put forward an option, but left himself open to further suggestions.*

leave word (with) someone: leave a message ~ *He wasn't at home, but I left word with his wife.*

left, right, and centre: from all directions ~ *Bullets were flying left, right, and centre.*

left-wing: in politics, a radical, liberal socialist

leftie/y: [informal] someone who supports left-wing ideals

leftover(s): uneaten food ~ *She feeds any leftovers to the dog.*

(give someone a) leg up: help someone climb up or over something ~ *Can you give me a leg up please?*

haven't a leg to stand on: be unable to prove something ~ *If you don't have a receipt, you won't have a leg to stand on.*

on its/one's last legs: 1) be very near to death; close to dying ~ *Our poor old dog is on its last legs.*

2) in bad condition/not working properly ~ *I think my old computer is on its last legs.*

3) extremely exhausted ~ *I was on my last legs as I approached the finish line.*

legless: very drunk/intoxicated; unable to stand

legal eagle: [informal] lawyer; solicitor

legit: legitimate/genuine ~ *My excuse is legit—I've been sick with the flu all week.*

lemon: a new product that doesn't work properly/is faulty ~ *The car I bought is a lemon—it's broken down four times in two months!*

lemon squash: lemon-flavoured soft drink

lend a hand: help someone to do something ~ *Could you lend me a hand to move this?* *also: lend a hand to someone

lend an ear: listen intently/compassionately ~ *She's always there to lend an ear.*

lend itself to something: be suitable for something ~ *His voice lends itself to opera.*

to a lesser degree: not as much/less strong than something else ~ *She was influenced by her father and, to a lesser degree, her mother.* *also: to a lesser extent

the lesser of two evils: the least unpleasant of two options ~ *The lesser of two evils—having a tooth pulled or root canal therapy?*

let alone: that something is less likely to occur than something else; that you are less likely to do something ~ *He can't even boil an egg, let alone cook a meal.*

let someone be: [spoken] a way of telling someone to stop annoying/disturbing another person ~ *Let her be—she's too upset at the moment.*

let bygones be bygones: forgive and forget past grievances ~ *We've known each other for too long to let this ruin our friendship. Let's let bygones be bygones and start afresh.*

let down: 1) allow the air to escape from something ~ *Someone let down the tyres on my car.*

2) gradually lower something ~ *The crane driver carefully let down the load.*

let someone down: fail/disappoint someone by not doing what's expected of you ~ *Many families felt they'd been let down by the politician's empty promises.*

let someone down gently: tell someone bad news without upsetting them too much

let (h)'er/it rip: [spoken] start a motor and continue with full power ~ *Just turn the key and let 'er rip!*

let fly: verbally attack/insult someone ~ *I asked an innocent question and he just let fly at me for no reason.*

let go: release one's emotions ~ *She found it hard to let go after her father died.*

let it all hang out: act freely/uninhibited ~ *I'm so looking forward to the weekend—I'm going to just let it all hang out.* *also: let loose

let it be known: [spoken] to make sure people are aware of something ~ *Let it be known that I took no part in their scam.* *also: let it be said

let it go: resist doing something ~ *There's nothing you can do about it—just let it go.* *also: let it be; let it ride; let it slip

let loose: do something spontaneous, in an uncontrolled way ~ *She let loose a loud scream.*

let something loose: release something ~ *They'll let the bird loose when its wing heals.* *also: turn loose

let's just say . . . : [spoken] that you are not going to reveal any more information ~ *Let's just say that Steve had nothing to do with it.*

let someone off: receive no punishment ~ *I was lucky, Mum let me off lightly for coming home late.* *also: get let off

let off easily/lightly: receive minimal punishment ~ *I was let off lightly with a stern lecture.*

let off steam: get rid of pent up energy/emotion ~ *He's so angry he's gone for a run to let off steam.*

let on: reveal information ~ *1a) I wasn't going to let on that I already knew about it. 1b) Don't let on that you know her.*

let oneself go: neglect one's appearance/standards ~ *He's let himself go over the past few years.*

let oneself in for: agree to doing something without knowing what's involved ~ *She has no idea what she's letting herself in for.*

let slip: inadvertently reveal a secret ~ *She let slip about the surprise party.*

let someone have it: physically or verbally attack ~ *When Sam arrived home in the early hours of the morning his father let him have it.*

let someone in: allow entry ~ *I had to wait for somebody to let me in.*

let someone in on: share a secret with someone ~ *Don't you think we should let her in on our little secret?*

let the cat out of the bag: mistakenly/carelessly reveal a secret ~ *It was going to be a surprise, but my brother let the cat out of the bag.*

let the side down: betray/disappoint a group of people one is part of; underperform ~ *Their poor performance let the side down.* *see also: let someone down

let through: permit/allow someone/something to move through a crowded space/a doorway ~ *1a) This is an emergency—please let us through! 1b) The doorman won't let you through if you don't have a ticket.*

let up: ease in intensity ~ *The rain didn't let up for three days.*

to the letter: precisely/exactly ~ *You should follow the instructions to the letter.*

letterbox: mailbox; postbox

level off: 1) become more level/smooth ~ *You need to level off the floor before putting the carpet down.*

2) stop fluctuating ~ *The workload should level off next week.*

level out: to resume a more level course/path ~ *The road started to level out at the base of the hills.*

level playing field: a situation that is fair to everyone/that shows no favour ~ *The ruling allows everyone to compete on a level playing field.*

level (to the ground): demolish/raze a building ~ *The blast was so big it levelled several other buildings.*

on the level: be honest/truthful ~ *Look, I'm on the level.* *also: level (with someone)

try one's level best: try very hard/do one's best ~ *I can't guarantee it, but I'll try my level best.*

level-headed: showing good judgement; being sensible; acting calmly in difficult situations ~ *By remaining level-headed, he was able to save his own life, as well as the lives of ten other people.*

level-pegging: in an equal position in a game/competition ~ *The horses were level-pegging for nearly the whole race.*

The Liberal Party of Australia: this major centre-right political party competes with the centre-left Australian Labour Party

have something/someone licked: 1) overcome a difficult situation ~ *Another five minutes and we'll have it licked.*

2) defeat someone in a competition or game ~ *They soon had the other team licked.*

lick and a promise: a quick, superficial clean ~ *Short of time, I gave it a lick and a promise.*

lick into shape: improve something/someone's quality/ appearance/performance ~ *She was confident he could lick the team into shape.* *also: whip into shape

(get) licked: be defeated in a game/competition beaten ~ *We were soundly licked.*

lickety split: do something as quickly/fast as possible ~ *He ran away—lickety split!*

lie about/around: 1) recline lazily ~ *Mike did nothing but lay about all weekend.*

2) left carelessly/casually ~ *He always leaves his clothes lying around his bedroom floor.*

lie about something: speak an untruth ~ *1a) He lied about his whereabouts! 1b) I would never lie about something like that.*

lie ahead/before: 1) an unknown future happening/event ~ *After what's happened I don't know what lies ahead.*

2) exist in front of someone/something ~ *A small clearing lay ahead of us.*

lie back: relax with one's feet up; recline ~ *When I get home I'm going to lie back and relax.*

lies behind: 1) the reason/cause of someone doing something ~ *I don't know what lay behind her decision to quit.*

2) positioned/placed behind something ~ *Not many people know there's a secret passage behind the wall.*

lies beyond: of something found/located on the other side of something ~ *1a) A stream lies just beyond the clearing. 1b) She sometimes wonders what lies beyond the universe.*

lie down: lie prone (with feet up) ~ *Why don't you lie down if you're tired?*

lie in wait: stay hidden/concealed waiting to ambush someone/ something ~ *The attacker lay in wait for his victim.*

lie through one's teeth: tell an outrageous lie ~ *She was lying through her teeth when she said she didn't know him!*

pack of lies: something written/spoken to be completely untrue ~ *The statement he gave to the police was a pack of lies.*

lie-in: time spent lying awake in bed before you get up ~ *I enjoy a lie-in on Sunday mornings.*

the life and times of . . . : a biography; an account of someone's life and lifestyle ~ *The book gives an in-depth look at the life and times of one of Australia's greatest artists.*

(the) life of the party: a person at social events who is amusing/exuberant/lively ~ *Stan, as usual, was the life of the party.*

bring to life: arouse/energise/awaken someone/something; make realistic ~*1a) A coat of paint will bring the room to life. 1b) In just one month he'd brought the sad, neglected garden to life.*

for dear life: do something using all your strength/determination to avoid danger/injury ~ *Alan hung on for dear life until he was rescued.*

for life: for a very long time; until one's death ~ *They vowed they would love each other for life.*

for the life of me: [spoken] that you cannot understand or remember something ~ *1a) I can't for the life of me remember where I put it. 2) Oh, for the life of me I can't understand these instructions!*

full of life: having vitality/liveliness/exuberance/energy ~ *She's not one to be sad and moody, she's busy and full of life.*

lead/have a hard life: to have had a difficult life ~ *Growing up in abject poverty, the children have had a hard life.*

as large as life: [spoken] when you encounter/see someone you have only seen in pictures or on the TV ~ *I couldn't believe it, I turned the corner and there, as large as life, was my idol.*

larger than life: someone who attracts attention because they are imposing or impressive ~ *Smith was a larger-than-life character both on and off the court.*

late in life: do something in one's life that is later than usual ~ *She began her writing career rather late in life.*

not on your life: [spoken] never; under no circumstances ~ *Are you going skydiving with them? Not on your life!* *also: not on your Nellie

put your life is in someone's hands: allow someone else to be responsible whether you live or die ~ *It was a risky operation and he knew his life would be in the hands of the surgeon.*

put your life on the line: risk dying/death to achieve something ~ *You literally put your life on the line doing this job.*

take one's (own) life: commit suicide

take someone's life: kill someone ~ *The accident took her life.*

(lead/live) the life of Riley: have an easy/uncomplicated life ~ *Now that they're rich, they live the life of Riley.*

(do something) to save one's/someone's life: have no ability to do something ~ *1a) I can't run to save my life. 1b) She couldn't cook to save herself.* *also: to save one's/her/himself

this is the life: [spoken] it's what you say when you're enjoying relaxation time ~ *Ahhh . . . this is the life—relaxing in the sun all day with nothing to do!*

true to life: representing events; something that is real/true ~ *The landscape painting is true to life.*

Life-Line: charity organisation

lifeline: 1) something you depend on to get help/assistance ~ *Her mobility is limited, so essentially the telephone is her lifeline.*

2) a rope you throw to someone who may be drowning

lifelong: remaining in a particular state all through one's life ~ *Theirs has been a lifelong friendship.*

lifesaver: 1) one who is helpful ~ *Thanks for helping us—you're a lifesaver!*

2) a lifeguard at the beach or public swimming pool

life-size: representing the true/actual size of something/someone ~ *There, just inside the door, was a life-size cardboard cut-out of the actor.*

lift one's game: improve one's performance; behave in an acceptable manner/way ~ *You'll lose your place on the team if you don't lift your game.*

lift the lid on: reveal/make public previously unknown information ~ *After a lengthy investigation, authorities lifted the lid on their corrupt work practices.*

lift up: 1) (physically) raise something/someone upwards ~ *Could you help me lift this up?*

2) make someone feel better ~ *Her kind words lifted me up when I was feeling down.*

give someone a lift: take someone somewhere in your car ~ *I gave him a lift to the airport.*

lift-out: a removable supplement in a magazine/newspaper

light up: 1) make/become bright or light ~ *Fireworks lit up the whole sky.*

2) ignite with a flame ~ *Let's light up the barbie!*

3) feel happy/bright ~ *Her presence lights up their lives.*

light years: greatly advanced/futuristic ~ *The company has technology that's light years ahead of the competition.*

bring to light: make something known ~ *I'd like to bring to light the time and effort Sue has put into this project.*

in light of: because of ~ *In light of the situation, the meeting has been postponed.* *also: in view of; in the light of

make light of: treat as unimportant ~ *He made light of the fact that he failed the exam.*

out like a light: to quickly fall asleep ~ *As soon as he lay down he was out like a light.*

shed light on: make something clear/easy to understand ~ *The survivors were able to shed some light on what went wrong.*

light-fingered: someone who steals goods from shops ~ *Light-fingered thieves have cost the business thousands of dollars.*

light-footed: quick on one's feet/nimble ~ *The light-footed thief easily escaped being caught by police.* *also: light on (his/her) feet

light-headed: giddy/dizzy ~ *The carnival ride made me feel light-headed.*

light-hearted: glad/cheerful/unburdened ~ *The story takes a light-hearted look at a mostly serious issue.*

lighten the load: assist someone with a task/job ~ *I was grateful to them for their help—they really lightened the load.*

lighten up: [spoken] a way of telling someone to be less serious about something ~ *Lighten up, will you—it's supposed to be a friendly game of tennis.*

like a bear with sore head: grumpy/bad-tempered ~ *Be wary, the boss is like a bear with a sore head today.*

like a stunned mullet: astonished/surprised (a mullet is a fish and the saying alludes to the goggle-eyed stare, and sometimes gaping mouth, of a fish that has been recently caught and made unconscious) ~ *I couldn't believe what he said. I stood there like a stunned mullet.*

like crazy: enthusiastically/madly ~ *We ran like crazy to catch up with the others.* *also: like mad; like the clappers

like death warmed up: to be/appear in poor health ~ *Are you okay? You look like death warmed up.*

like fun: [spoken] definitely not/not at all/never ~ *I'm going to get a tattoo. Like fun you will!*

. . . like it was going out of fashion: consume/do something quickly, or much more than people normally do ~ *He ate like it was going out of fashion.*

like two peas in a pod: for two people to look like each other ~ *It's easy to tell you are brother and sister, you're like two peas in a pod.*

the likes of: species/types of a similar kind ~ *We don't want the likes of them living around here.*

to one's liking: pleasing/acceptable to someone ~ *That type of music is not to my liking.*

li-lo: an inflatable rubber or plastic air bed/mattress

limo: limousine

line of work: type of vocation/job ~ *What line of work are you in now?*

line someone up: 1) convince/prepare/recruit someone to do a job ~ *I've got someone lined up to help you.*

2) convince someone to be someone else's date ~ *I've got a date lined up for you.*

line up: arrange in formation; form a line ~ *1a) He had all the equipment lined up on the bench. 1b) I'd like everyone to line up over here please!*

line up (with): 1) join a queue ~ *Please line up with everyone in group A.*

2) something aligning with something else ~ *Make sure this edge lines up with that edge.*

all along the line: at every stage/moment; all the while ~ *We've had problems with the project all along the line.*

(the) end of the line/road: 1) terminus/stopping place ~ *This is the end of the line for this bus service.*

2) final conclusion/outcome ~ *If he doesn't get elected it will be the end of the line for the candidate.*

down the line: at a later date/stage ~ *We'll review the project somewhere down the line.*

in line: be standing/waiting in a queue ~ *I've been waiting in line for ages!*

in line for/to: likely to receive an award/promotion/position ~ *She's in line for an award.*

in the line of duty: while working ~ *The policeman lost his life in the line of duty.*

in line with: conforming to limits/guidelines ~ *The company intends to keep its prices in line with the competition.*

on the line: 1) connected on the telephone ~ *Tim, I've got Fred on the line, and he wants to speak to you.*

2) something to be at risk ~ *I'd be putting my job on the line if I did that.*

(be) out of line: fail to conform to standards; have the wrong attitude ~ *You were way out of line saying those things about him.* *also: step out of line

step out of line: misbehave/not behave as expected or ordered to ~ *She stepped out of line when she called them incompetent.*

wait in line: stand (one behind another) in a queue ~ *He had to wait in line to be served.*

linger about/around: be slow to go away/disappear ~ *The odour lingered around for hours.* *also: loiter/mooch around/about

linger on: continue for a long time ~ *Party guests lingered on for another hour or so.*

the lion's share: the largest part/portion ~ *He's second in charge, which means he does the lion's share of the work.*

bite one's lip: refrain from showing a reaction; saying something ~ *I was tempted to argue back but I bit my lip.*

give lip: contradict/talk back to someone ~ *He's in trouble for giving the teacher lip.*

give someone a fat lip: punch someone in the mouth

lick one's lips: anticipate in delight ~ *He licked his lips at the sight of the feast laid out on the table.*

my lips are sealed: [spoken] that you will not say anything/that you will keep a secret ~ *I won't say a thing. My lips are sealed.*

tight-lipped: uncommunicative; restrained ~ *He remained tight-lipped about the government's new proposals.*

lippie/y: lipstick

listen here: [spoken] a command for someone to listen carefully to what you have to say ~ *Now, listen here. I've told you before not to do that!*

listen in: 1) eavesdrop ~ *Let's talk in here, I don't want anyone listening in on our conversation.*

2) listen without contributing to a conversation ~ *My supervisor will be listening in on the interview.*

listen out for something: listen carefully for a sound you are expecting ~ *Listen out for the baby in case he wakes.*

listen to reason: listen and be influenced by good advice ~ *I tried to convince him not to go, but he wouldn't listen to reason.*

listen up: [spoken] to get someone's attention ~ *Listen up, everyone, the bus leaves in five minutes, so please take your seats.*

(a) little bit: 1) a small amount of something ~ *I'll only have a little bit of pie, thank you.*

2) slightly ~ *I'm a little bit upset about what happened today.*

little by little: *see: bit by bit; in stages

little wonder: said when something is not surprising ~ *It's little wonder you're sick, with all that you ate last night.* *also: small wonder

live and breathe something: be very enthusiastic/passionate about something ~ *She lives and breathes horses.*

live and learn: become wiser through a bad experience ~ *Well, I now know not to ever do that again. You live and learn.*

live by: act/behave accordingly to a set of principles or beliefs ~ *You are expected to live by the house rules.*

live something down: that other people will not forget/will always talk about a past mistake you made/something embarrassing you did ~ *I'm so embarrassed—my friends will never let me live this down.*

live beyond one's means: spend more money that you receive as a wage

live within one's means: spend no more than one receives as a wage

live (from) hand to mouth: have just enough money to live on; have no spare cash

live it up: indulge oneself ~ *I'm going to live it up if I win!*

live like pigs: to live in squalor

live off the land: be self-sufficient; exist on food you can grow or food you can hunt

live through: endure something; survive a difficult period/situation ~ *He lived through two world wars.*

live to see the day: be alive when something new/shocking/surprising happens ~ *I can't believe it's happened. I thought I'd never live to see the day.*

live to tell the tale: survive an ordeal/a dangerous situation ~ *He was attacked by a shark and lived to tell the tale.*

live up to: be as good as expected or promised ~ *Her performance didn't live up to expectations.*

live with oneself: deal with one's guilty conscience ~ *I don't think I could live with myself if I had done that.*

live with something[1]: continue to suffer from; accept something you did ~ *It's something he'll have to live with for the rest of his life.*

live with something[2]: suffer from; be haunted by something not of your doing ~ *She finds it difficult to live with the fact that he'll never return.*

lived-in: homely; well-used; worn from constant use ~ *After a few days camping, his new clothes soon had that lived-in look.*

liven up: enliven/energise/invigorate ~ *The flowers certainly liven up the room.*

beat the living daylights out of: severely attack someone *also: beat the hell out of

scare the living daylights out of: to frighten someone ~ *He jumped out from behind the door and scared the living daylights out of me.*

Lizard: Of the 3,000 lizard species distributed throughout the world, more than 520 can be found throughout Australia. They range in size from 6 cm to 3 m long. The five main families of lizards are geckos, legless or snake lizards, dragon lizards, monitor lizards/goannas, and skinks.

loaded: rich; wealthy ~ *By the look of their house I'd say they are loaded.*

loads: plenty/heaps of something ~ *I've got loads of homework to do.*

(take) a load off one's mind: bring relief from anxiety/worries ~ *Their assistance has taken a load off my mind.* *also: weight of one's mind

use your loaf: a way of telling someone to think carefully before doing something; to use common sense ("loaf" refers to someone's head) ~ *Think about what you're doing. Use your loaf.*

loaf about: be idle/lazy; do nothing ~ *I've been loafing about the house all day.*

loafer: 1) style of men's shoe

2) one who is idle or lazy

loan shark: a money lender who charges an extremely high rate of interest

on loan: lent/borrowed for temporary use ~ *The book is on loan from the library.*

lob up: arrive unexpectedly/uninvited ~ *This cute stray dog lobbed up on our doorstep wanting to stay.*

local: 1) someone who lives in a particular place ~ *Locals were outraged that the library would be demolished.*

2) a pub in your neighbourhood that you visit often ~ *You'll find him down at the local.*

lock someone away: put someone in jail ~ *Thankfully he will be locked away for the rest of his life.* *also: lock someone up

lock something away: put something in a secure place ~ *Everything of value is locked away in the safe.* *also: lock something up

lock yourself away: stay in a space/room where you can be alone ~ *She's locked herself away in the bedroom so she can study.*

lock horns: argue/fight with someone ~ *We lock horns whenever we discuss politics.*

lock in: put someone/something in a room/space and lock the door ~ *I accidentally locked the keys in the car.*

lock, stock, and barrel: everything ~ *We moved all the equipment—lock, stock, and barrel!*

lock up: lock doors/a door ~ *Can you lock up before you leave?*

(a) lolly: confectionary; candy; a boiled sweet

do one's lolly/nut/narna/top: have an angry, vocal outburst ~ *I did my lolly when I found out.* *see also: lose it

(be) long: a time period ~ *1a) I'm going to the shops—I won't be long. 1b) How long will you be?*

long haul: a long period of time ~ *They worked well over the long haul.*

long in the tooth: old ~ *Old Jim's getting a bit long in the tooth.*

long neck: a type of beer bottle that has a long, thin neck

long on: do/have too much of something ~ *He's long on charm and short on manners.*

(a) long shot: attempt to do something even though you may not succeed ~ *It's a long shot, but I'll ask him anyway.*

long time, no see: [spoken] form of greeting; what you say to someone you haven't seen or met with for a while ~ *Hi Cathy, long time no see.*

before long: soon ~ *Before long you'll be up and walking again.*

(it's a) long story: [spoken] a way of letting someone know that what you've got to say is long and complicated ~ *What happened yesterday? It's a long story, but...*

cut/make a long story short: [spoken] that you will tell a shortened version of the story ~ *To cut a long story short, she got arrested.*

(have a) long talk: have a serious discussion with someone ~ *You and I need to have a long talk about your behaviour.*

have a long way to go: 1) that a lot more work needs to be done before something is completed ~ *This section's finished, but we've still got a long way to go with it.*

2) that there are many more miles to travel ~ *We've come this far, but we've still got a long way to go.*

in the long run: at some time in the future ~ *It's an expensive outlay, but it saves money in the long run.*

not by a long shot: not in any way ~ *Not by a long shot did they accrue enough points.*

not long (ago): recently; a short time earlier ~ *I'd not long washed the car when it began to rain.*

take a long, hard look at something: consider a problem/issue very carefully and decide how to deal with it ~ *They ought to take a long, hard look at the way they do business.*

any longer: added time or length ~ *1a) I can't wait any longer for them. 1b) If her hair was any longer it would reach her knees.*

no longer: formerly/previously ~ *1a) I no longer smoke. 1b) They no longer live here.*

long-winded: containing/using too many words ~ *It was a rather long-winded answer to a simple question.*

loo: [informal] toilet/lavatory/dunny ~ *She's gone to the loo.*

look after: be responsible/care for someone/something ~ *Steve's going to look after my dog while I'm away.*

look ahead: consider/think about what is likely to happen in the future ~ *They need to look ahead to when they retire.*

look alike: of someone/something to look like someone/something else ~ *1a) They all look alike to me. 1b) The sisters look very much alike.*

look around: 1) carefully observe your surroundings ~ *We spent the afternoon looking around the shops.*

2) search for something specific ~ *I looked all around for it but didn't find it.*

look at: 1) closely examine/observe something ~ *You ought to get the doctor to take a look at that nasty cut.*

2) consider something so you can make a decision ~ *You're looking at roughly $2,000 to repair it.*

3) read something ~ *I'd like to look at the report.*

4) direct your vision at something/someone so you can see them ~ *Look at that!*

5) [spoken] used when giving an example that proves that what you said is true ~ *It's still not a safe area. Just look at the trouble they had there last week.*

look at you: [spoken] used for telling someone that you're surprise/impressed by their appearance or by what they're doing ~ *Look at you. You look fabulous!*

look away: direct one's gaze elsewhere ~ *1a) She looked away to hide her embarrassment. 1b) It's not a pretty sight. You might like to look away.*

look back: turn and look behind you ~ *She looked back and waved a final goodbye.*

look back (on): 1) recall a time or event in the past ~ *I often look back on those days and start laughing.*

2) (said in the negative) to not recall the past ~ *He took the job offer and has never looked back.*

look bad/good: for something/someone to be considered bad/good ~ *1a) It'll look bad if you don't go and visit them. 1b) I think she did it just to make herself look good.*

look beyond: look past/to a point farther than someone/ something ~ *You have to look beyond the fence to find it.*

look for: try to find someone/something ~ *I've been looking for that for ages.*

look forward to: be excited/pleased about something that is going to happen ~ *I'm really looking forward to going on holiday.*

look here: [spoken] interjection to get someone's attention when you're angry/annoyed at something they've done ~ *Look here, I'm not responsible for what happened!*

look high and low: search everywhere ~ *I've looked high and low, but I still can't find them.* *also: search high and low

look in (on): briefly visit someone to see how they are ~ *I'll look in on you on my way home to see how you are.*

look into (it/the matter): find out more information about something ~ *They heard my complaint and promised to look into it.*

look like: 1) resemble someone/something ~ *She certainly looks like her mother.*

2) have the appearance; give the impression ~ *2a) You look like you've been crying. 2b) It looks like it might rain.*

look lively: [spoken] a command to be attentive/move quickly ~ *Look lively—the boss is coming!* *also: look sharp

look (like) a million dollars: look or feel extremely good ~ *1a) Wow, you look a million dollars in that dress. 1b) All it needs is some minor repairs and a paint of coat and it'll look like a million dollars.*

look on: watch an activity without participating ~ *Unfortunately they could only look on in horror as the building burned.*

look on as: regard/consider someone/something ~ *He's looked on as a role model by his peers.**also: look upon

look on the bright side: see good things in an unpleasant situation/issue ~ *Look on the bright side—think of all the money you'll save.*

look out: [spoken] alert/warning of impending danger ~ *Look out, it's about to fall!*

look out for: 1) be attentive to someone/make sure they're okay ~ *She's always looking out for her little sister.*

2) watch for someone/something specific ~ *2a) I was told to look out for a red truck. 2b) I'll look out for you when I get there.*

look someone in the eye: look directly at someone ~ *1a) He looked me in the eye and told me he didn't do it. 1b) I'm so embarrassed I don't think I'll be able look her in the eye again.*

look someone up and down: carefully look at/scrutinize someone ~ *The doorman looked us up and down before letting us in.*

look the other way: 1) turn your head in the other direction ~ *I didn't see it because I was looking the other way.*

2) deliberately ignore something illegal/bad happening *see: turn a blind eye

look to: 1) seek advice/assistance from someone ~ *I always look to my father for advice.*

2) promise to ~ *Their proposal looks to reduce costs by at least twenty per cent.*

look(s) to be: has the appearance/characteristic of something ~ *1a) The summary looks to be correct. 1b) He looked to be about thirty years old.*

look through: 1) read something ~ *I'll look through the report later.*

2) see beyond something ~ *You'll be able to see it if you look through that window.*

3) search for something ~ *I've looked through the cupboard, but I can't find it.*

4) fail to recognise/pretend not to see someone ~ *He walked right past, but looked straight through me.*

look up: 1) for a situation to improve ~ *After many setbacks, things are finally looking up.*

2) search for particular information ~ *I looked up your number in the phonebook.*

3) visit someone ~ *I'm going to look up some old friends when I get to Melbourne.*

look up to: respect/admire someone ~ *The students in his class all look up to him.*

look where you're going/what you're doing: [spoken] interjection to tell someone to be careful ~ *Look where you're going. You nearly walked into the post!*

(to) not look twice at: look quickly at someone/something without much consideration ~ *I never looked twice at him when we were at school.*

. . . not looking good: [spoken] that the outcome will most certainly be disastrous/bad ~ *Firefighters are working hard to save the homes, but it's not looking good.*

not much to look at: not attractive ~ *It's not much to look at, but it's spacious and functional.*

looks like a drowned rat: describes someone who is thoroughly wet/bedraggled ~ *He came in from the rain looking like a drowned rat.*

(have a) look see: investigate something happening ~ *I'd better have a look see at what the kids are up to.*

by the look(s) of: how someone/something appears/seems ~ *You need a good sleep by the looks of you.*

the look(s) of: the appearance of someone/something ~ *1a) I don't like the look of those dark clouds. 1b) I like the look of that.*

(a) look-in: an opportunity/chance to participate in something ~ *The opposition played so well we hardly got a look-in.*

(be on the) lookout for: watch for/be alert to something/someone specific ~ *Police are on the lookout for a second person suspected of being involved in the robbery.*

(a) looker: an attractive person (usually a female) ~ *She's going to be a real looker when she's older.*

loose cannon: a person whose actions are unpredictable/ uncontrollable ~ *He's too much of a loose cannon to be in charge.*

loose change: coins given as change ~ *The cashier was out of notes so she gave me ten dollars in loose change.*

loose ends: unfinished business; an unresolved problem ~ *I'll join you after I tie up a few loose ends here.*

at a loose end: to be restless; have little or nothing to do ~ *1a) She's been at loose ends ever since her husband died. 1b) My son's been at a loose end most of the holidays.* *also: at loose ends

break loose: 1) be freed from fastening/escape confinement ~ *1a) The boat broke loose from its mooring. 1b) The prisoner broke loose from his shackles.*

2) explode/emerge violently/noisily *see: all hell broke loose

let loose: 1) set something/someone free to run/roam ~ *We came home and let the dogs loose from their confines.* *also: turn loose

2) emit a loud, sudden sound ~ *She let loose an ear-piercing scream.*

on the loose: free; at large; unrestrained ~ *There's a monkey on the loose in the zoo.*

loosen up: become relaxed ~ *These exercises are designed to loosen up tense muscles.*

loot: illegally obtained money ~ *The crook refused to tell the police where he hid the loot.*

Lord Howe Island: Lying approximately 600 kilometres northeast of Sydney, is World Heritage-listed Lord Howe Island. Forming part of the state of New South Wales, it is less than two hours flying time from Sydney—the closest island getaway from Sydney. Because of its significant natural beauty, it is regarded as the most beautiful island in the Pacific.

lose face: suffer humiliation; lose one's reputation ~ *He didn't admit the mistake because he didn't want to lose face.*

lose it: become upset/angry; lose control of one's emotions ~ *I lost it badly during the funeral service.*

lose one's cool: become angry or physically violent ~ *1a) My opponent tried to intimidate me, but I never lost my cool. 1b) I don't know why I did that. I just lost it.* *see also: lose one's head; lose it

lose one's marbles: [informal] become insane/crazy (often said humorously) ~ *He must be losing his marbles if he thinks that'll happen.* *also: lose one's mind

lose one's touch: lose one's special skill/ability ~ *I used to be able to play golf quite well, but I seem to have lost my touch.*

lose one's train of thought: to forget what you were thinking ~ *What was I saying? I've lost my train of thought.*

lose out (on): miss an opportunity/chance; not get the same benefit ~ *He trained hard because he didn't want to lose out on being chosen for the team.*

lose sight of something: 1) be distracted from the main goal/interest ~ *We mustn't lose sight of the objective.*

2) be no longer able to see something ~ *The policeman lost sight of the suspect in the crowds.*

lose sleep over: to worry excessively ~ *It's a minor problem, nothing to lose sleep over.*

lose the plot: 1) [humorous] behave irrationally; do something silly ~ *I can't believe he did that! I think he's losing the plot.*

2) no longer be able to follow what's being said ~ *I lost the plot on page ten.*

lost cause: something/someone that will never improve/succeed ~ *Our plan to rebuild is now a lost cause.*

lost in thought: engrossed in one's own thoughts ~ *Sorry, I wasn't paying attention to what you said; I was lost in thought.*

(he/she/they've) lost me: [spoken] 1) lose interest/faith ~ *After doing that, he's lost me as a supporter.*

2) misunderstand/be confused with what someone is saying ~ *He lost me in the first two minutes of the speech.*

the lot: all/everything ~ *The rotten thieves took the lot.*

loud and clear: clearly heard/understood/expressed ~ *Yes, we can hear you loud and clear.*

out loud: in a way that others can hear ~ *I'll read it out loud so everyone can hear me.*

lounge around: pass the time idly; recline/rest ~ *After a busy morning I lounged around watching television all afternoon.*

lousy act: a despicable/contemptible action ~ *What he did was a lousy act.*

lout: an uncouth/aggressive male

love: affectionate term of address ~ *What's the matter, love?*

loved ones: people you love (usually family) ~ *Following the disaster, everyone wanted to know if their loved ones were safe.*

lovey-dovey: openly affectionate (in public) ~ *They've been married for all this time and they're still lovey-dovey.*

lowdown: the facts; relevant information ~ *The coach gave the players the lowdown on the game plan.*

low-down: unfair/mean ~ *It was a low-down act.*

low-key: moderate/understated ~ *They want a low-key wedding.*

any luck: This is the same as asking, "Did you have any luck?" ~ *Any luck? No, they'd sold out.*

as luck would have it: that something happened by chance ~ *As luck would have it, the bus arrived just as I got to the stop.*

bad luck: [spoken] expression of sympathy at someone's misfortune ~ *Bad luck you lost the game.*

beginner's luck: unexpected success attained by someone doing something new ~ *Talk about beginner's luck! Are you sure you haven't played this before?*

do something for luck: do something in the hope you will become lucky ~ *I wear this for luck whenever I'm competing.*

down on one's luck: to be suffering from an unlucky/bad period ~ *I was down on my luck when I was offered a job.*

Lady Luck: fortune/chance personified

never know your luck: to not realise what luck you might have ~ *You should enter the lottery—you never know your luck!*

(to) not believe your luck: surprised/pleased at your good fortune ~ *I couldn't believe my luck!*

press/push your luck: make an attempt to gain further advantage ~ *You're pushing your luck asking for more money.*

the luck of the draw: that something happened as a result of chance/that you have no control over ~ *We missed out on a prize, but that's the luck of the draw.*

try one's/your luck: take a chance; try to achieve something ~ *I'm going to try my luck at the casino.*

with any luck: used when hoping something will happen ~ *With any luck, the renovations will be finished by then.*

worse luck: [spoken] unfortunately/alas ~ *I have to work all weekend, worse luck.*

lucky break: an opportunity/chance ~ *Getting this job was the lucky break I needed to advance my career.*

lucky dip: a random/hidden sample; a game where the prizes are concealed in a box; lottery ~ *The lucky dip at the fair is the favourite for children.*

lucky duck: describes someone who has had good fortune ~ *The lucky duck won a trip to Hawaii!*

lumbered with: be burdened with something ~ *How come I always get lumbered with all the lousy jobs?*

lump sum: the total amount of money ~ *He received a lump sum payment when he retired.*

lure away: draw/entice away from something ~ *They used food to lure the menacing dog away.*

lurgy: a cold or flu (usually preceded by "dreaded") ~ *I've been in bed with the dreaded lurgy all week.*

lurk around: wait in hiding ~ *Police were called to investigate someone lurking around in the bushes.*

lurks and perks: job privileges/extra benefits ~ *One of the lurks and perks of working for an airline is heavily discounted airfares.*

Lyrebird: Of the two species, the superb and the Albert's lyrebird, it is the superb which gives the family its name. When spread out in display, its spectacular tail fans out to resemble a lyre, an ancient Greek musical instrument. They are capable of imitating almost any sound, including humans, trains, chainsaws, car alarms, and horns. They can be found in small, specialised forests along the coastal strip of New South Wales.

M

Macca's: McDonald's—fast food outlet

mad about: obsessed/infatuated with something/something ~ *1) He's mad about sports cars. 2) Likes him? She's mad about him.*

mad as a meat axe: silly/crazy/strange (usually said humorously) ~ *Have you heard his ramblings? He's as mad as a meat axe.* *also: mad as a hatter; mad as a cut snake

go mad: 1) become crazy with boredom ~ *I'd go mad living in a high-rise apartment.*

2) start behaving aggressively ~ *He just went mad and started bashing the door.*

3) become extremely excited ~ *The band stepped onto the stage and the crowd went wild.* *also: go crazy/wild

go mad on: get angry with someone ~ *Mum went mad on me for coming home late.*

like mad: do something very quickly and with effort ~ *I've run around like mad all day.*

. . . must be mad: that someone is stupid to do/have done something ~ *He must be mad to want to do that.*

made for: perfectly suited ~ *This dress seems made for me.*

made to measure: custom fit to exact measurements ~ *The curtains are made to measure.* *also: tailor-made

made up: 1) be wearing makeup/cosmetics ~ *The actors were all made up and ready to appear on stage*

2) assembled; put together ~ *I've already made up the guest bed.*

made up of: consisting of ~ *The human foot is made up of twenty-six bones.*

have got it made: to be in an envious/ideal situation ~ *Lucky him, he's got it made!* *also: made in the shade

not made for: be unsuitable ~ *The bike is not made for riding on rough roads.*

madhouse: a state of confusion/chaos/disorder ~ *It's a madhouse here at Christmas.*

mag: magazine

Magpie: native Australian bird

main drag: the main street that runs through the centre of a town ~ *The bank is on the main drag next to the cinema.*

make a break for: run towards something ~ *It started to rain so we made a break for the nearest shelter.* *also: make a run for

make a clean sweep of: 1) win overwhelmingly ~ *The team made a clean sweep of the competition.*

2) eliminate/remove unwanted things; start afresh ~ *... decided to make a clean sweep and start a new life as an honest citizen.*

make a difference: to have a positive/good effect ~ *Your contribution has made a difference to their lives.*

make a face: grimace/distort one's face ~ *She made a face the first time she tasted lemon.*

make a habit of: do something habitually ~ *I make a habit of checking the house is locked before I leave.*

make a liar out of one/someone: prove one/someone wrong ~ *That's not true. He's twisted the truth and is trying to make a liar out of me!*

make a mess of things: ruin/spoil something ~ *I don't trust him to do the job. He always makes a mess of things.* *also: make a hash of

make(s) a million: earn a large amounts of money ~ *He made a million by investing in real estate.*

make a mountain out of a molehill: exaggerate the importance of something; turn a minor issue into a major issue ~ *It's not that bad. You're making a mountain out of a molehill.*

make a move: 1) make a start; begin; do something ~ *I should make a move on the assignment.*

2) depart; leave; go ~ *I'd better make a move or I'll be late.*

make a pass at: make an amorous advance ~ *I couldn't believe it when he made a pass at me!*

make a pig of one/his/herself: eat greedily; overeat ~ *1a) He has no table manners; look at the way he's making a pig of himself. 1b) I can't eat anything else—I made a pig of myself at dinner.*

make a point: state an idea/fact/opinion that is part of a discussion ~ *1a) I'd like to make one more point before I conclude. 1b) okay, you've made your point.*

make a point of: 1) do something habitually ~ *I always make a point of locking the house before I leave.*

2) take particular care to do something ~ *I'd like to make a point of thanking John and Jenny for their efforts.*

make a quid: 1) become wealthy through hard work ~ *He's made a quid as a builder.*

2) earn a living ~ *It's hard to make a quid doing that sort of work.*

make as if: appear to begin an action ~ *She made as if she was about to speak.*

make believe: pretend that something is real ~ *The kids like to make believe they live in a castle.*

make do: improvise by utilising what is/isn't available ~ *We'll have to make do until we can afford a new one.*

make every penny count: be careful how you spend your money; stick to a budget ~ *The budget's tight, so we have to make every penny count.*

make for: 1) proceed/move towards something ~ *As soon as we got there the kids made for the surf.* *also: make a beeline for

2) make something possible ~ *Airbeds make for a comfortable camping trip.*

make good money: earn a substantial living ~ *He makes good money as a plumber.*

make hard work of something: do something in a difficult/ laborious way ~ *You're making hard work of that. Here, let me show you an easier way.*

make head or tail of: comprehend/understand something ~ *1a) I don't know why they did that—I can't make head or tail of it. 1b) It was so confusing, no one could make head or tail of it.* *also: make anything of it; make it out

make headway: to progress ~ *1a) With all the interruptions, I'm not making any headway with this report. 1b) We've had some setbacks but we're making headway.* *also: make progress

make it: 1) arrive somewhere ~ *Hurray, we made it!*

2) achieve success/fame/wealth ~ *After years of hard work and sacrifices he's finally made it as a professional musician.* *also: make it big; make the big time

3) be able to be present at a particular event ~ *Sorry, I can't make it this Saturday*

make it through: persevere/survive a difficult time ~ *He made it through the week without having a cigarette.*

make history: do something memorable enough to influence the course of history ~ *Their epic flight made history.*

make mincemeat (out) of: beat/destroy/win convincingly ~ *The fighter made mincemeat out of his opponent.*

make something/it out: discern/perceive something ~ *I can't quite make out what it says.*

make off with: take/steal something and leave/depart quickly ~ *A thief made off with my handbag.*

make one false move: make an unwise/careless decision that could be dangerous or unpleasant ~ *He has to be very careful—one false move would mean certain death!*

make one's blood boil: cause one to be enraged ~ *That just makes my blood boil!* *also: make someone/one see red; make one feel sick

make one's blood run cold/curdle: cause intense fright/fear ~ *I heard a sound that made my blood run cold.* *also: make your hair curl; make your hair stand on end

make one's mark: achieve success/fame/ambition ~ *She's made her mark as a writer.*

make one's/someone's day: be a source of happiness/make someone happy ~ *Your kindness and generosity have made my day!*

make one's way: 1) proceed with purpose ~ *You'll have to make your own way home.*

2) prosper/progress without help ~ *He's made his way in life.*

make oneself scarce: stay hidden/out of sight to avoid a situation ~ *They usually make themselves scarce whenever it's time to help in the kitchen.*

make or break: something that decides either failure or success ~ *The decision will either make or break me.*

make out: 1) cause someone to believe something that's not true ~ *She made me out as a liar.*

2) pretend ~ *He tried to make out that he was mad.*

3) fill out a document such as a cheque ~ *To whom do I make out the cheque?*

4) touch/kiss/cuddle in a sexual way ~ *A couple were making out on the lounge.*

5) progress in a particular way; succeed (usually used in question form) ~ *How's Amy making out in her new job?*

make sense: be comprehensible/understandable/reasonable ~ *1a) This report doesn't make sense. 1b) I can't make sense of the question.*

make a spectacle of oneself: do something stupid/embarrassing (wittingly or unwittingly) ~ *She'd had too much to drink and was making a spectacle of herself by dancing on the tables.*

make someone squirm: embarrass someone ~ *The all-revealing autobiography will most certainly make some people squirm.* *also: squirming in their seats

make something/someone out of something: transform/alter something/someone ~ *1a) She makes the most wonderful cushion covers out of scrap material. 1b) Time spent in the army will make a man out of you.*

make something out of nothing: make something into a problem when it's not ~ *Nothing happened. She's just making something out of nothing.* *also: make something out of it

make something up: invent/concoct a story ~ *It's not really true. I just made it up.*

make someone up: apply makeup ~ *I've hired professional beautician to make me up for the event.*

make the grade: reach the desired standard to succeed in something ~ *Jim wanted to be a professional musician, but didn't make the grade.*

make the most of: use to the best advantage ~ *We made the most of the sunshine and had a picnic by the river.*

make up: when two or more people settle an argument and become civil again ~ *They didn't talk to each other for days, but they've since made up.*

make up for lost time: 1) compensate for time wasted ~ *We had to work quickly to make up for lost time.*

2) do something that you didn't have the opportunity to do previously ~ *I never had the chance to travel when I was young, so I'm making up for lost time.*

make waves: cause trouble ~ *Just go in, do your work, and don't make waves.*

make way (for): 1) yield/move aside to allow passage ~ *We stopped to make way for the mob of cattle crossing the road.*

2) make progress/advance ~ *We've had to remodel parts of the factory to make way for the new machinery.*

make-believe: something imagined/pretended ~ *He lives in a make-believe world.*

(have) the makings of: possess the ability or qualities needed to become a particular type of person/thing ~ *She has the makings of a great musician.*

man: [spoken] interjection of surprise/anger/admiration ~ *Man, that was exciting!* *also: man, oh man

man enough: be/not be courageous to do something difficult ~ *He's not man enough to confront them.*

man/woman/person in the street: the average/ordinary person ~ *Politicians in power seldom listen to the man in the street.*

man of God: spiritual leader/follower of God

man of few words: a man who says very little/who's not conversational ~ *He's a man of few words and it's difficult keeping a conversation going with him.*

man of his word: a man who's trustworthy/dependable ~ *You can trust him to do it. He's a man of his word.*

man on the land: a farmer/primary producer/grazier ~ *If you want to find out how the drought affects food prices, go and talk to the man on the land.*

man's best friend: dog/dogs

man up: stop being a coward and start being brave ~ *He ought to man up and tell the truth.*

a ladies' man: a man who attracts and enjoys the company of women ~ *He's got a reputation of being quite a ladies' man.*

a man of . . . : a man possessing particular abilities/qualities ~ *He's a man of integrity.*

a man's man: a man who enjoys associating with other men and does manly/masculine activities ~ *Ross is a bit of a man's man, you're more likely to find him at the footy rather than the ballet.*

iron man: a male athlete of remarkable durability/endurance

my good man: a term of endearment between two gentlemen friends ~ *My good man, how are you?* *also: my good fellow

new man: reformed in appearance/attitude ~ *He's a new man now that he's out of jail.*

the man for the job: the right person to do something ~ *I think Andrew's the man for the job.* *also: your man

yes man: a man who always agrees with more powerful people because they want those people to like them

man-to-man: an open/honest/frank discussion ~ *I need to have a little man-to-man talk with Ken about his recent behaviour.*

he-man: strong/virile/macho man who likes to show he's strong ~ *He thinks the way to attract females is by being a he-man.*

all manner of: many different people/things ~ *There was all manner of goods for sale.*

in a manner of speaking: somewhat true; in some sense ~ *I am, in a manner of speaking, in charge.*

manner of: sort/type of ~ *What manner of person would do such a thing?*

manual (car): a car that has a clutch and gearstick (as opposed to an automatic)

many a time: frequently/often ~ *I've walked these trails many a time.*

marg: margarine

mark down: reduce the price/cost of something ~ *Kids shoes were marked down to ten dollars.*

(the) mark of . . . : a particular quality of a person or thing ~ *Integrity is the mark of a good leader.*

mark up: increase the price of goods ~ *Prices are regularly marked up in the tourist districts.*

miss/hit the mark: not achieve/achieve the intended result ~ *The escalating carnage on the roads was proof the "drive safely" campaign was missing the mark.*

black mark: regarded/remembered with disfavour ~ *Missing a deadline means a black mark on your record.* *also: blotch

leave a/your mark: have a strong/noticeable and lasting effect on something/someone ~ *The retiring headmaster has left his mark on all the students in the school.*

on the mark: correct ~ *Your answer was right on the mark.* *also: spot on

on your mark(s): [spoken] used to instruct participants in a race to ready themselves in the correct starting position ~ *On your marks, get set, go!*

(be) in the market for: looking to buy/purchase ~ *She's in the market for a new car.*

on the market: available to buy ~ *We've put our house on the market.*

master the art: perfect one's skills ~ *I never quite mastered the art of cooking the perfect sponge cake.*

Marsupial: A mammal with a pouch, in which its tiny baby grows and feeds. Most of the 140 species of Marsupials found in Australia are found nowhere else in the world. Marsupial species include Kangaroo, Wombat, Koala, Numbat, possum, bandicoot, wallaby, Tasmanian Devil, and Quoll.

match up: when two things have the same or equal qualities ~ *Their stories don't match up.*

be no match for: be less effective/powerful; not as good as someone/something ~ *He tried his best, but he was no match for his opponent.*

meet your match: encounter/meet someone equal in skill/talent ~ *I thought I was a good player, but it seems I've met my match.*

mate: 1) a friend/pal ~ *They've been mates for a long time.*

2) general term of address ~ *G'day, mate!*

maths: mathematics

a matter of doing something: used to say what action needs to/should happen ~ *1a) It's simply a matter of knocking out this wall. 1b) Reducing the road toll is not simply a matter of installing more speed cameras.*

a matter of interest: something of concern ~ *The results are a matter of interest to everyone in the industry.*

(a) matter of life and death: a critical, serious issue/circumstance ~ *1a) Please hurry—it's a matter of life and death! 1b) It's not a matter of life and death if we don't finish this today.*

(a) matter of opinion/choice/preference/taste: concerning one's/someone's opinion ~ *Which tastes better is a matter of opinion.*

(be a) matter of principle: concerning one's morals or personal beliefs ~ *He resigned as a matter of principle.*

(a) matter/question of time: that something is certain/sure to happen at some time in the future (sometimes preceded by "only") ~ *It's only a matter of time before somebody hurts themselves doing such a stunt.*

a matter of urgency: that something should be done very soon ~ *They need to contact us as soon as possible. It's a matter of urgency.*

as a matter of fact: [spoken] in fact/actually ~ *As a matter of fact, I do like it.*

as a matter of interest: [spoken] to say that you're asking because you're curious ~ *As a matter of interest, how much did you pay for it?*

in a matter of . . . : only a few seconds/minutes/hours/days/weeks etc. ~ *It was all over in a matter of minutes.*

another matter: used to indicate that something is very different from the situation/topic you've just discussed ~ *It seems like a good idea, but whether the others agree or not is another matter.*

(it) doesn't matter: [spoken] a way of telling someone that everything is okay ~ *I'm sorry I forgot to tell you. It's okay, it doesn't matter.*

the fact/truth of the matter: the truth ~ *The fact of the matter is they shouldn't have been there in the first place.*

for that matter: used to show that the second remark you make; something/someone mentioned later is just as important ~ *No, I've not told him, or anyone else for that matter.*

no matter: [spoken] regardless of; despite ~ *1a) I'll always be there for you, no matter what. 1b) Call me when you get there, no matter what time.*

no laughing matter: that something is very serious and should not be any less serious ~ *The offence they committed is no laughing matter.*

take matters into your own hands: deal with a situation yourself because others have failed to do so ~ *Locals took matters into their own hands and provided security for the event.*

matter-of-fact: without emotion; straightforward; literal; relating to facts ~ *He described it in a matter-of-fact manner.*

may well: 1) that something may be true/possible ~ *1a) She may well not want to go by herself. 1b) That may well have been the case, but things are done differently now.* *also: it might be

be that as it may: nevertheless; despite that ~ *Be that as it may, I still don't like him.*

(to) mean business: to be earnest/serious about what you say or do ~ *We could tell by the look on his face that he meant business.*

mean by: convey a meaning by words or deeds ~ *1a) What do you mean by that? 1b) I didn't mean anything by it.*

mean anything/something: 1) be familiar/have knowledge of ~ *Does this mean anything to you?*

2) hold sentimental value ~ *It may not look like much, but this old jacket means a lot to me.*

(have a) mean streak: a (hidden) characteristic where one quickly becomes angry/violent ~ *He seems likeable, but he has a mean streak and can be quite nasty at times.*

mean(s) well: have good intentions ~ *She sometimes gives the wrong advice, but she means well.*

means of communication: the method of sending/receiving information ~ *Please get the message across by any means of communication.*

meant to be: destined to exist/happen/be ~ *1a) It just wasn't meant to be. 1b) She was meant to be a dancer.*

mean to do: intend/not intend to do something ~ *Sorry, I didn't mean to hurt you.*

means of transport: vehicles used for transport ~ *They got there using various means of transport.*

a means to an end: a way of achieving/getting what you want ~ *It's not an ideal job, but it's a means to an end.*

by all means: [spoken] of course/definitely/certainly ~ *By all means, take some.*

by any means/manner: to any extent/in any way ~ *We are not, by any means, finished.*

by means of: by using the thing specified; with the help/use of ~ *They entered by means of an open window.*

man/woman of means: someone who is wealthy ~ *You could tell just by the look of him that he was a man of means.*

meant for: designed/destined for a certain purpose ~ *1a) The hard drive is meant for storing files. 1b) I knew they were meant for each other.*

measure out: 1) determine the measurement of something ~ *We measured out the area where the pool was going.*

2) weigh or measure a small amount of something from a larger amount ~ *Combine it and then measure out a ½ cup of sugar.*

measure up (to): qualify/meet requirements ~ *I'm not confident they'll measure up to the challenge ahead.*

beyond measure: without limit; in excess ~ *What they suffered was beyond measure.*

for good measure: in addition ~ *I'll add a bit more fruit for good measure.*

meat pie: A pie filled with meat and/or other savoury ingredients. It's a common convenience food and is consumed in great quantities at footy games. It's almost always topped with great quantities of tomato sauce.

meet someone halfway: reach a compromise ~ *I met her halfway and gave her a ten percent discount.*

meet up (with): meet as arranged or unexpectedly ~ *I met up with Cathy at the shops.*

megabucks: a large sum of money ~ *It would have cost them megabucks.*

Melbourne: the capital city of the state of Victoria

Melbourne Cup Day: The Melbourne Cup is the main racing event that takes place at the Flemington Racecourse in Melbourne, Victoria. So popular is the event that it is better known as Melbourne Cup Day—Australia's best-known horseracing event held on the first Tuesday of November every year. It's also known as "The Race That Stops the Nation." More than 100,000 people usually attend the race day. Local races are also held throughout the country on this day, and when the main race of the day occurs at the Flemington Racecourse it is televised on screens at racetracks across Australia. The race is televised live to an audience of about 650 million people worldwide. Many people stop what they are doing shortly before 3 p.m. to watch or listen to the main race via television, Internet, or the radio. The day is observed as a public holiday in Victoria and in the ACT. In other parts of Australia, some people plan a day off work in advance to attend the local races. At the races, people dress up—many women wear their best or most colourful hats and dresses, with some participating in fashion parades on the field. Marquees are set up for VIP guests, including local, national, and international celebrities who attend this festive event. Many offices across Australia stop work closer to the time of the main race. Activities include office parties that feature hat and dress competitions, staff lunches at restaurants, and afternoon teas where a television is available so workers can watch the main race. Bets are made on this day—even those who usually do not bet try their luck with a small wager or entry into a sweep, which is a lottery in which each ticket holder is matched with a randomly drawn horse.

Melbournian: a resident of Melbourne

melt away: disappear gradually ~ *It didn't take long for the snow to melt away.*

(have a) memory like a sieve: to be forgetful ~ *I knew you'd forget. You've got a memory like a sieve.*

mend one's ways: reform; be better behaved ~ *He decided he'd mend his ways once he got out of jail.*

mental block: a sudden inability to recall something specific ~ *I've got a mental block and can't think of his name.*

mess about/around: 1) waste time doing unimportant things ~ *We haven't got time to mess about, this has to be finished soon.*

2) act/behave in a silly way ~ *She was in trouble for messing around in class.*

3) spend time doing things in a relaxed manner *also: muck/fool about

mess around with: 1) have illicit sexual relations ~ *She suspected her husband was messing around with another woman.*

2) associate with; keep company with someone ~ *She usually spends Saturday afternoons messing around with her friends.*

mess with someone: argue with someone/make them angry ~ *I wouldn't mess with them if I were you.*

mess with something: become involved in something dangerous ~ *Some of them had been messing with drugs and alcohol.*

be in a mess: be in a confused, troublesome state ~ *1a) His life's a mess since the divorce. 1b) What a mess you've got yourself into!*

make a mess: create a dirty/messy environment ~ *He's making a mess in the kitchen.*

make a mess of things: make a lot of mistakes/errors when you're doing something ~ *She made a mess of the report.* *also: mess up

miffed: offended/annoyed ~ *I was pretty miffed when he didn't return my call.*

mighty: huge/impressive/powerful ~ *We put in a mighty effort to finish on time.* *also: almighty

miles away: 1) far away in distance ~ *They'd be miles away by now.*

2) to be daydreaming/lost in thought ~ *Sorry, could you repeat that? I was miles away.* *also: million miles away

(be) miles out: miscalculate something ~ *He was miles out in his estimate.* *also: miss by a mile

for miles: a long way ~ *You could see for miles from the top of the cliff.*

go the extra mile: make a special effort to do something; do more than expected ~ *Jim is a great salesman who always goes the extra mile to help the customers.*

milk bar: local shop/general store that sells ice creams, lollies, milk, newspapers, bread, milk shakes, and a small selection of grocery items

mill about/around: move aimlessly (usually whilst waiting) ~ *Everyone milled about the foyer waiting for the rain to ease.*

go through the mill: experience difficult or unpleasant circumstances ~ *She's been through the mill the last few months.*

put through the mill: test someone's mental/physical capabilities ~ *It was tough work. I feel as if I've been put through the mill.*

run-of-the-mill: unordinary/mundane ~ *It was a run-of-the-mill weekend.*

million to one: very slim/remote chance or opportunity ~ *You've got a million to one chance of ever finding it.* *also: one-in-a-million chance; Buckley's chance

look/feel a million dollars: to look/feel great ~ *Wow, you look a million dollars!*

one in a million: rare/extraordinary ~ *... the most generous person I know—he's one in a million.*

thanks a million: [spoken] a way of giving thanks ~ *Thanks a million, I couldn't have done it without your help!*

mince/mincemeat: ground beef

mince (one's) words: to say exactly what one means; be forthright ~ *Steve is a gruff boss who doesn't mince his words.*

make mincemeat out of someone: utterly defeat/destroy ~ *He made mincemeat out of them.*

(the) mind boggles: expressed when a situation or subject is difficult to comprehend ~ *Then he ate it whole! The mind boggles.* *also: boggles the mind/mind-boggling

mind one's p's and q's: be careful what one says; be on one's best behaviour ~ *Remember to mind your p's and q's tonight when you're with them.*

mind over matter: where the power of the mind overrides physical barriers ~ *Having the courage to do it is but mind over matter.*

mind you . . . : [spoken] used to make a point about a subject/add further information; just so you know/to let you know ~ *1a) He won easily, but mind you, he has played this before. 1b) They were always well dressed, but mind you, they were wealthy.*

mind/watch your step: 1) [spoken] a way to warn someone to be careful where they're walking ~ *Mind your step—the floor's slippery.*

2) [spoken] reminder for someone to watch how they behave ~ *You'd better watch your step when you work for him, he's a tough boss.*

frame/state of mind: mental state/mood ~ *1a) See what frame of mind he's in before you ask. 1b) I'm not in the right frame of mind to talk about it.*

give someone a piece of your mind: angrily scold/berate someone ~ *I gave her a piece of my mind when she got home.*

go over something in one's head/mind: think repeatedly about something that happened ~ *I've been going over it in my head, and wondered if I could have done something differently.*

have a good mind (to): threaten to do something ~ *I've a good mind to not let you go to the party after what you did.*

have on your/my mind: be thinking about something in particular or many things ~ *1a) Our holiday plans are on my mind right now. 1b) You seem distracted. Do you have something on your mind? 1c) Sorry I forgot to phone you—I've got a lot on my mind right now.* *also: have your/my mind on something

have a mind/will of its/her/his own: 1) operate/move/work in an unexpected way ~ *This shopping trolley has a mind of its own.*

2) think independently/make your own decisions ~ *I can't convince her otherwise, she has a mind of her own.*

have/keep an open mind: consider all options/other people's opinions ~ *I told them I'm keeping an open mind on the matter.*

have something/someone in mind: consider something/someone as a possibility/choice when making a decision ~ *1a) What colour do you have in mind? 1b) Who do you have in mind for the job?*

in one's mind: in one's opinion; as one sees it ~ *In my mind he's perfectly capable of doing the job.*

in the back of one's mind: in one's memory (not in one's immediate thoughts) ~ *Something in the back of my mind told me they were wrong.*

in two minds (about something): be undecided on which action to take ~ *I'm in two minds as to whether or not we should go.*

have the presence of mind: have the ability to think/act clearly/sensibly under duress or in an emergency ~ *Mary had the presence of mind to immediately phone for help.*

keep/bear in mind: remember something for future reference ~ *Keep in mind the fact that not everyone will be able to attend.*

keep one's mind on something: pay attention to what one's doing ~ *Keep your mind on the job, because it's easy to make mistakes.*

make up one's mind: decide on something; make a decision ~ *Which dress to buy? I can't make my mind up.*

mind keeps wandering: when you keep thinking of other things ~ *I couldn't concentrate, my mind kept wandering.*

mind goes blank: be momentarily unable to think of a specific thing/word ~ *I can't think of his name. My mind's gone blank.*

out of one's mind: crazy/deranged ~ *1a) Where have you been? I've been out of my mind with worry! 1b) Are you out of your mind?*

get something out of your mind: forget about something ~ *It was an experience I can't get out of my mind.*

(have a) twisted mind: have a sinister/strange/peculiar way of thinking ~ *You'd have to have a twisted mind to do that.*

mind-bending/blowing: something amazing/incredible ~ *It was a totally mind-blowing experience!*

in mint condition: as new; in very good condition ~ *The old car was in mint condition.*

Minties: Generations of Australians have, and still do, enjoy these delicious hard, chewy mints. In 1922, young confectioner James Stedman invented Minties and began mass producing them. These iconic mints are still made to the original recipe of glucose, sugar, water, and mint flavour. Each Mintie is individually wrapped in wax paper and packaged in bags. Roughly 500 million Minties are consumed each year.

bag of misery: sad/dispirited ~ *He's been nothing but a bag of misery since the divorce.*

put someone out of (their) misery: free someone of mental/ physical suffering ~ *1a) Put me out of my misery—tell me the surprise! 1b) They had no choice but to put the suffering animal out of its misery.*

mishmash: a confusing jumble/mixture ~ *It was a mishmash of colours*

miss by a mile: fail to reach/hit/make contact with a target ~ *He tried for the bull's eye, but missed by a mile.*

miss out: lose an opportunity/miss an experience ~ *1a) Buy the tickets today or you'll miss out. 1b) She missed out on going to the concert.* *also: miss the boat

miss the point: fail to understand/comprehend something ~ *You're missing the point. It's not that you can't go to any party, you can't go to* that *party.*

(doesn't) miss a trick: see all/everything; be aware of everything happening ~ *We can never fool Mum; she doesn't miss a trick.*

give it/something a miss: to not partake in an activity ~ *I don't feel well. I think I'll give the party a miss.*

near miss: a lucky escape; a narrowly avoided collision ~ *He's still shaken from the near miss earlier in the day.*

wouldn't miss it for anything/the world: [spoken] said about an event you want to attend ~ *I go every year. I wouldn't miss it for anything.*

missing link: 1) an important fact/knowledge that makes something complete ~ *The new evidence provided the missing link in the investigation.*

2) an absent/missing person needed to complete a series ~ *He's the missing link in our family tree.*

(the) missus: outdated term for one's wife ~ *How's the missus and the kids?*

mix and match: choose different items/ideas/colours and assemble them/put them together ~ *We provide a range of clothing that you can easily mix and match.*

mix up: put/assemble something in a different sequence/order/logic ~ *I often mix up my exercise routine to make it more interesting.*

mixed bag: a variety/assortment of things or people ~ *There was* a *mixed bag of people there.*

mixed up in/with: be involved in/with ~ *I don't want you getting mixed up with that crowd.*

mixed up: confused; emotionally unstable ~ *The poor boy's been a bit mixed up since his father died.*

mix-up: a state of confusion/misunderstanding ~ *Sorry I'm late, there was a mix-up as to the starting time.*

mob: 1) collective name for any group of people ~ *The whole mob is coming over this weekend.*

2) collective term for a group of kangaroos

mobile: mobile phone

mod cons: modern conveniences such as washing machines, TVs, dishwashers, and air conditioners ~ *The house is equipped with all the mod cons.*

moggy: domestic cat

Mondayitis: (humorous) A fictitious illness given as an excuse for not wanting to go to work/school on Mondays. You're most likely to be afflicted after a particularly enjoyable weekend.

at a moment's notice: without advance warning; almost immediately ~ *Emergency workers are ready for service at a moment's notice.*

at the moment: at present; right now ~ *I'm busy at the moment—I'll do it later.*

for the moment: for now; at this time ~ *We're safe for the moment.*

in a moment: very soon ~ *I'll be there in a moment.*

not a moment too soon: almost too late ~ *He was rescued from the burning vehicle, and not a moment too soon.*

one moment/just a moment: [spoken] request for someone to wait a short time ~ *1a) I'll be back in just a moment. 1b) One moment, please, while I check the booking.*

the moment . . . : as soon as; instantly ~ *The phone rang the moment I left the room.*

money is no object: that there's no limit to what you can spend ~ *Money is no object for them.*

be in the money: to suddenly have lots of money (often following a windfall) ~ *We won the lottery. We're in the money!*

dirty money: money gained from criminal activities

made of money: to have an endless supply of money ~ *I can't afford that. You must think I'm made of money!*

not made of money: [spoken] used to say that you can't afford something when someone asks you to pay for it ~ *I can't afford that. I'm not made of money, you know!*

for my money . . . : in my opinion ~ *For my money, he's the best player to come along in twenty years.*

(have) money to burn: to have so much money that you spend it on things you don't need ~ *She has got money to burn after receiving a bonus paycheck.* *also: cash to splash; money to throw around

on the money: accurate/correct ~ *She was on the money when she said they'd win.*

marry into money: marry someone whose family is rich ~ *She married into money and has never worked a day in her life.*

my money's on . . . : [spoken] said when announcing a certain winner/a certain outcome ~ *My money's on the Tigers to win.*

pay good money for: to pay a lot for something ~ *I paid good money for that, so please be careful with it.*

put/pour money into something: invest money into a project/ business for future profit ~ *No one's willing to pour money into the project with the economy the way it is.*

put your money on something: 1) bet on something ~ *I put my money on the Giants to win.*

2) used to emphasise that something is certain to happen ~ *They'll accept the offer. You can put your money on it.*

money-spinner: something profitable ~ *The annual fete is a good money-spinner for the school.*

moneybags: [informal] a wealthy person ~ *I'm sure old moneybags over there can well afford it.*

monkey around: engage in mischief ~ *The kids are monkeying around outside.* *also: fool around

monkey bars: children's playground climbing equipment *also: jungle gym

monkey business: mischievous/frivolous behaviour ~ *They're up to some sort of monkey business.*

Monkey Mia: Located 850 kilometres north of western Australia's capital city Perth is World Heritage landmark Monkey Mia, one of the world's premier natural dolphin sighting areas. Located at Dolphin Beach in the heart of Shark Bay, Monkey Mia has attracted schools of dolphins to its shores for more than forty years, and it is the only place in Australia where dolphins visit on a daily basis.

monster(s): [informal] badly behaved children ~ *Oh, those little monsters, look what they've done!*

month of Sundays: a long time ~ *I haven't seen them in a month of Sundays.*

moolah: [informal] money ~ *Did you bring enough moolah?*

moosh: [informal] one/someone's face or mouth ~ *The ball hit him smack in the moosh.*

mop: the hair on one's head ~ *He sports a thick mop of hair.*

mop something up: clean a spillage with a mop

mop up after: clear/clean up liquid/spillage ~ *Residents are still mopping up after the flood.*

more often than not: usually/mostly ~ *More often than not he stops for a beer on his way home.*

more than one can poke a stick at: to have plenty/enough of something ~ *They've got more money than you can poke a stick at.* *also: more than enough

moreish: food so delicious that you want more ~ *The chocolate was so moreish, I ate the lot!*

morning sickness: a feeling of nausea when pregnant

mosey around: stroll/saunter/wander about ~ *We spent the morning moseying around the market stalls.*

mosey on: leave/depart ~ *Well, it's about time we mosey on home.*

moth-eaten: material/clothing that has been eaten by moths ~ *This moth-eaten old coat needs to go in the bin.*

mouth off: talk back/speak impudently ~ *He was in trouble for mouthing off at the teacher.*

by word of mouth: of information to pass from person to person ~ *News of the event spread by word of mouth.*

down in the mouth: sad/unhappy ~ *He's been down in the mouth ever since.*

have a big mouth: be tactless; reveal secrets ~ *Tom's got a big mouth—he went and told everyone about the party!*

make one's mouth water: of something seen or smelled that appeals to one's senses ~ *The aroma of bread baking is making my mouth water.*

take the words out of one's mouth: say what someone else was about to say or was thinking ~ *I was just going to say that, but you took the words right out of my mouth.*

watch one's mouth: [spoken] to tell someone not to be rude; use bad language ~ *1a) Hey, watch your mouth! 1b) You should watch your mouth when you're in their company.* *also: watch your tongue

mouthful: a word or sentence that is difficult to pronounce ~ *His name's a mouthful.*

mouth-to-mouth: emergency mouth-to-mouth resuscitation; the act of breathing air into the lungs of a non-breathing person *also: kiss of life

mouth-watering: appetising ~ *The restaurant had a selection of mouth-watering desserts.*

move ahead of: advance beyond someone/something ~ *Police moved ahead of the protestors in order to prevent a riot.*

move about/around: travel from place to place ~ *He moves about the country looking for work.*

move away from something: distance oneself from a place or person ~ *1a) Move away from the edge! 1b) Move away from each other if you can't stop arguing!*

move heaven and earth: do everything possible; use all means to achieve results ~ *I vow to move heaven and earth to find out who was responsible.*

move house: begin to live in a different location ~ *We're moving house next month.* *also: move away

move in(to): occupy a living/work space ~ *We're moving in to our new house next week.*

move in on: impose on someone; become involved in; interfere with ~ *Police began to move in on the rowdy protestors.*

move in the same/different circles: associate; socialise with like-minded/similar people ~ *We don't know each other that well because we move in different circles.*

move in with: occupy/live in the same living space as someone else ~ *She's decided to move in with her boyfriend.*

move it: a [spoken] order to hurry up ~ *Come on—move it!*

move off: of a vehicle to begin moving ~ *Check the traffic before you move off.*

move on: 1) stop doing/discussing one thing and begin doing/ discussing another ~ *Let's move onto the next topic.*

2) leave one place to go to another ~ *We stayed in Melbourne for three days before moving on to Adelaide.*

3) to forget about a bad experience and continue on with your life ~ *He's in his twenties now, and has moved on from his angry teenager stage.*

move through: make a passage; travel from one place to another ~ *He moved quickly through the crowds to avoid capture.*

move up: change your position so as to make more room for someone/something else ~ *Could everyone please move up to the back of the bus?*

move up in the world: improve one's social status ~ *She's certainly moved up in the world since she started working there.* *also: step up in the world

move with the times: adapt/change one's lifestyle/behaviour to the changing situation ~ *They've moved with the times and introduced online purchasing.*

(the) movies: the cinema; films shown on TV or at the cinema ~ *Would you like to come to the movies with us?* *also: the pictures; flicks

mow the lawn: the process of using a lawn mower to cut grass

mozzie: mosquito

much of a muchness: of two things similar/almost the same ~ *I can't tell the difference. They're much of a muchness to me.*

muck around with: 1) interfere/tamper/tinker with something ~ *Who's been mucking around with this?*

2) associate/socialise with ~ *They're always mucking around together.*

muck something up: ruin/spoil something ~ *I just tidied the kitchen, please don't muck it up.* *see also: mess up

muck up: misbehave ~ *The kids mucked up in class.*

muckraking: seeking out and publicly exposing a scandal involving politicians ~ *It was just the usual muckraking going that goes on in parliament.*

muddle through: succeed despite lack of preparation ~ *I managed to muddle through the test.*

muddled up: 1) be in a confused state ~ *I was so nervous I muddled up my speech.*

2) a state of disorder/mess ~ *He muddled up the cards.*

mug: 1) one's face

2) one who is easily duped/tricked ~ *You're a mug if you believe that.*

3) hit/bash someone to rob them ~ *He was mugged in a back alley.*

mug shot: police photograph of a criminal ~ *The victim viewed some mug shots to see if he could identify his attacker.*

muggy: hot, humid weather

mulga: remote inland bush area ~ *He lives out in the mulga somewhere.*

mull over: ruminate/consider something ~ *I'll mull over the idea tonight and let you know tomorrow.*

keep/stay mum: keep a secret ~ *I'd like you to keep mum about it.* *also: mum's the word

mumbo jumbo: language/ritual designed to confuse ~ *He spoke a whole lot of mumbo jumbo.*

munchies: between-meal snacks ~ *We brought lots of munchies for the journey.*

(get) the munchies: have food cravings ~ *I've got a bad case of the munchies!*

murder: a particularly unpleasant/difficult task or job ~ *Working in that heat was murder.*

Murphy's Law: a law of nature to mean that if anything could possibly go wrong, it will

music to one's ears: news that's pleasing ~ *That you arrived safe and well is music to my ears.*

muso: musician

a must: something that certainly must be done/fulfilled or seen/visited ~ *1a) Having the right qualifications is a must for this job. 1b) A bridge climb is a must if you visit Sydney.*

mutt: another name for dog

my/my, my: an exclamation of astonishment/surprise/pleasure or dismay ~ *1a) My, what a beautiful flower! 1b) My, my! She looks gorgeous! 1c) My oh my! What are we going to do?!* *also: my goodness/my word/my oh my

my foot: [spoken] exclamation of scorn/disbelief ~ *1a) My foot he earns that much each year! 1b) She said it takes four hours to get there? My foot it does!*

my oath: absolutely yes ~ *1a) My oath I'll be there! 1b) My oath I will!* *also: bloody oath

N

nail someone: catch someone and prove them guilty of a crime ~ *Police have yet to nail the main suspect.*

nail something down: fix/attach with pins/nails ~ *You should nail it to the floor to stop it slipping.*

nail something home: emphasise/highlight a fact/point ~ *The graphic advertisement nailed home the dangers of drink-driving.*

nail someone to the wall: threatened punishment ~ *If I find the person who did this I'd like to nail him to the wall.*

nail-biting: a situation that causes suspense ~ *It was a nail-biting experience.*

namby-pamby: one who is spineless/indecisive/weak *also: wishy-washy

name of the game: the essential element; ultimate aim ~ *In this industry, the name of the game is to provide excellent customer service.*

by name: to use the name of someone/something ~ *1a) The principal knows all the students by name. 1b) He asked for you by name. 1c) I only know of him by name; I've never met him.*

(go) by the name of . . . : who is called . . . ~ *She is a singer who goes by the name of Giselle.*

call someone names: to verbally insult someone ~ *He tries to upset me by calling me names, but it doesn't worry me.*

get a bad name: a reputation that something/someone has ~ *That type of behaviour gives students a bad name.*

make a name for oneself: become well-known/famous ~ *She's making a name for herself as a talented artist.*

to one's name: having in one's possession (usually money) ~ *She doesn't have a dollar to her name.*

what's his/her name: used when you momentarily can't remember someone's name ~ *We have to go to what's his name's place to pick it up.*

nan/nanna/nanny: grandmother

nanny goat: female goat

nap: a short daytime sleep ~ *The tired child had an afternoon nap.* *also: catnap/doze/siesta/kip

(get) caught napping: be off guard/unawares ~ *The goalie was caught napping and the ball slipped through his fingers and into the net.*

narrow escape: narrowly avoid something happening to you/doing something ~ *We had a narrow escape when the car in front of us skidded and crashed.* *also: near miss; close call

narrow margin: not much ~ *They won by a narrow margin.*

nasty piece of work: a loathsome/despicable/offensive person

natter: informal talk ~ *We get together once a week for coffee and a natter.* *also: gossip; chatter

natter away: talk non-stop/continuously ~ *We nattered away for hours.*

nature strip: a council-owned grass strip in front of a house between the road and the footpath or fence

neat as a pin: orderly/tidy ~ *Her house is always as neat as a pin.*

neck and neck: exactly even/equal in a race or competition ~ *The horses were neck and neck as they approached the finish line.*

neck of the woods: vicinity/region/area ~ *What brings you to this neck of the woods?*

breathe down someone's neck: closely watch what someone is doing ~ *I can't work with you breathing down my neck!*

put one's neck on the line: put oneself at risk for the benefit of others ~ *You ought to be grateful that I'm putting my neck on the line* *to help you.* *also: stick one's neck out; risk one's neck; lay one's neck on the line

need a kick up the bum/pants: that someone needs to be reprimanded for their actions ~ *What he needs is a good kick up the bum.*

needless to say: obviously ~ *Needless to say I was excited about winning.*

nerves of steel: of being fearless/confident ~ *It take nerves of steel to swim with sharks.*

lose one's nerves: lose one's courage/bravery ~ *I came close to asking her for a date, but I lost my nerve.*

nerve-racking: something that causes someone to be worried/anxious ~ *The interview was a nerve-racking experience.*

nervous wreck: to be extremely worried or apprehensive about something ~ *I've become a nervous wreck waiting for the results.*

nervy: nervous ~ *He was very nervy just before the operation.*

nervy turn: a nervous episode

nest egg: money invested ~ *They had decent nest egg saved for their children.*

never mind: [spoken] a way of telling someone that they shouldn't worry about trivial, unimportant things ~ *1a) Never mind about losing your balloon, I'll get you another one. 1b) Never mind what Jill said, she's only trying to provoke you.* *also: not to mind

never too old: expressed to say that one is able to try/attempt ~ *You're never too old to learn.*

never-never: remote desert area

new blood: a different group of people with new/fresh ideas ~ *They need some new blood in the team to boost performance.*

new lease on/of life: to have renewed vigour/enthusiasm/energy for something ~ *The experience has given her a new lease on life.*

new one on me: [spoken] expressed when hearing surprising information ~ *The company is expanding overseas. Really, that's a new one on me.* *also: news to me

New Zealander: a citizen of New Zealand *see also: Kiwi

what else is new: [spoken] that specific information is not new; that something has happened before ~ *The price of petrol is going up again. So, what else is new!*

new-fangled: new/novel ~ *Have you seen those new-fangled bicycles?*

next best (thing): second in order of preference

next on the cards: [spoken] a way of asking what is to be done now ~ *We've finished this. What's next on the cards?*

next port of call: a stop included on an itinerary ~ *Our next port of call is Hawaii.*

what next: [spoken] cry of despair to mean "what else can go wrong?" ~ *First, the car broke down, now this! What next!?*

next door: a neighbouring/adjoining premises/room ~ *Sorry, you have the wrong house. Craig lives next door.*

next-door neighbour: person/people who live next door to you ~ *Luckily, our next-door neighbours are very nice people.*

nick: 1) steal/pinch ~ *He nicked my pen!*

2) gaol; prison ~ *Steve ended up in the nick.*

3) condition; state of being ~ *It's old, but it's still in good nick.*

nick off: 1) [spoken informal] a way of telling someone to go away ~ *Nick off, will you—you're annoying me!*

nick in: go into a place for a short time ~ *They nicked into the pub on the way home.*

nick out: go somewhere for a short time ~ *I'm nicking out for a minute.* *also: nick away

in the nick of time: at a critical moment; just in time ~ *They were freed just in the nick of time.*

Nightjar: Heard but rarely seen, the nocturnal white-throated nightjar is the biggest and darkest of Australia's three species of nightjars. The bird comes out at night to feed on insects close to the ground, but it is well camouflaged, making it difficult to see. They are common in eastern Australia's coastal ranges from central Queensland to Melbourne.

night of nights: the pinnacle, most important social event of the year/on the calendar ~ *The event is considered television's night of nights.*

night on the town: a night of celebration at more than one entertainment venue ~ *They had a night on the town to celebrate.*

nightie: night dress/wear/attire

nightlife: entertainment venues ~ *The city boasts a great nightlife.*

night owl: a person who goes to bed/stays up until late at night

nightmare: a difficult ordeal ~ *Sorry I'm late, the traffic was a nightmare.*

nincompoop: [informal] an idiot/fool/numb-skull/nit-wit

nine till/to five: daily work hours ~ *I work nine till five on Thursdays.*

nineteenth hole: (for golfing enthusiasts) the bar at the clubhouse

(a) nip in the air: it's cold ~ *You might need warm clothes, there's a bit of a nip in the air.* *also: nippy

nip it in the bud: stop something bad from progressing ~ *That sort of behaviour needs to be nipped in the bud.*

nitty-gritty: the essence; the basic essentials of an issue ~ *They got down to the nitty-gritty of who will be doing what jobs.*

no brains: lacking intelligence; forethought

no deal/dice: [spoken] refusal ~ *I've heard your offer, but no deal!*

no chance: no possibility ~ *1a) Do you think he'll agree? No chance! 1b) There's no chance of ever finding it.*

no fear: [spoken] certainly/absolutely not ~ *No fear! You'd never get me jumping out of a plane.*

no holds barred: without restrictions/rules ~ *It was a no holds barred contest.*

no ifs (ands) or buts: [spoken] that no complaints/objections/ compromises will be accepted ~ *These are the rules, and there will be no ifs, ands, or buts!* *also: no buts about it

no less/more than: an equal amount/degree/level/quality than something ~ *1a) It should take you no less than an hour to complete the job. 1b) It was no less than 40ºC in the shade.*

no stranger to: be familiar with a situation/experience ~ *I grew up on a farm, so I'm no stranger to riding horses.*

no such luck: [spoken] unfortunately/unluckily ~ *I believed this would be the end of the saga, but no such luck.*

no such thing: that something does not exist ~ *There's no such thing as fairies and goblins.*

no two ways about it: of having no choice/option ~ *There's no two ways about it—you're going to the dentist!*

no worries: Widely used in Australian speech, and often referred to as the national motto of Australia, "no worries" has the same meaning as "no problem," "that's alright," "sure thing," or "no problem." It represents friendliness, good humour, optimism, and mateship in Australian culture. ~ *Thanks for doing that. No worries!*

. . . like nobody's business: in an extreme way ~ *He eats like nobody's business.*

get/give someone the nod: get/give permission; say yes ~ *We finally got the nod to begin building our house.*

nod off: fall asleep ~ *She nodded off half way through the boring speech.*

noggin: one's head *also: noodle

no-hoper: an incompetent person; one who has a slim chance at success; a social outcast ~ *I'm not sure what'll become of him. He's a bit of a no-hoper.*

no-man's land: an area/space that is uninhabited/remote/ambiguous ~ *We took a wrong turn and found ourselves in no-man's land.*

no-no: something strictly prohibited/disallowed ~ *Riding without a helmet is definitely a no-no.*

no-nonsense: direct/practical/businesslike ~ *She takes a no-nonsense approach to parenting.*

none other than: that very person/thing ~ *The letter was signed by none other than the president himself.*

none the wiser: ignorant of something ~ *Jim was none the wiser to the prank.*

none the worse (for): be unaffected/unharmed by something ~ *They were none the worse for the ordeal.* *also: none too worse

none too: not very ~ *She was none too pleased with their behaviour.*

nong: fool/simpleton (said affectionately) ~ *Why did you do that, you silly nong?*

nope: [informal] no ~ *Do you know what time they're arriving? Nope.*

be/get up someone's nose: irritate/annoy; be irritated/annoyed by someone ~ *Jim really gets up my nose.*

have a nose for: 1) have an ability to detect/seek something out ~ *She has a nose for a bargain.*

2) be successful doing something ~ *No wonder his company is growing, he has a nose for business.*

keep one's nose clean: stay out of trouble/behave ~ *He's keeping his nose clean to avoid going to prison again.*

keep one's nose out: [spoken] a way of telling someone not interfere/meddle in someone else's business ~ *Just keep your nose out of my business!*

look down one's nose at: consider someone less important/not good enough ~ *There are some that look down their noses at the less academic students.*

on the nose: 1) smelly/malodorous ~ *These prawns are on the nose. Don't eat them.*

2) exact/precise ~ *Your cost estimate was right on the nose.*

3) distasteful; suspicious ~ *Their offer seems a bit on the nose to me.*

plain as the nose on one's face: very obvious ~ *Their love for each other is as plain as the nose on your face.*

poke one's nose in: intervene/interfere in issues that don't concern you ~ *She's always poking her nose in where it doesn't belong.*

powder one's nose: to use the bathroom ~ *Excuse me while I go and powder my nose.*

put/get/have one's nose out of joint: be resentful; insulted/ slighted ~ *Mark got his nose out of joint when his friend was promoted.*

thumb one's nose at: show disrespect/contempt for something ~ *He thumbs his nose at the road rules by continuing to speed.*

turn one's nose up: reject/spurn/refuse something ~ *She turned her nose up at our job offer.* *also: turn up one's nose

nose around: snoop/pry/meddle ~ *They were found nosing around our front yard.*

nosey parker: a person who meddle/snoops/pries ~ *Our neighbour is a nosey parker—she always knows everyone's business.* *also: sticky beak

no hope in hell: to have no hope at all of succeeding/doing something ~ *We have no hope in hell of getting there on time.* *also: haven't a hope in hell; Buckley's chance

not again: [spoken] expression of frustration at something bad happening again ~ *Not again! That's the second time this month the car has broken down.*

not (half) bad: of someone/something ordinary/mediocre/ passable/satisfactory ~ *Hey, this cheap wine is not half bad.*

just not cricket: [spoken] what you say about something you think is unfair/unjust ~ *Mate, you can't do that - it's just not cricket!* *also: not the done thing

not for all the tea in China: [spoken] never! ~ *I would never sell it, not for all the tea in China.* *also: not for love or money; for all the world; not for quids

not fussed: [spoken] said when you'd be satisfied with any choices offered to you ~ *Either the black or the red's okay. I'm not fussed.*

not fussed about: [spoken] said about something you don't really like ~ *It's okay, but I'm not that fussed about it.*

not half: [spoken] used to emphasise that you mean "yes" ~ *Are you interested in football? Not half!*

not if I can help it: [spoken] never; only if one can prevent it ~ *He won't be going. Not if I can help it.*

not much chop: of something below standard; unsatisfactory ~ *The food was not much chop, but the service was good.*

not one's cup of tea: not to one's liking/taste ~ *I know you like it, but it's not my cup of tea.* *also: not one's scene/thing

not on: unsatisfactory; unacceptable ~ *That you stay out until 4 a.m. is just not on!*

not on your nellie: [spoken] never ~ *Not on your nellie will I agree to that!*

not right in the head: [informal] mentally unsound ~ *He was doing some pretty crazy things. I'm sure he's not right in the head.* *also: not the full quid

not short of a dollar: wealthy ~ *I don't know why they're always looking for bargains, it's not as if they're short of a dollar or anything.*

not the end of the world: a reassurance that everything will be okay/that it is not as bad as it seems ~ *Don't cry, it's not the end of the world.*

not what it's cracked up to be: not reaching the anticipated; expected standard/quality ~ *It's claimed to be a miracle cream, but it's not what it's cracked up to be.* *also: not so hot

(not) within cooee: out of calling distance; far away ~ *You won't find any within cooee of here.*

not worth a brass razoo: having no value; worthless ~ *I thought it was antique, but it's not worth a brass razoo.* *also: not worth a crumpet/cracker

notch up: accrue; accumulate ~ *Our team notched up another win on Saturday.*

nothing between the ears: having no brains; thoughtless/stupid ~ *Why he would do that, I don't know. He mustn't have anything between his ears.* *also: nothing up top

nothing but . . . : just; only ~ *1a) I've done nothing but eat all day. 1b) When it comes to wine, he drinks nothing but the best.*

nothing doing: 1) [spoken] no; absolutely not ~ *"Nothing doing" was Mum's reply when I asked if I could go to the party.*

2) that nothing is currently occurring ~ *We drove through the town, but there was nothing doing.*

nothing much: 1) that little or nothing is/has occurred ~ *Nothing much has happened since then.*

2) nothing special ~ *How was the show? Oh, it was nothing much.*

nothing new: that nothing has changed/is still the same ~ *The trick he's attempting is nothing new.*

nothing to do with: not be connected/associated with someone/something ~ *1a) That has nothing to do with what we're talking about! 1b) I want nothing to do with him.*

nothing to hide: forthright/honest ~ *Ask me whatever you want, I've nothing to hide.*

nothing to it: that something is simple/easy/straightforward ~ *Is it difficult to do? Nah, there's nothing to it!*

nothing to something: that something is not true ~ *There's nothing to the rumours being spread about him.*

for nothing: 1) for no apparent reason/purpose ~ *He hit him for nothing.*

2) free of charge ~ *I got all this food for nothing.*

next to nothing: hardly any/very little of something ~ *1a) It cost next to nothing. 1b) They've done next to nothing to fix the problem.*

think nothing of something: 1) regard as easy/natural ~ *1a) Thanks for that. Think nothing of it. 1b) I saw some police cars there earlier, but I thought nothing of it.*

2) do something without hesitation/thought ~ *They think nothing of throwing their rubbish on the ground.*

escape one's notice: to go unnoticed; fail to be seen ~ *Your letter seems to have escaped my notice.*

hand in one's notice: officially resign from a job ~ *I just found out Sally handed in her notice today.* *also: give one's notice

now and again: occasionally ~ *I see her every now and again.* *see also: every once in a while

now I've seen it all: [spoken] that there's nothing that you haven't seen ~ *A car that turns into a plane? Now I've seen it all!*

now, now: [spoken] mild reproach; sympathy/concern ~ *1a) Now, now—that's not a nice thing to say! 1b) Now, now—you'll be okay.*

now or never: now is the time to do something (or it can't be done) ~ *It's now or never, so make up your mind.*

NSW: the state of New South Wales

NT: Northern Territory

in the nuddy: in a state of undress; naked ~ *Mary sleeps in the nuddy.*

null and void: invalid ~ *The certificate he produced was null and void.*

Nullarbor Plain: Stretching about 1,200 kms east to west between South Australia and Western Australia is the Nullarbor Plain—a treeless, flat, arid/semi-arid area immediately north of the Great Australian Bight. It is the world's biggest piece of limestone and occupies an area of roughly 77,200 square miles. One can cross the plain by car using the Eyre Highway, or the Trans Australian Railway runs directly through the Nullarbor.

Numbat: The numbat is a small marsupial found only in Western Australia. Sized at just under 30 cm long, it has a pointed nose and a bushy tail the same length as its body. Its colours vary from reddish-brown to grey with white bands. It has a prominent stripe running from the tip of its nose to the base of its round-tipped ears, and it feeds on termites and ants.

number-cruncher: [informal] an accountant

one's/someone's number's up: that one's time has come to die ~ *When he pulled out a gun I thought my number was up.*

nursing home: a private institution providing the elderly or the infirm with residential accommodation and health care *also: aged care facility

nut/nutter: 1) [informal] crazy/mad/insane; eccentric/foolish *also: nut case; nutty as a fruitcake

2) an expert/enthusiast ~ *He's a bit of a car nut.*

do one's nut: have an angry outburst ~ *She did her nut when she saw the damage to the car.*

hard nut to crack: 1) not easily swayed ~ *You might have trouble convincing her. She's a hard nut to crack.*

2) a difficult problem to solve ~ *This puzzle is a hard nut to crack.*

(be/go) nuts about . . . : be smitten/infatuated with someone/something ~ *He's absolutely nuts about her.*

nuts and bolts: practical/basic details ~ *I had to learn the nuts and bolts of running the business.*

in a nutshell: concisely; in a few words ~ *That's it in nutshell.*

O

ocker: a crude, uncultivated Aussie male

Blue-Ringed Octopus: The blue-ringed octopus lives in shallow coral/rock pools of Australia. Although it is only the size of a golf ball, it is considered one of the world's most poisonous creatures. Its poison is powerful enough to kill an adult human in minutes. It is not an aggressive creature, but when threatened it flattens out its body to hide, and its normal pale colouring changes to display electric-blue rings that light up as a warning. If you ever find one, just look at it. Don't *ever* touch it or pick it up. It hunts small crabs or small wounded fish, catching its prey by dispensing poison saliva. If it is threatened, stepped on, or handled, it will bite the victim, injecting a stronger poison from another gland. There is *no* known antidote.

odd bod: a strange/eccentric/weird/peculiar person *also: oddball

odd jobs: a variety of casual tasks/jobs done in the home ~ *He makes money doing odd jobs for people in the neighbourhood.*

odds and ends: a random collection of miscellaneous items/ articles ~ *I don't have much to buy, just a few odds and ends.* *also: odds and sods

odds are against someone/something: that the chances of success are slim ~ *You can try, but the odds are against you.*

against all odds: succeed/survive despite adversity ~ *She survived the ordeal against all odds.*

at odds: in a state of disagreement ~ *They were at odds with each other over the colour scheme.*

by all odds: undoubtedly; by far ~ *He is, by all odds, the smartest boy in the school.*

oddly enough: strangely/unusually ~ *Oddly enough, all the doors were locked.* *also: strangely enough

odds-on: of having a better chance of winning /succeeding ~ *Pete's horse is odds-on favourite to win.*

be/go off one's rocker: [informal] become crazy/insane ~ *She must be off her rocker if she believes that.*

off work: absent from work for a length of time ~ *Linda's been off work sick, all week.*

off and on/on and off: intermittently ~ *1a) I slept on and off last night. 1b) It's been raining off and on all day.*

off/up and running: 1) [spoken] by the race caller at the start of a horse race ~ *And they're off and running for race two!*

2) of having begun/started, and doing well ~ *Their new business had a shaky start, but now it's up and running.*

off colour: ill/sick ~ *Are you alright? You look a bit off colour.*

off one's face: heavily under the influence of alcohol/drugs ~ *He was so off his face he had no idea where he was.* *also: off one's tree

off to a flying start: to begin well (in a race/competition) ~ *They got off to a flying start.*

off one's food: lose one's appetite ~ *I don't think he's well, he's been off his food for a few days.*

off one's hands: something now out of one's control; out of one's jurisdiction ~ *I'm glad that matter is off my hands.* *also: out of one's hands

off one's own bat: do something independently; at one's own instigation ~ *The decision to donate the money was done off her own bat.*

off the beaten track: somewhere remote/secluded ~ *You have to go way off the beaten track to get there.* *also: out of the way

(go) off the boil: become less successful ~ *Her game started going off the boil after the second set.*

off the hook: 1) when a telephone receiver is not in place properly ~ *I often leave the phone off the hook while I'm working so I don't get disturbed.*

2) escape punishment ~ *I'll let you off the hook with a warning this time.*

off the mark: incorrect/inaccurate ~ *His prediction was way off the mark.*

off the rails: [informal] start behaving in an unusual/dysfunctional way ~ *After what she's been through, I'm not surprised she went off the rails.*

off with the fairies: [informal] in a confused state; out of touch with reality ~ *She's been off with the fairies since taking that new medication.*

offbeat: unconventional/different ~ *He has a somewhat offbeat humour.*

off-chance: a remote possibility ~ *I'll ring him at work on the off-chance that he's still there.*

off-load: dispose/get rid of something ~ *They had to off-load all the passengers because of engine problems.*

2) unload; pass/give to someone else ~ *I off-loaded it all to the charity store.*

off-peak: a period with less usage/activity ~ *We take holidays in the off-peak season to avoid the crowds.*

off-sider: an assistant/helper ~ *I could never have done it without my trusty off-sider, Greg.*

back off: [spoken] command to move away/retreat ~ *Leave him alone. Back off!*

eye something/someone off: look/stare longingly at ~ *She eyed off the new season's fashions in the shop windows.*

laugh something off: to dismiss as trivial/unimportant ~ *He laughed off any suggestions he might soon retire.*

pull something off: succeed under difficult circumstances ~ *I don't know how he pulled it off, but he managed to get front row seats to the opera.*

(be) put off: be repelled/repulsed ~ *I wanted to eat there, but was put off by the dingy interior.* *also: off-putting

rip off: 1) trick/swindle/cheat/exploit ~ *Don't buy anything from him, he'll rip you off.*

2) steal/pinch/take ~ *I left my camera in the car and somebody ripped it off!*

rip-off: an inflated price/charge ~ *They're charging $200 for that? What a rip-off!*

see off: farewell someone at the point of departure ~ *My best friend saw me off at the airport.*

set off: begin a trip/journey ~ *We aim to set off at the crack of dawn.*

well off: wealthy/affluent ~ *I don't know what work he does, but he's fairly well off.*

send-off: a celebration to wish/bid someone a safe journey/ venture ~ *My family gave me a wonderful send-off.*

oh boy: [spoken] exclamation of surprise/delight/dismay ~ *1a) Oh boy—a new car! 1b) Oh boy, we're in trouble now!*

oh no: [spoken] expression of disappointment/dismay ~ *Oh no—I've forgotten the tickets!*

oh yeah:1) [spoken] [informal] said when you remember something; oh, yes ~ *Oh, yeah—I remember that now!*

2) hostile way of asking someone "is that what you think!" ~ *1b) Oh yeah? We'll see about that!*

oi: [spoken] [informal] shouted to gain someone's attention ~ *Oi! What are you doing in here?* *also: hey!

old as the hills: very old ~ *This thing is as old as the hills.*

old biddy: [informal] old woman

old boy/man: affectionate term for husband/father/elderly man

old chook: [informal] old woman

old codger: [informal] strange, eccentric old man

old dear: affectionate term for elderly mother/grandmother/ aunt/woman

old flame: past lover

old girl/lady: [informal] affectionate term for wife/mother/elderly woman

(an) old hand (at): skilled/experienced/well-practised at doing something ~ *Allan will show you, he's an old hand at fixing tractors.*

old hat: old fashioned; out-dated; familiar ~ *Most teenagers think that style of music is old hat.*

old timer: [informal] old man

old wives' tale: traditional belief not based on fact ~ *Don't believe that, it's just an old wives' tale.*

oldies/olds: [informal] one's parents ~ *The oldies are going away this weekend—I'll have the house to myself.*

on a high: in a state of happiness/euphoria, either naturally or drug-induced ~ *1a) I'm still on a high since winning. 1b) He's on a high right now from the drugs he took earlier on.*

on a roll: experience a period of successes/luck ~ *Six straight wins! I'm on a roll!* *also: on a winning streak

on a shoestring: exist; do something with very little money ~ *She's been living on a shoestring she lost her job.*

(go) on about: 1) dwell on; talk tediously about something ~ *The salesman just went on about how great the product was.* *also: harp on

2) [informal] what do you mean/what are you saying? ~ *What are you on about?*

on and on: endlessly ~ *She talked on and on.*

(be) on at: nag/berate ~ *1a) Mum's always on at me to clean my room. 1b) I've been on at her to stop smoking.*

on behalf of: as the agent of; speaking for someone ~ *On behalf of the organisation, I'd like to thank everyone for their support.* *also: on someone's behalf

on cloud nine: euphoric/elated ~ *She's been on cloud nine ever since she heard the news.*

on edge: irritable/anxious ~ *I've been on edge waiting for the exam results.* *also: on tenterhooks

on for young and old: a situation where a minor scuffle escalates to a brawl involving many people ~ *Someone pushed someone else and it was on for young and old.*

on hand: nearby; readily accessible ~ *The boss is on hand to answer any questions.*

on the one hand: from one point of view/standpoint ~ *On the one hand, I'd prefer to leave on Friday...*

on the other hand: from another point of view/standpoint ~ *... but on the other hand, if we leave on Saturday morning there'll be less traffic.*

on offer: goods; options available to purchase or use ~ *The catalogue will tell you what specials are on offer.*

on one's feet: 1) to have overcome difficulties ~ *I've been laid up sick, but I'm back on my feet again.*

2) to stand/be standing ~ *The crowd were quickly on their feet cheering.*

on one's knees: to plead/beg ~ *He regretted his actions and was on his knees asking for forgiveness.*

on one's mind: thinking about something ~ *Sorry, I forgot to call you, I've had a lot on my mind this week.*

on paper: 1) in writing ~ *We need to formalise the agreement on paper.*

2) in theory ~ *Their proposal looks good on paper.*

on record: of something legally/publicly recorded ~ *Fatalities from road accidents last month were the lowest on record.*

on skid row: living an impoverished/destitute existence ~ *His excessive drinking and taking has landed him on skid row.*

on special: on sale; at a reduced cost ~ *I'll buy it when it's on special.*

on the blink: malfunctioning; out of order ~ *My washing machine is on the blink.*

on the blower: an old-fashioned way of saying you're talking on the telephone ~ *He's on the blower to Jim right now.* *also: on the bugle

on the breadline: living in poverty ~ *He's been living on the breadline since losing his job.*

on the dot: at a stated/expected time ~ *It closes at 3 p.m. on the dot.* *also: on the knocker

(be) on the grog: (to) be drinking liquor/alcohol ~ *He's been on the grog all night and now he's flaked out on the lounge.* *also: on the turps

on the hop: unprepared/surprised ~ *The new road rule caught many motorists on the hop.*

on the hoof: mobile/walking ~ *After resting in the shade, the cattle were now on the hoof looking for some grass to eat.*

on the mend: recovering ~ *He's not completely healed, but on the mend.*

on the move: active/mobile/afoot ~ *Finally, the traffic's on the move again!*

on the quiet: do something secretly; without making much noise ~ *He's been dieting on the quiet.*

on the rampage: run amok; rush about causing destruction ~ *Angry protesters are on the rampage through the city.*

on the receiving end: to be the recipient of something unpleasant ~ *She suddenly found herself on the receiving end of his anger.*

on the rise: increasing ~ *The number of assaults in the area is on the rise.*

on the rocks: 1) ruined; likely to fail ~ *Within two years their marriage was on the rocks.*

2) a drink served with ice ~ *I'll have a scotch on the rocks, thanks.*

on the run: 1) fleeing; escaping from arrest ~ *The fugitive is still on the run.*

on the scrap heap: useless; no longer wanted ~ *The policy was on the scrap heap before it was ever implemented.*

on the sly: covertly/secretly ~ *He was making bets on the sly.*

on the spur of the moment: without premeditation; on impulse ~ *We bought it on the spur of the moment.*

on the streets: exist with no place to live ~ *After coming into financial difficulties he had no choice but to live on the streets.*

on the take: someone in authority taking bribes/being corrupt ~ *It was soon discovered that the official was on the take.*

on the up and up: to be progressing/doing well ~ *After a slow start, business is finally on the up and up.*

on the warpath: angry; vengeful ~ *Watch out! The boss is on the warpath!*

on the way out: 1) becoming less popular/successful ~ *That is a fashion trend that's on the way out.*

2) while leaving/exiting a place ~ *I was on my way out when the phone rang.*

on the whole: generally ~ *On the whole her school grades are quite good.*

(be) on to: close to discovering/finding something/someone ~ *1a) They claim they're on to something big. 1b) You can't hide much longer, the police are on to you.*

on top of: 1) in control of a situation ~ *It took firefighters two hours to get on top of the raging inferno.*

2) in addition to ~ *On top of all that I had to prepare a meal for everyone.*

3) covering someone/something ~ *The beam fell on top of him.*

4) coming immediately after ~ *We had record low temperatures on top of the highest monthly rainfall.*

once again/more: happen/do again ~ *1a) I don't want to have to tell you once more to do it! 1b) Once again, you've defied my order.*

once and for all: conclusively; for the last time ~ *1a) I'm telling you once and for all - keep quiet! 1b) I hope to resolve the matter once and for all.*

once in a blue moon: very rarely ~ *We go to the opera once in a blue moon.*

once in a while: occasionally; sometimes ~ *I see her on the bus every once in a while.*

once upon a time: 1) a long time ago ~ *Once upon a time I used to like him.*

2) used to begin children's stories/fairy tales ~ *Once upon a time there was a beautiful princess.*

at once: immediately ~ *Come here at once!*

all at once: 1) all at the same time ~ *They came in all at once.*

2) suddenly ~ *All at once the rain stopped.*

just this once: on this occasion ~ *Just this once, I'd like you to do what I asked!* *also: for once

give someone the once-over: quickly look at someone and make a judgement ~ *He gave him the once over and let him through.*

give something the once-over: perform a quick clean ~ *He quickly gave it the once over.*

one after another: in succession; in sequence ~ *They watched with delight as the penguins jumped into the water one after another.* *also: one by one

one and all: everyone ~ *Welcome one and all!*

one and only: 1) the only/exclusive opportunity/chance to do something ~ *It's my one and only chance to be selected, so I'd better do it right.*

2) one's beloved ~ *She was my one and only true love.*

the one and only . . . : [spoken] used to introduce someone ~ *Please welcome on stage the one and only, Michael Bublé!*

one of these days: soon; sometime in the future ~ *I'll get around to fixing it one of these days.*

one of us: [spoken] that someone is considered to be of the same group ~ *Your initiation was successful. You're one of us now.*

(have) one too many: to have drunk too much alcohol ~ *He's had one too many by the looks of him.*

(be) one up (on): be at an advantage ~ *He thinks he's about to win, but I'm one up on him.*

as one: in agreement ~ *We are as one when it comes to environmental issues.*

at one with: relaxed/at peace with the environment ~ *I'm at one with nature in these mountains.*

be one for doing something: to like doing something ~ *I'm not one for partying all night.*

for one: to emphasise that you hold a specific view on something (even if no one else does) ~ *I, for one, would not allow it.*

one-eyed: 1) to be biased in favour of someone/something ~ *He's very one-eyed when it comes to politics.*

2) having only one eye ~ *In the next scene, the main character encounters a hideous, one-eyed monster.*

one-night stand: a casual sexual encounter ~ *He can never commit to a serious relationship, he has only ever had a succession of one-night stands.*

one-off: a once only occurrence; anything done/made once only ~ *1a) The painting is a one-off. 1b) The retired singer gave a one-off performance for charity.*

one-of-a- kind: the only item of a particular type/classification ~ *It's a one-of-a-kind diamond, the likes of which have never been seen.* *also: one of a kind

one-sided: prejudiced/unfair/partial ~ *The one-sided argument was going nowhere.*

one-tonner: a small truck/utility vehicle weighing one ton

(have) a one-track mind: think about/focus on one topic to the exclusion of all others ~ *You've got a one-track-mind. I wasn't referring to that!* *usually refers to being obsessed with sex

one-hit wonder: a musician/group known mainly for a single success/hit

only just: 1) by a small amount/degree ~ *He only just beat me.*

2) a short time ago ~ *We've only just got here—and you want to go home?*

if only . . . : [spoken] expression of regret; of wishful thinking ~ *1a) If only I hadn't done that. 1b) His health would improve if only he'd stop smoking.*

'onya: [spoken informal] good on you ~ *'onya Jack—you played well!*

oodles: excess quantities of something ~ *Relax, we've got oodles of time.*

oomph: energy/vigour/enthusiasm ~ *The speech is a bit dull. You need to put a bit more oomph into it.*

oops: [spoken] what you say when you make a mistake/have a mishap ~ *Oops—I spilt it everywhere!*

oopsie daisy: [spoken] what you say to a child if they stumble *also: ups-a-daisy

open day: a day when an organisation or school/university opens its doors to the public to showcase what's on offer

open house: 1) a period of time where prospective buyers can view a house or unit for sale

2) a day/time where your house is open to friends/relatives/guests who may wish to visit

open up[1]: 1) reveal one's innermost thoughts/feelings ~ *It took a long time for him to open up about what he'd witnessed.*

2) for a business to begin operating ~ *There's a new coffee shop opening up next door.*

3) cause to open/become open ~ *A beautiful valley opened up before us.*

4) open from a folded position ~ *The petals slowly opened up as the sun rose.*

open up[2]: [spoken] urgent command for someone to open the door ~ *Open up—I know you're in there!*

open one's eyes: confront the truth ~ *It took a grim prognosis to finally open his eyes to the fact that he should have stopped smoking years ago.*

open out: become wider ~ *The land beyond the mountains opens out to a vast plain.*

the open road: a stretch of road between towns where progress is unimpeded ~ *It wasn't long before we hit the open road.*

out in the open: visible/exposed/known ~ *1a) We camped out in the open. 1b) Now's your chance to get any issues out in the open.*

the open: any place that is exposed/outside/not confined

wide open: to the fullest extent ~ *1a) The wind blew the door wide open. 1b) She stood staring in amazement, her eyes wide open.*

with open arms: welcome/receive someone with warmth/ hospitality ~ *They welcomed him with open arms.*

open-and-shut case: a matter that's easy to prove/settle ~ *It is an open-and-shut case that needs no speculating.*

open-hearted: candid/kind/generous/sincere

open-minded: unprejudiced; receptive to new ideas ~ *You can talk to him about almost anything, he's very open-minded.*

(for) openers: to begin with; first of all ~ *For openers, we need more funding.*

(be) of the opinion: believe something ~ *They were of the opinion that admission is free.*

(have a) difference of opinion: mild quarrel/disagreement ~ *We had a difference of opinion as to whose job it was.*

in my/his/her/their opinion: I/he/she/they believe . . . ~ *In my opinion, they shouldn't go.*

second opinion: advice from another person ~ *I'd advise you to get a second opinion before making a decision.*

op-shop: charity store

opt out: choose not to participate in something ~ *She opted out of the next stage of the event.*

or else: 1) [spoken] verbal threat ~ *Be there or else!*

2) otherwise; alternatively ~ *We could eat lunch now and see the movie later, or else we could see the movie now and eat later.*

someone/thing/how/where or other: one besides/other than the one mentioned ~ *1a) Someone or other will collect the tickets. 1b) I'll get there somehow or other. 1c) We're leaving sometime or other on Tuesday. 1d) I put it somewhere or other in the garage.*

or so: thereabouts/approximately ~ *One hundred or so people attended.*

order of the day: the order of business; agenda ~ *So, what's the order of the day?*

2) the prevailing state of things ~ *Back in the '80s, big shoulder pads were the order of the day.*

Order! Order!: [spoken] command to restore calm in a meeting or debate

order someone around/about: tell someone what to do ~ *Since he was promoted he's been ordering everyone about.*

by order: in accordance with directions from the proper authority ~ *The fine is imposed by order of the court.*

in order: 1) in a state of readiness/preparation ~ *Everything's in order for her arrival.*

2) appropriate/desirable ~ *I think a nice refreshing swim is in order.*

in order that: so that (something can happen) ~ *In order that an agreement can be reached, we all need to cooperate.*

in order to: with the intention/purpose of achieving something ~ *1a) We arrived early in order to secure front row tickets. 1b) In order to fully understand why it's happened, we need to look back in time.*

in the order of something: approximately ~ *We had to pay something in the order of $10,000.*

in working/running order: working well ~ *The motor is in perfect running order.*

out of order: 1) not arranged correctly; not in sequence ~ *The page numbers are out of order.*

2) not working/operational ~ *The lifts are out of order.*

3) behavior that's unacceptable ~ *Your little rant was out of order.*

of the highest order: of the highest degree/quality ~ *The job requires technical skills of the highest order.*

among others: that what you've mentioned is one characteristic/ example of something ~ *She is, among other things, a fine pianist.*

the other day/night/week: an unidentified day in the near past ~ *Oh, I saw her at the shops the other day.*

other than: 1) except for someone/something ~ *Who else other than Jane is going?*

2) in addition to someone/something ~ *What subjects other than science are you doing?*

out and about: time spent outside the home ~ *1a) I don't seem to get out and about as much as I'd like to. 1b) It's good to see you out and about.*

out in the mulga/never-never/sticks: away from civilisation; in a remote place ~ *He lives out in the sticks somewhere.* *also: out bush

out in force: present in large numbers ~ *Police will be out in force during the event.*

outta: [informal] out of ~ *Let's get outta here!*

out of character: behave/act in a manner that's inconsistent with one's usual behaviour ~ *Her actions are completely out of character.*

out of depth: 1) in water too deep to stand in ~ *She's not a strong swimmer, so she never goes out of her depth.*

2) beyond the limits of one's capabilities ~ *When he started talking about ionization, I knew I was out of my depth.* *also: out of someone's league

out of hand: out of control ~ *With the arrival of aggressors, the peaceful protest soon got out of hand.*

out of it: disoriented/confused/dazed (often as a result of taking drugs or alcohol) ~ *We found him lying there, really out of it.*

out of kilter/plumb/whack: out of alignment/order; not working properly ~ *You're getting back pain because your spine is out of kilter.*

out of mind: crazy/silly/stupid ~ *1a) I'm going out of my mind with worry! 1b) Swim here? Are you out of your mind? This river is full of crocodiles!*

out of pocket: at a financial disadvantage ~ *I was left out of pocket after a day at the races.*

out of practice: no longer adept/skilled at a task due to neglect ~ *I used to play tennis, but I'm seriously out of practice.*

out of reach: physically or financially unattainable ~ *1a) I tried to get it, but it was just out of reach. 1b) On my wage, a sports car is out of my reach.*

out of the blue: unexpectedly; appearing to come from nowhere ~ *I'd been thinking of her, when out of the blue she phoned me.*

out of the ordinary: unusual/remarkable/unexpected ~ *His artwork is a bit out of the ordinary.*

nothing out of the ordinary: normal/usual/expected ~ *Their performance was nothing out of the ordinary.*

out of the question: [spoken] not worth considering; not possible ~ *Turning back is out of the question.*

out of this world: extremely good/fantastic/great ~ *The cheesecake Fiona makes is out of this world!* *also: off the planet

out of touch: in rugby league/union, for the ball to be outside the playing field

out of touch with someone: out of contact/communication ~ *I've been out of touch with them for a few years.*

out of touch with something: no longer up to date with recent developments ~ *He's out of touch with the latest techniques.*

out of the way: 1) in a remote location/area ~ *It's a nice location, but it's a bit out of the way.*

2) finished with/disposed of ~ *Well, I'm glad we've got that job out of the way.*

(not be) out of the woods: emerge from a perplexing/difficult/dangerous situation; not quite fully recovered from a health risk ~ *1a) We're over the immediate financial problems, but we're not out of the woods yet. 1b) He's recovered enough to go home, but he's not yet out of the woods.*

out of work: unemployed; having no job ~ *The company folded, leaving many people out of work.* *also: out of a job

(be/go) out on a limb: lacking support; vulnerable/exposed ~ *You'll be putting yourself out on a limb if you file that complaint.*

out on one's ear: dismissed; thrown out in disgrace ~ *You'd better behave or you'll be out on your ear.*

out with it: [spoken] command for someone to tell the truth/reveal all ~ *Come on—out with it! Tell me what really happened.*

fall out with someone: no longer speak to someone because of an argument/disagreement ~ *We fell out over something trivial.*

(the) outback: remote/unpopulated area ~ *. . . a tour company that provides the ultimate outback experience.*

outhouse: an outside toilet independent from the main house/ building

over and above: in addition to something ~ *The result was over and above what was anticipated.*

go over something: 1) practice/repeat something so as to master it ~ *Let's go over the opening scene again.*

2) clean something quickly ~ *It'll only take a minute to go over the carpet with the vacuum.*

3) review/check something ~ *It's best to go over your work in case you've missed something.*

4) conduct a search ~ *Police went over the crime scene looking for clues.*

to be over (it): to have had enough of something ~ *1a) I've organised this event for the past ten years—I'm over it! 1b) I'm so over hearing their arguments.*

over and over: repeatedly ~ *They played the same song over and over.*

over my dead body: [spoken] that something will never happen ~ *You'll do that over my dead body!*

over one's/someone's head: 1) beyond understanding/ comprehension ~ *The joke went right over my head.*

2) seek a higher authority ~ *I'd prefer it if you came to me about any issues than for you to go over my head.*

over the hill: be considered too old for something; past your prime ~ *He may be fifty, but he's not yet over the hill yet.*

over the moon: very excited/pleased ~ *I'm over the moon about my exam results!*

over the top: excessive; exaggerated ~ *He sings well, but his acting is sometimes over the top.*

over time: gradually ~ *I became more skilled over time.*

over with: finished/done/completed ~ *Let's get this over with so we can go home.* *also: over and done with

ow: [spoken] exclamation of pain ~ *Ow, that hurts!*

Tawny Frogmouth Owl: The tawny frogmouth hunts at night, remaining very still on a low perch waiting for the food to come to them. They catch their prey in their beaks, and occasionally will drop to the ground. They spend the day roosting on a dead log or low tree branch and are difficult to spot because of their excellent camouflage. They stay very still, their feather colours perfectly matching its surroundings, effectively looking like the tree it's roosting in.

own up (to): confess to something ~ *1a) She never owns up to her mistakes, she just blames everyone else. 1b) He decided to own up to what he did.*

P

P-plate: the letter P displayed on the front and rear of a vehicle to indicate the driver has a restricted license

P-plater: a driver who has a restricted license

pace around/about: walk around anxiously/nervously ~ *We paced around nervously waiting for any news.* *also: pace back and forth/up and down

pace oneself: do something at a steady rate ~ *If you don't pace yourself you'll tire too quickly.*

at one's own pace: do something at a speed you're comfortable with ~ *The course allows students to work at their own pace.*

at a snail's pace: do something very slowly ~ *We trudged up the hill at a snail's pace.*

change of pace: vary/change one's routine/lifestyle (either more or less) ~ *We're enjoying a welcome change of pace at work.*

gather pace: increase momentum ~ *The skiers soon gathered pace on the steep slope.*

go through the paces: demonstrate how well you can do something ~ *The coach watched the team go through its paces in preparation for tomorrow's game.*

keep pace: 1) proceed at the same speed ~ *I had trouble keeping pace with the lead runners.*

2) progress/develop at the same rate ~ *In this business, it's vital to keep pace with the competitive market.*

set the pace: determine the rate at which others proceed ~ *Out in front, he set the pace for the other runners.*

pack away: put something back in a container and store it ~ *It's your job to pack away the equipment.*

pack one's bags: prepare to leave after a disagreement ~ *He was told to pack his bags and go!*

pack (it) in: 1) stop functioning ~ *This old computer has finally packed it in.*

2) finish a job/task ~ *We've done enough for now. Let's pack it in for the day.*

3) retire from a sport ~ *He's finally packed it in after twenty years as a professional golfer.*

(a) pack of . . . : a group regarded with contempt ~ *They're a pack of idiots.*

pack a punch/wallop: 1) have a powerful influence/effect ~ *Wow, this chili sauce really packs a wallop.*

2) to have a forceful punch ~ *He really packs a punch.*

pack someone off: send someone away ~ *We packed off the kids to camp for the week.*

pack them in: attract a big audience to a venue ~ *She doesn't perform very often these days, but she still packs them in when she does.*

pack up: put things/equipment away/into containers ~ *It took us twenty minutes to pack up.*

packing death/it: be very afraid/scared ~ *It was so scary! I was packing death.*

packed out: of a venue filled to capacity ~ *With such a big attraction, the stadium was packed out.*

(cost) a packet: a large amount of money ~ *It's costing me a packet to send her to uni!* *also: a mint; the earth; a pretty penny

Paddle Pop: First introduced in 1953 and one of the best-known ice cream brands in Australia, the Paddle Pop is a milk-based ice cream on a stick. It is manufactured by Streets and it is their biggest selling and most popular ice cream on the market. The wooden stick from which it is eaten is called a paddle pop stick. The most current flavours are rainbow, chocolate, caramel, and banana.

paddock: a fenced field found on a farm mainly used for grazing livestock

paddock basher: an old, unregistered vehicle used on and around a farm *also: bush basher

long paddock: a stock route or roadside area used to graze sheep and cattle in dry times

paddy wagon: police prisoner lock-up vehicle/van ~ *The offender was taken away in a paddy wagon.*

(be a) pain in the bum/butt/neck: [spoken] someone/something considered annoying/boring/tedious (most often said humorously) ~ *1a) Stop being a pain in the bum! 1b) This job's turned out to be a pain in the neck.*

be at pains to do something: make careful effort to do something ~ *Authorities were at pains to stress that no one would paying extra for the service.*

pair off/up: form a pair for romantic interest; to do something together ~ *All the trainees were paired up with an instructor.*

paint the town red: celebrate freely; have a good time; go on a spree ~ *We painted the town red when the exams finished.*

palm off: give something away ~ *He tried palm off his old golf clubs to me.*

pan out: develop ~ *Let's see how things pan out before making a decision.*

panic merchant: one who worries excessively over minor issues

pantry: a small room off the kitchen used to store food and/or utensils

caught with one's pants down: 1) be caught unprepared for something

2) be caught in an embarrassing situation

paper: newspaper ~ *He sat in the sun reading the Sunday paper.*

par for the course: typical/usual; to be expected (good or bad). The literal meaning in golfing terms is the expected number of times a player will hit the ball to get it in all the holes. ~ *1a) It's becoming par for the course that job applicants take a personality test before being interviewed. 1b) What management did doesn't surprise me. It's almost par for the course lately.*

above par: better than average/usual ~ *The results are above par.*

under par: not up to standard ~ *I played well under par.*

on par with: equal to someone/something ~ *Our products are on par with what the competition has to offer.*

part and parcel: a necessary but unavoidable aspect of a situation ~ *Dealing with angry people is part and parcel of the job.*

part of: some but not all of something ~ *Part of the roof collapsed.*

part company/ways: go in different directions; do things separately ~ *They'd been travel companions, but it was now time to part company and go their separate ways.*

part with: relinquish/surrender something ~ *I could never part with them.*

for the most part: mostly ~ *For the most part, the weather was favourable.*

have/plays a part in: be involved in and influence an activity/ situation ~ *Community backing plays a part in the program's continuing success.*

in part: partly; to a lesser extent/degree ~ *He's responsible in part for what happened.*

look/dress the part: have the appearance of being suited to a particular role/job/situation ~ *1a) She looks the part for this role she auditioned for. 1b) In this business you have to look the part if you want to be noticed.*

on someone's part: done/experienced by someone ~ *It was quick thinking on Sam's part.*

bit part: a small/minor role in a play/performance ~ *I've a bit part in the play.*

take part (in): participate in something ~ *I've been invited to take part in the discussions.* *also: be a part of

the better part of something: almost all of a period of time ~ *It took the better part of an hour to finish the job.*

these parts: in this area ~ *Not much happens in these parts.*

party animal: someone who enjoys parties and who parties hard

party pooper: one who dampens everyone else's enthusiasm/ enjoyment

be a party to: participate/be involved in a dishonest activity ~ *He insists he wasn't a party to the robbery, and his alibi proves it.*

come to the party: take part in or be involved in something; to meet certain requirements ~ *I asked them if they could help our cause, but they wouldn't come to the party.*

the party's over: the fun/happy time has ended (and the serious work begins) ~ *Now sentenced to prison, the party's over for the career criminal.*

throw a party: have/arrange/hold a party ~ *They threw a huge party to celebrate.*

pass around: circulate/distribute something ~ *The pictures were passed around for all to see.*

pass away: to die

pass as/for: be accepted as/appear to be ~ *She could easily pass for someone ten years younger.*

pass down: transfer something (knowledge/information) to a younger generation ~ *1a) It's a tradition that has been passed down for many generations. 1b) She passed her collection of antique dolls down to her youngest daughter.*

pass muster: be up to standard in an examination or inspection ~ *The report didn't pass muster.*

pass off: to present as other than what is believed ~ *1a) He passed himself off as security staff to gain entry. 1b) They tried to pass it off as an original.*

pass on: 1) give someone an illness/infection ~ *I think you've passed your cold on to me.*

2) give someone something that someone else has given you ~ *Could you pass this message on to Phillip?*

3) pass a disease on to your offspring through your genes ~ *The faulty gene is carried by and passed on through females.*

pass out: lose consciousness; faint ~ *Some passed out in the heat.*

pass the buck: avoid responsibility by passing it to someone else ~ *She's now trying to pass the buck when the problem is clearly hers.*

pass the time: keep occupied/busy while waiting ~ *He reads the paper to pass the time when travelling to work.*

pass the time of day: have a short conversation with someone ~ *They often pass the time of day chatting over the back fence.*

pass the torch: give responsibility to someone else ~ *In his resignation speech, the company director revealed he would be passing the torch to his son.*

pass through: travel/move through a place for a short period ~ *We passed through most of the small towns.*

pass up: fail to act; to not take advantage of an opportunity ~ *It's an opportunity you can't pass up.*

pass with flying colours: succeed easily ~ *I passed with flying colours!*

past it: no longer able to do what you used to do ~ *She wants to revive her singing career, but she's past it.*

pat someone on the back: congratulate/praise someone for doing something ~ *She deserves a pat on the back for all the work she's done for us.*

patch up: 1) mend a relationship after a disagreement ~ *It's good to see you two have patched things up.*

2) do a quick repair job on something ~ *For now I'll patch it up until I can fix it properly.*

3) provide basic medical treatment ~ *All we could do was patch up her injuries until help arrived.*

bad/rough/sticky patch: a difficult or unpleasant period of time in your life ~ *Similar businesses are also going through a rough patch right now.*

bald patch: an area on one's head where no hair grows

in patches: in some areas/aspects ~ *The grass has regrown in patches.*

not a patch on: inferior/not as good as something ~ *This cleaning liquid is not a patch on similar products.*

pavlova: a popular dessert made from meringue, whipped cream, and fruit

pay back: return a favour/money/something owed ~ *Thanks for the loan. I'll pay you back tomorrow.*

pay someone a compliment: compliment someone ~ *He paid me a compliment by saying how much he liked the work I've been doing.*

pay dividends: that an investment will yield financial rewards ~ *Shareholders received over $5,000 in paid dividends.*

pay for itself: that the money you save when you invest in something is greater than the amount you originally spent/invested ~ *It paid for itself in under three months.*

pay heed: comply/obey ~ *He knows what he's talking about, so pay heed to his advice.*

pay(s) off: that something you do now will provide good results/be beneficial in the future ~ *All that extra training I did is beginning to pay off.*

pay something off: repay all the money you borrowed to buy something ~ *I'm hoping to have the house paid off by next year.*

pay one's (own) way: be financially independent ~ *He's earned enough money to pay his own way for an overseas trip.*

pay one's respects: honour someone after their death ~ *Many came to the funeral to pay their respects.* *also pay one's last respects

pay someone a visit: go and see someone/something ~ *I think I'll pay Amy a visit today.*

pay the price/penalty: suffer the consequences ~ *1a) If you abuse your health now you'll pay the price when you're older. 1b) I'll see that you pay for what you did.* *also: pay for (it)

pay top dollar: the highest price for something ~ *It's good quality—you can expect to pay top dollar for it.*

pay through the nose: pay too much for something ~ *I had to pay through the nose for it.*

pay up: pay money that's owed ~ *The insurance company is refusing to pay up!*

(it) pay(s) to . . . : that you should do something because you will be rewarded/benefited ~ *Profits have risen the past two months. It certainly pays to advertise.*

be at peace with: in a state of contentment/tranquillity ~ *They are now at peace with each other.*

keep the peace: prevent an argument ~ *I'm always trying to keep the peace around here!*

peak-hour: the time(s) in the day where traffic is most congested because large amounts of people are going to or from work ~ *It's usually a fifteen minute drive, but in peak-hour it can take up to forty-five minutes.* *also: rush hour

pearler: good/great/impressive ~ *I think it's a pearler of an idea!*

pearly whites: one's teeth ~ *Smile. Show me your pearly whites.*

pearly gates: the supposed gateway to heaven

peck at one's food: eat very little at any given time ~ *She only pecked at her food.*

pecking order: social hierarchy ~ *As a junior clerk, he's low in the company's pecking order.*

peckish: hungry ~ *I'm feeling bit peckish. What's to eat?*

peek through 1) take a quick/furtive glance ~ *A young child was peeking at us through the curtains.*

2) become slightly visible ~ *The sun began peeking through the cloud cover.* *also: peep/peer through

peel off: 1) remove by peeling; remove (wet or tight) clothing ~ *She peeled off the tight Lycra costume.*

2) go in a different direction to those you are with ~ *At that point, some riders peeled off the main pack.* *also: peel away.

peepers: one's eyes ~ *The first thing you notice are his big blue peepers.*

peeping Tom: voyeur/snoop who gets sexual pleasure from secretly watching others (expressly, a man who looks through people's windows at night)

peeved: irritated/annoyed ~ *I was peeved when the car broke down for the second time in one week.*

penny to one's name: to have no money; be broke ~ *I haven't got a penny to my name right now.*

penny dropped: suddenly realising/understanding something ~ *I watched, confused by their actions, then the penny dropped.*

penny for your thoughts: [spoken] a way of asking someone what they're thinking about ~ *You've been quiet all morning. A penny for your thoughts.*

penny pincher: someone who is especially careful spending money

spend a penny: go to the toilet (derives from the old-fashioned practice of charging a fee to use public toilets)

pent-up: 1) emotions not released/repressed ~ *His pent-up anger exploded in a violent outburst.* *also: bottled up

2) confined ~ *We've been pent- up in our cabin for days waiting for the rain to stop.*

pep pill: a stimulant drug

pep talk: a speech aimed to boost confidence/enthusiasm/moral ~ *The team was well behind in points at halftime, so the coach gave the players a pep talk.*

pep up: make more lively/interesting; invigorate/inspire ~ *He needs to pep up the speech to make it more interesting.*

perk up: 1) gain/regain energy ~ *Her visits always perk me up.*

2) to vomit

Perth: capital city of the state of Western Australia

perv (at): stare at lustfully ~ *He had a good perv at her breasts as she walked past.*

pet hate: something that annoys you greatly but doesn't necessarily annoy others ~ *My pet hate is ill-mannered people.*

peter out: lose momentum; diminish gradually ~ *Her enthusiasm for the game was petering out.*

petrol: fuel/gasoline

petrol station: *see: service station

petrol tank: fuel storage compartment in a vehicle

petty cash: small amounts of cash kept by businesses for incidental purchases

Brush-Tailed Phascogale: The brush-tailed phascogale is a tree-living marsupial carnivore, characterised by its bushy black bottlebrush tail. Weighing in between 110 and 230 grams, it has grey fur, conspicuous black eyes, and furless ears. These little tree dwellers feed on cockroaches, ants, spiders, insects, and beetles, and feed mainly at night. They make their leaf-lined nests in tree holes. Their distribution is patchy across Australia, but they are mainly found in ironbark forests in the state of Victoria. The brush-tailed phascogale and the red-tailed phascogale, found in Southwestern Australia, are endangered species due to habitat loss, tree clearing for agriculture, predation by cats and foxes, and fires that destroy their nest sites.

phew: /fju/ [spoken] 1) expression of relief/amazement/surprise ~ *Phew—we made it!*

2) used to indicate how hot it is ~ *Phew, it's hot in here!*

3) used to indicate how smelly something is ~ *Phew! That stinks!*

phone: telephone

physio: physiotherapist/physiotherapy; physical therapist ~ *I had to have physio on my knee following surgery.*

pick someone's brain: ask a lot of questions so as to gain information/advice ~ *Go and pick Carol's brain. She knows all about the stock market.*

pick a fight: start/initiated an argument ~ *She picked fights with everyone today.*

pick a fine/good time: choose the wrong moment/time to do something ~ *You picked a good time to go to the beach. It's starting to rain.*

pick and choose: select carefully/fastidiously ~ *Team selectors had a broad selection of players to pick and choose from.*

pick at: 1) eat a small amount of food ~ *She just picked at her food.*

2) pull/pluck at with one's fingers ~ *She nervously picked at a loose thread.*

pick of the crop/bunch: the best of something from a group ~ *The dancers they chose are the pick of the crop.*

pick holes in: find faults/flaws in something ~ *The group began picking holes in his theory.* *also: pick apart

pick a lock: open a lock without using a key ~ *He picked the lock with a piece of wire.*

pick on: 1) tease/bully; treat unfairly ~ *Jackie was a small, puny child who was often picked on at school.*

2) target/single out to perform an unpleasant task ~ *The teacher always picks on me to run errands.*

pick one's way: walk/go carefully so as to avoid hazards ~ *They picked their way through tangled debris.*

pick out: 1) distinguish; discern from the surroundings ~ *His bright orange cap made him easy to pick out from the crowd.*

2) select/choose ~ *She picked out a colourful scarf.*

pick to pieces: criticise sharply ~ *The police picked his alibi to pieces.*

pick someone's pocket: steal something from someone's pocket

pick up: 1) gather/collect ~ *He picked up the rubbish.*

2) casually acquire ~ *I picked up a great bargain at the markets.*

3) acquire knowledge by learning or experience ~ *She picked up the language very quickly.*

4) take on passengers ~ *The overcrowded bus was unable to take on any more passengers.*

5) purchase something ~ *I'll pick up some takeaway on the way home.*

6) take something in your hand ~ *Please pick that up!*

7) accept a charge/cost ~ *Dad kindly picked up the bill for our meal.*

8) acquire an illness/sickness ~ *She picked up a virus from somewhere.*

9) continue an activity/conversation after an interruption ~ *We picked up where we left off when the rain stopped.*

10) improve ~ *The housing market is gradually picking up after a long slump.*

11) discover ~ *The dog soon picked up the scent.*

12) increase speed/momentum ~ *The wind is beginning to pick up.*

13) of electronic equipment to receive a signal ~ *Rescuers were able to pick up the boat's distress signal.*

14) win something ~ *The movie is tipped to pick up four awards.*

15) meet someone and take them somewhere in your car ~ *I'll pick you up outside the school at noon.*

16) make a casual acquaintance in anticipation of sexual relations ~ *He tried to pick up at least three women that night.*

pick up on: become aware of something; notice something that's not obvious ~ *1a) No one's picked up on the fact that the statements contradict each other. 1b) Dad's always picking up on my grammar.*

pick up the pieces: recover from a misfortune; restore to normality ~ *He's only just begun to pick up the pieces since his wife died.* *also: pick up the threads

pick up speed: gather momentum; gradually increase speed ~ *The train picked up speed on the downhill run.*

take/have one's pick of something: have the option to choose exactly what you want ~ *We had our pick of seats in the near empty cinema.*

pick-me-up: a tonic; stimulus; refreshing drink

pics: pictures/photographs ~ *I've got some great holiday pics to show you.*

in a pickle: in a difficult situation ~ *I'm in a bit of a pickle with this.*

picky: fussy/finicky ~ *She's a picky eater.*

picnic: easy/enjoyable ~ *This section of the expedition is a picnic compared to what we've endured.* *also: walk in the park; piece of cake

no picnic: a difficult task/job ~ *It might look easy, but believe me, it's no picnic.*

picture of health: to be in good health; look healthy ~ *She's a picture of health now that she's stopped smoking.*

pictures: cinema/movies

piece by piece: in stages; by degrees ~ *We got the equipment there piece by piece.*

piece of the action: be involved in a popular activity/benefit ~ *Many fans turned up at the event, all wanting a piece of the action.*

piece together: assemble/put together ~ *Police are still trying to piece together the events leading up to the murder.*

go to pieces: emotionally break down; lose one's mental composure ~ *She fell apart when her husband died.*

in one piece: uninjured/undamaged ~ *Amazingly, he emerged from the wreckage in one piece.*

speak one's piece: express your opinion ~ *I felt so strongly about it I had to speak my piece.* *also: speak one's mind; say one's piece

take a piece out of: severely reprimand someone ~ *Dad took a piece out of me when he found out what I'd done.*

pie in the sky: false optimism; a plan/idea unlikely to occur ~ *His plans were dismissed as pies in the sky.*

pig out: eat greedily; excessively ~ *Having not eating all day, she totally pigged out at dinner.*

piggy bank: a small, personal moneybox to keep coins

piggyback: be carried on the shoulders or back of another person ~ *She loves being piggybacked by her father.*

pig-headed: obstinate ~ *It will be hard to convince her otherwise. She's so pig-headed.*

pike out: renege/back out of an agreement/arrangement ~ *We were ready to go ahead with everything when they piked out on us!*

pile in/out: enter a space in large numbers in a disorderly manner ~ *The doors opened and everyone piled in.*

pile on: increase something by weight or amount ~ *1a) I piled on the weight over the summer holiday. 1b) Authorities are piling on the pressure for the government to act.*

pile up: 1) accumulate/gather ~ *Bills are beginning to pile up.*

2) arrange into stacks/piles ~ *Books were piled up everywhere.*

pile-up: a major accident involving multiple vehicles

the pill: oral contraceptive

on the pill: using contraceptives ~ *She was on the pill.*

pill-popper: someone who takes drugs/medication regularly

pillow slip: removable pillow cover *also pillow case

PIN: Personal Identification Number – security number used in banking transactions

pin down: 1) understand/define clearly ~ *I can't seem to pin down the exact cause of the problem.*

2) force someone to give precise information; make a firm decision ~ *I can't pin him down on his decision.*

3) physically hold someone on the ground or a surface so that they cannot move ~ *Bystanders pinned down the suspect until the police arrived.*

pin it on someone: lay blame ~ *The suspect tried to pin the theft on someone else.*

pin one's hope on: put one's trust/hope in something/someone ~ *They're pinning their hopes on authorities finding their son alive.*

pull the pin: stop/end something ~ *The company pulled the pin on the project due to lack of funds.*

feel the pinch: experience the effects of having less money ~ *With the economy in such bad shape most people are feeling the pinch.*

at a pinch: do something under circumstances/with difficulty ~ *It holds ten people at a pinch.*

pinky: the little finger or toe

pins and needles: a tingling sensation in limbs caused by lack of circulation ~ *I've pins and needles in my hand.*

pipe down: [spoken] request to be quiet ~ *Will you kids pipe down!*

pipe up: begin to speak/play ~ *1a) At first there was no response, until a lone voice piped up from the back of the room. 1b) And then the band piped up.*

piping hot: extremely hot (food/drink) ~ *There's nothing like drinking piping hot soup on a winter's day.*

Piping Hot: an Australian brand of surf wear

pipped at the post: narrowly beaten/defeated ~ *The horse led the race all the way, but was pipped at the post.*

pissed: (slang) drunk/intoxicated

pissed as a fart/newt: (slang) very drunk/intoxicated

pissed off: (slang) very angry ~ *He was so pissed off at them.*

pitch in: 1) help to do something ~ *If we all pitch in we'll get the job done on time.*

2) donate money to a common cause ~ *Everyone pitched in to buy Sally a present.*

the pits: a truly awful/horrible action/event ~ *1a) Living there was the pits. 1b) This job is the pits!*

PJs: pyjamas *also: jammies; jim jams

place someone's face: to recognise someone but not remember how you know them or where you know them from ~ *I recognise her, but I just can't place her.*

all over the place:1) scattered ~ *We found little bits of paper all over the place.*

2) to many different places ~ *My job takes me all over the place.*

3) without order/poorly planned ~ *This report is all over the place.*

(act) as if you own the place: that someone thinks they are in charge/important ~ *He tries to tell everyone their job as if he owns the place.*

be no place for: an unsuitable place for someone/something ~ *This is no place for young children.*

change places: swap/trade positions with someone ~ *I'd never want to swap places with someone in that role.*

have friends in high places: know influential people who can help you get what you want ~ *I have friends in high places who will promote your cause.*

have no place: of something to be unsuitable for a situation ~ *There's no place for that type of behaviour here.*

in the first place: 1) before now; earlier ~ *What made you move here in the first place?*

2) as the first of several reasons ~ *I don't think she should be allowed to go because, in the first place . . .*

in place: 1) in the appropriate position/order ~ *Make sure everything's in place before the guests arrive.*

2) in use/operational ~ *The show can't begin until all the security measures are in place.*

in places: in some but not all areas ~ *Snow fell in places.*

in place of: instead of something/someone ~ *Buses will be used in place of trains.*

lose your place: 1) no longer have a position in a queue/line ~ *I lost my place when I went to the toilet.*

2) to not know which page (in a book) or the point in the text to continue reading ~ *I dropped the book and lost my place.*

out of place: not suitable for a situation/setting ~ *1a) I feel a bit out of place here. 1b) This furniture wouldn't look out of place in your apartment.*

place of residence/business: the place you live/conduct business

place of worship: a building such as a church where religious ceremonies are held

take pride of place: be in the most important position ~ *It takes pride and place on the sideboard.*

take one's place: resume one's usual/specified position ~ *Okay, everyone, take your places.*

take someone's place: be a substitute for someone ~ *Carol will take your place while you're away.*

take the place of: be used instead of something else ~ *Robots could never take the place of real people.*

plain English: language that is easily understood/that does not use difficult words or jargon ~ *The school is well known for its plain English policy.*

plain Jane: a female with an unremarkable appearance

plain luck/stupidity: that something is/was completely lucky/ stupid ~ *It was plain luck, I guess.*

plain old: something basic/uninteresting ~ *Plain old bicarb soda will get rid of the stains.*

plain and simple: that the truth is just as it seems ~ *My actions were stupid, plain and simple.*

plain truth/fact: that what you're stating is true—even though it may be offensive ~ *The plain truth is she's not well liked.*

plan of attack: an agenda/scheme for attaining an objective ~ *Our initial plan of attack is to lure private investors.*

plan on . . . : intend to do something ~ *1a) What do you plan on doing about it? 1b) I hadn't planned on this many people coming.*

go according to plan: happen as intended/arranged ~ *Luckily, everything went according to plan.*

plant a/the seed: something that puts an idea/thought in someone's mind ~ *It was an inspirational success story that planted the seed for the career course I'm following now.*

plastered: drunk/intoxicated ~ *He came home plastered.*

bring a plate: a request to contribute food at a social gathering

Platypus: With its duck bill and webbed feet, the platypus is a unique Australian animal. The platypus and the echidna are the only species of monotremes (egg-laying mammals) on earth. Reproduction takes place once a year, and the female lays between two and four eggs. When the young platypus is born it feeds on milk from the mother, which is excreted from glands under the skin and which ends up on the mother's fur. Only the male has venomous spurs on its hind legs which are used to defend itself. The venom is strong enough to kill a small dog, or cause extreme pain to humans. The platypus is found throughout eastern Australia. They live alongside rivers and make their burrows in the riverbanks. They use their webbed feet for swimming and their bills to stir up the mud on the bottom of the lake or river to collect freshwater insects, which they will consume when they return to the surface. Feeding is mostly done at night. The platypus shuts its eyes when swimming, and uses electroreceptors found on the bill to find their food. They range in length from 30 cm to 45 cms, and the tail is approximately 10 to15 cm in length. Their woolly furred coat has three different layers, providing good insulation. They have an average lifespan of twelve years, and there is no official name for a baby platypus.

play along: pretend to cooperate/be interested ~ *I was happy to play along with his charade.*

play around: 1) commit adultery ~ *He accused his wife of playing around.*

2) behave in a silly way ~ *2a) We ought to stop playing around and get back to work. 2b) The kids are playing around on the swings.* *also: fool around

play around with: tamper/fool/mess with something ~ *1a) Don't play around with that spider, it might bite you. 1b) You should never play around with explosives!* *see also: fool around with

play at: 1) engage/participate in a deceitful/secret act ~ *I don't know what she's playing at by saying that, but I'll find out.*

2) pretend to be someone else or involved in a situation ~ *The kids are playing at being shopkeepers and customers.*

3) show little interest in doing something ~ *I think she's playing at studying accountancy.*

play ball: cooperate/work together ~ *The federal government refuses to play ball with state government on the issue.* *also: come to the party

play it cool: appear nonchalant; remain composed ~ *We'll have to play it cool until the deal is signed.*

play with a full deck: be sound of mind (said humorously) ~ *I'm not certain he's playing with a full deck.*

play down: understate the quality/importance of something ~ *The finance minister played down reports the government was running well over budget.*

play by ear: play a musical instrument without reading the music ~ *She never learnt to read music, she plays by ear.*

play (it) by ear: improvise; act/plan according to the situation ~ *I don't know what we'll be doing when we get there, we'll just play it by ear.*

play the game: act according to the rules; play fairly ~ *Surprisingly, it's the larger corporations that are willing to play the game.*

play games: be deceptive; tell half-truths ~ *Stop playing games and tell me what really happened!*

play God: act/behave in a superior manner ~ *Many accused the scientists involved in cloning practices of playing God.*

play right/straight into one's/someone's hands: act/respond as expected to someone's advantage ~ *By negotiating with them we'll be playing right into their hands.*

play hard to get: pretend to be disinterested in someone's amorous advances so as to make them more interested in you ~ *She says she's too busy to go out with him, but she's playing hard to get.*

play havoc with: severely hamper/interrupt something ~ *The wind played havoc with our attempts to erect a tent.*

play a trick/prank: subject someone to a mildly mischievous /playful hoax ~ *Hey, let's play a trick on Benny.*

play a part: 1) represent a character in a theatrical performance ~ *I play the part of the wicked aunt.*

2) participate in something that involves other people ~ *He was accused of playing a part in the riot.* *also: take part in

play possum: pretend to be asleep or dead ~ *He appeared to be sleeping, but I knew he was playing possum.* *also: play dead

play it safe: act cautiously ~ *You should play it safe and take an umbrella.*

play second fiddle: play a subordinate/supportive role ~ *She took another part in the play because she would never play second fiddle to Susan.*

play silly-buggers: misbehave act/behave foolishly (said humorously) ~ *Will you two stop playing silly-buggers and help me here!* *also: act the goat

play the waiting game: delay an action/decision with the hope of gaining an advantage ~ *I'm happy to play the waiting game to get my preferred job.*

play up: 1) misbehave ~ *She's been playing up in school again!*

2) malfunction ~ *The motor's playing up.* *also: act up

play up to: impress/flatter in order to gain favour ~ *Some students play up to the teacher with the hope of getting a good report.*

bring into play: introduce something/put into motion ~ *Bringing new evidence into play at this stage of the trial is risky.*

(be) out-played: when the opposition/an opponent plays better than you ~ *You certainly out-played me today.*

out of play: when a ball has left the field of play or is considered dead

pleased as punch: very pleased ~ *She was as pleased as punch with the exam results.*

plod on: continue at a slow deliberate pace ~ *I'm happy just to plod along and enjoy the scenery.*

plonk: cheap wine ~ *He's quite happy drinking any old plonk.*

pluck up the courage: find one's courage ~ *He couldn't pluck up the courage to ask her out.*

plug away (at): doggedly persevere with a job/task ~ *How's the assignment coming along? Oh, I'm still plugging away at it.*

plug in: connect to an electrical outlet/power source ~ *You can plug the lamp in over here.*

plug up: become blocked ~ *The drain pipe plugs up from time to time.* *also: block up

speak with a plum in the mouth: a manner of speech using accentuating rounded vowel sounds, similar to the way upper British aristocracy speak. ~ *She thinks she's high class, the way she speaks with a plum in her mouth.*

plum pudding: A boiled or steamed pudding made with flour, butter, and dried fruit. Eaten at Christmas, it is also called Christmas pudding.

plumb forgot: to completely forget (used in the past tense) ~ *Did you call him? No, I plumb forgot.*

(a) plus: something advantageous/gained ~ *Not having such a long commute every day is a plus.*

pocket money: weekly allowance/spending money ~ *I give my kids five dollars of pocket money every week.*

point the finger at: accuse/blame someone ~ *Everyone was quick to point the finger at him for their financial problems.*

point in the right direction: direct someone ~ *1a) Could you please point me in the right direction of the post office? 1b) If you just point me in the right direction I'm sure I'll find it.*

point taken: [spoken] said when acknowledging/accepting a particular aspect of a discussion ~ *Point taken. How else can we address the issue then?*

point of view: one's opinion/viewpoint ~ *My point of view is that she should go to jail.*

point someone/something out: indicate something/someone; select from a group ~ *1a) You'll have to point her out, I don't know what she looks like. 1b) The teacher pointed out some errors in my work.*

point-blank: 1) direct/truthful/blunt ~ *He refused point-blank to tell me.*

2) with straight aim; directly ~ *He was shot point-blank in the chest.*

at some point: a time in the future ~ *We're going to have to reveal the truth at some point.*

at that/this point: a particular moment in time ~ *At that point she got up and left.*

at/on/to/reached the point of: the moment just before something might/will happen ~ *1a) By the time we got to summit Jane was at the point of exhaustion. 1b) We were on the point of losing all hope when they found him.*

beside the point: irrelevant ~ *I know they're selling for almost half price, but that's beside the point.*

(reach the) boiling point: reach a level of anger ~ *The announcement of further delays in the train service brought commuters' levels of anger and frustration to the boiling point.* *also: at breaking point (2)

(at) breaking point: 1) the moment at which something gives way under strain ~ *He began to panic when he realised the rope that was preventing him from falling was at breaking point.*

2) the moment at which mental/emotional stress gives way ~ *Tensions between them had reached breaking point.* *also: at the end of one's tether

case in point: a relevant example; for example ~ *A case in point is the recent spate of accidents that have occurred at the intersection.*

finer points: details ~ *Finer points on managing your money can be found in subsequent chapters.*

get one's point across: communicate an idea/opinion ~ *The best way to get your point across is to firstly state the main facts, otherwise your listeners will lose interest.*

get/come to the point: come to a conclusion; make a closing statement; reach the important part (of the story) ~ *Get to the point!*

good/strong/poor points: a particular quality/aspect ~ *1a) One of the good points of living here is a sense of community. 1b) Patience is not one of her strong points.*

more to the point: more importantly ~ *It's considered an unsafe destination. More to the point, it's recommended you avoid going there at all.*

no point in: no reason/purpose for doing something ~ *There's no point in organising a barbie on the weekend if it's going to rain.*

selling point: a feature of an idea; product used to promote/sell the product ~ *The fact that the house is close to the shops and the school is a good selling point.*

sore point: an issue/event that is difficult to talk about ~ *Don't mention anything about it. It's still a bit of a sore point with him.*

(a) sticking point: a subject/issue that cannot be agreed upon in a discussion ~ *How to divide it up is a sticking point with us.*

(at) the point of no return: a stage in an action/undertaking which can't be stopped or reversed ~ *As soon as you sign the contracts you're at the point of no return.*

to a (certain) point: to some extent; not completely ~ *I agree, to a certain point.*

to the point: expressed clearly/simply ~ *The letter was to the point.*

to the point of . . . : that something/someone is almost at a stage where it/they can be described as doing something/behaving differently ~ *1a) She was scared to the point of being paranoid. 1b) His actions were careless to the point of being dangerous.*

turning point: the stage at which a change occurs; a decisive action ~ *1a) It was a turning point in our lives. 1b) Winning the award ten years ago was a turning point in my career.*

vantage point: a position/place that offers a favourable view ~ *The cliff top offers the best vantage point to view the vast valley.*

poke around/about: 1) spy; snoop ~ *What are you doing poking about in here?*

2) spend idle/aimless time ~ *I spent the day poking around the museum.*

3) look for something by moving things about ~ *She was poking about in the drawer looking for a paperclip.*

pokies: poker/slot machine

polish off: finish quickly/easily; dispose of someone/something ~ *1a) I'll just polish off this task and I'll be ready.1b) We easily polished off the wine.*

pollies: politicians

Pommy/Pom: [informal] an English person ~ *The Aussies and the Poms are great sporting rivals.*

pooch: dog

pooh-pooh: dismiss/consider as impractical/foolish ~ *He pooh-poohed my idea!*

pool: swimming pool

pop/poppy: father/grandfather/pa

a pop: each (individual but similar) item ~ *At thirty dollars a pop, they're not cheap!* *also: a piece

pop around: visit someone ~ *1a) I'll pop around this afternoon to see you. 1b) I'm popping up to the shops for a minute.* *also: pop in/by/over/up; come by/around; stop in/by

pop the question: propose marriage ~ *She was hoping he would soon pop the question.*

pop up: appear/arise unexpectedly/materialise ~ *Tiny shoots are popping up everywhere.*

porn: pornography

porno: someone with an unhealthy interest in pornography ~ *I've heard he's a bit of a porno!*

pose(s) no danger: something that appears dangerous but is not ~ *The dog looks menacing, but he poses no danger to you.*

possie: position ~ *We managed to get a good possie to watch the fireworks.*

Possum: The common ringtail possum and common brushtail possum have adapted well to living in close proximity to humans and can be seen in suburban gardens. Their distribution covers Queensland, New South Wales, Victoria, and South Australia. About the size of a cat, it is grey in colour and has white patches behind the eyes and on its belly. It uses its long tail to climb and jump between branches, fences, and other structures and is able to use its forefeet to hold securely onto branches. It is nocturnal and feeds on a variety of leaves, flowers, and fruits. The male of the species can be heard at night when they make a loud hissing, territorial call. Native possum species in Australia are protected by Australian regulations.

post code: a series of digits in a postal address used as an aide in the sorting of mail. *also: area code; postal code

keep posted: inform/alert someone to the latest news/information ~ *I'll keep you posted on any new developments.*

postie: postman/woman ~ *The postie usually comes at 3 p.m.*

go to pot: be in a state of disrepair due to neglect ~ *The garden's gone to pot since the caretaker left.* *also: been let go

pot-belly: a rounded, protruding abdomen

pot-belly stove: a cast-iron rounded stove used for burning coal or wood

pot luck: random offering/choice ~ *1a) It will be a pot luck dinner tonight. 1b) Whether you'll win or lose is just pot luck.* *also: take pot luck

pothole: a depression in the road surface where the surface material has broken away

potter about/around: be busy in a slow, pleasant manner ~ *She spent the afternoon pottering about in the garden.*

pound away (at): hammer/beat/bat repeatedly (with force) ~ *He pounded away on the door for someone to let him in.*

powder room: women's toilet/restroom/ladies

power point: electrical outlet; wall-plug/socket ~ *You can plug it in to the power point over there.*

prang: car accident/crash; cause damage to a car ~ *I pranged the car last night.*

pre-loved*:* second-hand (goods)

press/push one's luck: extend (too far) one's fortune; chances ~ *You'd be pushing your luck asking for a loan.*

pressie: present/gift ~ *I can't wait to open my pressies!*

bow/yield/give in to pressure: act upon; be influenced by someone's demands/requests ~ *Authorities eventually bowed to pressure, announcing they would restore the building.*

under false pretences: lie about one's reason for doing something/being somewhere ~ *She was charged for obtaining money under false pretences.*

under the pretence: disguise one's illegal/false actions/intentions ~ *He entered the premises under the pretence of carrying out repairs.*

prey on someone: exploit; use someone to your advantage ~ *He preys on the elderly by overcharging them for simple repair work.*

pricey: expensive ~ *They're nice, but they're a bit pricey.*

pride of place: the highest; most important place/spot ~ *Her trophies takes pride of place in a glass cabinet.*

prim and proper: virtuous; demure; orderly ~ *I can't imagine her saying something like that, she's always so prim and proper.*

prime time: peak viewing time for television ~ *The advertisements will be aired on prime time television from tomorrow.*

privates/private parts: the genitals

pro: professional; expert

probs: problem(s)

not a/no problem: [spoken] a casual response to a request ~ *1a) Yes, I can do that for you. No problem! 1b) It's not a problem, I don't mind doing it.* *see also: no sweat; no worries

no prob(s): [informal] no problem(s) ~ *Yeah, no probs.*

promise the earth: make an excessive offer that cannot be fulfilled ~ *They promised the earth but gave nothing.*

promo: promotional (advertising) ~ *The store has a great promo going at the moment.*

prop up: support/sustain/hold/bolster something/someone ~ *1a) The old fence was propped up here and there by forked branches. 1b) His funny jokes certainly propped up her spirits.*

proper: absolute/complete/thorough ~ *She got drunk and made a proper fool of herself.*

prowl around: 1) move stealthily with intent ~ *He was seen prowling around in people's back yards.*

2) move stealthily in search of prey ~ *The cat prowled around the alley looking for food.*

on the prowl: actively searching for something/someone ~ *Police are on the prowl for the suspects.*

pros and cons: the reasons for and against something ~ *Weigh up the pros and cons before making a decision.*

p's and q's: one's language; manners *see: mind one's p's and q's

psyche oneself up: prepare mentally ~ *She normally has to psyche herself up before each performance.*

psycho: [informal] psychotic/psychopath ~ *1a) My dog goes psycho whenever that other dog goes near the fence. 1b) She's a bit psycho if you ask me.*

pub: public drinking house *hotel/drinking establishment

pub crawl: the practice of drinking at several different pubs/ establishments over a period of time

pudding: sweets/dessert; plum pudding

puffed (out): breathless; exhausted ~ *The steep hill climb left everyone puffed out.*

puff up: 1) become puffy/swollen because of an injury/infection ~ *The bee sting caused her hand to puff up.*

2) filled with air ~ *Wait for the muffins to puff up a bit more before taking them out of the oven.*

3) become filled with pride/arrogance; false bravado ~ *He puffed himself up so as to not appear intimidated.*

puke: [informal] vomit/heave/chunder/spew/chuck

pull a fast one/swifty: cheat/trick someone (usually for financial gain) ~ *He tried to pull a swifty by advertising them as brand name goods.*

pull a knife/gun: draw out a weapon in readiness for use ~ *He pulled a knife on him.*

pull a face: contort one's facial expressions ~ *The student was in trouble for pulling faces at the teacher.*

pull around: move by pulling ~ *The kids pulled each other around in the wagon.*

pull away: withdraw; move away from ~ *1a) The car pulled away from the curb. 1b) He tried to kiss her and she pulled away.*

pull down: 1) destroy; demolish ~ *They're going to pull down the old house.*

2) bring to a lower level ~ *She pulled the blind down to darken the room.*

pull in: 1) to arrive or stop somewhere ~ *We pulled in around midnight.*

2) reach a destination ~ *We got there just as the train pulled in.*

pull off: 1) succeed despite adversity ~ *They managed to pull off the deal.*

2) get away with doing something risky ~ *Only you could pull off a stunt like that!*

3) move/steer a vehicle off a road ~ *We pulled off the road to rest.*

pull your head in: [spoken] a blunt way to tell someone to shut up ~ *Oh, pull your head in. You know nothing about it!*

pull one's socks up: improve your behaviour/attitude/work ~ *You'd better pull your socks up if you want good marks.*

pull out of: 1) withdraw from a commitment/situation ~ *An injury forced her to pull out of the tournament.*

2) leave/depart ~ *The train pulled out of the station on time.*

pull out all the stops: do everything possible ~ *They pulled out all the stops for the gala event.*

pull over: move to and stop at the side of the road ~ *The police officer instructed the driver to pull over.*

pull no punches: be upfront; truthful ~ *He pulled no punches with his review of the plan.*

pull rank: assert one's power/rank over someone to gain an advantage ~ *Be careful, he might try to pull rank on you.*

pull someone's leg: trick/tease someone ~ *I didn't really smash your car—I'm just pulling your leg.*

pull the other leg: said when you know someone is joking ~ *You are going mountain climbing!? Pull the other one.*

pull strings: exert influence for benefit/gain directly or indirectly ~ *I'll see if I can pull some strings and get you a ticket.*

pull the plug/pin on: discontinue/cease; prevent from happening/ continuing ~ *Producers pulled the plug on the program after ratings dropped off.*

pull together: make a joint effort ~ *The community pulled together to help those affected by the disaster.*

pull yourself together: regain one's composure ~ *I found it hard to pull myself together after the tragedy.*

pull through: overcome an illness/a difficult situation ~ *It's a complicated operation, but I'm confident he'll pull through.* *also: come through

pull to pieces: dismantle; deconstruct ~ *. . . came home to find the dog had pulled the couch to pieces.*

pull up: stop/come to a halt ~ *A car has just pulled up outside their house.*

pull up a chair/seat: [spoken] invitation for someone to sit down ~ *Pull up a chair and I'll explain it.*

pull the rug out from under: suddenly remove all assistance/ support from ~ *If they cut funds they'll be pulling the rug out from under the people that rely on the service.*

pull someone up (on something): rebuke ~ *The teacher pulled me up for wearing the wrong type of shoes.*

pull up stakes/stumps: depart/leave/clear out ~ *I don't know where they went. They just suddenly pulled up stakes.*

pull (one's) weight: do one's fair share of the work ~ *There's been complaints from others that you're not pulling your weight.*

pull the wool over one's/someone's eyes: trick/deceive ~ *You can't pull the wool over his eyes, he's much too clever.*

punch someone's lights out: [informal] punch someone unconscious ~ *If you don't shut up I'll punch your lights out!* *mostly said as a threat

beat someone to the punch: do something before someone else does ~ *I wanted to surprise her with the news, but my brother beat me to the punch.*

packs a punch: to have a strong/powerful effect ~ *This brew really packs a punch!*

roll with the punches: be able to cope/deal with difficulties ~ *You have to be able to roll with the punches if you want to be a politician.*

punch-up: a fistfight ~ *There's been a big punch-up between rival gang members.*

push ahead: continue doing something despite difficulties ~ *Despite fierce opposition, they're going to push ahead with the plans to redevelop the site.*

push ahead of: jostle to get in front of someone ~ *Most pushed ahead of the slower competitors.*

push around: 1) jostle; threaten someone ~ *1a) Some bullies pushed him around a bit. 1b) He likes to act big and tough, but don't let him push you around.*

2) move by pushing ~ *She pushed the baby around in the pram.* *also: shove around; push about

push aside: ignore; push out of the way ~ *He claimed his complaints were always pushed aside.*

push buttons: know/do/say exactly the right thing to get a reaction from someone ~ *My son knows which buttons to push to make me angry.*

push off: 1) of a boat to leave the dock/wharf

2) use your feet to propel yourself forward/upward ~ *Swimmers must quickly push off the wall after completing the turn.*

push on: continue/proceed after stopping ~ *He had no option but to push on despite being injured.*

push over: cause/make something/someone fall over/down ~ *Be careful—you almost pushed me over!*

push past: force one's way ahead/past someone/something ~ *They rudely pushed past us when we were standing in line.*

pushed for something: lacking in/having little of something ~ *1a) I'd like to lend you some money, but I'm a bit pushed for cash at the moment. 1b) I'm pushed for time right now, I'll do it tomorrow.*

push (up) against: press against; exert pressure against ~ *1a) They pushed a chair up against the door. 1b) The venue was so crowded that everyone was pushed against each other.*

pushing up daisies: [informal] dead (said humorously) ~ *You keep that unhealthy lifestyle up, mate, you'll soon be pushing up daisies.*

if/when push comes to shove: action will be taken if or when a situation becomes urgent/critical ~ *If push comes to shove we can use some of our savings.*

pushover: 1) someone who is easily influenced/overcome/ defeated ~ *They're ill-prepared, so beating them should be a pushover.*

2) a task/job easily done ~ *The exam was a pushover.*

pussyfoot around: be undecided about something ~ *I wish she'd stop pussyfooting around and decide which university she wants to attend.*

put a cork/lid on it: [spoken] humorous way to tell someone to be quiet/stop talking ~ *Oh, put a cork in it will you!*

put a damper on: make something less enjoyable/exciting ~ *The number of rules and restrictions put a damper on the event.*

put a stop/halt/end to: terminate; bring to an end ~ *Authorities tried to put a stop to the proceedings.*

put away: 1) save money for a purpose ~ *If you put a little away each week you'll soon have enough saved for the trip.*

2) consume food/drink readily/quickly ~ *He can sure put his food away.*

put someone away: confine to jail ~ *The judge ordered the murderer to be put away for life.*

put something down: put something/someone down on a surface ~ *You can put it down over there.*

put someone down: criticise/berate ~ *She's always putting him down.*

put (yourself) down: think less of your abilities ~ *You shouldn't put yourself down. Not everyone passed the exam.*

(have) something put down: kill an animal with a drug because it's old, dangerous, or ill ~ *We had to have our poor old dog put down.*

put (something) down to: that you think something has happened for a reason ~ *It can only be put down to bad luck.*

put forth/forward: make an offer/proposal ~ *She put forth her plan to the committee.*

put hairs on your chest: a humorous claim that eating/drinking something will make you strong/healthy ~ *Here, eat this, it will put hairs on your chest.*

put in: 1) submit an offer ~ *He put in a bid at the auction.*

2) make a recommendation ~ *I'll put a good word in for you.*

3) make a contribution ~ *We all put in for the present.*

4) spend time doing something ~ *I put in for overtime this week.*

5) plant something ~ *They've put in about thirty gum trees since then.*

put in an appearance: be somewhere/attend for a brief period ~ *He put in an appearance at the office then left.*

put in for: apply for a job/position ~ *I heard Chris put in for the job in marketing.*

put in writing: write something so as to make it official ~ *All formal agreements should be put in writing.*

put into effect/action/practice: begin a process/procedure ~ *We expect the new laws will be put into effect at the end of the week.*

put into words: express your feelings ~ *It's hard to put into words how I feel about what happened.*

put it: state or explain something ~ *1a) I'd rephrase it and put it a bit differently so the meaning's clearer. 1b) The topic is—ah, how do* *you put it—delicate. 1c) That's not how they put it! 1d) Put it this way—I'd rather she didn't come. 1e) It is, as Lisa put it, out of this world.*

to put it bluntly: used for warning someone that you are going to be honest, even though it might upset them ~ *The report, to put it bluntly, stinks!*

to put it delicately: say something tactfully ~ *They were discovered, to put it delicately, in an intimate pose.*

to put it mildly: speak inoffensively; without exaggeration ~ *He said, "You're nothing but a stinker," and that was putting it mildly.*

to put it another way: say something using different words ~ *To put it another way—he's run out of resources.* *also: to put it differently

put it on paper: write something down ~ *Best to put it on paper so you don't forget.*

wouldn't put it past someone: have no doubt that somebody is capable of doing/did something illegal/wrong ~ *I wouldn't put it past Tom to do a sneaky thing like that.*

put it to someone: make a suggestion/plan/course of action ~ *I'll put it to management and see what they say.* *also: put forth

put to rest: settle/finish a discussion; finalise an issue ~ *I'll be glad when we can put the whole sordid affair to rest.* *also: lay to rest

put something off: delay/postpone doing something ~ *We've put the barbie off until next weekend.* *also: put off doing something

put someone off: 1) cause someone to be discouraged/repelled/ repulsed ~ *1a) Don't let horror stories like that put you off going. 1b) Don't be put off by his rough appearance, he's actually a very friendly dog.*

2) delay meeting with/talking to someone ~ *Can you try to put Carol off if she calls? I don't want to speak with her just now.*

put someone off doing something: discourage from doing ~ *Don't let one bad experience stop you from trying again.*

put on: 1) put clothing/something on your body ~ *1a) It's cold out. You'll need to put on something warm. 1b) Here, put this hat on.*

2) apply to a surface ~ *It doesn't take her long to put her makeup on.*

3) pretend ~ *She's not sick, she's putting it on to stay home from school.*

4) host/organise an event ~ *The kids are putting on a concert at the end of the year.*

5) gain weight ~ *Joe's put on some weight since I last saw him.*

6) hire someone to do a job ~ *We had to put on three extra staff to deal with the workload.*

7) gamble ~ *I put $100 on Wild Ride to win.*

8) start cooking something ~ *I'll put the dinner on in a minute.*

9) become operational ~ *Could you put the light on please?*

10) play music through an audio system ~ *I'll go home and put on some quiet music.*

11) show/display your talent/skills ~ *The team put on another match-winning performance.*

12) cause something to affect someone/something ~ *Any reduction in funding will put pressure on the department.*

13) pass the telephone to someone so they can speak to the person calling ~ *Sam wants to talk to you. I'll put him on.*

put on airs: act as if you're more important/better than others ~ *She puts on airs to impress the boss.*

put on an act: pretend so as to deceive/be noticed/get what you want ~ *I'm sure he's putting on an act so he can stay home from school.*

put something on hold: delay doing something ~ *Because of what happened, we've had to put the plans on hold.*

put something over someone: outwit/cheat/trick/dupe someone ~ *He's always trying to put one over me, but I'm too clever for him.*

put one's back into something: use force/energy to do something ~ *If we put our backs into it we should be finished by lunchtime.*

put one's face on: to apply makeup/cosmetics

put one's feet up: sit down with your legs outstretched ~ *I'm going to put my feet up when I get home!*

put one's finger on something: [in the negative] to not fully know/understand what's different/wrong about a situation ~ *From* *what he said I knew something was not quite right, but I couldn't put my finger on it.*

put one's foot in one's mouth: unknowingly make an embarrassing/tactless remark ~ *I really put my foot in my mouth when I asked him about his wife. I didn't know she'd left him.*

put (one's) hand up: raise your arm to say something or to be noticed/counted ~ *1a) I put my hand up to help. 1b) Put your hand up if you know the answer.* *also: put up one's hand

put one's hand in one's pocket: (unwillingly) spend money ~ *It seems I'm forever putting my hand in my pocket during school holiday time.*

put/bury/stick one's head in the sand: ignore important issues/ problems ~ *Don't just bury your head in the sand—do something about it!*

put one's heart into something: do something enthusiastically; with sincerity ~ *She's put her heart into this project.*

put someone's mind at ease/rest: cause/help someone to stop worrying ~ *1a) I can put my mind at ease now I know they're safe. 1b) His reassuring words helped to put her mind at rest.*

put one's mind to something: be mentally strong; concentrate fully on the task ~ *I could have done better in the exam if I'd put my mind to it.*

put one's thinking cap on: think hard/seriously about something ~ *If we put our thinking caps on we should be able to work it out.*

put oneself out: make a considerable effort to do something at one's own expense ~ *Are you sure it's okay? I don't want you to put yourself out just for me.*

(be) put under: be anaesthetised ~ *I'll have to put you under to mend the fracture.* *also: be put to sleep

(be) put out: 1) be inconvenienced/troubled ~ *I don't want you to be put out by our visit.*

2) be offended/annoyed ~ *I was put out by their rude behaviour.*

put out: 1) extinguish ~ *It took firemen two hours to put out the fire.*

2) publish/issue/release information ~ *The couple put out a statement denying rumour of a split.*

3) extend/stretch ~ *I instinctively put my arm out to stop myself from falling.*

put out feelers: find other people's opinion of something before making a decision ~ *I'll put the feelers out as to where we'll meet.*

put one's back/shoulder/joint out: to injure/sprain ~ *He put his back out lifting a cabinet.*

put the word out: tell people about something ~ *He quickly put the word out that she'd had the baby.* *also: spread the word

put paid to: end/finish something ~ *An injury put paid to his sporting career.*

put in(to) place: in the correct position/order ~ *We rushed around and put everything into place before the guests arrived.*

put someone in their place: remind someone of their position/rank ~ *A sharp reprimand soon put the impertinent teenager in her place.*

put simply: [spoken interjection] when you want to simplify a lengthy explanation ~ *To put it simply, they're broke.*

put/set someone straight: correct someone by providing accurate information ~ *Thanks for putting me straight on that issue.*

put to shame: disgrace someone by displaying one's own superior skill/talent ~ *Frank, who's in his eighties, put everyone else to shame by being the first to reach the summit.*

put someone/one up: accommodate someone for a short time ~ *My cousin kindly put me up for a couple of nights.*

put someone up to something: encourage someone to do something act ~ *It was Ben who put him up to it.*

put the bite/squeeze/heat on: pressure someone to give you money ~ *We'll have to put the squeeze on Dad for the extra ten dollars.*

put (the) pressure on: strongly influence/affect something/someone ~ *This has put pressure on the government to change its policy.*

put the wind up someone: make someone feel worried/anxious about something ~ *Talk of redundancies has really put the wind up the employees.*

put things right: correct something; make amends ~ *1a) He wanted to put things right by donating his time to help the needy. 1b) The company's finances were in a mess, but the new financial director soon put things right.*

put together: build/assemble/create ~ *1a) They put together a team of experts to help tackle the immediate problems. 1b) The event was put together by a group of aspiring musicians.*

put to sleep: 1) subject something to euthanasia ~ *Her elderly and ailing cat had to be put to sleep.* *also: put down

2) subject someone to anaesthesia; cause to sleep ~ *2a) The anaesthetic put her to sleep in seconds. 2b) His long speech was putting everyone to sleep.*

put to the test: find out something/someone's capabilities ~ *1a) It's time to put my new invention to the test. 1b) Your knowledge of the subject will be put to the test.*

put someone through something: cause someone to experience/ do something unpleasant/difficult ~ *We were put through a series of rigorous tests.*

put something through something: test something ~ *The mechanic put the engine through various tests before finding the cause of the problem.*

put someone through school/college/uni: pay for someone's education ~ *I was lucky that my parents were able to put me through uni.*

(be) put through the wringer: undergo/experience an extremely difficult ordeal ~ *I felt as if I'd been put through the wringer by the time I'd finished.*

(be) put through (to): be connected (on the phone) to the person you wish to speak with ~ *Could you please put me through to Sandra?*

put through paces: demonstrate a variety of skills to test ability ~ *1a) The rider put her horse through its paces before the judges. 1b) The coach put the players through their paces.*

put two and two together: draw conclusions from existing indications/evidence ~ *We put two and two together and discovered who was responsible.* *also: add two and two together

put up: 1) build/erect something ~ *We had to put the tent up in the rain.*

2) provide funds in advance ~ *Dad put up half the money for the car.*

3) offer for sale ~ *They've decided to put their house up for sale.*

4) provide lodgings for ~ *I'll put you up for the night.*

put up with: tolerate/bear/endure (without complaint) ~ *1a) I can't put up with that noise any longer! 1b) There's not much you can do, you'll just have to put up with it for now.*

put up or shut up: [spoken] blunt request to stop about something and take action ~ *You've been complaining about it for months. Either put up or shut up!*

put (it) upon: burden oneself ~ *He put it upon himself to organise the event.*

you're putting me on: [spoken] said when you think someone is tricking you ~ *They did what? Oh, you're putting me on!*

putty in one's hands: of someone to be compliant; easily influenced ~ *He's so madly in love with her he's like putty in her hands.*

Q

QLD: the state of Queensland

quack: [informal] medical doctor

quads: quadruplets - four babies born at one time

quad bike: a four-wheeled motorbike

Queenslander: 1) a resident or native of Queensland

2) house style designed to have a cooling effect against the hot Queensland sun

question mark: expressing uncertainty/doubt ~ *A question mark hangs over his future as a professional player.*

queue up: stand in a queue/line; form a line/queue ~ *Customers were queuing up out the door and up the street.*

quick as a flash/wink: very quickly ~ *Quick as a flash he grabbed it and disappeared.*

quick march: [spoken] request to hurry up/move quickly ~ *Come on, quick march—let's go!* *see also: hop to it

quick off the mark: quick to react/do something ~ *Sally's always quick off the mark answering the questions.*

quick smart: at once; promptly ~ *You'll need to do it quick smart!*

quickie: a hurried/quick/short sexual encounter involving intercourse

quid: Australian currency before decimalisation; [informal] dollar

do for a quid: the job you do to earn money ~ *What do you do for a quid?*

cost a quid: cost a substantial amount of money (usually said as an understatement) ~ *That would have cost them a quid or two.*

not the full quid: [informal] unintelligent; mentally defective ~ *He's not the full quid.* *also: missing a few kangaroos in the top paddock; not the full loaf; not playing with a full deck; a sandwich short of a picnic

(not) for quids: never/under no circumstances ~ *I wouldn't live there for quids.*

not worth a quid: worthless ~ *That old car Tim's got for sale is not worth a quid.*

make a few quid out of: make a bit of money ~ *It's not a very profitable business, but he makes a few quid out of it.*

(make/earn) a quick quid/dollar: to make money without much effort, often dishonestly ~ *He was nothing more than a con-man wanting to make quick quid out of scamming vulnerable residents.*

wouldn't be dead for quids: [spoken] happy with life/to be alive ~ *What a great life—I wouldn't be dead for quids.*

be quiet: [spoken] used to tell someone to stop talking/making a noise ~ *Please be quiet!*

quit harping: [spoken] a way of telling someone to stop whinging/complaining ~ *Oh, will you quit harping on about it!*

quit it: [spoken] blunt request for someone to stop/cease doing something ~ *Just quit it, will you!*

quite a few: a reasonable/considerable amount ~ *There's quite a few left.*

Quokka: Found in Western Australia on Rottnest Island near Perth and in small groups in bushland around Perth, the quokka resembles a small wallaby. It has small, rounded ears and brownish-grey fur. They thrive in a warm climate and live in tall grasses in the bushland. They feed at night on native grasses and leaves, and can survive long periods without water.

Quoll: Quolls are furry, carnivorous marsupials with long tails, pointed noses, and have brown to black coloured fur with distinctive white spots. Early settlers to Australia called them native cats because of their similarities with European animals. There are four species of quoll: the spotted-tail, northern, eastern, and western. Once only one species of quoll inhabited most parts of Australia, but now the numbers have declined dramatically due to habitat loss and introduced species such as foxes and domestic cats. Like most Australian mammals, quolls actively hunt at night, with the smaller quolls eating frogs, birds, lizards, and insects, and the larger quolls eating birds, reptiles, bandicoots, possums, echidnas, and rabbits. The eastern quoll is found only in Tasmania, the north quoll in tropical north Queensland, the western quoll in southern Western Australia, and the spotted-tail quoll along the East Coast.

R

RAAF: Royal Australian Air Force

a race against time: (be) in a rush to do something ~ *With his injuries worsening, it became a race against time to get him to the hospital.*

race off: 1) leave/depart quickly ~ *Realising he was late, he raced off home.*

2) [informal] seduce someone

race off with: snatch and steal ~ *He came into the shop and raced off with as many expensive items as he could carry.*

race through: 1) perform a task rapidly ~ *Eager to go out on a date, she carelessly raced through her work.*

2) run/move through a place ~ *The fierce fire raced menacingly through the treetops.* *also: rush through

not be out of the race: have an equal chance of achievement ~ *We may have suffered a set-back, but we're not out of the race yet.* *also: be still in the race

not in the race: have no possibility of winning ~ *Most of the competing businesses are not in the race to secure the market because their products and services are inferior.*

human race: mankind; all people as a group

(the) races: a series of horse races that happen at one place on a particular day ~ *I won $200 at the races!*

rack and ruin: in a state of neglect/disrepair ~ *The house has gone to rack and ruin.*

rack off: 1) [spoken] strong command to go/leave ~ *Just rack off, will you!*

2) leave/depart quickly ~ *They racked off school at lunchtime.*

rack up: amass/tally/accumulate ~ *1a) Last season she racked up fifty points for the team. 1b)We racked up hundreds of kilometres.*

Rafferty's rules: have no rules ~ *He plays by Rafferty's rules.*

rag: a newspaper of poor quality

rag trade: the clothing manufacturing business

from rags to riches: a person's rise from extreme poverty to extreme wealth ~ *1a) They hit the lottery and went from rags to riches. 1b)Theirs is a true rags-to-riches story.*

rage: an entertaining social event/occasion ~ *The party was a rage!*

all the rage: something popular/fashionable ~ *Shoulder pads were all the rage in the eighties.*

take a rain check: refuse/decline an offer and suggest you'll take it up at a later date ~ *I'll have to take a rain check on your dinner invitation. I'm rather busy right now.*

raining cats and dogs: raining steadily and heavily ~ *We can't go out now, it's raining cats and dogs.*

rainy day: a (future) time of financial need ~ *She's saving for a rainy day.*

raise/sound the alarm: alert people to impending danger ~ *It was Nick who raised the alarm.*

raise (one's) eyebrows: facial expression (make the eyebrows go higher) to show surprise/interest/disbelief ~ *His outrageous comments caused many raised eyebrows.*

raise a family: rear; bring up ~ *It's a struggle raising a family on one salary.*

raise one's glass: drink to someone's health

raise hell: cause/provoke trouble ~ *He raised hell with the injustice done to him.*

raise/lift hopes: to feel/make someone feel that what they expect/hope to happen will happen ~ *Don't tell him about it until it's been confirmed. I don't want to raise his hopes.*

raise a laugh: cause others to laugh ~ *His weak jokes didn't raise a laugh.*

raise the question: put forward for consideration ~ *Tim raised the question of what would happen if he quit.*

raise the roof: 1) make a lot of noise ~ *The lively music raised the roof.*

2) complain loudly ~ *He's going to raise the roof when he finds out.*

raise a smile: cause someone to react by smiling ~ *Frank's attempt at comedy barely raised a smile.*

raise one's voice: speak loudly and angrily ~ *I would rather you didn't raise your voice.*

rake in: earn/acquire large quantities of money ~ *The company raked in millions of dollars in profits.*

rake over the coals: severely reprimand someone ~ *Their wayward son was raked over the coals for behaving badly.*

rake up: 1) revive; mention a past event that someone might not want to talk about ~ *He tried to rake up any scandalous stories involving his political rival.*

2) use a rake to clear leaves/debris on the ground ~ *They raked up all the leaves into a huge pile.*

3) accumulate ~ *I managed to rake up enough money for a deposit.*

rally around: gather in a group to offer support to someone ~ *Friends and neighbours rallied around the family.*

ramble on: talk endlessly so as to bore your listeners ~ *I've no idea what he's rambling on about.* *see also: go on about

rank and file: ordinary members of an organisation; people who form the major part of a group (excluding leaders) ~ *A new leader was voted in by the rank and file members of the company.*

rant and rave: speak in a violent/angry manner ~ *He ranted and raved at first, but soon calmed down.*

rap across/over the knuckles: 1) strike/hit someone's knuckles

2) light punishment ~ *The punishment they gave him was akin to a rap across the knuckles.*

rare as hen's teeth: so rare as to be almost non-existent; very rare ~ *Please don't lose them. They're as rare as hen's teeth.* *also: scarce as hen's teeth

raring to go: eager/ready to proceed/begin ~ *She's all packed and raring to go.**also: ready and raring to go

rash vest: Commonly known as a rashie, these short- or long-sleeved shirts, made of spandex and nylon or polyester, are used for water sports and an array of outdoor sports and activities. Its main purpose is to prevent chaffing and irritation to the skin while surfing or by impact with surface water or waves. Rashies also have an ultraviolet protection factor to offer protection from the harsh Australian sun.

rat race: continual/tiring competitive routine; frantic pace ~ *They were looking forward to retiring and getting out of the rat race.*

rats: a mild expletive *see also: darn

give a rat's arse: [offensive slang] *see also: give a toss/give two hoots

ratbag: an unpleasant or disagreeable person; troublemaker ~ *1a) That ratbag Frank used my car without asking me. 1b) I wouldn't put it past him to do something like that, he's a real ratbag!* *also: ratfink

rattle around: 1) cause to make a rattling noise whilst moving around in an area/space ~ *There's something rattling around in the back of the car.*

2) occupy a space that's too big ~ *Poor dear, all he's done is rattle around in that old house since his wife died.*

rattle off: recite/utter/perform rapidly and effortlessly ~ *She could rattle off the names of all the students in all the classes.*

rave about: extravagantly/enthusiastically praise/review something ~ *She can't stop raving about her new boyfriend!*

rave on: talk non-stop/endlessly/tediously ~ *What are your raving on about?* *also: babble on

raving lunatic/idiot: someone acting as if they were completely mad ~ *He's behaving like a raving lunatic!*

raw talent: powerful, impressive talent ~ *It was a display of raw talent, the likes of which hadn't been seen for a long time.*

raw deal: an instance of unfair/unjust treatment ~ *The changes means some workers will be getting a raw deal.* *also: the rough end of a pineapple

in the raw: naked; without clothes *see also: in the nuddy

razzle-dazzle: excitement/theatrics; bright/showy appeal ~ *A little bit of razzle-dazzle will liven up the performance.*

RBT: Random Breath Testing, a roadside test conducted by the police to measure the amount of alcohol a person has consumed/ has in their system

read between the lines: read what is implied; detect an unexpressed/obscure meaning ~ *Reading between the lines, I'd say they've got marital problems.*

read into something: interpret meanings/actions not inferred ~ *I read too much into her behaviour.*

read someone like a book: easily understand someone's motives/character; anticipate what they might think, say, or do ~ *I know you're lying because I can read you like a book.*

read someone's mind: know intuitively what someone is thinking ~ *I knew you were going to ask me that because I can read your mind.*

read the riot act: remind someone of the consequences of their actions ~ *Dad read me the riot act before letting me go to the party.*

read through: (to) read all of something ~ *I'll read through the report tonight.*

read up on: acquire information by reading ~ *I'm reading up on the countries we'll be visiting.*

take as read: assume something (without the need for further discussion) ~ *I'll take it as read that you all agree.*

you wouldn't read about it: [spoken] a way of expressing disbelief/incredulity ~ *What happened at the meeting last night? Oh, you wouldn't read about it.*

good and ready: thoroughly ready ~ *I won't do it until I'm good and ready.*

face up to reality: accept the state of things as they exist ~ *You have to face up to reality and accept that he's never coming back.*

in reality: actually/ in actual fact ~ *Theoretically it was easy enough to do, but in reality, it was very difficult.*

really: [spoken] expression of annoyance or surprise ~ *1a) Oh, really? 1b) Really—did you have to say that?*

reckon: suppose/think/conclude ~ *I reckon we'll get there first.*

for the record: 1) [spoken] that what you're about to say is to be officially recorded/noted and made public ~ *What I'm about to say is for the record.*

2) make sure you understand me; let me make myself clear ~ *For the record, I didn't vote for her.*

go on record: state one's views publicly ~ *He went on record as having no knowledge of their plans.* *also: for the record

off the record: not for publication ~ *He warned the reporter that those comments are to remain strictly off the record.*

red light camera: a permanent camera fixture set to record drivers who proceed through a red traffic light

red light district: an area of a city where there are brothels

red tape: excess official rules and formalities ~ *Red tape held up the application process.*

Redback Spider: Widespread across Australia and commonly found in habitats ranging from urban areas to bushland, the redback spider is one of Australia's most recognisable species. In the bush, they nest under logs and rocks and they can be found in undisturbed machinery, outdoor furniture, and in dry places around buildings. The mature female—jet black with a variable red stripe on her spherical abdomen—rarely leaves the web and is not aggressive, but is likely to bite when a part of one's body comes in contact with her. A bite from the spider may be life-threatening, so urgent medical treatment is advised. An effective anti-venom is readily available at any hospital emergency room. The spiders mainly feed on insects, and sometimes lizards and mice, and the tiny male will be eaten by the female after mating. Spiderlings, which emerge after two weeks, will be dispersed on the wind, thus recolonising in faraway places.

reel off: recall/repeat information from memory ~ *He easily reeled off all the items on the list.*

ref: referee

refrain from doing something: try to stop doing something ~ *1a) Please refrain from smoking in the building. 1b) I refrained from telling her what I really thought about the situation.*

rein in: keep under control ~ *She fought hard to rein in her emotions.*

(have) free rein: have permission to do a particular job the way you think best ~ *I have to follow some guidelines, but I'm given free rein in regards to the use of graphics.*

hold/take over the reins: be in control of something ~ *She takes over the reins next week.*

refuse point blank: refuse outright/completely ~ *He refused point blank to do it.*

rego: motor vehicle registration ~ *When's the rego due?*

rego check: when a mechanic inspects a vehicle for road worthiness before it can be re-registered

(a) regular: a regular customer ~ *He's been a regular at the café for years.*

rellies: relatives ~ *All the rellies were there.*

remind (oneself) of: to appear similar in looks and mannerisms ~ *You remind me of my uncle.*

rep: representative (travelling salesman/company representative) ~ *She's a sales rep for an electronics firm.*

repeat on oneself: when food makes you burp/belch; have an aftertaste ~ *My spicy lunch is repeating on me.*

repeat yourself: say or write the same thing ~ *1a) Listen carefully to the instructions. I don't want to have to repeat myself. 1b) Grandma often forgets what she's said and repeats herself.*

resort to: what you are forced to do when no other options are available ~ *Having missed the last bus and with no money for a cab, they resorted to walking home.*

R&R: rest and relaxation ~ *She's enjoying a bit of R&R at the moment.*

rest assured: [spoken] expression of reassurance ~ *You can rest assured we'll find the people responsible for the attack.*

rest on something: consider/ponder something ~ *I'll rest on it overnight and give you an answer tomorrow.*

resting place: a place where a person or animal can rest ~ *The hiker went in search of a resting place.*

restroom: toilet; bathroom; public toilet; ladies; gents

rest up: rest so as to recuperate/recover ~ *Let's rest up. I'm exhausted.*

rest with (someone): be someone's responsibility ~ *The final decision rests with the members of the board.*

at rest: 1) inactive/motionless ~ *Blood pressure is best taken when the patient is at rest.*

2) asleep/dead

3) calm/tranquil ~ *If you're worried, see a doctor and put your mind at rest.*

come to rest: come to a stop/stop moving ~ *The car skidded across the road and came to rest on the grass verge.*

final resting place: one's burial place

returned soldier: a soldier who has served overseas/abroad

revs: revolutions of an engine/motor per minute

rev up: speed up; accelerate ~ *The race car drivers revved up their engines before the start of the race.*

rev-head: motorsport enthusiast *also: petrol-head

no rhyme or reason: lacking sense/meaning/logic ~ *There's no rhyme or reason for doing it.*

rib someone: make fun of; tease; ridicule in a friendly way ~ *My friends rib me all the time about my lack of height.*

riddled with: spread throughout/filled with ~ *1a) His story is riddled with inconsistencies. 1b) The door was riddled with bullet holes.*

ride around: move/travel about as a passenger ~ *The kids love to ride around the neighbourhood on their bikes.*

ride out: endure/sustain successfully ~ *With nowhere to shelter, we had little choice but to ride out the storm.*

ride up: of clothing, a belt/restraint to move higher (out of position) ~ *This too-small jacket keeps riding up my back.*

let something ride: not take action on something; leave it as such ~ *I let his derogatory remarks ride.*

ridgy-didge: genuine; original ~ *It's a ridgy-didge boomerang.*

rig up: erect; assemble as a temporary measure ~ *We rigged up some coloured lights for the party.*

rig something: manipulate dishonestly (to gain an advantage); fraudulently tamper with ~ *The race was rigged.*

right: total; proper; absolute ~ *He's a right idiot!*

right as rain: 1) in good health ~ *Rest for a few days and you'll be as right as rain.*

2) okay/in good order ~ *I had some repair work done on it, and it's been as right as rain ever since.*

right around: fully encircling something; a full circumference ~ *1a) The snake curled itself right around my arm. 1b) You need to turn it right around so it faces the opposite direction.*

right away/off: at once; without delay; immediately ~ *I'll do it right away.* *also: right/straight off the bat

right behind someone: to back/support them ~ *I'm right behind you in whatever career choice you make.*

right on: 1) [spoken] exclamation of encouragement/support; an enthusiastic agreement

2) exact; correct; true ~ *You're estimate was right on.* *also: spot on

(be) right on someone's arse/bum/bottom: [informal] be driving close to the car in front ~ *I couldn't make the turn because there was someone right on my bum.*

right on target: correct/accurate ~ *This month's financial budget was right on target.*

right slap bang in the middle: exactly in the middle/centre ~ *You can't miss it. It's right slap bang in the middle of the city.*

right royal: absolute/total/proper ~ *This is one right royal mess you've got us into!*

(the) right way up: 1) facing right side up; not upside down ~ *Stand it the right way up or it might leak.*

right wing: have/hold conservative political views

God-given right: a perceived right to do what you want ~ *He thinks it's his God-given right to play loud music all night.* *also: divine right

right mind: [spoken] sane/rational/sensible ~ *No one in their right mind would want to attempt that!*

make all the right noises: indicate one's approval; say what you're expected to say ~ *They certainly made all the right noises indicating they liked my presentation.*

(a) step in the right direction: an action taken that will bring good results ~ *It may not solve all their problems but it's a step in the right direction.*

too right: [spoken] definitely/unequivocally ~ *Too right I'll be there!*

you right: [spoken] a way of asking if someone if they're alright/okay/in need of help ~ *You right, mate? Do you need some help?*

rightly or wrongly: that something is true/factual though but not justifiable ~ *Rightly or wrongly, we have to abide by the new regulations.* *also: right or wrong

rightly so: [spoken] that a decision/action is justified ~ *Everyone complained about the changes—and rightly so!*

(I) don't rightly know/can't rightly say: [spoken] that you're unsure if something is true/correct or not ~ *Is what John said true? I don't rightly know.*

right-side up: 1) correctly orientated ~ *Luckily my phone landed right-side up.*

2) with the top facing upwards ~ *Please place the box right-side up.* *also: right way up

right(y)-oh: [spoken] expression of agreement; a way of saying yes/alright/okay (used at the end of a conversation) ~ *1a) Righty-oh then, I'll see you tomorrow. 1b) Right-oh, I'll be there soon.* *also: rightio; righty-ho

riled up: extremely annoyed/angry ~ *Her comments got me all riled up!*

ring: *see: phone/call

ring a bell: of something/someone that appears familiar or reminds you of someone/something ~ *1a) No, that name doesn't ring a bell. 1b) Something about the picture rings a bell, but I don't know why.* *also: strike a chord

ring around: call a succession of people on the telephone ~ *I'll ring around and let everyone know what's happened.*

ring true: seem genuine/honest/sincere ~ *Her story rings true.*

ring (someone) up: call someone on the telephone ~ *I'll ring them up when I get home.* *also: call; phone

ringer: 1) a farm worker who specialises in working with cattle

2) a sheep shearer who can shear sheep the quickest

ring-in: a (last-minute) fraudulent substitute ~ *There was an uproar when it was discovered the winning horse was a ring-in for another.*

riot: someone/something/a situation that causes hilarity/ amusement ~ *His new girlfriend is a riot!*

(a) rip: an ocean undertow; a tidal under-current ~ *The main role of a life-saver is to help swimmers caught in a rip.*

rip into someone: severely attack/criticize someone ~ *She ripped into me in front of everyone!*

rip up: tear into pieces/shreds ~ *He ripped up the contract.*

let rip: get very angry about something ~ *When she found out about it, she just let rip!* *also: let fly

(get) ripped off: be cheated/defrauded/swindled/tricked ~ *They were ripped off by a fraudulent investment scam.*

rip something off: steal something ~ *Cars in this area get ripped off all the time.*

rip-roaring: boisterous/exciting ~ *We had a rip-roaring time!*

ripper: splendid/excellent/fantastic ~ *1a) We had a ripper time! 1b) It was a ripper of a party! 1c) You little ripper—he won!* *also: corker/beaut

rise above something: to not allow something to affect/influence your behaviour ~ *She rose above those who criticised her work to became a well-known artist.*

rise (up) against: challenge/confront/rebel ~ *1a) The angry citizens began rising up against the oppressive regime. 1b) He rose up against his attacker.*

rise and shine: [spoken] a cheery wake-up call ~ *Wakey, wakey—rise and shine!*

(a) rise in . . . : an increase in something ~ *1a) He predicted a rise in petrol prices. 1b) There's been a rise in the number of people using the service.*

rise to one's feet: to stand ~ *The audience rose to its feet, cheering and clapping.*

rise to the occasion: 1) do what is expected/needed at the time ~ *The company rose to the occasion by providing financial help.*

2) meet a challenge ~ *He was at a disadvantage but he rose to the occasion and came third.* *also: rise to the challenge

rise to the top/surface: ascend from below and break the surface ~ *1a) The bloated animal carcass rose to the surface. 1b) Watch as the cream rises to the top.*

rise up (above): 1) ascend ~ *The mist rose up out of the valley.*

2) ascend higher than something ~ *2a) The balloon rose up above the tree. 2b) We watched as the big yellow moon rose up above the horizon.*

get a rise out of someone: (humorously) tease someone so as to provoke a response ~ *I tried telling some funny jokes, but I couldn't get a rise out of him.*

give rise to: cause to occur/exist/happen ~ *Her death gave rise to an unprecedented outpouring of grief.*

risk one's neck: do something risky ~ *I'm not prepared to risk my neck for anyone.*

at risk: exposed to danger/harm ~ *. . . a sport that puts you at risk of serious injury.*

road hog: a reckless driver who occupies a part of two lanes ~ *The road hog in front won't let me pass!*

road sense: show good judgement/awareness when driving/walking/cycling on the road ~ *He's too young to walk there by himself, he has no road sense.*

road train: a series of linked trailers pulled by a truck, used for transporting goods

by road: travel (in a vehicle) on a road ~ *It's a four-hour journey by road.*

go down that road: choose a particular action ~ *Some of his friends urged him to take drugs, but he didn't want to go down that road.*

(be) in the road: be positioned so as to obstruct someone's passage/vision ~ *I can't see the TV because your head's in the road.* *also: in the way

on the road: 1) travelling in a vehicle for a long distance or for a long period of time ~ *The band has been on the road for a month now performing in many cities.*

2) moving from place to place because you have no permanent home ~ *The work he does means he's often on the road for months at a time.*

on the road to recovery: in the process of recovering from an illness/injury ~ *She's doing well after surgery and is on the road to recovery.*

one for the road: [spoken] an alcoholic drink consumed quickly before you leave a place) ~ *Would you like one for the road?*

middle-of-the-road: of popular music having a wide appeal ~ *The station mainly plays middle-of-the-road music.*

roam around: wander aimlessly ~ *The child was found roaming around the streets.*

roar off: leave noisily in a vehicle ~ *He roared off in anger.*

roaring success: something that was very successful ~ *The event was a roaring success.*

give someone a roasting: subject to criticism/ridicule ~ *The performance was given a roasting.*

rock on: continue celebrations ~ *Some left at 1 a.m., and the rest of us rocked on until 3 a.m.*

rock on down/over/up: go/travel to a place ~ *1a) We're having a party tonight, why don't you rock on over? 1b) As soon as you get to my house, we'll rock on down to the pub.*

rock the boat: say something to upset the status quo; destabilise a situation ~ *Now, don't rock the boat by saying something stupid.*

rock up: arrive unannounced; make a surprise visit ~ *There's no real starting time, just rock up whenever you want.* *also: roll up

roll along: of something to progress smoothly ~ *Things are rolling along nicely.*

roll around: move by rolling ~ *1a) Marbles were rolling around everywhere. 1b) His eyes were rolling around in his head.*

roll by: of time to pass/elapse ~ *Years rolled by and when I saw him again he was old and frail.*

rolling in the aisles: of an audience in a theatre to laugh uncontrollably/wildly ~ *Her performance had them rolling in the aisles.*

roll off: 1) be produced in a factory ~ *The latest model should be rolling off the assembly line next month.*

2) recite volubly ~ *A barrage of expletives rolled off his tongue.*

rolled into one: combined ~ *It's a mattress and sleeping bag all rolled into one.*

roll over in one's grave: that someone who is dead would be offended by something happening/said ~ *He'd roll over in his grave if he knew they were demolishing the house.*

roll up: arrive at an event ~ *There's no set time, just roll up whenever you want.*

roll up one's sleeves: prepare for hard work ~ *Knowing what had to be done, he simply rolled up his sleeves and got to it.*

rolling in dough/money/cash: to have a lot of money ~ *They must be rolling in money if they can afford a house on the harbour foreshore.*

(I'm) ready to roll: [spoken] said to indicate that you're go somewhere ~ *I'm ready to roll—let's go!*

Rolls/Roller: Rolls-Royce car

Rolls-Royce of: top class/quality product ~ *It's the Rolls-Royce of computers.*

romp home: easily win a race or competition ~ *Our team romped home to win a spot in the semi-finals.*

romp in the hay: humorous term for sexual intercourse

romp in: *see: romp home

'r on/ron: later on ~ *I'll see you 'r on!*

roo: kangaroo

roof over one's head: a place to live ~ *We don't have many luxuries, but at least we have a roof over our heads and food on the table.*

under the same roof: in the same house/building ~ *They were living in crowded accommodations, with two or more families under the same roof.*

under one's roof: in one's home ~ *As long as you're living under my roof there'll be no swearing.*

room to move: plenty of space ~ *We had a large office with plenty of room to move.* *also: elbow room; room to swing a cat

root out: remove/eliminate a person or thing that is causing problems ~ *Authorities are determined to root out corruption within the organisation.*

rooted to the spot: *see: glued to the spot

rope someone in: persuade/lure/entice someone to participate in something ~ *I was roped in to doing it.*

ropable: very angry/livid/furious ~ *She was ropable when she found out what they'd done.*

rort: 1) take unfair advantage of something ~ *He knew how to rort the system.*

2) an illicit/dishonest scheme ~ *The cash prize giveaway scheme was a rort.*

rose among thorns: something gentle/soft among something rough/thorny (usually said of the only female in the company of men)

Rosella: Rosellas are colourful parrots native to Australia, from the family *Platycercus*, which means "broad" or "flat-tailed." They inhabit bushland, farmland, and suburban parks and gardens on the coastal fringes. They cannot be found inland or in the outback. Of the four species, the crimson rosella perhaps has the most distinct markings, with a bright crimson-red body and deep blue wings with pale blue outer feathers. Rosellas nest in high tree hollows and feed on eucalyptus seeds, grasses, insects, and tree blossoms. They are easily attracted to seed trays placed in gardens and can easily become familiar enough with humans to eat out of their hands.

come up roses: produce a successful/favourable result ~ *We've had a few setbacks, but everything's come up roses.*

no bed of roses: an unpleasant/difficult situation (said in the negative) ~ *The task ahead of you will be no bed of roses.*

put/have a rose in one's cheek: to have a healthy glow/ appearance ~ *Here, this will put a rose in your cheeks.*

rot: 1) [spoken] exclamation of scorn/ridicule/contempt ~ *What a lot of rot!*

2) nonsense; rubbish ~ *He's talking rot.*

rot away: decompose (and fall away) ~ *The timber supports had rotted away.*

rot in hell: be forever cursed/damned ~ *I hope they rot in hell!*

(the) rot sets in: when a situation begins to worsen ~ *The rot set in when communication broke down.*

rot your socks: [spoken] expression of disappointment/disgust ~ *That this area has been overlooked once again for transport upgrades really rots your socks.*

rotten sod: morally despicable ~ *He's a rotten sod the way he treated her.* *also: rotter

rotten to the core: totally despicable; having no morals ~ *I'm glad that creep is in jail—he's rotten to the core!*

rough around the edges: an unsophisticated/unrefined but likeable person ~ *He's a nice guy, but a bit rough around the edges.* *also: rough diamond

rough as guts: 1) of a machine not running smoothly ~ *This motor needs tuning—it's running as rough as guts.*

2) uncouth/crude

rough guess: a quick estimation ~ *At a rough guess, I'd say four hours.*

rough it: be without the usual conveniences/comforts ~ *Jack's been roughing it in the bush for a week.*

(be) rough on: treat harshly ~ *1a) I don't know why they were so rough on him for a minor offence. 1b) This dirt road is rough on the car's suspension.*

rough road: a difficult period/passage of time; difficult circumstances ~ *It will be a rough road for many people until the current financial crisis is over.*

rough someone up: use physical violence against someone ~ *He roughed up his rival as a warning.*

rough stuff: physical force/violence ~ *It's almost certain there'll be some rough stuff when those two teams meet on the field.*

rough trot: difficult circumstances; bad luck/misfortune ~ *She's had a rough trot, poor thing.*

rough-and-ready: makeshift; unpolished, but complete and ready for use ~ *It's a bit rough and ready, but it'll do the job for now.*

rough-and-tumble: 1) playful wrestling ~ *The brothers often engage in a bit of rough-and-tumble.*

2) busy activity done in a forceful way ~ *He thrives on the rough-and-tumble of politics.*

round (of drinks): a custom where each individual in a group takes turns to buy a drink for everyone else in the group ~ *This round's on me.*

do/make the rounds: 1) go from place to place ~ *I've done the rounds of all the bookshops in the area, but no one has a copy of the book you're after.*

2) pass from person to person ~ *There's a rumour doing the rounds that Ted's leaving next week.*

(all) year round: operating/continuing throughout the whole year ~ *They're open all year round.*

(a)round about: approximately ~ *It's going to cost 'round about $50 per person.**also: roughly

round and round: in circles ~ *We drove round and round looking for the house.**also: around and around

round figures/numbers: numbers adjusted to the nearest ten

round up: 1) gather people/things/animals in one place ~ *His trusty working dogs quickly rounded up the stray cattle.*

2) increase an amount to the next highest number

go round the bend/twist: go crazy/insane ~ *I can't remember where I put them. I must be going round the bend!*

roundabout: a circular road junction in which the traffic moves in one direction, around a central island

rouse on: reprimand/scold someone ~ *I roused on her for being late.*

RSL Club: Returned Services League, a national institution honouring returned service men and women

RSPCA: Royal Society for the Prevention of Cruelty to Animals. This national association is the leading authority in animal care and protection, and its aim is to prevent cruelty to animals by promoting their care and protection.

RSVP: an indication (on a letter or invitation) to please reply **repondez s'il vous plait* (French)

rub off on: a skill/interest/quality learned or passed on without effort ~ *His love of music has rubbed off on his children.*

rub salt into the wound: make a difficult situation worse ~ *Losing her was bad enough, but to rub salt into the wound, she started dating the handsome school captain.* *also: rub someone's face in it; rub it in

rub up the wrong way: annoy/irritate someone without intending to ~ *His attitude rubs me up the wrong way.*

rubber: eraser

rubber cheque: a cheque that "bounces"; a dishonoured cheque

rubber duckie: an inflatable rubber boat

rubberneck: sightseer/tourist who takes a curious look at something ~ *Rescue efforts were hampered by people rubbernecking at the accident scene.*

rubbish: 1) trash/garbage

2) worthless talk; nonsense ~ *Don't believe anything he says. He's talking rubbish.*

rubbish bin: trash can/garbage bin

rubbish someone: attack strongly ~ *Critics were quick to rubbish his theory.*

ruffle someone's feathers: aggravate/annoy/irritate/someone ~ *His comments certainly ruffled a few feathers.*

rug up: wear warm clothing ~ *It's cold outside, you'd better rug up when you go out.*

Rugby League: a popular code of football played in Australia

Rugby Union: another popular code of football played in Australia

rule of thumb: an approximate/general rule/principle or procedure based on experience as opposed to a specific or scientific estimate or calculation ~ *A rule of thumb is to turn the oven off ten minutes before the specified cooking time.*

rule with an iron fist: to rule with absolute control/authority ~ *The department has a high staff turnover because the manager rules it with an iron fist.*

rule out: eliminate; stop considering something as a possibility ~ *The police ruled her out as a suspect.*

rule the roost: be the boss/leader of a group ~ *She's not the boss at work, but at home she rules the roost.*

rummage around: move things haphazardly whilst searching for something ~ *He rummaged around in the pantry looking for something to eat.* *also: rummage through; search through

rummage sale: *see: garage sale

rumour has it . . . : [spoken] unconfirmed facts; hearsay; general gossip ~ *Rumour has it that you won an award.* *also: word has it . . .

rump steak: beef steak from the hind quarters

rumpus room: an informal recreation room in a house

run a comb through one's hair: comb one's hair ~ *He quickly ran a comb through his hair before running out the door.*

run a fever: have a high body temperature (from an illness or sickness) ~ *I'm taking him to the doctor's, because he's running a fever.*

run a mile: do anything to avoid a situation ~ *At the mere mention of the words "hard work," he runs a mile.*

run a red light: proceed through an intersection against a red stop light

run a tight ship: control a business/organisation in a strict/firm manner ~ *John runs a tight ship, so be prepared to work hard.*

run across someone/something: meet; find unexpectedly ~ *1a) I ran across Sue at the conference. 1b) Did you happen to run across any good books at the flea market?*

run aground: of boats/ships to get stuck or stranded on the river/sea bed ~ *Many boats have run aground on that sandbank.*

run all over someone: be more skilled/adept; defeat easily/out-play ~ *The Tigers ran all over the Bears in last night's final.* *also: walk all over someone

run amok: behave/act dangerously or wildly ~ *A gang of drunken youths ran amok through the city centre.*

run/cast your eye over something: briefly look at something without paying attention to the details ~ *Could you run your eyes over my report?*

run around: go busily from place to place ~ *1a) I've been running around everywhere looking for you. 1b) He's tired from running around after the kids all morning.* *also: race around

run around with: spend time; keep company with someone ~ *Who do you run around with at school?*

run away: 1) escape/flee ~ *She ran away from home when she was a teenager.*

2) [spoken] request to go away ~ *Run away, will you, I'm busy!*

run(s) deep: strong and well established ~ *Resentment between them runs deep.*

run down: 1) unfairly criticize someone ~ *If you keep running her down, she's never going to gain confidence.*

2) hit and knock someone down with your car ~ *He was run down as he was crossing the road.*

run dry: become empty of water ~ *Because of the drought, many rivers and streams have run dry.*

run for: stand as a nominee/candidate for an authoritative position/role ~ *She's running for mayor.*

(give) a run for your money: be close competition ~ *I won the race, but my competitors certainly gave me a run for my money.*

run for cover: flee to shelter/safety ~ *We ran for cover when it started hailing.*

(make a) run for it: escape; flee ~ *He escaped and made a run for it.*

run hot: 1) successful/doing well ~ *Right now his acting career is running hot.*

2) (of the phone) to be active/busy ~ *The phones have been running hot since we placed the job advertisement.*

run(s) in the family: an ability/trait/quality that passes from generation to generation ~ *Mathematical ability seems to run in our family.*

run into: 1) (costs/figures) total; amount to ~ *Repair costs have run into the thousands.*

2) incur debt ~ *He's seeking financial help because he's run into debt.*

3) meet someone by chance ~ *I ran into Chris at the shops today.*

4) collide with something ~ *The car behind ran into the back of me.*

run its course: continue naturally until finished ~ *The doctor advised me to rest until the illness had run its course.*

run late: behind time/late ~ *1a) The bus is running late again! 1b) Sorry I can't stop and talk, I'm running very late.*

run like clockwork: to happen smoothly or exactly as planned ~ *The event ran like clockwork.* *also: go like clockwork

run low: of a supply of something to be nearly used up ~ *Water supplies are running low.*

(a) run of good/bad luck: a continuation/series of good/bad fortune ~ *I had a run of good luck coming home. I got all the green lights.* *also: streak/string of good/bad luck

run off: leave/depart suddenly ~ *He was last seen running off down the road.*

run off one's feet: excessively exhausted/weary/tired from busy activity ~ *It's good to sit down. I've been run off my feet all day.*

run off with: 1) pinch/steal/ pilfer something and run away ~ *The dog's run off with a sausage off the barbie!*

2) elope ~ *Did you know Brad's run off with Sally?*

(a) run on something: a period of great demand for something ~ *Because of the hot weather there's been a run on air conditioners.*

run on the smell of an oily rag: of a motor/engine to operate efficiently/use little fuel ~ *You won't need to spend much on petrol with this car, it runs on the smell of an oily rag.*

run out: 1) use all of something ~ *We quickly ran out of money!*

2) in the game of cricket, for a batsman to be dismissed

run out of steam/puff: suddenly lose energy; become exhausted/ weary ~ *He soon ran out of puff walking up the steep slope.*

run out on someone: abandon; desert someone in a time of need ~ *He ran out on me when I told him I was pregnant.*

run rings around someone: do something much better than someone else ~ *She runs rings around her opponents.*

run short of: have an insufficient supply of something ~ *Watch your spending—you don't want to run short of cash.*

run smoothly: operate/function without difficulties/delays ~ *Thankfully, the event ran smoothly.* *also: go off without a hitch

run something/someone down: unfairly criticize/belittle someone/something ~ *It seems he can't do anything right—she's always running him down.* *also: run into the ground

run someone ragged: make someone weary/exhausted by making them work too hard ~ *The coach ran us ragged at training tonight.* *also: run someone off their feet

run something past/by someone: briefly inform someone of something without revealing all the facts ~ *1a) I have to run the plans past the boss first. 1b) Could you run the plans by me again?*

run the risk (of): take a chance knowing the possible outcome/ result ~ *If you stray off the track you run the risk of getting lost.*

run the show: be in charge of an activity/organisation ~ *1a) Don't complain to me—Dave runs the show! 1b) Just who's running this show?!*

run through: 1) rehearse/practice quickly ~ *We'll need to run through the procedure again before we begin.*

2) use up quickly ~ *Jobless, she ran through her savings fairly quickly.*

run up: 1) accumulate a bill/debt ~ *We easily run up big phone bills speaking long distance.*

2) make something hastily ~ *It won't take her long to run up some curtains.*

run up against something/someone: encounter difficulties/ problems ~ *We ran up against a formidable opponent in our last game.*

run with it: adopt/accept a particular method/idea ~ *I think we should run with Jeff's plan.*

runners: *sports/tennis shoes; sandshoes; sneakers

do a runner: run away to avoid paying for something or to avoid capture ~ *The suspect did a runner, but was found a short time later.*

runner-up: second place; high-ranked; non-winning contestant ~ *We were runners-up in the tournament.*

running battle: an on-going disagreement/argument ~ *I'm having a running battle with them over noise complaints.*

running scared: in a state of fear/panic ~ *He's been running scared ever since some gang members threatened him.*

runny nose: mucous-like nasal discharge; a symptom of a common cold or allergy

(the) runs: [informal] diarrhoea

run-in: 1) angry dispute ~ *She's upset because she had a run-in with her boss.*

2) an unpleasant encounter ~ *This is not the first time he's had a run-in with the law.*

runabout: a small motorboat *also: tinny

rural setting: an area away from cities and towns ~ *They live in a delightful rural setting two hours from Sydney.*

rush through: 1) quickly move through an area ~ *Shoppers looking for a bargain rushed through the doors as soon as they opened.*

2) process something in a hurry ~ *The new law was rushed through parliament.*

rush-hour: *see: peak-hour

rust away: to dissolve into rust ~ *The guttering had rusted away.*

rust bucket: a rusted/dilapidated car ~ *He drives an old rust bucket.*

rustle up: get/make something quickly ~ *1a) He's trying to rustle up supporters for his candidacy. 1b) He quickly rustled up something for dinner.*

rusted through: completely eroded/rusted ~ *The car's bumper has rusted through in many places.*

rusty: out of practice; below standard ~ *I haven't played for a long time so I might be a bit rusty.*

(be) stuck in a rut: be in a situation that is difficult to get out of or change ~ *He was tired of being stuck in a rut made so he made some drastic lifestyle changes.*

S

SA: the state of South Australia

sack: one's bed

hit the sack: go to bed ~ *I came home and hit the sack.*

sad sack: someone who is morose/sad ~ *I don't know what's wrong—he's been a sad sack all day.*

saddle up: put a saddle on a horse in preparation to ride ~ *Why don't we saddle up and go for a ride?*

safe and sound: in good health/condition; unharmed ~ *1a) I snuggled up safe and sound in the warm bed. 1b) Your goods arrived safe and sound.*

safe as houses: very safe/secure ~ *Your money will be as safe as houses if you invest with us.*

safe bet: something that is certain to happen ~ *It's a safe bet they'll accept your proposal.*

safe in the knowledge: assured/secure/content knowing something ~ *I'll sleep better safe in the knowledge that they're safe.*

in safe hands: for someone/something to be cared for/looked after by someone trustworthy ~ *Your child will be in safe hands. The staff here are very experienced.*

(be) on the safe side: do something as a precaution ~ *We're going to take some spare equipment just to be on the safe side.* *also: play it safe

sail through: 1) move/travel through a land opening on a ship/boat ~ *Spectators watched as the Tall Ships sailed majestically through the heads.*

2) complete a task; easily succeed in something ~ *I sailed through the maths exam.*

salt of the earth: person/group of people held in high regard by others ~ *Sam's dedicated and hard-working—true salt of the earth.*

Salvation Army: an international charitable, evangelical organisation. *also: Salvos/Sallies

the same as: identical to something/someone ~ *1a) My car's the same as yours. 1b) I'm leaving at the same time as you.*

(the) same again: [spoken] said when ordering the same drink as the previous one ~ *I'll have the same again, thanks.*

same difference: that one thing is no different from another; the difference is not important ~ *Whether the red or the blue - it's the same difference.*

the same old, same old: of a dull/boring routine/habit that never changes ~ *Has anything exciting happened lately? No—everything's just the same old, same old.*

(the) same to you: [spoken] that the same comment applies (to the speaker) ~ *1a) I hope you do well in the exam. Thanks, Lisa, same to you. 1b) You're the rudest person I've ever met! Same to you, pal!*

all/just the same: act despite what happened/what was said ~ *1a) He said he'd done it, but I'll check it just the same. 1b) Some bits of the movie were boring, but I liked it all the same.*

all the same with: equally acceptable; that it makes no difference ~ *1a) We ought to leave soon if it's all the same with you. 1b) Sure, we can leave then—it's all the same with me.*

amount(s) to the same thing: that several different actions will produce the same outcome ~ *It matters not who does it, it amounts to the same thing.*

(a) sandwich short of a picnic: [informal] lacking in intelligence *also: have a few screws loose; have a few kangaroos loose in the top paddock

sanger: sandwich

save the day: do something that solves a problem ~ *We thought we'd go hungry, but James saved the day by bringing enough food and drinks for everyone.*

save up: accumulate/stash/save money ~ *I'm saving up to buy a car.*

saved by the bell: relieved of a difficult situation by a timely intervention ~ *The lesson ended before I got to do my speech. Saved by the bell!*

saw through something: cut with a saw ~ *Rescuers had to saw through a heavy beam to free him.*

. . . says it all: that something/someone's appearance expression shows clearly how they feel/what the situation is ~ *1a) The look of joy on his face says it all. 1b) The number of vacant shops here says it all.*

say no more: [spoken] that you understand the unspoken message and that you don't want to hear any more details ~ *You saw them getting into a taxi together? Say no more.*

say one's piece: openly express one's opinion ~ *I've said my piece, now I'll leave.*

say the wrong thing: say something inappropriate/improper/unsuitable ~ *I usually get nervous in job interviews and end up saying the wrong thing.*

say this/that for someone: used for admitting/confirming something good about someone ~ *He conned everyone, but I'll say this for him, he did it in a charming way.*

say when: [spoken] a way of telling someone when to stop doing something ~ *1a) I'll fill your glass—you just say when. 1b) I can't judge how much to trim, so you'll have to say when.*

(one) can't say (something): a polite way of saying you don't know something ~ *I can't say I've heard that expression.*

have one's say: have the opportunity to express one's view/opinion ~ *1a) Please be patient—there's time for everyone to have their say. 1b) Don't ask us why they changed the plans. We didn't even have a say in the matter.*

have something to say about something: express how one feels about something ~ *Dad will certainly have something to say about this.*

have something/nothing/a lot to say for yourself: be willing/ unwilling to talk or express your ideas ~ *1) I don't know who she was, but she had plenty to say for herself. 1b) He might be shy—he didn't have much to say for himself at the meeting. 1c) I heard what happened—what have you got to say for yourself?*

having said that . . . : [spoken] used when you're introducing an opinion that is in contrast to what you've just said ~ *I love the autumn leaves on the trees in my garden. Having said that, I hate the mess they make when they fall.*

I say: [spoken] 1) exclamation of delight/surprise/dismay ~ *I say, that's a stunning piece of jewellery!*

2) used to attract attention; introduce a new topic ~ *I say, what time is the plane due?*

3) express one's opinion ~ *I say we see the show then have dinner.*

if I may say (so): [spoken] used to introduce a personal comment ~ *1a) I thought your performance was spectacular—if I may say so. 1b) If I may say, your attitude stinks!*

I'll say: [spoken] emphatically "yes" ~ *It's cold isn't it? I'll say!*

I must say: [spoken] to be honest ~ *Well, I must say, I've never heard of that happening like that.*

I wouldn't say no to . . . : [spoken] that you would like what's been offered ~ *I wouldn't say no to another glass of wine.*

let's say . . . : [spoken] introduces speculation/a suggestion/an estimation ~ *1a) Let's say we go out tonight. 1b) We'll need—let's say, five loaves of bread.*

not to say: [spoken] used to further describe what you've just said ~ *I'm upset, not to say devastated, by the news.*

that is (not) to say: in other words ~ *1a) I've been re-appointed interstate—that is to say I'll be leaving this office. 1b) I'm moving interstate, but that's not to say I won't ever see you all again.*

to say nothing of: used to introduce further information to a previously mentioned subject ~ *The damage the storm caused here was minor, to say nothing of the destruction it caused further inland.*

to say the least: without exaggeration ~ *The suffering they experienced was horrendous to say the least.*

you don't say: [spoken] 1) expression of surprise at what someone has told you ~ *I heard they're getting married. You don't say!*

2) used to express that you are not surprised/unimpressed by what someone has told you (often said sarcastically) ~ *You know the sun rises in the east. Oh, you don't say.*

scallywag: rascal; naughty but likable person

scamper away: run away nimbly/with agility ~ *The rabbit scampered away when he heard us approaching.*

scare away: frighten (away from) something/someone ~ *If you make too much noise you'll scare away the fish.* *also: scare off

scare the wits out of: frighten someone ~ *Aargh! You scared the wits out of me!*

scared stiff: to be so frightened that you can't move ~ *I'm scared stiff of spiders.*

scaredy-cat: coward

scatterbrain: a disorganised/flighty person ~ *Jim is too much of a scatterbrain to be in charge.*

behind the scenes: 1) out of public view; in secret ~ *A lot more work went on behind the scenes than most people imagined.*

2) not heard or seen by the audience of a play or film ~ *His tireless work behind the scenes helped make the show a success.*

come on the scene: become known; be involved in a situation/ activity ~ *1a) He was an actor who first came on the scene in the seventies. 1b) All was going well until Jane came on the scene.*

make a scene: publicly display emotions; cause upset; be loud/rude with other people ~ *When she saw him at the bar with another woman she went over and made a scene.*

not your/one's scene: not something you/someone likes doing ~ *Loud dance parties are not my scene.* *also: not my cup of tea

schnoz: one's nose

school of thought: doctrine; belief/system of beliefs held by a particular group ~ *There a few schools of thought on how the species died out.*

schooner: 425 ml beer glass used in pubs and bars in NSW

sci-fi: science fiction

scone: /skɒn/ a small quickbread made of oatmeal, barley, or wheat, and baking powder prepared individually in rounds. They are a main component of a Devonshire tea.

Scone: /skōn/ a rural NSW town

scoop up: lift up with a scooping action ~ *Shoppers scooped up the bargains.*

scorcher: a very hot day ~ *It's been a scorcher of a day.* *also: sizzler

score something: 1) obtain illegal drugs

2) succeed in acquiring something ~ *I managed to score tickets to the concert.*

3) gain points/favour ~ *You'll score brownie points with Dad if you wash his car.*

keep score: keep a record of the score in a game

know the score/story: be aware of all the facts/details of a situation/issue ~ *You know the score: if you don't do your homework you can't go to the concert.*

scout around/about: search for something ~ *John put up the tent whilst I scouted around for some firewood.*

scram: *see: beat it

scrambled eggs: eggs beaten and cooked in a pan to a firm but soft constituency

scrape the bottom of the barrel: 1) use the last remaining reserves ~ *I've just enough money to buy it, but I'll be scraping the bottom of the barrel.*

2) call upon/utilise someone/something because there are no alternatives ~ *You really are scraping the bottom of the barrel by asking Jenny to go with you.*

scrape by: make do/barely manage one's existence ~ *He somehow manages to scrape by on a lousy wage.* *also: scratch a living

scrape through: succeed (only just) ~ *I scraped through the exam by two marks.*

scrape together: amass/produce with difficulty ~ *They managed to scrape together enough money for the trip.*

scrape up: remove from a surface by the act of scraping ~ *It took ages to scrape up all the hardened mud off the floor.*

scratch around: search/hunt for something ~ *He's scratching around in the drawer for a pen.* *also: scrounge around

scratch away: scrape; rub off by scratching ~ *The dog has scratched away all the paint from the door.*

scratch a living: struggle financially/to make a living ~ *They could do with some help, they're only just scratching a living.*

scratch the surface: superficially reveal the full extent/potential of something discovered ~ *The new findings have only scratched the surface of the potential it has to cure certain illnesses.*

(not) up to scratch: (not) sufficient/adequate ~ *The work they did was not up to scratch.* *also: second-rate

scratchie: a lottery ticket card played by scratching a designated area to win a cash prize

(a) scream: a hilarious/funny situation/person ~ *Paul's new girlfriend is a scream!*

scream blue murder: shout/protest/complain very loudly ~ *1a) Commuters screamed blue murder when train fares were increased again. 1b) The child screamed blue murder when I tried to take his toy away from him.*

(be) screaming for something: in great need of something ~ *My car is screaming to be washed.*

screw around: [coarse slang] be sexually promiscuous ~ *She's never in a permanent relationship, she just screws around.*

screw something/someone up: 1) mismanage/ruin/bungle something ~ *In doing that, you've screwed up the whole project.*

2) rumple/crinkle/crumple something ~ *She screwed up the letter in anger!* *also: scrunch up

screw you: [vulgar slang] strong/harsh expression of contempt/ annoyance

screwy: strange/odd/eccentric/peculiar ~ *There's something screwy about the deal.*

scribble away: write furiously ~ *The students scribbled away so as to finish the exam on time.*

scribble down: write quickly ~ *A witness managed to scribble down the get-away car's licence plate number.*

scrub away: wash/clean by scrubbing ~ *It's going to take some time to scrub that dirt away.*

scrub up alright/okay: to make someone/something to look presentable, after a good clean ~ *I may not look much in my dirty work clothes, but I scrub up okay.*

scum/scumbag: [informal slang] an offensive/despicable person

sea change: change of lifestyle

sea legs: the ability to keep one's balance on a moving ship ~ *I didn't get my sea legs until two days into the cruise.*

all at sea: *see: at sixes and sevens

seal a bargain/deal: confirm/reach an agreement ~ *We had a celebratory lunch to seal the deal.*

seal off: barricade/cordon off an area; close tightly ~ *1a) The entrance was sealed off. 1b) The swelling sealed off his throat.*

seal someone's fate: decide the (sometimes unpleasant/ unsuccessful) future of someone/something ~ *The rash decision he made sealed his fate.*

seal up: tightly secure; encase ~ *1a) The food is sealed up inside the container. 1b) The envelope needs to be sealed up before you post it.*

sealed with a kiss: written and sent with love and care (in love letters) *also: SWAK

search me: [spoken] expression which means "I don't know" ~ *Where could it be? Search me!*

sec: second (unit of time) *see: just a sec

second best: someone/something that is not as good as others/is not what you wanted ~ *She knows what she wants, and she won't settle for second best.*

get/have a second bite at the cherry: have another opportunity/ chance to achieve something ~ *He missed out this time, but he will get a second bite at the cherry next month.*

second nature: instinctive trait/tendency/habit ~ *Surfing is second nature to me.*

give something a second thought: to not think about something ~ *I'm sorry, I forgot to do it. I never gave it a second thought.*

have second thoughts: change your opinion; start to doubt something ~ *I'm having second thoughts about going.*

on second thoughts: [spoken] to indicate a change in one's decisions/actions; a change of mind ~ *On second thoughts—I will go!*

second to none: above all; the best ~ *The service we offer is second to none.*

(get one's) second wind: have renewed energy/vigour (after a rest) ~ *I thought I would have to retire from the race, but I got my second wind and went on to finish.*

second-guess something: 1) criticize someone's actions/an event after it has occurred ~ *It's easy to second-guess the coach's decisions, but he's not to blame for the team's loss.*

2) guess/anticipate an outcome/result ~ *It would be impossible to second-guess the judge's decision.*

seconds: 1) merchandise with minor faults; imperfect goods ~ *You'll always find a good bargain at a seconds clothing shop.* *also: factory seconds

2) a second helping of food ~ *I'm still hungry—may I have seconds?*

see about (doing) something: attend to something ~ *1a) Can you see about arranging transport home? 1b) I'll see Richard about getting the tickets to the play.*

see (someone) around: notice someone in different places ~ *I don't know which department he works in, but I see him around here often.*

see you around: [spoken] farewell, know that you'll see that person again in the same vicinity

see as: 1) considered as ~ *Their actions were seen as a direct threat.*

2) visualise/imagine ~ *I can see you as being a community spokesperson.*

see the back of someone: to no longer have to deal with/associate with someone unpleasant ~ *He's overstayed his welcome. I'll be glad to see the back of him.* *also: see the last of someone

see double: see two of everything (because of a visual disturbance) ~ *1a) I've been seeing double ever since the accident. 1b) I didn't know she had a twin working here. I thought I was seeing double!*

see the error of one's ways: accept and understand what you did wrong and make amendments ~ *It took a threatened jail sentence for him to finally see the error of his ways.*

see for dust: see someone that makes a hasty departure (as to stir up dust) ~ *As soon as she knows Jack's in town you won't see her for dust.*

see for yourself: [spoken] invitation to prove to someone that what you've just told them is true ~ *It's empty! See for yourself.*

see the glass as half empty: take a pessimistic view of a situation; think negatively

see the glass as half full: take an optimistic view of a situation; think positively

(now) see here: [spoken] interjection expressing a protest; calling attention to a command/statement ~ *Now see here! I did nothing of the sort!*

see how things are: that you will assess a situation before making a decision ~ *I'm not happy about letting you go at this stage. I'll see how things are in the morning.*

see the light: 1) finally understand/comprehend something clearly ~ *I finally saw the light after the concept was explained more fully.*

2) begin following/believing in religion ~ *Through her writing she hoped others would see the light about religion.*

see the light of day: that something should never be seen again in public ~ *I've worn this tattered old jacket for the last time. It will never see the light of day again.*

see/have one's name in lights: become famous/well-known for your work in stage/theatre/music ~ *She's wanted to see her name in lights ever since she was a little girl.*

see someone off: go with someone to the place/point of exit; say goodbye to; take leave of someone ~ *1a) My family and friends came to the airport to see me off. 1b) They saw us off at the door.* *also: wave off

see one's way clear (to do something): consider then agree to do something ~ *Do you think you can see your way to finishing the report by tomorrow?*

see reason: become realistic ~ *Charlie's finally seen reason and stopped smoking.*

see red: became enraged/infuriated ~ *I saw red when I heard what she'd done.*

see the point: understand something ~ *I just don't see the point of going.*

see the sights: look at/visit places of interest ~ *I'm off to see the sights.*

(be) seeing someone: be romantically involved with someone ~ *Now's the time to ask her out. She's not seeing anyone right now.*

see someone about something: have a pre-arranged meeting with someone to discuss something in particular ~ *1a) I'm going to see the doctor about this cough. 1b) What does the boss want to see you about?*

see someone coming (a mile off): recognize a person who is easily duped/tricked ~ *You paid a hundred dollars for that? They must have seen you coming.*

see someone out: go to the door with the person/people leaving/departing ~ *1a) Thank you for coming—I'll see you out. 1b) It's okay, I can see myself out.*

see someone through something: support/sustain through difficult times/long periods of time ~ *1a) She's a true friend who saw me through a long illness. 1b) They'll have enough food to see them through the winter.*

see something coming: be prepared for/expect something to happen ~ *It's no surprise they're separating. We all saw it coming.*

see something through: complete a task; fulfil a commitment ~ *Despite setbacks he's determined to see the project through.*

see stars: be dazed; see flashes of light after hitting your head

see to it that . . . : be certain/make sure of doing something ~ *Please see to it that you lock the door after I leave.*

see things: 1) to have an opinion on something ~ *At first they opposed the changes, but they're finally seeing things our way.*

2) believe you see something that's not there ~ *I thought I was seeing things when I saw you. I didn't realise you'd come back.*

see things differently: have a different perspective/opinion on something ~ *That's your opinion. I see things differently.*

see through (someone): not be deceived by; realise someone's true intentions ~ *1a) You can't fool me. I can see right through you. 1b) We can see through your charade, Peter.*

see to (something): take action/responsibility for doing something ~ *1a) I'll see to their dinner. 1b) I'll see to it that it gets sent.*

see someone for who they (really) are: to better understand someone ~ *. . . provided the opportunity to see her for who she really is.*

see what someone is made of: find out what someone can achieve ~ *This will show us what he's made of.*

see what I care: [spoken] a way of saying that you don't care what someone does (often a pretence) ~ *Go ahead and leave—see what I care!* *also: see if I care

see you: 1) meet with again; encounter ~ *When will I see you again?*

2) [spoken] used for saying goodbye to someone who you expect to see soon ~ *Bye, Jo. See you.*

see ya: [informal] see you (2)

as far as I can see: to the best of one's belief/understanding ~ *As far as I can see, there's no reason they can't go.*

as I see (it): in my opinion ~ *As I see it, she's innocent.* *also: the way I see it

can't see for looking: fail to see what you're looking for because you've trying too hard to see it

(I'll) believe it when I see it: [spoken] said when you don't believe something will happen until it does happen ~ *The government promised income tax cuts, but I'll believe it when I see it!* *also: seeing is believing

(go to) see a man about a dog/horse: humorous way of saying you are going to the toilet; keeping an undisclosed appointment ~ *He has gone to see a man about a dog.*

I see: [spoken] said to let someone know that you're paying attention to and understand what someone is saying ~ *Here, this is how it's done. Oh, I see.*

I'll/we'll see: [spoken] maybe/possibly ~ *Can I go to Jane's party next week? I'll see.*

I'll/we'll see about that: [spoken] a way of saying that you're not going to let someone do something they intend to do ~ *So, he wants to go skydiving does he? Well, I'll see about that!*

I don't see why not: [spoken] a way of saying that something's possible ~ *Can I go to Jane's party next week ?I don't see why not.*

let me see: [spoken] said when you're thinking/trying to remember something ~ *1a) Let me see. It must have been at least two years ago. 1b) Let's see—if we leave at 5:00, we should be there by 8:00.* *also: let's see

wait and see: all will be revealed/obvious later on ~ *1a) Let's wait and see what the weather's doing first. 1b) I can't tell you. You'll just have to wait and see.*

you see: [spoken] 1) used to emphasise a point when explaining something difficult/do you understand ~ *You can't let on that you're coming. It's a surprise you see.*

seeing that: inasmuch; because; considering; since ~ *Seeing that you're here early, let's eat before we go.*

(have) seen better days: of something to have visibly aged compared to when it was new ~ *The old car has certainly seen better days.*

have seen worse . . . : accept something as it appears; to previously witness something more extreme/terrible ~ *1a) The only accommodation on offer wasn't good, but I've seen worse. 1b) The storm we had today was pretty bad, but I've seen a lot worse.*

(it) remains to be seen: that something remains uncertain/unclear ~ *It remains to be seen what will become of her.*

(be) seedy: to feel ill/sick/nauseous ~ *I'm still feeling seedy after last night's party.*

seep away: to slowly pass out of and away from something ~ *I could feel my last ounce of strength seeping away.*

seize something: grab/take something (with an upward movement) ~ *She seized up her child out of harm's way.*

seize (the/an) opportunity: take advantage of an offer ~ *She seized the opportunity of a free trip.* *also: seize on

seize up: suddenly stop working/moving; freeze ~ *The rusty old gears on my bike have seized up.*

self-made: be successful/wealthy by one's own doing/efforts ~ *He's a self-made millionaire.*

sell off: reduce the price to sell quickly ~ *They had to sell off the excess stock to avoid going bankrupt.*

sell one's soul: do anything; go to great lengths; act immorally in order to succeed ~ *He'd sell his soul to gain status within the organisation.*

sell someone out: betray someone ~ *I thought I could trust him to do business with, but he sold me out!* *also: sell down the river

sell up: put one's house and possessions up for sale ~ *We're selling up and moving interstate.*

(put the) hard sell: a method of persuasion ~ *She put the hard sell on me to go into business with them.*

Sellotape: adhesive/sticky tape

send something away/off: dispatch; cause to leave/depart ~ *1a) I sent it away for repairs. 1b) We send the kids off to camp every summer.*

send back: return something/someone ~ *Dissatisfied with his meal, he sent it back to the kitchen.*

send away for: write to an organisation to order something ~ *I sent away for their latest catalogue.*

send flying: cause something to be knocked/scattered about with force (often accidentally) ~ *The collision sent him flying.*

send for: summon someone to come to you; arrange for something to come to/be delivered to you ~ *1a) I've sent for Peter, he should be here soon. 1b) His injuries were severe so we sent for an ambulance.*

send in: 1) submit documents/forms to a particular place ~ *1a) Don't forget to send in your entries by June 30. 1b) I've yet to send in my application.*

2) send someone/people to a place ~ *Reinforcements were sent in to help control the protestors.*

send off: 1) eject/dismiss a player from a game for violating the rules ~ *He was sent off for striking an opponent.*

2) arrange for someone to go somewhere ~ *We've sent them off to the beach for the day.*

3) post something ~ *I sent it off yesterday.*

send packing: dismiss someone abruptly ~ *A security guard sent the unruly lads packing.*

send(s) shivers up one's spine: said of something that causes excitement or great fear ~ *1) That music sent shivers up my spine. 1b) The sight of a big, hairy spider sent shivers up my spine.*

send on: forward/convey something (received) to another place/to someone else ~ *Mum's going to send our mail on to the new address.* *also: forward on

send someone up: satirise/mock/mimic someone ~ *He had a talent for sending up almost any famous person.*

send word: inform someone ~ *Could you send word of the change of venue?*

(a) sense of . . . : a strong feeling of belief about oneself/about something ~ *1a) I have a great sense of pride at seeing my life's work recognised. 1b) Steve felt a strong sense of foreboding; he decided not to go.*

sense of direction: an ability to navigate (even in unknown places) ~ *I'm sure I'll find it, I've a pretty good sense of direction.*

sense of humour: the trait/ability to express/appreciate humour; see the humour in something ~ *No matter how bad the situation, she never loses her sense of humour.*

sense of smell: to perceive the scent of something ~ *Dogs are used to detect things unseen because of their acute sense of smell.*

bring to one's senses: cause someone to think rationally/clearly ~ *He's crazy for wanting to do it, but no one can bring him to his senses.*

come to one's senses: begin to think rationally/clearly; recover consciousness ~ *1a) She finally came to her senses and quit smoking. 1b) The anaesthetic is wearing off and he's coming to his senses.*

common sense: the ability to make sensible/rational decisions; make good judgements ~ *. . . provided a common sense approach to the problem.* *also: horse sense

lull into/give a false sense of security: make someone feel they're safe ~ *The people that invested in the dodgy scheme were lulled into a false sense of security.*

in a/one sense: in some way/manner; according to one explanation/view ~ *His report states that there are other options, and he's right in a sense.*

in every sense: in every possible way/manner ~ *His report is correct in every sense.*

not make (any) sense: not understandable; incomprehensible ~ *Her account of the event doesn't make any sense.*

make sense of (it): be unable to comprehend/understand something ~ *1a) I can't make sense of her writing. 1b) We can't make sense of it all!*

sixth sense: keen intuition; power of perception; send/receive information beyond the realm of the five senses ~ *I knew something like this would happen—I had a sixth sense about it.*

take leave of one's senses: become irrational/unthinking ~ *You're going to do what? Have you taken leave of your senses?*

serve as: of something to be used for a particular purpose other than the main or original purpose ~ *1a) The office serves as a guest room. 1b) This tragedy should serve as a reminder not to speed on the roads.* *also: serve a purpose

serves someone right: that one's punishment/misfortune is deserved of the action ~ *It serves you right for getting sunburned, you didn't wear a hat or put on any sunscreen.*

serve a sentence: spend time in prison ~ *She's serving a life sentence for murder.*

serve time: hold office for a normal period; spend time in in prison; spend time in an apprenticeship ~ *1a) He's serving time at a* *maximum security facility. 1b) The out-going captain served for ten years.*

serve well: be useful/beneficial ~ *A restful holiday will serve you well.* *also: do well to

serve up: *see: dish up

give someone a serve: reprimand/scold/rebuke ~ *He left a terrible mess—so I gave him a serve when he got home.*

service station: petrol station/motor garage

servo: service station

set about doing something: begin/start to do something; deal with something ~ *It's time we set about finding a solution.*

set (the) alarm bells ringing: something alerts someone to a problem/danger ~ *His symptoms set the alarm bells ringing for the doctor.*

set apart: make noticeable ~ *Her positive attitude set her apart from the other candidates.*

set aside: reserve/keep for a specific reason/purpose ~ *This wine should be set aside for a special occasion.*

set someone back: 1) to cost someone an amount of money ~ *The repairs set me back two hundred dollars!*

2) to hinder/delay progress ~ *Repair work set us back two hours.*

set down: place/put into a position ~ *1a) Could you set it down over there? 1b) The house was set down in a pretty valley.*

set eyes on: see; catch sight of something/someone ~ *1a) I hope I never set eyes on her again! 1b) She fell in love as soon as she set eyes on him.*

set for life: in a favourable position; financially stable ~ *They sold the business and they're set for life.*

set forth: 1) propose; present for consideration ~ *He set forth his proposal to the client.*

2) depart/set out/start out ~ *After an unexpected delay, they were finally able to set forth on their exciting journey.*

set in: 1) to begin (for a duration of time) ~ *1a) I think the rain's set in. 1b) If you don't keep the wound clean, infection will set in.*

2) be apparent/beginning to happen ~ *Evening had set in by the time we arrived.*

set in concrete: of something firmly established/difficult to change ~ *The company's guidelines are set in concrete.*

set something in motion: begin/start a process ~ *She set in motion her career plan.*

set in one's ways: keep the same habit; do the same things every day ~ *You can't convince her to do things differently, she's too set in her ways.*

set off/out: start/begin to leave ~ *We made camp then set off on foot to explore the surrounds.*

set sights on: have a future goal/plan ~ *She's set her sights on becoming a dancer.*

set out: 1) begin/set in motion a plan ~ *After finishing his degree he set out to become a successful architect.*

2) begin a journey/course ~ *We're setting out at the crack of dawn.*

3) lay/position in a pattern; in order ~ *Jim had already set the equipment out on the table.*

set sail: begin/start a journey on a boat/ship ~ *We set sail tomorrow.*

set someone off: cause someone to be excited/upset ~ *Ever since then, any sudden loud noise sets him off.*

set something off: 1) initiate/trigger off ~ *Authorities are unsure of what set off the riot.*

2) perfectly complement/complete something ~ *That hat sets off the outfit nicely.*

set something/things right: correct something/a situation to the way it should be ~ *There's unrest and disharmony within the company, and it's my job to set things right.*

set the scene: 1) describe a situation/something about to happen ~ *Let me set the scene by describing how we came to live here.*

2) arrange/make possible ~ *By going against current clothing styles, the designers set the scene for others to try to copy their ideas.* *also: set the stage

set the record straight: tell the truth about something ~ *I need to set the record straight about what happened earlier today.*

set the tone: alter/establish the mood of a situation ~ *The sad news set the tone for the rest of the day.*

set someone up: 1) frame someone; make an innocent person appear guilty ~ *Authorities now have evidence to support his claim that he was set up.*

2) lay/arrange plans; a meeting/date with someone ~ *When no one else but Steve showed up at the restaurant I realised we'd been set up for a blind date.*

3) equip someone; provide for ~ *Tom's parents helped set him up in his new apartment by giving him some old furniture and household goods.*

set something up: 1) arrange/prepare something for operation/ use ~ *1a) We'll set the tables up over there. 1b) I've set up a meeting with them for next week.*

2) establish/create something ~ *The organization set up a charity fund.*

set the wheels in motion: *see: set in motion

set to work: begin a task/job ~ *They set to work cleaning up the mess.* *also: set about

set the world on fire: cause a great sensation; be sensationally successful ~ *It's predicted their music will set the world on fire.*

set up shop: establish a business ~ *The business has grown tenfold since they set up shop in the sixties.*

settle a score: fulfil an obligation/make even/avenge a wrong ~ *It's believed whoever shot him was settling a score with a rival.*

settle down: 1) abate; become calm/orderly ~ *It took ages to settle the kids down.*

2) become grounded; have an established lifestyle ~ *I'm not sure he's ready to settle down to married life just yet.*

3) make oneself comfortable in place/position ~ *After a busy day I was glad to settle down in front of the TV for the evening.*

settle for: accept; be satisfied ~ *He expects the best, and won't settle for anything less.*

settle up: pay one's debts to another ~ *Finally, I was able to settle up my account with them.*

it's all settled: [spoken] indication that a decision has been made ~ *It's all settled then—we'll do it this way.*

seven seas: the oceans and seas that are navigable ~ *They're off to sail the seven seas.*

seven-year-itch: a period of time in a union/marriage where couples get bored with the relationship and (typically) seek out someone else

sew up: stitch together (with needle and thread) ~ *I can easily sew that up.*

2) conclude/complete proceedings ~ *We hope to have the deal sewn up next week.*

shack up (with): [informal] live together without being married

shades: *see: sunnies

shake a leg: [spoken] a way of telling someone to hurry ~ *Come on, it's time to go, shake a leg!*

shake off: rid/free oneself of something/someone unwanted ~ *I can't seem to shake off this cold.*

shake up: 1) arouse; motivate; activate ~ *Shake it up before consuming.*

2) upset mentally/physically ~ *He's still a bit shaken up after the incident.*

3) cause beneficial changes within an organisation ~ *A new coach was brought in to shake up the under-performing team.*

(the) shakes: nervous trembling caused by a fright/nervousness or by the effects of drugs or alcohol

Shaky Isles: [informal] New Zealand

a crying shame: a great misfortune ~ *It's a crying shame it's going to be demolished.*

shape up: 1) improve one's performance/behaviour ~ *You'll have to shape up if you want a place on the swimming team.*

2) develop/evolve ~ *It's shaping up to be a long, hot summer.*

shape up or ship out: [spoken] command to improve one's performance/behaviour or leave ~ *That's the third time this month you've failed in your duties. You'll need to shape up or ship out!*

in/out of shape: in good/bad physical condition/health ~ *1a) I'm trying to get in shape for the marathon. 1b) I can't believe how out of shape you all are!*

in any way, shape, or form: in any way (at all) ~ *I have not, in any way, shape, or form, been associated with them.*

in many (different) shapes or forms: in many types/ways ~ *These days, cars come in many different shapes or forms.* *also: many shapes and sizes

in the shape of . . . : state exactly who or what you're referring to ~ *Relief from the heatwave came in the shape of a wild storm.*

take shape: to develop/appear as a distinctive form ~ *1a) Our plans are beginning to take shape. 1b) Our new house is finally taking shape.*

the shape of things to come: a style/form that is likely to develop in the future ~ *This innovative design is the shape of things to come.*

(as) sharp as a tack: very astute/intelligent ~ *She may be ninety-five years old, but she's still as sharp as a tack.*

she's right/she'll be right: [spoken] idiom indicating that a situation is not ideal, but good enough ~ *There's some structural damage, but she'll be right. It's nothing that can't be fixed.*

2) a situation is under control and you don't need the help that was offered ~ *She's right, mate—I can manage it.*

shed: The term mostly refers to any building that is not a residence and that may be open at the ends, sides, or both. Sheds can be elaborate or simple, small or large, and these days are mostly made from high-tensile steel sheeting. They are used for various purposes, including lawn mower and yard equipment storage, miscellaneous storage, or as a potting shed, and they appeal to the culture of "blokes" who do woodwork, metalwork, or DIY (do-it-yourself) projects in them.

shelf life: the period in which consumables are suitable for consumption ~ *Heat-treated milk has a longer shelf life than fresh milk.*

sheila: old-fashioned/informal word for girl/woman ~ *Who's that sheila you were with last night?*

shell out: pay for something; hand over cash/money (usually unwillingly) ~ *I had to shell out another forty dollars for postage.* *also: fork out

shelve something: put aside/away to be considered at a later date ~ *In light of what's happened, we've shelved our holiday plans.*

shemozzle: a confused situation/affair; a mess; an uproar; a disturbance ~ *Due to poor preparation and planning, the whole event was an absolute shemozzle.*

shenanigans: mischief/pranks ~ *What shenanigans have you kids been up to?*

shifty: someone devious/dishonest/evasive/sly ~ *Be careful doing business with him, he's a bit of a shifty character.* *also: shady

shilly-shally: procrastinate; dawdle ~ *If you hadn't shilly-shallied we wouldn't have been so late.* *see also: dilly-dally

shimmy up: ascend; climb quickly ~ *He shimmied up the tree to escape his pursuer.*

shindig: 1) a noisy quarrel/row ~ *Our attention was turned to the shindig happening outside.*

2) a party or festive gathering ~ *We're having a bit of a shindig next weekend. Would you like to come?*

shipshape: organised/tidy/neat/in order ~ *We should make sure everything's shipshape before they arrive.*

give someone the shirt off your back: display great kindness/ generosity; lend assistance ~ *He's so generous—he'd give anyone the shirt off his back.*

shirty: annoyed/angry ~ *I asked him a simple question and he got shirty with me!*

(don't) give a shit: [coarse slang] care in the least; be unconcerned ~ *1a) I don't give a shit what happens! 1b) Who gives a shit?*

in the shit: [coarse slang] in deep/big trouble ~ *I'm going to be in the shit when Dad finds out I failed my exams.*

no shit: [coarse slang] 1) expression of contempt; acknowledgement of something obvious ~ *The sun rises in the east, you know. No shit!*

2) an expression of disbelief ~ *You did what? No shit!*

3) truthfully/honestly ~ *No shit, I know nothing about it.*

shit a brick: [coarse slang] expressed when scared/frightened/ worried ~ *Shit a brick, mate. Are you okay?* *also pack(ing) shit; scared shitless

scare the shit out of: [coarse slang] frighten someone; be frightened ~ *Don't sneak up on me like that. You scared the shit out of me.* *also: shit oneself

tough shit: [coarse slang] bad luck; have no sympathy for someone ~ *Tough shit you're in trouble with the police. I warned you not to speed.* *also: stiff shit

treat/get treated like shit: [course slang] treat or get treated poorly/badly ~ *1a) She treats him like shit. 1b) I'm going to confront him if he insults me again. I'm tired of being treated like shit.*

(when the) shit hits the fan: [course slang] when the situations worsens; when trouble begins ~ *I don't want to be there when the shit hits the fan.*

shit-stirrer: [coarse slang] someone who makes trouble for someone ~ *Pay no attention to him—he's just a shit-stirrer.*

get/give the shits: [coarse slang] become angry/annoyed ~ *1a) He gives me the shits the way he acts sometimes. 1b) She easily gets the shits.*

shithouse: [coarse slang] unpleasant/despicable ~ *This is a shithouse movie!*

2) outside toilet

built like a brick shithouse: [coarse slang] (of a man) being well-developed/muscular ~ *You wouldn't want to pick a fight with him. He's built like a brick shithouse.*

shitty: [course slang] 1) angry; bad-tempered ~ *He's been shitty ever since his girlfriend left him.*

2) wretched/miserable ~ *I had a shitty day at work!*

shivers: [spoken] mild exclamation of amazement/surprise/ annoyance/disbelief ~ *1a) Shivers it's cold! 1b) Shivers—what a mess!*

(a) shocker: something that startles; horrifies; disappoints ~ *1a) Her new hair style is a shocker. 1b) It's a shocker of a movie.*

shoddy: cheap/poor quality; run-down/shabby ~ *It collapsed because of shoddy workmanship.*

be in someone's shoes: be in the same (often unpleasant) predicament/situation as another ~ *1a) If I were in your shoes I'd say something about it. 1b) It's up to Frank to explain the situation. I wouldn't like to be in his shoes.*

fill someone's shoes: fulfil someone else's job/role/position to the same standard ~ *She's done a splendid job. It's going to be difficult to find someone else to fill her shoes.*

shonky: 1) illicit; crooked; underhanded ~ *They offered me a shonky deal.*

2) shoddy; of poor/dubious quality ~ *The only room available was at a shonky little motel.* *also: dodgy

shoo: [spoken] a way of telling someone to go away/get lost ~ *Go away. Shoo!*

shook up: upset/anxious/worried ~ *She's all shook up from the accident.*

shoot daggers at someone: look angrily or accusingly at someone ~ *I'd obviously said something wrong when I saw Jill shoot daggers at me from across the room.*

shoot someone/something down in flames: refuse to accept an idea/plan; soundly beat in an argument/debate ~ *1a) What I thought was a reasonable suggestion was shot down in flames. 1b) The government's plan would have been shot down in flames if it had been proposed earlier.*

shoot from the hip: speak frankly/directly ~ *She doesn't mean to offend, it's just that she tends to shoot from the hip.*

shoot off: quickly leave/depart/go ~ *I have to shoot off down to the bank before it closes.*

shoot one's mouth off: boast/exaggerate; talk excessively about something you know little about ~ *He's always shooting his mouth off about how good he is at the game, when in fact he's only a mediocre player.*

shoot oneself in the foot: say or do something that will make a situation worse for yourself ~ *I think I've just shot myself in the foot by refusing his offer.*

shoot the messenger: blame or become angry with the person bearing bad news ~ *Don't shoot the messenger. He's not the one who issued the order.*

shoot through: depart/go in haste and leave behind unfinished business ~ *When the police finally found out where the suspect was hiding they were too late—he'd already shot through.*

shoot up: 1) increase quickly in size or amount ~ *1a) You've shot up since I saw you last. 1b) The angry flames were shooting up into the air.*

2) the act of injecting an illegal drug into one's veins

shop around: compare the price of something before buying it ~ *It's worth shopping around to find the best bargains.*

shoplift: steal goods (from a shop) ~ *She was caught shoplifting.*

shoplifter: one who steals goods from a shop *also: petty thief

shore up: *see: prop up

(get the) short end of the stick: be unfairly affected in a situation ~ *When it comes to being assigned the worst jobs around here, I seem to always get the short end of the stick!* *also: draw the short straw

short and curlies: [informal] pubic hair

have someone by the short and curlies: to have power over someone ~ *We can't do much. They've got us by the short and curlies.*

short of: 1) except/other than ~ *Short of replacing the motor, there's not much I can do.*

2) without reaching a particular position/place ~ *The runner collapsed with exhaustion just short of the finish line.*

short of breath: breathless/panting ~ *We were rendered short of breath not long into our ascent.*

short on: lacking in something ~ *He's good looking, but short on manners.*

short and sweet: surprisingly/pleasantly short ~ *The meeting was short and sweet.*

in the short term/run: (for) a relatively brief period/time ~ *The repair will hold for the short run, but eventually the whole thing will need replacing.*

at short notice: without much warning ~ *I was asked to work at short notice.*

(be) cut short: of something to stop earlier than expected/before it is finished ~ *Her career as a dancer was cut short when she permanently damaged her knee.*

be caught short: be temporarily short of money; something at a critical time ~ *I have emergency funds available in case I get caught short.*

for short/short for: as an abbreviation ~ *1a) Just call me Will, for short. 1b) Typo is short for typographical error.*

go short: to not have enough of something ~ *Here, take some extra supplies. I don't want you to go short.*

in short: briefly ~ *In short—we lost.*

in short supply: lacking in/less than needed ~ *Because of the drought, many fruits and vegetables are in short supply.*

the long and the short of it: the essential facts/points ~ *The long and the short of it is we're in financial trouble.*

make short work of something: finish/complete; deal with something quickly ~ *The hungry boys made short work of the meal.*

nothing/little short of . . . : strongly displaying a particular quality ~ *The results are nothing short of amazing.*

pull up short: cause someone to pause/stop abruptly ~ *The driver pulled up short to avoid hitting him.*

(to have) a short fuse: be quick to anger (over minor issues) ~ *He's a good boss, but be warned, he has a short fuse.* *also: short-tempered

sell short: fail to recognise the full value/worth of someone/something ~ *1a) I know you can do the job—don't sell yourself short. 1b) She's capable of doing good work—don't sell her short and take her off the team.*

stop short: suddenly stop doing something (for an obvious reason) ~ *She ran to greet James, but stopped short when she realised it wasn't him.*

stop short of doing something: to almost do something then decide not to do it ~ *She was furious, but stopped short of firing him.*

short-arse: [slang] an affectionate term (amongst friends) for someone who is short in height ~ *He may be a short-arse, but he sure can run fast.* *also: shortie

shorts: short pants

(a) shot in the arm: a boost of vigour/energy/confidence ~ *A glowing review was the shot in the arm she needed.*

(a) shot in the dark: 1) an unsubstantiated guess ~ *At this stage, any attempt to predict an outcome would just be a shot in the dark.*

2) a hopeful attempt ~ *It might be a shot in the dark, but as I see it, the only way out is to go over that ridge.*

shot to pieces: damaged/injured/destroyed ~ *1a) Because of that, my holiday plans are shot to pieces. 1b) My nerves are shot to pieces.*

(a) cheap shot: an unfair criticism; unsporting verbal attack ~ *The remark about her playing ability was a cheap shot.*

big shot: an important/influential person ~ *He thinks he's a big shot since he got promoted.*

give it your best shot: do something to be best of your ability ~ *I didn't do very well, but I gave it my best shot.*

like a shot: do something eagerly and quickly ~ *She bolted out of there like a shot.*

take a shot at something: 1) try/attempt something (often for the first time) ~ *I've never done it before, but I'll take a shot at it.* *also: give something a shot/whirl

2) attempt to hit a target with a missile ~ *He turned and took a shot at his pursuer.*

shotgun wedding: a forced/hurried wedding precipitated by pregnancy

shoulder the blame: accept responsibly ~ *You can't expect them to shoulder the blame for what happened.*

shoulder the burden: deal with something ~ *He was shouldered with the burden of arranging the funeral.*

(a) shoulder to cry on: listen sympathetically to someone's troubles ~ *She's a good friend who's always provided a shoulder to cry on.*

shoulder to shoulder: 1) stand close together/side to side ~ *Houses along the beachfront stand shoulder to shoulder.*

2) work in united effort/support someone ~ *Total strangers stood shoulder to shoulder clearing the wreckage.*

give/get the cold shoulder: be unfriendly to/ignore someone/be ignored ~ *1a) I don't know what I said or did to upset him, but he gave me the cold shoulder at the party. 1b) Home late again without an explanation, his wife gave him the cold shoulder.*

have a chip on one's shoulders: be resentful; remain angry over perceived grievances ~ *He's still got a chip on his shoulders from an argument they had last month.*

rub shoulders with someone: mix socially; come into social contact ~ *We rubbed shoulders with the rich and famous at last night's gala dinner.*

shrug one's shoulders: up and down movement of the shoulders used to indicate that you don't know the answer to something

shout someone: pay for something (especially drinks); buy something for someone ~ *1a) I'll shout this round of drinks. 1b) Dad shouted us a meal at a fancy restaurant.*

shout down: silence someone by shouting loudly ~ *When the speaker tried to justify his actions he was shouted down by the angry audience.*

shout from the rooftops: tell everyone very loudly how happy/ proud you are about something ~ *When she agreed to marry him, he wanted to shout it from the rooftops.*

(a) shouting match: an argument that escalates and becomes vocal ~ *The mild debate soon turned into a shouting match.* *also: slanging match

nothing to shout about: of something not be especially exciting or good ~ *The movie was nothing to shout about.*

shove it: [spoken] rude exclamation of dismissal/refusal/contempt ~ *Shove it! I'm not doing that!*

shove off: 1) leave depart ~ *We'd best be shoving off.*

2) [spoken] a terse way to tell someone to go away ~ *Just shove off!*

show around: guide/lead someone through a place; give a guided tour ~ *Come in, I'll show you around.*

show of hands: of a vote/decision indicated by people raising their hands ~ *We'll decide the course of action by a show of hands.*

show off: 1) act/behave so as to attract attention/be noticed ~ *My young daughter loves to show off in front of everyone.*

2) display something visibly/ostentatiously ~ *He's here to proudly show off his sporting medals.*

show one's face: revisit a place where one has done something shameful/embarrassing ~ *1a) I don't know how he can show his face here again after what he's done. 1b) They'd better not show their faces around here again!*

show one's hand: reveal one's plans; declare one's intentions ~ *I don't want to show my hand at this stage of the proceedings.* *also: declare one's hand

show one's true colours: reveal one's true personality/character (usually dark/unpleasant) ~ *I thought I knew her well, but in doing that she's shown her true colours.*

show someone the door: ask/order someone to leave ~ *Anyone who doesn't conduct themselves in a proper manner will be shown the door.*

show in: welcome someone into a room/building by opening the door for them ~ *A doorman was posted to show in the guests.*

show out: farewell someone out of a room/building by opening the door for them ~ *John's gone to show our guests out.*

show someone the ropes: demonstrate/explain how a job/activity is done ~ *Peter will show you the ropes.* *also: learn the ropes

show signs: become visible/obvious ~ *He's beginning to show signs of improvement.*

show of strength: a demonstration of power/force ~ *They were parading the troops as a show of strength.*

show someone a thing or two: impart one's knowledge/skills learned through practical experience ~ *Ex-professional racecar driver Larry could show you a thing or two about driving.* *also: learn a thing or two

show up: 1) arrive/appear ~ *1a) We waited for an hour, but he never showed up. 1b) The illness didn't show up in the blood test.*

2) become apparent/obvious ~ *The light background really shows up the darker colours.*

show someone up: outdo someone; embarrass in public ~ *That's not really his car. He's just trying to show you up.*

show who's boss: make clear who has more power/authority ~ *Don't let them get the advantage. Show them who's the boss!*

show yourself: [spoken] request to come out of hiding and reveal your identity ~ *Police ordered they come out and show themselves.*

for show: for appearances/decoration rather than use ~ *The shutters are for show. They're non-functioning.*

have something/nothing to show for (it): to have no results/advantage for doing something ~ *1a) I've been working for over an hour on this report and I've got nothing to show for it. 1b) What have you got to show for the work you did all morning?*

get/keep the show on the road: begin/continue an undertaking/journey ~ *We've a long trip ahead of us, so let's get the show on the road.*

(it) goes to show: proves/indicates/demonstrates that something is correct/true (often preceded by "just") ~ *He was spared serious head injuries. It just goes to show the importance of wearing a helmet.*

make a show of: do something to make a false impression ~ *He made a show of being upset.*

make a show of yourself: say something or behave in a manner that attracts attention ~ *Whatever you do, don't make a show of yourself in front of them!*

on show: being exhibited ~ *Flower arrangements are on show in the main hall.*

shrink: [informal] psychiatrist

shrinking violet: a shy/timid person

shrivel up: dry out; shrink; crease/wrinkle (through loss of moisture) ~ *The plants soon shrivelled up and died in the intense heat.*

shrug off: disregard ~ *He shrugged off reports that he was retiring.*

shush: [spoken] a way of telling someone to be quiet ~ *Shush everyone—I can't hear the TV.*

shut away: be in a place away/apart from other people ~ *She shut herself away in her room all weekend studying for the exams.*

shut down: 1) of a school/shop/industry/business to close permanently ~ *They shut down the factory after a series of workplace accidents.*

2) of a machine to stop operating ~ *Please shut down the computer when you've finished.*

shut in: confined; be in a place you cannot leave ~ *We shut our dog in the garage at night.*

shut off: 1) stop the flow of water/electricity ~ *You shut the water off by turning this lever.*

2) stop from operating ~ *How do you shut the alarm off?*

3) isolated; away from others ~ *The community is shut off by flood waters.*

shut someone up: quieten/silence someone ~ *Our budgie has been talking and whistling all morning. I can't shut him up.*

shut up: [spoken] strong/rude request for quiet ~ *Shut up, will you?*

shut up about: stop talking about something ~ *I wish she'd shut up about her new boyfriend.*

shut up shop: cease trading; close a business (either permanently or at the end of the day) ~ *The poor economy will force more business owners to shut up shop.*

shut-eye: sleep ~ *I didn't get much shut-eye last night.*

shy away (from): keep away from; avoid someone/something ~ *1a) I tend to shy away from spicy food. 1b) He generally shies away from strangers.*

sick as a dog: very sick/ill ~ *The food must have been bad. I was sick as a dog all night.*

sick and tired (of): weary/intolerant/tired of something ~ *I'm sick and tired of having to clean up after everyone.* *also: sick to death of; fed up/sick to the back teeth

worried sick: extremely/very worried ~ *Why didn't you say you'd be late? I've been worried sick about you all day.*

sickie: a day off work when you're not really sick

side by side: besides or near each other; in allegiance ~ *Side by side they marched.* *also: shoulder to shoulder

(from) side to side: from one side to the other side ~ *The huge waves tossed the small craft from side to side.*

side with: support one person/group ~ *I'm siding with you on this issue.*

. . . side of the story: someone's account/version of events ~ *This is a chance to tell your side of the story.*

be/get/keep on side with someone: favour/support/ be partial to someone ~ *1a) Remember, whatever happens—I'm on your side. 1b) If you want to keep your job, stay on side with the boss.* *also: side with someone

from/on all sides: from/in all directions/everywhere ~ *Attackers were coming from all sides!*

on the side: 1) extra; in addition to one's regular activity/job/ relations ~ *He works a regular job, and repairs bicycles on the side.*

2) (of food) served separately, but eaten together ~ *I'll have the steak, with a salad on the side.*

3) secretly—in regards to an illicit intimate relationship ~ *She's married and is seeing someone on the side.*

to/on one side: aside/out of the way ~ *Please put what you're doing to one side while I show you something.*

this side of: before a particular event/date/time ~ *He never wakes this side of midday.*

the wrong side of the tracks: the poor/disadvantaged part of town ~ *Despite growing up on the wrong side of the tracks, he became a very successful businessman.*

a thorn in one's side: an on-going cause of trouble/irritation ~ *The unfinished repair work has been a thorn in my side for months.*

sidle away: move furtively/unobtrusively (sideways) away from ~ *Hoping to leave unnoticed, he sidled away from the group and snuck out the side entrance.*

sidle up to: advance unobtrusively/furtively; move closer to ~ *1a) He sidled up to me and kissed me on the cheek. 1b) The boat quietly sidled up to the wharf.*

sift through: thoroughly examine all the parts/bits ~ *Detectives sifted through the evidence hoping to find the missing clue.*

sight unseen: accept/buy something you haven't seen ~ *They're buying it sight unseen.*

a sight: someone in a dishevelled/unkempt state ~ *He looked a sight this morning, unshaven and bleary eyed, and still wearing last night's clothes.*

(a) sight to see: something strange/odd (to be seen) ~ *It was a sight to see.*

(not/be) a pretty sight: describes something/someone unpleasant to look at (often said humorously) ~ *He's not a pretty sight after he's been drinking.*

a sight for sore eyes: a welcome sight; pleasing to look at ~ *Well, aren't you're a sight for sore eyes!*

(the) sight of . . . : the act of seeing something ~ *1a) He can't stand the sight of blood. 1b) Such is the infatuation she trembles at the sight of him.*

at first sight: when you first see someone/something ~ *1a) At first sight I thought it was a dead body. 1b) For them, it was love at first sight.*

have something in one's sights: have a goal/aim; attempt to achieve something ~ *He's trained hard and now has an Olympic medal in his sights.*

know by sight: to recognise someone but not know them ~ *I know him by sight, but I've never met him.*

on sight: immediately after you see someone ~ *He's been ordered to shoot intruders on sight.*

out of sight: unable to be seen/concealed ~ *1a) They were quickly ushered to a table out of sight of the paparazzi. 1b) He took off quickly, turned the corner, and was out of sight.*

out of sight, out of mind: that if something is not visible it will be quickly forgotten

the sights and sounds: the visual and aural experience of a place ~ *Experience the sights and sounds of this vibrant city!*

within sight of: any place visible from where you are ~ *The harbour is within sight of our office.*

sign away: relinquish one's claim or one's rights to something on a document ~ *1a) If you sign this you will be signing away all production rights. 1b) He signed away any claim on the estate.*

sign in: write one's name in an official list upon entering (a place) ~ *Anyone attending the conference needs to sign in at the front desk.*

sign(s) of life: 1) evidence that someone is alive ~ *When rescuers finally reached him, he showed no signs of life.*

2) evidence of existence ~ *They searched the derelict building looking for any signs of life.*

sign of the times: something that demonstrates changes in society ~ *It's a sign of the times that many small, independent suppliers are closing.*

sign off: 1) [spoken] ending to a (radio/television) broadcast

2) end a letter by writing your signature ~ *He signed off, "Yours faithfully, John Smith."*

3) [in business] show/indicate official approval that something is completed satisfactorily ~ *We can begin the project now the manager has signed off the application.*

sign on: employ/hire someone on a contract ~ *She's been signed on for two years.*

sign on the dotted line: formally submit one's name to a contract; agree to something ~ *Just sign on the dotted line and the house is yours.*

sign out: write one's name in an official list upon leaving (a place) ~ *Please sign out before leaving.* *also: sign someone out

sign over/away: relinquish ownership by signing an official document ~ *1a) He signed his property over to his son. 1b) By doing this you'll be signing away your right to participate in official proceedings.*

sign up: join an organisation/club/group ~ *I signed up for gym membership.*

sure sign: almost certain proof of something ~ *He was fidgety and sweating—a sure sign nervousness.*

silent cop: a fixed dome on the road designed to direct traffic flow in a certain direction (used in place of a policeman)

silly season: the Christmas holiday season

simmer down: become less agitated/excited; calmer ~ *It took a while for the kids to simmer down after all the excitement.*

sin bin: [in rugby league/union] an area (off the field of play) where players must remain for a specified time after committing a serious foul/penalty ~ *Player number twelve was sent to the sin bin for punching another player.*

sing along (with): sing a song with someone who's already singing/to a song playing ~ *She sings along with almost all of the songs this radio stations plays.*

sing out: call out loudly ~ *Just sing out when you're ready.*

sing to sleep: sing softly (to a baby or child) to help them go to sleep

sink (a few): drink (cans/glasses) beer ~ *He's at the pub sinking a few with Roger.*

sink in: come to realise/comprehend something ~ *1a) It took a while for it to sink in that she'd won. 1b) When will it sink in that I don't want to go out with you anymore?*

sink like a brick: to sink quickly (under the water) ~ *It was all we could do to watch the stricken vessel sink like a brick.*

sink money into: invest in a venture ~ *They sank almost all of their money into starting up the business.*

sink so low (as to): be so dishonest; without morals as to do something bad ~ *He sank so low as to steal from his mother to support his drug habit.*

sink or swim: fail or succeed (with little or no help) ~ *The parent company collapsed, leaving us to sink or swim.*

sink to/into: 1) lapse into a particular state ~ *Her injuries were severe and she soon staring sinking into unconsciousness.*

2) fall/sit or lie down ~ *2a) He sank to his knees in despair. 2b) All I want to do is go home and sink into a hot, deep bath.*

a/that sinking feeling: a feeling of foreboding/apprehension ~ *As soon as I heard the distress in her voice I got that sinking feeling.*

sit around: relax/sit idly ~ *We sat around watching TV all day.*

sit around something: sit around the perimeter of a table; sit in a circle ~ *1a) The table's big enough for everyone to sit around. 1b) We sat around the campfire telling ghost stories.*

sit back: relax in a reclining position ~ *I'm looking forward to sitting back and relaxing.*

sit by: do nothing when action should be taken ~ *We can't just sit by and ignore the problem!*

sit down: sit on a chair/seat

sit in for: temporarily replace someone ~ *I'm sitting in for the manager for a few days.*

sit in on: attend/observe without being actively involved ~ *He'll be sitting in on the meeting without contributing to it.*

sit on (one's hands): deliberate/delay making a decision ~ *They're sitting on their decision pending further investigation.*

sit on one's bum/arse/backside: [slang] be lazy; idle ~ *He's done nothing but sit on his bum all day watching TV!*

sit on the throne: [informal] a humorous way of saying one is sitting on the toilet

sit out: 1) endure to the finish (something unpleasant) ~ *We had no option but to sit out the storm.*

2) refrain from participating for a period of time ~ *I'm going to sit this dance out.*

sit tight: 1) wait patiently; remain in one place ~ *We just have to sit tight until help arrives.*

2) take no action while waiting for something to happen ~ *They decided to sit tight until the market recovers before selling the house.*

sit through: remain seated/in attendance; stay until the end of something ~ *1a) We had to sit through a couple of boring speeches. 1b) I doubt the kids will be able to sit through the entire performance.*

sit up (and take notice): suddenly become interested/alert ~ *The alarming statistics they provided made everyone sit up and take notice.*

(not) sit well/right: of something you find difficult to agree with/accept ~ *Their decision didn't sit well with shareholders.*

sitting duck: an easy target/victim; powerless/vulnerable ~ *My car broke down in the middle of the freeway, effectively making me a sitting duck.*

sitting pretty: in a good situation; living comfortably ~ *Retired and debt free, they're sitting pretty.*

six foot under: [informal] dead and buried

six of one, half a dozen of the other: [spoken] the same; no different ~ *It doesn't matter which route we take, it's six of one, half a dozen of the other.*

six pack: a six pack of beer *also: sixer/6er

(go for) a sixer: fall heavily ~ *I went for a sixer on the ice rink.*

sixty-four thousand dollar question: an important or difficult question that is almost impossible to answer ~ *How long will it take? That's the sixty-four thousand dollar question.*

size up: make an estimation; assess someone/something ~ *1a) Size up your options before making a decision. 1b) The boxers walked in circles around each other, sizing each other up.*

skedaddle: go/leave/depart quickly ~ *Gang members skedaddled when they heard the approaching sirens.*

skeleton staff/crew: the minimal amount of workers needed to operate a business ~ *We only have skeleton staff on weekends.*

(have a) skeleton in the cupboard: shameful family secrets ~ *You'd be hard pressed to find any skeletons in their cupboard.* *also: closet

skerrick: little or nothing of something ~ *There was not a skerrick of food in the fridge.*

skid row: derelict/poor/neglected district mainly inhabited by vagrants and down-and-outs ~ *After years of drug and alcohol abuse he's now homeless and living on skid row.*

skid lid: [informal] bicycle helmet

skim through: read something hastily ~ *I only had time to skim through the report. I'll read it in full later.* *also: skip through

skin and bone: a condition of extreme thinness; emaciation ~ *The harsh drought had reduced the sheep to skin and bone.*

no skin off (my) nose: [spoken] a way of saying one is unconcerned about something ~ *It's no skin off my nose if they don't take my advice.*

save one's skin: save oneself from harm/difficulty at the expense of others ~ *He didn't help save others from the sinking vessel, he seemed interested in saving his own skin.*

(have a) skinful: to have had as much as one can tolerate/endure ~ *I've had a skinful of their noisy parties.*

have a thick skin: be insensitive to personal criticism ~ *You have to have thick skin to work under her.* *also: thick-skinned

have a thin skin: to be sensitive to personal criticism ~ *Be gentle with your reproach—she's has rather a thin skin.* *also: thin-skinned

skinny-dip: swim naked/nude

skip town/the country: leave a place suddenly or secretly ~ *His sudden disappearance led them to believe he'd skipped town.*

skirt around: go around the edge of something ~ *The road skirts (around) the edge of the town.*

skirt the issue: avoid addressing/discussing problematic issues ~ *In a manner typical of most politicians, he discussed everything else but skirted the main issues.*

the sky's the limit: to have no limits/obstacles ~ *As to its potential, well, the sky's the limit.*

(to) skyrocket: price/amount/rate to increase rapidly ~ *House prices have skyrocketed in recent months.*

slab: a beer carton (containing twenty-four cans, tinnies, or stubbies)

slack off: 1) reduce gradually ~ *Trade is brisk in the mornings, but slacks off in the afternoons.*

2) become lazy/inefficient ~ *She was fired for slacking off at work once too often.*

slack(o/er/arse): [slang] one who is idle/lazy/negligent/ inefficient ~ *He has a reputation for being a bit of a slacker.*

cut someone some slack: ease restrictions; allow more freedom ~ *I studied hard all week, so Mum cut me some slack and let me go to party.*

take/pick up the slack: continue on with someone's unfinished work ~ *Jill went home sick, leaving Sally to take up the slack.*

slam someone/something: severely criticise someone/something ~ *Critics slammed the movie for being too violent.*

slam on the anchors/brakes: to brake/stop quickly ~ *I slammed on the brakes to avoid a collision.* *also: hit the anchors

slammer: [informal] prison/jail

slanging match: *see shouting match

slap (with): issue a legal fine or court order ~ *For his actions, he was slapped with a speeding ticket.*

slap and tickle: non-serious sexual activity

slap something on something: put something in/onto something without care ~ *1a) You'd best slap on some sunscreen before going out in the sun. 1b) He slapped some paint on the wall to hide the imperfections.*

a slap in the face: a rebuff/insult ~ *The decision to demolish the building was a slap in the face for those who campaigned to have it restored.*

a slap on the back: a gesture of congratulations/praise ~ *She deserves a slap on the back for the hard work she's put into making the evening a success.*

a slap on the wrist: a mild warning/punishment ~ *The sentencing imposed was but a slap on the wrist.*

slap-bang: precisely/exactly ~ *The bed was slap-bang in the middle of the room.* *also: right slap-bang

slap-happy: 1) cheerfully carefree/irresponsible ~ *The judge was getting tired of the defendant's slap-happy attitude towards the severity of the crime.*

2) giddy/dazed; mentally impaired ~ *He was last seen walking slap-happy down the middle of the road.*

slap-up: hastily/carelessly constructed/created ~ *Dinner on Friday nights is usually a slap-up meal.*

slapdash: reckless/hasty/careless ~ *It was a slapdash response.*

slapstick: violent/vigorous comedy

start/begin with a clean slate: begin something anew/afresh/ over again ~ *After serving time, Jack decided to start his new life with a clean slate.* *also: wipe the slate clean

slaughter: defeat soundly (in a game) ~ *We were sure we'd win, but instead we were slaughtered!*

slave away: toil; work doggedly at something ~ *I've been slaving away for weeks on this project, but getting nowhere with it!*

slave over a hot stove: toil/work hard in the kitchen ~ *I'd much prefer to cook on the barbie than slave over a hot stove.*

slave-driver: an employer who demands workers work excessively hard ~ *Be prepared to work very hard if you want to work for George, he's a slave-driver.*

sleaze bag: (someone) sleazy

sleep around: be sexually promiscuous; have more than one sexual partner ~ *She had a reputation for sleeping around.*

sleep something off: recover; get rid of by sleeping ~ *He spent a good part of the day sleeping off a hangover.*

sleep like a log/top: sleep very soundly ~ *I slept like a log last night and I feel great today!*

sleep on (it): consider a decision ~ *Let me sleep on it and I'll let you know tomorrow.*

sleep through: remain asleep through a noisy event ~*I slept right through the thunderstorm.*

sleep with someone: have a serious relationship; be sexually active with someone ~ *I know they've dated a few times, but I think she might be sleeping with him.*

sleepyhead: one who is tired/sleepy ~ *Come on, sleepyhead, time to get up.*

have something/a trick up one's sleeve: have a back-up plan ~ *Don't worry that it failed, I'm sure Steve's got a few more tricks up his sleeve.* *also: have a card/ace up one's sleeve

roll up one's sleeves: turn one's sleeves up (expose one's arms) in readiness for work ~ *There's a lot to be done, so let's roll up our sleeves and get working!* *also: roll sleeves up

slice up: cut into slices ~ *The chef expertly sliced up the ham.*

slice through: 1) easily cut through something ~ *It will easily slice through a pumpkin.*

2) move through something easily ~ *The yacht sliced through the waves with ease.*

slice of the cake/pie: a share of the benefits/profits ~ *He was expecting a decent slice of the pie for the work he'd done.*

slide around: slip/skid about (on a surface) ~ *Cars were sliding around everywhere on the icy roads.*

let something slide: ignore a mistake/take no action ~ *She wasn't being entirely truthful, but I let it slide.*

slip away: 1) leave/depart quietly/secretly ~ *They slipped away from the boring proceedings.* *also slip out

2) to die ~ *They found, in the morning, that she'd slipped away in her sleep.*

3) of time to elapse ~ *We need to get this finished before time slips away.*

4) become less strong/able ~ *He could feel his strength slipping away and wondered how long he could hold on.*

5) of an opportunity to be no longer available ~ *This time, I'm not going to let my chance of selection slip away.*

slip of a thing: a female of slight build ~ *She's only a slip of a thing, I'm amazed she managed to carry such a weight.*

slip one's mind: to forget something ~ *I meant to call her, but it slipped my mind.*

slip out: 1) say something you didn't intend to say ~ *I didn't mean to say that. It just slipped out.*

2) leave a place quietly ~ *He slipped out the back door undetected.*

3) of something to be removed from a place ~ *I don't know what became of it. It must have slipped out of the pocket.*

slip over: slip and fall ~ *I slipped over on the icy surface.*

slip up: make a mistake ~ *Hopefully there'll be no slip ups next time.*

slip through: move smoothly/easily/stealthily ~ *With only seconds to spare, the lithe feline slipped through a gap in the fence to escape it's pursuer.*

slip/fall through the cracks: to escape notice; be overlooked/ neglected ~ *The number of illiterate adults indicate that too many are falling through the cracks in the education system.*

give someone the slip: escape from one's pursuer/follower ~ *The nimble thief soon gave the police the slip.*

pink slip: a mandatory checklist carried out by authorised motor mechanics to prove a car is roadworthy for yearly registration

Slip, Slop, Slap: an Australia-wide sun-safe campaign aimed at educating people to protect themselves against the damaging effects of the sun. *Slip* on a shirt, *Slop* on some sunscreen, and *Slap* on a hat.

slippery as an eel: 1) someone who is crafty/cunning ~ *Be careful doing business with him—he's as slippery as an eel.*

2) hard to hold/grasp

slippery dip: playground slippery slide

slob: a slovenly/lazy/uncultured person ~ *I wouldn't have her as a housemate, she's too much of a slob.*

slob about: behave in a slovenly way ~ *He just slobbed about the house all day.*

slog: 1) hit/strike heavily ~ *Somebody slogged him from behind as he walked down the street.*

2) progress slowly at a heavy pace ~ *That hill climb sure was a hard slog.*

slog away (at): toil/work hard for a period of time ~ *We've been slogging away at it all day.*

slog it out: compete/argue until there's a winner ~ *The teams will be slogging it out next weekend.*

slope away (from): slope downward and away from something ~ *The lawn slopes gently away from the house towards the creek.*

sloppy joe: a non-zippered, cotton sweatshirt

sloshed: drunk/intoxicated *also: sozzled

slouch: an inept/lazy person

no slouch: someone who works hard and is not lazy ~ *1a) She's no slouch when it comes to hard work. 1b) He plays a good game of tennis, and he's no slouch at golf either.*

slouch hat: A style of felt hat, khaki in colour (with its brim pinned up on the right side), that was first worn by military forces in Australia in 1885. It's widely associated with Australian identities such as the slouch or digger hat, and it has become a symbol of courage and nationalism.

slow down: become slower/less active ~ *He was advised to slow down to reduce the risk of having a heart attack.* *also: slow up

slow going: the rate of speed at which progress is made ~ *This heavy work is slow going.*

slow off the mark: slow to act/react ~ *He won the prize because the other contestants were too slow off the mark.*

slow-coach/poke: someone slow to move/act ~ *Haven't you finished yet, you slow-coach?*

smalls: underwear

small change: coins/loose change/schrapnel

small hours: the hours after midnight and before dawn

small screen: television

small talk: casual/informal conversation

smart aleck: someone who thinks they know everything *also: smart arse; wise guy; smarty pants

smart cookie: an intelligent/clever person ~ *I'm not surprised Peta won the scholarship; she's one smart cookie.*

smash up: damage/destroy in a violent way ~ *He was too scared to tell his father the car had been smashed up.*

smashed: heavily intoxicated; drunk

smell a rat: suspect something is not what it seems ~ *He smelled a rat when he noticed discrepancies in their story.*

smile upon: regard favourably ~ *Let's hope the heavens smile upon us for our wedding tomorrow.*

all smiles: very happy ~ *She was all smiles when she learned the good news.*

smoke like a chimney: smoke heavily ~ *No wonder he's easily puffed. He smokes like a chimney.*

the big smoke: the nearest big city ~ *Some people in these parts have never been to the big smoke.*

smoko: a short work break where one smokes a cigarette

smooth as a baby's bum: [informal] very smooth; soft to touch *also: smooth as silk

smooth out: *see: iron out

smooth over: make a problem less serious ~ *Jim tried to smooth over recent media reports about his behaviour.*

smooth sailing: smooth/easy progress ~ *The worst bit's over, it should be smooth sailing from now on.* *also: plain/clear sailing

smooth someone's ruffled feathers: calm someone; make them feel less angry/upset ~ *I spent the morning trying to smooth his ruffled feathers.*

smooth talker: someone who uses flattery/charm to convince someone to do something they might not want to do ~ *He's somewhat of a smooth talker.*

smooth/easy ride: a difficult, arduous time (said in the negative) ~ *We succeeded, but it's not been a smooth ride.*

smoothie: a thickened milkshake consisting of milk, fresh/frozen fruit, crushed ice, and frozen yoghurt.

snag: 1) sausage

2) an unforseen drawback causing delay ~ *There's one small snag: it won't be ready until next week.*

3) obstacle/impediment

snake in the grass: one who feigns friendship then betrays you ~ *He put his trust in a despicable rat who, as he soon discovered, was a snake in the grass.*

snap out of (it): come to one's senses; quickly recover from an emotional state ~ *I wish he'd snap out of his bad mood.*

snap someone's head off: to react angrily ~ *When I broached the subject, she snapped my head off!*

snap to: act/react quickly ~ *When the commanding officer barks a command, you snap to.*

snap up: acquire; purchase quickly/hastily ~ *1a) I snapped up a bargain at the markets. 1b) She snapped up the last tickets to the concert.*

in a snap: almost immediately ~ *The new system means orders are ready in a snap.*

snappy: 1) brisk/energetic/lively ~ *That's a snappy tune you're whistling.*

2) fashionable ~ *He's rather a snappy dresser.*

make it snappy: [spoken] command/order for someone to do something quickly ~ *Say what you have to say, but make it snappy, I'm in a rush.*

snazzy: stylish/fancy/bright ~ *She completed the outfit with a snazzy hat.*

snazz up: decorate; make fancy ~ *Some colourful cushions and some bright prints will snazz it up.* *also: jazz up; smarten up

(get) snazzed up: dress brightly/appealingly ~ *The event is an opportunity to get all snazzed up.*

sneak peek: a secret/private viewing ~ *We were given a sneak peek at the new design.*

sneak around: move sneakily/stealthily/furtively ~ *Someone was discovered sneaking around the rear of the shop.*

sneak away: leave/depart quietly/secretly ~ *I don't want to stay for the duration so I'll try to sneak away early.* *also: steal away

sneak up (on): approach quietly/without notice; happen when least expected ~ *The kitten sneaked up on the butterfly, ready to pounce.*

2) The deadline to finish the report seems to have sneaked up on me.

sneakers: canvas shoes with rubber/soft soles

sneaking suspicion: premonition/hunch; a belief based on little evidence ~ *I have a sneaking suspicion he's not telling the whole truth.*

sniff around: investigate something ~ *I'll sniff around at work for more information.*

sniff/sneeze at: express dislike/contempt ~ *1a) Management sniffed at their proposal. 1b) Her work is nothing to be sneezed at.*

sniff out: locate by sniffing; search and discover ~ *1a) The dog is especially trained to sniff out drugs. 1b) She managed to sniff out a great travel deal.*

sniffer dog: a dog trained to detect drugs/chemicals/something out of the ordinary

(the) sniffles: an action in the nose (causing you to sniff) when you have a cold/the flu; when you're crying ~ *1a) I've not got a true a cold, mainly the sniffles. 1b) I've got the sniffles after watching a sad movie.* *also: snuffles

snoop around: investigate; search covertly ~ *I caught her snooping around my office.*

snooty: high-class; aloof; haughty *also: snobby/snotty

snooze: daytime nap/short sleep *also: cat nap; forty winks; shut-eye; nap

snowball: grow in size and become harder to control ~ *He caused a minor problem to snowball.*

snowed under: overwhelmed with a task/job/work ~ *I'll look at the report tomorrow, I'm a bit snowed under at the moment.*

Snowy Mountains: Nestled in southeast New South Wales and incorporating the 6,900 square kilometres of Koscuiszko National Park—the largest in New South Wales—is an area known as the Snowy Mountains, or Snowies. The highest point in Australia's Great Dividing Range, the Snowy Mountain region is home to the 2,228-meter high Mt. Koscuiszko, the highest peak on the Australian mainland. Around three million people visit this area every year to ski the snowfields, indulge in snow sports, go bushwalking, kayaking, fishing, biking, or trekking to the top of Mt. Koscuiszko.

This area is also home to the Snowy Mountains Hydro-Electric Scheme, the largest engineering project ever undertaken in Australia and one of the most complex hydro-electric schemes in the world. The scheme consists of sixteen major dams, a pumping station, seven power stations, and 225 kilometres of pipelines, tunnels, and aqueducts. The scheme provides water to farming industries as well as producing up to ten percent of all electricity needs for New South Wales and two other states.

snoz: the nose *also: snout

snuff it: [informal] to die

snug as a bug in a rug: cosy/snug

snuggle up to/against/with: cuddle; stand/lie close together ~ *She snuggled up to me for warmth.*

snuggle up under: become cosy/snug under a blanket/cover ~ *Content and ready for sleep, she snuggled up under the bedclothes.*

and so on: et cetera ~ *It lists the company policies and so on.* *also: so forth

or so: approximately/around/about ~ *It's two metres or so in height.*

so-and-so: 1) a person who's name is ignored/forgotten ~ *It's a gossip magazine that tells of so-and-so doing this or so-and-so doing that.*

2) used in place of a swear word to describe an unpleasant person ~ *I hope they catch the rotten so-and-so that did this.*

so be it: [spoken] expression of resignation/acceptance ~ *If that's what you want to do, so be it.*

so far, so good: [spoken] that progress is satisfactory ~ *How's the project coming along? So far, so good.*

so long: [spoken] farewell; goodbye

so long as . . . : 1) inasmuch as; since ~ *So long as you're driving to the shops, why not take me?*

2) provided that ~ *I'll lend it to you, so long as you return it.*

3) while; during that time ~ *We'll be here as long as required.*

so much as: an intensifier used as a dismissal; even ~ *He left without so much as a goodbye.*

so much for: a spoken indicator that signifies the finish/end of something ~ *So much for staying up late, I fell asleep half way through the movie.*

so that: in order that; with the consequence/result that ~ *1a) So that you can properly hear the speaker, it's best to sit up front. 1b) You ought to write down the directions so that you don't get lost.*

so what: [spoken] expression of disregard/contempt ~ *So what if we're late, it's not as if we'll be penalised.*

soak through: of a liquid to penetrate/permeate material ~ *The rain quickly soaked through his thin cotton shirt.*

soak up: absorb ~ *1a) She used a towel to soak up the water. 1b) They paused to soak up the marvellous view.*

soap opera: sentimental/melodramatic daytime television/radio serial concerning the daily lives of a (or the same) group of people

so-called: 1) commonly/aptly named ~ *They were so-called because of their long tails.*

2) supposed ~ *Her so-called friends never turned up to her party.*

soccer: *see: football

Socceroos: Australia's national soccer team

sock it to someone: deliver or receive a forceful punch/strike/ blow ~ *They were arguing and then he socked him right in the nose.*

wouldn't it rot your socks: [spoken] expression of disgust/ disappointment ~ *Wouldn't it rot your socks—all this bad weather when we're supposed to be going camping!*

soft in the head: crazy/foolish/silly ~ *He must be going soft in the head if he thinks they'll agree to that!*

soft job: a job that requires little physical/hard work ~ *She's found a nice soft sales job.*

be soft on someone: have an affection for someone ~ *He's been soft on her for some time now.*

(have) a soft spot for someone: continue to like someone who sometimes behaves badly but is not a bad person ~ *Most regard him as a rogue, but she still has a soft spot for him.*

soften up: 1) make softer ~ *A special oil is applied to soften up the leather.*

2) adopt a more kindly/gentle manner ~ *At first he was aggressive and bullish, but he soon softened up.*

3) be nice to someone so as to weaken their resistance ~ *The government's trying to soften up the public for the coming price hikes.*

soften the blow: to make a predicted difficult experience more pleasant ~ *Emergency funds have been made available to soften the blow for families affected by the disaster.*

softy: generous; kind-hearted ~ *He comes across as harsh and uncaring but he's actually a big softy.*

solid as a rock: strong/sturdy ~ *1a) Their marriage is as solid as a rock. 1b) It appears flimsy, but the old structure is a solid as a rock.*

somehow or other: in some way/manner ~ *We'll get there somehow or other.*

something: to an extreme degree ~ *My leg is hurting something bad.*

something else: someone/something quite remarkable/impressive ~ *The performance was something else.*

something else again: something remarkable/impressive but unrelated/not connected ~ *She's a fine athlete, but her skills as tennis player are something else again.*

something or other: an unknown happening ~ *I don't exactly know what, but there's something or other going on in the meeting room.*

something to do with: be connected in somehow/in an unknown way ~ *I'm not sure how it works, but it's something to do with a magnetic field.*

a little something: 1) a token gift ~ *I bought her a little something for helping us.*

2) a small portion of food ~ *I'm not hungry right now, I had a little something to eat before I left.*

the start of something: the beginning of a new trend ~ *Scientists predict this discovery is the start of something much bigger.*

you know something/what . . . : [spoken] used before giving your opinion or announcing something ~ *1a) You know what, you're right. 1b) You know something, I don't really want to go.*

son of a gun: 1) an unpleasant/mean man ~ *Their leader is one mean son of a gun.*

2) [spoken] when addressing a rogue/scamp that you admire ~ *Frank, you old son of a gun, what have you been up to?*

3) expression of surprise ~ *Son of a gun, how did that happen?*

break into song: to suddenly begin singing ~ *He should have taken up singing as a career, he's always breaking into song.*

for a song: very cheaply ~ *They bought the house for a song ten years ago.*

make a song and dance of something: fuss excessively about something so as to be noticed ~ *1a) It was a simple request, but he made such a song and dance about it. 1b) Her work was only mediocre, but she made a song and dance about how good it was.*

swan song: final farewell; act/performance before retiring ~ *This tour will be the great soprano's swan song.*

sook/sooky: a cowardly/timid person; one who cries easily ~ *1a) Come on, you big sook—jump in. It's not that cold! 1b) Jane gets a bit sooky when she's tired.*

sooner or later: at some time in the future ~ *He'll find out sooner or later.*

soothe away: *see also: ease away (2)

drown one's sorrows: try to forget one's problems/troubles by drinking a lot of alcohol *also: drown one's troubles

sort: 1) a particular type of person ~ *He's not the sort to pick a fight with anyone.*

2) an attractive female ~ *Pete's new girlfriend is a real sort.*

sort of: to some degree/extent ~ *1a) It's sort of a green-blue colour. 1b) I sort of like it.* *also: kind of; in a way

sort (out) the men from the boys: that a difficult situation or activity will show who in the group are brave/strong and who are not ~ *The tricky ascent will sort out the men from the boys.*

sort someone out: deal with; punish someone causing problems ~ *This time she left it to her husband to sort out their wayward son.*

sort out/through: 1) deal with a problem/issue/situation ~ *Why is it always me who ends up sorting out your problems?*

2) clear up a mess of paperwork by sorting/filing ~ *I can't leave until I've sorted through all the files on my desk.* *see also: work something out

of sorts: having some, but not all, the characteristics of something; a variation of something ~ *It's a motor of sorts.*

all sorts: all varieties/types ~ *They sell all sorts of sporting goods.*

my/your sort: the type of person/thing you like ~ *1a) I agree he's handsome, but he's not my sort. 1b) A South Pacific cruise, now that's my sort of holiday*!

nothing of the sort: [spoken] emphatic denial ~ *How dare you accuse us! We did nothing of the sort.*

out of sorts: be irritable or vaguely unwell without cause ~ *I don't know what's wrong. I've been out of sorts all day.*

(it) takes all sorts: that one should accept that people will do (what you consider) unusual or strange things or have strange habits ~ *That guy was wearing a skirt! Well, it takes all sorts.*

that sort of thing: an example of a much larger group ~ *They sell old wares, bric-a-brac, that sort of thing.*

so-so: mediocre/average/ordinary ~ *How was it? So-so.*

sound as a bell: in very good condition; healthy ~ *I went for a check-up, and I'm as sound as a bell.*

sound someone out: question someone to determine their opinions ~ *I'll sound out the others to see what they think.*

sound something out: pronounce each letter/syllable of a word ~ *The teacher sounded out the new word to help everyone spell it correctly.*

sounds like a bit of alright: [spoken] a way of saying you like what someone suggested ~ *A movie, then dinner and a show. Sounds like a bit of alright to me.* *also: sounds good (to me)

spag bol: spaghetti Bolognese

spare tyre: 1) a roll of fat around the waist/abdomen

2) an extra tyre for the car

spark off: cause to start happening ~ *The massacre is certain to spark off a new round of violence.* *also: touch off

sparkie/y: electrician

spat: a minor argument/quarrel ~ *It wasn't a serious argument, just a bit of a spat.* *also: tiff; lover's spat

speak a different language: describes others who have different beliefs/opinions/backgrounds/attitudes ~ *He's a nice enough bloke, but we speak a different language.*

speak about: mention/discuss something ~ *1a) I need to speak to you about something. 1b) What do you want to speak about?*

speak at length: talk for a long period of time ~ *The police questioned the suspect at length.*

speak down to: speak condescendingly ~ *He was a fair boss who never spoke down to his employees.*

speak for: speak on behalf of another/others ~ *I'm sure I speak for us all when I say that you'll be greatly missed.*

speak(s) for itself: for something to be so obvious that no further comment or explanation is needed ~ *The fantastic work he's done on the project speaks for itself.*

speak for yourself: [spoken] response directed at the speaker to mean "don't presume that everyone agrees with you" ~ *Speak for yourself! I for one am not happy with the changes within the organisation.*

speak highly of: 1) praise someone/something ~ *I can't speak highly enough of him.*

2) for a fact to reflect favourably on someone/something ~ *All the recognition the school received speaks highly of the principal.*

speak ill of: say something unfavourable/bad about someone ~ *They're such wonderful people—I can't imagine that anyone would speak ill of them.*

speak one's/someone's language: have the same beliefs/attitudes/ understanding as another ~ *Did you say fishing? Now you're speaking my language.*

speak of . . . : something/someone worthy of mention ~ *1a) There's only one other person to speak of, and that's John, who has worked tirelessly throughout the project. 1b) There's nothing exciting to speak of.*

speak of the devil: mention someone's name who suddenly appears/enters ~ *Speak of the devil—here's Bob now.*

speak the same language: share similar opinions/views/ideas; have the same likes and dislikes ~ *We understand each other's needs because we speak the same language.*

speak one's mind: be forthright; talk freely; speak out ~ *No one ever wonders what she's thinking because she easily speaks her mind.* *also: speak out

speaking of . . . : [spoken] interjection used to steer the conversation in another direction though related to the subject being discussed ~ *Speaking of John, I saw him last week at the beach.*

speak out: speak strongly/fearlessly or publicly ~ *Previous threats by their tormentors made them too scared to speak out.*

speak of something: show clearly that something happened/ existed ~ *Her vast collection of ornaments spoke of her love of cats.*

speak up: 1) speak so one can be heard ~ *Don't forget to speak up when it's your turn to say something.* *also: talk up

2) [spoken] interjection asking someone to speak louder ~ *Speak up, we can't hear you.*

speak(s) volumes: that a person's appearance or manner tells a lot about them ~ *His appearance speaks volumes.*

be not/not be on speaking terms: that two people are not speaking with each other because they've had an argument ~ *Sadly, they've not been on speaking terms since the fallout.*

nothing/none to speak of: have little or nothing worthy of mention ~ *1a) We sat mostly in silence, because there was nothing to speak of. 1b) We've had virtually no rain to speak of this winter.*

generally/broadly speaking: used when expressing an idea that is usually true, but not in all instances ~ *Generally speaking, most of the patrons are responsible drinkers.* *also: mostly

so to speak: in a manner of speaking ~ *His ideas were a bit over the top, so to speak.*

be spoken for: for someone/something to be promised to someone else ~ *Nearly everyone here is spoken for.*

specs: spectacles/ eyeglasses

speed camera: a permanent fixed-site system that uses a camera and a vehicle monitoring device to detect and identify vehicles travelling over the legal speed limit

speed away: quickly move/drive away from something ~ *The car sped away from the kerb.*

speed up: to happen/move faster ~ *1a) We decided to speed up the process so we could finish on time. 1b) It's not a good idea to speed up when passing a speed camera.* *also: speed something up

speedo: speedometer; speed gauge in a vehicle

Speedo: a brand of swimwear such as those used for competitive swimming or diving. The popularity of this iconic Australian brand has led to the use of its name to refer to any type of racing suit regardless of the maker (always referred to in the plural). ~ *He wears Speedos under his boardies.*

spell: 1) a short, indefinite period of time ~ *He had a spell in jail earlier this year.*

2) a short rest from work/activity ~ *I think I'll sit down for a spell.*

3) to relieve someone at work by taking a turn ~ *Here, I'll take over while you have a spell.*

4) a period of a particular type of weather ~ *We're in for a wet spell this summer.*

spell disaster: predict/indicate disaster/a tragedy ~ *This drought could spell disaster for farmers.*

spell trouble: signify future trouble; be the cause of possible problems ~ *1a) This information we just received could spell trouble. 1b) This latest scandal could spell trouble for the government.*

spell out: 1) [spoken] to say/explain clearly because someone has not understood ~ *For the last time, NO, you can't go! Do I have to spell it out for you?*

2) write or say the letters of a word in the correct order ~ *I'm often asked if I could spell out my surname.*

spend up big: spend extravagantly ~ *If I ever win the lottery, I'm going to spend up big.*

(to) spew up: to vomit ~ *She's been spewing up all day.* *also: chunder

spewing: be extremely angry ~ *He was spewing when he heard what they'd done.* *also: spitting chips

spewy: to feel so sick as to want to vomit; be inclined to vomit ~ *I've been a bit spewy today, so no dinner for me, thanks.*

spice up: 1) make something more lively/exciting ~ *The director told me I need to spice up my performance.*

2) make drink/food spicier ~ *This food needs some spicing up.*

spick-and-span: very neat and tidy ~ *She soon had the house looking spick-and-span.*

spicy: scandalous; risqué ~ *She got involved in a spicy romance when she was in Italy.*

spiffed up/spivved up: *see: dressed to the nines

spiffy: something unusual/unique/interesting ~ *He got dressed and topped it off with a spiffy hat.*

spike someone's drink: an illegal and dangerous act where a substance is covertly added to someone's drink in order to drug them

spill the beans: knowingly or unknowingly reveal/divulge a confidence/secret ~ *Okay, who spilt the beans on my little secret?*

(go for) a spin: take a short ride in a car/vehicle/motorbike ~ *Jim is taking me for a spin in his new car.*

spin a yarn: tell an unlikely or exaggerated story/tale ~ *I'm not sure the story he told us was true. I think he's spinning a yarn.*

spin out: of a car/vehicle to rotate and skid out of control ~ *I rounded the corner and spun out on the wet road.*

in a spin: dizzy/bewildered/confused ~ *All that information has left my head in a spin.*

spirit away: carry away mysteriously ~ *Detectives found the evidence had been spirited away from the holding area.*

spit and polish: a thorough cleaning/polish with attention to order/appearance ~ *I gave it a bit of spit and polish and it came up like new.*

spit it out: [spoken] a way of encouraging someone to say what they're having trouble saying ~ *Come on, spit it out—what is it that you have to tell me?*

spit the dummy: a sudden and unreasonable display of childish anger ~ *He spat the dummy when he heard what they'd done.* *also: throw a temper tantrum; have a fit

spit up: cough out/expectorate/spit out ~ *Alarmingly, he suddenly began spitting up blood!*

spitting image: mirror image; an exact likeness of someone ~ *You're the spitting image of your mother.*

splash around/about: play and splash in water ~ *The kids happily splashed about at the water's edge.*

make a splash: attract a lot of attention ~ *She made a splash with her debut performance.*

split hairs: argue over unimportant details; make unnecessary distinctions ~ *Let's not split hairs, five dollars is not a big margin.*

split one's sides: laugh merrily/heartily ~ *We nearly split our sides laughing.*

split second: a fraction of a second; an instant ~ *In a split second it was gone!*

split the difference: pay half of the cost; the average of differing estimates ~ *Let's split the difference, which means we each pay ten dollars.*

split up: 1) finish/end a relationship/marriage ~ *Did you hear that John and Sue have split up?*

2) divide equally ~ *We split the winnings up between us.*

3) go/move in different directions ~ *We'll have a better chance of finding them if we split up.*

splitting headache: a severe/throbbing headache ~ *I'll have to lie down, I've a splitting headache.*

spoilt rotten: extravagantly indulged to the detriment of one's character ~ *She's been spoilt rotten all those years, now she expects everyone else to do everything for her.*

sponge off: live at someone else's expense; freeload ~ *He still lives at home and sponges off his parents.*

be a sport: [spoken] what you say to encourage/convince someone to be admirable; do something they may not want to do ~ *Would you be a sport and finish this for me?* *also: be a good sport

good sport: one who accepts defeat/loss/teasing cheerfully; someone admirable ~ *We played a devious trick on him, but he was a good sport about it.*

poor/bad sport: one who doesn't readily accept defeat/loss ~ *No one wants to play with her anymore because she's such a bad sport.* *also: bad/poor loser

spot check: a random/selective examination ~ *A spot check was done on all the safety equipment.*

spot on: exact/precise ~ *Your prediction was spot on!*

bright spot: a pleasant happening/occurrence amidst unpleasant happenings ~ *The only bright spot in their lacklustre performance was a stunning try just before halftime.*

in spots: occasionally; here and there ~ *The rain fell only in spots.*

hot spot: a place where there's lots of violent activity/unrest

be put on the spot: be asked a question that's awkward/ embarrassing to answer ~ *He put me on the spot when he asked me if he could come.*

sore spot: a subject that evokes emotion ~ *I wouldn't question her just yet. It's still a bit of a sore spot for her.* *also: sore point

weak spot: 1) lacking in mental or physical strength; a flaw ~ *Saying no to chocolate cake is my weak spot.*

2) a liking/fondness for something/someone ~ *She has a weak spot for defenceless animals.*

on the spot: 1) where one stands ~ *I'm standing on the exact spot where the event took place.*

2) at the same place something is happening ~ *Firemen were on the spot in minutes.*

3) immediately ~ *He was fired on the spot for stealing.*

4) without leaving the position you're in ~ *We ran on the spot to keep warm.*

spout off: utter angrily at length/to excess ~ *1a) He can spout off for hours about it. 1b) She was spouting off about how unfairly she was treated. 1c) He's spouting off about catching the biggest fish.*

spread across (one's face): of an expression to slowly appear on someone's face ~ *A shy smile slowly spread across her face.*

spread around: be broadcast ~ *News of their engagement soon spread around town.*

spread out: 1) unfold or open out, especially over a flat surface ~ *She spread out the picnic blanket on the soft grass.*

2) diffuse; move outward ~ *Searchers spread out so as to cover the entire area.*

3) splay; widen ~ *The dealer spread the cards out on the table.*

4) have people/things stationed in many parts of a large area ~ *Forces are now spread out over most of the country.*

5) disperse over an area or time ~ *It would be easier if the course was spread out over one year instead of six months.*

6) a large area of land that you can see before you ~ *The couple stood gazing in awe at the vast valley spread out below them.*

spread on thick: exaggerate a story/situation ~ *He was spreading it on a bit thick with the story about how heroic he was.*

spread yourself thin: try to do too many things at once

spread through: move through an area; become larger ~ *The fire quickly spread through the building.*

spread like wildfire: move quickly ~ *The news spread like wildfire throughout the small community.*

spread your wings: start to live independently; experience new things ~ *The overseas job offer will allow him to spread his wings.*

spring a leak: develop a leak ~ *The sight of a small water spout in the middle of the yard meant only that the garden hose had sprung a leak.*

no spring chicken: someone well past youth; an old person ~ *I'm amazed he can lift it! He's no spring chicken.*

spring something on someone: surprise someone by telling them something ~ *1a) I won't tell her the good news now, I'll spring it on her later. 1b) A request to speak at the meeting was sprung on me only minutes ago.*

spring to mind: of an idea/thought to occur to someone ~ *Nothing significant springs to mind when I look at that picture.*

spring up: 1) develop/appear suddenly ~ *New shopping centres are springing up everywhere.*

2) energetically arise from a seated position to a standing position ~ *She sprung up out of the chair when her name was called.*

sprout up: of a seedling to sprout ~ *Tiny shoots were sprouting up everywhere.*

spruce up: clean/tidy something; groom/dress oneself nicely ~ *1a) She quickly spruced up the house before the visitors arrived. 1b) He looks handsome when he's all spruced up.* *see also: smarten up

spud: potato

spunk: courage/spirit ~ *It would have taken a lot of spunk to do that.*

squander away: thoughtlessly waste/use up something ~ *1a) With his lifestyle it didn't take too long to squander away his inheritance. 1b) She squandered away her wages on clothes.*

square deal: an honest/fair deal or transaction ~ *You'll always get a square deal with that company.*

square meal: a healthy/nutritious/substantial meal ~ *You should eat at least one square meal a day.*

square up: pay/settle an account/bill ~ *I'll give you ten dollars and we'll be all squared up.*

square up to someone: bravely face/tackle something/someone ~ *It was time to square up to his opponent.*

square peg in a round hole: a misfit ~ *She doesn't appear suited to this type of work, it's like she's a square peg in a round hole.*

fair and square: 1) honestly/justly ~ *We won fair and square.*

2) in an exact spot on the body ~ *The ball hit me fair and square on the chin.*

square-eyes: 1) derogatory term for someone who wears glasses

2) humorous term for someone who watches too much television

squash down: compress/pack something down ~ *It'll fit if you squash it down.*

squatter: one who illegally occupies a vacant building

squawk: complain noisily ~ *Everyone's squawking about the new tax increases.*

squeaky clean: 1) without fault/unblemished ~ *1a) Mary has lost her squeaky clean image. 1b) My driving record is squeaky clean.*

2) extremely clean ~ *This will make your hair squeaky clean.*

squeeze through: force (by compressing/flattening) through a narrow/tight space ~ *Thieves entered the premises by squeezing through an open window.*

tight squeeze: of having restricted space because of overcrowding ~ *1a) It was a tight squeeze in that small room. 1b) It's going to be a tight squeeze fitting all that equipment in here.*

squillions: an obscene amount of money

squirrel away: save/hoard for future use ~ *She's squirrelled away some emergency money.* *also: stash away

(have a) squiz(zy): a casual/brief look at something ~ *1a) Yeah, come over and have a squizzy. 1b) I'm just nicking next door to have a squiz at Jack's new car.*

(a) stab (at something): an attempt at doing something ~ *I've never done this type of work before, but I'll have a stab at it.*

stab in the dark: an uninformed guess; estimation ~ *It's just a stab in the dark, but I think this might be the answer to your problem.* *also: wild guess

to (have a) stack: to crash a bicycle ~ *I stacked my bike on the way home and damaged the gears.*

stack on: increase in weight ~ *I've stacked on the weight since leaving work.*

stack the deck: arrange playing cards to your advantage ~ *He began to wonder if the deck was stacked.*

stack up: 1) compare to; measure up to/against ~ *Their team didn't stack up to the opposition.*

2) appear truthful/plausible ~ *His story wasn't stacking up.*

stag night: a party for men only, especially for a man before he gets married

set the stage: make possible/likely to happen ~ *The negotiations set the stage for future meetings.*

the stage is set: that the conditions/circumstances are ready for something to happen/occur ~ *The stage seems set for negotiations to begin.*

at some stage: in the near future ~ *You're going to have to confront her at some stage.*

be/take centre stage: the centre of attention; the most noticeable person/thing in a situation/at an event ~ *My car will take centre stage at the motor show.* *also: hold the stage in

stages: *see: bit by bit

at this stage of the game: at this point/place in the process/ workings; right now ~ *It's too late to change the plans at this stage of the game.*

stagger about: move unsteadily/totter (as if drunk) ~ *Disorientated, he staggered about in the dark.*

stamp of approval: approval/acceptance ~ *It's got my stamp of approval.*

stamp out: end something by taking firm action ~ *It's their duty to stamp out corruption.*

stand alone: something/someone having no support ~ *I stand alone in my decision.*

stand around: stand/stay in one position doing little or nothing ~ *1a) Don't just stand around—do something! 1b) There was little we could do but stand around and wait.*

stand by: 1) watch something happen and not be able to take action/assist ~ *Helpless to do anything, they could only stand by and watch as the disaster unfolded.*

2) be resolute; uphold one's beliefs ~ *Right or wrong, I'll stand by my decision.*

3) provide emotional support to someone ~ *I'll stand by you no matter what.*

4) be ready for action ~ *Helen is standing by to answer your questions.*

stand corrected: to admit you are wrong ~ *I stand corrected on my earlier statement.*

stand firm/fast: 1) refuse to change your mind on something ~ *I stand firm on my pledge to provide financial assistance.*

2) remain in the same position/place ~ *Amazingly, the makeshift shelter stood fast against the gale-force winds.*

stand for (something): 1) represent; mean ~ *The sculpture stands for freedom.*

2) tolerate; allow ~ *I won't stand for that type of behaviour.*

3) try to get chosen for a position in office ~ *He intends to stand for mayor next elections.*

stand idle/empty: the condition/state of a building ~ *1b) Most of the restaurants in this once-thriving district now stand empty. 1b) The old factory has stood empty for nearly fifty years.*

stand in: be someone's substitute ~ *Can you stand in for Frank when he's away?*

stand in line: join the end of a queue ~ *We stood in line for thirty minutes to get tickets.*

stand in someone's way: 1) impede someone's progress ~ *Please move, you're standing in my way.*

2) stop someone from doing something ~ *Don't let me stop you, I won't stand in your way.*

stand in the way (of something): hinder/impede/block something happening ~ *1a) A minority group is standing in the way of the land development.*

stand like a shag on a rock: completely alone/exposed (a shag is a sea bird) ~ *Where have you been? I've been standing here like a shag on a rock for half an hour!*

stand on one's own two feet: needing no help/assistance; be independent/self-sufficient ~ *He's had to stand on his own two feet since leaving school.*

stand/hold one's ground: 1) remain resolute in one's opinions/ beliefs ~ *She stood her ground and refused to sign despite his bullying tactics.*

2) refuse to retreat in an attack ~ *A small group of warriors stood their ground against the attacking force.*

stand out a mile: be easily seen; prominent/conspicuous ~ *You stand out a mile in that orange hat.* *also: stands out like a sore toe/thumb

stand out from the crowd: be noticeably different; remarkably superior ~ *Of all the performances, yours stood out from the crowd.*

stand over: watch/supervise closely ~ *It's as if she's checking on my work the way she watches over me.*

stand someone doing something: be intolerant of someone's actions ~ *1a) How can you stand that terrible noise? 1b) I won't stand any more backchat from you.*

stand someone in good stead: a skill/qualification that will be useful in the future ~ *Your experience in this field of work will stand you in good stead.*

stand someone up: intentionally fail to meet someone at pre-arranged time/place ~ *I'm not sure if she's late or has stood me up.*

stand stock-still: stand completely still ~ *Upon seeing us, the animal stood stock still then retreated into the darkness.*

stand the test of time: 1) be enduring/worthy/true ~ *I can't imagine this fashion trend standing the test of time.*

2) remain in good working order over time ~ *This grand old clock has certainly stood the test of time.*

stand(s) to reason: appear likely to be true; be obvious/clear ~ *It stands to reason that if you go out in the rain you'll get wet.*

stand the strain: tolerate adverse conditions/situations ~ *She resigned because she couldn't stand the strain of working under such a tyrant.*

stand trial: appear in a court of law to be judged ~ *He's been charged, and will stand trial next month.*

stand up: 1) prove to be correct/true ~ *The contract wouldn't stand up in a court of law.*

2) rise from a sitting position; be standing ~ *Could everyone please stand up?*

stand up and be counted: make your opinion/support for something be known publicly ~ *Those who were brave enough to stand up and be counted were arrested.*

stand up for: defend/support something/someone that is being criticised ~ *1a) You must stand up for what you believe in. 1b) I stood up for him because he was struggling to defend himself.*

stand up to: confront something/someone fearlessly/courageously ~ *He's not afraid to stand up to anyone.*

as it stands: *see: as is

from where someone stands: according to a particular person's understanding/viewpoint ~ *From where they stand, a new shopping complex will certainly put them out of business.*

know where you stand: be sure of what someone thinks about you/what's expected of you; be certain of your rank/position ~ *1a) He's quite strict, but everyone knows where they stand with him. 1b) She was blunt in her report, but at least I know where I stand.*

still stands: of a record/offer/law to remain as such ~ *1a) Despite what's happened, our offer still stands. 1b) His record still stands today.*

stare up at: look upwardly at something ~ *They stood transfixed staring up at the enormous rainforest trees.* *also: gaze up

stark: utter/absolute/complete ~ *You'd have to be stark raving mad to attempt that stunt.*

starkers: naked/nude *also: stark naked; in the altogether; in the bollocky; in the buff; in the nuddy; in the raw

start afresh/anew: make a new start ~ *He intends to start afresh when he gets out of jail.*

start back: 1) begin a return journey ~ *It's time we started back.*

2) resume working/studying after a break ~ *I start back at work next week.*

start from: begin doing something at a particular point in time ~ *Starting from tomorrow, I'm on a diet.*

start from scratch: start from the very beginning/from nothing ~ *1a) Everything was ruined, so I started again from scratch. 1b) I made it from scratch.*

start off: 1) begin doing something ~ *She started the proceedings off by fielding questions from the audience.*

2) cause someone/have cause to react again ~ *Just one look at his goofy expression was all it took to start us off laughing again.*

start off on the wrong/right foot: have a good/bad beginning; make a good/bad first impression ~ *1a) Being prepared for a job interview will start you off on the right foot. 1b) I started off on the wrong foot by being late on the first day of my new job.*

start on: 1) begin work on something ~ *We'll soon be starting on the next stage of the project.*

2) begin to berate someone ~ *Don't start on Sally, she had nothing to do with it!*

3) begin dealing with someone ~ *When I've finished here I'll start on showing you how it's done.* *also: make a start on

start out: begin a journey ~ *They started out at dawn.* *also: start off (1)

start out/off as: begin in a particular way/manner/status ~ *1a) The day started out sunny and hot, but now it's cloudy and cold. 1b) I started out liking the job, but now I don't really like it.*

start over: 1) begin doing something from the beginning ~ *I lost count and had to start all over again.*

2) begin career/lifestyle again ~ *I'm glad to be financially secure, because I'm too old to start over.*

start out from: begin a journey from a particular place ~ *We start out from Melbourne.*

start something: 1) instigate an argument/fight ~ *She's argumentative—always starting something.*

2) cause/create/instigate something untried/untested/unknown ~ *You might be starting something there with that crazy dance move.*

start (something) up: 1) start an engine/motor ~ *Start her up, let's see how it sounds.*

2) begin operating a business venture/organization ~ *We plan on starting up a café.*

starting point: the place something begins/starts ~ *Sydney's the starting point of the race.*

starting to get to one/someone: beginning to affect one/someone ~ *The pressure is starting to get to him.*

start with something: 1) at the start ~ *We started with $100 and now we have fifty.*

2) as the first thing ~ *We'll start with a few easy questions.* *also: start out with

get someone/one started: 1) cause someone/have cause to react ~ *Don't get him started on that topic, you'll never shut him up.*

2) cause/help someone begin something new ~ *It was her cousin that helped get her started in the publishing industry.*

the start of something big: the commencement/beginning of a new trend or method/manner/way of doing something that has an impact/is recognised world-wide ~ *The recent discovery of a more accurate treatment could be the start of something big.*

get started: begin doing something ~ *1a) okay, let's get started. 1b) She can't wait to get started in her new job.*

to start with: used as a beginning/to introduce the first point to support an argument ~ *1a) To start with, you're not trained to do that. 1b) I'll give you some easy questions to start with.* *also: to begin with

station: a large sheep or cattle farm

stay up: 1) remain awake; not in bed ~ *We stayed up all night watching TV.*

2) remain in a fixed/upright/horizontal position ~ *These pants won't stay up unless I wear a belt.*

staying power: one's stamina/endurance ~ *He certainly has a lot of staying power.*

steady on/up: *see: hold your horses

(a) steal: bought cheaply/at a bargain price ~ *At only ten dollars it's a steal.*

steal someone's heart: win someone's affection ~ *It took just one look from the little puppy and he'd stolen our hearts.*

steal someone's thunder: take the credit/praise for something someone else did ~ *They used Janet's idea and turned it into a successful marketing campaign, stealing her thunder.*

steal the limelight: get more attention that anyone/anything ~ *Her performance stole the limelight.* *also: steal the show

(all) steamed up: 1) become angry/upset ~ *Look, you're getting all steamed up over nothing.*

2) become clouded with steam ~ *The bathroom was all steamed up.*

steel oneself: mentally/physically prepare for something unpleasant ~ *You'd best steel yourself for some bad news.* *also: brace oneself

steeped in: immersed; infused in ~ *The area is steeped in history.*

steer away: direct/turn away from ~ *The car skidded but I managed to steer it away from oncoming traffic.*

steer clear (of): avoid someone/something ~ *1a) That part of town is dangerous—I'd steer clear of it if I were you. 1b) Steer clear of Lisa, she's in a bad mood.*

step aside/down: relinquish/resign from one's position/post ~ *It was time to step aside and let his son take over the business.*

step back: 1) move backwards away from something ~ *Please step back from the edge of the platform.*

2) pause to consider the next stage ~ *I stepped back from the project to see what had been done and to get some fresh ideas.*

3) go back in time ~ *When you walked in, it was like stepping back forty years.*

step forward: reveal/identify oneself; volunteer to do something ~ *1a) So far, no one's stepped forward to claim responsibility. 1b) Tony stepped forward and offered his help.*

step in: 1) intervene in a dispute ~ *I stepped in when there was a threat of physical violence.*

2) act as a replacement ~ *The deputy director is stepping in to take his place while he's on leave.*

3) make a brief/informal visit ~ *Pete stepped in to see how I was.*

step inside: enter a place ~ *Could you step inside my office for a minute?*

step into someone's shoes: replace someone; take over someone's position/role/duty ~ *She should step into my shoes for a week to see how difficult the job really is before being so critical.* *also: fill someone's shoes

step it up: [spoken] directive to increase the pace; improve something ~ *Come on, step it up. We haven't got all day!*

step/tread on: put one's feet on something/someone ~ *1a) I stepped on something sharp. 1b) Ow! You trod on my foot!*

step/tread on someone's toes: knowingly/unknowingly upset/ irritate someone ~ *He's trying to prove himself, but is stepping on everyone's toes in the process.*

step on it: [spoken] directive to go faster/hurry ~ *I'm in a bit of a rush—could you step on it?*

step out: go outside; be absent from for a short period of time ~ *He's just stepped out to get a coffee.*

step outside: [spoken] threatening invitation by one to another to settle the matter, presumably to fight ~ *Why don't we step outside and settle this?*

step up: 1) increase/advance ~ *We had to step up production to keep up with consumer demands.*

2) come forward ~ *She stepped up to the microphone to deliver her speech.*

step up to the plate/mark: take responsibility for doing something ~ *It's up to authorities to step up to the plate and take control of the situation.*

a step up from: a higher level/stage in a process ~ *This apartment is a step up from the dingy little flat we previously occupied.*

be/keep/stay one step ahead: be better prepared; have advanced knowledge ~ *He thought he'd made good his escape, unaware that the authorities were one step ahead of him.*

have a spring in your step: walk with energy/happiness ~ *Excited at being here, she walked with a spring in her step.*

keep in step: walk/dance/march at the same pace/rhythm as others ~ *It's hard keeping in step with him because he has such a long stride.*

out of step: to have ideas that are not like those of other people ~ *The methods used are out of step with recent changes.*

stew over/on it: 1) think about/consider something at length ~ *He stewed over the options all weekend.*

2) fret/worry ~ *You can't change what happened so it's no good stewing over it.*

stew in one's own juices: suffer the consequences of your actions ~ *He left her to stew in her own juices.*

in a stew: in an agitated/anxious state ~ *She's got herself in a right royal stew over nothing!*

stick around: remain/stay in a place ~ *Let's stick around for a bit and see what happens.*

stick at/with it: persevere with something ~ *I don't particularly like my job, but I'll stick at it for a while.* *also: stick it out

stick by: remain loyal to; support someone ~ *I'll stick by you, no matter happens.*

stick in one's mind: remain in one's memory; be remembered ~ *I've got that new song stuck on my mind.*

stick like glue: firmly adhere/stick to ~ *I can't get it off—it's stuck like glue.*

stick one's neck out: take a risk because you believe in something ~ *I know I'm sticking my neck out in saying the application will be approved.*

stick one's nose in: pry; interfere ~ *She's always sticking her nose into someone else's business.*

stick out a mile: be prominent or easily seen ~ *Her pink hair sticks out a mile.* *also: stand out like a sore thumb/toe

stick to something: 1) do something that you promised/decided to do ~ *I'm determined to stick to this diet.*

2) continue to follow the same way/path ~ *We'd best stick to the route we know so we don't get lost.*

3) stick to doing something you're familiar with/you know about ~ *I'd rather stick to this way of doing it.*

4) talk about one thing only ~ *Don't tell me anything else, just stick to the facts.*

5) adhere to something ~ *It's stuck to the wall.*

stick together/to someone: 1) stay close another person/other people ~ *Let's stick together for safety.*

2) support/uphold each other ~ *We're sticking together no matter what.*

stick to your guns: remain resolute/firm in one's beliefs/ideas ~ *Ignore anyone who tries to argue otherwise. Just stick to your guns.*

stick through: penetrate through something ~ *All I could see was a dog's nose sticking through the hole in the fence.*

stick something up: 1) affix/fasten something in a prominent position ~ *I'll stick the newsletter up on the noticeboard.*

2) hold something up high; raise something ~ *She stuck her hand up in the air to get their attention.*

stick up for: defend/support/speak in defence of someone ~ *Don't worry if they question you about it. I'll stick up for you.*

make something stick: make something accepted/agreed upon ~ *The authorities didn't have enough evidence to make the charges stick.*

stick-in-the-mud: someone predictably conservative who lacks imagination/enthusiasm ~ *He'll never agree to the changes, he's too much of a stick-in-the-mud.* *also: wowser

the sticks: a remote area ~ *I can't remember exactly where, but it's somewhere out in the sticks.*

sticky: 1) [of the weather] warm/humid/muggy ~ *These are the hot, sticky days of summer.*

2) a quick (curious) look at something ~ *Let's take a walk and have a sticky at the newly renovated house.*

stickybeak: one who's curious ~ *Our cat wants to know everything we do. She's a real stickybeak.*

(have) sticky fingers: likely to steal ~ *He's one to watch if he comes into the shop, he's known to have sticky fingers.*

sticky situation: a difficult/awkward situation

stiff drink: a strong alcoholic drink (to settle one's nerves) ~ *I need a stiff drink after all that.*

stiff/tough cheddar: [spoken informal] rude way to show lack of sympathy ~ *Stiff cheddar! You can't have your own way all the time!* *also: stiff shit; tough titties

stiffen up: become stiff/rigid/tense ~ *1a) My knees stiffen up if I sit for long periods. 1b) Alone in the house, she stiffened up when she heard strange noises.*

stinks of: indicative of something else ~ *The story stinks of a cover-up!*

. . . stinks to high heaven: to have a highly offensive odour ~ *Phew, it stinks to high heaven in there!* *also: on the nose

make a stink: cause an uproar/fuss ~ *I can't believe they made such a stink over nothing!* *also: kick up a stink

a stinker/stinking hot: a very hot day ~ *1a) What a stinker of a day it's been. 1b) It's been a stinking hot day.*

stir up a hornet's nest: cause great upset to a large number of people ~ *An investigation into the company's business practices has stirred up a hornet's nest.*

stir someone: humorously tease to invoke emotion ~ *There's not really a big hairy spider on your back. I'm just stirring you.*

stir something up: 1) agitate/stimulate ~ *He sang a few racy tunes to stir up the audience.*

2) displace/move ~ *Strong winds easily stirred up the sand.*

(be) a stir/stirrer: one who stirs someone ~ *Don't be such stirrer!*

cause/create a stir: arouse interest/excitement or trouble/ commotion ~ *1a) His comments caused quite a stir. 1b) It seems he set out to deliberately create a stir.*

stir-crazy: become slightly mad/crazy by being confined inside a small space for too long ~ *The kids are going stir-crazy at having to stay indoors.*

stitch up: *see: sew up

stock up on: purchase a large amount of something for future use ~ *They stocked up food and drink for the camping trip.*

stock up (with): increase/accumulate a supply of something ~ *We're stocked up with enough firewood to see us through the winter.* *also: store up

stockman/stockperson: Someone who looks after cattle or sheep on a large property known as a station. A stockman is responsible for treating illness/injuries and all manner of care of the animals. It's also a stockman's job to inspect, maintain, and/or repair fences, gates, and yards. The head stockman is responsible for a number of workers and a range of station operations including staff training and repair and maintenance of property structures. Stockmen traditionally ride horses and are aided by a stock whip and working dogs.

(be) stoked: extremely excited/thrilled/pleased ~ *I'm absolutely stoked you're coming!*

stoke up: tend to/feed a fire; cause a fire to burn more intensely ~ *He stoked up the fire to warm the room.*

(to) stomach something: tolerate/bear/endure something unpleasant ~ *I'm not going to be able to stomach this for much longer.*

have the stomach for . . . : be brave enough to do something unpleasant ~ *She hasn't got the stomach for that sort of work.*

stone the crows: [spoken] expression of surprise/amazement or frustration ~ *Stone the crows—look who's here!*

stone-broke: having no money ~ *I can't afford it, I'm stone-broke.* *also: stone motherless broke; stony-broke

stone-cold sober: not affected in any way by alcohol ~ *I've not had a drop to drink. I'm stone-cold sober.*

stoned: under the influence of illegal drugs ~ *He's pretty much stoned most nights.*

stoned out of one's head/brain: to be heavily under the influence of illegal drugs ~ *He was so stoned out of his brain he didn't know his name.*

stone's throw (away): a short distance ~ *1a) I only live a stone's throw from the shops.1b) The school is only a stone's throw away.*

stop at nothing: do everything in one's power to achieve something ~ *1a) So intent is he that he'll stop at nothing to achieve his career goals. 1b) They'll stop at nothing, including murder, to get what they want.*

stop something's tracks: 1) prevent someone from continuing along a track/path ~ *The sight of a deadly brown snake across the path stopped me in my tracks.*

2) halt progress ~ *Ugly protests have stopped construction in its tracks.*

stop dead in one's tracks: come to an abrupt halt when walking because of fear ~ *We all stopped dead in our tracks when we heard the terrifying scream.*

no stopping someone/something: be unable to prevent someone from doing something ~ *Once they'd worked out a plan there was no stopping them.*

stop-out: one who stays out late/all night

stop-work meeting: a workplace meeting (during working hours) structured to discuss industrial matters with employees

store away: put in storage (for later use) ~ *Excess stock is stored away in a warehouse.*

storm out/off: leave angrily ~ *1a) I heard raised voices then saw her storm out of the meeting. 1b) He stormed off in a huff.*

a storm in a teacup: a small issue/problem that's made worse than it is ~ *They're creating a storm in a teacup. It poses no danger at all to anyone's health.*

take by storm: 1) gain quick success in a particular place ~ *The show took New York by storm.*

2) attack and capture by force/surprise ~ *Enemy troops took the building by storm.*

talk/sing/dance/cook up a storm: do/say something energetically ~ *Those two can certainly dance up a storm.*

the calm before the storm: a period of calm/quiet before an active/busy period ~ *We've got lots of visitors coming, so I'm having a quiet cuppa and enjoying the calm before the storm.*

weather/ride out the storm: continue unharmed by a difficult/ troublesome situation/period ~ *They were sufficiently prepared to ride out the financial storm.*

story: 1) excuse/alibi; lie ~*1a) Late again! What's your story this time? 1b) Have you been telling stories again?*

2) a true account of a current situation ~ *What's the story with Jeff? I heard he was leaving.*

a cock-and-bull story: an obviously false/far-fetched account ~ *He told me some cock-and-bull story about owning houses in three countries.* *also: tall story; tall tale; a likely story

another story: expressed when one has more to say; that there is more to the story ~ *There was the time I got stuck in a lift, but that's another story.*

end of story: [spoken] expressed when one has made a statement that is not to be challenged or contradicted ~ *You're not going—end of story!*

it's/that's my story and I'm sticking to it: [spoken] used after you tell a story that may or may not be credible ~ *I definitely saw a fish with two heads. That's my story and I'm sticking to it!*

(it's) the same old story: used to describe a bad situation that repeats itself ~ *It's the same old story—he comes home late, she gets upset, and they argue.*

sob story: an excuse intended to arouse sympathy/pity ~ *She told me some sob story about her husband leaving her, but in fact she was the one who left him.*

tell stories: to fabricate/invent an account of an event ~ *She's telling stories. That's not what happened.*

stow away: put something in storage; store something ~ *Life jackets are stowed away in here when not in use.*

stow-away: one who conceals themselves in a transport vehicle in order to obtain free transportation ~ *Upon further inspection, more stowaways were found in the engine room.*

straight away: immediately ~ *I'll come straight away!*

straight from the horse's mouth: directly from the source ~ *I got the information straight from the horse's mouth.*

(on) the straight and narrow: behave in an honest/moral way ~ *She's kept on the straight and narrow since leaving prison.*

straight out/off: directly; candidly ~ *I told her straight out what I thought of the plan.*

straight out of/from/to: directly; immediately ~ *1a) He copied it straight from the book. 1b) She was straight out of school when she got the job. 1c) I got straight to the point.*

straight through: move/travel without stopping/interference/ directly ~ *1a) This train goes straight through to Central Station. 1b) Please put all calls straight through to me. 1c) The bullet went straight through his shoulder.*

straight up: used to show you're honest/forthright ~ *I'll tell you straight up that it won't be easy.*

(as) straight as an arrow: very straight ~ *This outback road runs straight as an arrow for 100 kilometres.* *also: straight as a die

get things/it/this straight: make clear; clarify the facts ~ *1a) Let's get things straight—you take directions from me only, and no one else! 1b) Let me get this straight—you're coming here first, then you fly to Brisbane, then you go on to Darwin?*

go straight: reform after leading a life of crime ~ *He wants to go straight when he gets out of prison.*

play it straight: do something in earnest; without jokes/trickery ~ *You know I usually make a joke of everything, but I'm playing it straight this time. I really do mean it.*

see straight: be unable to see clearly ~ *He's had too much to drink and can't see straight.*

think straight: think/not think clearly ~ *I can't think straight with all this noise!*

straight-laced: excessively moralistic/prudish/formal ~ *My father is so straight-laced he'd never let me go.*

straighten out: 1) settle/put right ~ *We need to straighten out the misunderstanding.*

2) help someone improve their bad behaviour ~ *I'll talk to him and see if I can straighten him out.*

straighten up: 1) make tidy; put in order; make or become straight ~ *I only had time to quickly straighten up the room before the guests arrive.*

2) stand up straight

strange as it is/as it seems/it appears: [spoken] in a way that is difficult to understand ~ *Strange as it seems, this little device is the most important component of the motor.*

strangely enough: in a surprisingly unusual way/manner ~ *I expected the water to be cold, but strangely enough it was very warm.* *also: strange to say

strap up: fasten (a cloth/bandage) in the manner of a strap ~ *The doctor advised me to keep my ankle strapped up for a week.*

strapped for cash: lacking in/short of money ~ *Could you lend me $20 until next week? I'm a bit strapped for cash.*

lucky streak: a series of wins when gambling ~ *I had a lucky streak playing cards and won the jackpot.*

streaker: one who runs naked across a public space (usually in front of a crowd of people at a sporting event)

streets ahead: superior; better than; more advanced ~ *Their new product is streets ahead of the competition.*

down the street/road: not far in distance ~ *They live just down the road from the school.*

stretch away: extend away from something ~ *The flat plain stretched away as far as the eye could see.*

stretch a/the point: be flexible; agree to; give latitude ~ *To say that he did a great job would be stretching the point.*

stretch one's legs: stand; walk around after a period of inactivity ~ *I'm going for a walk to stretch my legs.*

stretch one's luck: do something in the hope of extending one's good fortune ~ *I agreed to do give you this much—don't stretch your luck and ask for more.*

stretch the finances: something that puts stress/a strain on your resources/finances ~ *This unexpected expense is going to stretch our finances.*

stretch the friendship: extend/strain the limits to one's tolerances to the point of jeopardising the friendship (often said in humour) ~ *You want me to help you do what?! Boy, that's stretching the friendship a bit.*

stretch the truth: make an exaggeration ~ *He's stretching the truth if he said the fish he caught was that big.*

at a stretch: 1) with difficulty/effort ~ *I could do it at a stretch.*

2) at any one time ~ *They worked in silence for hours at a stretch.* *also: at a push

not by any stretch of the imagination: as much as anyone could imagine; is imaginable ~ *I don't know how, by any stretch of the imagination, they failed to see it.*

strewth: [spoken] mild oath; expression of surprise/alarm ~ *1a) Strewth, what was that? 1b) Stewth, it's hot in here!*

strides: trousers/long pants/daks

strike a bargain/deal: reach an agreement; successfully negotiate ~ *They were able to strike a bargain after intense negotiations.*

strike a chord: evoke/arouse an emotion with someone/something ~ *His heartbreaking story struck a chord with everyone who heard it.*

strike back: 1) retaliate ~ *The enemy struck back with a devastating bombing attack.*

2) equal the score in a game/competition ~ *Down six points, the Tigers struck back in the second half with a spectacular corner try.*

strike down: 1) cause someone to fall as if by striking ~ *The car careened off the road, striking down two pedestrians.*

2) cause someone to die/become seriously ill ~ *He was struck down by a mystery virus.* *also: strike down something

strike home: profoundly affect one's emotions ~ *It suddenly struck home that she would never see him again.* *also: hit home

strike it lucky: to have sudden/unexpected success ~ *The author struck it rich when her book became a bestseller.*

strike me lucky/pink/dead!: [spoken] expression of complete surprise/amazement ~ *Well, strike me dead—look who's here!*

strike(s) one: impress upon; appear/seem ~ *1a) Does he strike you as being wealthy? 1b) He strikes me as being very kind.*

strike out: fail; be unsuccessful ~ *I tried to buy tickets for the show, but I struck out—they'd all been sold.*

strike it rich: acquire wealth suddenly/unexpectedly ~ *She bought a lottery ticket and struck it rich.*

strike something up: cause to begin; begin/start something (typically a conversation) like a friendship or the playing of a band ~ *1a) They quickly struck up a conversation. 1b) We arrived just as the band was striking up the first tune.* *also: strike something up

go on strike: stop work; refuse to work because of a dispute with management ~ *Workers went on strike when negotiations broke down.*

strine: humorous exaggeration of the broad accent of Australian English ~ *Can you speak strine?*

string along with: go with; join someone for a short time as a convenience ~ *I'll string along with you if that's okay.*

string someone along: falsely maintain someone's interest; deceive someone ~ *I discovered he'd been stringing me along the whole time—he never intended to marry me!*

string someone a line: deceive someone with an untruth ~ *He strung her some sob story in the hope she'd take pity on him.*

string someone up: 1) kill by hanging

2) an angry threat ~ *I'd like to string them all up for what they did.*

(a) string of: 1) a set/sequence of similar items threaded together on a thin cord/line ~ *The outfit was complemented by a magnificent string of pearls.*

2) a sequence of similar events ~ *There's been a string of burglaries in that suburb over the past month.*

string out/along/across: arrange/hang something in a long line ~ *Colourful lanterns were strung out between the trees.*

string out: prolong; draw out ~ *... strung out negotiations as a delaying tactic.*

be strung out: tense/nervous/stressed ~ *She's strung out and acting out of character.*

string words/a sentence together: use words in the right order so as to be understood ~ *1a) I wasn't fluent in the language but was able to string together some sentences. 1b) He was drugged to the point where he couldn't string two words together.*

control/hold the purse strings: control the finances in a business/marriage ~ *You'll have to speak with Dan. He controls the purse strings.*

have/keep someone on a string: have/maintain control over someone ~ *He's been kept on a string for the entire marriage.*

have more than one string to your bow: to have other skills/ talents ~ *A degree will add another string to her bow.*

(have) no strings attached: unconditional ~ *The offer is genuine. It comes with absolutely no strings attached.*

pulls the strings: control others; make decisions (usually secretly) ~ *I think his position in the organisation is a ruse, and that someone else is pulling the strings.*

strip away: 1) remove in layers ~ *The contractor stripped away layers of paint to discover beautiful hardwood timber.*

2) uncover/reveal ~ *He stripped away the façade, which revealed a culture of violence.*

(be) stripped of: be deprived of rights/privilege/rank ~ *And because of his actions he was stripped of his duties as school vice captain.*

strip off: 1) tear off/pull a garment/covering ~ *He stripped off his shirt and dived in.*

2) remove one's clothes ~ *We stripped off for a swim.*

in strips: (of cloth/paper) in narrow pieces ~ *The old paint was peeling off in strips.*

stroke of genius: a clever/inspirational idea/act/decision ~ *Your idea to make it a feature wall was a stroke of genius.*

stroke of luck: an instance of good luck ~ *It was a stroke of luck that I found it.*

at the stroke of . . . : at a precise point in time ~ *We arrived on the stroke of 2:00.*

have/suffer a stroke: to experience sudden unconsciousness/and or paralysis due to a blockage/interruption of the blood supply to the brain

stroll around: walk casually ~ *We strolled around town all afternoon.*

stroll through: walk casually through an area/space ~ *We took a stroll through the Botanic Gardens.*

strong language: bad/abusive/offensive language; swear words ~ *He used some rather strong language to make his point.*

strong point: one's particular talent/ability/skill ~ *Maths are not my strong point.*

stroppy: of being bad-tempered/angry/difficult/cantankerous ~ *He's usually stroppy on Monday mornings.*

struggle through: perform a task with difficulty ~ *She struggled through the exam.*

struggle with: have difficulty managing/coping with/handling something ~ *We struggled with all the equipment we had to carry.*

strut your stuff: display/exhibit one's talents/abilities ~ *The Monaco Grand Prix is the place where the best Formula One drivers strut their stuff.*

stubby: a small, squat bottle of beer (usually 375 mls) *also: stubbie

stubby holder: an insulated cylinder made of foam designed to keep your stubby or can of beer cold *also: stubby cooler

stuck at/in/for: be in an unpleasant/unavoidable situation or a place you can't escape from ~ *1a) I'm stuck for time right now. I can come later today though. 1b) We were stuck in traffic for half an hour. 1c) He hates being stuck at home all day.*

stuck fast: unable to move/be moved ~ *It's stuck fast, I can't open it.*

stuck on someone: infatuated/attracted to someone ~ *They met last month and she's been stuck on him ever since.*

stuck on something: 1) fixed/locked in to an idea/purpose ~ *I'm stuck on the idea of extending the house.*

2) stumped/puzzled ~ *I got stuck on the second question.*

stuck with: be burdened with; deal with someone/something ~ *1a) I always seem to get stuck with the lousy jobs! 1b) Annie got stuck with Jack as her date.*

stuck for words: be rendered speechless ~ *I couldn't believe it—I was stuck for words!* *also: at a loss for words

get stuck in (to it): begin doing something/eating with enthusiasm ~ *1a) I can't wait to get stuck into my new job. 1b) okay, there's lots to do. Let's get stuck into it.*

(a) study: a home office

stuff around: *see: fool around

stuff it: [spoken slang] intensive expression of anger/disgust/frustration ~ *Stuff it, I've left something important behind!*

stuff one's face/oneself: eat greedily/to the excess ~ *Jim couldn't eat dinner after stuffing his face at the party.*

stuffed: *see: buggered

stuff up: [informal] ruin/bungle/spoil something ~ *I'll have to re-do this bit—I stuffed it up.*

(a) stuff-up: a bungled/ruined/spoiled event/situation ~ *Everything went wrong—the whole event was a stuff-up.*

stuffy: 1) airless; lacking in ventilation ~ *It's stuffy in here, let's open a window.*

2) a blocked nose/respiratory passages ~ *This is good for treating a stuffy nose.*

stumble across/on/upon: meet/find by accident ~ *1a) The hikers stumbled on a ruined castle. 1b) We stumbled across Helen in the library.*

stumble along/over/on: move with difficulty because you're tired/ill ~ *1a) The tired, cold hikers stumbled wearily along the path. 1b) The runner stumbled across the finish line and collapsed.*

stumble over: fall/nearly fall ~ *I stumbled over a protruding tree root and fell flat on my face.*

stumble through: make a mistake/falter (while speaking) ~ *Suffering a severe case of stage fright, he stumbled through his speech.*

stumbling block: obstacle/impediment that obstructs/blocks progress ~ *A serious injury was a major stumbling block in his sporting career.*

stump(s): three cylindrical posts that support a bail that are placed together at the end of a wicket in the game of cricket

(be) stumped: (be) unable to understand/explain something ~ *Her odd behaviour has everyone stumped.*

stump someone: [in the game of cricket] a manner of dismissing a batsman

stunner: describes someone/something very attractive (often a female) ~ *His new girlfriend's a real stunner!*

sub: submarine

such and such: someone/something unspecified/unknown/ undetermined ~ *They're meeting at such and such pub in the city.*

. . . sucks: something deemed worthless/disliked/woeful ~ *This movie really sucks!*

suit one/someone down to the ground: that something is appropriate/adequate/acceptable in every way ~ *That job would suit you down to the ground.*

suit yourself: [spoken] expression to mean do as you want/please in a situation where choices are made ~ *I've warned you of the dangers, so suit yourself if that's what you want to do!*

sum up: make a quick assessment/estimate of someone/a situation ~ *1a) Within minutes I summed her up as honest. 1b) He summed up the situation before making a decision.*

thinks the sun shines out of their arse/backside: [coarse slang] to admire someone so much they can do no wrong/have no bad qualities

sunbake/sunbathe: to lie in the sun so as to get a tan

Sunday best: one's best clothes/clobber (refers to the time when people had only one good set of clothes that were reserved for social outings on Sundays) ~ *He was there, all dressed up in his Sunday best.*

Sunday driver: an overly careful, slow driver who usually only drives on Sundays

sunnies: sunglasses

sunscreen/block: cream/lotion applied to the skin to prevent sunburn

sunshine state: nickname for Queensland

Sunshine Coast: a popular tourist spot on the mid-Queensland coast

super-duper: excellent; great; fantastic ~ *We had a super-duper time!*

superiority complex: of someone to have an exaggerated feeling of being superior to others

sure: [spoken] a remark that indicates you doubt/disbelieve what someone is saying (often said with a facial expression of raised eyebrows and a slow nodding of the head whilst uttering a drawn-out "suuuurrre") ~ *1a) Sure it is. 1b) Sure you do.*

sure as hell/rain/eggs: [spoken intensive] absolutely/certainly/undoubtedly ~ *I'm sure as hell not going to touch it!*

sure enough: as expected ~ *I thought that would happen, and sure enough it did.*

sure of oneself: having excess confidence; of being overly certain of one's/someone's abilities; of having a high self-esteem ~ *She's a lot more sure of herself since she completed the course.*

can't say for sure: [spoken] to indicate uncertainty ~ *I can't say for sure what time I'll be leaving.*

make sure: be certain; leave no doubt ~ *Make sure you close it properly.*

quite sure: [intensive] to be very certain of something ~ *1a) Are you quite sure you want to do it? 1b) Yes, I'm quite sure.*

sure-fire: certain to succeed/perform as expected ~ *Their new product is a sure-fire winner.*

(to) surface: reappear after a time in hiding ~ *1a) Detectives are waiting for him to surface again so they can arrest him. 1b) She went into her bedroom on Friday night and didn't surface until 3 p.m. on Saturday.*

on the surface: to all intents and purposes; as appears/seems ~ *On the surface she's a tough business woman, but deep down she's very caring.*

(the) surf: the ocean waves as they break on the shore ~ *They ran down the beach and jumped in the surf.*

(to) surf: ride a wave with/without a surfboard

surfer/surfie: one who surfs *also: (surf)board rider

surfie chick: a female surfer

surf lifesaver: beach lifeguard/lifesaver who patrols the beach and rescues people who get into trouble when swimming in the surf.

surf's up: [spoken] what you say when the waves are big/suitable for riding

body surfing: the act of riding a wave to the shore (without a surfboard) using the force of the wave to for propulsion

surfboard: a long narrow, elongated, pointed fibreglass board (with fins) used to surf

suss: something/someone doubtful/suspicious/iffy ~ *His story sounds a bit suss to me.*

suss out: investigate something ~ *1a) Let's suss out this old building. 1b) Her account of the incident sounds a bit iffy. I think you should suss it out.*

swag: a canvas bundle pack containing essentials/rolled up bedding *often used when travelling in the bush by foot

swag of: a large quantity/amount ~ *Police found a swag of stolen goods at the property.*

swagman: An outdated term for a transient, temporary worker who travelled from farm to farm. They would typically seek work in towns and on farms as they travelled through. Their meagre possessions were rolled up and carried in a swag. *also called: swaggie; sundowner; tussocker

swallow: 1) accept/believe without questioning ~ *They didn't swallow my excuse.*

2) endure/put up with something unpleasant ~ *The bad reviews were hard to swallow.* *also: a bitter pill to swallow

swallow one's pride: humble oneself ~ *She could do nothing but swallow her pride and admitted she wrong.*

swallow up: 1) devour; gobble up ~ *The food was quickly swallowed up by the hungry crowd.*

2) envelope/enclose as if by swallowing ~ *Our boat was soon swallowed up by the towering waves.*

swallow something down: to swallow something ~ *Here, swallow this down.*

swallow something hook, line, and sinker: to be thoroughly convinced something is true ~ *They swallowed your excuse hook, line, and sinker!* *also: swallow it

swallow whole: to eat something as a whole/intact ~ *. . . caught the fish in its mouth and swallowed it whole!*

swallowed words: retract a statement; admit you were wrong ~ *I was forced to swallow my words when the show turned out to be a success.*

swanky: stylish; luxurious; fancy; ostentatious ~ *We went to a swanky nightclub.*

swarm around: gather in large numbers around something (as in bees) ~ *The young party guests swarmed around the clown.*

swear at: direct bad/abusive language at someone ~ *They stood there swearing at each other.*

swear blind: [spoken] convince oneself/others of one's own beliefs ~ *1a) I swear blind I saw you at the party. 1b) I swear blind I put the keys in the bag!*

swear by: 1) have conviction in/reliance on ~ *I swear by this recipe.*

2) be sure of; have reliable knowledge of something ~ *I think they're responsible, but I can't swear by it.*

swear someone in: administer a legal/official oath ~ *She was sworn in as mayor.*

swear off: give up/renounce/abstain from ~ *I've sworn off cigarettes for good!*

swear to . . . : [spoken] conviction of one's solemn honesty/ truthfulness ~ *I swear to God I didn't do it!*

sweat blood: work strenuously/intensely ~ *I sweated blood to get that built.*

sweat like a pig: sweat profusely ~ *I've only been at this for five minutes, and I'm already sweating like a pig.* *also: sweat buckets

sweat it out: 1) wait anxiously/endure suspense ~ *She had to sweat it out for a month before getting the results.*

2) endure something unpleasant ~ *There wasn't much we could do at the time other than sweat it out.*

no sweat: *see: no problem

sweat on (it): await nervously for something to happen ~ *I'm sweating on the package arriving today.*

sweat over: work hard using/doing something ~ *1a) He's been sweating over a hot stove all afternoon. 1b) I've been sweating over the report all morning.*

(don't) sweat the small stuff: [spoken] a way of telling someone to not worry about insignificant things

break into a sweat: begin to sweat profusely (often because you're anxious) ~ *I broke into a sweat when I realised I was being followed.* *also: break into a cold sweat

get into a sweat: be in a state of anxiety/stress about something ~ *He's getting into a sweat about tomorrow's exam.*

work up a sweat: cause to sweat by physical exertion ~ *It seemed an easy exercise at first, but we quickly worked up a sweat.*

sweep away: 1) destroy/eliminate something ~ *Raging flood waters swept away everything in their path.*

2) affect emotionally ~ *I was swept away by his incredible story of hardship.*

sweep under the mat/carpet/rug: hide a problem instead of dealing with it ~ *She could no longer sweep her son's drug habit under the mat.*

sweep someone off their feet: impress/overwhelm emotionally ~ *1a) She was quickly swept off her feet by the handsome stranger. 1b) He wanted to do more than impress her, he wanted to sweep her off her feet.*

sweep through: move swiftly/intensely through an space/area ~ *A fire swept through the valley and burnt everything in its path.*

sweep (something) up: clear an area/space using a broom/brush ~ *1a) Could you sweep up this mess? 1b) He swept the crumbs up off the floor.*

sweet: [spoken] a way of saying okay/good/alright ~ *Jack's coming as well. Oh, sweet.* *also: sweet as

sweet tooth: have a fondness/desire for; a liking of sweet foods

sweets: a sweet dish/last course of a meal such as desserts/ pudding ~ *We had strawberry ice cream for sweets.*

sweet-talk: use flattery to convince someone to do something ~ *They tried to sweet-talk me into doing it.* *also sweeten someone up

sweeten up: make food sweeter by adding sugar

sweetener: an artificial sweetening agent (replacing sugar)

swell up: become swollen/expand abnormally ~ *Her injured ankle soon began to swell up.*

swim around: swim casually/aimlessly ~ *It's relaxing to sit and watch the fish in the aquarium swimming around.*

swim like a fish: describes someone who can swim very well ~ *She's only three years old and already swims like a fish.*

swing around: turn abruptly to face the other way ~ *She swung around at the sound of her name.*

(take a) swing at: try to hit something/someone using a curved movement of your arm ~ *He took a swing at me but missed.*

swing by: briefly visit a place ~ *1a) I'll swing by the office and collect it. 1b) Swing by later and we'll have a chat.*

swing into action: quickly begin/start doing something ~ *1a) Soon the guests will be arriving, we'd better swing into action. 1b) Fire crews swung into action as soon as news of the fire reached them.*

get in/into the swing of things: become familiar with; become involved in something ~ *The work was easy once we got into the swing of things.*

not enough/no room to swing a cat: a very small space

swing both ways: be sexually attracted to either gender

swing(ing) vote: a vote that could go to any number of candidates in an election ~ *The political party was hoping to get enough swinging votes to win the election.*

swing(ing) voter: a voter who may not be affiliated with/show favour to any particular party

swirl around: for something to rotate/circulate ~ *1a) All the leaves were swirling around in the wind. 1b) He swirled her around the dance floor.*

swish around: for liquids/fluids to rotate ~ *Julie swished the cool water around in her mouth.* *also: swirl around

switch around: exchange/interchange/swap someone/something ~ *A staff shortage forced me to switch some of the workers around.*

switch off: lose interest in something; stop paying attention ~ *I switched off when she started talking about her love life.*

hit the switch: press/turn the switch on quickly/suddenly ~ *He hit the switch and the machine swung into action.*

switched on: alert; up-to-date; excited ~ *1a) I get switched on by that kind of music. 1b) I think he'll agree to the proposed changes, he's pretty switched on.*

sworn enemies: people who hate/are hostile to each other ~ *They'll never reconcile their differences, they're sworn enemies.*

Sydney: the capital city of the state of New South Wales

Sydney Harbour Bridge: iconic Sydney landmark

Sydneysider: one who resides/lives in Sydney

(it's) all systems go: that everything's ready for something/an activity to begin ~ *I just need to install one final component and then it's all systems go.*

buck the system/trend: attempt to change the way of doing things ~ *Don't ever try because you'll never buck the system.* *also: beat the system

get it/something out of one's system: 1) rid yourself of a bad/negative emotion by expressing it to make yourself feel better ~ *We had a good talk and I got what was bothering me out of my system.*

2) do so much of something that you don't want to do it any more ~ *I got the travel bug out of my system by going on a long journey.*

3) to get rid of something from your body by process of natural elimination ~ *It can take several hours to get rid of the alcohol in your system.*

T

ta: thank you

ta-ta: goodbye

tab: a bill for a meal/drinks in a restaurant

pick up the tab: pay a restaurant bill/tab ~ *I'll pick up the tab this time.*

TAB: Totalisator Agency Board—a government and privately operated betting agency for betting on horse races that can be found throughout the towns and cities of Australia

tabby: any domestic cat that has a coat featuring distinctive stripes, dots, lines, or swirling patterns, usually together with a mark resembling an *M* on its forehead

clear the table: remove the eating utensils and dishes from the dining table ~ *Could you please clear the table?*

set the table: prepare the table for a meal ~ *All we had to do was to set the table before the dinner guests arrived.*

turn the tables: reverse the situation advantageously ~ *Outplayed in the first half, the Blues turned the tables in the second half to win by two points.*

wait on tables: serve food to diners at a restaurant ~ *I waited on tables to help pay my university fees.*

tack on: add something extra ~ *A surplus charge was tacked on at the end of our bill.*

flat as a tack: 1) totally deflated ~ *He got out and found the rear right tyre was as flat as a tack.*

2) emotionally drained ~ *She's been as flat as a tack since the relationship ended.*

tacky: 1) lacking in style/quality ~ *The outfit was a bit too tacky for the occasion.*

2) distasteful/offensive ~ *He made some tacky remark about her breasts.*

tad: a small amount/degree; slightly ~ *The shoes are a tad small, I'll need the next size up.* *also: titch/touch

tah-dah: an expression used to attract attention or announce/declare a visual surprise or perform a physical act. It could be saying "look at this," "here it is," or "look at what I've done." Said either before or after the act, it is a spoken version of a musical fanfare. *1a) Tah-dah! I baked you a birthday cake. 1b) Tah-dah, I did it!*

tail someone: follow someone secretly to see what they're doing/where they're going ~ *Detectives tailed their quarry, hoping he'd lead them to other persons of interest.*

chase one's tail: be unsuccessful; achieve very little ~ *I've been working on this problem for weeks, but at this point I think I'm just chasing my tail.*

have one's tail between one's legs: retreat in a state of rejection/humiliation ~ *She left the court with her tail between her legs after suffering a humiliating loss.*

(be) on someone's tail: drive close behind someone ~ *No less than three police cars were on his tail.*

the tail end of something: the very last part of something ~ *1a) I managed to catch the tail end of the concert. 1b) Luckily we received only the tail end of the storm.*

turn tail: flee in fright; suddenly leave ~ *When he saw his tormentors up ahead, he turned tail and went back home.*

tail-ender: the last runner in a race ~ *The tail-enders are now coming into view.*

tailgate someone: drive too closely to the vehicle/car in front

tailor-made: made for a specific purpose/to precise measurements ~ *Catering for specific industries, the program offers tailor-made courses.* *also: tailor made for

Taipan snake: A stealthy hunter with an extraordinarily fast and accurate bite and growing up to three metres in length, the Taipan is Australia's largest venomous snake. Its common name is the Coastal Taipan because it is found along the Queensland coast and in some areas of the N.S.W. coast, living in grasslands, coastal heaths, cane fields, and grassy beach dunes. The inland Taipan can be found in parts of Central Australia. Its colours range from light olive to dark russet to almost black in some parts of Northeast Queensland. The bite from this snake is severe and potentially lethal.

take a bit of doing: requiring considerable hard work/effort ~ *It's repairable, but it might take a bit of doing.* *also: take some doing

take a deep breath: pause to compose your thoughts (to give you courage) ~ *The passenger took a deep breath before jumping out of the plane.*

take/have a breather: have a rest ~ *I've been working solidly for an hour now. I need to take a breather.*

take a dim view of something: disapprove of ~ *They took a dim view of the government's new policies.*

take a fancy to: begin liking someone/something ~ *He's taken a fancy to her.* *also: takes a liking/shine to

take a hammering: suffer/receive a sound defeat/beating/abuse ~ *Our house took a hammering in the storm.* *also: a beating

take a toll (on): the damage/bad effects caused to someone/something by something ~ *1a) Years of heavy smoking have taken a toll on his health. 1b) The war has taken a toll on both sides.*

take a leaf out of someone's book: follow someone's good example ~ *I should take a leaf out of your book and start exercising.*

take a load off one's feet: rest/sit with one's feet up ~ *Here, sit down, take a load of your feet.*

take a trip: go to a place; travel ~ *We're taking a trip overseas next year.*

take a turn for the worse: for a situation to deteriorate ~ *Unfortunately the weather took a turn for the worse, forcing us to abandon our hike.*

take a tumble: fall over ~ *He was coming first when he took a tumble.*

take after: 1) resemble in temperament/appearance/character voice ~ *It's easy to see that you take after your mother.*

2) follow by (either good or bad) example ~ *He's taking after his uncle by entering into a career in journalism.*

take apart: disassemble ~ *I had to almost take the whole engine apart to find the problem.*

take around: take someone to a place; show someone the premises ~ *I'll take you around to Dan's house if you don't know the way.*

take as gospel: believe to be undeniably true ~ *Don't take everything she says as gospel.*

take away: 1) remove from a place ~ *Take it away from me!*

2) remove something abstract ~ *The medicine will take away the pain.*

3) deduct/subtract; minus ~ *Ten take away five equals five.*

4) cause to remember the past ~ *Hearing this tune takes me away back to my childhood.*

take back: 1) retract (something said) ~ *I'd like to take back what I said earlier. I spoke in haste and didn't mean it.*

2) retrieve; regain possession ~ *I've come to take back my things.*

3) return something ~ *We need to take the books back to the library.*

take care: 1) [spoken] alert to be careful doing something ~ *Take care when crossing the road. 1b) Bye-bye, have a good trip, take care!*

take care of: 1) deal with; attend to something ~ *Don't worry, I'll take care of it.*

2) watch over; be responsible for ~ *My aunt will take care of the children while we're away.*

take charge: assume command/control ~ *I want you to take charge while I'm away.*

take down: 1) put in writing ~ *The officer took down my details.*

2) bring from a higher to a lower position ~ *Just take the picture frame down an inch.*

3) dismantle ~ *We took down the decorations.*

take/bring/knock someone down a peg or two: lower someone's self-esteem; humble someone ~ *The surprise loss took them down a peg or two.*

take effect: 1) produce the desired result/reaction ~ *The medication, at last, has taken effect.*

2) become operational ~ *The new law will take effect on Friday.*

take exception to: express offence to/at; argue against ~ *I took exception to the personal questions they asked.*

take five/ten: take a short break/rest for five or ten minutes ~ *Take five, everybody.* *also: take a break

take flight: 1) start flying; become airborne ~ *We watched mesmerised as the majestic bird took flight.*

2) flee/escape quickly ~ *The robbers heard the approaching police sirens and immediately took flight.*

take for: 1) mistakenly consider ~ *1a) I took him for his brother. 1b) At first, the victim was taken for dead.*

2) regard someone as something ~ *He's not well educated, but don't take him for a fool.*

take for granted: 1) underestimate the value/worth of someone ~ *He takes for granted everything his mother does for him.*

2) assume/consider something as forthcoming/true/real ~ *I took it for granted you were coming.*

take heart: 1) regain one's spirit/courage ~ *Although the house was destroyed by fire, she took heart that no one had been injured or died.*

2) soften one's resolve; have a capacity for feeling/sympathy ~ *The man took heart and let the shivering wet stray dog inside.*

take something to heart: 1) consider/regard seriously ~ *With the amount of carnage on the roads, it seems many drivers are not taking the safe driving campaigns to heart.*

2) take seriously; consider as a personal attack ~ *You wouldn't last long in this job if you took to heart to every bit of criticism that came your way.*

take heed: listen and pay attention ~ *Take heed of your father's advice before making a decision.*

take hold: 1) become firmly established ~ *The roots had well and truly taken hold.*

2) assume control ~ *Troops stormed the building and took hold of the post.*

take hold of: seize/grasp something ~ *Here, take hold of my hand for support.*

take ill/sick: become suddenly ill/sick ~ *He took ill soon after lunch.* *also: fall ill

take in: 1) look at/view a place ~ *I am going to Italy to take in the sights of Venice.*

2) understand; absorb (mentally) ~ *I suggest you sit down because what I'm about to tell you will be hard to take in.*

3) receive as a guest; provide shelter ~ *She sometimes takes in borders to help with the expenses.*

4) deceive/swindle/fool someone ~ *She was taken in by his easy charm.* *see also: fall for

5) be filled with liquid ~ *Unfortunately, by then waves were breaking over the side and the boat quickly started taking in water.*

6) reduce in size (clothing) ~ *The pants need taking in at the waist.*

take into consideration: consider something before making a decision ~ *In sentencing, the judge took into consideration the defendant's clean record.*

take into (one's) own hands: personally deal with a situation/problem ~ *After weeks of inaction they took matters into their own hands and did it themselves.* *also: take matters into one's own hands

take (it): 1) endure something unpleasant ~ *This pain is intolerable. I'm not sure I can take it for much longer.*

2) presume ~ *I take it you'll be coming to the party.*

take it away . . . : [spoken] signal for a musician to begin playing ~ *We're ready to begin, so take it away, George!*

take it from me: believe/accept as true ~ *Take it from me, you'll need a jacket.*

take it in one's stride: cope/deal easily with an unpleasant/difficult event ~ *In this job you need to take criticism in your stride.*

take it or leave it: accept/reject unconditionally ~ *This is my offer—take it or leave it.*

take (it) out of someone/one: use up/exhaust energy ~ *Hours of hard work has taken it out of me.*

take it out on: vent one's own anger ~ *I'm not the cause of your anger, don't take it out on me.*

take kindly to: be attracted/receptive to ~ *I didn't take too kindly to her comments.*

take lying down: submit to harsh treatment without resistance ~ *I refuse to take her taunts lying down.*

take measures: do something to accomplish a purpose ~ *I took measures to ensure something like this would never happen again.*

take notice (of): pay attention to ~ *Take no notice of him—he's looking for attention.*

take off: 1) imitate/mimic satirically ~ *He's very good at taking off Jimmy Durante.*

2) (to) ascend ~ *The plane took off from runway two.*

3) enjoy rapid success/popularity ~ *The idea took off quickly.*

4) reduce the cost of something ~ *The store took ten dollars off the total price.*

5) have time away from work ~ *I'm taking two weeks off at Christmas.*

6) leave a place ~ *Jim got in his car and took off in a hurry.*

7) discontinue manufacturing/selling a product ~ *They took it off the market because of safety issues.*

take off one's/someone's hands: assume responsibility for something; relieve someone of their burden ~ *I'll be happy to take the kids off your hands for the afternoon.*

take off with: steal/pinch; go/leave/run away with ~ *1a) Hey—he's taken off with my bicycle! 1b) Who's taken off with my pen?*

take offence: be offended by; object to someone's actions/words ~ *I took offence to his criticism.*

take on: 1) compete against/oppose (in a competition) ~ *Next week, the Bears will take on the Tigers in what should be a thrilling final.*

2) assume/adopt responsibilities/offices/duties ~ *She will take on a new role within the organisation.*

3) engage/hire ~ *We usually take on extra workers over the Christmas break.*

4) tackle/undertake; accept a challenge ~ *If he wants to fight me, tell him I'll take him on any day.*

5) assume a certain form/aspect ~ *The actress has gone overboard with plastic surgery and has taken on the appearance of a doll.*

take on the chin: accept punishment/defeat/suffering without complaining ~ *There was little else she could do but to take the insults on the chin.*

take one's hat off to: acknowledge/congratulate ~ *1a) I take my hat off to him, I didn't think he'd do it. 1b) What a fantastic performance—I take my hat off to you!*

take one's time: act/move at a leisurely pace ~ *1a) We took our time getting there. 1b) She's certainly taking her time with it.*

take out: 1) remove/extract ~ *The surgeon took out her appendix.*

2) cause to leave ~ *The teacher took the children out of the building to a safer area.*

3) obtain by legal/official process ~ *The only recourse was to take out an injunction on them.*

4) escort someone ~ *Tony's taking her out to dinner on Friday.*

5) destroy in an armed attack; murder/kill ~ *Combat pilots took out half the enemy platoon in a surprise raid.*

take over: assume responsibility/control ~ *John's going to take over from you at 2 p.m.*

take part: join/participate ~ *Sally will be taking a big part in the proceedings.*

take place: occur/happen ~ *The meeting will take place in the hall.*

take root: become rooted/firmly established ~ *Once this plant takes root it will be difficult to remove.*

take sides: support a particular person/group/faction; show bias ~ *The teacher took sides, believing their version of events.*

(be) taken to the cleaners: lose most/all of your money/assets through a bad investment/gambling ~ *1a) Nearly everyone who invested with them has been taken to the cleaners. 1b) I got taken to the cleaners in last night's poker game.*

take (someone) in hand: be responsible for guiding/assisting someone ~ *The teacher asked Sarah to take the new student in hand until she gained confidence.*

take for a ride: 1) convey someone in a vehicle (for recreation) ~ *Mandy's going to take me for a ride in her new car.* *also: take for a spin

2) trick/swindle/cheat/deceive someone ~ *Mate, no such thing exists. You've been taken for a ride!*

take someone to task: challenge/scold/reprimand/criticise ~ *The boss took me to task over inappropriate remarks I made at the meeting.*

take steps: initiate/begin an action ~ *She took steps to make sure the mistakes made would never happen again.*

take stock (of): 1) make an inventory ~ *Before I order more parts we need to take stock of what's in the warehouse.*

2) review one's situation/prospects ~ *At first light were they able to take stock of their new surroundings.*

take that: [spoken] a final angry/verbal/physical retort or retaliatory remark in an argument/fight scene in a movie script

take the bait: to be tricked/conned/fooled/deceived/provoked ~ *Detectives set the trap and waited for the suspect to take the bait.*

take the blame: assume responsibility for wrong doings/mistakes ~ *He protested his innocence. He wasn't going to take the blame for something his brother did.* *also: take the rap

take the bull by the horns: confront a problem and deal with it promptly/quickly ~ *She took the bull by the horns and confronted him about it.*

take(s) the cake: be the most outrageous/disappointing/ outstanding ~ *The outrageous excuse she gave really takes the cake.*

take the floor: arise to address a meeting/deliver a formal speech ~ *I now call upon John to take the floor.*

take the law into one's own hands: attempt to administer the law; seek personal justice ~ *Two members of the public took the law into their own hands by capturing and detaining the offender.*

take the mickey out of someone: good naturedly tease/mock someone so as to deflate their ego; lighten a serious situation ~ *Tom took the mickey out of me by claiming that I'd won because I was the only competitor.*

take the plunge: make a decision to do something after considering it for a long time ~ *1a) I've decided to take the plunge and buy the business. 1b) John and Sue are finally taking the plunge and getting married.*

take the rough with the smooth: accept/tolerate the good with the bad in a situation ~ *It won't be an easy job. You'll have learn to take the rough with the smooth.*

take the sting out of something: ease/lessen something unpleasant ~ *A bonus incentive should take the sting out of new tax increases.*

take the wind out of one's/someone's sails: challenge/deflate someone's ego/confidence; feel less confident/determined ~ *1a) She took the wind out of his sails by turning down his offer to marry him. 1b) I was prepared for an argument, but he took the wind out of my sails by apologising and giving me a bunch of flowers.*

take to: 1) go to a place (for safety) ~ *Everyone took to the hills to escape the floodwaters.*

2) have recourse/reason to do something ~ *He took to drinking after his wife died.*

3) develop a habit/practice of ~ *He's taken to having a daily swim to help with the recovery.*

take to like a duck to water: adapt naturally/easily to something ~ *He took to surfing like a duck to water.*

take turns: alternate; do something one person after another ~ *We usually take turns driving on long trips.*

take up: 1) consume/use up; occupy ~ *The current project is taking up most of my time.*

2) resume/begin again ~ *The professor took up the conversation from where they left off.* *also: pick up

3) develop an interest in ~ *She recently took up golf.*

4) enter into a profession ~ *He's taken up nursing.*

5) shorten (clothing) ~ *You'll need to take up the hem.*

take up with: begin to associate; become friendly with ~ *She took up with some members of a book club.*

take your pick: [spoken] invitation to choose something ~ *They come in a variety of colours—take your pick.*

take with a grain/pinch of salt: be sceptical/doubtful/unbelieving ~ *I took her version of the events with a grain of salt.*

take something the wrong way: fail to understand something correctly; think someone is criticizing whey they're not ~ *1a) You've taken it the wrong way. The complaint is against the department, not you. 1b) Even the mildest suggestions are taken the wrong way.*

take you up on: accept an offer/challenge ~ *I am not prepared at this stage to take them up on their offer to buy the business.*

someone's take on something: one's opinion/view of something ~ *What's your take on the topic, Toby?*

take-away: food sold for consumption away from the premises; a fast-food shop that sells such food ~ *1a) Let's have take-away tonight. 1b) The take-away shop down the road sells hamburgers.* *also: takeaway; take away; take-out; food to go; fast-food

take-off: *see: send someone up

(be) taken aback: surprised/shocked ~ *I was somewhat taken aback by his angry response.*

(be) taken in (by): be fooled/tricked ~ *She was taken in by his good looks.*

(it) takes one to know one: that the person who criticises has similar faults to the one being criticised ~ *She called me an idiot, but it takes one to know one.*

(it) takes two to tango: that two, not one person is responsible for a bad situation ~ *She blames him for her predicament, but it takes two to tango.*

do whatever it takes: do everything possible to get results/to succeed ~ *They're doing whatever it takes to prevent it from happening again.*

have what it takes: have the influence/skills/intelligence to do something ~ *1a) He's got what it takes to do the job. 1b) I haven't got what it takes to be a professional dancer.*

(it) takes all kinds: said when one should accept other peoples differences/habits no matter how strange/odd ~ *His behaviour was quite bizarre—but I guess it takes all kinds.*

tart: promiscuous woman; prostitute

get tarted up: dress up in a provocative way—with too much make-up and skimpy clothing ~ *I saw his sister last night, all tarted up and giving all the guys the come-on.*

that takes care of that: [spoken] uttered when an arduous job/task is completed ~ *Well, that takes care of that. What's next to do?* *also: that's that; that's the end of that; take care of

tell tales: 1) report malicious stories/trivial complaints to someone in authority ~ *If you've come to tell tales, I'm not interested in hearing them.*

2) tell exaggerated stories ~ *Jim has been telling tales again about an encounter with a bear.*

tell a tale: recount a story/the narrative of an event ~ *The reporter was told an amazing tale of courage and bravery.*

tell its own tale: be obvious/revealing without further explanation ~ *The devastation before them told its own tale.*

tall tale/story: an exaggerated story that is difficult to believe ~ *The old man told tall tales of monsters and dragons.*

talk about: 1) discuss something ~ *1a) Let's talk about something else. 1b) What did you talk about?*

2) [spoken] interjection used to add emphasis to a statement ~ *Talk about hard work—I'm bushed!*

talking about . . . : [spoken] interjection to steer the conversation in another direction ~ *Talking about snakes, I read the other day that . . .*

know what one is talking about: speak informatively/ knowledgeably ~ *1a) I learned so much. This guy certainly knows what he's talking about. 1b) Going by this report, I don't think she knows what she's talking about.* *also: talk sense

talk/answer back to someone: reply rudely to what someone (with authority) says ~ *1a) Please do as I ask and don't talk back! 1b) I couldn't believe it when he answered back to the teacher.*

talk behind someone's back: make derogatory/scandalous remarks about someone in their absence ~ *It's not nice to say that about Jane. You shouldn't be talking about her behind her back!*

talk dirty: speak suggestively about sex/sexual acts ~ *Melissa loves it when he talks dirty.*

talk in riddles: talk in a way that is confusing/difficult to understand ~ *I don't understand what he's saying—he's talking in riddles.*

talk it/something over: discuss something with someone ~ *1a) I'll have to talk it over with my boss first. 1b) I'd rather not talk about it over the phone.*

talk of: mention of something ~ *There's been talk of a takeover.*

(be the) talk of the town: be the subject of gossip/conversation (for good or bad) ~ *Their romance is the talk of the town.*

talk one's head off: talk endlessly ~ *We talked our heads off all night.*

talk one's way out of something: use persuasion to avoid something or gain access somewhere ~ *1a) He tried to talk his way out of a speeding fine. 1b) They somehow talked their way into the private party.*

talk someone into/out of doing something: convince/persuade into doing something ~ *1a) I talked her into coming with us. 1b) He wanted to go, but I talked him out of it.* *also: talk someone round

talk (some) sense into someone: help someone think logically/ reasonably ~ *He's determined to go ahead with this stupid stunt. I hope I can talk some sense into him before he hurts himself.*

talk shop: talk about work/business matters in a social situation, to the exclusion of any other topics ~ *Others broke off from the group who couldn't help but talk shop.*

talk someone through something: explain something in detail/step by step ~ *I have a rough idea of how it's done, but I'll need you to talk me through the process.*

talk to someone about something: 1) reprimand/lecture someone ~ *I need to talk to you about your behaviour.*

2) confer with someone ~ *I'll have to talk to my boss about it first.*

talk through one's hat: talk rubbish; without regard for truth ~ *When he said this was going to be easy, he was talking through his hat.*

talk turkey: have a serious/frank business discussion ~ *I quite like your marketing ideas. Why don't come by tomorrow and we'll talk turkey.*

talk till/until you're blue in the face: talk convincingly without the desired result/to the point of exasperation ~ *I talked till I was blue in the face, but he still wouldn't listen to reason.*

(can) talk under water: describes someone who has a lot to say/who talks non-stop ~ *I'm sure that guy could talk under water. He never shut up the whole time.* *also: talk in wet cement; talk the leg off an iron pot

(be) all talk: empty promises; boasting ~ *1a) I can't imagine he'll go through with it. He's all talk, no action. 1b) I know for a fact he didn't catch all the fish that day. He's all talk.*

. . . now you're talking: [spoken] interjection to show enthusiasm/approval ~ *Dinner at a French restaurant? Now you're talking!*

talking point: subject that causes discussion/argument ~ *Their romance has been the talking point among everyone at the office.*

(like) talking to a brick wall: that the person you're talking to is not listening ~ *1a) Asking her to do it is like talking to a brick wall. 1b) I feel like I'm talking to a brick wall whenever I ask you to do something.*

give someone (a) talking to: severely reprimand/scold someone ~ *His mother gave him a big talking to when he got home.*

(it's been) good/nice talking to you: [spoken] phrase at the end of a conversation when saying goodbye ~ *Bye, Stella—it's been good talking to you.* *also: talk to you soon

talk/speak out of turn: say something you shouldn't have ~ *I know I'm talking out of turn, but what you're proposing is quite wrong.*

you can't talk: [spoken] rebuff to remind the speaker that they too are guilty of a similar misdeed ~ *You can't talk. You've run a few red lights in your time.*

tanked: (full) of alcohol; drunk/intoxicated ~ *He was pretty much tanked by the time we got there.*

tarred with the same brush: to believe unreasonably that one person/group shares the same bad traits/characteristics as another/others ~ *Teenagers in the town shouldn't be tarred with the same brush because of the reckless actions of some.*

tart up: 1) dress oneself up so as to look attractive ~ *Barbara quickly tarted up for the evening.*

2) embellish/decorate ~ *It's liveable. It just needs a bit of tarting up.*

Tasmanian Devil: It was the early European settlers who were haunted at night by the spine-chilling screeches and haunting growls that gave *Sarcophilus harrisii* the common name of Tasmanian devil. A state icon and wholly protected, the Tasmanian devil is found only in the wild in the state of Tasmania. It is the largest of the living marsupial carnivores, and it is Australia's only specialised mammalian scavenger. It was once widespread across mainland Australia, but it disappeared with the introduction of the dingo. It resembles a small but robust dog, and it has large, strong teeth and powerful jaws which allow them to eat every part of their prey, including the bones and the hide. It feeds on anything from birds and insects to wallabies, possums, and wombats. It has a bad reputation, but it is actually quite timid. The terrifying sounds it makes is usually only an intimidating bluff. They are not dangerous to humans, but will defend themselves if attacked.

Tassie: Tasmania; pertaining to Tasmania ~ *We're going to Tassie for our holidays.*

(a) taste/dose of one's own medicine: to give someone the same bad treatment as they have given you/others ~ *The story's about a* *woman who gets a taste of her own medicine when the guy she falls in love with jilts her for another woman.*

(a) taste for something: develop a desire to eat/drink something or experience something ~ *1a) He developed a taste for travel after his first overseas trip. 1b) I have a taste for hot spicy food.*

in bad/poor taste: be offensive/vulgar/rude ~ *Most of his jokes were in bad taste.*

leave a bad taste in one's mouth: to have an unpleasant memory of something ~ *His off jokes left a bad taste in my mouth.*

tatt(s): tattoo(s)

tea/coffee break: a short workplace break

tea towel: cloth used in the kitchen *also: kitchen towel

teach someone something: learn/cause someone to learn through a bad/unpleasant experience ~ *I forgot to bring the sunscreen and got burnt. That'll teach me remember to bring everything next time.*

teach someone a lesson: take revenge; punish someone ~ *I'd like to teach him a lesson for the way he treated her.*

(that will) teach you: [spoken] said to someone who has suffered for doing something they shouldn't have done ~ *I fell out and sprained my ankle. Well, that'll teach you not to climb trees.*

teacher's pet: a student favoured by the teacher, henceforth who is disliked by other students ~ *She is precious little teacher's pet—gets away with everything!*

team up (with): join someone/a group in order to do something together ~ *Mark and Jim will be teaming up for a charity match in June.*

tear across/through: move quickly from one side of a place to the other ~ *The weatherman watched helplessly as the tornado tore through the township.*

tear apart: 1) cause great upset worry ~ *Their heartless action is tearing him apart.*

2) cause arguments that damages relationships ~ *All the mudslinging and backstabbing is tearing the government apart.*

3) separate two people who are in a close relationship ~ *They vowed nothing would tear them apart.*

4) destroy/damage something by breaking into pieces ~ *Everything was torn apart by the blast.*

tear around: move about hurriedly/excitedly/recklessly ~ *1a) I've been tearing around like a mad thing tidying the house before everyone arrives. 1b) He came tearing around the corner and nearly knocked me over.*

tear at: 1) cause distress ~ *News of their plight tore at his heart.*

2) pull at; attack with force ~ *2a) Strong winds tore at our clothing. 2b) The dog tore at the bone.*

tear away: remove oneself/someone reluctantly/unwillingly ~ *1a) I had trouble tearing the kids away from the playground. 1b) I couldn't tear myself away from the mesmerising sight.*

tear down: demolish something ~ *All these old buildings will be torn down to make way for a housing development.*

tear into someone: strongly criticise/berate ~ *The boss tore into Tony when he found out what he'd done.* *also: tear strips off someone

tear into: do something with gusto ~ *The kids tore into the party food.*

(to) tear one's hair out: to be extremely worried/frustrated about something ~ *This puzzle's got me tearing my hair out.*

tear off: travel quickly/recklessly ~ *Jim tore off down the street in anger.*

tear something off something: remove by pulling/with violent force ~ *1a) The hiker tore off his T-shirt and dived into the water. 1b) Many houses had their roofs torn off by damaging winds.*

tear one's heart out: of something to cause sadness/heartache ~ *It tore my heart out to see such suffering.*

tear up: tear paper/material into small pieces ~ *The manager said the contract was useless, then tore it up right in front of me.*

tear /tɪə(r)/ up: for tears to well in one's eyes ~ *I started tearing up as I listened to her sad story.*

burst into tears: to suddenly begin crying ~ *She burst into tears when I told her what had happened.* *also: burst out crying

in tears: to be crying ~ *I was in tears when I heard what happened.*

move someone to tears: bring someone to the point of crying ~ *Their story moved me to tears.*

not shed a tear: to show no emotion/not cry ~ *He never shed a tear the whole time.*

reduce to tears: cause someone to cry by belittling/insulting/teasing ~ *Their cruel insults reduced him to tears.*

teary: 1) watery-eyed/tearful ~ *They said a teary goodbye to each other.*

2) inclined to cry/weep ~ *She's been a bit teary of late.* *also: teary eyed

tear-jerker: a sad story (book or movie) that makes one cry ~ *It's a bit of a tear-jerker, so bring some tissues.*

tech: technical college

tee (something) up: arrange/organise something ~ *I've teed up a meeting with them tonight.*

teeny-weeny: tiny/minute ~ *It's only a teeny-weeny spider.* *also: teensy-weensy/itsy-bitsy

armed to the teeth: fully prepared or equipped/armed with weapons ~ *They were armed to the teeth.*

scarce as hen's teeth: exceedingly rare; hard to find; non-existent ~ *Taxis at this time of night are as rare as hen's teeth.* *also: thin on the ground

by the skin of one's teeth: barely/only just ~ *1a) They won by the skin of their teeth. 1b) He escaped death by the skin of his teeth.*

(be) cutting teeth: for a baby/young child to have teeth emerging through their gums

get one's teeth into something: attempt a challenging task with energy enthusiasm ~ *The course offers subjects you can get your teeth into.*

give one's eye teeth for something: do/give anything to have something ~ *1a) I'd give my eye teeth to have been there. 1b) She'd give her eye teeth to go with them.*

grit one's teeth: 1) accept a difficult/unpleasant situation ~ *My foot was hurting like hell, but I grit my teeth and finished the race.*

2) clench/grind one's teeth in anger/frustration/determination ~ *I grit my teeth in silent anger and continued working.*

like pulling teeth: have difficulties extracting information from someone ~ *Trying to get him to talk about it was like pulling teeth.*

sink one's teeth into: become actively/totally engrossed/involved in ~ *I like a book you can sink your teeth into.*

teething problems: unforseen problems/difficulties in the early stages of a project ~ *The few teething problems we had have since been resolved.*

tell about: divulge information to someone ~ *Did you tell Jack about it?*

tell me about it: [spoken] expression to mean you are well aware of what someone tells you because you've had the same experience ~ *The leg of the trek over the mountain is tough going. Tell me about it. I almost didn't make it.* *also: you're telling me; don't I know

tell apart: be able/unable to see the difference between one thing/person and another ~ *They're so alike I can't tell them apart.* *also: tell which is which; who's who; one from the other

tell by: identify someone/something by a distinguishing manner/mark/appearance ~ *1a) I can tell by looking at you that you're not well. 1b) You can tell Sally by her bright red hair.*

tell it like it is: speak frankly; describe a situation honestly (without omitting any details) ~ *I know some of the things I said made you uncomfortable, but I had to tell it like it was.*

tell me: [spoken] used to encourage someone to talk about something specific ~ *So tell me, how did you go in the interview?*

tell a mile off: be able to easily recognise/realise something ~ *1a) With that bright red hat, I can tell you a mile off. 1b) You could tell a mile off she was lying.*

tell of: speak of someone/something ~ *Did I tell you of the time I . . . ?*

tell off: rebuke/reprimand someone ~ *I told him off for being rude.* *also: tell where to get off; where to go

tell on someone: inform someone of another's misdeeds (often used by children) ~ *I'm going to tell on you.*

tell (the) time: 1) be able to read time from a watch/clock ~ *She learnt to tell the time at school.*

2) keep/report the accurate time ~ *This clock runs slow—it doesn't tell the right time.*

tell me another one (lie): [spoken] used when you know someone is not being truthful ~ *Come on, do you think I believe that story? Tell me another one.* *also: pull the other one

tell someone where to put/what to do with something: [spoken] angrily reject something ~ *I told them what they could do with their offer.* *also: tell where to stick it

as far as one can tell: judging by what one knows/sees/the available information ~ *As far as I can tell, there's only some minor damage.*

I can't begin to tell you . . . : [spoken] used to indicate that you cannot express your feelings ~ *I can't begin to tell you how much this means to me.*

I couldn't tell you . . . : [spoken] used when you don't know the answer to something ~ *I couldn't tell you the number of times that's happened to me.*

I (can) tell you: [spoken] used to emphasise a statement ~ *1b) I tell you, I'm sick of this lousy weather! 1b) I can tell you now, you won't be going anywhere unless you change your attitude.*

I told you so: [spoken] used to emphasise that you were right/correct ~ *See, they have got a new car. I told you so!*

pray tell: a [spoken] interjection/plea for the speaker to reveal more about something ~ *What, pray tell, is that?*

telly: television ~ *What's on telly tonight?*

temp: temporary/casual employee ~ *We've called in a temp to replace Tracey.*

temper, temper: [spoken] said as a reminder to someone to subdue their anger

(throw a) temper tantrum: a display of anger expressed by screaming, crying, and foot stomping ~ *My young daughter threw a temper tantrum in the supermarket.* *also: hissy fit; throw a fit; spit the dummy

tempt fate: do something that's risky/likely to fail ~ *You shouldn't temp fate by saying we'll win.*

(be) tempted to do something: a way of saying what you're considering doing/what you think should be done ~ *I'm tempted to report the matter to the authorities.*

tend to: 1) be likely to do something/think about something in a particular way ~ *1a) I tend to think of it as a waste of time. 1b) I tend not to go there at night. It's too dangerous.*

2) care for/manage/attend to someone/something ~ *She spent the day tending to her garden.*

terror: troublesome/naughty child ~ *Their youngest child's a little terror.*

thank heavens: [spoken] exclamation of relief ~ *Thank heavens you got here when you did.* *also: thank goodness; thank God; thank your lucky stars

thanks a lot/million: [spoken] thank you very much ~ *Thanks a lot. I really appreciate your help.*

thanks a lot: [spoken] sarcastic response to something done or said that was unwelcome or unwanted ~ *Gee, thanks a lot for telling everyone our secret!*

thanks for nothing: [spoken] sarcastic reply/response to receiving help that had the opposite effect/was not forthcoming ~ *You're too late, we've finished the hard work. Thanks for nothing!* *also: no thanks to you

that does it: [spoken] what's said when you reach the limit of your patience/tolerance ~ *That does it, I'm not putting up with your rudeness any longer. I'm leaving!* *also: that's it!

that is . . . /that is to say: used to clarify meaning; in other words ~ *1a) Jane suggested we have dinner and then go to the movies, that is if you are free that night. 1b) I understand why he did it—that is to say I don't agree with what he did.*

that/it figures: [spoken] that something is not surprising/to be expected ~ *He's spent all his money and now he's asking us for a loan. Well, that figures!*

that'll be the day: [spoken] expression of disbelief; that something will most likely never happen ~ *She says she wants to help with the housework. That'll be the day.*

that's it/about it: that there's nothing left to do/say; it's all over/finished ~ *1a) That's about it—there's nothing more to pack. 1b) That's about it—that's all that happened.*

that's done it: [spoken] expression of annoyance when something goes wrong; to indicate the limit of one's tolerance/patience ~ *1a) That's done it. Now it's truly broken 1b) That's done it—you blew your chance. You won't be asked again!*

that's life: [spoken] expression of resignation; acceptance of a situation ~ *Not everyone is blessed with good looks, but that's life!*

that's that: [spoken] said to indicate finality/the absolute end of something said or done ~ *1a) Well, that's that—the job is done! 1b) I'm not doing it and that's that!*

that's the trick/shot/way: [spoken] words of encouragement; that someone is doing the right thing ~ *That's the way to do it. That's the trick!*

. . . at that: 1) furthermore; in addition ~ *They live in a nice house, a small one at that.*

2) regardless ~ *I don't want to say anything more about it. I'm going to leave it at that.*

(and) with that . . . : immediately after doing something ~ *He blew her a kiss, gave a little wave, and with that walked off into the night.*

thataway: in that direction (used in conjunction with a hand signal) ~ *They went thataway.*

there goes . . . : [spoken] when witnessing something being destroyed/damaged ~ *Well, there goes the roof.*

there goes somebody: [spoken] as you watch someone move/drive past you ~ *There goes Scott in his new car.*

there goes nothing: [spoken] of a failed effort/missed opportunity; yielding nothing ~ *All the work I put into the application and I missed the deadline. There goes nothing.*

there and then: on the spot; immediately ~ *He signed up then and there.* *also: then and there

there, there: [spoken] said to calm/comfort/console someone ~ *There, there, everything will be alright.*

there you are: [spoken] expressed when handing someone something they've asked for/bought ~ *There you are. This is the book you wanted, isn't it?*

you've got me there: [spoken] when you don't know the answer to something ~ *How much does it weigh? You've got me there.*

thick: [derogatory] dim-witted/stupid ~ *Are you thick or something? I told you not to go there!* *also: thick as two planks; thick as a brick

(as) thick as thieves: good friends who do everything together and share confidences ~ *Those two are as thick as thieves—where you see one you'll see the other.*

thick and fast: at a rapid rate and at great numbers/amounts ~ *Bargain hunters came through the doors thick and fast.*

in the thick of: (be) heavily involved in something ~ *It started with an innocent comment, but she soon found herself in the thick of their argument.*

get something through/into your thick skull/head: [spoken] expression directed at someone who is having trouble realising/understanding something ~ *Get it through your thick skull that she doesn't want to see you anymore!*

lay it on thick: exaggerate an emotion/experience/speech ~ *I know you wanted to convince him, but you didn't need to lay the sob story on so thick.*

through thick and thin: stay with; endure hardships; support someone through easy and/or difficult times ~ *Their relationship has been strained at times, but they've stuck together through thick and thin.*

thin down: 1) become slimmer/thinner ~ *She's really thinned down since I last saw her.*

2) dilute a liquid with water ~ *You need to thin down the soup a bit.*

thin on the ground: scarce/few in numbers (in a particular area) ~ *Aussies in this part of the world are thin on the ground.*

thin on top: [informal] balding ~ *Geez mate, you're getting a bit thin on top.*

thin out: become less dense; spread out ~ *We can go faster once the traffic thins out.*

out of thin air: appear suddenly; from nowhere/nothing ~ *1a) I don't know where it came from. It appeared out of thin air. 1b) She made up the story from thin air.*

skate on thin ice: to be in/put oneself in a risky/precarious situation ~ *You'll be skating on thin ice if you ask him for any more favours.*

spread oneself thin: to be doing so many thing that you can't devote enough time to each one ~ *I realised I was spreading myself too thin, so I resigned as team manager.*

vanish into thin air: disappear without a trace ~ *I turned around and he'd vanished into thin air!*

things are looking up: that a situation/conditions are improving ~ *Things are looking up now that I have a job.*

thing of the past: something that no longer happens/is no longer popular ~ *Looking up a number in the phonebook is almost a thing of the past.*

a good thing: a wise decision ~ *It's a good thing we brought an umbrella, it's starting to rain.*

sure thing: [spoken] interjection to say okay/alright/yes ~ *I'll do that for you. Sure thing.*

a sure thing: something certain to happen/succeed ~ *One sure thing: with a change of government will be an increase in taxes.*

all things considered: [spoken] after everything into account ~ *All things considered, we had a good result.*

(you've/they've) got another thing coming: be deluded/ mistaken ~ *If she thinks she's going to use my car all weekend she's got another thing coming!*

any old thing: anything (not necessarily old) ~ *1a) It's not just any old train, but the Orient Express! 1b) Just wear any old thing.*

as things stand: as the situation is ~ *As things stand there's nothing more we can do.* *also: the way things are (going)

(be) on (to) a good thing: to be in a pleasant/profitable situation ~ *He's on a good thing with that little shop of his.*

(I've got) better things to do: there are more enjoyable/important/better ways to spend your time ~ *I've got better things to do than listen to your complaints!*

(don't) do things by halves: put a lot of effort into doing something; do something well ~ *I didn't expect you to do all that. You know me, I don't do anything by halves.*

do one's/his/her/their own thing: do exactly as you please; whatever interests you ~ *My children mostly do their own thing on the weekends.*

. . . except for one thing: excluding something in particular ~ *I like it except for one thing—the colour.*

for one thing: [spoken] one reason; an example ~ *Why can't I play outside? Well, for one thing, it's raining.*

have a good thing going: have an ongoing arrangement/plan that is beneficial/serves one's purpose ~ *They have a good thing going with the community vegetable garden.*

how's things (with you)?: informal greeting meaning "how are you?" or "how is life?" ~ *Hi, how's things?*

interested in only one thing: focused on/concerned about one issue/subject one thing ~ *Our cat is interested in only one thing—sleeping!*

not know the first thing about: to know nothing about a particular subject ~ *Don't ask me about it. I don't know the first thing about fixing cars.*

make a big thing of something: place a great deal of importance on something ~ *It's only a minor injury and she's making a big thing of it.* *also: make a thing out of; make a big deal about

of all things: surprisingly; amazingly ~ *I thought John didn't like sports, but he's learning tennis of all things.*

(just) one of those things: an unavoidable, often uncontrollable occurrence ~ *I don't really understand why it happens; it's just one of those things.*

one thing after another: a succession of unfortunate events ~ *I couldn't have been worse. One thing after another went wrong!*

(with) one thing and another: a way of explaining that you failed to do something because you were busy doing everything else ~ *What with one thing and another, I forgot to phone them.*

(if it's not) one thing it's another: a way of complaining that if one thing doesn't go wrong another thing will ~ *Last week we had a burst water pipe, now the washing machine needs fixing—if it's not one thing it's another!*

have (got) a thing about: have a strange/unreasonable like/dislike of something ~ *She's got a thing about tattooed men.*

have a thing going with someone: to have a love affair/romance with someone ~ *I think Bill and Sue have got a thing going.*

the very thing: exactly that ~ *That's the very thing I've been looking for.* *also: just the thing

the funny thing is/was: [spoken] used to say you think something is strange ~ *The funny thing is that he didn't seem to realise it was missing.*

the thing is . . . : [spoken] a polite way to introduce a fact/excuse/explanation ~ *1a) I'd love to go sailing, but the thing is I get seasick. 1b) Yes, I did my homework, but the thing is I left it at home.*

thingummy/thingamabob/thingamajig: what you call something when you don't know/can't remember what it's called ~ *What's that thingamajig sticking out there?* *also: whatchamacallit; whatsits; thingy

feel/be thingy about something: feel uncomfortable about a situation ~ *I'm a bit thingy about you having to walk through there at night.*

think again: reconsider something ~ *A hefty fine should make her think again about wanting to speed.*

think aloud/out loud: speak one's thoughts as they occur ~ *What did you say? Nothing really, I was just thinking out loud.*

think back: recall a past time/event ~ *It makes me think back to when we lived in London.*

think better of: decide not to do something after reconsideration because the original decision was unfavourable ~ *I thought better of eating the chocolate cake.*

think big: plan ambitiously/on a grand scale ~ *He's thinking big, as in a week-long event.*

think little of someone/something: have a poor opinion of them/it ~ *Experts on the panel thought little of Dan's theory.*

think something over: consider something ~ *Give me the weekend to think it over.*

think something up: concoct/invent/devise ~ *I don't know what our act will be, but we'll think up something.*

think through: consider something (before making a decision) ~ *I'll think it through and let you know tomorrow.*

think twice: think carefully before making a decision/taking action (because you're aware of the dangers/problems) ~ *1a) I'd think twice about swimming there. 1b) He doesn't think twice about getting behind the wheel even if he's been drinking.*

think the world of something/someone: regard highly; admire; be fond of ~ *He thinks the world of his Aunt Jean.*

I think not: a way of disagreeing/saying no ~ *Are you going to go? I think not. I'm really tired.*

just think . . . : [spoken] used when asking someone to imagine/consider something ~ *Just think—we could be famous!*

that's what you/they think: [spoken] a way of saying you strongly disagree with someone ~ *They're of the opinion that you're going to drive them there and back. Well, that's what they think!*

. . . thinks he's God's gift to women: a man who has delusional thoughts about being irresistible to women

thinks only of him/herself: describes someone who is selfish ~ *I'm not surprised she didn't offer to help. She only ever thinks of herself.*

to think that . . . : [spoken] expression of surprise when realising/imagining something ~ *1a) To think that you lived two streets from me when we were kids is amazing! 1b) To think that she'll be representing Australia makes me very proud.*

(I) got to thinking: ponder something and come to a realisation ~ *After hearing about Jack's predicament, I got to thinking about how we can help him.*

(I) wasn't thinking: [spoken] used as a reason for doing/saying something you shouldn't have ~ *I don't know why I did that. I wasn't thinking.* *also: wasn't thinking straight

get/give the third degree: a long, intense interrogation ~ *Dad gave me the third degree when I came home late from the party.*

thirsty work: physical work that induces great thirst ~ *You'll need lots to drink. It's thirsty work.*

this and that: various/unspecified items/events/facts; everything and nothing ~ *1a) What sort of work have you been doing? Oh, a bit of this and that. 1b) I usually add some wine, a bit of this, and a bit of that. I don't really stick to the recipe.* *also: this, that, and the other

this minute: [spoken] immediately/right now ~ *Come here this minute!*

thong(s): a sandal, commonly made of rubber, held on the foot by a strip that fits between the first and second toes

a thousand and one: many/numberless; exaggerated amount ~ *There's a thousand and one reasons why you shouldn't go.*

give something some thought: consider something ~ *1a) I've given it some thought, and have decided to approve your application. 1b) To tell you the truth, I haven't given it much thought of late.*

don't give it another thought: [spoken] used to tell someone not to continue to worry about something they've apologised for (often used to indicate the close of discussion on the topic) ~ *Nothing came of it, you didn't let anyone down, so don't give it another thought.*

food for thought: anything that provides mental stimulus; something to think about ~ *Her suggestions gave us some food for thought for the next project.*

never thought to . . .: [spoken] used when you fail to consider something ~ *I never thought to ring Steve.*

spare a thought for somebody: used to tell someone that they should think about someone who is in a bad situation ~ *You think this is bad? Spare a thought for all the people who don't even have access to running water.*

that's a thought: [spoken] an expression of approval of a suggestion/idea ~ *We could cut this bit off and make a new opening underneath. Now, that's a thought.*

thrash about/around: move in a violent/convulsive way ~ *1a) He lay there, thrashing around in pain. 1b) The kids had fun thrashing about in the water.*

thrash out: debate/discuss something thoroughly so as to reach a decision ~ *I left them to thrash it out.*

be/get thrashed: suffer heavy defeat in a contest ~ *He beat me at tennis, but I thrashed him in a game of squash.*

threads: clothes/clothing ~ *Nice threads.*

a three-ring circus: a situation of uncontrolled, confusing activity ~ *It was a three-ring circus in there. Everyone was busy doing nothing.*

thrilled to bits: elated/thrilled/excited/extremely pleased ~ *They were thrilled to bits with the results.* *also: tickled pink

be at each other's throats: argue angrily/bicker ~ *It's a wonder they're still together. They're always at each other's throats.*

cut one's own throat: cause/bring about one's own failure ~ *You'd be cutting your own throat if you sell them for that price.*

(have a) frog in your throat: have a sense of an uncleared throat ~ *I'm not coughing because I have a cold, it's a frog in my throat.*

(a) lump in one's throat: a tight feeling in your throat caused by strong emotion (usually sadness) ~ *I get a lump in my throat whenever I hear that song.*

shove something down someone's throat: 1) force someone/one to swallow/eat something ~ *I managed to shove some food down my throat before I left.*

2) force someone to accept information ~ *They shoved that subject down our throats at school.* *also: ram down throat

through and through: completely/thoroughly ~ *1a) He's a Tigers fan through and through. 1b) I've read it through and through and still can't understand it.*

(be) through with: finished with someone/doing something ~ *1a) Take your things and go. I'm through with you! 1b) Are you through with your tirade?*

throw around: carelessly toss/cast something/someone about ~ *. . . came in and started throwing all my things around the room.*

throw away: 1) dispose of something ~ *I'm going to throw all this junk away.*

2) to waste something; fail to make use of ~ *If you turn them down you'd be throwing away a once-in-a-lifetime opportunity.*

throw caution to the wind: do something despite the risks ~ *... threw caution to the wind and jumped in.*

throw a game: lose a game deliberately/on purpose (usually as a bribe)

throw one's hands up in the air: give up in despair (as a sign of resignation) ~ *Unable to convince him otherwise, I threw my hands up in the air and walked away.*

throw one's hands up in horror: a physical reaction at being shocked/horrified ~ *She threw her hands up in horror at the scene before her.*

throw in: include (as an extra) with something being sold ~ *They're throwing in a carry case with every unit purchased.* *also: throw in to the bargain

throw in the towel/sponge: quit; admit defeat ~ *His energy depleted, he reluctantly threw in the towel.* *also: throw hand in; give up

throw oneself at someone: attract the attention/admiration of someone; attempt to seduce someone ~ *Women throw themselves at him wherever he goes.*

throw out on one's ear: physically eject someone ~ *Any sign of trouble and you'll be thrown out on your ear.*

throw into confusion/disarray/chaos: cause disruption/confusion ~ *1a) A power outage in the auditorium threw everyone into confusion. 1b) The strike has thrown the airline industry into chaos.*

throw in at the deep end: make someone do a job/task without first preparing them or offering any help ~ *They threw me in at the* *deep end on my first day by putting me in charge of customer complaints.*

throw off: 1) recover from/resist a disease/illness ~ *He rested in an effort to throw off a nasty cold.*

2) emit; give off ~ *2a) The rose bush threw off a heavenly scent. 2b) We need to have the fans going all the time because the machinery gives off a lot of heat.*

3) quickly remove/discard ~ *He threw off his towel and dived into the water.*

throw off the scent/track/trail: purposely mislead/divert away ~ *They tried to throw him off the scent by saying she'd moved overseas.*

throw off balance: 1) cause/be caused to falter and/or fall ~ *A strong gust of wind threw me off balance.*

2) confuse/disorientate/upset someone ~ *The speaker was thrown off balance by a difficult question.*

throw open: 1) make accessible ~ *The owner has thrown open the doors, giving the public access to a magnificent collection of rare artefacts.*

2) open something that was closed ~ *The maid threw open the windows to clear the stuffy air.*

3) make available for someone to participate in ~ *The discussion was then thrown open to the audience.*

throw out: 1) see throw away (1)

2) discard/reject ~ *The committee threw out our proposal.*

3) remove from office or a place of learning ~ *3a) He was removed from office for misappropriating funds. 3b) Josh was thrown out of school for taking drugs.*

4) force to leave/expel ~ *She was thrown out of the meeting for disruptive behaviour.*

5) cease to consider ~ *The judge threw out the case due to insufficient evidence.*

throw a punch: punch someone ~ *He threw a punch, but missed.*

throw someone: say something confusing/surprising ~ *He threw me completely when he said he wouldn't be coming to stay.*

throw/put a spanner in the works: do something that obstructs/hinders/alters a procedure/plan ~ *Their sudden withdrawal from the competition really threw a spanner in the works.*

throw together: 1) of a particular situation that causes people to meet and get to know one another ~ *We were thrown together by chance at a work conference.*

2) hastily assemble/arrange ~ *I had to throw a meal together for some unexpected guests.*

throw up: 1) to vomit ~ *I don't know what she ate, but she's been throwing up all night.*

2) cause to rise ~ *2a) His father threw the ball high up into the air. 2b) The Jeep barrelled along the dirt road, throwing up dust and rocks.*

3) construct hurriedly ~ *We threw up a shelter to protect us from the rain storm.*

throw (one's) weight around: act as if you have a lot of authority; use your position/power to get what you want ~ *Bill likes to throw his weight around, but mostly everyone ignores him.*

throw yourself into something: 1) start doing an activity/task with vigour/enthusiasm ~ *With renewed energy, she threw herself into her homework.*

2) jump into something (water) with intent ~ *He threw himself into the raging river in an effort to save her.*

thumb a ride: hitch-hike; persuade the driver of a passing vehicle to take you somewhere ~ *Steve thumbed rides to make his way across Europe.*

thumb through something: quickly turn the pages of a book/magazine ~ *I thumbed through a gardening magazine while I waited.* *also: leaf through

all thumbs: to be clumsy/uncoordinated (especially with one's hands) ~ *I'm all thumbs when it comes to sewing.* *also: all fingers and thumbs

give/get the thumbs up/down: expression of satisfaction/approval or refusal/rejection; that all's okay/not okay ~ *Our proposal has been given the thumbs up!*

twiddle one's thumbs: fidget; pass the time inactively ~ *Well, don't just sit there twiddling your thumbs. Get to work!*

(be) under one's thumb: under someone's control/influence ~ *He's been under her thumb for years.*

thunderstruck: shocked/amazed ~ *We were all thunderstruck when they were both declared winners.*

(a) tick: a very short time; a moment ~ *I'll be with you in a tick.* *see also: (just) a sec; any tick of the clock

tick all the right boxes: fit the criteria; meet expectations ~ *I'll consider it. It certainly ticks all the right boxes.*

tick away: of time to pass, especially when you're waiting for something to happen ~ *Minutes ticked by, and still nothing.*

tick off: scold/berate/reprimand ~ *I got ticked off for being late.*

tick over: 1) (of an engine) to idle ~ *There doesn't seem to be anything wrong with the engine. It's ticking over nicely.*

2) (system/business) working/operating at minimum level ~ *Mary is keeping things ticking over until Dan gets back.*

what makes somebody/something tick: what makes someone/ something do what they do ~ *I've often wondered what makes her tick.*

ticker: one's heart ~ *You'll be pleased to know your ticker's in good shape.*

dicky ticker: weak/unhealthy ~ *He's got a weak/unhealthy heart.*

ticket: notification of a traffic offence ~ *She's been given a speeding ticket.*

have tickets on oneself: be conceited; have a high opinion of oneself ~ *He must have tickets on himself if he thinks she'll go out with him.*

just the ticket: exactly what's needed ~ *A nice hot meal will be just the ticket.*

tickety-boo: in order; doing well; alright ~ *He gave it a quick check to make sure everything was tickety-boo.*

tickle one's fancy: appealing/amusing ~ *1a) This style of music doesn't tickle my fancy. 1b) I think this birthday card will really tickle his fancy.* *also: do it for me; does nothing for me

tickle the ivories: (to) play the piano

tickled pink: overjoyed ~ *I was tickled pink when I heard the news.**also: tickled to bits/death

tiddly: slightly drunk ~ *We were all a bit tiddly.*

tide (one) over: support/help through a difficult period/ circumstance ~ *I've got just enough cash to tide me over until next week.*

tidy: 1) substantial/considerable ~ *1a) He earns a tidy sum. 1b) They made a tidy deal.*

2) neat/orderly

tidy up: make things tidy; put in order ~ *My son never tidies up his room.*

tie someone down: limit someone's freedom; encumber with something ~ *I was tied down doing extra work all weekend.*

tie in with: connected with something relevant ~ *His account ties in with what they told us.*

tie the knot: get married ~ *I heard they're tying the knot.*

tie up: 1) conclude/finalise something ~ *We hope to tie up the deal by Thursday.*

2) slow progress ~ *The accident tied up traffic for over an hour.*

3) be busy/occupied ~ *I've been tied up in a meeting all morning.*

4) of money to be secured in a deal but unavailable to use ~ *A lot of their money is tied up in the business.*

tie up loose ends: finalise minor unresolved issues/problems ~ *I have a few loose ends to tie up first.*

tied up in knots: experience physical symptoms due to worry/anxiety ~ *My stomach's tied up in knots worrying about it.*

tight corner/spot: a difficult situation ~ *1a) Recent changes to regulations have put me in a tight corner. 1b) He's good to have around if ever you're in a tight spot.*

tight squeeze: *see: squeeze

tighten one's/the belt: restrict spending ~ *With the economy worsening we've had to tighten our belts.*

tight-knit: closely integrated ~ *It's a friendly, tight-knit community.*

time after time: repeatedly; again and again; always ~ *Time after time he's been told not to do it.* *also: time and time again; time and again

time and a half: one and a half times the usual hourly rate ~ *They get time and a half for working Sundays.*

(ticking) time bomb: a situation that has a potentially damaging/ disastrous outcome in the future ~ *He's a heavy smoker and drinker, he doesn't exercise, and has a stressful job. He's a ticking time bomb.*

time flies: [spoken] used to say that time appears to have passed very quickly ~ *Well, time flies—I have to go now.*

time for . . . : the moment one has to do something; that something needs to happen ~ *1a) It's time for me to go now. 1b) It's time for a change of leadership.*

(the) time has come: [spoken] used to announce that it is time to do something ~ *The time has come for me to resign from the company.*

time immemorial: a time in the past that no one can remember/ has knowledge of ~ *It's a custom that's gone on for time immemorial.*

time someone in: record one's/someone's arrival time ~ *You were timed in at 10 a.m.*

time is money: [spoken] used to say that wasting time costs money ~ *Time is money. I can't afford equipment breakdowns.*

time is of the essence: [spoken] used to emphasise a need for haste in doing something ~ *Time is of the essence when performing this procedure.*

time is on your side: [spoken] that you have enough time to do something ~ *I don't have to be there until noon, so I have some time on my side.*

time is up: [spoken] when an allotted time has expired/run out ~ *Your time is up—stop what you're doing!*

time off: 1) a period of time free from work/employment ~ *I have some time off next week. I can do it then.*

2) a shortened prison sentence ~ *He got time off for good behaviour.*

(the) time of my/his/her life: describes a fantastic/wonderful experience ~ *We had the time of our lives!*

time waits for no one: a way of saying that something should be done now otherwise there won't be time

(only) time will tell: the result/answer will be revealed in the future ~ *I'm not sure if we made the right decision. Only time will tell.*

ahead of time: earlier than expected ~ *We arrived an hour ahead of time.*

ahead of one's/its/their time: more advanced/modern than anyone/anything ~ *A lot of the buildings he designed were ahead of their time.*

against time: do something quickly because you're not sure if you have enough time to do it ~ *There's much to be done and fewer workers, so we'll be working against time.* *also: race against time

all in good time: [spoken] a way of telling someone that something will happen very soon, and that they should be patient ~ *When will the buds open? All in good time, Alice, all in good time.*

any time soon: indefinite time in the future ~ *We have no plans to change it any time soon.*

any time now: very soon ~ *They'll be arriving at any time now.*

at a set time: at a particular/pre-arranged time ~ *Do we have to be there at a set time?*

at a time: in specified groups or numbers; separately ~ *1a) He eats them two at a time. 1b) The mourners filed past one at a time.*

at no time: never; that something did/should happen ~ *1a) At no time did I say I wanted to go. 1b) At no time should you enter without knocking.*

at one time: ago/in the past; once; on an occasion ~ *At one time he used to have really long hair.*

at one time or another: on occasions; occasionally (in the past) ~ *We encountered problems with it at one time or another.*

at the same time: simultaneously ~ *We arrived at the same time as everyone else.*

at this time: now; this particular time ~ *Sorry, but at this time I have to say no.*

behind time: late ~ *The train's running behind time.*

behind the times: out-dated; old-fashioned ~ *I'm a bit behind the times when it comes to technology.*

before my/your time: happen or exist before you were born/before you were able to remember it ~ *1a) That happened well before my time. 1b) That method of teaching was used before my time.*

bide (one's) time: wait for a favourable opportunity; continue in a place ~ *I'm biding my time here until I find the job I want.*

buy time: delay something; try to gain extra time ~ *He's buying time so he can finish the assignment.*

by the time: the time when something happens or should happen ~ *It had already started by the time we got there.*

do time: serve a specific amount of time in prison; serve a prison sentence ~ *He's doing time for robbery.*

for the time being: for now; meantime ~ *We'll wait here for the time being.*

for the umpteenth time: used to indicate a person/occasion/thing happens or comes after many others ~ *1a) For the umpteenth time, NO! 1b) She checked her watch for the umpteenth time.*

from time to time: sometimes; occasionally ~ *We visit them from time to time.*

give it time: [spoken] that you need to wait before something happens ~ *Your leg will get better, just give it some time.*

give someone the time of day: that you dislike someone so much that you wouldn't let them know what time it was if they asked; refuse to talk to someone because you think you're superior ~ *1a) She's so arrogant she wouldn't give you the time of day. 1b) He's a creep. I wouldn't even give him the time of day.*

go back in time: revisit the past ~ *To understand the significance of this discovery you have to go back in time about four million years.*

half the time: as often as not ~ *I don't know where he goes half the time.*

have a tough time (of it): face a lot of difficult problems ~ *1a) Did you manage to fix it? Yeah, I had a tough time of it though. 1b) She's been having a tough time lately.* *also: have a hard time; have a rough time

have time on one's hands: have not enough to do ~ *She has a lot more time on her hands now that the children have left home.*

not have a lot of time for somebody: to disapprove of someone and be unwilling to be in their company ~ *I don't have a lot of time for Tim.*

have a lot of time for somebody: like someone very much and that you want to be in their company ~ *I've got a lot of time for Michael—he always has something interesting to talk about.*

in due time: soon; at the appropriate time ~ *I'll get to that question in due time.* *also: in due course; in good time

in half the time: in much less time ~ *I'll help you with it and we'll have it done in half the time.*

in no time flat: very quickly ~ *We finished in no time flat.* *also: in less than no time; in no time at all

in time (to/for): at a set/specific time ~ *1a) I hope we get there in time. 1b) She was in time to catch the train.*

in one's own time: do something at your own pace ~ *The assignment can be done in your own time.*

(have a) whale of a time: to really enjoy yourself ~ *We had a whale of a time—it was so much fun!* *also: the time of my life/our lives

keep time: 1) of a timepiece to indicate the correct time ~ *This old watch no longer keeps good time.*

2) maintain a musical rhythm ~ *. . . kept time to the music by clapping their hands.*

3) to record/keep time in sports

keep one's eye on the time: be aware of what the time is ~ *Keep your eye on the time because you need to be back here at 2 p.m.* *also: watch the time

live on borrowed time: outlive reasonable expectations ~ *The treatment has given him some reprieve, but he's living on borrowed time.*

(a) long time: ages; an extended period of time ~ *1a) It's been a long time since I've seen one of those. 1b) I haven't seen her for a long time.*

lose time: take longer to do something ~ *We lost time when we took a wrong turn.*

lose track of time: be unaware of what the time is ~ *Sorry, I'm late. I was engrossed in a book and lost track of time.*

make good time: travel with no risk of being late ~ *We're making good time. It looks like we'll be there half an hour early.*

make time: allow time to do something particular ~ *No matter what's happening, I always make time to read to my children.*

mark time: 1) march on the spot/in place

2) wait idly for something to happen ~ *Mary is marking time until she starts uni.*

nine times out of ten: almost always ~ *He gets it right nine times out of ten.*

no time to lose: [spoken] do something without delay ~ *We only have an hour to complete it, so let's get started—there's no time to lose!*

no time to scratch oneself: be very busy ~ *We were so busy, I had no time to scratch myself.*

not before time: [spoken] response used to say that you think what's about to happen should have happened a long time ago ~ *They're going to upgrade the highway. And not before time!* *also: and about time too

of all time: used to make a comparison that something is the best ever ~ *She is possibly the greatest opera singer of all time.*

of all times: the worst of all possible times ~ *Oh, why did it have to rain NOW of all times?!*

on time: not late ~ *You need to be there on time.*

on your own time: do something outside working hours ~ *If you want to gossip on the phone, do it on your own time.*

be/run out of time: to have no time left to complete something ~ *1a) I tried to finish it, but ran out of time. 1b) You've just about run out of time.*

play for time: tactic used to stall/delay ~ *He's playing for time because he doesn't want to go to bed.*

take (the) time: make available a period of time to do/say something ~ *I appreciate you taking the time to do this.*

take time: [spoken] used to say that something will take a lot of time to do ~ *I can repair it, but it's going to take some time.*

take time out: stop a task/activity temporarily; make more time for leisure ~ *She took time out from her job to travel.*

take one's time: [spoken] used to tell someone not to hurry; to say that you did something unhurriedly ~ *1a) Take your time, I'm in no rush. 1b) We took our time walking along the beach.*

the whole time: continuously during a period ~ *She talked the whole time!* *also: all the while

there was a time . . . : [spoken] used to talk about things that happened/the way something was done in the past ~ *There was a time when deliveries were made using horse and buggy.*

tough time(s): periods of hardship ~ *He's helped me through some tough times.* *also: bad/difficult/trying/hard times

turn back (the hands of) time: go back (in time) ~ *The actress underwent plastic surgery in an attempt to turn back the hands of time.*

(be a) waste of time: that something done is/will be unproductive; do something for nothing ~ *1a) Going there was a waste of time. He wasn't home. 1b) It will be a waste of time washing the car today. It's going to rain.* *also: wasting your time

(to) waste time: spend one's allotted time idly ~ *We can't waste time sitting and talking, we've got work to do.*

waste no time: do something immediately/without hesitation ~ *She wasted no time in getting there.*

when the time comes: [spoken] at the appropriate time ~ *I'll most likely start crying when the time comes to leave.*

Tim Tam: Tim Tam is a brand of chocolate biscuits manufactured by Arnott's. A Tim Tam is comprised of two layers of chocolate malted biscuit separated by a chocolate cream filling and coated in a thin layer of chocolate. They are perhaps the most popular chocolate biscuits Australia wide—with approximately thirty-five million packs sold each year. Varieties of Tim Tams are available in Canada, the USA, Hong Kong, Indonesia, and Timor-Leste.

(give someone) a tingle/buzz: call someone on the telephone ~ *Give me a tingle when you get there.*

tinker with: *see: fiddle with

tinny/ie: 1) a can of beer

2) a small aluminium boat

crack a tinny: open a can of cold beer ~ *I cracked a few tinnies with Jonno.*

tiny tot: a young child; a toddler

(rubbish) tip: designated waste disposal area; landfill; the dump

tip off: give advance information; advise to ~ *Authorities were tipped off as to his whereabouts.*

tip of the iceberg: the evident portion; a small part of a much larger problem ~ *The corruption they uncovered is only the tip of the iceberg.*

tip the scales: 1) offset the balance in a situation ~ *They only needed two more votes to tip the scales.*

2) register a weight ~ *He tipped the scales at 150 kilos.*

tip up: tilt/overturn/invert/slant something ~ *You need to tip it up a bit more to get the right angle.*

tip-top: the highest quality ~ *1a) The car is in tip-top condition. 1b) She keeps in tip-top shape by exercising every day.*

tipsy: mildly/happily intoxicated/drunk ~ *We were all a bit tipsy.*

tit for tat: equivalent repayment/retaliation ~ *It's believed they're tit for tat assaults by rival gangs.* *also: an eye for an eye; a tooth for a tooth

tits/titties: [slang] a woman's breasts *also: boobs

a tizz/tizzy: 1) a state of anxiety; fluster ~ *He's in a real tizz about it.*

2) pretentious/gaudy ~ *She has a fondness for wearing tizzy clothes.*

tizz up: attempt to beautify in a tawdry manner ~ *Pauline tizzed herself up for the event.*

to a T: exactly/perfectly ~ *That jacket suits you to a T.*

to and fro: (of movement) toward and away from; in one direction and then in the other direction ~ *1a) The mother cradled her, rocking her to and fro. 1b) They were like ants toing and froing everywhere.* *also: back and forth; backwards and forwards

propose a toast: propose to drink in honour of/to the health of someone/something ~ *I would like to propose a toast to Jeff, for all the work he's put into this project.*

the toast of the town: someone admired/celebrated ~ *She was the toast of the town following her first solo performance.*

warm as toast: very warm/cosy ~ *My feet are as warm as toast.*

to-do: commotion/fuss ~ *What's all this to-do?*

toddle off: depart; walk in a leisurely way ~ *1a) They said their goodbyes and toddled off down the road. 1b) Well, I think I'll toddle off to bed now.* *also: toddle away

toddle about: walk unsteadily ~ *I watched with joy as my young nephew toddled about.*

toe the line: conform; do what is expected ~ *You'd better start toeing the line or you'll find yourself off the team.* *also: toe the mark

be/keep/stay on one's toes: alert; ready to act ~ *The teacher gives us mental exercises to keep us on our toes.*

makes your toes curl: something that causes an extreme reaction ~ *The very thought of it makes my toes curl.*

toey: nervous/edgy ~ *This wild weather is making the horses a bit toey.*

together: mentally stable; calm; composed ~ *I don't know how she kept it together under such trying circumstances.*

keep it together: remain focused/composed in difficult circumstances ~ *He kept it together throughout the ordeal and led us all to safety.*

together with: along with; and also something ~ *The shoes, together with a hat and scarf, make it an expensive outfit.*

tomfoolery: foolish/silly behaviour ~ *I suspect when they all get together that there'll be some tomfoolery going on.*

Tom, Dick, and/or Harry: any/everybody; multiple unspecified people ~ *Make sure you get a qualified tradesman. You don't want any Tom, Dick, or Harry messing with it.*

tons of/a ton: a large amount/number ~ *1a) I've a ton of work to do. 1b) We had tons to eat!*

weigh a ton: extremely heavy ~ *This weighs a ton!*

tone down: moderate; lessen; ease ~ *Could you tone down your language?*

(be on) the tip of one's tongue: when you know the word you want to say but you just can't remember it at that moment ~ *I know who she is—her name is on the tip of my tongue.*

(have one's) tongue in one's cheek: say something in humour but give the appearance of being serious ~ *I suspect that Sue had her tongue firmly in her cheek when she said she was the best looking woman in the room.* *also: tongue-in-cheek

bite/hold (one's) tongue: stop yourself from speaking ~ *I had to bite my tongue when she made those outrageous claims.*

bite your tongue: [spoken] strong rebuke to tell someone to say no more/to be quiet ~ *Oh, bite your tongue, will you!*

find one's tongue: be willing to talk; be able to express yourself after a shock ~ *She found her tongue at last and told them what happened.*

have a loose tongue: speak thoughtlessly/insensitively or in a way that causes embarrassment/indignation ~ *Be very careful what you tell her. She has a loose tongue.*

lose one's tongue: be unable to speak (temporarily) ~ *I was so nervous I lost my tongue.* *also: be stuck for words; tongue-tied

(can't) get one's tongue around: used to describe words/phrases that are difficult to pronounce ~ *Most Welsh place names are very difficult to get your tongue around.*

(has the) cat got your tongue: a way of asking someone why they aren't saying anything when they're expected to speak ("why aren't you speaking?") ~ *What's wrong? Has the cat got your tongue?*

keep a civil tongue in one's head: speak politely ~ *That man can't keep a civil tongue in his head!*

native/mother tongue: one's native/parent language ~ *She finds it easier to speak in her native tongue.*

rolls off the tongue: easy to pronounce/say ~ *It's not a name that rolls easily off the tongue.*

sharp tongue: said of someone who speaks critically/severely ~ *She comes across as a nice person, but she has a sharp tongue at times.*

slip of the tongue: a mistake/error in speech ~ *Sorry, a slip of the tongue. I meant fifty, not fifteen.*

speak with (a) forked tongue: distort the truth; tell lies ~ *The salesman is speaking with a forked tongue promising everything and delivering nothing.*

stick your tongue out at someone: The act of putting your tongue outside your mouth. It can be a sign of disrespect or, humorously, a way of proving some else wrong, a sign of bragging, or a flirty gesture.

start/set tongues wagging: to cause people to gossip; start people talking ~ *Her presence in the office is sure to start tongues wagging.*

watch/mind your tongue: [spoken] warning to someone to stop being rude/stop using bad language ~ *I don't like being spoken to like that, so you'd better watch your tongue, young lady!*

tongue-lashing: a severe scolding ~ *I got home late, and boy, did I get a tongue-lashing!*

tongue-twister: a phrase/sequence of words designed to be difficult to articulate and repeat. For example: She sells sea shells by the sea shore. The shells she sells are sea shells I'm sure.

too bad: 1) used to say that you're sorry/sympathetic about something ~ *That's too bad about your father being in hospital.*

2) [spoken] a dismissive response to someone's predicament ~ *If you don't like the colour, too bad. That's all they had.*

not too bad: better than expected; reasonably good ~ *1a) How are you feeling? Not too bad, thanks. 1b) This chicken risotto's actually not too bad.*

(have) too much on one's/someone's plate: to be too busy ~ *Sorry I can't help you with it, I've got too much on my plate right now.*

(the) too hard basket: an imaginary basket where tasks deemed difficult or tedious are placed ~ *Did they respond to your complaint? No. I think it went in the too hard basket.*

all/only too . . . : that something is the case to the extreme ~ *1a) You're all too kind. 1b) It was all too much for her and she had a nervous breakdown. 1c) I know only too well the difficulties they'll face.*

be only too glad/happy/pleased: willing to do something ~ *We're only too pleased to help.*

not too: not very ~ *His hearing's not too good.*

Tooheys: popular brand of beer

tooth fairy: an imaginary being that leaves money in place of a child's baby tooth that has fallen out

tootsies: toes (humorous) ~ *Oh, my tootsies are cold.*

top brass: the highest rank in a military organisation; the most important people in a governing body ~ *All the top brass were there.*

top dog: the most important person/leader of a group ~ *Go and talk to Jack. He's the top dog.*

top something off with something: finish up/conclude in a memorable way ~ *We topped off the holiday with a visit to Disneyland.*

top (something) up: replenish ~ *1a) The waiter topped up our wine. 1b) May I top up your glass?*

top something with something: decorate/adorn something by adding something else ~ *The sponge cake was topped with strawberries.*

top that: [spoken] verbal challenge when you've achieved something for someone to do better ~ *I got a hundred out of a hundred. Top that!*

at the top of one's lungs: shout/yell/scream/sing out very loudly ~ *She was screaming at the top of her lungs.*

not have much on top: a humorous way of saying that someone is bald/balding ~ *He hasn't got much on top any more.*

not have much up top: lacking intelligence; dim-witted ~ *He's a nice enough bloke, but I don't think he has much up top.*

(get/keep/stay) on top of things/something: 1) keep well-informed ~ *He reads the business section every day to keep on top of current economic trends.*

2) manage/control a situation ~ *I try to keep on top of the housework by doing just a little every day.*

on top of the world: elated; very happy ~ *I was on top of the world when he asked me to marry him.*

The Top End: a geographical region encompassing the northernmost section of the Northern Territory

Top Forty: an ever-changing list of the current, most popular songs in a particular genre ~ *The song has been number one in the Top Forty for the last three weeks.*

go topless: be without clothing on the top half of one's body ~ *She went topless to get an even suntan.*

topsy-turvy: upside down; in a state of confusion/disorder ~ *My life's a bit topsy-turvy at the moment, so I can't commit to anything.*

torch something: cause to burn; set on fire ~ *The thieves dumped and torched the stolen vehicle.*

torn between: (be) undecided ~ *She's torn between staying here or moving interstate.*

toss a coin: toss a coin into the air and guess which side (heads or tails) will land face up (used as a way of making a decision) ~ *1a) I'll toss you for it. 1b) Let's toss a coin to see who goes first.*

toss and turn: unable to lie still ~ *1a) I tossed and turned all night trying to get comfortable. 1b) He tossed and turned with worry.*

toss something around: 1) discuss in an informal way ~ *We tossed a few ideas around.*

2) to throw something/someone (around) ~ *2a) The kids went to the park and tossed the ball around. 2b) The waves tossed us around like matchsticks.* *also tossed about

toss aside: move something to one side and out of the way ~ *The rugby player tossed his challenger aside like a rag doll and kept running.*

toss away: casually discard something ~ *She carelessly tossed the wrapper away.* *see also: throw away

toss back: throw back with a quick light motion; drink quickly ~ *1a) Sally tossed back her head laughed heartily. 1b) Steve tossed back a scotch to calm his nerves.*

toss off: throw something of oneself ~ *I tossed off the blanket when it got too hot.*

toss out: eject forcibly; discard ~ *1a) The owner picked up the intruder and tossed him out the door. 1b) The driver carelessly tossed the wrapper out the window.*

toss someone for (something): flip a coin to decide something ~ *I'll toss you to see who goes first.*

toss together: assemble hastily ~ *I had to quickly toss together a meal for some unexpected guests.*

toss up: decide one of two options ~ *I'm tossing up whether to go today or tomorrow.*

toss something up: throw something into the air ~ *He tossed the ball high up into the air.*

argue the toss: dispute a decision ~ *It's useless arguing the toss after the goal was disallowed.*

full toss: [cricket] a bowled ball that reaches the batsman without bouncing

toss-up: an unpredictable result/outcome ~ *They both play at the same level so it will be a toss-up as to who will win.*

tot: small child

tot up: *see: add up

total(led): wrecked/demolished beyond repair ~ *She walked away from the crash uninjured, but totalled the car.* *also: write-off

touch base: confer/talk briefly with; renew a line of communication with someone ~ *I'll touch base with you later on in the week.*

touch down: for an airplane to land/reach/come in contact with the ground ~ *We touched down at 2 p.m.*

(a) touch of: something in small doses ~ *1a) I have a touch of the flu. 1b) You look like you've had a touch of sun. 1c) It just needs a touch of paint.*

touch on/upon: 1) verge on; approach ~ *The symptoms she displayed touched on a more sinister illness.*

2) briefly discuss/deal with a topic ~ *We only had time to touch on the issue at the meeting.*

touch the sides: a drink/liquid consumed (often in haste) that is insufficient to quench one's thirst/have the desired effect (said in the negative) ~ *That didn't even touch the sides. I'll have to have another one.*

not touch/go near with a ten-foot pole: refuse to associate with someone/something; avoid at all costs ~ *He's such a creep, I wouldn't go near him with a ten-foot pole.*

touch something up: improve; finish/complete by making minor changes/alterations ~ *It just needs a bit of a touch up here and there and it'll look like new.*

touch wood: [spoken] a superstitious interjection to keep bad luck away or for good luck to continue ~ *1a) I haven't dropped or broken any yet. Touch wood. 1b) We haven't had any problems with it so far, touch wood.*

at the touch of a button: used to indicate that something is possible by simply touching a button ~ *There is heating and air conditioning at the touch of a button.* *also: at the turn of a key; at the flick of a switch

(an) easy/soft touch: someone easy to take advantage of; easily persuaded to part with their money ~ *Dad's such a soft touch when we need extra cash.*

(have the) common touch: the ability of an influential/powerful person to relate with and appeal to the ordinary person ~ *She was well liked by everyone because she had the common touch.*

finishing touch: the final adjustment/action to complete something ~ *It just needs a few finishing touches and it's ready.*

in/into touch: (rugby/rugby league) when the ball connects with the touch line or goes over the touch line, either by being kicked there or carried there by a player

in touch with: 1) in communication with someone ~ *I'll be in touch with you later on in the week.*

2) conscious/aware of ~ *She is in touch with her emotions.*

lose touch with somebody: cease to be in communication ~ *I lost touch with them when they moved overseas.*

(have a) magic touch: possess a special skill/ability to do something well ~ *You've got a magic touch with babies.*

to the touch: when touched ~ *It's soft to the touch.*

(be) touched by something/someone: emotionally affected/ moved ~ *I was touched by her kindness.*

touch-and-go: describes an uncertain situation; a narrow escape ~ *His injuries were so severe, it was touch-and-go as to whether he would survive.*

touchy-feely: openly express love and affection through physical contact (often in a way that makes people feel uncomfortable) ~ *He's the touchy-feely type who often touches you on the arm or puts his arm across your shoulder.*

tough/tough luck: [spoken] used to indicate lack of sympathy for someone's problem ~ *That they've missed out is tough luck. They should have said something earlier.*

tough as nails: very tough ~ *The steak they served us was as tough as old nails.* *also: tough as boots

tough call: a difficult decision ~ *Deciding who gets the job will be a tough call.*

(a) tough cookie: a tenacious/aggressive person; someone emotionally strong ~ *1a) You'll find it hard getting him to change his mind. He's a tough cookie. 1b) It's amazing what she's endured. She's one tough cookie.*

(a) tough customer: someone who is difficult to deal with ~ *He's a tough customer to do business with.*

tough doing something: have difficulties doing something ~ *It's tough living out here.*

tough going: a passage/progress that is difficult ~ *1a) We got there eventually, but it was tough going. 1b) I find most of his books tough going.* (difficult to read)

tough love: be stern/strict with someone you care about with the intent to help them in the long run

(be) tough on: be very strict/severe ~ *The mayor promises to be tough on gun crime.*

(get) tough with (someone): deal with severely ~ *He's promised to get tough on repeat drink-driving offenders.*

tough something out: endure hardship/a difficult situation ~ *The owners can do little else but to tough out the recession.*

do it tough: experience difficulties/hardships ~ *They've been doing it tough since Jack lost his job.*

toughen up: become stronger/more resilient ~ *1a) A week working alongside that lot will toughen him up. 1b) Years of exposure to the sun has toughened up her skin like leather.*

tow away: move/remove by the act of pulling ~ *He came out to find his illegally parked car had been towed away.*

in tow: following/accompanying someone ~ *Negotiating the supermarket aisles with kids in tow is no easy task.*

toy with: 1) consider/think about before making a decision ~ *I've been toying with the idea of starting a business.*

2) thoughtlessly nervously handle/fiddle with an object ~ *Nicole toyed nervously with her rings as she waited for the results.*

toy with someone: tease someone's emotions; pretend to like someone ~ *She's convinced he loves her, but I think he's toying with her.*

track something/someone down: seek out; find where someone/something is ~ *Police are trying to track down the thieves.*

track record: a person's/organisation's past achievements/failures ~ *She was hired because of her track record in sales.*

on track: developing; making progress as expected/to schedule ~ *The project is on track and should be completed by the end of the month.*

on the right track: following the correct line of reasoning ~ *It's not the answer I'm looking for, but you're on the right track.*

on the wrong track: to be not following the correct line of reasoning ~ *He thinks the blame lies with them, but he's on the wrong track.*

back on track: operate/proceed again according to schedule ~ *There were a few setbacks, but we're finally back on track.*

lose track (of): 1) be no longer aware about something ~ *Sorry I'm late, I lost track of the time.*

2) lose contact with someone ~ *I've lost track of nearly all my school friends.*

make tracks: depart/leave ~ *It's late—we'd best make tracks.*

trackies: tracksuit

trackie daks: tracksuit pants

tradie: tradesman/tradesperson

trail away/off: of noise/sound to gradually fade ~ *His voice trailed off when he realized no one was listening.*

a trail of . . . : evidence of something that has passed ~ *1a) It was a monster hurricane that left a trail of destruction across the state. 1b) He dated a string of women and left, leaving a trail of broken hearts.*

traipse around/about: walk/wander/trudge slowly/aimlessly ~ *We spent the afternoon traipsing around the shops.*

traipse up and down: walk the length of an area from one end to the other ~ *We traipsed up and down the road looking for her lost dog.*

traipse through: walk a passage through a space/area ~ *We were forced to traipse through a muddy field.* *also: tramp through; trudge through

keep your trap shut: [spoken] a rude way of telling someone to keep quiet

tread carefully: be cautious/wary of offending/upsetting someone ~ *She's still sensitive about it, so I'd tread carefully when you're talking to her.* *also: tread lightly

tread the boards: perform on stage ~ *She's been treading the boards since she was a child.*

tread water: stay afloat in an upright position by moving one's legs in a walking motion

(a) treasure: regard as precious/valued ~ *Thanks for doing that. You're a real treasure.*

treat like dirt: treat someone badly ~ *He treats everyone like dirt.*

out of his/her tree: affected by either drugs or alcohol

trial and error: a method of solving problems that involves repeated varied attempts until success is achieved ~ *It was a procedure perfected by trial and error.*

tricks of the trade: a quick and/or effective way of doing things ~ *A trick of the trade to stop butter burning is to add two or three drops of cooking oil.*

(have a/few) trick(s) up my sleeve: have a secret strategy/skill/ability to use when necessary ~ *He might think he's outsmarted me, but I have a few tricks up my sleeve.*

bag of tricks: a supply of utensils/skills/techniques/methods ~ *I'll see what I've got in my bag of tricks.*

do the trick: do exactly what is expected ~ *1a) It's not the right tool but it should do the trick. 1b) I feel better now. A little nap did the trick.*

oldest trick in the book: an often-used/effective way of deceiving/tricking someone ~ *To say the cheque is in the mail is one of the oldest tricks in the book.*

take a trick: be consistently unlucky/unsuccessful ~ *Everything's gone wrong for me today—I can't seem to take a trick.*

the trick is . . . : [spoken] used when describing a useful/effective way/method of doing something ~ *If you want to wake up at the same time every day, the trick is to go to bed at the same time every night.*

up to his/her old/usual tricks: act/behave in the same bad way as before ~ *He hasn't reformed. He's still up to his usual con-artist tricks.*

use/try every trick in the book: use every possible method/means to achieve something ~ *I've tried every trick in the book to convince her to eat vegetables, but she still refuses.*

tried-and-true: dependable; proven; reliable; successful; trustworthy ~ *This is a guaranteed tried-and-true method for making scones.*

trim away: cut something away from something ~ *You need to trim away excess fat off the meat.* *also: trim off

trim, taut, and terrific: slim and fit ~ *She's trim, taut, and terrific after losing all that weight.*

trim down: become trim/slim ~ *He's trimmed down a lot since starting the diet.*

keep in trim: maintain a healthy weight/shape ~ *Betty keeps herself in trim by jogging.*

trip up: make/cause to make a mistake/falter/stumble ~ *1a) That last question tripped me up. 1b) Someone stuck out their foot and tripped me up.*

(a) guilt trip: prolonged feeling of guilt/remorse for a misdeed ~ *I'm on a bit of guilt trip for having forgotten her birthday.*

take a trip down memory lane: remember things you did/places you went in the past ~ *Looking at the photos was like taking a trip down memory lane.*

tripe: nonsense ~ *Those claims he made are just a load of tripe.*
*also: codswallop

trot along: run/walk quickly using short steps ~ *The mother duck led the way and all the chicks trotted behind her.*

trot out: 1) mention something regularly/habitually ~ *He trots out the same old jokes at every party.*

2) bring out/show for inspection

a good/bad trot: a period of good/bad luck ~ *She's had a bit of a bad trot.*

on the trot: in succession ~ *They won three games on the trot.*

the trots: [informal] 1) diarrhoea ~ *All that spicy food has given her the trots.*

2) a race meeting for trotting/harness horses ~ *I won a hundred dollars at the trots!*

trouble someone for something: [spoken] a polite way to ask someone to do/for something ~ *Could I trouble you for a drink of water?*

trouble oneself: bother to do something; concern oneself ~ *Don't trouble yourself to help me, will you!*

cause/make trouble: knowingly/unknowingly cause an upset ~ *They're out to cause trouble.* *also looking/asking for trouble

in trouble: due for punishment; in difficulty/danger ~ *She'll be in big trouble if her parents find out.*

(it's) no trouble: [spoken] a way of saying you're happy to do something for someone ~ *Are you sure you want to do it? Yeah, it's no trouble.*

save someone the trouble (of doing something): do something so someone else doesn't have to do it ~ *If I do it now, it'll save you the trouble of doing it tomorrow.*

take the trouble: make a special effort to do something ~ *She took the trouble to deliver it in person.*

truckie: truck driver

true to form: behave/act as expected ~ *True to form, George arrived late.*

true to one's word: do exactly what you said you'd do ~ *True to her word, she arrived on time.*

all too true: used to say that something is true, though you wish it were not ~ *Alas, the claims brought against him are all too true.*

too good to be true: for something to be so good as to be unbelievable ~ *The job sounds too good to be true.*

true-blue: faithful; staunch; loyal ~ *1a) They're true-blue supporters. 1b) A true-blue Aussie.* *also: dinkum

true-to-life: a play/book/description to be realistic ~ *It was a hilariously funny, true-to-life film.*

trump card: an advantage/resource reserved to be used at an opportune moment ~ *He hoped to use his previous experience in the field as a trump card.*

trumped-up: contrived; made up ~ *He was held at the police station on some trumped-up charge.*

try as I can/could/might: fail to do something despite repeated attempts ~ *Try as I could—I couldn't move it.*

try it on with someone: deliberately annoy/irritate someone so as to test their level of anger ~ *He's trying it on with the new teacher.*

try on: put on a garment to check the size ~ *Why don't you try it on to see if it fits?*

try out for: demonstrate how well you can do something so as to become a member of a team/get a part in a play/movie ~ *He's going to try out for the school rugby team.*

try someone out: employ someone for a trial period to see if they're suitable for the job ~ *I need an apprentice so I'm trying out a couple of would-be landscapers.*

try something out: experiment with/test something to see how/if it works ~ *1a) I think I can fix the problem, but first I want to try something out. 1b) She's trying out her new camera.*

try someone's/one's patience: to test someone's patience ~ *1a) A rude customer really tried my patience today. 1b) You're really trying my patience!*

tuck someone in/up: secure someone (a child) in bed by tucking the bedclothes under the mattress ~ *Even at age twelve, he still likes to be tucked in.*

tuck in/into: eat greedily/heartily ~ *The homeless man hungrily tucked into his meal.*

tuck shop: school canteen/eatery

tucked away: difficult to find/hidden ~ *We discovered a great little coffee shop tucked away in a back street.*

tucker: food

tucker-bag: an outdated term for a bag/box for storing food

tuckered out: exhausted/tired ~ *I'm all tuckered out after all that work.*

tummy: one's stomach

(be) tuned in: 1) be sensitive to ~ *It was an interesting topic and everyone was tuned in to what the speaker was saying.*

2) listen to/view a broadcast ~ *Be sure to stay tuned in.*

tune out: stop listening/paying attention ~ *By then, I'd already tuned out.*

tune up: 1) adjust a motor so it runs smoothly ~ *There was nothing much wrong, I just tuned it up.*

2) adjust a musical instrument to the desired pitch ~ *The orchestra was already tuning up.*

change one's tune: reconsider something; change your story ~ *He changed his tune when he realised there might be something in it for him.*

in/out of tune with: in/not in agreement ~ *They're out of tune with what the public wants and needs.*

to the tune of: the amount; extent of ~ *They profited to the tune of $10,000.*

turf out: discard; throw out ~ *Just turf out anything you don't want.*

(have) a turn: 1) be shocked/frightened ~ *News of the accident gave me quite a turn.*

2) an unexpected episode of bad health/illness ~ *He had a turn and had to go to the hospital.* *also: bad/funny turn

turn a deaf ear: deliberately ignore; pretend not to hear something ~ *The government often turns a deaf ear to what the public wants.*

turn against: stop supporting/liking someone and start disagreeing with/opposing them ~ *1a) As a result of the decision, many of his supporters turned against him. 1b) The whole family is against him now.*

turn around: change; cause to change direction ~ *We turned around and went back home.*

turn away: divert from a chosen course/passage ~ *The white car turned away at the last second to avoid a collision.*

turn away (from): stop looking at something ~ *The scene before us was so confronting we had to turn away.* *also: avert one's eyes

turn someone away: refuse entry ~ *1a) We were forced to turn customers away because we'd run out of stock. 1b) They tried to enter, but were turned away.*

turn something/someone back: cause to retreat; stop and go back ~ *The road up ahead was blocked and all the cars were being turned back.*

turn your back on: ignore/abandon/forsake ~ *1a) He started strongly, only to turn his back on the project six weeks later. 1b) I turned my back on her because she was so rude.*

turn/wind back the clock: revert back to how something was in the past ~ *You can't turn back the clock. You have to accept the situation.*

turn the corner: pass a critical stage in a process; to improve ~ *He's much better today. I think he's turned the corner.*

turn someone/something down: refuse an offer/request; issue a refusal ~ *They turned down our offer.*

turns heads: to be so attractive/noticeable that people notice and turn to look ~ *She turns heads wherever she goes.*

turn in: 1) give over/hand in ~ *The student turned in the assignment.*

2) deliver ~ *He turned himself in.*

3) go to bed ~ *I'm tired—I think I'll turn in.*

4) point inwards ~ *Notice how his feet turn in.*

5) make an entrance by turning (from a road) ~ *You can turn in here if you like.*

turn(s) into: transform/change appearance/manner ~ *1a) He turns into an idiot when he's been drinking. 1b) The home office can be easily turned into a guest room.*

turn of the century: the time when one century ends and the next begins ~ *My great grandfather was born at the turn of the century.*

turn of events: a sudden/unforeseen change in a situation ~ *There's been a dramatic turn of events in the bushfire crisis.*

turn off: 1) cease the activity/operation of something ~ *Who turned off the lights?*

2) cause someone to feel bored/no longer interested in something ~ *I got turned off by all the swearing.* *also: be/get turned off

3) leave the road you're driving on ~ *To get there, turn off the main road just after the bridge.*

turn on: 1) exude/display ~ *She knows how to turn on the charm.*

2) cause to begin the activity/operation of something ~ *To get a drink, turn on the tap.*

3) excite/cause to become excited/stimulated ~ *This music's turning me on.*

turn on someone: become hostile/attack someone ~ *He was patting the dog when it turned on him and bit him.*

turn something on someone: point a weapon at someone ~ *The deranged man shot four people then turned the gun on himself.*

turn on the waterworks: begin to cry (for the purpose of gaining sympathy) ~ *She turned on the waterworks to avoid punishment.*

turn one's hand to: begin a new task/activity/job; be able to do a task/activity skilfully/adeptly despite having no prior experience ~ *1a) She gave up nursing and turned her hand to teaching. 1b) He has such talent. He could turn his hand to anything.*

turn one's stomach: make someone feel sick ~ *The smell of rotten meat really turns my stomach.*

turn of phrase: a way of saying something/expressing oneself ~ *I've never heard that turn of phrase.*

turn out: 1) produce/make (by a manufacturing process) ~ *Seventeen million individual Swiss army knife parts are turned out at the Victorinox factory each year.*

2) become/result in/come to be ~ *It turned out to be a glorious day.*

3) point outwardly ~ *For the part, I need to turn my feet out like a penguin.*

4) to be proven/found/known ~ *4a) It turned out they already knew each other. 4b) As it turned out, we didn't need all that equipment.*

5) arrive/assemble for an event ~ *Hundreds turned out to see the spectacle.*

turn over: 1) invert ~ *Let's turn it over to see what's underneath.*

2) shift one's/the position by rolling from one side to the other ~ *She turned over in bed.*

3) surrender something ~ *The witness turned the evidence over to the police.*

4) do business to the amount/extent of ~ *The company turns over two million dollars a year.*

5) of an engine to rotate/cycle ~ *The engine won't turn over.*

turn over a new leaf: begin again/start afresh; shed a bad habit ~ *He's turned over a new leaf since coming out of jail.* *also: turn the page

turn (over) in one's grave: that a deceased person would be greatly displeased with something if they knew about it ~ *Your grandmother would turn in her grave if she knew what had happened.* *also: roll (over) in one's grave

turn to dust: be completely destroyed ~ *All our dreams have turned to dust.*

turn/look to: go to someone for support/help ~ *I have no family here and I didn't know who to turn to.*

turn to jelly: to suddenly feel/become weak through fear/ excitement/nervousness ~ *My legs turned to jelly when I saw the rickety bridge we had to cross.*

turn up: 1) increase the volume/intensity/speed ~ *Turn the music up.*

2) arrive/make an appearance ~ *2a) Some friends turned up unexpectedly. 2b) It's sure to turn up somewhere.*

(a) turn up for the books: an unexpected surprise/result/reversal of luck ~ *He did all that without being asked? That's a turn up for the books!*

turn up one's toes: [informal] to die

turn up the heat: apply increased pressure ~ *The runner turned up the heat on his rival by narrowing the gap between them.*

at every turn: everywhere; at every possible place or time ~ *We encountered problems with the project at every turn.*

(do someone) a good turn: do a favour/something helpful ~ *He did a good turn for the neighbour by mowing the lawn.*

(not) know which way to turn: to not know where to go/what to do/who to ask for help in a difficult situation ~ *I'd lost my job and had no money—I didn't know which way to turn.*

wait your turn: wait for others to do something before you get the chance/opportunity to do the same thing ~ *Wait your turn, everyone, you'll all get to see it.*

turnout: the amount/number of people gathered for an event ~ *We weren't expecting such a large turnout.*

turps: any alcoholic drink—especially beer

on the turps: (to have been) drinking alcohol ~ *Mark was on the turps all night, so I suspect he won't be here today.*

tut-tut: [spoken interjection] a mild rebuke; for shame ~ *Tut-tut—you broke it.*

tux: tuxedo

TV: television

twig: to suddenly realize/come to understand something ~ *It hasn't twigged with him yet that he's going the wrong way.*

twinkle-toes: someone who is quick/nimble on their feet (a dancer) ~ *No one's better on the dance floor than our old friend, Tom "Twinkle-toes" James!*

twists and turns: 1) a series of curves/bends in a river/road ~ *The river twists and turns, winding its way across the plain.*

2) a series of sudden changes in a storyline/plot ~ *It's a story that has more twists and turns than the Amazon River.*

twist around: wrap around; encircle something ~ *1a) The rope was twisted around his ankle. 1b) The river flows east then twists around and flows westward again.*

twist someone's/one's arm: coerce/persuade/pressure someone to do something ~ *1a) You won't have to twist my arm to convince me. 1b) He'll do it, but you might have to twist his arm.*

two by two: in pairs/side by side ~ *They came in two by two.*

two shakes of a lamb's tail: quickly/promptly ~ *I'll be there in two shakes of a lamb's tail.*

in two: in/into two halves ~ *He broke the stick in two.*

that makes two of us: [spoken] that someone has the same opinion of the previous speaker ~ *I have no idea how to do this. That makes two of us.*

Two-Up: Two-Up is an Australian gambling game traditionally played on ANZAC Day. Players gamble on whether the two coins thrown into the air by the "spinner" will both land either heads or tails. Pennies (old currency) are used to play Two-Up because they are the ideal weight and size to fly and turn in the air. It is a game that was originally played by the Diggers in the world wars.

type in: type information on a computer keyboard so it appears on the screen

type out/up: reproduce in type/print ~ *I have to type up the report.*

be/not be someone's type: describes someone who has qualities/characteristics you find/don't find appealing ~ *1a) John wants to go out with me, but he's not my type. 1b) Now that's my type of guy!*

U

U-turn: a turn made by a vehicle resulting in a complete change of direction

u-ey: U-turn *see also: chuck a u-ey

uh-oh: [spoken] used when something bad is about to happen/ when you make a mistake/when something has gone wrong ~ *1a) Uh-oh, it's about to fall! 1b) Uh-oh, I've broken it.*

Uluru: Uluru, also referred to as Ayers Rock, is a large sandstone rock formation situated in the Kata Tjuta National Park, 450 km southwest of Alice Springs in the Northern Territory in central Australia. It is often referred to as a monolith, but it is actually an inselberg, or island mountain, an isolated remnant still remaining after the slow erosion of an original mountain range. One of Australia's most recognisable natural icons, it is considered one of the great wonders of the world. It is sacred to the Pitjantjatjara and Yankunytjatjara Aboriginal people of the area. Visitors to the park can take guided walking tours around the rock and learn about its importance in Aboriginal dreamtime legend. The area around Uluru boasts many springs, waterholes, rock caves, and ancient Aboriginal rock paintings. Uluru is listed as a World Heritage Site.

umpteen: a large unspecified/indefinite amount; many times ~ *I've asked her umpteen times to clean her room, and she still hasn't done it.* *also: for the umpteenth time

under a cloud (of suspicion): suspected of doing something wrong ~ *She left under a cloud, accused of misdirecting funds.*

under arrest: in police custody ~ *Kevin is under arrest on a drink-driving charge.*

under consideration: being currently deliberated/discussed ~ *Jones is one of the players we have under consideration.*

under construction: in the process of being built ~ *The bridge is still under construction.*

under lock and key: secured; locked away ~ *All the important documents are kept under lock and key.*

under no/any circumstances: in no case; never ~ *1a) Under no circumstances are you to go. 1b) I wouldn't do that again, under any circumstances!*

under one's belt: 1) qualifications/attributes/achievements acquired ~ *She has twenty years of managerial experience under her belt.*

2) alcohol consumed ~ *He already had a couple of beers under his belt when we got there.*

under one's feet: in one's way ~ *I didn't get much work done because the kids were under my feet all day.*

under one's hat: keep a secret ~ *It's a surprise, so keep it under your hat.*

under one's/someone's nose: in plain/full view ~ *1a) There it is—right under your nose! 1b) They stole the goods right under the nose of the shopkeeper.*

under one's own steam: unaided; without assistance ~ *You won't need to arrange transport, I'll get there under my own steam.*

under one's/someone's skin: irritate/provoke/annoy ~ *His haughty attitude gets under my skin.* *also: get up (my) nose

under scrutiny: of being examined/watched closely/carefully ~ *Their business dealings are under scrutiny by police investigators.*

under someone's spell: captivated/enchanted by someone ~ *He fell quickly under her spell.*

under someone's wing: in one's protective/loving care ~ *He took the shy new student under his wing.*

under the/these circumstances: because of; given these conditions ~ *He had every right to be angry under the circumstances.*

under the counter/table: of goods bought or sold illegally ~ *The clerk was jailed for selling drugs under the counter.*

under the hammer: of goods sold/to be sold at auction ~ *The house is going under the hammer tomorrow.*

under the influence: intoxicated/drunk ~ *He was fined for driving under the influence.*

(go) under the knife: have a medical operation/surgery ~ *She is yet another celebrity to have gone under the knife for a cosmetic procedure.*

under the sun: everything that you can imagine or exists anywhere on earth ~ *He has the largest collection of guitars under the sun.*

under way: proceeding/in motion ~ *1a) The party was well under way by the time we got there. 1b) As soon as the others get here we'll be under way.*

(be/feel) under the weather: slightly ill; indisposed; hung over ~ *I'm sorry I can't come, I'm a bit under the weather today.*

under wraps: concealed; kept secret ~ *The new design will be kept under wraps until the official launch.* *also: undercover

undies: underpants/underdaks

go unchecked: continue/spread/grow unhindered ~ *1a) The weeds had spread unchecked through the garden. 1b) The drugs passed unchecked through two security check-points.*

uni: university

unsung hero: a person whose bravery/contribution is not yet recognised ~ *They are the brave unsung heroes of the war.*

unwritten law: an informal yet accepted rule/custom/code of behaviour ~ *It's an unwritten law in these parts to give way to livestock on the road.* *also: common law

up: This little word probably has more meanings than any other two-letter word in the English language. It can be used, and is listed in the dictionary, as an adjective, an adverb, a noun, a preposition, and a verb. Idioms beginning with up are listed below, and other entries containing the word can be found throughout the dictionary.

up a/the creek (without a paddle): to be in an extremely difficult/awkward situation/predicament ~ *If we lose this contract we'll be up the creek.*

(come) up against: facing; confronted with ~ *1a) He's up against a formidable opponent. 1b) We'd never come up against this type of problem.*

come up against a brick wall: be unable to continue/make progress because of a problem ~ *Detectives have come up against a brick wall with the investigation.* *also: hit a brick wall

up and about/around: mobile/active after a period of inactivity ~ *It's only a minor sprain, you'll be up and about in no time at all.*

up and away: of a plane/bird to become airborne ~ *The plane sped down the runway, then they were up and away!*

up and at 'em: [spoken] command/direction to get busy or get moving/going/working ('em meaning the task/job) ~ *Up and at 'em, everybody—we've work to do!* *also: up and at it

up and down: 1) backward and forward/back and forth ~ *The man paced up and down anxiously.*

2) from head to toe/top to bottom ~ *He looked me up and down suspiciously.*

3) (emotion) sometimes sad, sometimes happy ~ *He's been a bit up and down since his wife took ill.*

ups and downs: good and bad times ~ *We've had some ups and downs, but we're still together.*

up and down like a yo-yo: for someone to be constantly standing up then sitting down ~ *Will you relax! You've been up and down like a yo-yo all afternoon!*

(be) up for: 1) be eligible for; a possible choice ~ *I've seen how prepared he is. I know he's up for the job.*

2) want to do something ~ *Who's up for a game of snooker?*

up for grabs: available for anyone to take/win ~ *There are hundreds of prizes up for grabs.*

up for sale: available for purchase ~ *Their house is up for sale.*

up front: 1) payment in advance ~ *They want a fifty dollar deposit up front.*

2) honest/candid/straightforward ~ *He was very up front about it.*

up in arms: angry/outraged/indignant/agitated ~ *Everyone is up in arms over the proposed development.*

up in the air: unresolved; not settled ~ *We're not sure when we're moving, everything's up in the air at the moment.*

up one's alley: suitable for; in keeping with one's abilities/interests/knowledge/talent ~ *The job is right up your alley.* *also: up one's street

up oneself/him/herself: arrogant/smug/egotistical ~ *He's so up himself he thinks he deserves preferential treatment.* *also: full of oneself

(be) up there: have the same/equal recognition/status as similar others ~ *It was a performance that put him right up there with the best.*

up to: 1) engaged in; doing ~ *What are you up to?*

2) able/capable; fit for ~ *Dan's not up to the job.*

3) to a certain degree/point; as far as ~ *The flood water came up to the tops of the doors.*

4) the responsibility of someone ~ *It's up to you to tell them.*

5) indicating a maximum amount ~ *It could take up to ten years to recover.*

up to no good: doing/planning something wrong (often said humorously) ~ *By the look of them they're up to no good!*

up to one's neck/armpits/ears/elbows in: thoroughly consumed with; deeply involved in ~ *They're up to their necks in renovations.*

up to something: secretly planning something (good or bad) ~ *Those two are up to something.*

(get/wake) up with the birds/sparrows/crows: get out of bed/rise very early ~ *A seven o'clock start doesn't bother me—I'm usually up with the birds.*

up our/your/their way: the area in which one/someone lives (in a perceived northerly direction) ~ *Drop in and see us when you're up our way next.*

up yours: [spoken] a vulgar exclamation of contempt often accompanied by an obscene gesture

(on the) up-and-up: progressing/proceeding well ~ *He's a very talented musician whose career is on the up-and-up.*

use the bathroom: a way of saying you want to go to the toilet ~ *Excuse me, I need to use the bathroom.*

use strong/foul/coarse language: swear; curse ~ *Please don't use bad language in front of the children.*

use up: consume/expend/deplete ~ *They used up all the hot water!*

in use: currently occupied/busy ~ *Some older production methods are still in use today.*

(get) used to: accustomed to; familiar with something ~ *1a) I used to have to walk to school. 1b) We used to always play together at school. 1c) I can't get used to getting up so early.*

as usual/per usual: in a habitual/expected way ~ *1b) We're late, as usual. 1b) They continued on as per usual.*

not your usual self: thinking/acting/behaving differently ~ *Are you okay? You don't seem your usual self.* *also: feel out of sorts

the usual suspects: the people one would expect to see at an event ~ *Who was there? Oh, Steve, Dan, Grace—the usual suspects.*

ute: utility vehicle with a flatbed tray and a cabin that can seat up to four people

V

vamoose: leave/depart quickly ~ *The cops are coming—let's vamoose!*

vanish/disappear into thin air: disappear without a trace ~ *It's got to be here somewhere—it can't have just vanished into thin air.*

vanishing act: become un-contactable/unable to be found ~ *She does a vanishing act whenever there's work to do.*

VB: Victoria Bitter beer

Vee-dub: VW - Volkswagen ~ *He gets around in a beat-up old vee-dub.*

Vegemite: In 1922, a young chemist named Dr. Cyril P. Callister of the Fred Walker Cheese Company developed a remarkable spread from Brewer's Yeast, hence the birth of the Aussie icon Vegemite. This nutritious black spread, one of the world's richest sources of Vitamin B, is considered a national food and a cultural icon. It is mainly used as a spread for sandwiches and toast, and is also used to flavour soups and stews. The Vegemite product has been, and still is, a remarkable success story to this day.

veggies: vegetables

vent one's spleen: release one's anger ~ *The mayor used the meeting as an opportunity to vent his spleen on the media.*

(have) verbal diarrhoea: [humorous] to talk non-stop ~ *He had verbal diarrhoea. He didn't know when to shut up.*

very much so: [spoken] an emphatic yes to something; an indication that something's correct ~ *Are you enjoying yourself? Very much so.*

not very: (true) to a certain extent ~ *1a) The water's not very hot. 1b) I'm not very happy with it.*

vet: 1) veterinarian/veterinary surgeon

2) war veteran

vicious circle: a situation where efforts to solve a problem results in aggravating the problem further ~ *She is caught in a vicious circle of weight gain and dieting.*

in view: within a range of vision ~ *Willie wanted to keep his quarry in view.*

in full view: clearly visible ~ *The thief stole it off the shelf in full view of everyone.*

in view of . . . : in regard to; in consideration of ~ *In view of the fact that it is raining, the race has been postponed.*

on view: on exhibition; displayed in a place for public inspection ~ *The exhibit will be on view in Perth next month.*

with a view to: with the purpose/aim/intention of ~ *They've been sussing out the real estate with a view to moving here.* *also: with an eye to

Vinnies: St. Vincent de Paul, charity clothing/goods outlet

vocab: vocabulary

W

Big W: department/variety store, a division of Woolworths supermarkets

WA: the state of Western Australia

wacko: [slang] insane; mentally unsound; crazy *also: wacky

wade through: 1) walk (with effort) through water ~ *The survivors were forced to wade through the floodwater.*

2) read a lot of complicated/detailed information ~ *It took hours to wade through the report.*

waddya: [informal] what are/do you ~ *1a) G'day Jack, waddya doin'? 1b) Waddya want? 1c) Waddaya think of that? 1d) Waddaya reckon?*

waddayacallit: [informal] used when you cannot recall the name of something ; what do you call it ~ *We rode on one of those waddaycallit's at the fairground.* *also: waddaycallem; whatsamacallit; thingummy; whatnot

waffle on: speak vaguely/evasively ~ *He waffled on about nothing.*

wag school/class: be wilfully absent from ~ *Billy is in trouble again for wagging school.*

wait a minute[1]: [spoken] stop/halt doing something; pause momentarily ~ *1a) Just wait a minute, will you—I need to fix this first. 1b) Wait a minute—what's that strange noise?*

waaiit a minute[2]: [spoken] uttered in a drawn-out manner when one suspects something suspicious happening/when one has a revelation ~ *1a) Waaiit a minute—you're trying to trick me! 1b) Waaiit a minute, something's not quite right here.*

wait on hand and foot: take care of someone's every need ~ *I was laid up for a couple of days and my darling husband waited on me hand and foot.*

wait up: 1) a request for someone to wait so one can catch up ~ *Wait up! I can't run as fast as you.*

2) remain awake waiting for someone to come home/arrive ~ *I'll be home late, so don't bother waiting up for me.*

wake up: arouse from sleep ~ *1a) I woke up late today. 1b) Wake up, we have to leave soon.*

2) [spoken] way of telling someone to pay attention/become alert/rouse from lethargy ~ *Wake up, Smith! I asked you a question.* *also: wakey wakey; wakey wakey, rise and shine

wake up to oneself: adopt a sensible attitude; come to one's senses ~ *He'll find himself in jail if he doesn't wake up to himself.*

wake-up call: a sign/warning; a portent event that brings an urgent/dangerous situation/issue to immediate attention ~ *A heart attack was the wake-up call for him to take better care of his health.*

walk a fine/thin line: equally balance opposing ideas/groups ~ *The negotiator was walking a fine line between the hostage-taker and the police.*

walk ahead: walk in front/ahead of someone/something ~ *He walked ahead of the group so he could watch for danger.*

walk all over someone: 1) smother/dominate/exploit someone ~ *He's a tough businessman so be careful. He'll try to walk all over you.*

2) win easily ~ *They walked all over us.*

walk along: walk; move/travel on foot ~ *1a) I was walking along minding my own business when a dog attacked me. 1b) We walked along the beach to get to the headland.*

walk alongside: walk next to something/someone

walk around: wander/walk aimlessly ~ *We didn't do much, just walked around town.*

walk away (from): 1) suddenly leave/depart; abandon something ~ *You can't just walk away from your problems.*

2) survive an accident having little or no injuries ~ *How he managed to walk away from such an accident I'll never know.*

walk away/off with: 1) win (a prize) easily/unexpectedly ~ *Sally walked away with all the prize money.*

2) steal/pinch/pilfer ~ *I looked outside and saw someone walking off with my surfboard.*

walk back: return somewhere on foot ~ *I caught the bus there but walked back home.*

walk down (to): travel by foot in a southerly direction/downhill ~ *It's only a short walk down to the shops.*

walk in on: accidentally interrupt someone/something by entering a room ~ *I opened the door and accidentally walked in on a meeting.*

(a) walk in the park: easily done/accomplished ~ *This job's a walk in the park.*

walk into: 1) collide with; become tricked and/or trapped ~ *1a) He walked right into their trap. 1b) I walked into the door.*

2) enter a room/space ~ *All eyes were on us as we walked into the room.*

walk of life: occupation/career/profession/social class ~ *People from all walks of life attended the meeting.*

walk off: go for a walk to ease/reduce the effects of an illness/bad feeling ~ *She needs to walk off her bad mood.*

walk on air: in a euphoric/happy state ~ *He asked her to marry him and she's been walking on air ever since.*

walk on by: continue walking past something without stopping ~ *She hoped he'd notice her, but he just walked on by.*

walk on eggshells: try to be diplomatic/inoffensive ~ *He's very stressed at the moment, so I'm walking on eggshells whenever I'm with him.*

walk on tiptoes: walk on the tips of one's toes ~ *The dad walked on tiptoes so as to not wake anyone.*

walk out: leave angrily; (of workers) to go on strike ~ *Workers threatened to walk out if their needs weren't met.*

walk out on: leave/desert/abandon someone ~ *His girlfriend walked out on him.*

walk someone somewhere: accompany someone on foot ~ *Would you like me to walk you home?*

walk tall: be confident/self-assured/proud ~ *She could walk tall knowing she'd been proved innocent.*

walk through: instruct/lead someone through a complex process/procedure ~ *The stage director walked the actors through the scene.*

walk up to: approach someone ~ *He casually walked up and punched him in right in the face.*

walk with: 1) walk in a particular manner/way ~ *She walks with a limp.*

2) walk with someone ~ *I walked with him to the car.*

walk-a-thon: a fundraising event where participants are sponsored by people pledging money for walking a predetermined distance/course *also: walkathon

walk-in wardrobe: a large storage room for clothes/clothing

walking disaster: someone who is prone to mishaps/accidents ~ *John's injured himself three times in as many months—he's a walking disaster area.*

bang/hit one's head against a wall: [spoken] a feeling of frustration at trying to achieve the impossible ~ *I feel I'm banging my head against a brick wall by constantly asking my son to tidy his room.*

climb the walls: feel nervous/frustrated/annoyed/worried ~ *When they went missing we were practically climbing the walls.*

have one's back against/to the wall: be in a difficult situation with no means of escape/with limited options ~ *With their backs to the wall, they had little chance of winning.*

(the) writing is on the wall: a sign that indicates something/someone's demise/misfortune ~ *After four straight losses, the writing was on the wall for the team's coach.*

see the writing on the wall: realise/be aware of one's imminent demise/misfortune ~ *She didn't see the writing on the wall and was shocked when she lost her job.*

Wallabies: the national Rugby Union football team

waltz around: dance as a waltz ~ *He grabbed his wife and waltzed her around the room.*

waltz in: move with confidence/self-assurance ~ *She waltzed right in and tried to take control.*

wander along: a casual stroll/walk ~ *The hikers wandered along the meandering path.*

wander around: walk/stroll aimlessly or without purpose ~ *With little else to do we spent the afternoon wandering around town.*

wander away/off: casually walk away from something ~ *1a) When the excitement was over, the onlookers wandered off. 1b) The little girl wandered away from her mother.*

wanna: [informal] want to ~ *I wanna go home.*

want for nothing: to have everything you want or need ~ *She's very spoiled and wants for nothing.*

want the moon/earth: desire/want too much of anything

(be) wanted: of a criminal sought after by authorities ~ *He's wanted for murder.**also: a wanted man/woman

warm up: 1) of the air temperature to become hotter ~ *It was cold this morning, but it's really starting to warm up.*

2) prepare/practise for a sporting game/performance ~ *The players warmed up before the start of the game.*

The Warrumbungles: The combination of forested ridges, rocky spires, domes, deep gorges, and plenty of camping and visitor facilities make the Warrumbungles one of the most popular national parks in the state of N.S.W. The first European record of the Warrumbungle Mountains was by the explorer John Oxley in 1818 on his second inland expedition. He named the mountains Arbuthnots Range, but this name did not survive. Today the mountains are still known as the Warrumbungles, as they were known to local Aboriginal people before Oxley arrived. This word comes from the Kamilaroi language and is believed to mean "crooked mountains." The Kamilaroi are one of the Aboriginal language groups who have lived in the Warrumbungles for thousands of years. On July 12, 2006, this park was added to the National Heritage List.

warts and all: portray or describe something/someone including any faults/imperfections ~ *1a) It's a warts-and-all biography. 1b) She loves him, warts and all.*

wash away: 1) be carried away by water (liquid) ~ *Floodwaters washed away the bridge.*

2) clean something by washing in water ~ *The product promises to wash away stains.*

wash down: 1) drink (liquid) immediately after eating food ~ *She washed the cheese and bickies down with some red wine.*

2) cleanse/wash thoroughly (from top to bottom) ~ *They got home and gave the horse a good wash down.*

wash/wipe one's hands of: renounce/abandon/reject/dismiss ~ *He continues to abuse my hospitality so I've washed my hands of him.*

wash(ed) out: 1) colourless/faded ~ *All the colour has washed out of my jeans.*

2) exhausted/lacking in energy ~ *I'm feeling a bit washed out today after yesterday.*

3) rinse/cleanse with water ~ *You should wash the glass out before you use it.*

wash up: the act of washing used dishes/cutlery/kitchen utensils after a meal ~ *We don't have a dishwasher so we have to wash and wipe up.*

washed up: 1) of someone's career to be over/finished ~ *He had a successful music career, but now he's all washed up.*

2) carry or deposit something by means of water (ocean/river) ~ *Seaweed had washed up on the beach.*

wash-n-wear: wash-and-wear—clothing requiring minimal care/that can be easily washed and requires no ironing

washout: the cancellation/cessation of an event/sporting match due to excessive rainfall ~ *The tournament was a total washout.*

waste away: 1) dwindle away/wither ~ *He's wasted away all his inheritance.*

2) to lose a lot of weight/become thin ~ *She's is wasting away because she's not eating properly.*

waste one's time: use/expend one's energy in vain/fruitlessly ~ *I wasted all that time searching for you, and you've been here all along.*

go to waste: be unused/abandoned (therefore be discarded/ thrown away) ~ *I can't let all this food go to waste—please take some home with you.*

watch it/out: [spoken] alert to be careful/alert/aware/cautious ~ *Watch out—it's about to fall!*

watch over: guard/protect ~ *The nanny watched over the kids as they played.*

water down: 1) lessen the effectiveness/strength of something ~ *I was given the watered-down version of the story.*

2) dilute with water ~ *You need to water it down a bit. It's too strong.*

water under the bridge: said of a past event that cannot be changed/rectified ~ *We've had some major disagreements, but that's all water under the bridge.*

watering hole: 1) a natural hollow containing water ~ *All the animals came to the watering hole to drink.*

2) a favoured pub/bar ~ *You'll find him at his favourite watering hole.*

waterworks: 1) begin to cry in a way that seems false/unnecessary ~ *She often turns on the waterworks to gain sympathy.*

2) [informal] one's urinary system

wave a magic wand: solve a difficult problem; make the impossible happen ~ *I wish I could wave a magic wand and make all our troubles go away.*

wave aside: disregard; ignore; dismiss as irrelevant ~ *He waved aside the suggestion of a scandal.* *also: pooh-poohed; wave away

wave something around: raise something high and move it about so others can see it ~ *George waved around the winning ticket for all his friends to see.*

on the same wavelength: in harmony/accord/in agreeance with; of two or more people to think alike ~ *They work well together because they're on the same wavelength.* *also: on the same page

way back: 1) a far distance behind; at the rear/back of ~ *The queue went out the door and way back down to the corner.*

2) a long time ago ~ *Our friendship goes way back.*

way of life: cultural habits/behaviour/principles/lifestyle typical of a person or society ~ *It can take a while to become accustomed to a different way of life in a foreign country.*

way off: 1) in the future ~ *The departure date is a long way off yet.*

2) far (in distance) from a specific target ~ *The arrow she fired was way off the mark.*

3) far from knowing the facts/truth; wrong ~ *Your thoughts on it are way off.*

way out: 1) the exit (door); the route/path out of an area ~ *1a) Where's the way out?*

2) the means/way to resolve a problem/dilemma ~ *She lay awake all night trying to find her way out of the dilemma.*

(on one's) way out: do something as one leaves a place ~ *Could you please lock the door on your way out?*

no way: [spoken] not possible; (emphatically) no!; never! ~ *1a) There's no way I could ever do that! 1b) You want me to do that? No way!*

pave the way: make processes/developments/progress easier ~ *The results will pave the way for future development of the drug.*

(be) on its way out: in need of repair; broken down; becoming unusable ~ *This old computer is doing strange things—I think it's on its way out.*

way-out: unconventional; unusual; extreme ~ *Their music is a bit way-out for my liking.*

ways and means: the methods/resources of accomplishment ~ *There are ways and means of getting it done.*

(go) weak at the knees: be overcome by emotion (so as to want to collapse) ~ *I go weak at the knees whenever I see him.*

the weaker sex: condescending term for women/females (in general)

weakness for: a special/self-indulgent liking/fondness for something/someone ~ *I have a weakness for chocolate.*

wear: 1) believe/accept something/someone ~ *I didn't wear his excuse.*

2) put up with/tolerate ~ *I'm not going to wear this type of treatment any longer!*

wear and tear: the damage caused by constant/regular use/work ~ *1a) The rough roads around here cause wear and tear on a car's suspension. 1b) Playing contact sports often causes wear and tear on your joints.*

wear away: become eroded/diminished ~ *The writing has worn away over time.*

wear down: 1) reduce someone into submission by relentless badgering/pressure ~ *My pleading wore Dad down, and he relented and let me to go to the party.*

2) erode/rub/grind away by constant use ~ *The stone steps have worn down over time.*

wear off: for the effects of something to diminish/lessen ~ *The effect of the drug is starting to wear off.*

wear out/through: grind/rub a hole in something ~ *The legs of the heavy cabinet have worn through the carpet.*

wear to a frazzle: exhaust/tire someone; be exhausted/tired (physically or mentally) ~ *I'm worn to a frazzle looking after those kids all weekend.* *also: wear oneself down to the ground

wear the pants/trousers: be the one who carries the most responsibility/authority ~ *She wears the pants in the family.*

wears one's heart on one's sleeve: openly shows one's emotions ~ *My husband is not afraid to wear his heart on his sleeve.*

wear thin: 1) of a joke/explanation/excuse to becomes less effective because of overuse ~ *She's used that excuse so many times it's wearing thin.*

2) become more and more impatient (with someone/something) ~ *My patience is wearing thin with them!*

(the) worse for wear: 1) in poor health/condition (often as a result of drinking too much alcohol) ~ *He's a bit worse for wear after last night's party.*

2) damaged/injured/deteriorated/worn through constant use ~ *This old rug looking a bit worse for wear.*

weather permitting: if the weather allows (something to happen); if the weather is good ~ *We're having a barbie on Sunday, weather permitting.*

how's the/this weather: [spoken] 1) used to enquire about the weather ~ *How's this weather—isn't it cold?*

2) used to indicate a change of subject to an unimportant topic ~ *So, how's the weather?*

nice weather we're having: conversation filler ~ *Nice weather we're having.*

weatherboard (house): a timber house

weave through: move through a space/area by dodging/weaving ~ *The cyclist weaved through the halted traffic.*

wedgie: 1) a shoe with a wedge-shaped heel

2) a wedge-tail eagle

3) broad/wedge-shaped (hot) chips

weed out: remove/separate/eliminate (an unwanted element) ~ *They were sent in to weed out the troublemakers.*

week about: every alternate/second week ~ *We do duty there every week about.*

week after week: for many weeks (repeatedly) ~ *I've tried week after week to contact him, but I get no reply.*

week by week: every week ~ *He grew stronger week by week.*

week in, week out: week after week; every week ~ *1a) Week in, week out my job never changes. 1b) I see her here week in, week out.*

weeks on end: continue for multiple weeks in a row ~ *Sometimes he's away for weeks on end.*

dirty weekend: a weekend where two people/lovers/a married couple go away to be alone to have sex (said humorously) ~ *It's believed they went away for a dirty weekend.*

long weekend: a three- or four-day weekend involving either the Friday, Monday, or both

weekender: small holiday house/shack ~ *We're staying at a friend's weekender.*

weigh down: 1) to burden/oppress ~ *The problem is weighing her down.*

2) become bent over/bowed under weight; secure something with a weight ~ *You'll have to weigh it down with something or else it will blow away.*

weigh-in: when a boxer, jockey, or sportsperson has their weight recorded before and/or after an event

weigh into: contribute/add to; join in a discussion/debate; have one's opinions heard ~ *It began as a quiet discussion until everyone decided they wanted to weigh into the debate.*

weigh one's words: choose/consider carefully ~ *It was a sensitive issue so I had to weigh my words carefully.*

weigh up: ponder/assess something ~ *I'll weigh up the options before I make decision.* *also: weigh the pros and cons

(have a) weight problem: a polite way of saying someone is overweight ~ *She's had a bit of a weight problem all her life.*

carry weight: 1) have influence over someone ~ *Her arguments carry a lot of weight with management.*

2) have excess body fat ~ *I'll have to go on a diet, I'm carrying too much weight.*

(a) dead weight: the weight of an inert person or thing ~ *The dead weight of the animal was over 100 kg.*

pull one's weight: do one's share of duties/work ~ *Everyone in our household is expected to pull their weight.*

put weight on: gain weight ~ *He's put some weight on since I last saw him.* *also: put on weight

take weight off: lose weight ~ *I've taken some weight off in the last month.*

throw (one's) weight behind something: 1) use strength/power to do a physical task ~ *We could only move it after big John threw his weight behind it.*

2) use one's influence to support someone/something ~ *I was happy to throw my weight behind the campaign.*

work weight off: lose weight by exercising ~ *Larry has been jogging to work the weight off.*

worth its/one's weight in gold: very valuable; highly regarded ~ *Sally's been good to me—she's worth her weight in gold.*

weirdo: (long 'o' sound) [informal] a strange/eccentric/peculiar person ~ *He's nice enough, but a bit of a weirdo.*

welcome relief: much wanted/appreciated relief ~ *The rainstorm provided welcome relief from the heat.*

roll out the welcome mat: prepare to welcome visitors ~ *We've got visitors coming—we'd better roll out the welcome mat.*

wear out one's welcome: stay too long somewhere (where one has been invited); visit someone too often (so that they tire of seeing you) ~ *Don't stay all weekend or you'll wear out your welcome.*

well and truly: totally/completely/absolutely ~ *We're well and truly lost!*

well aware: have full knowledge/understanding of something ~ *I'm well aware of the facts.*

(keep) well away from: stay a distance from someone/something ~ *1a) Children need to keep well away from a hot stove. 1b) You'd better keep well away from me because I don't want to give you my cold.* *also: keep/stand well back

well done: 1) [spoken] an expression of praise ~ *You passed the exams. Well done!*

2) meat that is well/thoroughly cooked ~ *I don't like to see any pink meat—I like my steak well done.* *also: good for you!

well into: far along/into something; after a period of time ~ *1a) They partied well into the night. 1b) They didn't score any points until well into the second half.*

well out of: far out(side) of something ~ *The ball was well outside the boundary.*

well over: exceeding the expected/projected figure/amount/number ~ *1a) We raised well over $4,000 for the charity. 1b) Temperatures today reached well over thirty-five degrees.*

well said: a way of telling someone you liked their speech/commentary; equivalent to saying, "You said that very well." ~ *Well said! You made your point very clear.*

well then . . . : 1) [spoken] interjection used when one has considered a reply/response ~ *Well then, if that's what you want to do, let's do it.*

2) an interjection to begin/resume a conversation ~ *Well then, what did you think about that?*

well, well, (well): [spoken] expression of surprise/curiosity ~ *1a) Well, well, I never expected to see you here! 1b) Well, well, well, what have we here?*

well up: for liquid to pool ~ *Tears welled up in his eyes.*

well within: 1) in the scope/sphere of ~ *I'm well within my rights to contend the issue.*

2) inside the limits of time/distance ~ *The project was completed well within the expected time frame.*

as well: also; too; in addition ~ *1a) Jane's going as well. 1b) He's a good musician, and he can act as well.*

as well as: 1) equally; as much ~ *I didn't do as well as expected in the test.*

2) along/together with; including ~ *My sister came, as well as all her children.*

darn well: a forceful expression of annoyance/anger ~ *1a) You knew darn well what time you were to come home! 1b) I'll darn well do what I want!* *also: full well

do well (at): succeed/prosper ~ *1a) He's done well to have completed all that work. 1b) I'm confident he'll do well at university.*

get well: become healthy ~ *I hope you get well soon.*

go well: of a process/something to happen without problems ~ *1a) Good luck, I hope it all goes well. 1b) Although we lost, the game went really well. 1c) Fred's new car goes well.*

if all goes well: [spoken] said in the hope there are no problems/ delays in doing something/in something happening ~ *I should be back at 3 p.m. if all goes well.*

just as well: luckily; with good fortune ~ *1a) It's just as well I brought the umbrella, it's starting to rain. 1b) Just as well you got home when you did, or you would have been in big trouble.*

know full well: have full knowledge/awareness of something ~ *You know full well you should have called me first!*

may/might as well: should/ought to do something; of having no reason not to; having no alternate plan ~ *1a) If everyone's here we may as well begin. 1b) We may as well wait here for them.*

money well spent: said when one is pleased/satisfied with what they spent their money on; that they were getting value for money ~ *Having a pool put in was money well spent.*

oh well: [spoken] expression of disappointment/resignation ~ *Oh well, there's not much more we can do right now.*

take something well: readily accept criticism/bad news ~ *I thought he'd be upset when I told him the news, but he took it quite well.*

very well: 1) possibly/might have ~ *It could very well have killed him.*

2) (have) a clear understanding of something ~ *She knew very well she was supposed to come straight home.*

3) in excellent health ~ *How are you? Oh, I'm very well, thank you.*

4) have a good result/be successful ~ *James did very well in his exams.*

5) okay/alright—[spoken] said when one has considered a reply/response ~ *5a) Very well then, let's do it. 5b) Very well then—do what you want!*

could very well have: almost certainly ~ *The attack was so severe it could very well have killed him.*

well-adjusted: emotionally happy/healthy/sensible/sane ~ *She's a good choice for the job because she's well-adjusted.* *also: well-balanced

well-balanced: correctly adjusted/balanced/regulated ~ *He stays healthy by eating a well-balanced diet.*

well-heeled: prosperous/wealthy ~ *The business caters to well-heeled clientele.* *also: well-to-do

well-oiled: working/operating smoothly/efficiently ~ *They're playing like a well-oiled machine.*

well-preserved: showing little or no signs of aging ~ *She's well-preserved for someone eighty years old.*

well-spoken: articulate; speaking clearly/correctly/politely ~ *He's a very well-spoken young man.*

well-worn: 1) showing physical signs of overuse ~ *The old man's clothes were well-worn.*

2) a word/phrase being repeated/overused; having lost its meaning ~ *I'm tired of hearing his well-worn jokes.*

wet behind the ears: young and naïve/immature/inexperienced ~ *He's not yet familiar with the job—he's still wet behind the ears.*

the big wet: an extended/long rainy season in the northern tropical area of Australia

whack on/in: hastily apply; put on/in; do something ~ *1a) Whack on some sunscreen before you go out. 1b) I'll just whack it in the fridge.*

whack down: hastily/smartly put/place something down ~ *If you like you can whack your bags down over there.*

out of whack: out of sequence/order; unbalanced ~ *The door won't close because it's out of whack.*

whacked: 1) exhausted/tired ~ *That was hard work. I'm whacked!*

2) under the influence of drugs or alcohol *also: whacked out of one's brain

whacko: [informal] fantastic/great/excellent ~ *Whacko—you got the job!* *also: whacko-the-diddly-oh!

wharfie: wharf labourer

what's cooking: [spoken] a way of asking what's happening; what are you doing; what are the plans ~ *Hi guys—what's cooking?* *also: what's doing?

what about . . . : [spoken] a way of making a suggestion ~ *What about a game of cards?*

2) what someone's opinion of something is ~ *What about this one?*

3) concerning what? ~ *Fred, I need to talk to you. What about?*

what's your beef: a way of asking someone what they're complaining about ~ *We've always done it that way. What's your beef?*

what's eating (someone): [spoken] a way of enquiring why someone is angry/upset/troubled ~ *What's eating Cathy? She's hardly spoken to anyone the whole day.*

what for: [spoken] strong reprimand/scolding ~ *She said what? I'll give her what for when I see her!*

what for?: [spoken] a way of querying/questioning something ~ *I'm going to have another shower. What for? You had one two hours ago.*

what have you: incidental items that don't need mentioning ~ *All they had for sale were some second-hand books and what have you.*

what if . . . : [spoken] suppose; is it possible? ~ *What if we try it this way? It might work then.*

what's it to you: [spoken] a way of asking someone why they need to know something ~ *Why do you want to know? What's it to you?*

what of it: [spoken] an expression of scorn/indifference; so what! ~ *That's the fourth time you've called her today. So, what of it?*

what in the . . . : expression of exasperation/questioning (often spoken in surprise) ~ *1a) What in the blazes is that!? 1b) What in the world are you doing?* *also: what the . . . ; what the heck/hell is; what on earth

what's that got to do with it/anything: [spoken] used to ask someone the relevance/connection of an unrelated topic to the current topic ~ *We're having fish for dinner tonight. What's that got to do with anything?* *also: what's that got to do with the price of fish/eggs/milk

what's the catch: [spoken] response to a suspicious/dodgy/questionable deal ~ *You're letting me have it for nothing? What's the catch?*

what's the matter: [spoken] used to ask someone what is wrong/what the problem is ~ *What's the matter? Why are you crying?*

what's what: the true facts/situation; the visual identification of items ~ *1a) Everyone's telling me something different—I don't know what's what. 1b) There's so many identical electrical cables behind here I don't know what's what.*

what's with: [spoken] a way of asking about something; why someone is doing something ~ *1a) What's with all the empty boxes outside?1b) What's with all the noise?*

whatever: 1) (that) any choice/anything is okay ~ *Whatever you want to do is fine by me.*

2) [spoken] a rude way to express indifference (often preceded by "yeah") ~ *Would you prefer this one? Yeah—whatever.*

whatever turns you on: [spoken] said of something that pleases/excites/interests someone else, but not you ~ *I don't really like this music, but whatever turns you on.* *also: tickles your fancy; makes you happy; floats your boat

whatshername: [informal] what you call someone who's name one cannot immediately remember ~ *Oh—I forgot to tell you, whatshername's coming too.* *also: whatshisname; whosamabob

wheels: method/mode of transport; road vehicle ~ *Hey, I like your new wheels!*

wheel and deal: plot/scheme/instigate/negotiate (often immoral/shonky) business dealings/transactions, usually delegated to a smooth talker ~ *We leave all the wheeling and dealing to Chris.*

wheel away: move/push something on wheels ~ *The orderly wheeled the trolley away.*

wheelie bin: domestic/commercial rubbish bin with wheels

do/chuck a wheelie: a manoeuvre where a motorcycle rider quickly accelerates from a standing start, causing the front wheel of the bike to lift off the ground

whiffy: having a bad/offensive odour ~ *Phew! These shoes are whiffy.* *also: woofy; on the nose

while away: spend time idly (having nothing else to do) ~ *She read to while away the hours.*

while you're at it: [spoken] request for someone to do something for you while they are doing something else ~ *I'm going to make some coffee. Could you make me some tea while you're at it?*

whinger: one who is always complaining/whinging about something

whip around: turn around very quickly ~ *He whipped around to see what caused the loud noise.*

whip into shape: improve someone's health/condition/behaviour ~ *He's a good trainer—he'll whip you into shape in no time.*

whip something out: yank/jerk something out of a place/ somewhere ~ *He whipped his wallet out to pay for the goods.*

whip something up: 1) quickly prepare a meal/food/something to eat ~ *I whipped up some scones for afternoon tea.*

2) cause something to increase in volume/strength ~ *Strong winds whipped up the waves.*

3) arouse/incite interest/excitement ~ *The political candidate was busy trying to whip up support.*

whip through: perform a task quickly ~ *Hurrying to go out, she whipped through the housework.* *also: whiz through

whippersnapper: a confident/impertinent young person

whipper snipper: a motorised, hand-held device that uses a length of strong nylon to cut/trim grass/bushes *also: brush cutter

whirl around: rotate/turn very quickly ~ *He whirled her around the dance floor.*

whisk away: quickly remove something/someone away from an area/space ~ *He stopped and was whisked away in a waiting car.*

bells and whistles: extra fancy gadgets; add-ons ~ *His new motorcycle has all the bells and whistles.*

blow the whistle: expose; bring a stop to; halt mischief/wrongdoing of individuals/corporations ~ *Jim blew the whistle on the company's illegal activities.*

wet one's whistle: quench one's thirst; have a drink ~ *It was barely enough to wet my whistle.*

wolf whistle: an appreciative whistle usually directed by a man at an attractive woman ~ *She got a wolf whistle when she walked by.*

whistle-stop: a quick/brief visit/tour of a place ~ *We did a whistle-stop tour of Melbourne.*

(as) white as a ghost/sheet: pale/colourless due to shock ~ *1a) She turned white as a sheet when she heard the bad news. 1b) What's wrong? You're as white as a ghost.*

white elephant: a household ornament/article/utensil (of little value) that is no longer wanted/needed

white elephant stall: a market stall that sells white elephant goods

white lie: a small, insignificant lie told so as to not upset anyone (often preceded by "little") ~ *She told her mother a little white lie because she wanted to go to the party.*

White Pages: residential/business telephone directory

in black and white: written down; in print ~ *It's all there in black and white.*

whittle away: gradually reduce the size/amount/importance of something ~ *The ongoing expenses were whittling away at his savings.* *also: whittle down

whiz past: move very quickly ~ *It whizzed past me so quickly I didn't see what it was.*

whiz through: do something very quickly ~ *Sally whizzed through the housework before going out.* *also: zoom/zip through

as a whole: all things considered/included; in all ~ *As a whole, the concert went very well.*

the whole lot: everything; the entire amount/extent/totality/sum ~ *By the time I returned he'd eaten the whole lot!*

whoop it up: celebrate noisily/loudly ~ *They went out on the town and whooped it up.* *also: make whoopee/ie

whoopee/ie: [spoken] shout of exuberant joy/happiness ~ *Whoopee—I won!*

whoopee doo: [spoken] sarcastic remark that says "so what" ~ *Well, whoopee do!*

whoops: [spoken] expression of mild surprise; an apology ~ *1a) Whoops, I made a mistake. 1b) Whoops, I nearly dropped it.*

whopper: 1) large/big/huge ~ *1a) He caught a whopper of a fish! 1b) What a whopper!*

2) an outrageous lie ~ *Keith just told the biggest whopper ever!* *also: whopping big

(the) who's who: influential/important/outstanding people/person in a community/group/profession ~ *The who's who of the film industry will be attending.*

on a good wicket: to be in a good/pleasing predicament ~ *He's certainly on a good wicket with the job he's got now!*

on a sticky wicket: to be in a difficult/awkward predicament

wide awake: completely alert; aware ~ *I've been wide awake since 4 a.m.*

wide blue yonder: far away; a far off unspecified area/space (anywhere and everywhere) ~ *He just walked off into the wide blue yonder one day and never returned.*

wide of the mark: 1) inaccurate/incorrect ~ *Her comments are wide of the mark.*

2) far from/off (the) target ~ *His arrow went wide of the mark.*

wild about: greatly interested in; intensely enthusiastic about ~ *All the teenagers are wild about his music.* *see also: go wild about

wild and woolly: unkempt/lawless/uncultured ~ *He looked a bit wild and woolly after a month roughing it in the bush.*

wild goose chase: look/search for something that doesn't exist; be given incorrect information about where to find something ~ *After two hours searching, I realized we were on a wild goose chase.*

wild horses: said when one can't be persuaded/made to do something ~ *Wild horses couldn't tear me away.*

wildest dreams: something that one could never imagine/expect/hope for ~ *1a) Never in my wildest dreams did I think this would happen. 1b) The results were beyond their wildest dreams.*

go wild: get very excited; behave excitedly ~ *As he stepped onto the stage the crowd went wild.*

in the wild: in an open/uncultivated/uninhabited area/region ~ *We're also visiting a game reserve to see animals in the wild.*

run wild: act/behave in an unrestrained, unruly manner ~ *When we got to the beach the kids just ran wild.* *also: run riot

Willie Wagtail: Found throughout mainland Australia, but absent from Tasmania, the Willie Wagtail is the largest and most well-known of the Australian fantails. They have black plumage above and a white underside and are recognized by their black throat and white whisker marks and eyebrows. They are named thus because of the constant sideways wagging of the tail as they busily forage for insects in open habitats. They are very aggressive and territorial and will often chase and harass larger birds such as kookaburras. They are happy to live in and around human habitats, and are a common sight around gardens and parks and urban lawns.

willy-nilly: without formality/order/at random; whether it's wanted /desired or not ~ *1a) He threw his clothes into the suitcase willy-nilly. 1b) Names were chosen willy-nilly.*

willy-willy: small whirlwind that swirls dust and sand to a great height

win a few, lose a few: sometimes succeed, sometimes fail ~ *I'm not too worried. You win a few, lose a few.* *also: win some, lose some; can't win 'em all

win at: succeed/triumph at a competition ~ *I can never win at cards.*

win back: regain someone/something ~ *1a) He hoped to win back the money he'd lost in the card game. 1b) She was trying to win back his affection.*

win by a nose: win by a small margin; closely beat ~ *The horse came from behind to win by a nose.*

win hands down: to win without effort/easily/by a bigger margin ~ *I beat him hands down.*

win out over something: the most popular/successful choice between two or more options ~ *For our kids, pizza always wins out over hamburgers.*

win (over): gain the support/favour of; win someone/be won ~ *1a) Charles gave a performance he hoped would win over his critics. 1b) What a great idea. You've won me.*

win someone's heart: gain someone's affection/love ~ *He set out to win her heart.*

win the war against: fight and succeed against an overwhelming adversary ~ *Used regularly, this disinfectant will help you win the war against germs in the home.*

(a) no-win situation: for a person/persons to be in an awkward/ difficult predicament/situation where the only way out will be harmful/bad for that person or other people ~ *Sally will be upset if I go to Jack's party, and Jack will be upset if I don't go. I'm in a no-win situation.*

(a) win-win situation: a situation where everyone will benefit no matter what the result is ~ *The trial proved a win-win result for local residents and the supermarket giant.*

wind around: make wide turns/bends; twist/coil/turn around something ~ *1a) The bush track winds around the escarpment. 1b) To anchor it we wound the rope around the tree trunk.*

wind back: for a path/road/waterway to turn in a circle so that it goes in the direction from which it came ~ *It's here that the river winds back on itself and forms a delta.*

wind down: 1) slow the pace; operate/function at a less hectic pace; end; cause to end gradually ~ *The party wound down at midnight.*

2) the mechanical action of winding a handle to make something move down ~ *She wound down the window for some fresh air.*

wind through: of a path/track to twist/turn through an area ~ *The track winds through the tall trees.*

wind up: 1) *see: end up

2) the mechanical action of winding a handle to make something move up; tighten a spring so as to begin the actions of a watch/clock ~ *Please wind the window up.*

wind someone up: knowingly get someone excited/agitated/upset/ angry; tease someone; cause someone to react ~ *He's saying that just to wind you up.*

all wind: bluster; without substance; all talk, no action ~ *He never follows through with his threats. He's all wind.*

get wind of: hear/learn about; begin to suspect something ~ *He got wind of their plans.*

windbag: someone who talks excessively about nothing of interest

(go) window shopping: to look but not buy

wine and dine (someone): treat someone to a lavish/expensive meal ~ *He wined and dined her hoping to keep her attention.*

winning streak: *see: on a roll

wino: [informal] a destitute person or drunkard who drinks cheap wine

wipe away: clean something away ~ *He gently wiped away her tears.*

wipe down: clean (a surface) by wiping ~ *Don't forget to wipe down the kitchen bench when you're finished.*

wipe off: remove/tidy/clean something by wiping/rubbing ~ *1a) It's best to wipe off the excess paint. 1b) Wipe it off before it stains.*

wipe out: 1) eradicate; kill in large numbers ~ *A disease is threatening to wipe out the entire species.*

2) use/deplete materials/resources ~ *All that spending has wiped me out.*

3) eliminate/destroy; remove from existence/memory ~ *Time could not wipe out the terrible memories.*

wipe the smile/grin off one's/someone's face: a way of telling someone to be serious ~ *Wipe that silly grin off your face, Jones!*

wipe up: 1) clean/mop spilt liquids from a flat surface ~ *The maid wiped up the mess.*

2) dry (with a tea towel) wet crockery/glasses/cutlery ~ *If you wash up, I'll wipe up.*

wipe the floor (with someone): to easily defeat someone ~ *He didn't just beat him, he wiped the floor with him!*

wipe off the map: utterly destroy a place ~ *The force of the hurricane wiped the town off the map.*

down to the wire: to be decided at the last possible moment ~ *With only two minutes on the clock, the game is down to the wire.*

wise up: [spoken] a way of telling someone to stop being stupid/to act sensibly/maturely ~ *If you don't wise up you'll have us all in trouble.* *also: wizen up

(to) wise up to: face reality/the truth about something ~ *When are you going to wise up to the fact that smoking is bad for your health?*

become wise to: begin to realise/understand something ~ *The authorities soon became wise to the suspect's usual habits.*

wisecrack: a flippant/off-hand/facetious remark/retort ~ *Tim is upset because she made a wisecrack about his haircut.*

wish list: a list of things that one/someone wants very much/would like to have or do ~ *Owning a reliable car is at the top of my wish list.*

wishy-washy: watery/colourless; lacking in substance/purpose/ strength ~ *1a) He's too wishy-washy to be a leader. 1b) The colour's a bit bland, wishy-washy.* *also: namby pamby

with it: 1) mentally alert/competent ~ *I must be tired. I haven't really been with it all day.*

2) savvy/knowing; up-to-date ~ *He's a very with it guy who is always seen wearing the latest fashions.*

with a vengeance: attack/strike violently/excessively or with greater intensity ~ *The cold I had has come back with a vengeance.*

(are) you with me: [spoken] a way of asking someone 1) if they comprehend/understand what's been said ~ *It's a difficult concept to follow. Are you with me so far?*

2) if they support your plan/undertaking ~ *It's a risky venture but I can't do it on my own. Are you with me on it?*

withdrawal symptoms: the emotional/physical effects that occur when someone stops using substances like drugs/alcohol (often said humorously when one is denied other pleasures/habits)

wither away: shrivel/dry up ~ *The flowers quickly withered away in the hot sun.*

wolf one's food down: eat greedily/quickly ~ *He didn't say much. He just wolfed his breakfast down and left!*

Wombat: About the size of a pig and solidly built with short legs, these Australian marsupials are found in mountainous, forested, and heathland areas of Southeastern Australia and Tasmania. Their herbivorous diet consists of shoots, leaves, and roots. They use their powerful claws and rodent-like teeth to dig extensive burrow systems. Dirt is unable to enter their backward-facing pouch. During the day they sleep in their burrows—sometimes on their backs, with their feet in the air—and forage in the evening and throughout the night. They have no predators in their natural environment and are not afraid of humans. The three living species are the Common Wombat, the Northern Hairy-Nosed Wombat, and the Southern Hairy-Nosed Wombat.

cotton wool: wool in its natural state; wool gathered but unprocessed

dyed-in-the-wool: permanent; extreme; committed ~ *1a) She's a dyed-in-the-wool supporter. 1b) The changes to the policy are dyed-in-the-wool.*

woollens: clothing made from wool; warm clothing

woollies: 1) see: woollens

2) [informal] Woolworths, a national supermarket chain

woolshed: a free-standing farm building where sheep are shorn and where the fleece is packed for market/storage *also: shearing shed

won't take no for an answer: that one will not accept a negative answer ~ *You're coming out with us tonight, and I won't take no for an answer.*

word by word: one word at a time ~ *I re-read it word by word to make sure I understood it.*

word of honour: solemn vow/promise ~ *She gave him her word of honour that she would return.*

(hear) word from someone: have/hear/get/receive communication from someone/somewhere ~ *I just got word from them—and everything is okay.*

(a) word of warning: offer cautionary advice ~ *She gave me a word of warning about the new boss.*

wpm: words per minute (typing speed)

household word: a commonly/widely known word *also: household name

a play on words: a humorous/inventive way to use words/phrases (often used as a logo/business name). For example: The Mane Event (for a hairdressing salon)

a war of words: an angry argument ~ *They've had a war of words over the proposed changes.*

as good as one's word: true to one's promise; dependable (in keeping one's) promise ~ *1a) As good as his word, he presented ready to work. 1b) You can trust Sue to keep her word.* *also: keep one's word; true to one's word

beyond words: more than one can say/express, often preceded by grateful, thankful, shocked, or amazed ~ *I can't believe what they did. I'm shocked beyond words!* *see also: gobsmacked

eat one's words: admit that what one said was wrong ~ *Well, I'll have to eat my words. I didn't believe they could win.*

go back on one's word: renege; break a promise ~ *I don't want to go back on my word, but the situation has changed.*

have a way with words: be talented in using words effectively ~ *Aaron says things so eloquently. He has such a wonderful way with words.*

have a word in someone's ear: privately advise/warn someone ~ *She had a word in my ear about what to expect.*

have a word with someone: speak to someone privately ~ *I'll have to have a word with him about his behaviour.*

have words: to argue/speak angrily to someone ~ *I don't know what the problem was, but the two of them had words after the meeting.*

in other words: restate/say something in a different way/with clearer meaning ~ *There'll be celebrations tonight. In other words – we won!*

in so many words: directly/clearly/explicitly ~ *I told them in so many words that I wasn't interested.*

(be) lost for words: become speechless due to surprise/astonishment/amazement ~ *I couldn't believe what he was doing—I was lost for words.* *also: at a loss for words

(the) magic word: please or thank you ~ *Say the magic word and I'll get it for you.*

mark my word(s): [spoken] a way of reinforcing what you've said ~ *Mark my words, this will be the greatest invention of modern times.*

. . . or words to that effect: similar words meaning the same thing ~ *He said something about failing to attend, or words to that effect.*

put in a good word: say something positive/supportive about someone to a person in authority ~ *I'm trying out for the team, so will you put in a good word about me to the coach?*

put the hard word on someone: pressure someone into doing something ~ *1a) They'd only been together for a short time when he put the hard word on her. 1b) I put the hard word on Dad to let me use the car tonight.* *see also: put the bite; squeeze on

put words into one's/someone's mouth: claim/allege someone said/implied something one did not say at all ~ *I never said that! You're putting words in my mouth!*

(just) say the word: give the okay/signal to begin something/do something for someone ~ *1a) I'm ready to begin any time you say the word. 1b) If you need help at any time just say the word and I'll be there.*

send word to: get a message to someone ~ *I'll send word to you if there are any further problems.*

spread the word: tell others so they can tell others ~ *The meeting's next Monday, so if you see anyone, spread the word.*

take one's word for: believe/accept what someone says on trust ~ *I wasn't there, so I'll have to take your word for it.* *also: take someone at his/her word

too stupid/silly for words: very stupid/silly ~ *1a) He got drunk and his behaviour was too silly for words. 1b) This movie is too stupid for words.*

twist words: distort/restate/misrepresent someone's words ~ *That's not what I said. You're twisting my words!*

word for word: verbatim ~ *She copied it, word for word.*

four-letter word: any vulgar/offensive/obscene word that contains four letters

work like a treat/a charm: be effective; have the desired effect ~ *Your advice worked like a charm.* *also: work like magic; work like a dream

work against the clock: work quickly to finish one's work within a limited period of time ~ *Everyone was working against the clock to find them before nightfall.*

work alongside someone: 1) work with someone in the same place and for the same purpose ~ *That means she gets to work alongside some of the world's most famous actors.*

2) fight in a war; play in the same side/team; work in the same place ~ *Believe me, I know what she's like. I have to work alongside her every day.*

work amongst: do one's work among people/animals/things ~ *She became a zookeeper so she could work amongst lions.*

work around: do one's work whilst avoiding going near someone/something ~ *The table's too large to move, so we'll just have to work around it.*

work as: work in the capacity of something ~ *I used to work as a taxi driver.*

work away: keep/continue working at something ~ *The children are quietly working away on their school projects.*

works both ways: has a similar/equal effect or the same advantages/disadvantages as the other ~ *It works both ways—management needs to work as hard as the staff if they expect an increase in production.*

work one's bum off: [informal] work very hard ~ *I worked my bum off on that project.* *also: work one's arse/backside/butt off; work one's fingers to the bone

work its way out (of something): find/make its way out of being embedded somewhere ~ *The fish worked its way out of the net.*

work itself out: (of a problem) to be solved by itself ~ *It's only a small problem. I'm sure it'll work itself out.*

work of art: 1) a piece of artwork ~ *They had a grand home with some very expensive works of art hanging on the walls.*

2) anything created/made/done/performed with great skill ~ *Positioning the statue in itself was a work of art.*

work something off: 1) repay a debt through work rather than money ~ *I spent all weekend working off the debt I owe my father.*

2) do a physical activity to get rid of anger/tension ~ *Instead of yelling at everyone—go for a run and work off your anger.*

work on something: the act/process of doing a task/activity ~ *1a) Pete's out working on his car. 1b) It's not finished yet, but I'm working on it.*

work on someone: 1) for something to have the desired effect on someone ~ *This cream works beautifully on my dry skin.*

2) for a doctor/surgeon to treat someone ~ *Doctors worked on him for ten minutes trying to re-start his heart.*

3. try to convince someone of something ~ *Dad hasn't said I could go yet, but I'm working on him.*

work something out: 1) find a solution to a problem/dilemma; understand something ~ *1a) I can't work these instructions out. 1b) I can't work out why it won't go.*

2) come to an agreement with someone ~ *Surely we can work something out!* *also: work things out

work someone out: understand someone's thinking/thought process ~ *I don't know why she does those things—I just can't work her out sometimes.*

work out: 1) a physical exercise regime ~ *I get fit by working out at the gym.*

2) to conclude positively/satisfactorily ~ *2a) I hope everything works out for you. 2b) Somehow or other it all worked out in the end.*

work out for the best/in the end: for a bad situation/dilemma to finish/turn out alright ~ *1a) There was a lot of confusion at first, but it all worked out in the end. 1b) It was difficult at the time, but it worked out for the best.*

work someone over: intimidate/beat/bash someone ~ *Some thugs worked him over.*

work things out: come to an agreement; resolve an issue/problem ~ *You two should learn to work things out instead of arguing.*

work together: share the workload; work cooperatively with someone ~ *Let's all work together and get this job finished.*

work toward: make progress towards a goal/aim ~ *I'm doing some short courses, but I'm working towards a career in law.*

work through: progress/advance steadily through a task ~ *We're working through the problem and hope to soon have it fixed.*

work under: work in a non-supervisory role; have an immediate supervisor ~ *I work under Steve, who is the area manager.*

work someone up: prepare someone for a medical procedure ~ *Mr. Jones needs a full blood work-up before he goes to theatre.*

work (yourself) up: become worried/nervous/excited ~ *She got herself worked up before meeting him.* *also: get worked up ~ *She got all worked up over nothing.*

work up a thirst/appetite: get thirsty/hungry through physical effort ~ *1a) It won't take long to work up a thirst in this heat. 1b) I've worked up an appetite.* *see also: thirsty work

work (one's) way: move laboriously through/along/towards something/someplace; work laboriously on a job/activity ~ *1a) They worked their way along the riverbank to reach the cottage. 1b) He's slowly working his way through the heavy tome.*

work wonders: beneficial/helpful/effective; improve/cause improvement ~ *1a) The herbal tea has worked wonders. 1b) She's only been teaching here for a month and already she's worked wonders on the students.* *also: do wonders for

blue-collar worker: a worker engaged in manual labour

white-collar worker: a worker engaged in non-manual labour; an office worker

worlds apart: completely different ~ *They remain good friends, yet their lifestyles are worlds apart.*

(makes a) world of difference: describes something that greatly improves something/a situation ~ *Installing insulation has made a world of difference.*

for all the world: precisely; in every way ~ *The rock formation looks, for all the world, like a dinosaur.*

have the weight of the world on one's shoulders: carry a burden; have lots of worries ~ *It looks like Ian has the weight of the world on his shoulders with that long face.*

mean the world (to): that something/someone is very important in one's life ~ *My family means the world to me.*

(it's a) small world: [spoken] what you say when you discover that events/people are connected ~ *Oh, so your mother's friend, Jane, lives in the same street. Well, it's a small world!*

the (big) wide world: the scope of the entire world where one is vulnerable/unknowing ~ *He's lived with his parents for so long he wouldn't know what it's like out in the big wide world.*

the whole wide world: everything/everywhere ~ *You're the best in the whole wide world!*

the world over: covering the entire scope of the world ~ *Insects are found the world over.* *also: through the world; world wide

the world without end: forever

worm one's way into: gradually/subtly infiltrate/penetrate oneself into a favourable position/situation ~ *The homeless dog wormed his way into their home and into their lives.*

worm one's way out of: escape from a situation; avoid doing something by an artful/devious manner ~ *He's under arrest for fraud, but knowing him, he'll most likely try to worm his way out of it.*

worry about: fret/be anxious about someone/something ~ *1a) Don't worry about it—there's nothing you can do. 1b) I worry about him sometimes.1c) Everything's alright—you've got nothing to worry about. 1d) He worries about it all the time.*

worrywart: a pessimist; one who worries excessively

worth a bit/a few quid: worth a lot of money; expensive ~ *I don't know how much, but it would be worth a bit.*

(well) worth it: worthwhile/important/useful; rewarding (despite difficulties) ~ *1a) This is a view well worth looking at. 1b) When we saw the finished result we knew it was well worth the effort.*

worth one's while: worth time/effort/energy (to do something) ~ *1a) It's worth your while applying for the position. 1b) It's not worth my while going all that way for a half-hour meeting.*

wouldn't know someone . . . : would not recognise someone ~ *It's been a long time since I saw her I wouldn't know her now.* *also: wouldn't know her/him if he/she stood up in my soup; if I fell over him/her; from a bar of soap

wouldn't you (just) know it: [spoken] expression of dismay/annoyance/frustration/surprise ~ *I'd just finished washing the car,* *and wouldn't you know it—it started to rain!* *also: wouldn't that rot your socks

wow: [spoken] expression of amazement/astonishment/ pleasure/excitement ~ *Wow—what an amazing sunset!*

wow someone: impress/charm someone ~ *He wowed the audience.*

wrapped: very/extremely happy ~ *I'm wrapped that you got the award.*

wrap around: coil/twist; fold/drape/enclose something around something/someone ~ *The snake slowly wrapped itself around its prey.*

wrap/twist someone around your little finger: manipulate/ control someone by using charm ~ *Jane usually gets what she with her father—she's got him wrapped around her little finger.*

wrap something up: 1) enclose/encase with paper ~ *She lovingly wrapped up the present.*

2) complete/finish work on something; bring to an end/a close ~ *I should have the job wrapped up in a few days.* *also: wrap up something

wrap somebody in cotton wool: be overprotective of someone; restrict someone's independence ~ *If you wrap your children in cotton wool they'll never become independent adults.*

wrapped up in/with: engrossed/involved in/with something/ someone ~ *1a) He was so wrapped up in his work he failed to notice how late it was. 1b) She always gets herself wrapped up with everyone else's problems.*

wriggle out of: manoeuvre/extricate oneself from a situation/from doing something ~ *1a) As usual, he tried to wriggle his way out of doing the household chores. 1b) Jim tried to wriggle out of any involvement in the scam.*

wrinkle up: of a surface to become creased ~ *1a) He left his clothes wrinkled up at the bottom of the bag. 1b) The old man's face was all wrinkled up with age.*

wring one's hands: the action of squeezing each of your own hands when you're worried or concerned ~ *Marge was wringing her hands waiting for the news.*

wring someone's neck: an idle threat of physical violence (to twist someone's neck) as a means of reproach/reprove ~ *I'd like to wring his neck for the trouble he's caused everyone!*

wring something out of something/someone: obtain/extract information by applying mental force/pressure causing distress ~ *It took much negotiating to finally wring the truth out of the witness.*

wringing wet: soaked through; very wet ~ *I got caught in the storm and was wringing wet by the time I got home.* *also: sopping wet

write something off: 1) dismiss as insignificant ~ *She thought the teachers had written her off.*

2) announce that someone doesn't have to pay back a debt ~ *The president urged the banks to write off debts owed by poorer countries.*

3) deem worthless ~ *The insurance company wrote my car off.*

wrong in the head: [informal] insane/crazy

(be) in the wrong: legally/morally incorrect; to blame in error ~ *1a) I'll have to pay for damages to the other car because I was in the wrong. 1b) It takes courage to admit you're in the wrong.*

don't get me wrong: [spoken] a way of telling someone not to get upset with what you say; that you are making yourself clear ~ *1a) Don't get me wrong. It's not a bad idea, but I don't know if it will work. 1b) Don't get me wrong—I'm happy to help, I just don't know when I'll have the time.*

get it wrong: misunderstand something/what someone says ~ *1a) I hope I don't get it wrong this time. 1b) You've got it all wrong—that's not how it happened.*

go wrong: go amiss/fail; make a bad decision ~ *1a) If you follow the directions you can't go wrong. 1b) We've had so many problems, I'm hoping nothing else will go wrong. 1c) After the marriage broke down she wondered where it all went wrong.*

you're not wrong: [spoken] a way of saying you agree with someone ~ *Gee, it's hot! You're not wrong.*

what's wrong: [spoken] a way of asking what is the matter/problem; what happened ~ *1a) What's wrong—why are you crying? 1b) I don't know what's wrong with it.*

wrung-out: mentally exhausted/tired ~ *I'm wrung-out after all that work.*

X

x-amount: an unspecified/unknown amount quantity (used theoretically) ~ *Just say, for example, he earns x-amount of money.*

Xmas: [informal] Christmas

xox: represents kisses and hugs, written at the end of a personal letter

X-ray: a photograph of the body for medical diagnosis

x-rated: a film with this classification is sexually explicit/obscene

xxxx: represents kisses written at the end of a personal letter

XXXX: Fourex beer

Y

y'/ya: [informal] you ~ *1a) G'day, how y' goin'? 1b) Wadda ya doin?*

y-fronts: blokes' undies

yabber: chatter/talk *also: yack

yabbie/y: small freshwater crayfish

yachtie: yachting enthusiast

yahoo/yippee: [spoken] shout of cheer/happiness

yobbo/yob/yahoo: *see: bogan

yakka: work

hard yakka: strenuous work ~ *I'm bushed. That was hard yakka!*

yarn: 1) (a) tale/story (preceded by "spin") ~ *They sat around the camp fire spinning yarns.*

2) a chat/conversation ~ *Marj and I had a good old yarn across the back fence.*

yea big: a way of saying "about this big" (said using one's hands as a measure) ~ *The fish was about yea big.*

yeah: [informal] yes ~ *1a) Yeah, I wondered about that. 1b) Yeah, waddaya want?*

yep: [informal] yes (as a stand-alone reply) ~ *Is that what you want to do? Yep.*

year dot: a long period of time; for as long as anyone can remember ~ *They've done it that way since the year dot.*

year in, year out: year after year; each year ~ *You do the same old thing year in, year out.*

Yellow Pages: telephone directory advertising businesses and services

yes and no: [spoken] that you're undecided; in a way; sort of ~ *Did you have a good time? Yes and no.*

yet again: one more time; once again ~ *Petrol prices have risen yet again.*

as yet: until now; so far ~ *1a) They haven't arrived as yet. 1b) As yet, no arrests have been made.*

have yet to: that something that should have happened/been done has not ~ *1a) They have yet to arrive. 1b) He has yet to make a decision.*

yikes: [spoken] an exclamation of surprise/astonishment ~ *Yikes—what was that!*

yonks: a very long time ~ *I haven't seen her for yonks.* *also: donkey's years

you can say that again: [spoken] a way of saying that you agree with what someone said ~ *That was the worst movie I've ever seen. You can say that again!* *also: you said it!

you could have cut the air with a knife: [spoken] describes a very tense atmosphere ~ *You could tell they'd been arguing. You could have cut the air with a knife.*

you could have knocked me down with a feather: [spoken] an expression of utter surprise/astonishment ~ *When she told me what happened you could have knocked me down with a feather.* *also: you wouldn't read about it

you'll get yours: [spoken] a way of saying that revenge will be sought on someone ~ *You might be laughing now, but you'll get yours!* *often used humorously between friends *also: you'll keep!

young at heart: retain a youthful spirit no matter what one's age ~ *I may be ninety, but I'm still young at heart.*

young gun: a brash/confident/assertive young man

young'un: a child/youngster ~ *The young'uns will be coming with me later on.*

you're on: [spoken] what you say when you'll accept a bet/wager/ challenge ~ *Do you want to bet? okay, you're on!*

yours truly: oneself ~ *It was painted by none other than yours truly.*

Yowie: Australia's equivalent of the Himalayan yeti or the North American bigfoot or sasquatch, the mythical Yowie is a huge ape-like creature that supposedly inhabits the bush, particularly in the eastern Australia states. Yowie-type creatures are common in Australian Aboriginal legends.

yum: [spoken] what you say when you like what you're eating ~ *Yum, that was delicious!* *also: yummy; yummo

Z

zap: [informal] cook/heat food in a microwave oven

zebra crossing: pedestrian crossing indicated by broad, white stripes

zero in: accurately approach a target ~ *The hungry eagle zeroed in on his prey.*

zilch/zero: nothing ~ *I put all that effort for zilch!*

zillion: a large unspecified/indeterminate amount/quantity ~ *I wouldn't do that in a zillion years.*

zip up: close a zipper ~ *Could you please help me zip this up?*

zippy: fast/energetic/lively ~ *It hasn't got a powerful engine, but it's pretty zippy.*

zits: pimples/acne

zombie: appearing to be lifeless; apathetic; looks/behaves as if on automation ~ *I didn't get much sleep last night and I'm like a zombie today.*

zonked: utterly exhausted/weary ~ *I'm zonked—I'm going to bed.*

zoom across: move/travel rapidly across something ~ *The jet zoomed across the sky.*

zoom around: move/travel quickly about the place ~ *I've seen her zooming around town on a zippy little motorbike.*

zoom in (on): 1) focus; concentrate one's attention on something ~ *Once they'd identified the problem they were able to zoom in and fix it.*

2) move quickly/rapidly on something ~ *The giant eagle zoomed in on its prey.*

3) view an image in close range (by use of a zoom lens on a camera) ~ *The photographer zoomed in for a close-up shot.*

zoom off: leave/depart in a hurry ~ *The police zoomed off in a hurry.*

zoom through: complete/finish something very quickly ~ *I zoomed through the exam.*

zzzs: used in writing to indicate someone is snoring/sleeping

Review Requested:
If you loved this book, would you please provide a review at Amazon.com?
Thank You

CPSIA information can be obtained
at www.ICGtesting.com
Printed in the USA
LVOW07s2318021217
558435LV00001B/134/P

9 781618 975447